Noch einmal sei es euer Morgen, Götter.+

+Once more be it your morning, gods. - R M Rilke

Also by Tom Stacey

NOVELS
The Brothers M
The Living and the Dying
The Pandemonium
The Worm in the Rose
Deadline
Decline
(under the *nom de plume* Kendal J Peel)
The Twelfth Night of Ramadan

COLLECTED LONG SHORT STORIES
Bodies and Souls

INDIVIDUALLY PUBLISHED LONG SHORT STORIES/NOVELLAS
The Same Old Story
The Tether of the Flesh
Golden Rain
Grief

TRAVEL and ETHNOLOGY
The Hostile Sun
Summons to Ruwenzori
Peoples of the Earth (20 vols. deviser and supervisory editor)

CURRENT AFFAIRS
Today's World (editor)
The Book of the World (deviser and supervisory editor)
Immigration and Enoch Powell

SCREENPLAY
Deadline

TRIBE

This work is dedicated to

Arthur Syahuka-Muhindo, scholar and
academic, who knows much more than I
and if I have it wrong will forgive me.

TRIBE

The Hidden History of the Mountains of the Moon
An Autobiographical Study

Tom Stacey

STACEY INTERNATIONAL

Which of my friends is it impossible not to thank
with pipes and shawms? Meriel Carruthers, my
dedicatee Syahuka-Muhindo, Zostine Kiongozi,
Wilfrid Grenville-Grey, Angela Landels (who also
did the portrait on the jacket), Henry Maas, Lise
Schiemann, Ruth Spriggs...

TS

First published November 2003

Second impression December 2003

STACEY INTERNATIONAL
128 Kensington Church Street
London W8 4BH
Tel: +44 (0)207 221 7166; fax: +44 (0)207 792 9288
E-mail: enquiries@stacey-international.co.uk
Website: www.stacey-international.co.uk

Printed and bound in UK by Biddles Ltd

ISBN: 1900988 763

CIP Data: A catalogue record for this book is available from the
British Library

Contents

PART III
King Over the Water: 1982-200?

A Foreword

This book is precise and scrupulous as to what the author has observed and thought and gathered in from others but it is not scholarship. There are indeed fine scholars, a hardy handful, on matters concerning the Bakonzo people and their habitat – scholars with whose work I have long been acquainted and who will have contributed in varying measure to what is contained in my narrative. These include the dedicatee of this book, Arthur Syahuka-Muhindo, a Mukonzo patriot who is in the first place a political scientist; and, next, Kirsten Alnaes, anthropologist and dear friend, for whose remarkable thesis on the spirit-singing of the Bakonzo she was awarded her Doctorate by the School of Oriental and African Studies at London University; Dr Yona Balyage, the Mukonzo historian; Dr Henry Osmaston, David Pasteur, and the late Guy Yeoman, each in their way specialists on the higher reaches of the mountains; and Professor Nelson Kasfir, the American political economist.

I have not usually sourced the information the reader will find in *Tribe*. Where the source is not manifestly my own or my companions' interlocutors or my own observations, be assured that all purporting to be fact which I have put down on paper *has* a source such as I, canny old investigator, claim with confidence to be sound. My stalwart friend Zostine Kiongozi Tumusiime, forty years my junior, was resident at my family home for a year when I was at work on *Tribe*, while he was in London studying the arcane universe of the computer. I cannot count the times Zostine has thrown light on my own notes taken on Ruwenzori over the years, or gently adjusted my interpretations.

The full story of the Kingdom of Rwenzururu, 1962-82, will surely be written one day, drawing on the documents preserved by Yolamu Mulima, former prime minister of that Kingdom, and on the memories of members of the recently formed Rwenzururu Veterans' Development Association. That precious future account may very likely put right some things I have written, notwithstanding my earnest striving for accuracy. There will be further and fuller studies of the Bakonzo as a people and of Ruwenzori as mountains. My hope is that *Tribe* will spur the next wave of formal research into that extraordinary region of central African habitat and in particular into Rwenzururu: the independent and defiant Kingdom of those days warrants it; the constitutional Kingdom many of us look to in the future assuredly needs it. Bakonzo scholarship is young but it is vigorous, and the mountains' mines are rich.

   Tribe remains a subjective contribution to the story of the Bakonzo of Ruwenzori and, I hope, to understanding the human condition. It is *wilfully* subjective. This is not only because I am truly unequipped to be a scholar of my Bakonzo brethren: my personal intimacy, however vivid, is patchy and episodic; my grasp of the language, best in 1954, has dwindled as interpreters have surrounded me with my own language. It is subjective because my belief is that the truth of anything is attained only subjectively: the underrunning will of man is – by love, submission, commitment and desire as creature and as spirit, simultaneously and integrally – to seek and be found by his wholeness. That is a guided subjectivity. My purpose will have been to take my reader by the hand into the mountains and let go of the hand there.

TS Spring 2003

Dramatis Personae

A list of principal figures which occur in the story of *Tribe*. Readers should be aware that in Bakonzo usage, where a name comprises a tribal appellation coupled with a name of Christian or non-Bantu origin, the order in which they are spoken is arbitrary. For instance, Syayipuma Augustine might just as well answer to Augustine Syayipuma. Tribal names usually comprise a traditional name which tells something about the child's birth (*e.g.* that it is firstborn), coupled with another 'given' name for more precise distinction. Thus, shared names which occur repeatedly – like Bwambale, Mukirane, Baluku, Masereka – do not indicate relationship. Quite frequently, full names are not given in the text and so do not occur in this list.

In this list, names have been ordered alphabetically according to the usage most commonly occurring in the text. With non-African names, the surname determines its position in the order.

Abruzzi, Luigi, Duke of (1873-1933) – explorer and traveller; aka
    Prince of Savoy
Alnaes, Kirsten – Norwegian anthropologist
Amon Bazira – leader of (rebel) NALU (National Army for the
    Liberation of Uganda); former Ugandan minister
Amos Kambere – Mukonzo Member of (Ugandan) Parliament
    (1981-86)
Apollinaris Kithende – Mukonzo politician and M P
Barnabas Bamusede – Mukonzo administrator
Batulomayu Kasiraho – Rwenzururu runner; later judge
Timothy Bazarrabusa – Mukonzo sophisticate and
    administrator. Later, Ugandan High Commissioner
    in London
Yokasi Bihande – Mukonzo administrator
Godfrey Binaïsa – Ugandan President
Bonifasi (Bonnë) Baluku –Rwenzururu patriot
Dr Henry Bwambale – Mukonzo academic
Charles Wesley Mumbere – eldest son of Isaya Mukirane,
    successor as King (Omusinga) of Rwenzururu,
    entitled Irema-Ngoma (Keeper of the Drum). *Aka*
    (as a child) Kisembo (the chosen one)
Cheyne, Colonel W E (Bill) – Commanding Officer of
    the Ugandan army in 1963

Christine (or Christina) Mukirania – wife, later widow, of Isaya
   Mukirane (hence Queen, and Queen Mother)

Christopher Tabaan Mbalibula, self-styled Kibanzanga – second
   son of Isaya Mukirane, currently MP for Busongora South

Emin Pasha (1840-92) – administrator of Equatoria. *Aka* Eduard
   Schnitzer

Erisa Kironde – a Muganda; travelling companion of the author in
   early 1954. Later, a leading Ugandan citizen

Ezironi Bwambale – Mukonzo politician

Fanehasi Bwambale, self-styled Kisokeronio – Mukonzo rebel
   leader

Frederick Lugard (1858-1945) – empire-builder and administrator

Furaha Cristabel – daughter of Omusinga Charles Wesley

George Rukidi (1904-65) – King (Mukama) of Toro

Gerisoni Ndambireki – Rwenzururu minister; later, judge

Ibrahim Linkoni *see* Linkoni

Ibrahimu Ndyanabaïsi – son of Semwiri Bukombi, brother-in-law
   of Isaya Mukirane

Idi Amin Dada – soldier, erstwhile Ugandan President

Irema-Ngoma see Charles Wesley

Isaleri Kambere – Mukonzo village chief and Church teacher

Isaya Mukirane – author's companion on his
   1954 journey; later President, then
   Omusinga (King) of Rwenzururu

Johannis Mpanya – Mukonzo elder

Kabalega (c1850-1923) – Bunyoro king

Kabila, Laurent – Congolese rebel; later President

George Kahigwa – senior son of Semwiri Bukombi. A Mukonzo
   elder

Kapoli (executed 1921) – Mukonzo rebel

Kasagama – familiar name of the (future) King (Mukama) Daudi
   Kyebambe of Toro (1885-1928)

Yeremiah Kawamara – Baamba leader

Khavaïru – Buswagha regional chieftain

Khyawatawali – prospective bride of Khavaïru

Kigoma – author's companion on his 1954 journey. The name,
   implying Drum, is given to a child born under a full moon

Richard Kinyamusitu – the name adopted (from *omusitu*,
   forest) by the Mukonzo warrior and longtime
   Rwenzururu army commander

Kisokeronio see Fanehasi

Dr Crispus Kiyonga – Ugandan cabinet minister; later National Resistance Movement Commissar and WHO administrator

Kule – eldest son of Khavaïru

Kunihira – a 'neglected' wife

Rev. Liminya – Rwenzururu Church of Uganda priest

Linkoni, Ibrahim, aka Abraham Lincoln (born Bahamba Kaleba) – Mukonzo administrator

Loice Bwambale – Mukonzo politician and MP

Luigi di Savoia, Prince *see* Abruzzi

Yusufu Lule – Ugandan President

Peter Mupalya – Mwamba political activist

Maate (a shortened form of Mazereka, indicating a third-born boy) – a Mukonzo sage

Maate – a Mukonzo smith

Blasio Maate – teacher, Rwenzururu patriot and, later, District Commissioner

John Maate – a high mountain guide

Milton Apollo Obote – (former) Prime Minister, later President (twice) of Uganda

Mudenge John – mountain guide

Christine Muhindo – political activist, widow of Vito Muhindo

Muhongya Yeremiya – Rwenzururu premier

Ibrahim Muhonjya – a (Muslim) kinsman of Charles Wesley

Mukirane – *see* Isaya or Seylversta

Muruli Mukasa – Ugandan Minister for Security

Yolamu Mulima – Rwenzururu premier

Mumbere see Charles Wesley

Yowere Museveni – Ugandan President; former Minister of Defence (Museveni, a coinage from 7th Bn KAR in which his father served)

Ronald Mutebi – Kabaka of Buganda

Yolana Mwambalha – Rwenzururu regent; former parliamentary Speaker, and Finance Minister

Nyamutswa (executed 1923) – Mukonzo sorceror and rebel leader

Rönson, Bent – Norwegian peacemaker

Ruhandika (c1860-1930) – northern Konzo chieftain

Samwiri Mukirane – Rwenzururu premier

Semwiri Bukombi Mulwahali – chiefly son of Ruhandika

Seylversta Mukirane – author's companion in 1963

Stanley, H M (1841-1904) – explorer, empire-builder

Augustine Syayipuma – Mukonzo cultural specialist

Arthur Syahuka-Muhindo – Mukonzo political scientist; lecturer at
    Makerere University
Tibamwenda (executed 1923) — Mukonzo rebel
Balwana Timeseho - Rwenzururu preacher
Vito Muhindo – Mukonzo political aspirant
Williams Sibibuka – third son of Isaya Mukirane
Bishop Zebedee Mazereka – Mukonzo Church of Uganda cleric
Zeuliah Biira – former Queen consort and wife of
    Omusinga Charles Wesley

And some acronyms:

ADF	Allied Democratic Front
BLHRS	The Bakonzo Life History Research Society
NALU	National Army for the Liberation of Uganda
NRM	National Resistance Movement (the political system under which Museveni's government of Uganda operates)
UNLA	Uganda National Liberation Army (*i.e.* Ugandan army under the Obote regime)
UPDF	Uganda People's Defence Forces (*i.e.* Ugandan army, under the NRM government)

A Note on the Vernacular

Let no reader be daunted by the occasional vernacular. The use of some vernacular is inescapable. For example, there is no English term for the vast xylophone of Bakonzo musical culture. So we must say *endara*. Yet at times I indulge myself, and for the music which should be near the reader's ear sometimes I will use the vernacular where an English equivalent *is* available. We are together in Africa. So do not furrow at these words: if you need to recall a precise meaning, a glossary is printed at the end of the book.

In another region of the vernacular, a tiny mastery is called for. This involves elementary Bantu patterns in the association of people and speech with places or types or ideas. A little guide to such usage also appears at the end of the book.

PART I

THE MOUNTAINS OF THE MOON: IMMEMORIALLY TO 1962

Mountains as Dream

The mountains pull me back. I cannot always tell whether they are real. Sometimes they are decidedly not: that is when I dream them, and I know I do not dream them as they are. Yet even if I also dream them, they *are* real, for I have climbed into them, have brought influence to bear upon them, have on at least two occasions tried to foster peace among the people whose homeland they provide.

The realm of the peaks lies beyond and above the territory of the people. That further highland realm is beyond issues of good and evil, beyond the strains of humanity, or the wickedness or the triumph of men. It is a sacred realm, allocated by the people who are by inheritance its guardians – the Bakonzo tribe – to their

spirits, the snow-spirit Nzururu, and progeny Kitasamba, spirit of thunder, storm and lightning. If you require to protect your highland compound from Kitasamba's lightning,  bury elephants' teeth upright in the earth so that the grinding edge of those molars lies, as above, flush with the soil.

We of the wide world know Rwenzururu as Ruwenzori, or by its preferred East African form, Rwenzori. The mild confusion entered with H M Stanley in 1888, when he first placed the name and position of the massif on a white man's maps. He took the name for the mountains he heard on the lips of the people he found himself among on the southern shores of Lake Albert, when, some fifty or sixty miles to the south of his party, the snow peaks were briefly released from cloud to capture his astonished sight. Some of the informants of his expedition could well have been Bambuti pygmies who to this day inhabit the forest below the northern foothills, or members of the Baamba people, the Bakonzo's lowland neighbours and co-habitants on the north and north-west perimeter of the mountains.

Stanley's eyes were not the first of his expeditionaries' to fall upon them. A few weeks previously, on April 20, the mountains had capriciously revealed their heights to his medical officer, Tom Parke, on an excursion to the lakeside with another Englishman of Stanley's team. Parke realised that he was indeed gazing upon ice and snow on summits which straddled the equator – even though his African companions (from Zanzibar) declared it was surely salt glittering there. The compulsive glory-hogger Stanley brushed Parke's report aside, making out that the fellow had been gazing at quite other hills, and far too low for the presence of snow, though he might have glimpsed, at best, a momentary, freakish scattering of distant hail...

They reluctantly unveil themselves, those white peaks. You could be at hand for a year in the plains to the east or the forests to the west and know nothing but the proximity of a dark, bluish mass and a conflation of cloud.

The mountains come and go.

How *could* a man at their feet have an inkling what lies up there – above and beyond? It is a world entire, mist-swirled, of grotesquely gigantised plantlife, the unique and only home of twenty-five species of reptiles, fifteen of mammals, of the brilliantly plumed turaco and seventeen other birds, of scores of species of grub and insect. They come and go in the imagination. I can dream Ruwenzori as one mounting to a high wild region, the air thinned, vegetation sparse, a ragged skyline of snow-blown rock, yet still inexplicably a remnant of human presence among which I have some function.

Or am I up there in pursuit of silence? Of inviolability? Waking, I am at once aware that this is not the place I am truly acquainted with. My dream has taken me exploring in my sleep. Yet despite my better knowledge, the dream has insisted: it is Ruwenzori. When I was growing up, my first craft was writing poems, and to explore was a kind of calling. What remained on earth to explore? The craft and the vocation could come together as a state of mind: a man can explore himself as soul.

Where the map stops another map begins.
Have no doubts, my traveller: only the conjectural
Contains certainty.
A boy

Perusing grandpa's atlas, the places he knew intimately were
Blank spaces. Beyond, where contours faltered, miners
Slaved in galleries. In their upper reaches
Rivers of dots were thoroughfares:
Bargees naked to the waist called out in a babble
He fully understood. Greetings. Wares. Prices.
                                                    Look
From this high scarp on the long peace of the land,
Look upon her hills and hollows, and amid them
Other hills, myriad, intricately watered,
Quilted by cultivation, by habitance.

Here descend, sir, by these raw rock nullahs
That conies have crossed alert for eagles,
Come down on strong feet into her first groves.
Listen – the first of her laughter in the orchards,
And gurgle of water.
                                    Where the map stops
You have made discovery.

And now, explorer, forward,
For you have entered on a boundless act of faith.

    I did not reach Ruwenzori until I was twenty-four. I came to it, surprisingly for an Englishman, from Congo-side, as Stanley had on that 1888 journey; for although the border was to be fixed by the colonial powers to run along the highest peaks, the greater part of the massif (70 miles long and 40 wide) lay in British-administered Uganda, rather than Belgian-administered Congo. It was mapped, of course, although a fair amount of it by aerial survey rather than by ground surveyance, and there were surely gulches and ravines never yet entered by recording Man. And in contradiction of the poem, I did not actually come down upon its inhabited spurs and ridges from above, even though that would have been fancifully possible had I first made a bee-line ascent by the scarcely inhabited, precipitous Congo flank, breasting the snows and at length descending to the populated contours Uganda-side. Had I done so I would have found Ruwenzori's heights to be indeed home to conies – the mountains' unique species of hyrax, emperor among guinea pigs, *dendrohyrax arboreus Ruwenzorii*: a plump six or eight pounds of flesh and fur, feast for an eagle... and, occasionally, the

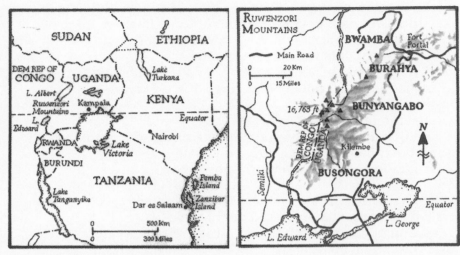

high-ranging Ruwenzori black leopard. However, on that first journey in the mountains, 1954, with Isaya Mukirane, he and I did cross the high forested spine of the range below Karangora peak at the northern end, ascending from Bwamba and thus coming down into the inhabited foothills of Bunyangabo – myriad, intricately watered, quilted by cultivation, by habitance. Yet the very day I write this, in January 1999, I have news from Bunyangabo which does not tell of peace, but of the gratuitous murder last week of six defenceless Bakonzo by terrorists raiding from the very uplands by which Isaya and I descended.

The Bakonzo claim that once upon a time they smelted their own copper from the mountains' ore. Maybe they extracted it at Kilembe, where the English came to mine it open-cast from the 1940s to the '70s. Nearly half a century ago the Bakonzo presented me with a pair of their ancient copper beads, which they said proved their forgotten mining and smelting culture since no other east African people has such beads, and these beads are not Arab. Indeed I know them as ardent smithies. Yet they would never have mined in *galleries*.

Nor are the rivers of Ruwenzori of a breadth and languor for barges. Only the Semliki river, snaking northwards from Lake Edward and into the Ituri forest for some 250 miles of river-route below the steep western heave of the massif, to lose itself in Lake Albert two day's trek beyond the northernmost foothills and one thousand feet lower than its effluence – only that broad, urgent, hidden stream might carry a barge. There is little human presence besides Bambuti pygmies within ready reach of the Semliki's banks – flitting figures, hunters and gatherers, borrowing much of the Mba and something of the Konzo lingo but seldom the blood and not the boats. I know that forest: jungle is my old, old ground – and I have just a little familiarity with its Bambuti. Meanwhile, the only Konzo boats I know of are dugouts such as they have made immemorially to fish from and spear hippo in Lake Edward and the Semliki headwaters. I own such a complex hippo spear, with its metal head designed to separate from its wooden shaft and fibrous float as the stricken beast dives. I have partaken of their hippo meat, right there in their southern foothills, with Idi Amin, when he was a mere deputy Company Commander. I was thirty-three then, called back to mediate between Uganda's newly independent government and Rwenzururu's secessionist kingdom I had inadvertently inspired, and which Captain Idi Amin Dada and his British senior officers and their troops had been assigned to suppress.

Now I am, I suppose, an old man, in my seventieth year. I have recently returned from Ruwenzori, where once again I was in the business of assisting in restoring the long peace to the land, on this occasion in the company of the heir to the dynasty of tribal kingship which, likewise, I had inadvertently played a part in initiating among the Bakonzo. The Omusinga (*King*) Charles Wesley Mumbere, Irema Ngoma (*Keeper of the Drum*), had suddenly been recalled to Kampala, conjured back out of fourteen years of anxious self-exile in Washington DC, fourteen years of struggling for a living as a hospital menial. It was a gamble by the Ugandan President, Museveni, that this Charles, in his personifying the secret *embitha* of his people, might secure an end to the latest and most dreadfully vicious of the wars that have beset these mountains, my Ruwenzori, in the memory of men.

Part of what I shall tell is how it has all turned out, even though at the actual moment I write this sentence, I do not yet know.

When our black Charles Wesley, King-over-the-water, received his summons from Kampala through a perverse twist of regional history, he and I had been in touch as normal: he in Washington, I in London. There had been little warning. On the telephone I said, 'If you felt you would like me to be at your side, Charles, I would do my best to make that possible.' 'That is verra kind,' he responded in his characteristic high drawl of tender surprise. He had not leapt at the half-offer. Charles is not a leaper. Two days later a fax arrived from Washington in the familiar rounded hand and regal style: 'From Omusinga Charles Wesley Irema Ngoma. Dear Tom, Since you have referred to the chance of being able to accompany me on my return to Uganda and my people, I cordially invite you on this visit. The details of my flight to Kampala will be faxed to you as soon as they are confirmed. Yours, Charles.'

I rang back to assent. I quipped, if quip it was, 'If they want to get you, they'll have to get me too.' We knew that there were enemies at home in Uganda, in the mountains, those of habitual ruthlessness; and below the mountains too, those accustomed to power. And that there were friends also, of course, in greater numbers: we could not yet know how many, Africa so volatile. Neither of us knew what awaited.

Within two weeks we were to be back in the foothills, in the tumult of it all – the welcoming ecstasy, throngs so vast, drumming and dancing and rippling endara-xylophone; cabals, sortilege, menace and machinations; wickedness and triumph; the prowling and pouncing guerillas. All that was in the teeming lowlands. Up there behind lay highland farms and ridge-top villages, abandoned in fear of the terror which, higher still, lurked in caves and forest camps; all this habitable territory known intimately to the Bakonzo and some of it known also to me – and to precious few others, unless they be military men on fleeting patrol. In and above was that further Ruwenzori, not inhabited since not habitable, a lost world, being too cold, precipitous, densely overgrown, storm-blown, or else ice-bound. The greater part of this other Ruwenzori is to this day untrodden by men; and if any man is there, he cannot be other than fugitive, explorer, or both.

ii

H M Stanley

Between that April 20 and May 24 of 1888, being the first two recorded sightings by Western eyes of the glaciered summits of Ruwenzori, H M Stanley had met a slight, myopic Jewish Bavarian convert to Islam. Stanley had journeyed in dreadful hardship across what he called 'darkest Africa' to rescue him.

Emin Pasha was an employee of the Khedive of Egypt, a country which since 1882 had been under overall British governance. Yet already from the 1870s, the titular ruler of Egypt had depended on a few remarkable Europeans to supervise the country's vast southern hinterland of the Sudan and to free it of the slave trade, as the great powers of Christian Europe eccentrically required. One such proconsul, General Charles Gordon, was murdered in Khartoum, and his garrison massacred, in 1885, by the God-crazed Sunni Mahdists, who seized control of the entire Sudan north of the Nile marshland known as the Sudd. The undefined 'Sudanese' territory to the south was at that time administered under the hand of Eduard Schnitzer, *aka* Emin Pasha, and his Egyptian and Sudanese janissaries, still loyal to the Khedive and trained by the crude, tried disciplines of the British army. Emin Pasha had thus become marooned in an empire of his own, incorporating a territory comprising (on a map of today) all of Southern Sudan, much of northern Uganda, and swathes of the Central African Republic and north-eastern Congo. This was Equatoria: a mythic, savage, unclassifiable demesne. It straddled the Nile's headwaters.

To the north, all contact was severed with Egypt by the power and presence of the ferocious Mahdists. To the south and east, contact with the British east African base on Zanzibar island had been severed north of Victoria Nyanza by the murder on the orders of the Kabaka of Buganda of Bishop Hannington and his newly converted Baganda Anglicans, and by the famed belligerence of the Masai tribe between the great lakes and the coast. For some three years almost nothing had been heard of Emin Pasha except that he was still master of his territory, a sort of latter day Prester John, albeit no Presbyter.

The indomitable Stanley, 'breaker of rocks' as Swahili-speakers

knew him, born out of wedlock, raised in a workhouse, one-time newspaperman, rooter-out of Livingstone and now, at 52, veteran of the penetrators of Africa's illimitable darkness, accepted the sponsorship of King Leopold of the Belgians and the Imperial British East African Company to attempt the relief of Emin Pasha by an astonishing route, namely from the west, by the Congo river, from its mouth on the Atlantic ocean. Eight years previously Stanley himself had explored the river's course from the reverse direction – downstream, east to west – threading together the territories he passed through with so-called 'treaties' with letterless chieftains such as to embolden him to 'offer' the entire abstraction of threaded darkness he named *Congo* to the metropolitan power of his choice. In London, the grandees had kept this formidable oick, this chippy Welsh-American, this abandoned work-house bastard and imperial visionary, hanging about. So he had crossed the water to a lately-conjured little nation state without a colony or explorer to its name, and offered his gift, half the size of the continent of Europe, to Belgium. King Leopold accepted it as his personal property.

And now, in 1888, Leopold was only too pleased to have his new estate further penetrated and explored, whatever the pretext. So

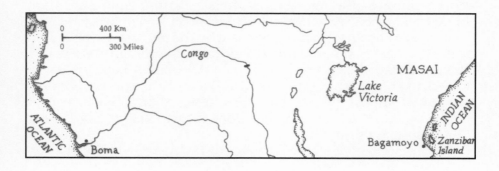

money was found for the egregious Stanley to recruit the bulk of his expeditionary force of several hundred in Zanzibar, and to sail with them half way round the African continent by way of the Cape to the Congo's estuary. He depended on the most powerful of the Omani ex-slavers of Zanzibar to recruit his local porters. The style and methods of Tippu Tib and his Zanzibaris were to characterize the administration of Leopold's private tropical empire, which he himself never got around to visiting. The Congo Free State became infamous for the brutality of its tyranny.

As for the Congo river, to which Stanley had so impressively returned, the pace of the river (as he knew) for the first 350 miles from its mouth left him no choice but to porter his weapons, ammo, and stores. At that point occurs a swelling in the belly of the mighty snake, above which it is free of rapids for 1,100 miles. From the time of his earlier expedition that spreading out of the river's course had been known as Stanley Pool. I have myself been acquainted with it on and off for nearly half a century, and with its natives, in turmoil or sullen acceptance of life's mess. From this eponymous Pool, in 1888, Stanley proceeded upstream in no less than four commandeered steamers, one called *Peace*, another re-named the *Stanley*, with barges in tow. He carried a single Maxim gun, latest invention of Europe's manufacturers of invincibility, with its unprecedented rapid-fire bullets on a belt. Branching off

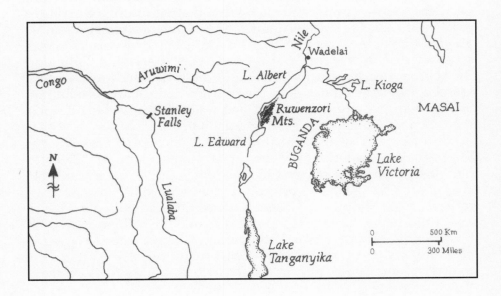

11

into a westward flowing Congo tributary, where the great river's upstream course loops south, he left 133 of his expedition at the foot of that tributary's first rapids. This was the site at which a 'rear column' of 270 more men, plus the bulk of the stores and ammunition destined for Emin Pasha, were to be consolidated after being ferried up the Congo mainstream while Stanley, always up against deadline, pushed on with 260 men. Ahead of him were a further three hundred and fifty miles of struggle by canoe and jungle paths until at last he could emerge into the savannah country west of Lake Albert: the southerly perimeter of Equatoria.

At the lake at last, on April 24 1888, far from his 'rescuing' Emin Pasha Schnitzer, it was the Pasha himself who sent his well-appointed 'smoke boat' – his steamer, the *Khedive* – the length of the vast water, the size of Wales, to fetch Stanley north for restoration amid the good order and relative ease of his southern Equatoria headquarters at Wadelai, on the Albert Nile, flowing from the lake. At this point Stanley was some two hundred miles north of Ruwenzori.

His assignment was, at all costs, to escort Emin Pasha out of a predicament which, in the long term, was deemed by the powers of Europe to be untenable. He saw no choice but personally to trek back to gather up that substantial remainder of the expeditionary force he had left at the riverside base below the first rapids of the Congo's tributary (the Aruwimi) by which he had come, together with the 'rear column' and the stores that should by then have reached the base from the Atlantic. So trek he did. Virtual disaster greeted him at the riverside base. Of the 133 men he had left there, sixty were dead or dying, mostly of fever or starvation. Dragging the remnant eastwards by the jungle route he had already twice crossed, plus the survivors of the pitifully reduced 'rear column', proved a nightmare. His hair turned white. Such was his despair that at one point he was carrying poison to destroy himself with.

As for Emin Pasha, by the time Stanley once more broke free of the privations and gloom of the forest route in January 1889 and had pushed on the remaining 150 miles to Lake Albert, all had also changed. The Pasha's prized, white-uniformed troops had mutinied, the Mahdi's dervishes had attacked from the north, and his authority in Equatoria was at an end. Even then, it was all Stanley could do to persuade the Sudan-struck doctor to agree to be conducted out to the east coast with the remnant of his followers; and as the caravan set out by the only route by which it might avoid Muslim territory to the north and east, namely southwards, the two men were scarcely on speaking terms . Once they were far enough southwards, they could swing eastwards below Lake Victoria, giving a wide berth both to Buganda and, with luck, the warrior Masai. Thus the first stretch of this journey took Stanley beneath the western flank of Ruwenzori. The Bakonzo and their mountains were to encounter their first ever white men.

Let us follow the motley of rescuer and rescued moving upriver along the forested valley of the Semliki river. The mountains reared to their left. Gravely weakened by dysentery and managing only two or three hours' march a day, Stanley kept up his assiduous geographic note-taking and measurements and probing of the unknown. One of his surviving lieutenants on this testing expedition, W G Stairs, had handled his driving, driven master with a nicely-judged combination of forbearance and respect. It was young Stairs whom Stanley sent on an excursion into the area of the central peaks of the entirely unknown massif heaving into the clouds.

Stairs set out from their camp on the eastern bank of the Semliki by a north-western ascent. He took with him a selection of the expedition's fittest Zanzibaris – forty of them; and no others. He did not consider attempting to consult, let alone to engage the services of, any Bakonzo of the higher settlements. Of them he recorded only that the tribesmen tried to warn the party against further ascent by shouts and the blowing of horns. There is no evidence that Stairs paused to consider why the tribesmen should make such a warning – that to penetrate this territory, for example, might in some way be an act of sacrilege, inviting retribution.

Stairs led on upwards through the belt of bamboos, which rings the entire massif at about 9000 feet, and on into the broad contours of giant heathers fifty feet in height, trailing their bearded lichen. Among those tree-heathers the going gets tougher. One must sometimes hack one's way, and at one's feet the heather roots are slimy and treacherous under their mosses, concealing a hollow region of dark morass. Making fire in such damp is not easy. Two of Stairs's men were inadequately clad.

He reaches 10,677 feet. Ahead, three deep ravines – the first that of the Bakoka torrent, in our subsequent judgment – intervene between the exploratory party and twin peaks on which snow lay. These are surely the summits of what we have since come to name

Kraepelin Peak and Mount Emin, the most northwesterly of the six clusters of glaciered tops that comprise Ruwenzori's highlands. It is an evilly hostile place. Stairs turns and swiftly descends, pursued by cold and swirling mist, by the furious grandchild of Nzururu. He will have got no view of the highest cluster, six miles or so to the south, crowned by Margherita at 16,763 feet. However, within two decades Stairs shall have a peak named after him, in the southernmost cluster, at 15,000 feet. And he has got back down with no less than 38 species of highland Ruwenzori plant for the myopic ex-emperor of Equatoria , botanist extraordinary, to break his sulk and attempt their identification.

As for Henry Stanley, his unaccustomed frailty notwithstanding, he is fascinated by Ruwenzori. Its peoples impress him. He remarks the richness of their soil and the enterprise and variety of their produce. He reports banana (plantain) groves clothing the slopes, and tobacco, maize, beans, 'colocassia' (a variety of taro), and yams. (Did he chance upon the fact that highland Ruwenzori yams induce a tickle in the throat that lowland yams never do?) He notes: 'In no part of Africa may be seen such an abundance of food.' Such is true to this day, for Ruwenzori soil still is fecund and the farming skilled, supporting the most productive peasant farms in central Africa when the mountains are at peace.

On June 5 1889, the day before Stairs left for the interior highlands, Stanley had met his first Bakonzo. 'At the first village the advance guard encountered men who unhesitatingly resented their intrusion, and began hostilities... So we pressed armed bands' – the rifle being the instant and infallible answer to the spear – 'up to the mountains, and the skirmishing was brisk.' There was no call for the Maxim gun, which was anyway rusty. Shortly, a Mukonzo elder emerged to sue for peace. 'He came in and said he had come to throw himself at the feet to be slave or saved. The trumpeters sounded to cease firing... This chief and his friends were the first representatives of the Ukonjo [Bakonzo] we had seen, and the devoted mission of the chief instantly won our sympathy and admiration.' The next day, Stanley notes, 'Ruwenzori, called already Bugombowa, Avrika and Viruka, by the forest tribes [i.e. pygmies], became now known as Ruwenzu-ru-ru.'

So it was, to the Bakonzo, and is. *Rwenzururu*. Their word, their place. Their snows. Their deity.

Stanley was a broad-brush man of anthropology, which could not be said to exist as any sort of science in 1889. (Malinowski was a five-year-old in Warsaw.) He vaguely supposed that those dwelling where the climate was cold would be paler-skinned than those bred in the hot plains or the steamy jungle. He was surprised to find the Bakonzo even darker than the lowlanders (they are not: their skin pigment is indistinguishable from any other Bantu peoples'). The Bakonzo, he recorded, 'are round-headed, broad faced, and of medium size. They affect circlets manufactured of calamus fibre, very slender, and covering the ankles by hundreds. The chiefs are also distinguished by heavy copper or brass wristlets. The women's neck decorations consist of heavy iron rings coiled spirally at the ends.'

When I arrived among them two and a half generations later I would wonder how the rings were got round the slender necks in the first place: the answer was that they were slipped over head when the women were mere children. As for the appearance of the Bakonzo, I would have had more to say: specifically that they are, on average, stocky, notably sturdy, and significantly shorter than the plainland tribes on the east side of the mountains – Banyankole, Banyoro, Batoro – who are tall and elegant, especially among the lordly castes. Peruse for a moment the tribal map on page 24. Each of those tribes has in its time made vassals of the Bakonzo, the squat little fellows in the mountains, in their monkey-skins and bark-cloth, putting up with the cold heights of their strange place, difficult of access and secret of route. I am by way of telling, therefore, of a vassalage which has been physiognomic and geographic no less, perhaps, than political and demographic – all those three plainland tribes possessing greater stature, greater numbers and ranging, open-sided territory.

The dominance of the Banyankole was a past history. But the rampaging power of the Banyoro to the east of Ruwenzori, under their king Kabalega, was evident enough to Stanley, once he rounded the southern perimeter of the mountains. From the Arabs of the coast and Zanzibar, Kabalega had got himself firearms, originally to do the Arabs' bidding as to the gathering of slaves and ivory. Reputedly he had 1,500 pieces – rifles, double-barrelled shotguns, and carbines: Henry-Martinis, Sniders, Jocelyn and Starrs, Sharps. The Bakonzo to the north of the mountains, Stanley had heard, had been robbed by Kabalega of 'vast herds of cattle'. Oh, this was an old story, the vassalage of the Bakonzo.

To the east of the mountains, the heartland of Banyoro power, Stanley's route took in only the flatlands of the extreme south-east, and the salt industry at Katwe , where the Bakonzo's neighbours the Basongora predominate – and it was Kabelega's depredations upon *them* that Stanley reports. Yet I can vouch that Kabalega brought fear and servitude to any lowland Bakonzo on the east of the mountains, for in 1954 on a ridge in Bunyangabo I was brought a bent, grey Mukonzo crone with vivid stained Nyoro weals cut in a skilful curve from her ears across her cheeks. As a girl she had been captured and enslaved by Kabalega's musketeers.

As for the Batoro and the Bakonzo, by that date, a measure of ascendancy on the part of the Batoro had been acknowledged by the Bakonzo – or if not of Batoro in the generality at least of the aristocracy that defined them. The 'Batoro' were something new. They had come into being a mere half century before Stanley clipped their territory at Katwe on Lake George by the defection of Kaboyo, a son of the nineteenth Bito-Mukama of the Banyoro, whose heartland lay far to the east. With his rustled herds of Bunyoro cattle, the prince Kaboyo established his breakaway realm centred upon the hillock of Kabarole, close to where Lugard would subsequently site his jeriba at Fort Portal. He proceeded to accept the allegiance, first of the small Basongora community of cattle herders in the plains beneath the south-eastern slopes of the mountains; next, of the Baamba, below the northern and northwestern foothills. But tribute was also received at Kabarole from Bakonzo from the northern slopes of Ruwenzori, and I dare to presume that in return for such allegiance, not at first willing, lowland Bakonzo of distinction received their gifts of Batoro cattle. For no Bantu people were by tradition herders of cattle.

In the next chapter I shall view this in the broader context of evolving demography in interlacustrine Africa. For without that broader context, the chaos of modern times is uninterpretable. The Bakonzo's *irksome* vassalage by the Batoro lay in the colonial future, and in the tale of this book was to lead us into our long drama.

Now in the 1880s the surging ambitions of King Kabalega had brought together the Batoro and Basongora in common defensive cause. A month before Stanley arrived at the ancient salt works at Katwe, in June 1889, he had heard the name of a 'king' of the northern Bakonzo, Ruhandika...that self-same same 'king' whose son, in 1954, put me together with his son-in-law, Isaya Mukirane,

16

father of Omusinga ('king') Charles Wesley.
Here is the line of descent :

Chief Ruhandika
|
Semwiri Bukombi 'Mulwahali'
|
Christine = Isaya Mukirane, Omusinga (king)
|
Omusinga Charles Wesley, Irema Ngoma (Keeper of the Drums)

In reality, this Ruhandika was chief of the branch of the substantial Swagha clan occupying the northern reaches of the mountains, and who, in the face of the Banyoro threat, had emerged to champion the generality of northern Bakonzo.

What Stanley did not know was that Ruhandika had by then already given shelter in his mountains to the infant heir to the kingship of the devastated Batoro. That devastation had taken place only a year or two previously, on the other side of the mountains from where Stanley was then camped. Toro's omukamaship had fallen vacant, and rival sons of the late Omukama Nyaïka were struggling over the succession. In subduing his quarelling Toro kinsmen, Kabalega had systematically exterminated the entire male line of Toro royalty except for the tiny child Kasagama, whose mother had spirited him away to the mountains. The strong shoulders of Ruhandika had personally carried the infant Toro prince to his place of refuge. Kabalega was emperor of the plains; but he did not rule the mountains. He despatched envoys up by the mountain paths – hazardous paths – up past that belt of savannah where none chose to live because it had become a No Man's Land: a region whose evacuation has recurred repeatedly in the Konzo story, a shield of emptiness.

The envoys found their northern mountain chieftain. *Was Ruhandika, King of the Bakonzo,* they required to know, *willing to be ruled by the mighty Kabalega, Omukama of the Banyoro, and live under his protection?* Ruhandika replied that he could make no such concession, because the royal Toro child Kasagama had fled to him in trust and still survived under his, Ruhandika's, pledged guardianship.

So Kabalega summoned Ruhandika out of his mountains and

down to Bulyambosi. As an alternative to war, Ruhandika consented to the summons, descending with a small entourage in their monkey-fur skins and bark-cloth cloaks. The same invitation as before was put to him: *will you not, for the sake of peace for your people, accept my authority and my protection*? The Konzo leader repeated that he would not. Kabalega looked at him out of his scarred face and bade him rest for a few days in his palace. To honour the Bunyoro warrior king, so he did.

Ruhandika was a big man for a Konzo, bold and bearded, not accustomed to fear. But now he got word from a friend, Katamara, a Mutoro soldier, that Kabalega intended to have him secretly done away with. That next night Ruhandika and his Konzo companions slipped out of Kabalega's palissaded encampment and made for the hills under cover of darkness. Then, still before dawn, Katamara raised the alarm in the Banyoro camp. Kabalega roared for his captains. A force of his swiftest warriors was assembled before sun-up to set off in pursuit of the Konzo recalcitrant by the steep and dangerous paths. Ruhandika had taken the *high* route over the northern backbone of the mountains. Yet of course his pursuers could track him. He heard their sounds as they mounted the trail below, and then the cries as stragglers of his own party were overtaken and slaughtered. Already he had reached that height of nine thousand feet where the forest trees were hung with bearded lichen and the first bamboos grew. He traversed the spine of the range, and began the descent into his own heartland by the high Kyogho valley which feeds the stream named the Humia: in a hut beside that very stream this account of it all was to be retailed to me by Ruhandika's son Samwiri well over half a century later as if it had occurred the previous week.

Ruhandika reached his own spur and compound and sounded the drum. On the instant the whole mountainside knew: this was war. His men raced together out of their huts on spur after spur. Meanwhile, Kabalega's pursuing soldiery came down from the high pass through the forest towards the multiplying sound of drums.

The drums abruptly ceased, and in utmost silence Ruhandika deployed his spearmen in the tall grasses and vegetation beside the track along the precipitous flank of the Kyogho valley. Kabalega's men broke from the cover of the high forest at a run. The Konzo spearmen crouched with their square, black, wicker shields. Ruhandika gave a whoop and the spearmen flung themselves on the enemy. Most of Kabalega's force were killed on the path, a few driven over the sheer edge into the ravine itself, others ran for their lives up by the way they had come, into the forest where the bearded lichen blew. Kyakimwa, mother of Ruhandika, made a spell and through the intervention of Kitasamba a hailstorm broke on the heights, chilling most of that remnant to death.

Such defiance of the authority of Kabalega was unprecedented. Meanwhile the infant Batoro prince Kasagama and his mother were secured in the fastness of Ruhandika's territory, where the Bakonzo chieftain hid him in the cave Ekaleyaleya, three ridges to the south of his headquarters. The Konzo waited for the inevitable retribution. It was not long in coming. Kabalega reassembled his askaris for the thrust into the mountains. He placed in command the general Kakabwa. The invading force moved into the northern foothills, crossing to the western side of the range and reaching a bluff above the settlement of Bukundu. It was empty of people. From there they followed Bakonzo tracks to the spur village of Ebupomboli, which was also evacuated. From their concealment across the gulley, Ruhandika and his spearmen watched them, resolved to avoid open battle with so great an army mustered in war-paint.

That night Ruhandika crossed the forested gully and stole up on the sleeping soldiers. Moonrise was his chosen moment. The Bakonzo fell on their victims. The bewildered Banyoro scattered in disorder, many fleeing down the steep flank of Ebupomboli ridge into the Tokwa valley. The Konzo on the spur rolled boulders down on the invaders, breaking their painted limbs.

Thereafter, doubtless to avoid a third attempt to recapture the infant prince, Kasagama was smuggled to Ankole, south of Banyoro territory, whence he was in due course taken in by Mwanga, the wayward Kabaka of the Baganda, in Kampala. By this slender thread the Bakonzo had thus preserved the royal line of the Batoro, and punctured Kabalega's reputation of intertribal invincibility.

Of all this heroic saga in the mountains neither Stanley nor Emin had any inkling, passing a year later beneath Ruwenzori in 1889. Indeed no written record of it was made for another sixty-five years, when as I have said I noted it down from the account given me by Ruhandika's son, Samwiri, as translated by Samwiri's son-in-law, Isaya Mukirane. That first record was made by lamplight in a hut above the Humia on a spur or two away from Ebupomboli itself. What you have just read is the first printed record.

When H M Stanley arrived at Katwe, on the shore of Lake Edward just below Ruwenzori to the south-east, in July 1889, Kabalega himself, it seems, had returned to his Nyoro heartland at Hoima. Katwe's salt industry did trade with those from as far distant as Lake Albert to the north and Rwanda to the south – that is, a span of some two hundred miles. It was a newly-acquired possession of economic significance for Kabalega. But the sheer reputation of the white man's fire power had persuaded the Banyoro forces, under Kabalega's henchman Rutaro, to withdraw from the place, at least for the time being. The Basongora and Bakonzo who worked the deposits for barter-trade greeted Stanley and his cortège with exultation, as liberators. Stanley had had with him for several days a Mukonzo chief, whom he calls Bevwa, manifestly forging a strong respect for the man, which was reciprocated. With this Bevwa (whose appellation I can approximate to no Konzo name I've encountered – though there is an Mbiwa) were 150 Bakonzo, and some Basongora. Now the very core of the saltworking community evidently occupied the three islands of that bay of Lake Edward just west of where the channel enters from Edward's northern annexe, Lake George, and locatable in the sketch-map on page 115. The Banyoro had omitted to subdue these islands.

As Stanley tells it, certain of these islanders now approached the village of Katwe cautiously by canoe, despatched by their chief Kakuri [whom Bakonzo knew as Kakuli] to find out what manner of white-led force this was that so alarmed the Banyoro as to scatter them by their mere approach. The canoemen were told, but at once sought further proof of these strangers' authority. 'Burn the town of Katwe,' they commanded, 'so that there shall be nowhere for the Banyoro invaders to re-establish themselves at our lakeside.' Stanley duly fired the hutments on or by the shore – to the loud cheers of the islanders in their boats.

'I believe you,' their spokesman called out, 'to be of the Wanyavingi, now. Sleep in peace, and tomorrow Kakuri shall come with gifts to give you welcome.'

Stanley records how Bevwa, chief of his Bakonzo, then 'stood on a canoe which was in the lake and asked, "Ah, you children of Kakuri, the great chief of the sea, do you remember how Kwaru-Kwanzi came to defend the land from Wara-Sura [i.e. Abali-Sura – Banyoro – literally 'stranger-raiders'] robbers? Lo! Kwaru-Kwanzi, a true son of the Wa-nyavingi, is here again. Rejoice, my friends, Rutaro and his thieves have fled, and all the land will rise as one

20

man to follow in pursuit of them."'

This speech evoked applause and drumming from the islanders in their boats, and renewed assurance from the leading islander present that the chief Kakuri would meet Stanley with gifts of gratitude on the morrow. The islanders' six Banyoro captives – snatched in the scamper of retreat on Stanley's approach – were joyfully done to death that very evening.

But who were these 'Wa-nyavingi'? Bevwa looked at Stanley hard. 'They are tall, big men with long noses and a pale colour who came, I have heard from the old men, from somewhere beyond Ruwenzori. You came from that direction. Therefore, you must be of the Wa-nyavingi...'

I know Nyavingi – the 'g' is soft – to be the name of a female deity so subtle and secret to the Bakonzo that it is uttered only with the severest caution. Charles's father Isaya Mukirane, later to become the first Omusinga of Rwenzururu, had vouchsafed it to me, as a mark of privileged trust, towards the end of our long tramp through the mountains in 1954; and approaching the dire climax of the novel seeded by that tramp, *The Brothers M*, my principal African character, a stranger to the mountains, is himself vouchsafed the name in utmost confidentiality by the book's main Mukonzo character Kigoma whom I built out of the person of Isaya Mukirane. Nyavinji is a will-o'-the-wisp, everywhere and nowhere, a terrific sorceress for good or ill. Once she was human, now not quite, yet listening in across the fire, beyond the bark-cloth arras. It was years after all of that novel was written that I came across the same name, mysterious for other reasons, in Stanley's account of his interchange with the Mukonzo chief, Bevwa. Before this book is done I shall have attempted to win clarity as to any connection between tall, pale men and this Nyavingi (or Nyavenji, in my own original transcription, or Nyabingi as favoured by Konzo writers today) by consulting such a Konzo scholar of his own culture as Syahuka Muhindo.

The lake-island chief of the salt industry, Kakuri, was 'a physically fine man', as it emerged the following day when gifts were exchanged with Stanley. He appears to have been not a Musongora but a Mukonzo in blood and language if not in common acceptance (at that time) of the tribal name of *Konzo* . He was of that lacustrine wing of our people, masters of fishing and hippo-hunting on Edward and George, and saltmen... albeit under the shadow of their kinsmen's mountains. Shadows bind, cloud

21

presences bind.

Stanley paid tribute to Bevwa and his tribal retinue. As his column proceeded east, and out of Busongora and the long awareness of our mountains on June 25th, 1889, he recorded this note: 'Our Wakonju (Bakonzo) and Wasongora friends begged permission to return. Each chief and elder received our gifts, and departed to our regret. Bevwa and his Wakonju were now eighty-five miles distant from their homes, and their good nature, and their willingness and unobtrusiveness had quite won our hearts.'

So was my heart to be quite won two and a half generations later, in the early '50s of the century now just passed. Not a lot had changed for the Bakonzo by that time of my arrival, for there was not so much as a road into the mountains, or any school in the mountains except at the southern perimeter where the missionaries had entered at Katwe in customary unChristian rivalry, and put the boys into trousers and made breasts a source of pudency. Elsewhere it was still bark cloth and monkey-skins for warmth; and still the curse of a taller Nilotic-led part-pastoral tribe on the plains lording it – no longer the Banyoro, but the Batoro. We shall come to that...as we shall also come, most recently, to the militant recrudescence of the star and sickle, Islam ascendent, in our region.

As for the mountains he left behind him and never to have penetrated himself, of all the wonders of his explorations and all his geographic reportage nothing else roused the Breaker of Rocks to such lyricism. 'On the morning of this day [May 9, 1889], Ruwenzori came out from its mantle of clouds and vapours, and showed its groups of peaks and spiny ridges resplendent with shining white snow; the blue beyond was not that of the ocean – a purified and spotless translucence. Far to the west, like huge double epaulettes, rose the twin peaks... and from the sunk ridge below the easternmost rose sharply the dominating and unsurpassed heights of Ruwenzori proper, a congregation of hoary heads, brilliant in white raiment; and away to the east extended a roughened ridge, like a great vertebra – peak and saddle, isolated mount and hollow, until it passed out of sight... The guides – for we had many now – pointed with the spears vaguely, and cried out "Ukonju".'

Mark him again, on June 12th: 'We had a magnificent view of Ruwenzori just before sunset one evening during our halt... A large field of snow, and snow-peaks beyond the foremost line, appeared in view. During the whole day our eyes had rested on a long line of dark and solemn spurs, their summits buried in leaden mist, but soon after 5 p.m. the upper extremities of those spurs loomed up one after another, and a great line of mountain shoulders stood out; then peak after peak struggled from behind night-black clouds into sight, until at last the snowy range, immense and beautiful, a perfect picture of beautiful and majestic desolateness, drew all eyes and riveted attention, while every face seemed awed...

'The superb Rain-Creator or Cloud-King, as the Wakonju fondly termed their mist-shrouded mountains [did they really?], fill the gazer with a feeling as though a glimpse of celestial splendour was obtained... The rapt faces of whites and blacks set fixed and uplifted in speechless wonder towards that upper region of cold brightness and perfect peace, so high above mortal reach, so holily tranquil and restful, of such immaculate and stainless purity, that thought and desire of expression were altogether too deep for utterance.

'What stranger contrast could there be than our own nether world of torrid temperature... with its savagery and war-alarms and deep stains of blood-red sin, to that lofty mountain king, clad in its pure white raiment of snow, surrounded by myriads of dark mountains, low as bending worshippers before the throne of a monarch on whose cold white face were inscribed "Infinity and Everlasting!" These moments of supreme feeling are memorable for the utter abstraction of the mind from all that is sordid and ignoble, and its utter absorption in the presence of unreachable loftiness, indescribable majesty, and constraining it not only to reverentially admire, but to adore in silence, the image of the Eternal. Never can a man be so fit for Heaven as during such moments, for however scornful and insolent he may have been at other times, he now has become as a little child, filled with wonder and reverence before what he has conceived to be sublime and Divine.'

Soledad en Dios in those very heights. What will Ruwenzori not do? The Breaker of Rocks as a little child, on his knees before his Maker, spilling his confessions. I, too, can wax Wordsworthian. But I know Ruwenzori from closer to, from – let us say – within, knowing its barbarity, its violence and caprice; I have set death up there in fiction, and seen it there in fact; and from among its Bakonzo, in their storms and griefs, their boon and their joy, how their mountains have inspired them and riven them. As shall be told.

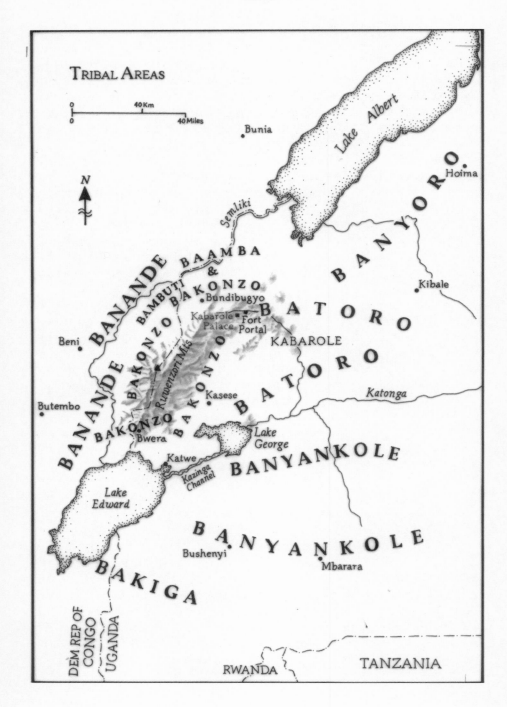

TRIBAL AREAS

0   40 Km
0   40 Miles

N

Lake Albert

Bunia

Hoima

BANYORO

Semliki

BANANDE

BAAMBA
&
BAKONZO

BAMBUTI

Bundibugyo

BATORO

Kibale

Beni

BAKONZO

Kabarole
Palace

Fort
Portal

KABAROLE

Ruwenzori Mts

BATORO

Butembo

BAKONZO

Kasese

Katonga

BAKONZO

Bwera

Lake
George

Katwe

Kazinga
Channel

BANYANKOLE

Lake
Edward

B A N Y A N K O L E

BAKIGA

Bushenyi

Mbarara

DEM REP OF
CONGO
UGANDA

RWANDA

TANZANIA

iii

Celts and Picts

In the end, or the beginning, Uganda became the 'protectorate' of our reluctant Queen – the last Queen before the present – in June 1894. That was the month in which one of my grandfathers was preparing for his finals at Oxford, and the other was about to go up to Cambridge. This younger one died at 78 in the year Uganda was handed its independence in 1962. Thus we may say that the period of colonial authority lasted just about as long as an ordinary adult English lifespan: no more than that.

For years Fort Portal, Toro's only town, below Ruwenzori, was little more than a jeriba of the unexpected white intruders, one of a chain of six garrisons established by an urgent, acerbic Englishman curing himself of a broken heart. This was Frederick Lugard in 1891, when he was not the Queen's man but the young quasi-military employee of the all-but-bankrupt Imperial British East Africa Company, engaged on the pre-colonial scramble for that segment of the unknown continent. During the next decade the mountains and their highland peoples were lost and half forgotten in their mists and inaccessibility.

In the previous chapter I touched upon the broader demographic context of our private kingmaking saga. The arrival of us whites in Uganda, with our guns, our bibles, and soon enough our treaties, flags, courts of law and boundaries, suspended what had been a pervasive and invasive demographic change that had been under way in this part of Africa for centuries. It suspended it for as long as colonial power was in place, and not much longer. For it has today resumed. I speak here of the prevailing of the authority of certain groups of Nilotic or Hamitic gene and culture upon those of Bantu gene and culture.

The anthropologist of today's academia will furrow the brow over the terms 'Nilotic' and 'Hamitic'. He or she will insist that they correspond to no dependable linguisitic, physiognomic, social, cultural, or territorial category. He/she is correct. Yet it is a faddish sort of correctness, suggestive of those who have come so to scrutinise the brush strokes as no longer to see a picture. In our island two thousand years ago, what, please, infallibly distinguished Pict from Celt? Were they not both woaded, both subservient to the heavenly bodies through the divination of their stone circles? A newly colonizing Roman might sometimes be hard put to say in the presence of a Pictish-looking fellow speaking Celt, or a bevy of what seemed to be Celts engaged in sacrificial ritual at a winter solstice, which was which. But the Picts and Celts would have no problem. A Celt is one who in the presence of a Pict knew himself to be a Celt, and a Pict is one who in the presence of a Celt knew himself to be a Pict even if he did not talk about it. As we know, the Celts prevailed, and not in the first place by conquest.

At much the same time as the spread of the Celts was spelling the apparent disappearance of the Picts in the British isles, so also in the fertile land between and around the vast lakes of east-central Africa the agriculturalist Bantu migrating from western Africa's Atlantic littoral was spelling the disappearance of the hunting and gathering aborigines. Like the Picts, these aborigines were not wiped out in battle; but the will to hold to their old identity seeped away. In fragments of territory – usually forested and difficult – there were those who have to this day clung to the pristine identity, and as best they can to pristine ways: the Wandorobo of Kenya and Tanzania, the tragic Ik in the Uganda-Sudan borderland hills, and the Bambuva and Bambuti pygmies of the Congo's eastern jungle, right up to the perimeter of Ruwenzori. Where a people loses the will to be itself, it will not survive as a people. Some may disperse and then be lost by degrees in a new identity, others will stay and by degrees adapt to the ways and *mores* of the dominant culture, often persisting as a subservient caste within that new society and culture and gradually accepting assimilation into the superior caste as and when it may be made available to them through intermarriage or grants of status.

Thus it next was, during these more recent several centuries, that a people of a different kind, driving long-horned cattle, began to penetrate the settled, agricultural, Bantu communities of the Africa of the Great Lakes. These newcomers were Hamitic herdsmen – tall (as are all cattle folk) and paler than the host community; Noah's descendants, through his son Ham and Ham's son Cush, according to mythologies of the Semites (who were

26

themselves progeny of Ham's brother Shem). Their beasts were of Asian provenance. They were a long-faced folk, fabricants of iron, wearers of cloth, ritualisers of meat and milk, indicative of Ethiopia's Oromo (or Galla) people of today and linkable by evidence of craft and symbol to the ancient civilisation of Egypt; complex in organisation, yet nomadic. They came, seemingly, as grazers rather than conquerors; but their lofty confidence and a sweep of skills won them an undeniable awe and honour; and wherever in highland equatoria the tsetse spared their herds and they were minded to stay, the Bantu cultivators adhered to them, bringing their produce, tributes, sometimes persuading them into their own tribal communities as a caste of aristocrats. They are here today as *Hima*, carrying in their name the Semitic consonantal hint – the *Hay/Ha* and the *Mem/Mim* of Hebraic and Arabic alphabet; and persisting in caste or social strain and sometimes as ethnic units in that broad swathe of upland Africa amid the lakes. These people are always associated with the ownership and herding of cattle. There is evidence of the Nilotics, in their various tribes, learning their cattle skills and dietary practices of milk and blood from the Hima. It is reasonable for us to assume that these same sons of Ham brought the trick of iron to our part of Africa, by the Nile route, overlaying a stone culture with a few key tools wrought in complex furnaces built in regions where ferrous ore and enough trees for charcoal were jointly available. Such a region was the Rift which carried the equatorial Nile and its Semliki tributary juxtaposed with Ruwenzori.

Yet in recent centuries the more pervasive ascendancy from the north among the agricultural Bantu fell not to the Hamites but to the Nilotes. The Nilote differs from the Bantu not by his pallor but his blackness – not infrequently ink-black – and as a rule is tall (like the Hamite), handsome, narrow-nosed, moving with grace, and martial when so required. Nilotes seem to have spilled forth across the African map from that region south of the Nile *sudd* where Emin Pasha came briefly to preside. The authority of both (originally Hamitic) Hima and (Nilotic) Bito is sometimes distinguishable in the dominant social grades of various largely Bantu tribes of the region – including Baganda, Banyoro and Batoro – where Bito provide the ruling caste. Or else, amid inextricably mixed communities, those of Nilotic physique, bearing and tradition constitute the dominant ethnic presence – as the minority Tutsi among the Hutu villeins of Rwanda and

27

Burundi, producing a feudalism of the blood. Or else such Nilotics came to stand forth – proud, separate, and militantly dominant among their deferential Bantu neighbours as cattle-herding pastoralists like the Masai and the Luo of Kenya and Tanzania.

Upon this progressive assertion of instinctive Nilotic (and precursive Hamitic) dominance, the arrival of the Europeans at the end of the 19th century imposed a suspension. We British and the Germans (replaced soon enough – in 1919 – by us in Tanganyika, and by the Belgians in Rwanda and Burundi) built a dam in history and delayed the stream, more or less for the span of my maternal grandfather's adult life. The Masai caught the plague, were displaced from their grazing, and watched in sullen isolation the advancement of the Kikuyu and the Kamba under the white man's aegis. The Banyoro's Nilotic leadership was at length beaten in the field, thanks in no small degree to that single Maxim gun, oiled anew and sputtering efficient death, that H M Stanley had humped all the way across Africa from one ocean to the other . The Germans conceded the reality of Tutsi social and economic authority over their Hutu, while bludgeoning the entire native community into obedience. Half a century later, in 1961, the Germans' Belgian successors launched Ruanda-Urundi into independence, without the least preparation, on the basis of one-person-one-vote democracy. This reversed the instinctive social order at a stroke. The consequence has been serial massacre, by one group or the other of one group or the other, ever since. This sustaining tragedy will touch our story.

In colonial days the Nilotes, by and large on account of their aloofness, missed out on the literacy, the mission teaching, the administrative posts and the appropriate European lingo. But history has a way of overflowing dams. Once more the Nilotes are regaining ascendancy. East Africa's most capable and successful President of recent times, albeit designated *Hima* (by quirk of tribal nomenclature), is a Nilotic. He is an ethnic and *quondam* political brother of the Tutsis who prevail (and will continue to prevail) in both Rwanda and Burundi, and much of eastern Congo. I speak of Museveni of Uganda.

Those who would follow my tale deserve to be aware of these soft, significant but inexact distinctions: which are the Celts and which the Picts. For the Africans on African soil know. *They* know, and have known immemorially.

And sketching the demographic subcurrents that prevailed then

28

and prevail again now, a century on, I shall also point to a parallel religious resumption in our region. For whereas in the 1880s and '90s the Muslim Mahdists and dervishes, menacing and penetrating from the north the lands and tribes among whom Protestant and Catholic missionaries were scrapping for souls, were checked and repulsed by colonial troops, so today has fundamentalist Islam resumed its militancy, even in our very mountains, our Ruwenzori. Last week (as I write these particular words in early 1999) sixty-nine Bakonzo died from Muslim-provided AK47 bullets in the territory where Ruhandika once presided.

I tell you such things for a purpose. Why should you be denied the *setting*, in history, in geography? – that is, in time and space; or for that matter, outside time and space. Moreover, this is *my* account of the place I know, and of the people I know and love. I shall take you there by my own route.

What then, meanwhile, of the mountains, my Ruwenzori, brooding under cloud, brooding under rain, as H M Stanley at last reached Zanzibar in November 1889? For how long were those lowland Bakonzo to the east and south of the mountains, down to the salt lake at Katwe, to be free from the scourge of Kabalega of the Nilotic Banyoro and his general, Rutaro? Not long, for Kabalega's bush telegraph was always swift and sure. Yet help was at hand – help that was to contain an ominous penalty. It was young Fred Lugard of the Imperial British East Africa Company, with an army of Ganda and Sudanese, who broke the power of Kabalega and his Muslim supporters from the north. It was Lugard who brought back to Toro the child-chief Kasagama of the Batoro from Kampala, where he had found refuge after fleeing first into the Ruwenzoris under the protection of the Konzo chieftain Ruhandika, and then holing up in Ankole.

There in Kabarole-Fort Edward (soon to be renamed Fort Portal) Lugard installed Kasagama as King Daudi Kasagama Kyebambe VI of a generously delineated Toro, to be a block to any renewal of Banyoro expansion or irredentism; for the Batoro are the ethnic cousins of the Banyoro, and as we have noted, the royalty and aristocracy of both tribes are similarly drawn from Nilotic Bito and Hima stock. Lugard promised the young king, on the word of an Englishman, that the British would guarantee his authority. Into that Kingdom he threw the Ruwenzori mountains, no doubt

29

unthinkingly, on the hearsay that some sixty years previously the little people up in the hills had paid tribute in surplus crops to Kasagama's ancestor, the Nyoro prince Kaboyo. The royal boy grew up to inherit a 'confederacy' (in the parlance of the 1894 Agreement) under the flag of Toro. He bestowed on Ruhandika, who had saved his life and bloodied his enemy, the Lutoro title of Omulemonsozi, Master of the Mountains. He had a street in Fort Portal named after him: it is thus named to this day. He gave him a fine drum, and beside it Ruhandika drove his ceremonial spear into the ground. The drum was sounded on grand occasions, such as the coronation of Kasagama's son as King George Rukidi, in 1924. But when Ruhandika Omulemonsozi came to die, no figure of comparable standing in Konzo society emerged to take his place; and there was no office of paramountcy to fill.

For we should note that mountain societies do not readily make for the collective figurehead. Steep-sided valleys divide communities, centralized authority eludes them. Among the Konzo, each spur's community was familiar with the compounds further up or further down the same rib of land, or the communities occupying spurs on either side – for they would encounter one another collecting water at the streams which served as their common boundaries. To maintain familiarity with those dwelling five or six spurs away would entail much hard descending and ascending. A sense of *operative* unity among those living fifty or a hundred spurs distant was not easy to envisage. Ponder the Swiss, in their alpine valleys; search Kirghizia: Kings do not grow there. Nor are they called for unless and until there is a communal threat, or a grievous collective handicap. It is a matter of communication. In Ruwenzori a federation of a dozen or so spurs – not more – made for a clan elder. Rarely, a few clan elders decided for communal protection upon a leader among them, and a small 'King' briefly emerged: such was Ruhandika, grandfather-in-law of my companion Isaya, first Irema Ngoma and Omusinga, pivot-figure of this history.

For the Bakonzo, what Lugard did in Toro in 1891 was to replace the capricious, bellicose overlordship of the distantly-headquartered Banyoro, which they could escape amid their complex highlands, with the less violent but more pervasive, disdainful and proximate suzerainty of the Batoro. The Bakonzo might be prepared to accept the Mukama himself, I was to learn later, but not the courtiers, not the nobs and placemen who usurped the official, colonially-administered chieftainships in the Bakonzo community.

Three years later, 1894, Lugard's free-lance commercial (and Protestant) satrapy north and west of the greatest of the lakes, from which he had seen off the Germans, the Mahdists and the French, fell into the old Queen's lap as the British 'protectorate' of Uganda. The creation of the Toro kingdom in the remote west was confirmed in the agreements of 1894 and 1900. They tied in that two-thirds of Ruwenzori that lay in British Uganda under the rule of the Batoro's King Kasagama – addressed as 'Mukama', 'Lion', 'Sun', 'Moon', 'Father of Orphans', 'Dispeller of Darkness' – on his thatched hilltop palace at Kabarole. At that same site I paid my visit to his son, King George, half a century later, in 1954. In his airy mesh-windowed reception room, a half-circular chamber and still thatched, his Ministers came and went on their knees, backing thus towards the door. A signed photograph of his recently departed namesake, of the line of Windsor, George VI, stood in a frame. George of Toro and I discussed cricket. He was a large, expansive man, strong in the neck and shaven-headed, rich in progeny and also in household servants, paid in kind. One of his daughters was to be chosen by Idi Amin twenty years later as that dictator's Minister of Foreign Affairs, at which she – the fine-boned, long-legged Elizabeth – was adroit.

King George's eyes popped at my intention to go into the mountains to live with the Bakonzo. In his eighteen years of rule, no one else had come to him with such a bizarre intention. He told me it would be cold, uncomfortable, and the food inferior. I said I did not mind. I explained that nothing was known in the outside world of the Bakonzo: the Batoro were famous, the Baganda were famous, people had written books about them, studies had been published. But on the Bakonzo, nothing. King George did not think that surprising, since three years earlier, on a royal visit to Harugali, sub-country headquarters in the north-west mountains, when someone had the nerve to ask him why the Bakonzo were not given chieftainships in their own area, he had riposted, 'Baboons are not given chieftainships.'

I was young, of course, and impulsive. The young know not what they seek. Or seek the impossible. So the King and I turned back to the Tests – Denis Compton, Learie Constantine... The Ministers came and went, on their knees.

I had had to call on this King George, Mukama of Toro, because the Konzo were his subject people. History and the British had made them so. Four out of the seven Sazas – counties – that comprised the Toro Kingdom, contained substantial populations of Bakonzo. There were only twice the number of Batoro in his Kingdom as there were Bakonzo, according to the 1948 census. Yet apart from the palace retainers of Konzo origin, King George knew them little. He was not built for steep ascents on foot. Since the lowland roads were made, he had better acquaintance with the much less numerous Baamba and Basongora who lived below the mountains rather than in among them – although Bwamba proper was an awkward place of gulches. All of the saza chiefs were, of course, Batoro; as were virtually all of the gombolola – sub-county – chiefs. Only at miruka – parish – level were Bakonzo usually permitted to be headmen in their own territory. What the Dispeller of Darkness did know of his Bakonzo subjects was they were damn slack payers of their poll tax, levied on the head of every family in his kingdom. By the Toro 'treaty' with the British, formalised between Sir Harry Johnston and Kasagama in 1900, ten per cent of the tax take went to maintain the Toro palace with its few score of princes and princesses, courtiers, soothsayers, askaris, craftsmen, cooks and varlets. Royalty must have its panoply, and the ethnic lords of east Africa rise inspirationally to that requirement. Someone had to pay for it, and statutorily most of the traditional ruling caste of the Batoro were excused the annual levy.

To the remote Bakonzo in their ridge-top compounds, under the high forest rim, whether they paid up or dodged it, the poll tax surely irked. It might not be heavy – a few hens, a basket of millet – yet what of the principle? What right had these white men to lump the mountains in with the 'kingdom' of the Toro? Batoro knew nothing of the mountains, and never of their own accord entered them. What did any Mukonzo, in those heights above Fort Portal, benefit from this tax? Not a road, not a school, not a dispensary existed in the mountains. A rumour might reach them that around the Toro fort itself, a town was growing, with those wondrous amenities of the Wazungu-white man's style of life. It was a rare Mukonzo who ventured there, in his monkey-furs, or his goatskin, smelling of hut-smoke, uncertain of the argot, squat, puckered and afraid. Such 'baboons'. Even the distortion that the plainland outsiders gave to the name – Konjo, rather than Konzo – bore a connotation in the Swahili patois of something other, sickly and unblessed.

iv

The Duke Summits

Let us return to the chronology of exploration.

The mountains lay back, beyond the reach of outsiders, engendering dreams, making their rains, their hail, their ice and snows at the summit clusters, clamped in cloud, or cresting – above the cloud and beyond the sight of man – amid clear heavens; and ever, as Aeschylus had written, 'nourishing Egypt with its snow', by the flow of the Nile.

Let us not hurry past the classical reference. For the ancient Mediterranean, astonishingly, knew of our mountains and had picked a name for them: mountains 'of the moon'. Intrigued by the seasonal flooding of a lower Nile that snaked out of the desert to water the immemorial civilisation, classical antiquity heard rumours: mighty lakes, it was said, and a range of snowy mountains in the heart of unknown Africa, gave birth to the life-giving stream. Aeschylus' comment about the 'snows' that fed the Nile was dropped as if it were common knowledge. Scholars of late seventh century BC Attica would cross to Egypt for educational finish. One such was Solon, who brought back to Athens the story of Atlantis: we may speculate that a century or so later Aeschylus gathered up Egyptian reports of these tropical snows. A generation on, Herodotus vouchsafes the name, (τα οὐρεα της σεληνης) – the Mountains of the Moon – which, with the lakes, were the ultimate watershed. Doing his own research, he sailed up the Nile... for about one seventh of the theoretic distance the journey would have entailed.

Solon's teachings were surely in the ear of Plato who taught Aristotle; and Aristotle wrote of those speculated mighty lakes. So also – in the century after Aristotle (the third BC) – did Eratosthenes of Cyrene (north-east Libya), the great geographer who calculated with fair accuracy the circumference of the earth and was called in by Ptolemy Euergetes to supervise his celebrated library along the coast at Alexandria. So also, in the next century, Hipparchus, the

33

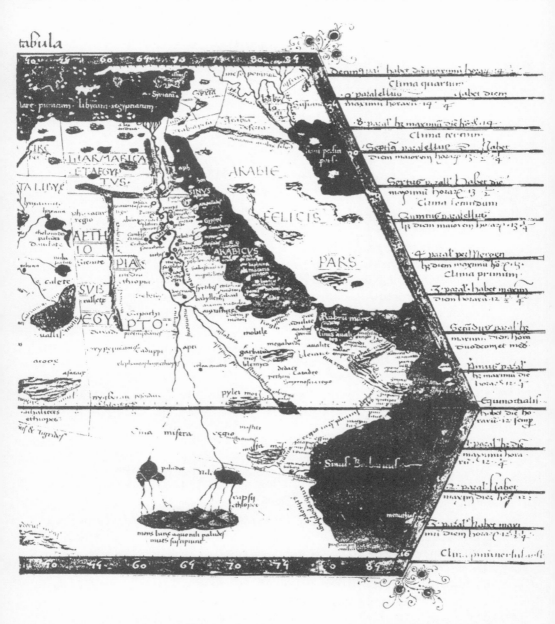

astronomer-geographer and inventer of trigonometry. Hipparchus paved the way for the work of the Alexandrine geographer Ptolemy Claudius (*c.* AD 90-168). Late mediaeval European geographers attempted to draw the map of Africa originally devised by Ptolemy, using the co-ordinates and sites listed in his surviving writings. These had reached the West from the Arabs, for whom the geographies of El Qeludi (=Claudius) had served as a

34

merchant marine aid for centuries. In his siting of the Mountains of the Moon ('Mons Lune' in the mediaeval Latin at the foot of the map above), Ptolemy may have considered the testimony of a Greek merchant named Diogenes, quoted in the contemporary seafarer's handbook *Periplus of the Erythrean Sea*. Diogenes plied the trade route to India. He called at the East African port of Rhaptum ('Raptum') – which plausibly fits today's Kenyan site of Malindi, just south of the outflow of the Galana river. Diogenes reported snow-covered heights twenty-five days' march inland from Rhaptum. This would point to Kilimanjaro (which provides no waters for the Nile), Ruwenzori lying some two months' march further westward. As to the 'Rhapsi' Aethiopians (Africans) in the mountains' vicinity to which Ptolemy refers, we can but speculate. The word means 'stitched'. Pygmies stitch leaves for garments; pygmies are there today. They were there when we ourselves – let us recall – we of this narrative retreated from those heights, not reaching the glaciers yet sighting them, with Stanley's lieutenant, W G Stairs, in June of 1889. Stairs knew, of course, as Stanley knew, what they were in the presence of: the two-millennium myth.

Two years later, 1891, the next genuine attempt at summiting was made by one of the members of Emin Pasha's revisitation of the region. Emin Pasha returning? Yes indeed. The appetite for empire-carving of this curious figure was not satiated. The Pasha, recalling his German-speaking provenance, and responding to the colonial ambition of the young Kaiser for a nation that cannot be said to have existed when he was born a Schnitzer, switched allegiance from the England-manipulated Egyptian Khedive and teamed with the adventurer Herr Carl Peters at Bagamoyo, Germany's Tanganyikan coastal base which was a-scurry with thrusting counts and grafs. He and Peters would beat Great Britain to possession of Uganda and that entire region of the continent north and west that headwatered the white Nile. And so the pair of them seemed to do, dashing to Kampala to secure a treaty with the hectic Mwanga, Kabaka of Buganda, heartland of the colony-to-be. All that was then required, in May of 1890, was for the Kaiser to make this Protectorate official, his, and Germany's.

But the Kaiser's foreign minister had been affronted by his master's coup, seven or eight weeks earlier, which had ended the career of the maker of modern Germany, Bismarck. He tipped off Lord Salisbury, Prime Minister to the Kaiser's grandmama, Queen-Empress Victoria, as to the urgent plea from Kampala via Bagamoyo.

And Salisbury, on the instant, put before the Kaiser a proposal that his instinct told him would tweak the Kaiser's fancy. Thirty-eight miles out in the North Sea from Cuxhaven lay a tiny island, which eighty years previously Britain had annexed from Denmark as a smuggling base wherewith to breach Napoleon's all-Europe blockade of Britain. Heligoland had suddenly acquired importance for Germany with the imminent opening of the Kiel Canal. Britain, proposed Salisbury, would swap this atoll for German claims in central Africa north of the 1° parallel south of the equator.

The Kaiser took the bait. Salisbury explained to his old Queen, tetchy at the idea of 'giving up what one has had', that Britain had thus exchanged a North Sea pimple a mile long and six hundred yards across for 100,000 square miles of Africa. Hence the northern border of today's Tanzania runs in a straight east-west line at 1°S across Lake Victoria, and hence the Kaiser threw back a gift of territory, doubling or even tripling his East African possessions, into the face of a man whose collateral descendants were presumably hunted down in Bavaria, fifty years on, for *vernichtung* in the gas chambers of his successor, Adolf Hitler.

Even still the Pasha was not quite done. That next year, 1891, in flawed health and half blind, he re-entered for the second time the region that obsessed him – at the head of a new free-lance expedition. His aim was to mobilise once more the Sudanese troops he had left behind him at Lake Albert on Stanley's insistence two years previously (as we have already described). In this he failed: his old troops clung to their Egyptian loyalty; and not long afterwards Emin Pasha, seated at his verandah table near the River Lualaba (which the Congo river becomes in its upper reaches) was to be tipped arsy-versy on to the floor, have his bearded chin thrust back and his throat slit on the orders of a slippery chief.

A protégé of the Pasha's, however, a certain Dr Franz Stuhlmann, had detoured from that 1891 expedition as it passed beneath Ruwenzori to become the first European since W G Stairs in 1889 to penetrate the region of the peaks.

Stuhlmann approached the mountains from the side of the Pasha's returning route to Lake Albert – the Congo side and the Semliki valley. In an excursion of five days he ascended by the northern flank of the major valley of the western fall of the range, the Butawu valley. Then he crossed the Kanyamwamba torrent to follow the ridge dividing it and the Kamusoso. This was the route by which I took my own half-fictional characters, the 'brothers' of my novel *The Brothers M*, plus Kigoma (Isaya Mukirane), in their flight from Belgium's colonial policemen. That invention stemmed from my own journey into the heights in 1954. Dr Stuhlmann, by contrast, had taken with him no Bakonzo. He reached 13,200 feet, and surrounded by giant groundsels of twenty feet and a floor of alchemilla left a record there of his achievement in a bottle. Ahead of him reared the sheer walls of the Mount Stanley cluster, snow-laden and swirled with fog and containing – unknown to Stuhlmann – the highest peaks of the entire massif. There was no question of his continuing further.

For the first years of Uganda's formal administration by Britain, it fell to the British – climbing out of Toro on the east – to probe and reconnoitre the high fastness of Ruwenzori: Scott Elliot in 1895, Moore and Sir Harry Johnston in 1900, Wylde and Ward in 1901, Fisher and his wife in 1903, and David and Dawe in 1904. Administrators, missionaries, soldiers. Moore was the first to discover, and exploit, the skills, knowledge and endurance of Bakonzo, and David the first to reach a glacier. But the first true mountaineering expedition intent on the summit was that of Freshfield and Mumm in 1905.

They are stormed and rained out. They have with them a Swiss guide, Moritz Inderbinnen, a kind of Sherpa Tensing of his day who had climbed in the Caucasus and Himalayas. He had never known such assault of weather. 'It is Kitasamba,' he might have overheard their Bakonzo murmur to one another. 'It is Kitasamba's season.' (It was November.) 'It is Kitasamba's season and very near to Kitasamba's place.' The name Kitasamba may be rendered in English as *Spirit Lord who does not climb* – since he occupies the highest pinnacles of his mountains, the fortress of his progenitor, Nzururu, *Snow*. Kitasamba is the intervener, the inspirer. His is the pink crepuscular glow on the highest bare rock and glacier and snowfield. Yet equally he is tempest, he is freezer of man. He can bring fertility to womb, or he can stop the womb. He is tender; he is hard; the threatener and the soother. From Kitasamba flows that by which men and women made expression to him before they found words and thus always beyond words – men upon the *endara*-xylophone, *eluma*-flute, *ekhinanga*-harp, *enzenze*-fiddle, *enyamwulera*-recorder, *akayamba*-rattle, and the drum (*Ngoma*); and women and men also in song, or musical *olwimbo*-ballad, performed antiphonally between one singing group and another, or between humankind and spirit-medium. All this is Kitasamba's, and Kitasamba demands homage and burnt offerings.

The expedition backs out and down. So also does its immediate successor, headed by A F R Wollaston and R B Woosnam, backed by the British Museum but not the Konzo spirits. Yet the contest for the highest peaks, whichever they may prove to be, is on. For such is the *daimon* in the European.

Outstandingly the two worst colonial powers in tropical Africa were those newest to nationhood. In the Congo, Belgium progressed from incompetence through vicious brutality to a deadening managerial condescension. From their earliest days of colonisation, the Belgians gave the Bakonzo a taste of their style. In 1897, a missionary of the Church Missionary Society named A B Lloyd who was given a brief assignment to Toro (via Zanzibar) decided to make his way home by traversing the Ituri forest and descending the Congo river. The start of his route took him into the Congo immediately south of Ruwenzori, crossing the Nyamugasani river (at that time the presumed border), and heading west for the Semliki. There beneath the mountains he was making for the Belgian post of Karimi when, walking through a plantation of yams, he 'came upon 60 or 100 women, all with hoes, cultivating... Close at hand was a native soldier with a rifle... acting as guard. I inquired where all these poor creatures had come from, and I was told a sad, sad story – alas! not an uncommon one in the Belgian Free State. A Wakonjo [Bakonzo] chief had been told to do some work for the Belgians, and when he had refused soldiers were sent, and upon the least resistance the men were shot down and the women captured as slaves and made to work. It was a sad sight to behold these poor creatures, driven like dogs here and there, and kept hard at their toil from morning till night. One of the Belgian soldiers told me there had been many killed, including the chief, and when I said what a terrible thing it was, he merely laughed and said... "They are only heathen."'

Not much had changed in the spirit of the place when I crossed much of it overland in 1954. Six years later (1960) the Belgians launched their possession into an 'independence', without a single native graduate, secretly intending to continue to run the place puppet-mastered by Brussels through their white-officered paramilitary Force Publique. The plan collapsed with the Force's mutiny on day four (July 4, 1960). Within forty-eight hours I was

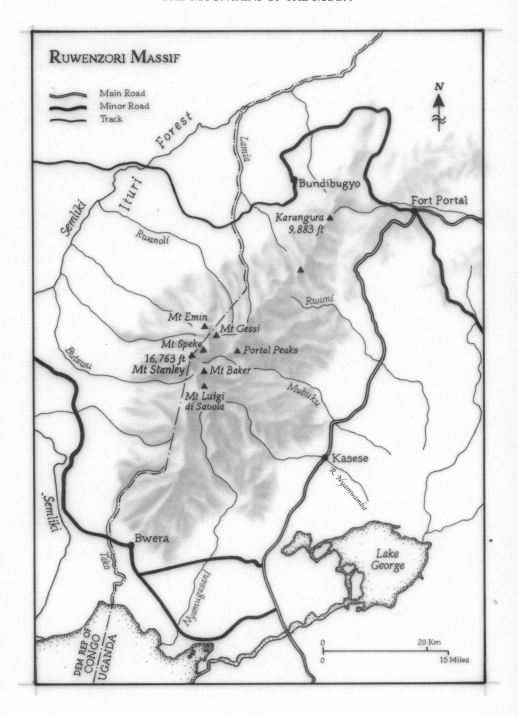

RUWENZORI MASSIF

Main Road
Minor Road
Track

Forest

Ituri

Lamia

Semliki

Bundibugyo

Fort Portal

Rwanoli

Karangura
9,883 ft

Rwimi

Mt Emin
Mt Gessi
Mt Speke
16,763 ft
Mt Stanley
Portal Peaks
Butawu
Mt Baker
Mt Luigi
di Savoia

Mubuku

Kasese

R. Nyamwamba

Semliki

Tako

Bwera

Lake
George

Nyamugasani

DEM REP OF CONGO
UGANDA

0   20 Km

0   15 Miles

N

there for my newspaper to follow the events on the ground thereafter by the hour for a period of several weeks. The country has never to this day recovered – a reality that will return to haunt our present story.

The Germans entered Africa rowdy and arrogant, mocking their own Rhenish Fathers, in today's Namibia, in Kamerun (Cameroon), Togo, and in German East Africa (Tanganyika, Rwanda and Burundi), blundering into provoking rebellions to which they responded with wholesale slaughter. The Herero of South West Africa were scheduled for *vernichtung*, extermination; the native death toll after the Maji-Maji rebellion in Tanganyika, from the machine-gun, the rope, and starvation compounded by displacement and drought, ran into hundreds of thousands. Germany's episode of colony-holding will touch our story indirectly.

Western Europe's third newcomer to nationhood with African ambitions, namely Italy, was humiliated in the field of battle against the Ethiopians (at Adowa, 1896), though they were to cling on in the Horn of Africa until Mussolini's self-inflation eventually put paid to their political presence on that continent for keeps. However, there now steps on to our physical proscenium, the territory of the mountains, an Italian of cold command, whose family had produced the first king of a united Italy.

One wonders whether Luigi Amedeo di Savoia ever actually saw himself as an 'Italian'. For he was a mountain Prince in his own right, and a mountain Duke to boot. As Prince of the Savoy his nominal territory comprised much of the southward curving Alps, and as Duke of the Abruzzi his nominal territory contained the highest peaks – topping 9,000 feet – of the Apennines. He had already summited Mount St Elias, at 15,000 feet, in the Yukon, and had been turned back (by frostbite) in an attempt on the still unconquered North Pole. Word now reached him of the as yet stubborn mysteries of a massif of remotest Africa few of his countrymen would have heard of, except as the fabled *Montes Lunae* of their classical memory: Ruwenzori.

The Prince assembled a vast expedition around a team of eleven Italians: three geophysicists, a photographer and his mate, a doctor doubling as zoologist, four Alpine guides, and a cook. Three hundred Africans, no less, were recruited to porter their stuff from Lake Victoria to Fort Portal. There the Prince paid court upon Kasagama, whose kingdom comprised the mountains; black royalty honoured by white royalty. From Kabarole-Fort Portal the

vast caravan winds its way to Ibanda, forty miles to the south and into the foothills, the start of the tested route to the heights from the eastern – 'British' – side. Here he was among the Bakonzo, of whom he recruited 80 for the first three legs of the ascent to the rock shelter of Bujongolo, above the bamboos, the expedition's base camp. Of these 80, it seems fifteen were selected for porterage into the heights – pictured on this page – in turn to be reduced to nine for the last assaults.

A year or so later, the Prince had his grandly published account of his expedition ghosted for him by a Dottore who was not actually on the journey and refers to the Prince throughout as 'SAR', Sua Altezza Reale. His Royal Highness really hadn't the time, he explained personally in the preface, to write books. Given the meticulousness of his planning and organisation, the lordly expense, the assiduity of his trigonometry and cartography, and the vigour of his assaults on the peaks, this disdain for putting his own pen to paper is a surprise and a disappointment. He and his

Italians – only the Italians, as it turns out: no Africans – wrap up the main peaks, all 17 of them, between June 10 and July 17, an appropriate season for mankind in our mountains. On June 18 (1906), on the summit of the highest peak of all, at 16,736 feet, the Prince unfurls a small Italian flag personally given to him before he set out by Queen Margherita, consort of his kinsman King Vittorio

Emmanuele III, third of united Italy's ill-fated monarchy. He names after her, *Margherita,* a peak hung magnificently with snow-laden cornices of ice. A sea of cloud stretches beneath, for infinity.

Margherita thus crowns the already-named Mount Stanley cluster. In the summit cluster immediately to the north, Mount Speke, Victor Emmanuel is accorded a peak. Just south of Margherita, the Prince allows his own name, Luigi di Savoia, to be bestowed on a summit at 15,179 feet, glaciered and colonnaded with snow-festooned ice. I report with sorrow that today, ninety-six years on, your glacier, Luigi, has melted away. Global warming has seen to that. Victor Emmanuele, irretrievably discredited by the dictator he backed, Benito Mussolini, abdicating in 1946 at the age of seventy-seven – had a glacier named after him by this explorer-cousin of his, in the Emin cluster of peaks at the northern end of the highlands: both Umberto and his glacier are gone today.

So the Prince conquers Ruwenzori. Two scientific volumes, contributed to by various of his expeditionaries, soon appear on the mountains' zoology, botany, geology, petrography and minerology. There are some fine photographs... The European *daimon* is assuaged. And the natives? They win a few lines. Those he assembled or inherited (as it were) from Freshfield and Mumm, he considered tough, somewhat jut-jawed, shaven-headed, or shorn in odd designs, and here and there with light beards. The cold and rain and sun had tanned their skin to leather. They wore armlets or leglets of metal or woven fibre, and a rag at the loins. Several slung fur bags round the neck for their tobacco and pipe. One wore a hyrax-fur cloak, another a leopardskin. They were clever on the climb with their sticks. There were no Christians among them, naturally. They were not redeemed. They were, after all, *portatori*. Yet was it not they, Prince, who had given the names to the streams, the gullies, the crags, the waterfalls, the species of mammal and plant for which you and your friends had as yet had no word in your own language? And to the twin pinnacles you could not climb, Kitasamba and Nyabibuya?

But they were *portatori*. They themselves carried no names in the Prince's explorational notes or recollections. Very well, they knew the paths, had *made* the paths, through the forest, the bamboos, the tree-heathers. They knew the twists of the weather, could find their route in the fog. So what? They were *portatori*.

The Prince notes among his porters a 'veritable terror' of the region of the peaks and an intense reluctance to follow him over to the western, Congo, side of the summits' watershed. He does not reflect on this *vero terrore*. He is not the reflective sort. And if I were to have told him – if I were to have explained (making an echo) that this place of greatness, power, glory, splendour and majesty, patrolled by fog, was the very dwelling of Nzururu, and his progeny Nyabibuya, the incarnational figure of birth and continuance, and of Kitasamba the intervener, who spake by the soothsayers – I think I would not have distracted him from his theodolite. If I had mentioned that to cross the heights to the Congo side, *it could mean nothing other than that one had violated the sanctum of Him Who Cannot Climb Higher,* he would at length have turned on me his regal frown of cold disdain. And in the nomenclature of all those peaks, which was now complete, none would bear the name of Stacey.

v

The First Rebellion 1919-21

So our mountains could rest awhile. Or, at least, seem to rest. White authority in Toro had no direct contact with Ruwenzori's true people. These hardy little folk dwelt too remotely and inaccessibly. In Fort Portal resided the District Commissioner for the Toro kingdom. He was administrator, judge and treasurer. From his white tribe came a police chief (an Assistant Superintendent), an agricultural officer, and the first missionaries, Protestant and Catholic, who ran up their churches in mud and wattle, one for each Jesus-version, and linked to each church a school. The missionaries included a doctor (and his wife), who built a hospital at Kabarole and, later, a scattering of dispensaries. A road soon pushed through the bush, for 240 miles, from Kampala. Far to the east, a railway from the coast at Mombasa, begun in 1896, had climbed into the Kenya highlands and within ten years reached the oceanic Lake Victoria at Kisumu. From Kisumu it was just a day's steaming in a 'smoke-boat' to Jinja, Uganda's lake port. Soon, a railway was to link Jinja to Namasagali, the first navigable point on the Victoria Nile northwards – navigable for a stretch. Joe Chamberlain, Colonial Secretary, visited Uganda by the railway from the coast. In 1908 young Winston Churchill, Under-Secretary of State for the Colonies, visited Uganda by way of the Nile, dreaming railways, like Rhodes – Cape-to-Cairo. (It remained a dream.)

The mountains brooded. From time to time, reaching Fort Portal, adventurous white visitors would make their way south – a mere thirty miles' march to where the Mubuku torrent reaches the plain – and mount the valley to the village of Bugoye. There Konzo porters would be recruited to accompany us Wazungu – whites – up by the Mubuku and off by its northern tributary, the Bujuku, to the region of the Stanley peak cluster, there to assault the glaciers and the top-most summit, if Kitasamba complied: four hard days up, three down: no deviations, no sojournings, presuming to render the inaccessible accessible as the Manichean wazungu will insist upon. The fibrous bands by which the loads were supported, indented the tops of the skulls of those Bakonzo hardies most practised as porters. For all the rest of the mountain realm, the habitable and the non-habitable, Ruwenzori brooded.

The tax demands came to men in their compounds on the spurs via the hierarchy of appointed chiefs: the saza (county) chiefs, Batoro all, put there by the District Officer, in consultation with King Kasagama; the gombolola (sub-county) chiefs, Batoro all except one, the ageing Ruhandika; the parish chiefs picked reluctantly from the indigenous folk – Bakonzo, Baamba – for their willingness to extract the tax and implement the hunting prohibitions. When none compliant were to be found, a Mutoro would be awarded even the miruka – parish – chieftainship, with its useful fee and patch of land. Each miruka chief had a couple of headmen on his staff.

Most of the cultivable land in the kingdom was divided into fiefs by King Kasagama, and only he and his seven county chiefs held freeholds. In Bwamba in the mountains' north, the first Mutoro saza chief grew rich in ivory. The poll tax levied by the colonial government, was shared (in small measure) with the Toro king. But there was also levied busulu, the peasant's tribute for his right to hoe, six shillings a year, going to the Batoro lords of the land. The language of administration, the language of authority, the language of any chance of advancement, was Rutoro.

The vassal peoples, three fourths Bakonzo, one fourth Baamba, brooded in their mountains, in their foothills, in the craggy tectonic rift of Bwamba. The alien abstract *money* crept in. For what benefit was this money subscribed? Not any that they knew. Cash-crops – coffee, cotton – were proposed: out of good soil an abstract unconsumable to be cultivated for abstract currency to meet demand for and by an abstract power.

Mountain people are bred to independence, to ultimate self-sufficiency, to a very natural, geographic defiance of unwarranted intrusion, by weather, beast or man. Ruwenzori mountain dwellers ring an impenetrable and illimitable inner fortress. Knowledge of this is no less in the legs than in the psyche. What is Fort Portal to Fort Rwenzururu? Had not the Bakonzo ambushed Kabalega's askaris a generation earlier on the forest heights of Karangura, as the Banyoro sought the Mutoro child-prince Kasagama hidden in the mountains by their chieftain Ruhandika? Did the Konzo warriors not kill them by the score and scatter the rest to perish of cold?

Out of such discontent a spirit of revolt took shape in Bukonzo proper, the county of the extensive southern foothills, a mazy landscape of heights and dips, groves and streams, mounting to the north in ever more majestic tiers to the ultimate fastness. Its agriculture is rich. Konzo tradition tells of the first violent protest in 1911 and the pursuit of the rebels into the uplands and their drowning in the torrent Nyamugasani. That stream rises beneath Luigi di Savoia and tumbles into a series of dark and unexpected forest lakes before emerging into delectable uplands, quilted with cultivation, and at length emptying itself into Lake Edward. Its estuary is beside the salt lake of Katwe of which I have written already, when Stanley passed by. But by now Katwe's crater lake, with its commercial treasure, extracted immemorially by our Konzo-Bakingwe, had become the private property of the King of Toro who had his own agent installed there, by arrangement with the British. May we not mourn these unknown freedom-fighters?

Three names of martyrs to the sputtering cause reach us from 1915: Nkwirakaghe, Kalikura and Kindongi. By that date, England was at war with Germany, once more invaders of France, and colonial lords of Tanganyika, half of Lake Victoria, Rwanda – a mere forty miles southwest of our mountains – and Burundi beyond. The entire world order was in jeopardy. In German East Africa, a tiny army under General Paul von Lettow-Vorbeck, with a starting complement of 261 compatriot officers and NCOs and not a single reinforcement to come from the fatherland, began hostilities with raids upon Uganda. It was to harry and elude a British force ten times its size for the entire four-year campaign. The British colonial authorities were in no mood to tolerate refractory tribalism in mountain backwaters. The three disrupters, whose names are recorded only in Konzo oral tradition, met death on the sly – 'liquidated' is Syahuka's word; no questions asked – at the hands of the Toro agents of authority, perhaps that ambitious subgroup of largely Konzo blood, the so-called Banyabindi, historically inveigled into Kitoro allegiance by offers of petty authority or by their upbringing in the households of Batoro nobles or even of the Dispeller of Darkness, the Toro king himself.

The gallant von Lettow's mercurial raiders were at times surely not so very distant from our mountains. Some four decades later, after another German war, I attended upon a spur chief in Bunyangabo on Ruwenzori's eastern flank – a figure of dignified antiquity, his magnificent white head with its cataracted eyes like a dying fire built on a rock. His name was Musabaho. I wondered at the frayed wide-shouldered tunic, cornflower-blue and military in cut – until its single button of tarnished brass caught my attention. The button bore the relief of an eagle. This chiefly regalia had been the tropical dress-uniform of one of Lettow's officers. In 1918, before that Great War was won in Europe, and the British in Fort Portal were distracted and thin on the ground, a certain Mukonzo from Buhira, Congo-side, across from Bwamba, named Nyamutswa Kihokolho, emerged to confront the ageing Ruhandika's readiness to toady to Batoro royalty and comply with their encroachments. His followers carried spears, and smeared their ox-hide shields and their own skins with castor oil.

Then in 1919 a young Mukonzo chieftain, Tibamwenda, born to authority in the southern lowlands in Kiringa-Kalingwe village between the rivers Nyamugasani and Kanyampara, cast the die. The spirit of the goddess Nyabibuya got into him. Personally riled by Batoro high-handedness, so I was to learn, and primed by a meeting with Nyamutswa, he speared a Mutoro to death. The call went out to fellow Bakonzo throughout their territory to defy the interlopers and poll tax-gatherers, the land-expropriators and the whole apparatus of colonially-foisted Kitoro authority. From one end of the mountains to the other the effect was electric. Of a sudden, no Fort Portal-appointed chief was safe. A few died by the spear. A Konzo patriotism gripped the mountain peasantry. The District Commissioner in Fort Portal, his presumption of docility shattered, faced an emergency. A few additional Colonial soldiery – mostly so-called 'Nubians' from Uganda's north – were hurried in. Tibamwenda rallied the south and Nyamutswa the rest, with his lieutenant Kapoli who Roland-like summoned the spearman from the spurs with his horn. (Here is a picture of such a horn – to be blown sideways.)

The rebels made their redoubt in the southern foothills

straddling the wild frontier. There – Judased, so the story runs, by Tibamwenda's younger brother, for Toro money – they were snatched as they slipped back from the Congo, and manacled. They were tried in Fort Portal on charges of murder, treason and cannibalism by a white judge and two white 'assessors', which is to say (most likely) planters or traders of respectability, and condemned to death. Against this sentence they appealed, in the light of their political grievances, to the East African Court of Appeal. Their appeal, heard on purely legal grounds, was dismissed. So they were hanged, in 1921, right there on their home ground, and dumped together in the same pit beside Kagando where the Nyamugasani river meets the plain and their fellow patriots had been 'liquidated' by drowning. A bleak monument stands there today: a kind of shrine. Scarcely a mile away the half-finished Tom Stacey Primary Boarding School, of mud bricks, crumbles, abandoned.

The colonial brow of the time furrowed. How had they erred, that this rebellion flared so quick among the hill dwellers? I sense a regret among white tribe's representatives. Young James Elliott, a doctor's son, aged 23, arrived as a Colonial Service cadet in Fort Portal in 1920. He encountered the Bakonzo in his recreational activities – shooting buffalo and elephant and lion, all of which abounded. In an unpublished memoir he writes of 'the Bakonjo, who live on the foothills and lower parts of the Mountains of the Moon' as 'by far the more reliable, stolid and pleasant people' who ' dislike the Batoro intensely, which dislike is mutual.' He found his new charges in Toro 'a lazy lot, with the exception of the Bakonjo.' In 1923, to the protests of the lords and nobles of Toro, the Mukama's *busulu* tribute from the peasantry (including the Bakonzo) was declared illegal. Food and grain was distributed to Bwamba, where there had been much disturbance and resulting hunger – a challenging exercise in such remote and difficult territory, for there was to be no road into Bwamba until 1938. Arrangements were put in hand to delineate precisely the forest and mountain frontier with the Belgian Congo , where a set of rules and responsibilities of one flag gave way to another's. Surely those wayward Konzo could grasp that (given patience) the light of literacy, the order of law, the boon of commerce, the shield of medicine, the saving helmet of Jesus, would eventually penetrate to benefit even the remotest...

Let us not suppose that Tibamwenda and his fellows rebelled

and died because of this and that – because of tax or economics or agronomics or whatever. They died for the inner liberty to be the people they most intimately knew themselves to be. As I write this passage at our millennium's turn, do I not hear just such a clamour all around us – from Scots, Kurds, Kosovars, Québécois, Tibetans, East Timorese and women? As for our Konzo: where do they line up in justification of grievance? What had imperially endorsed vassaldom done to them? Indeed, it was a soul-cry for the legitimacy of the idea of themselves. Here was blood, genetics, physiognomy, language, a lilt of speech, a method of life, a highland vocabulary of technique and trick, a history, genealogy, mythology, cosmology; a cosmology of place, genius of place, sanctuary of gods, an Olympus, Valhalla, the fount of rain, anvil of thunder, source of life, a hunter's paradise. They were orphaned of the joy and clarity to be themselves here, in their Rwenzururu, of excitation at the thought of themselves beating in the heart, of the beauty of their feet upon their mountain paths, the pure power and elixir of their innocence under their snows, Nzururu. They were stripped and orphaned.

Nothing had changed for them by those deaths, other than that they retreated inwards: into the fortress of their mountains and the bastion secrets of their spirit community. Such steep paths no others knew. In the aftermath of the Tibamwenda rebellion a Commission of Enquiry ended the arbitrary awards of land to – and by – the Toro king and his Bito aristocracy. In the Konzo lowlands, outbreaks of cholera occurred. The tsetse fly so ravaged the remaining Konzo herds that cattle-owning by Bakonzo ceased to be any part of their culture.

From their Fort Portal headquarters, successive District Officers would strive honourably for a radiating advancement. A road was pushed southwards through the plains below the mountains to the salt deposits at Katwe. By the Thirties' end, the first Christian missionary spur reached the southern lowland community. A few Konzo catechists were appointed. A tendril of road from Fort Portal had reached round the massif's northern perimeter to Bundibugyo in Bwamba, above the Semliki and the great Congo-side forest of Ituri and its Mbuti pygmies. Lowland agriculture began to reach a wider market. By the end of the Forties, in the Kabarole-Fort Portal region, King George was prevailed upon by the British administrator to insist that each of his sub-county/gombolola chieftains in Bakonzo or Baamba areas should subsidize the primary education of a minimum of two pupils from one or other of those two tribes. The schools were of course Toro schools, and the medium of instruction the Rutoro language. Certain names we shall shortly encounter were of those first chosen for this fraught privilege in the Toro plain.

vi

1954 I am Admitted

We are commonly drawn to the primal. We ascribe to the savage a nobility and to the primitive a purity. Over-educated, rich in distraction, soft-living and petty vice, we speak of something that has gone, yet might still be recovered to redeem us.

> Who are these we come across fur-capped
> At the roadside, staved, suspicious, wrapped
> Against an adversary we are not acquainted with exactly -
> Wary of lowlanders, never first to speak,
> Yet responding to our greeting and (in the basic mode)
> Sharing our lingo?

> If not in line of time our ancestors,
> Surely it is these that took our past
> Up by the sunless tributary gullies,
> Difficult to pass and single file for goats,
> To what were once pastures in most parched
> High summertime, and settled there above
> The treeline, not for a season,
> But to live and die.

Where have I swept you, my reader – into what other wild mountain region of illiterate peasantry (such as we are all descended from)? To Atlas? Tibesti? The Caucasus? The Pamirs?

> The younger men trespass down,
> With a few hides and artefacts of bone.
> For a single day, or a day and a night's unrest
> Lodged at the town's edge, their zest
> Gone absent, narrow-eyed, observing little,
> Watchful for exploitation, trickery and the derision
> Of our children.

Then they are away again for another year, on foot,
Squatting at the roadside to regroup their hearts,
Rising hesitantly as our vehicle decelerates,
Swart, monkey-faced, smelling of old smoke,
Uncertain if to smile or be on guard
Upon the currency (for ornament), salt, tobacco,
Peppers and white sugar in the warm
Darkness of their clothing.

On our return they are gone, we suppose
Moved off between high grasses on a trail we never noticed
Still half a day's tramp to where the mountains start
And their legends of precipitous routes by tree-cramped
Torrent. Then the bared steeps where their turf huts
Crouch windowless against the cold
That slays their frail each winter, an adversary
We are not acquainted with
Exactly.

　　　　　Were these not they of the simple life
Whom we townsmen, sophisticates, *boulevardiers,*
Affect to envy?

We are not so distant from Ruwenzori, from its people, from their fears, their dream-songs. My spirit-singing Konzo friends will permit me my own dream-songs. Bakonzo are seldom fur-capped – though this occurs. They make artefacts of ivory, rather than bone – specifically horns, for warring, and music, but never to sell to outsiders. There is no 'high summertime' as such, Ruwenzori being equatorial; no pattern of transhumance to meet the seasonal shift between heavy and sparse rain. And though their huts crouch against the cold, and at times a dense decaying thatch becomes a habitat of its own for living plants and small animals, Bakonzo peasantry do not fabricate them of turf.

The young Englishman closing upon Ruwenzori from the west in 1954, in search of the primal and the pristine, was not to know such things yet.

In the previous four months of travelling he had not slept any night under the same roof as another white. There had been times, I suppose, when he could have been mistaken for a townee, sophisticate, *boulevardier.* His last school report five or six years earlier had cautioned against dilettantism. Such a caveat was less apt than it might have seemed at that moment: as a much younger child, the Grampians of Perthshire prioritized the soul that claimed him. Turning twenty, an ensign in Malaya in the uniform of the white King George, he had chosen to spend his leave finding and attaching himself to a group of Temiar aborigines in the jungle. This had set off something which was to have no particular end in him and ought not to have an end: namely, a renewal of his claim on immortality by means of such intimations as he might recollect or gather in of atavistic innocence. On this early brush with the primal he had already published a day-by-day account, his first book. And now at 24, he was commissioned to write his second, on any theme such as might recapture the readers of the first and add to their number.

He has left behind him in London a young wife of scarcely credible beauty, and two infant daughters. A Muganda, just graduated in anthropology from Cambridge, has – with the blessing of several friends they shared – accompanied him on an erratic trans-African perambulation by Land Rover, feet, dugout, river-boat, and bus from the lower reaches of the River Congo. Entering Uganda from the Belgian Congo, the two companions part at the foot of the mountains. The Muganda knows next to nothing of the Bakonzo. He knows only: *They have never been studied. And they alone live in the mountains.*

So precisely for that negative attribute and that positive attribute Ruwenzori and its people have become Destination... and through the forty-eight years of exploration between that date and the present day have remained, I daresay, Destination: a site at which to engage in the serious process of unlearning, of learning afresh.

Naturally I speak of exploration as a venturing of mind as much as of body, albeit a person's body providing the housing of the mind, and the physical and mental influencing one another, for better or for worse, as the soul alone may assay.

Of those who would explore, there are perhaps the driven and the drawn. Of the driven are the Stanleys and the Burtons: of the drawn, the Raleighs and the Donnes. The requirement to be elsewhere, *ailleurs,* for its own sake (do I hear an echo of Arthur Rimbaud in Harar?), will not suffice: it may be flight wrapped in disguise. Nor will being *first there* quite suffice for its own sake –

even if, surely, there is a legitimate excitement at the tracing of the Nile to its sources or the Alph (sacred river) through its measureless caverns. The valid requirement is to dare: venture body, venture mind – let body, at times, take mind venturing – into what is not known, not readily predictable, possibly beyond one's coping, to the edge, *terrore vero*, fear and trembling. Emulate the mountaineers. Take risks. Taking care, take risks. Then there is a chance, *there is a chance* you may know your own soul, and you shall not have lived in vain.

Long since it has struck me, in quite another context, that simultaneously to be journeying and at destination is the paradox characteristic of love. But to write that yet is to anticipate.

I was root-tired and homesick, that August of 1954, crossing the Semliki and entering Uganda for the first time. Yet the new book had been commissioned – I had taken an advance from the publisher – and I knew that, for all our exploits and for all its unprecedentedness, my journey with Erisa Kironde through six little-known countries of colonial Africa and into this seventh would be neither the book I wished to write nor a book that could be written. Erisa and I had parted in crisis. If I were to write of a journey through forgotten Africa in terms of the death of a comradeship between black and white, I would have destroyed him and shamed myself. For I had become unwittingly and personally embedded in the neurosis overwhelming him, rooted in the implacabilities of planetary, and also very local, history.

Erisa was a Muganda sophisticate of high education. Throughout his four years at Cambridge he had become a mascot to those fellow undergraduates outraged by the very premise of British colonial presence in Africa: mascot and darling. Britain's outgoing Prime Minister of 1951, Clement Attlee, had appointed as Governor of Uganda the Labour Party's most distinguished Fabian ideologue of how the British empire should evolve in peace and justice to the speedy self-determination of subject territories. In three years of taking up his role, the enlightened Sir Andrew Cohen (later my friend) found he had no course but to deport the Kabaka (King) of Buganda at the cost of igniting a Baganda patriotism that threatened to make the heartland of the colony ungovernable.

To Erisa, the paternalism of the condescending Left had come to seem more outrageous than any white supremacist tyranny of the

Right. We had arrived from England at Brazzaville, on the Lower Congo, with Erisa convinced of the superiority of all other colonial regimes to that of the British. The ensuing months with me in Moyen Congo, Gabon, Spanish Guinea, Caméroun, Oubangi-Shari and the Belgian Congo, shattered that conviction. The backwardness and servitude of his fellow Africans were pitiable. We had entered Conrad's Africa, a continent of darkness, disease, witchcraft, barbarism and arrant colonial authority exercised unobserved with casual brutality. On the edge of unexplored territory (designated as such on the latest French map) late at night, paddling by *pirogue*, we had chanced upon a riverside village (containing not a single child, since gonorrhoea robbed the wombs) where the tragic remnant had opened a grave and were engaged in human necrophagy out of an enamel basin.

From the day we arrived in Africa to the day we crossed the border with Uganda, we found no commercial hospice catering for whites which would also accept a black. Within minutes of our entering the Leopold II hotel in Stanleyville a Belgian planter had knocked Erisa to the floor in the foyer. Three weeks later in Irumu much the same occurred in a roadside bar – to teach *me*, no less than him, for the impertinence of our partnership. To have become so dependent on me (four years his junior) for his survival in his own continent, let alone his ability to reach home, had privily broken him up. On our reaching Uganda, the population's lightness of being was instantly manifest, and to Erisa it was the last straw. At the Mountains of the Moon Hotel in Fort Portal, we were welcomed as two guests on equal terms, as a matter of course, by literate, open-faced Africans. What had survived of Erisa's *raison d'être*? What was his Africa? Where lay the battle now? He was wracked and speechless. I had no possible means of helping.

We stayed in the hotel the one night: a rambly, single storey, wood-built place of verandahs and frangipane. In the morning, on a grass verge, we divided the contents of our packs, he to go on to his own people in Kampala, I to the still unseen mountains brooding under their cloud. This separation of our meagre belongings was itself a dreadful ordeal. Three or four small implements of critical utility which I had been sharply mourning since their disappearance, one by one, in the latter weeks of our journey were exposed there in the pit of his rucksack – a multi-purpose penknife and the like exposed as confiscated fetishes of an abominated dominance. Could I write of any of this retrogression towards contagious magic? Not by any conceivable device or skill... until (so to speak) my second journey to the mountains, a literary one, when I would weave Erisa out of fact into fiction. Erisa in the flesh is now dead.

Meanwhile, to write was my function and my livelihood, my daughters' rusks. I must surely write on a theme out of reach of this demonic stain: on the Bakonzo and their mountains.

I was to reach Bwamba's capital village of Bundibugyo in the personal Land Rover of the Dispeller of Darkness. This was the outcome of the meeting I have described on page 31 above. Another outcome was the Mukama's advice first to call upon a Mukonzo in Fort Portal of rare gifts and standing. This was Timothy Bazarrabusa. His name is given because he too plays a critical part in this story, beyond the present moment. I wrongly suspected his name derived, by common transposition of consonants, from Barabbas; and I noted that unlike his presumed namesake, a zealot Hebrew, Timothy Bazarrabusa had for the time being detribalized himself. He had been born into a Konzo family in the service of the Toro aristocracy, and was given a Kitoro name which actually means that this was a child of whom nothing would become. His father had crossed from that greater body of Konzo-speaking people (the 'Banande') in the Congo lowlands, immediately west of the mountains. Converting to Roman Catholicism, the father secured his freedom from slavery: he became a Catechist, halfway to priesthood, and the family rose by energy, grace and brains amid the host Batoro community. Young Timothy Bazarrabusa won the hand of a Mutoro 'princess' of the Omukama's kin who bore him a family. When she died, he married further 'out': a Muganda girl, daughter of no less than the Kabaka of Buganda's treasurer. By dint of these various qualities, not least sheer sweetness of temperament, he had risen to become an inspector of schools in the Western Province, and very soon – surely to his surprise – was appointed a Cross-bench Member in Uganda's embryo parliament, Sir Andrew Cohen's Legislative Council. His career does not stop there, as we shall discover.

Here, now, was a man of about forty, with large fanned upper teeth which diminished a passing chin: the firm quality of the face thus shifted forward into a muscular, almost horizontal, lower lip. At once on meeting I recognized him as an exceptional. I recall his avoiding precision as to 'Konzo' roots, while acknowledging he 'knew something of the mountain people'. Later I came to reflect on this imprecision. Timothy Bazarrabusa was of the blood and language, but not of the mountains; he was a sophisticate, what the Belgian chose to call an *évolué* – not of Africa's primality of which the mountains were a bastion-relic. If in my presence he was self-detribalized, it was out of no shame but to ameliorate a gratuitous handicap. Imagine it thus: that if by good luck, from your Kentish backwoods, you secured a place at grammar school in south London, had shone there, and gone on to collect a degree at the LSE, you would be aware of not favouring your chances of selection for a Parliamentary seat by gratuitously declaring your parents to be a pair of gypsies. The upper orders would be dubious; the lower, appalled.

For had I not already got some inkling of what it was to be a Mukonzo here, in the northern Toro plainland? That previous evening, my third in Fort Portal, walking into the town from the Anglican mission where I had cadged lodging, I heard music in an alleyway coming from a gramophone. It was tribal music (pygmies' music, lifted from a musicologist's tape). I heard live African chortling. I turned aside to see. A handful of lanky Batoro lounged in a circle between the backyards of Indian dwellings, and in their midst a ragged old man – a little fellow – dancing with odd jerking assertions of spine and stomach muscle, and hopping movements with little feints, gyrations, stampings and flicks of the elbow. He was hamming it up, for the laughs and the pennies. Yet he was also intent upon it, on his own performance and on the thrumming, patternless puffing of many weak reeds in concert and the drums coming thinly from the wind-up gramophone and its unexpected disc. He wore a goatskin – you did not see such a garment in town. He was skinny, and as crazy as they all wished.

After watching, I enquired.

'Oh – a Mukonjo,' said a chortler.

'What's he doing down here in Fort Portal?'

Why should they know? This was a 'Mukonjo', with no whys and wherefores, no recognisable place among ordinary people...

Bazarrabusa's office was of lime-washed mud, erected on a foundation of a dozen or so courses of bricks left over from the building of the Anglican deanery on the next hill. He had visited, he said, certain of the *backward* parts beneath the mountains, in Bwamba. He would give me three letters: and proceeded to write them there and then. Two were to Bakonzo: Samwiri Mulwahali, and Isaya

Mukirane. The long reach of the prophets of ancient Israel: Samuel... Isaiah. Just a few lines to each prophet. (Bazarrabusa himself was emphatically *New* Testament, carrying a first name of Timothy.) I have no record of these two letters, neither of the words nor of the language employed, whether Lukonzo or Lutoro: that I regret, since my note to Isaya would be seen today, perhaps, as a seminal fragment of Ruwenzori history. The third letter, and first for presentation, was to the saza chief in Bundibugyo, capital village of Bwamba county – a Mutoro, naturally: of this I did keep record. In pencilled English it read: *The bearer, an anthropologist, wants to find something about the Bakonjo. If you can help him in any way, please do so.*

Bazarrabusa said, 'Mind that you take enough of clothes when you go upon the mountains. It is very cold, and some have been gripped by the coldness and died.' He smiled. His teeth seemed to spread at the movement of his lips like a mechanical toy.

I was not an anthropologist – but then, nor was Malinowski when he entered the Pacific. I had very briefly shared the life of a group of Lower Strata Temiar of Malaya, witnessed their shamanism, and had read all that had been written of that country's forest aborigines. I had with me a book entitled *Notes and Queries on Anthropology*, compiled by the Royal Anthropological Institute, no less, sitting in committee. I had to be *something*. 'An explorer' was insulting to any native; 'a writer', an invitation to creative paralysis; 'a journalist' (which I already partly was), a mark of Cain; 'a student of the human condition'... come, come.

With letters in my pocket, I accepted the offer by the Mukama of Toro, King George, of his Land Rover and his driver to carry me to Bundibugyo. And thus I would arrive among the Bakonjo, in my innocence and unwittingness, in the chariot of the oppressor.

How could I have known? I knew nothing, nothing beyond that there were these mountains, this fabulous terrestrial event of which rumour had reached the ancients of the Mediterranean, word seeping from Egypt, as I have told here already, of remote snow-sources for the Nile, peaks which dwarfed men – dwarfed men's imagination so that there was need to invoke the extraterrestrial, *luna*-goddess, Selene: *her* place, *her* mountainscape. Ever since our coming south by lorry-bus on Congo-side from Irumu (where Erisa was assaulted by white settlers), the mountains had been somewhere proximate, a presence, a monumental barrier. On our entering Uganda between the massif and the rift-lake Edward they were an unseen presence, to our north; on our coming north to Fort Portal, an unseen presence to the southwest. All we had seen were foothills, waves tumbling out into the plain as from huge combers guessed at in the far beyond. To this presence, a people attached: that is all I knew.

So now in the royal Land Rover, with the canvas roof rolled back, I sat alongside the liveried driver, my left hand dangling over the door panel and my fingertips aware of the paintwork of this petty King's coat-of-arms, presumably devised by an Englishman half a century or so earlier after George's father had been re-installed in *his* father's raped palace. Look at the map, reader. See the grey baboons close to the murram road waking suddenly and, screaming in alarm, hobbling like crippled beggars (their dexterity alarming) off the

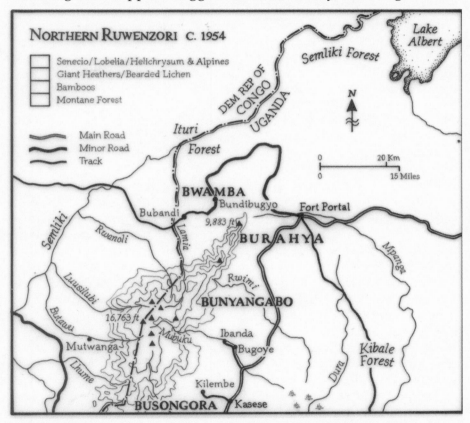

The highest contoured area shown is 14,500 feet or higher, comprising permanent snow and glacier. In descending order, the contours indicate vegetational zones beginning at 12,500 feet, 10,200 feet and 8,300 feet.

rocks into the tumbling sea of grasses. See the goatherds, each alone, alerted by the noise of the engine – a vehicle was a rarity – standing up all but invisibly in the reed-grasses amid their flocks, watching any wisp of the road within view for who or what we were.

As for my view, vistas open northwards suddenly, each a route to Lake Albert, itself too distant for visibility yet emanating lightness. Valleys fall away steeply. Batoro women lengthened by head-borne burdens – figurines of essential grace – step back into high grasses at our approach. There are their bee-hive huts, stuck among shady plantain groves. Then fewer villages, then none: a no-man's land. Small lakes whose shores are barren disfigure the landscape. At length we top a rise and the endless forest is flung down beneath me westwards. This is Ituri, which H M Stanley had crossed in unrelenting self-punishment three times, and its secret, sluggish waterways. Close by, below, across a mile of savannah by the jungle's edge, fumes rise into still air from Earth's molten core, reminding of hell and creation's tectonic split that runs interminably north-south below us: these are the sulphur springs, Sempaya. And still to my left, as the road swings south towards its fifty-mile half-circuit's end, the foothills mount in tiers to the defending ramparts of invisible glaciers.

Baboons and snow.

A Ruwenzori storm was threatening but there was still sun when we pulled up outside the sharply squared-up thatch and bamboo office of the saza chief of Bwamba. Squared-up too were beds of scarlet canna, and the gravel paths were brushed. The squared-up courtroom stood beside. Square was the colonial shape, and round the native. We had reached the capital village of the Baamba, a tribe of no more (then) than thirty or forty thousand, occupying the jumbled lowlands northwest of the mountains. They lived, and live, in a workable symbiosis with the hardier and more numerous Bakonzo who did not marry into them and took for granted their readiness to provide menial labour. The two peoples shared a resentment at the suzerainty of Toro, which my smart grey (squared) royal-crested Land Rover proclaimed.

I noted at the time how a Mutoro chief of these parts was inclined to address his ethnic inferiors: '*He will draw his head up and back, and put his hands on the back of his hips. When he has finished speaking to the Mukonzo/Mwamba, he will look past him as if to say tartly, "That will be all".*' In just such a manner, then, this particular saza chief – after scanning Bazarrabusa's brief letter and learning the addressees of the other two letters – turned to a Mukonzo youngster he had summoned into his presence.

Now this Mukonzo youngster was his assistant part-time clerk, Ibrahimu Ndyanabaïsi, and very soon I was to understand that he was the son of Samwiri Mulwahali and the brother-in-law of Isaya Mukirane. He was sixteen then. We shall not lose sight of him. This young Ibrahimu of 1954 had a rudimentary working English. Our *saza* chief bade him to conduct me to the other two addressees of Bazarrabusa's letters: his father and his brother-in-law. Ibrahimu had me climb back into the Land Rover: the road itself could still serve us.

Look at the picture of him there, on page 211: the quick offer of friendship therein, a bonny lightness to the face, the 'innocent trickster's charm', I noted on the day 'of the idle child to whom charm comes too easily'. By that I suppose I meant instant likeability, again and again enabling him to dodge existence's *terrore vero*, which would reach him in its time. We took the gravel and mud road that trundled and lurched its last twelve miles to Bubandi. People on the way to Bubandi's market cluttered the narrow track, each with produce for the barter market. It came on to rain. We pegged down the Land Rover's canvas top. The travelling rain mist blindfolded the mountain steeps, darkened the plantain patches and palled with grey the elephant grasses. All of a sudden the world was struggling for its light. The tributary gully to the Lamia ahead was obliterated. Only a channel of illumination reached us from behind, northwards, an orange ray from Lake Albert way. The swift storm had scattered the people with their burdens to shelter in plantain groves, under roof-lips.

We proceeded. All of a sudden the Land Rover drew up.

'My brother-in-law lives in that place,' said Ibrahimu. He referred to Isaya.

Two hundred yards from the road stood a mud house, square, with a metal roof. The rain teemed, the noise of the water increasing violently. Chickens fled incoherently for shelter, heads stuck forward. We ran from the Land Rover, heads stuck forward, for the shelter of the tin roof. We arrived panting, heavily wet, between the mud wall and the skirt of falling water. Lizards whipped away at our coming.

Ibrahimu said, half-way between a question and statement, 'I think you do not have an umbrella.' It was a well-honed announcement, shaped by the Norfolk English Reader, for African

Schools, Book IV. Moreover, I did not have an umbrella, and was not of that order of person to enter upon weeks of sojourn with the Bakonzo of Ruwenzori with an umbrella.

The house appeared to be empty. The door, of narrow bamboo, in a double layer, was bolted and padlocked. There was scarcely a purpose in knocking.

'I think the door is bolted,' Ibrahimu offered, as if again quoting from his Norfolk English Reader.

'Where is your brother-in-law?'

'He is not here. He is not coming.'

Ibrahimu knew that already. We made the dash through the rain because I seemed a rain-defying type. He thought he had followed me here and I thought I had followed him.

I felt a profound futility in my soggy bush jacket with humped side pockets stuffed with a note book, revolver rounds, compass, lens hood, water sterilizing tablets and the rest. My pistol hung impotently on its own belt, with the cloth-covered water bottle. What was my purpose here? A book for the sake of a book? There were many books. A study for the sake of a study? There were so many studies, even if none of the Bakonjo.

'Where *is* Isaya Mukirane?' I demanded.

'My brother-in-law.'

Ibrahimu was using me as a gym horse for his English vocabulary.

'Where is he?"

'He is up.' It was obvious he had known from the start.

Why should I, soaked and marooned under this cascading roof, have come to this place at all? For an idea? *What* idea? Was it for these storm-ridden people, *up* and beyond on the high ridges, by the sunless gullies, to provide the idea? To carry me somewhere beyond? Why should they? Who was I that they should do this? Moreover, to where beyond?

And what had I to bring *them*? Salt, tobacco, aspirin, tea, white sugar, and scarcely enough condensed milk for the fortification of one week's quota of mugs of tea. (I was short of money, pinching pennies.) And their first sustained white presence, their own Munyavenji, from out of the encroaching world; young, without any official brief, yet vaguely sanctioned – by virtue of race or class – by the remote system; empistolled yet benign; undemanding yet obscurely impatient for whatever might happen... It was to be days before Isaya would be found. I have a

full chronicle of them, but we should not loiter.

The Mukama's vehicle bounced and jollied us on to Bubandi market. There the sun swept out, flinging life back into the jumble of open-air commerce conducted by the bibis from the mountains in their goatskins and barkcloth with great panniers of wheat, and cumbrous strings of green plantains and earthen jars for sale. How they did all stir at the portentous Land Rover! and the sting taken out of the bargaining. But almost at once I disembarked my kit on to the mud – my rucksack and attached poncho, my rifle-case – and dismissed the Land Rover back to where it came from, to Kabarole-Fort Portal, its kingly stable, and they perceive me – *who*? – to be alone. I was carefully noticed. Alone; nonetheless, Ibrahimu was with me, barefoot, in his educated shorts.

A first night, right there, in the house of the parish chief, a Mwamba. Then we returned on foot to Isaya's lowland house, by the road. It was occupied now by his wife, Ibrahimu's senior half-sister, who was sweeping the compound at the front door. They greeted in the drawn-out, pause-laden Lukonzo manner; antiphonal, naturally; as monks recite psalms, rhythmic inwardness in the silences, the seeds of chant in the drawling vowels; the other granted time to consider what manner of newcomer you may be. *'Wawukire'* – the day's first greeting –

'E, nau [spoken as *hay, now*] *wawukire.'*

'Kuti?' (How's life?)

'Eneyho!'

'Wahino-wundi?' (And things?)

'Nimirembe.' – the hummed syllable, gravid, contemplatively resigned.

'Oneyo?' – ('You okay?') the central vowel weighted with acknowledgement of the immeasurable significance of the passing show.

'E, nganeyo.'

It was a greeting that rocked, like a moored boat on a tide.

At length Ibrahimu enquired: 'Has Isaya returned?'

'He is on the mountain,' she answered, bunched up. 'He is cutting wood for building.' He had been expected down, and evidently was delayed. Isaya's wife had with her two infants, a boy of two years and a girl of a few months, and a female companion. Since my presence there was surely official and ominous we were offered neither hospitality nor accommodation. The older infant was Charles Wesley, though I had no knowledge at that moment of the name either of mother or offspring. And let us not, with our hindsight, hurry past this lady with the strength in her face. For she is the self-same Christine Mukirania beside whom, forty-four years later – Queen Mother, widow, womb and repository of royal lineage – I was to be seated in a Ugandan presidential Mercedes in cavalcade through the crowds and drums and ululation behind the self-same Charles Wesley, garlanded on his triumphal ride out of Entebbe airport bound for Kampala after his years of exile. Let past and its future interpenetrate...

I proposed at once that we should go up by the route Isaya would descend by, to intercept him if he was on his way. So by stages we mount to the ridge of Bukangama, house of Ibrahimu's father Samwiri Mulwahali, that figure of eminence for whom I have a letter in the hand of Bazarrabusa. We move rapidly up through densely occupied territory of first Baamba and now Bakonzo compounds, by mud paths and over streams, through plantain groves, in heavy equatorial heat, elephant grasses brushing our faces with furry, yellow seed-heads on stems arched by the weight of their fecundity. I have insisted upon carrying my own pack as a point of old principle, but Ibrahimu has taken the folding campbed attached to it, counter-insisting that he must share my load on his own head. On our final steep ascent to Samwiri's spur, two women in goatskins with great jugs of plantain beer atop, skedaddle away from this newcomer with his white-skin deformity to conceal themselves and watch us.

On the ridge top, here was a new round house in skeletal structure of sprung reeds lashed around two poles, awaiting grass as thatch from its builder, George Kahigwa, eldest son and Ibrahimu's half-brother by Samwiri's first wife. I learned that Isaya, though evidently not present, was assisting in this construction. A few paces on ahead rose another new dwelling, but square, with a man on the roof fitting corrugated iron sheets. Below, directing, was an older figure to whom Ibrahimu knelt in greeting – a son greeting a father.

Samwiri was a man of fifty – a late-arriving child of his father Ruhandika and his mother, as implied by his name *Mulwahali* ('he who comes from afar' i.e. born after prolonged childlessness). This 'Isaac', treasured thread of the honoured line, wore a long loose white shift, a kind of galabiyya with tent sleeves. I recorded this description: 'a large man (for a Mukonzo), with a big mouth, and wearing an expression which told of a natural wielding of authority that was in some way hobbled. The result was a curious incompletion: a big man *curtailed.*' After a few words of explanation, with Ibrahimu translating, I passed across my letter. Samwiri had no English: Lutoro, Lukonzo and Swahili would have been his tongues. Of course, I knew nothing yet of this one being the son and heir of a famous chieftain, twice humiliator of the forces of Kabalega of the Banyoro, shelterer of Kasagama, infant prince of Toro, in whose son's Land Rover I had been carried to Bwamba. I was ignorant of all these figures of history, as I was ignorant of the fact that up to six years previously Samwiri had held the highest administrative rank open to a Mukonzo, as sub-county chief in succession to his father, but had been stripped of that office by the (Mutoro) saza chief over a high-handed decision to order the judicial beating of a miscreant without due processes of trial.

Ibrahimu told me at once: 'My father says it is Isaya you must find.'

But where? He was still *up*, cutting his building wood.

I learned that Isaya's true house was further up, as indeed was Samwiri's. From where we stood we could see Samwiri's round house, on Buhundu spur. Isaya's true house, also presumably round, was above that, on Kasulenge.

I was settled under the partial roof. The roofer dropped his cigarette on me. I moved. Samwiri cursed the man. I took tea. It struck me that Bakonzo of significance possessed two houses, the square and round, the official residence and the true hearth, the lower and the higher. And also that the true hearth, the higher, grew most naturally out of the native soil, while the square house, inviting angles and even tin, took more a-building, and the dropping of cigarettes and cursing. From time to time Ibrahimu and I drifted out on to the compound to scan for Isaya approaching. Ibrahimu would crouch to the hard earth of the path's edge and bounce his summons off the scooped ground. Samwiri performed the yell even louder. No Isaya came. It grew suddenly dark.

'Do you eat cock or hen?' Ibrahimu enquired. The appropriate answer was *Yes*, since I was being offered not a gender alternative but a fuller than usual nomenclature of the *genus* chicken.

So in a gaunt unfinished chamber I ate alone a hen of unprecedented rubberiness, including its ovaries and its head and the stock thereof to season a wadge of millet dough, *obundu*, of the consistency – and probably the taste – of warm putty. I slept in my sleeping bag on a corrugated surface of woody reeds, since Samwiri was proud of his sleeping platform raised off the ground where the rats ran.

To wait for what shall be is black, to hurry and harry the future is white. Since the only certainty was that sooner or later Isaya would return to wife and children, I as a future-harrier descended next day to Isaya's roadside house, the square one, where on this occasion we were admitted and provided with another pliable cock-or-hen, the women keeping me at a safe distance. In the morning Ibrahimu and I once more set forth.

We were approaching a tope of plantains at a point where the mountainside flattens to drop more gently towards the interminable rainforest when I spotted approaching at a brisk pace a small dark man in a shirt and shorts. At twenty paces I could see he was worried. This was a king coming. Unknown to him or to me, this was a king coming.

I shook his hand. Isaya Mukirane, *Wabukire*. The shirt was tattered and the dark blue shorts cut down from a former owner's cheap suit. He wore black, broken walking shoes, and no socks. (He had bought the shoes from an Indian cobbler in Kampala for

17.50 shillings.) Patches of pale discoloration on his skin were early evidence of malnutrition.

I handed him Bazarrabusa's letter. A faint glow of relief found a place behind his frown. He had heard that very morning how a white 'officer' was searching for him. Though he knew of no further misdemeanour, he supposed it must mean trouble. There were regulations on tree felling.

'Where is your wood?' I asked.

It was still lying where he had cut it, he said.

'Then let me come with you to bring it where it is needed.' My proposal was unexpected. It was unprecedented in its very mode, as between white and black.

Okay. Indeed, we could together fetch part of it.

This was a task that would come to occupy much of the remainder of the day.

So the three of us emerged out of the lowland plantain groves and mounted towards Buhundu. The grasses were grey-green and shone like the sea, moving in waves under the strokes of the wind, and the white scrub bushes were crests to the waves. Steeply above us, beginning at 8,000 feet, spread the dark pall of the highland forest. Twenty or thirty miles to the south of us, under a joyful sky, snowy tops of the Emin cluster briefly revealed themselves. Yet the heights are never long at rest, and will not let men rest.They proclaim flux. I think of the mountains in their clouds also as waves, and the peaks the truly dangerous combers I have written of.

I made a note that very day of a 'despair' in Isaya that my friend Syahuka-Muhindo has since spoken of as the 'anguish' such as was to drive him to achieve what he did. But I would say to good Syahuka that I was *there* at this critical moment of Isaya's inner history, and of the Bakonzo's history, inner and outer, and that the line between despair and anguish is not a distinct one. Syahuka-Muhindo scarcely knew him: he was a boy when Isaya died. Despair is of course the ultimate negative, since without hope there is no action and no access to amelioration. And yet not to have confronted despair, not to have contemplated that abyss, is very likely to be deprived of that ensuing faith which endures in all circumstances. The polarities *are* the root of all of us, in the further ground.

What I can vouch for – can indeed trace in my own detailed reportage – is that when Isaya and I first met he saw no way forward, neither for himself nor for the people he belonged to, nor indeed for anything he might uphold in the face of an indifferent and impervious world; but that when we parted, it was otherwise: what had intervened was week upon week of galvanization of bodily and mental endeavour to meet the requirements of the task we had chosen for ourselves. We may even say a saving vision had been hinted, a rosy glow on Nzururu's daring heights fleetingly glimpsed whensoever Kitasamba would concede it. I was greeting a man at his nadir of private despair; I left him possessed of a sense that whatever the ubiquity of injustice, Justice was indestructible – an ultimate Theodicy. This was the lifting of despair lifted to an Isaian anguish.

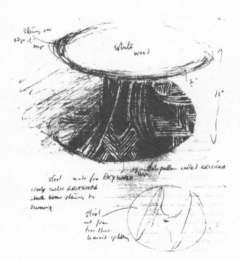

I wrote that day, 'His face tells of his isolation. He is a man alone. I watch him regulating the regard he gives when addressing others as if by conscious effort of the brain.' These same eyes (so I recorded) evince a confusion of pride and guiltiness when we pass the skeletal structure of the new round house for his brother-in-law George Kahigwa, it being of the primal design, not the colonial. I persuade him that this is, already, the moment for him to explain to me the traditional method of construction. He responds with a complaint that I have given him no time to prepare for the study of Bakonzo life and history (such as was becoming the vaguest theme of my possible book). I could have counter-protested that I could not have dared form any such intention until I had met him. Surrendering to this logic, he begins his explanation; and in my big notebook beside me as I write now are the detailed drawings I made that day of the method of round-house construction – and the stool I sat on to make them.

Some of the trimmed saplings he had cut are intended for his own new square house by the road. These I proceed to carry down by the steep paths; but as we approach the gentler ground of plantain groves and denser settlement, the implacable hieratics of race have him forbidding me to be seen engaged in such a task, and then and there he commandeers a pair of Baamba to carry the poles. A softer understanding arises between us, both from my acceding thus to his authority as from his own toleration of my eccentric disdain of colonial presumptions.

vii

At Work with Isaya

No note survives of my proposing to him that he should be my dragoman and co-researcher into the *moeurs* and mythology of his own people, on a long march through most of the length territory. What we did together was not so much planned as allowed to emerge. I was to write a book: it was to be about these people in this place: it could not presume to be anthroplogical in an academic sense: it would simply hold to the truth about what I might learn of these people, and – juxtaposing these of the simple life with us citizens, sophisticates, *boulevardiers* – perhaps prompt another truth. Thus there was an interior brief, without parameters.

Nothing awaiting the act of creation is predictable, unless in dreams. In the end, after the failures, the literary brief would be fulfilled – more or less to my satisfaction – in *The Brothers M* . As a published piece of work, that was to be six years later. But that work of fiction, set here in these mountains, was only the start of what was to prove the assisting in the generating of kings, hoisting a standard, meliorating rebellion, skeining out a dynasty. All that I accepted on entering those Bwamba hills of northern Ruwenzori was that there were no parameters. Isaya's and my intentions grew in our hands and under our feet.

From that first day we were intensely at work. At some point within those first few hours he dropped the remark 'when I start teaching again...' with the intention to mislead me into supposing that he had the option to teach again. He had no such option. Already I knew he had received a letter, several months previously, confirming his 'resignation' as a primary school teacher in the Toro system; that he had been jostled and harried into the 'resignation' after establishing a name for himself in his two years of service as an intractable subordinate. His career had come to a stop six months previously when the effort of finding him a post proved too much for the educational Department. He was 'advised' to go

70

home and wait for word of a further appointment. Then a letter was delivered to him formally accepting his resignation from the teaching profession – a resignation he had never tendered. Bazarrabusa had confided that much to me already. So I let Isaya's false hint go through to the wicket-keeper. Weeks later he did tell me about that letter – the sting of it. We had come to trust one another utterly by then. As to Timothy Bazarrabusa, Isaya reckoned the senior man had sacrificed him in fear that he, Isaya, might confirm the vulgar suspicion that his fellow tribesmen were, after all, *njo*, blighted, in the Swahili connotation of the sound.

Isaya had spent four years training as a teacher, first at the local Toro teachers' training college at Nyakasura and then at the training college ten miles outside the national capital of Kampala. It was unprecedented to find a Mukonzo at such a place – this bandy little fellow from some backward people in an unknown territory. Among those clannish students from among such dominant peoples as the Baganda, Acholi, Teso, Banyankole and Banyoro, Isaya *was* the one with the blight. If he were to have any regional intercourse with a fellow student it would only be with a Mutoro – and in the other's language, naturally. His first appointment was to a school at Mbarara, Ankole territory.

The one thing which had singled out Isaya from all his tribe was a refusal to endure the smart of vassalage to their plainland neighbours which the British had endorsed. This refusal he combined with a conviction that the scheme of knowledge brought by those same British was sacrosant. The contempt his fellow student teachers pretended for their colonial-devised course affronted him. For he knew it to be hollow. He took up his appointments only to witness the duplicity and venality of headmasters (from other tribes) who over-crowded the classes for the capitation fees they got, fudged the curriculum, and stayed away from their posts for days in succession while they cultivated a cotton cash crop over the hill. In his mudwalled room with his two European shirts, his blue trousers (cut down), his 17.50 shilling shoes, his Testament (in English) and his young wife, grand-daughter of Chief Ruhandika, Isaya yearned for and mourned for his own people in their distant mountains... in their ignorance, their purity and their biding strength. Iron was entering the soul.

From Mbarara, lastly, to Toro, where his persecution was more vividly personal and ethnically precise. He survived a year or two, in whichever primary school it was. Then he was sent home: he had to go, though it was edged with private catastrophe. Six years earlier the people of Kasulenge, his own high spur (where Ruhandika had hidden Toro's royal heir in the cave of Ekaleyaleya) had seen their boy go forth, the chosen one – chosen out of the smallest clan – to go *down*, into the other world, that of the plainsmen, the master tribes, Baganda, Banyoro, Batoro and the rest. Six years – four in the training, two in the faltering execution of the role, then this failure in a manner piercingly vivid in his own eyes. We seldom perceive the secret goads of our fellows. The sin which impels another man to sainthood is minuscule to the rest of us. An eyebrow raised in disdain seeds in the future rebel an absolute requirement of power.

Recall, recall that long evening with Isaya Mukirane – could it have been my very first in that company? – in the squared house, still incomplete, of his father-in-law Samwiri on Bukangama spur, the four of us in conversation in the smoke of the slow fire, and the comfort of plaintain beer: Samwiri son of Ruhandika, Isaya, young Ibrahimu and I. We had the light of my paraffin lamp – paltry light, enough for me to jot an *aide-mémoire* to jog me in the morning, but not so bright as to button back the private chagrin from soft confession. We must have begun with the writer of my letter of introduction, Timothy Bazarrabusa. I have a note of a summary aside to me from Ibrahimu, after Isaya and Samwiri had been discussing him in Lukonzo. '*We do not know him.*' What is best learned is intimately learned, from glimpse and hint that does not always make it to outright statement.

Samwiri had gotten primary *and* secondary eduction (in Toro) and as a boy had served as clerk to his illiterate father's subcounty-gombolola chieftainship. On Ruhandika's death he inherited it, the sole Mukonzo to exercise formal authority on even that modest, subcounty scale. It survived until 1948. Then occurred the incident of the Konzo miscreant whom Samwiri ordered to be judicially chastised. There were doubts as to the fellow's guilt; questions were raised as to Samwiri's legal rights; the case was discussed by the local government authority which found Samwiri technically at fault, and fined him several humiliating shillings. Bakonzo feelings were roused this way and that, and a white man out of the office of the District Commissioner in Fort Portal raised the issue of Samwiri's continuing suitability. It was not the first controversy surrounding Samwiri. There was a story around of his use of an old-fashioned, not to say mediaeval, method of extracting the truth from captured thieves – namely, strapping them to a bedframe and lighting a fire beneath. King George of Toro claimed to have told him his role was to protect not fry his people. I learned this through enquiring the meaning of his younger son, Ibrahimu's, Konzo name 'Ndyanabaïsi', and was given the translation as 'son of the one who eats with his opponents'. On my enquiring further, the young man himself told me it recalled a time when his father, although unpopular among his subjects, was of necessity – as chief – recipient of their hospitality. An alternative Mukonzo of standing was sought for what was an unquestionably majority population of Bakonzo in the hills above Bundibugyo, but none seemed to qualify, least of all in the command of the written word. So a Mutoro was put in Samwiri's place.

Outside our hut it had long grown dark. A low drum persisted meditatively from somewhere on a ridge beneath us. We had already been provided separately (as a gesture of respect) a heavy meal of glutinous ovundu – millet porridge – on a grass plate, and portions of a rubbery chicken in a coiled, sunbaked bowl made exquisite by the rolling around of its outer rim (when soft clay) of a green seed-pod stem of a certain grass, *embatama*. I scooped the salty stock into my mouth by making clumsy cups of the grey dough, with my palm and thumb. I had been treated to the gristly ovaries and dared not return them uneaten. All that the Batoro's king Toad in his wicker-and-daub palace on Kabarole hill had warned about the mountain-dwellers' comestibles was already confirmed: the indigenous grub was lousy. I would stick with it, I knew, relying on sheer hunger to oblige appetite: to eat native was a matter of Stacey principle learned in Malaya. My host group and their women ate the rest of the arthritic bird in the cooking hut. Now we were on stools around the fire in the middle of the hut, twisting the long logs into the embers, enough to keep the warmth up and the smoke down. We were at 6,500 feet here. A grin played around Samwiri's broad mouth as he told of his misfortunes and of his people's loss of their own authority: a grieving grin at life's futility, at smudged history, glory erased. The banana beer loosened him, and the telling diffused the pain. Isaya, frowning, was translating. I was being slowly accepted into the bosom of them, listening, holding on to the narrative, in sympathy, wholly attentive. All at once Isaya said, 'That is why we hate the Batoro!'

I was white, an outsider, yet young, bearing no baggage, neither goods nor attitude, an outsider entering within, eyes smarting from their smoke, a fourth log halfway into the embers, lineaments of face picked out by the same Rembrandt lamplight as theirs, coming out of Congo-side not Uganda-side and thus dissociated, a kind of arbiter and yet of course of the intruding civilisation's mystic power with its guns and Jesus and tyrannous literacy, its gross ignorance and its alien wisdom. The paraffin flame made impenetrably deep the vertical gullies of persecution between Isaya's eyebrows. He had entered a long speech of his own. The beer, and age, and the end of the day had brought his father-in-law into a bleary silence, staring into the fire. Now spoke the young ex-teacher, the only such Mukonzo at this region of the mountains, not out of his twenties yet driven into redundancy and retirement among a people yearning for the new Light of whiteness. The Batoro oppressors cast the Bakonzo as inferior. The Bakonzo here had no schools of their own. Whenever – against the odds – they got to attend a school (to be taught in the medium of English and Rutoro), they proved smarter than the Batoro. The Batoro were lazy, the Bakonzo diligent. The Batoro wilfully kept them down. Why, this very fellow Ibrahimu here, Isaya's brother-in-law, had swiftly mastered standard Secondary II, only to be persistently failed by his Mutoro headmaster who, aware of the boy's chiefly heritage, would frustrate his entry into a higher school and his passport to advancement. Ibrahimu's elder half-brother George Kahigwa on the next spur had been permitted his ascent up the educational ladder in line with his abilities only by virtue of his father then holding the gombolola chieftainship.

Already by that night I found I had the means in me to dissolve for an instant those parallel ruts of persecution on Isaya's brow.

The drum below had ceased. Samwiri on his stool had propped his heavy back against the mud wall partitioning our section of the hut from the women's. He had drifted into boozy somnolence. I began to put together my camp bed – a strip of canvas with sprung steel legs in three shallow Ws. It served to keep one's body and rats apart, if only by inches. It struck me that in history one civilisation has prevailed over another by little more than inches.

Before we awake that next morning, I wish here to make a Jesus-point that readers at this moment of our own English history need to have explained. It concerns the missionary factor in Africa, such as our *bien pensants, boulevardiers,* affect to deride as crabbing, paternalist, guilt-breeding and destructive of the vibrant innocence of an antique symbiosis between native man and his native environment. Christians came to lay one set of myths, of alien provenance, upon another, of indigenous aptness.

I am not of this view. And it is important to reflect where the truth lies because Isaya was the product of mission education and Anglican adherence, in a country in which competitively proselytizing Christianity had led to its very creation and the colonial presence. Isaya believed. Many a fellow Ugandan believed; and believes still.

He believed on account of the light the gospel brought his soul. I venture to say that pre-Christian Africa was no less soul but with little light. Pre-Christian Britain was much the same. The converts of Patrick or Columba or Augustine Cantuar could no more go back on the light their souls had been brought by the message of the gospels than the converts of Bishop Hannington, the Reverend Alec MacKay, or the White Fathers of Uganda. The first whites to arrive in Buganda witnessed daily executions for ridiculous offences at the whim of a Kabaka revelling in absolute power. Large numbers of young men were ritually sacrificed – bludgeoned to death – as propitiation or thank-offerings to the spirits. Sickness was the consequence of magic. To be childless meant forfeiture of *being*. Life was short; capricious death everywhere. The Lukonzo name *Mukirane* was given to a child born after the death of its immediately preceding sibling: it was an all too common appellation. When at length I came to write the novel *The Brothers M* to which the journey in Ruwenzori in 1954 gave birth, the plot hinged on the maternal Konzo aunt of my central Ganda character having been ejected from the community of her fellow Bakonzo in the southern Ruwenzori foothills – to die in exile for an 'offence' she had no option to avoid. I shall soon come to describe the real events from which the story was drawn, as recorded by me in the village of Kituti. Isaya beside me struggled to explain the precise cause of that dark cruelty. He did not condone it, nor precisely condemn it. He regretted it, in the mood of regretting what was unavoidable in the circumstances. The circumstances were that these fellow Konzo of his were living in the mountains and encircled by many dangers and caprices of place and weather. Storm, cold, fog, beast, torrent and declivity threatened them, and from all these, and illness too, frail Konzo man had as yet no protection whatsoever but to keep on bargaining terms with those spirits which have such threats in their ordnance of misfortunes. He himself might be able to place his trust in Jesus, but those who as yet knew not Jesus could hardly be left naked.

Christianity to Isaya *was* light amid this shot dark. It was an affirmation of the true justice, at least in the end, 'as it is in heaven'. It was also often visible kindness, for the incoming missionaries were truly good people, a living sacrifice; it was medicine, in no respect dependent on magic. It was an alternative and superior cosmology, soaring even above the mountains' snow, above Nzururu, above Nyamuhanga with all his wives, subsuming them all, presided upon by a triune majesty that incorporated the bleeding, dying, wickedly misjudged failure Jesus, the discarded cornerstone. It was most vividly *other*, and purveyed by the *wa-*zungu, us whites, with overwhelming technology and very soon the apparatus of colonial authority. This Christianity therefore was a liberation at the cost of a certain liberty, the inner at the expense of the outer. This same race of whites who brought the gospel of love and hope had confirmed the paramountcy of Toro over Rwenzururu, printed the sacred word of Jesus-God in Rutoro not Lukonzo, and ordained a system of enlightenment through education which could find no employment for the only Konzo from the northern end of the mountains qualified to teach.

I, Tom Stacey, 24, had sought out this man, in the heart of his fortress homeland – I a *mu*-zungu, harbinger of the new dispensation yet not of its apparatus, beholden to none (except a wife and two infants in 14a Bolton Gardens, SW5); bold, determined, fatigued, strong in the legs, linguistically hobbled, imbued with the certainties of youth, as ignorant as my still empty notebooks, deceptively poor, yet with the appropriate talismans of the dominant culture: camera, pistol, penknife, battery torch, malarial prophylactic, compass, map (drawn from quite recent aerial photography of Ruwenzori) and the ability to read it. I carried no Christian scriptures, yet knew the stories, hymns and purport of the Message. Insofar as I was culturally intelligible to Isaya, it was in the primal, pre-Pentecostal context – fellow heir to the liberation that had touched him, yet alongside him amid his people in their mountains without brief, without judgment. A few weeks later Isaya was to entitle me *musabuli*, which carried implications of open-ended responsibility, yet changed nothing at the time. I asked Isaya to translate the word for me, and he replied, *He who is lifting them out who are sinking down into swamps*, among

which swamps (inspired by the 69th Psalm) he included both his own personal Slough of Despond and the apparently inexorable slide to extinction of the Bakonzo, politically and ethnically, in Greater Toro. Nine years after the present journey was done, I took a close look at a copy of the New Testament newly translated by the Catholic fathers of Beni, in the language of the more numerous 'Banande', so-called, resident in the lowlands of the Congo side of the border to the south-west of the mountains, who share the tongue and the blood of Ruwenzori's Bakonzo. There at once my eye fell on the word *Musabuli* as that used for 'Saviour' and

'Redeemer' throughout the text. Whatever the relative poverty of the Bantu vocabulary, I read it with alarm: I resolved to confine my self-view to the role purely and simply *vis à vis* the victims of swamps. The reader will understand why today, with the Lukonzo Testament widely known among a prevailingly literate people of over half a million on the Uganda side of the border and a less literate three million beyond it, I do not refer to my first, king-bestowed honorific unless it be in utmost privacy.

In the morning we awoke on Harugali spur to a report that a Mwamba had died of cold in the mountains, somewhere beneath the peak of Karangura, crossing on foot from Fort Portal. The issue arose at once: what was to be done with the body? It could not be abandoned where it was, beside a known forest route, as a haunt of spirits: it must either be buried, or carried down to Bundibugyo-side. Either way it was a problem and a task for the Bakonzo, since the Baamba would now be too full of fear to mount themselves to such a hostile, blighted place. I put it to him that if any here from Samwiri's compound were to go up to deal with this death, I would accompany them. I was free of the authority of spirits.

Within hours, a group of us assembled. We reached a high Konzo spur named Ngogo, and slept there. A sturdy, thick-built uncomplaining fellow had by now been formally attached to us, as a porter and one versed in the highland tracks. He was called Kigoma, signifying 'Drum' and by the love-labour of metaphor *of the Moon*, and so given to an infant born under a full moon - and by prophetic instinct given by me to the character built out of Isaya when I came to write *The Brothers M*. This good hod-man was to accompany us throughout our entire journey during the coming months. He possessed formidable strength in his bandy shanks. No physical challenge daunted him.

I noted the cold at Ngogo. The huts of this upland settlement, just below the forest perimeter at approximately the 8000 foot contour, were clad with the sheath leaves of bamboos, which exclusively comprised the forest above us between the contours of approximately nine to ten thousand feet – a barrier, as we have noted earlier, not readily penetrable by men except where they have hacked out a track or can slip through by a stream's bed. We were above the plantain level here. Millet and highland yams, and wheat too, were the strong crops. There were coarse-fleeced sheep, brown-black in colouring. They and the goats ruminated in the three-fourths darkness beyond our fire and our lamp's range. An apprehension hung over our frail prospective funereal delegation, and indeed the villagers we were among, one of whose number had chanced upon the body of the Mwamba two or three days earlier. He had not inspected the corpse, yet knew the victim to be an itinerant Mwamba. The dead man sat in all our speech and our ruminant thoughts. That lowland tribe, it seemed, were for ever fearful of the heights, and not accustomed to the Konzo discipline of never pausing when Kitasamba struck with hail or rainstorm but to keep on the move, moving down. That spur's medicine man had joined us in our hut, an old, poxed fellow in a ragged shirt of blue, and with his fibre string-bag containing his striating tools and animal and herbal powders for rubbing into his incisions. He had Isaya's respect. I had encountered medicine men already in my crossing of the continent, and medicine women also, had noted their powers, and was inclined to read evil into them. Evil there could be, yet by no means necessarily, and I was to learn that what I first read in their faces as maleficent was not that but *inward*. Before they were done with me on this journey, these Bakonzo will have come to me in dawn-light, and one man with such skills as this fellow will have made three parallel nicks with his Konzo-made razor each side of my breastbone above the sternum, and rubbed into the little wounds the ash of burned leopard fur. Why? To give me a long life of sustained energy. The cuts' stains are still visible on my old skin, and something of leopard-energy still with me.

There is a night-note concerning Isaya in my diary entry covering that date. On this high spur a new hut built by the chief's sons had been given over to us. But the meal was wickedly late in coming, and exhaustion was closing me down. I guessed the lateness was caused by the women's struggle for perfection over a narrow fire. I stepped out into the compound, where the night wind was bitter off the mountains. The sky was of an exquisite clarity, our moon a thin crescent. The bamboo sheath-leaf huts, six or seven of them, were great white artichokes in the starlight. Far below – six thousand feet – the pall of the jungle stretched away into infinite darkness. White in the same starlight rose the tendrils of smoke from out of the region of jungle nearest to the mountains' base where the Semliki invisibly coiled its waters northwards to Albert Nyanza. A twisting line of night mist betrayed its course, like a discarded girdle – that's the river's name in Lukonzo: *akalemba*, belt. The smoke tendrils were of the last fires of that night's encampments of the Bambuti pygmies, with whom the lower dwelling Bakonzo and the Baamba did barter in jungle produce, and sometimes mated. I wrote of that distant nocturne that 'you could feel it under your hands, like a toy landscape in our blankets at night.'

We had no bed-blankets here but barkcloth. I had my sleeping bag, army surplus, and a second one – which Erisa Kironde had used – I had lent to Isaya for these high places. I knew that this small dead-attending expedition-within-an-expedition was troubling to Isaya, although he acknowledged the need for intervention and was relieved (I felt sure of this) by my personal spirit-immune participation. I re-entered our hut, amid the tang of its bamboo smoke, and settled on the brand new stool, shaped like a narrow-waisted cotton spool, which had been sent for specially that very evening from the stool-carver on a spur below. The old mutahwa-doctor of the string bag of charms and ritual implementa had retired, but the young man who found the body when hunting in the forest was still present. I fought sleep long enough to do justice to the yams and cassava and a rubble of stewed chicken that at last were brought. Yet when sleep was finally permitted, it did not come easily and was ruckled. Kigoma, Isaya, and I were sharing the hut as a bed chamber. 'The goats go on ruminating' – I recorded – 'after the lantern is put out. I lie awake with the tickle in the throat left by the mountain yams. The fire all but gone. It is cold. Some of the bamboo sheath leaves of our thatch are absent. Wind flows through the holes and shifts the straw over by the door. There is a door of yellow reeds. I can hear the twitching of the straw. Is it wind or rats? I am unsuitably alert and the mind dashing out with the night wind into a thousand places where neither mind and body would take it during the day. Isaya stirs, and sharply moves in his straw' – he had nested his sleeping bag in a pile of dry fodder. 'He cries out. It is 2 a.m.' Kigoma seemed not to hear him. Isaya continued to talk rapidly in Lukonzo, but in his sleep. Then he shifted his sleeping position, as if brushing consciousness and fell into quiet sleep.

At 4 a.m. I was again not quite asleep. The wind still invaded through the far side of the hut. Starlight crept in by the door, otherwise it was all dark. Isaya called again. I shone my torch. He sat up and leaned forward in his sleeping bag, his eyes wide open, staring downwards. A rat scuttled off from the region of his feet in the sleeping bag. Then he rolled sideways, and lay in a crouch. He was out of his bag from the waist up. His shirt was open. He was asleep throughout. Marks of blood on his shirt can only have come from protective cuts made on his chest by the medicine man. Beside him lay the little red notebook I had provided to help him plan our activities. I shone my torch towards gaps in the hut's cladding. I caught pairs of red eyes of rats on the earth floor. The wind flowing in was already the wind of morning.

Let me not be supposed immune from the primitive terror of these fellow men, making our gods, imputing to them deeds, ascribing to them speech, vengeance, authority, which had snuffed out the light of one of us, a frail Mwamba, by hail and funk on his mountain. To assuage these gods we had been drawn up to this high forest edge, to bury the evidence of our unacceptable mortality. I look back, writing this account in the comfort of my house in Kensington from where this Sunday I am about to set out to read the lesson at St George's, Campden Hill, from that passage of *The Acts of the Apostles* which tells of Paul's 'proclaiming' with authority to his audience of Athenians that 'Unknown god' to whom they have already erected an altar. Forty-six years ago with no such authority I had ascended this mountainside to lay a ghost and bury a body.

When I awoke it was full daylight. Isaya was writing carefully in his red notebook, sketching out our itinerary when this diversion was done. I stepped outside and stood where the flattened earth of the compound reached the lip of the Ngogo spur. The ground fell steeply away. Behind me, Ruwenzori's heights blocked the reach of the sun. Below lay half the world, nothing between us and that which five thousand feet beneath reached into infinite distance westwards and north. The hills past Bunia, north-west, had hills beyond them. Directly below, on our side of the hidden Semliki and within a mile of the mountain's base, dark trees began to dot the savannah, and as they approached the perimeter of the rain forest, became ever more numerous as if they were a crowd of people hurrying across the plaza to lose themselves in the revolutionary masses.

We set off at a brisk pace, I immediately following the young hunter who found the body, and his dog. We entered the forest within a matter of minutes. We have between us only the two tools, Konzo-smithied, one a short-handled hoe with its blade like the Queen of Spades' spade set at right angles to the short wooden haft; the other a probing hook, *omoöso*, with its crescent head given a cutting edge on the inner curve. The highland forest here was not dense. At a certain altitude, trailing lichen began to appear, eerily festooning the outer branches and resembling the weeds of the dead and a conjuror of fog. It was wet underfoot from the heavy rain and Isaya, behind me, was slithering where it was steep in the new gym shoes he called his 'tennis' I bought for him as his choice at Bundibugyo. All our companions wore skins of goats or velvet monkeys (stitched into bags that hung from the neck), or civets. Isaya's 'tennis' gave him status, becoming an early item of regalia rather as the black-and-white colobus monkey-skin that I was soon to be presented with became an item of my regalia, culture-crossing, the two of us.

The body was pointed out to me at a distance of thirty feet, half-sitting half-lying against a tree. We could smell it. The fellow must have left the track to seek his place to give himself up to Kitasamba and die. I crossed to him alone, briskly. The eyes were open, the jaw slack: a young chap. I was surprised we had beaten the carrion-eaters to him. Rats go with human habitation; vultures go with savannah. Cats would do their own killing. The serval does not range so high. Only the ants were at work. The grave I dug – it was mostly I – was far too shallow for proper protection from future scavengers. Grave-digging is half a day's work for any professional, even with a heavy spade and no roots. There are no Konzo spades. The corpse was barefoot, in a grubby shirt and shorts. He was a young mother's son chancing his luck, on a shortcut from Kabarole. Here was his bundle, containing Ugandan coin on a ringlet of fibre. I lowered the awkward corpse into the mean cavity in its rigor position and glairy water from his mouth spilled onto my trousers and wrist. The earth barely concealed him. I wiped my hands and contaminated arm on the wads of moss. He was not my first dead – at nineteen, I and my platoon had carried back victims of my own Sten in Malaya, for purposes of identification. This Mwamba was my first quiet one. I recalled the sudden meaninglessness of body, implying a conceit to life. Bantu Africa accords every living creature a shadow woven into the creature of flesh which not so much *has* a shadow as *is also* shadow. The shadow supervenes, tapping the species Man into an ancestral ground of being which has sustained a person in life, and by which that person will have in turn contributed to the ancestral line. The line can blur between the living and the dead. The Mwamba, though young, was known to have offspring. His fragment of earthly goods I laid with the body. I presumed a contagion by things associated with the ill-starred, but I did not bury his good stick. While I was at work the young hunter had made a shrine, a foot high, of bamboo sheaths, and left wrapped food there – for propitiation, or, maybe, for Kalissia, for the hunt's god. They were quiet and respectful.

While I was photographing the grave, fog came down and across like a black garment over body parasites with sudden darkness. I watched the needle of my daylight meter plunge to nil. My companions were restless. Isaya brought me a young bamboo he had cut, telling us not to use the Mwamba's staff. We hurried on down – all the way to Ebupomboli, a central spur and parish

headquarters, just across the valley from Isaya's own spur of Kasulenge. We stayed there many days, I asking questions, taking notes, photographing, listening, observing and bonding.

viii

Take the Drum...

The Bakonzo claim common ancestry with the Baganda? I mentioned this the other day to the Kabaka of the Baganda, Ronnie Mutebi, when he was about to meet Charles Wesley, Omusinga of the Bakonzo, for the first time. The Kabaka knew of no such agnatic link. Theirs was an official meeting of two Cultural Leaders, prompted by the President of the Republic himself as a gesture of acknowledgement of Charles's role. Museveni had personally introduced into the constitution the provision – Clause 146 – for the recognition of tribal royalty, provided it represented the will of the relevant 'culture' (to talk of 'tribes' in Uganda these days is thought to be rattling spears and is politically incorrect). By this clause the young Kabaka himself had returned to his capital at Budo, Kampala, in 1993, to the tumultuous delight of most of his six million 'cultural' subjects. The 600-year-old office of Kabaka had been nominally abolished by President Obote in 1966 after his troops shelled and stormed the palace and sent Ronnie's father, King Freddie, fleeing for his life. Two years later King Freddie, a former officer of the Grenadier Guards, was poisoned to death in his East London refuge on the orders – so I have been personally assured by Idi Amin – of the highest authority in Kampala, thus orphaning a pair of sons of whom Kabaka Ronnie is the single survivor.

Just previous to that recent encounter in Kampala of December 1998 between the two tribal leaders, Omusinga Charles had himself been tumultuously welcomed back by his half-million people in Rwenzururu, at various intimate ceremonies and a series of open air rallies, seldom attended by fewer than 30,000 and addressed in masterly style by Charles and by my less masterly self and others. We were by way of restoring a mere two-generation dynasty, founded by Isaya no earlier than 1962, and in abeyance since Charles, then on a scholarship in the US, discretely decided upon regarding himself as an exile from the year 1987. We will come to all that heady drama.

What I need to tell at this point is that after returning from burying the luckless Mwamba and while lodged at Ebupomboli with Isaya, Ibrahimu, and certain of the elders of that spur cluster, I learned of a time long ago when two brothers, Kaganda and Kakonzo, fought over a chicken. The Konzo story runs that a polecat had seized and killed a chicken. The boys' father heard of this and despatched the boys to recover the body of the bird. Kaganda refused: but Kakonzo set forth, found it, and brought it home. It was cooked for the family supper in the usual fashion. The idle Kaganda picked out from the pot the wing, the leg, and the succulent ovaries, that delicacy which had already tested my gastro stamina. Kakonzo remonstrated at this unjustifiable greed. Thus the brothers fell out, and went their separate ways.

In a moment I shall revert to the route that Kakonzo took, while first recording another version of the ancient quarrel which Isaya and I were to gather up some weeks later in the southern hills of Ruwenzori from a wise old woman who also assured us that her Konzo ancestors were of the same stock as the Baganda. They were residents, she said, of the Sese Islands of Lake Victoria, members of a craft clan of boat builders, Bakonzo-Amato. Kakonzo, the elder of a pair of siblings, instructed his brother Kaganda to make a new kind of boat, of clay. Off they sailed in two boats, Kakonzo's of wood, Kaganda's of clay. Sure enough, the clay boat began to sink, and Kaganda to drown. On being rescued by his brother, Kaganda remonstrated at his being instructed to make so daft a vessel. So they fell out and went their ways. A third, less goonish, version has a flavour of Old MacDonald's farm. When the same two brothers' father died, Kaganda wanted to kill a bull. Kakonzo said not a bull but a ram. This Kaganda refused, and proposed a goat, which Kakonzo objected to, suggesting a hen. Kaganda agreed. But when it came to dividing up the cooked fowl, they succeeded in scrapping over which should get the damned ovaries.

All three versions have Kakonzo walking out, and the consensus of those we heard is that, setting forth from their islands of western Lake Victoria, Kakonzo's group migrated to the region of the next great lake, westwards, known to our sooth-sayers as Mwita Njike, 'the killer of locusts' – that is, too broad for a locust swarm to attempt a crossing and survive. To us today it is Lake Edward, its eastern shore in today's Uganda, and western shore in

Congo. They settled in a region they named for the quantity of fallen trees in the region, Eisale, a word deriving from the Lukonzo *emesale,* firewood. A small town of Eisale exists today in that west-of-Edward region of Congo, inhabited by Bakonzo co-tribalists; and before our tale is told we will find Isaya a captive there. Konzo tradition speaks of the people multiplying at Eisale, and of a certain seminal village lying back from the lakeshore, which I noted as Bukove, which is Bukobi in modern orthography, meaning 'ingenious people'; for they carved fine dug-out canoes and stools, and the full range of iron implements and spears – more for hunting than for battle. They were master hunters of the hippopotamus, piercing the beast in the heart with a spear whose shaft fell away to release a float attached by long twine to the head. By means of that float they could trace their prey wherever in the lake's depth it had submerged to die. From Bukobi the ancestral folk spread north to the Semliki basin, where they befriended the pygmies, and thence to Ruwenzori. Repeatedly Isaya and I were to hear speak of of the fountainhead village of Bukobi.

Isaya used to run through with me a list of terms and linguistic formations shared by Konzo and Ganda tongues. We should not give too much weight to the mythic association, yet it is worth noting a recurring Bantu experience that when tribes attain to a certain number, somewhat greater than ten thousand, elements of the ruling élite find cause to divide, with the defecting group establishing its own dynastic structure in new territory. Thus the Banyoro spawned the Batoro, as we have told; and much further

south in Africa since the eighteenth century the Nguni spawned the Zulu which spawned the Matebele. It is possible that ancestral *participants* of the two peoples, Ganda and Konzo/Nande, may have split in ancient times, dwelling adjacently until further divided by the southward-pushing Nilotic or Hima peoples of which I have already written. An elder of Kitolu in Ruwenzori's south spoke of forty-one generations having elapsed since the mythic quarrel –

86

say, seven or eight centuries.

Now my prime informant at Ebupomboli, old Maate, tells me of a more recent ancestor, Kibiniru, who led the hardy into occupying the slopes and steeps of Ruwenzori. He was their patriarch, Maate insists, their Moses, setting forth from Bukobi. This Kibiniru sprinkled his kith and kin along the southern and western flanks of the range. Why, it was Kibiniru himself who brought from Bukobi the seed of the first *olutegha* tree ever to grow up here – the *olutegha* that produced the dense yellow fibre from which are manufactured the armlets that adorn the upper arm and lower leg of every Mukonzo woman and, not so long ago, in the days of Bukobi, was the tribal currency. Look, here across the compound is the armlet weaver, at the entrance of his hut, bracing the armlet circle against a forked stick gripped by his clasped feet: the most honoured of all the spur-dwelling craftsmen after the smithie... It was this Kibiniru's sister's husband, Kibinduka, who brought his people to these *northwestern* slopes. There ensued some sort of armed, territorial scrap with the Baamba, who retreated lower. Kibinduka begat Baragassa, who begat Barongo, who begat Mutoke, who begat this very Maate. Isaya declared this Maate to *be* 'a pedigree'.

Does Maate-the-pedigree mean to imply that the Bakonzo have been occupying these mountains a mere four or five generations of a people who, as a rule, conjoin in matrimony in their teens? It can hardly be so, with their crowded pantheon of *mountain* gods, and panoply of lore and techniques intimately adapted to and drawn from the fact and mystery of *Ruwenzori.* How had they names for so many reptiles, mammals, birds and grubs living only in these mountains in or above the high bamboos? Isaya and I were to collect several such mountain genealogies and ancestors of the various Konzo clans that occupy the range, tracing each one father to son – Mutolovo begetting Missalala, ancestor of the clans Baswagha, Bahira, Abatangi, Abahambu, Avakira, and Abasu – grouped, so I seem to have noted, as Babundu people; meanwhile Missalala's brother Ngununu, of these very spurs where we were ,had begotten Boranda, who begat Malumbe, who begat Khingora, who begat... and all at once we are among us, the living, in our smoky huts and a precarious *now*.

These days of the early 21st century Konzo scholars themselves chart the migrations of the past century or two. The clues lie in the oral traditions of the clans, and indeed in the very origins of the clans which indicate the pioneering of new territory up the mountains under an ancestor of special authority, or of exceptional skills in certain crafts like smithing or hunting or development of high altitude crops like millet or wheat, or the clearance of forest. The sites fixed in folk memory as points of provenance – like Bulega in the Semliki basin northwest of the mountains – tell of an element of what would become Ruwenzori mountain folk pushing southwards from west of Lake Albert, or their being pushed by the spread of the Nilo-Hamitic Lugbara. Possibly technology and even a genetic element enter from that very quarter. The Lugbara were fine tool-makers in iron. Man and man alone cleared Ruwenzori slopes of forest, for the habitance of agricultural folk. It is a daunting task, with iron axe-blades in a high steep place. Why should man wish to colonise *up*? The epidemic scourges. In 1905 the first colonial records told of the devastation in lower Bwamba and along the Semliki of sleeping sickness. People died like flies; but the tsetse fly which carried that plague did not itself survive above six thousand feet. Unaware of the role of the fly, the people at last knew that the contagion spared those living high. The heights were not the refuge of the weak: no, they naturally selected the smart, the hardy, the pioneers.

These people remembered their pioneering ancestors: who made whom, just as we all require to, that son from that father, ultimately to God the father making Adam and rounding out a mate for him. Here in Ruwenzori the ultimate ancestor of all was and is Nyamuhanga, whose very name combines the reproductive *Nya* with *hangi*, the roaming, ranging, ubiquitously flowing spirit, which *mu* brings to personal enduring life. How alike we are, rooting the here and now in the eternal; and by the same requirement finding fixity in the flux. Here was Ruwenzururu. Water and rock. Bantu principle of personhood *ntu* and of sex is ever water; and of indestructibility it is rock. Here was water, spilling water; deluging water, icy water, solid icon water, dangerous, glittering, blinding, unendurable water; corniced, cloud-piercing, exquisite water; and here rock, a rock majesty, a vast metropolis of rock, tectonic phenomenon, rift and collision, metal-yielding rock, servant and master, tool and altar. At the edge of this very compound, Ebupomboli, lay two mystic stones brought and set there by Kibiniru, staking the Konzo claim to this territory.

There is a deal to tell you, as Isaya brought me in, and I conducted him, on our joint exploration of his *terra*, his *patria*, amid whose people past and present we, in coming weeks, would weave a certain unity and he (in a handful of years) would make a flag. I recorded it all, in notes and drawings, and backed it all up with photographs, building before the eyes of my guide a kind of sacred archive: of history, legend, craft, crop, flock, ritual, magic, poisons, spells, the society of spirits, the society of men, of birth, initiations, marriage, death, of things past and things to come, of low forest and high forest, of bamboos, giant heathers, deadly bogs, declivities and coombs, of secret caves and gulches, high torrents and sudden mountain lakes, of spur and pinnacle, moraine and naked rock, hail and thunder, fog and snow and colonnades of ice; of man and beast, man and forest, man and weather, man and mountain, man and *place*; and *this* man, of this place, these people, whom I was at work with, intently, day upon day, moving, asking, listening, making record of – for the hermeneutics of future generations, as it has turned out – Isaya Mukirane himself. I have scarcely begun to bring him alive for you, reader (though I soon shall), for he was scarcely discernible yet to me on those early spurs – Bukangama, Kasulenge, Harugali, Ebupomboli, Kazimba again – but lay there concealed alike to himself as to me, awaiting exposure like a stool foetus-curled in the virgin log, the dug-out in the tree-trunk: unexcavated, unrevealed, the sleeping king.

For this we need tools of metal, and here at Kazimba itself is the smith of the highland Bwamba ridges. See the picture of him, the

force and focus of the man, endowed with the sanctity of craft. And allow me to dwell awhile on metal here in Ruwenzori, and indeed beyond. For with iron, let us understand, came a massive move in the frontiers of our ancestors' power and pride, and nowhere more massive than in sub-Saharan Africa for which there was no intervening age of bronze. Here our ancestors – if not in line of time, yet of our genes, *homo sapiens, homo habilis, homo fabricans* – passed in an evolutionary instant from stone to iron, and thus from dependence upon grubbing and the trap to settlement, hoe and coulter, sowing and reaping, the felling of trees, the clearance of a living and a planting space, the styles of permanence, innumerable artefacts in the marriage of wood and iron, to plough, delve, cut, shave, chisel, gouge, pierce; articles of adornment, treasure, music, rhythm, chase, and war. The Bakonzo assured me they *always* had metal and knew not only how to work it but to smelt it. Geology helps to bear them out: the tectonic Rift at our feet betrays the presence of the crust's ore. So does the ancient pottery of precisely our region of this rift and mountainous event in interlacustrine Africa. Finds of what has come to be known regionally as Urewe ware provide unmistakable clues of iron smelting, through the presence of charcoal, slag, tuyères and furnace bricks. Tuyères are those pipes of pottery through which air is bellowsed – necessarily for a day and a half at a stretch – into the charcoal-heated furnace in which the ore is at length obliged to release its liquid metal. Various sites yield incontrovertible evidence of smelting iron in our region in the first centuries AD; another site, a mere three or four days' trek south of Ruwenzori, in northern Rwanda, indicates smelting in progress a thousand years before that. The copper beads presented to me in Ruwenzori that year, according to the Konzo donor's own oral inheritance, were fashioned of metal smelted from the mountains' own rock, generations before the Europeans came to Kilembe in the eastern foothills 'making their holes and holes', as Isaya phrased it. Copper, as you will know, smelts out at a mere 1100 degrees centigrade, while iron needs 1500 degrees. Interestingly, despite presence of copper ore, and not all of it buried, mid-African archaeology yields up no copper utensils of indigenous origin: only the rare ornament, and the copper ingots cast as currency by Luba-Lunda empire a thousand years ago along the Lualaba river, three hundred miles to the south-west. Iron, it seems, was the first metal mastered here, copper the after-thought; and unless those Rwandan carbon tests deceive, iron came by spontaneous development of the smelting foundry.

Our smith at Kazimba, Maate Muhesi, is aware that there was at least one foundry in his forebears' times (and his is an hereditary profession): it – the furnace – was the womb, he describes it, where metal was gestated. Chippings of red ore were collected from the scree and the talus around the high lakes, and brought down for sale. The *eribwe*-bellows worked by Maate's son, I think, are womanly in their fullness and roundness: he works them with the frenzied insistency of a drummer, standing with two vertical smoke-and-sweat stained *esyomango*-poles which drive the oxygen by way of the *eribwe's* doubled goatskin bags and internal wooden tubing out through the clay *engere*-spout, to sustain the fierce white of the charcoal's heat. A great basket of charcoal stands just inside the forge hut, at whose entrance Maate works. See the smithy's powerful arm with the veins in full relief; see the upper lip thrust forward in concentration; see the gleam of sweat under the hair of his lip, the nostrils clenched upon the focus of the task; the parallel brackets to the corners of the mouth as is characteristic of all those whose creative demand is that of eye and hand and muscular precision. He is fashioning the crescent blade of an *omoöso*, for which there is no English word. He has all the metal he needs from abandoned motors, such as he sometimes saw (prior to abandonment) moving like ants, three or four thousand feet below through Baamba grasslands. Here in his forge lies an axle, here a big end. Yet a mere two generations earlier such scrap, originating from the profligate factories of the whites or the East, was surely rarer. Metal for hoes, spears, razors, neckrings was treasured. When the Arabs came, scouring for slaves and ivory – the old folk remember – the men would prise the *ebiwoliro*-rings from the necks of their womenfolk and hide them. This would split the metal, making it impossible to restore them to the necks of their former owners. Instead, after repair in the forge, the neckrings would be passed to a female child approaching puberty whose head still allowed the hoop of metal to pass. There by God's grace it would remain until death. Here in the picture is just such an *ekiwoliro* of which I write, its sinews framed and twisted by the hand and eye of this very Maate Muhesi.

Years later I heard of a Konzo furnace smelting iron in operation in the hills of southern Busongora, on the other side of the mountains. It was sited in and up from the village of Muhokya, which lies a few miles south where today mining engineers extract cobalt from the vast mounds of tailings from a previous, mid-twentieth century, British-managed copper mine at Kilembe. My informant from Muhokya, Ibrahim Muhonjya, remembered talk in his youth of the foundry, having been in operation when his own grandfathers were growing up – that is to say, in the first two decades of the 20th century. Then it 'disappeared'. However, there is an inhabited spur up there still named Buthale – a word that straddles 'ore' and 'furnace', in the upland parish of Kyanjuki or Kalongo, just below the upper forest's perimeter. Muhonjya would take me up there, he promised, when the region was free of guerillas, to show me the ore diggings. When Isaya ruled the mountains and came to designate the eight counties of the Kingdom, he gave the name of Buthale to that high saza comprising the region above Muhokya; and I speculate now whether this was not in honour of a Konzo source of metal providing the spears to Tibamwenda's rebels (*see* page 47 *ff*) which on colonial orders was destroyed and razed in or around 1920. One day soon I shall mount with my friend Muhonjya to probe the undergrowth for clues of slag, furnace-linings and tuyères. There is a factor here of tribal pride, since foundrymen are half-way to gods; they made a partnership with dumb creation, wrested out what was latent there in ochred rock... Even smiths are few now, in our long-disrupted mountains.

As for our smith, Maate, in 1954, enter his vulcan hut. It is dark with sooty blackness, thick with heat and charcoal fumes; fantastically cobwebbed; and under the roof goatskins hang ready to replace bellow bags. Here is cow horn for rubbing on red-hot spear-heads and blackening them for better malleability, here the *ekiriba*-waterpot for plunging in the fashioned glowing iron and harden it. Since this Maate makes also the hafts and handles of his tools, the earth floor is a litter of wood shavings. A large bundle of bamboo *oboükoko*-sheaths lies at hand, to draw down from for repair of the hut's skin. Maate's anvil is a smoothed volcanic rock; another rock props his heel as he squats to hammer out his art.

Isaya and I, in partnership, set off to move across the interminable ridges of Bwamba, each cultivated spur with its dark torrent, Akakoko and the Sindira, Ekawoön and the Ngüutu, Ebitama and the Kuka, Kasanse and the Nyahuka, Kaleyaleya and the Ngite, Massule and the Luko, Kasulenge and the Nyalulu, Kazemba and the Bibu, Ngogo and the Torkwa, Bumate and the Bimara, Buhundu and the Kyogho, and over the pass in the forest where the Mwamba died, into the *saza* of Burahya, on the east side of the Ruwenzori range at its northern end. Emerging from the

92

upper forest in the early eastern light we did indeed look down on the long peace of the land, and what I was to write as poetry – the 'hills and hollows, and then amid them other hills, myriad, intricately watered, quilted by cultivation, by habitance,' – gathered names! Kitonya, Bunalia, Sibahikwa, Khibwa, Mitumba, Butini, Bunyangabo... How we worked! And how we warmed to the task.

'*October 7. Overhear Isaya singing, inward melisma, "Jesus lives. No longer now..."*' [the Easter hymn], in the Rutoro version, naturally, for there was no Lukonzo translation: it goes on: 'no longer now/can thy terrors, death, appal us; Jesus lives! by this we know/thou, O grave, canst not enthral us. Alleluia.' I was not Jesus as such, but Isaya had by then already entitled me *musabuli*, in recognition of my resurrectional effect, the lifting-up-out-of-the-swamps office, as to himself from his former blank despair and as to the Bakonzo themselves, in their tribal occlusion – *his* Bakonzo for whom this Musabuli had travelled an incalculable distance to make a study of, an enduring record, this long-nosed, pale Munyavinji from the fountainhead of the master civilisation. I had released the Jesus-factor that lay in him: an obligatory hope, a right to worthwhile martyrdom.

My honorific *musabuli* seemed to precede me as we worked our way southward, spur to spur, by way of deep gully to deep gully, the four of us – Isaya, brother-in-law Ibrahimu, the strong sinewed Kigoma, and I. We whites know of a grace peculiar to native black Africa, so that when we speak of Africa a softness enters us, remarking to one another, 'So you, too, like to be in Africa?' Africa at peace finds our peace: peace to peace. Many a gesture has it: a woman bending to lift an infant from the ground: tenderness and endurance that grace consummates. When I tread in my lumpish boots on Isaya's foot, it is *he* who exclaims 'Sorry', since on the instant he is sorrowing for my regret on his behalf. Grace tells him that his own pain is negligible to my discomforture at my own clumsiness. Africans do not judge, that they may not be judged. Whatever you can give in quietness and simplicity, they have grace to receive and magnify. What I had brought to the Bakonzo – my will to delve the roots of them – Isaya was magnifying. On Bunyangabo spur we settled for a while.

What I was learning from and with Isaya was unity. Here I was penetrating the premise of what was to become Isaya's and my joint endeavour, which is to say: the meaning of tribe. Where there is

93

meaning, there is light, and where light is, righteousness shall be found lying there curled and ready to awake. In the fact of tribe there resides that which may uniquely make for righteousness in the fragile soul of man. Let us perceive and honour. Amid these innumerable ridge-tops and steep valleys, these ascents and descents, the slippery tracks in the treacherous boots, the wild storms and sudden breaks of sun, amid the smoky nights, the interminable palavers, the meditative pipes passed from mouth to mouth, amid the listening and observing, the noting and photographing and drawing – Isaya and I working *as one* all day and half the night – there could not be but further exploration: the inner, interpretative discovery. As in my own inadequate words, put on paper later, 'where the map stops / You have made discovery,

>   And now, explorer, forward,
>   For you have entered on a boundless act of faith.'

Somewhere in these early weeks of trek and sojourn, sojourn and trek, the 'boundless act' was entered upon, Isaya and I together: we were moving, driving ourselves forward, at destination all the way – this people, this place. This was the 'boundless act' that was to take Isaya into rebellion, kingship and early death, and the passing of the tribal sceptre to his son Charles Wesley; it was to take me into the wrestle of the composition of *The Brothers M*, into my attempt to restore the 'long peace of the land' in 1963, into my sustaining of allegiance to the Bakonzo throughout the intervening generation, and into being at Charles's side on his return from long exile, to assist in his restoration as Omusinga.

This 'premise' and this 'faith' I write of are therefore of race and place: of the righteous force and function of collective identity, both as to the single community and to the communion of communities. We have in our vaunted 'West' two generations of glib muddle-headedness and facile politics to sweep aside before we can touch truth here.

As I recall it, the very first Article of the United Nations' Charter of Civil and Political Rights declares the right of all peoples of the earth to 'self-determination'. What, then, defines this 'self' that the drafters of that document postulated? Allow me to delve the instincts of those eminent and liberal-hearted dignatories who made the Charter and remind the modern reader that any man's ultimate self or singularity is nothing if not within God. Or shall we say that self stands at the 'still point of the turning world' in the presence of God upon the ground of its nothingness? For that nothingness – to crave a moment's excursion – we may borrow Gregory of Nyssa's *apatheia* or Meister Eckhart's *abgeschiedenheit* ('self-emptiedness' in my private rendering), or Paul's declaration to the Galatians that he 'lives and yet does not live', or with John of the Cross who opened to his Lord the poignancy of his isolation, *vivo sin vivir en mi*, 'I am alive without life in me.' In the territory of Nzururu and Nyabibuya, Kitasamba and Ndyoka, Nyamuhanga and Nyabinje, I venture to draw from Christian perception, since such was Isaya's inheritance also in any pondering the sanctity of self in which men and women are rooted, and no less apt on this high spur. Beset by many a hazard, hail threatening our fragile huts, sickness stalking us, we cling to our mountainside, our precipitous hour, our ever vulnerable exiguous human presence, fortified only by the primal divinity of collective ancestral right to this place. Moreover, if these people are to be truly of my own heart – something other than a topic of study or an exotic source of life's lesser dramas – I can surely allow myself to see and know and care for them in the context of my own cosmology.

Before the previous rains there had occurred on this present mountain spur the death of a certain Kabale. A blight of sickness and foetal miscarriage descended upon his family. First there was consultation with the omutahwa, the healing medium, and then engagement in the healing ritual – *obubadwa* – of nocturnal communication in song with the afflicting spirit Ndyoka and his hirelings. This gift of Kitasamba – song and music generally – plays a critical role in Bakonzo life, for it refines thought and expression, it is gentling and cajoling of hostility (be it from spirit or men), it releases imagination and invokes humour, it may give to a spirit his own voice and so release his pent hostility. Such song is invariably antiphonal, between singer-medium and chorus, the one leading the other into discourse, even argument – even *protest*. Yet sung protest is acceptable protest. There is beer to drink and a beast to sacrifice. Returning to Ruwenzori with Charles Wesley the other day, to restore him to his Omusingaship, we were repeatedly caught up in all these components of Konzo tradition, binding in the ancestors, strengthening their power to counter-strengthen the living. The sheep and heifers slaughtered by or for Omusinga

Charles, were slaughtered in obeisance to the *megara* of this very one here, Isaya, my late companion, Charles's father... In Bunyangabo in 1954, he was initiating me.

To confirm the lifting of the curse – to ensure, as Isaya put it with a mock gravity, Christian to Christian, 'no more troubles from Mister Kabale' – an eluma dance was to be held, at which inescapably I would be guest of honour. Whatever function of 'musabuli' I might so far have earned my title for, in the estimation of Isaya, I was being brought into the centre of these people as a man among men.

In Konzo society, the men ruled the roost: they made the decisions, owned the property, built the homes, hunted the game. The women were not bold – not yet. *They* would regard me cautiously, returning from their cultivation strips of millet or wheat, babies on their rumps or mounting from the lower spurs with great baskets of plantains or cassava supported on their backs by fibrous bands across the crowns of their skulls. They eyed me as I sat on a stool in the compound writing my notes. I would hear the rhythm of their clinking neckrings and bangles pause as they paused to regard me. The older women eyed me from the cassava mortars, or through chinks in the hut walls, scraping the obundu-porridge bowls. They eyed me from the paths; and sometimes on the cultivation strips, bent horizontally at the hip, they would eye me as they sowed seed. Heavy breasted young mothers emerged from the mouths of huts tentatively, like rock fish. From within her hut, squatting at her fire and her clay pot on three stones, the armlet-weaver's wife eyed me. I knew of one woman lying sick in her hut, her child dead within her, and of how she was eyeing with her ears, if only the silence around me.

There was a big drum out on the compound – it was often so. With the eluma dance in prospect, a tiny boy came at it with a couple of sticks and rattled the mountainside. A matter of seconds; then silence. Now the big boys came at it, and two or three stayed at it sustainedly. When the men displaced them, the elaborate oratory of the drum began in earnest. Three eluma flute-players were out there. The compound was crowding with children. Some of the older ones were evicting the brown sheep. Men were approaching from other ridges, in groups; others, already assembled, held back at the compound edge. Just beside me, someone was stretching out a sky-blue kid goatskin to dry in the sun, making a popping sound as the pegs that were to clamp it to the hard earth pierced the hide: it was to be a child's cloak. Its early death (Isaya explained) was the consequence of being taken down to the market, finding no buyer, and on its 'growing tired' climbing the mountainside, the gods took it.

Giant earthen jars of banana beer were set there, beside the drums – two or three of them now – on their trestles. Here were assembled precisely eleven eluma (reed orchestra) players, each enclosing in the right hand a tiny single-noted *erirenga*, a reed gloved with plaited grass stained alternately dark, chequering it, and bearded with a tuft of colobus fur. Each *erirenga* was pitched to a different note, so that between them they climbed a chromatic scale, over-topping the octave by a tone or two. The flautists revolved in a shuffling circle, blowing antiphonally, sounding forth like a concertina played by an idiot, obsessively jerking open and squeezing the instrument as the keyboard hand blindly shifted across the stops, drunk from his own inspiration. The reeds, presages of eternity cut from the Congo's rainforest, were provided by Bambuti pygmies. I remembered then the sound on the record playing in the lane in Fort Portal, and perceived at once the pygmy influence reaching into these high cols, by blood and secrecy, by the low road.

As the circling pipers crossed before the drummers, they concertedly bent towards them in obeisance. Isaya explained, 'They are receiving life.' And so too the circling dancers. One who had been with us for days, with a humorously elongated upper lip, gyrated out from the throng to posture before me with exaggerated turns, calling out 'Musabuli!', then returned to his fellows, each with hands held forward, arms half bent, in utter concentration and urgency in their staccato stamping, and jerking twists of the loins in bark cloth, slaves of the drumbeat, the rattle-rhythm, the *erirenga* breath-rhythm. Women in their goatskins and ankle rattles joined the dance, in their own circling and individual rotating, yet exchanging no glances with the men. The sexual dissipation was nil, for was not the seed half-sacred? That which was reproductive was in bond between dancers and ancestors for the fleet collision in recumbent dark of the *male* and *female* resting perpetually in the tribe.

Wait, now. 'They are receiving *life*,' said Isaya. What did he mean by 'life'? He was putting into English the Lukonzo *omilimu*, a term which has all the torque of the Saviour's promise to bring his followers 'life' more abundantly – that is, inwardly and eternally.

Hence such grave intensity: this was not dance but prayer. It was the conjuring of that force, *ntu*, inherent in the species man, which by ritual and invocation bind the living and the dead, reconciling them (when so required), straddling ancestry and progeny, balming and embalming present life with contentment and enduring wisdom. Hence the attribute of the elder, that honour accruable among the Bakonzo – as among other Bantu people – by the old. The elder is closer to the dead and by virtue of his acknowledged age a better conduit of this essential 'life', inner no less than outer. This *omilimu* is the source of his persuasiveness: persuasiveness both ways – on behalf of the living to the ancestors, and on behalf of the ancestors to the living. Let us enhance *omilimu* by judicious sacrifice. Besides the kid, we killed a sheep (at least one), and ate most of it, vicariously for ancestors, putting out a portion in small shrines on steep, hidden places for the actual palate of ancestors, where only they would find it. This *eluma mabina* continued virtually without pause for two days and nights.

Isaya held himself ever so slightly aloof, yet utterly engaged with these, his people. He and I were the executors of this conjuring, and were intently at work upon every aspect of it, sharing the plantain brew, smoking the communal petiole-stem pipe of the older men, taking sacrificial meat, Isaya in his white buttoned mzungu's shirt and velvet-monkey bag, I in my bush jacket and colobus skin, worn over one shoulder like an abbreviated toga. Nothing missed us, my notes cramming the paper – all the lesser music and song spawning in the huts away from the compound and the thrashing drums, and suddenly private, in intimacy with the ancestral presence. Here in a hut is the *ekhinanga*, the primal lyre, with eight strings, plucked upright – harpwise – and its sounding box, sheathed in goatskin, nestled into the groin. Its music is secret liquid. And in another hut, here, the *enzenze*, the two-stringed fiddle, a hybrid of musical contrivance, dug with devotion out of a hardwood *omwamba* core – maybe mahogany – never more than one tiny instrument from any one tree for spiritual reasons, since the living arboreal entity was and is the genetrix of that particular *enzenze's* music, and for ever contributor to the song that it will accompany: the spirit song. Here are drawings of these intruments – the *enzenze* unique, I daresay, to our Konzo, Isaya's folk. Here in my notes is every name of every component – stem, strings, bridge, frets, sound chamber; how each part was fastened and fitted, how it is held, nursed in the hand and plucked. Isaya and I have teased it all out from the musicians. I would have you take such an *enzenze* from my Konzo cabinet, in England now, and putting its sounding gourd to your nose, have you scent Konzo hut-smoke from 7000 feet and half a century ago, and hear in your ear the tiny buzz of that strange fiddle.

For we are touching now the heart of a certain people where the secret collective *embitha* vow is about to be seeded. I began, some paragraphs ago, to lay forth, to innerly explore (driven or drawn) this dilemma of *homo sapiens'* existence – that to be accorded consciousness is to be pivoted at the crux, the *vero terrore* of his isolation; how he is blessed and cursed by this accident of consciousness that dignifies Man – Mukonzo or Englishman alike – beyond all the rest of living creation, since none can bear that nullity of the pure 'I' but must seek refuge in the diffusion of it: diffusion by love or willed surrender. By virtue of that same accident of consciousness, and of its consequence just described, we frail beings of the passing flesh have presumed a vast presumption – namely that God has made us in his own image. Hence the polar counterpoint of our nullity, that in our nothingness we are heirs to all. Hence our shared agnatic Adam, living metaphor, cleaved to his Eve, and Eve to her Adam, and they made their ragged family, the tiller murdering the shepherd, but the third boy, Seth, assuaging that doubled grief. Hence those fragile few and lonely folk, gone from their Eden and their innocence, simultaneously cleaved to their creator, Nyamuhanga, in obeisance, awe and sacrifice, at first in a degree of dark and terror and then in a measure of such light as could also be named Love.

God of gods, how we run to you for safety.

See then this two-way amelioration of man's nullity, the two-way route of escape from his 'still point': let us say, the inward radiation and the outward radiation, an elemental geometry of concentric circles, multi-dimensional, on the one hand within the laws of space and time and on the other *shedding* laws of space and time. 'They are getting *life*', said Isaya, of his fellows circling that drum. That 'life' was outer and inner, which our geometry should demonstrate as divided and also as one – divided, as it were, by the crux of a figure-of-eight which nonetheless, at the merest twist, opens crux-less as a perfect circle. Picture it.

Take the drum itself: that drum of the drumming had everywhere

accompanied Isaya and me in the mountains, and indeed had been constantly in my ears all these preceding months in Africa. In that myriad beat and fleeting art was always prayer – prayer or half-prayer let loose to whoever had ears to hear it, spirit or men, spoken with the hands (mere mortal hands) or handheld drumsticks upon the hide of a goat, slaughtered (with ritual) for the purpose, and tautened across the hollow of a tree, an *omwamba* – not any tree, but a tree of knowledge, chosen and blessed – for it to yield its astonishing service, mutter and frenzy, sorcery, proclamation; wood and hide and mortal flesh, hands and feet, inner and outer; and the feet moving in circling obeisance on this exiguous spur of high Rwenzururu.

Perceive the 'still point' as the invisible spirit within the drum: the tether point of awareness of the *I*; see those shunting feet of dancers (a little drunk), the twirling pelts of sacrificial beasts and sacrificial trees that clothe man's nakedness, as straining out from the pivotal nothingness of acknowledged self. Men *must* lose themselves amid each other in the world about them and amid whatever made them and all creation: they must love, worship and make art for one another, and for him from whose table they are not worthy so much as to eat the crumbs that fall.

The distinguishing indelibility of our kind is self-awareness. I dare repeat myself. Adam gave the game away by clothing himself. When God saw these 'dressings' (as Isaya would have called them), he protested, 'Who told thee that thou wast naked?' Thereafter was no going back. All his life a man must work to round out identity: subsuming the 'I' in his immediate kin upon whom survival was

mutually dependent in his lair and hunting ground. So the primal collective expands – from mate and offspring to huddled compound, clan and tribe. The agnatic line and link makes circles of common ancestry, widening into the past, and again widening (by progeny) into the future. Thus, circles of spirit. For there is also the inheritance of place, of territory: stream, grove, saddle and spur; fecund ground, damasked cultivation, teeming plains and game-haunted, dappled forest. For us Konzo there is also uniquely *mountain*, and all its majesty and caprice, its thunder and fog.

The sacredness is in the *round*: round sun, round moon, moon-drum, round universe, round hut, round hearthstone, round pot upon the fire, round drop of water, round seed, round womb. The circles ripple out infinitely; yet men cannot sustain the infinite 'without' any better than they can withhold the nullified 'within'. Men must cling to dimension. For all us men, our circles must crave circumference, defined and recognisable, and hence sustained as 'folk', a language, 'home', 'land', a place, a spirit of place, a cosmology, a myth, a ritual, a humour, style and odour, each ringed within its invisible girdle named 'people', 'tribe', 'culture', 'heritage' – the binding and inspiring *we* such as bears the throb of life and common rhythm of the feet. There *has* to be tribe; there has to be tribe if there is to be life, *omilimu*.

Tribe, then, is that which, of the innumerable concentric girdles that permit any man acknowledgement of his being, gives him on this earth his most holy allegiance, for which he would most readily risk his own bodily manifestation of being, thus winning lasting honour among his fellows, and in the sight of the sanctities of place and history, and of inheritance and blood, and also in the sight of the Father of infinite inwardness and outwardness. From this righteous need of collective allegiance, understood well and subtly met, a person goes forth to his or her humble grandeur. Let it be I, let it be you, let it be Isaya, let it be Kigoma, let it be Ibrahimu; let it be Abraham clinging to his conviction of chosenness for his and his Sarah's progeny (by that terrifyingly slender link of Isaac), in *their* Canaan. Let it be that same progeny whose protective Yawe-Nyamuhanga was to speak by the mouth of that earlier Isaya, 'Comfort ye, *my people*, comfort ye', *as* a people, self-defined, and – in course of their history, by the message of one of their number (perceived and acknowledged by himself and a handful of his blood-fellows, as that tribe's Messiah) – was to offer Light to the world even as remotely as Ruwenzori. From *that* people and from *that* Canaan the Word went out to those of other tribes: Angles, Saxons, Bakonzo. That is why I wrote a little earlier in this chapter of the 'righteous force and function of collective identity, both as to the single community and to the *community of communities'*. For by the affirmation of this collective identity palpable in his own kind, man is permitted to live his little gift to the illimitability of those girdles, concentric upon his bare feet on the bare earth of Bunyangabo spur, to embrace his neighbouring communities, even Batoro, even Banyoro... a veritable 'nation' of tribes in the capricious construct of us white colonialists a century and a decade ago; and so embrace mankind, and so creation, all things, visible and invisible.

I, English, am an elder of the Bakonzo now, a double tribesman. So be it; so life is lived.

Isaya and I had more of Rwenzururu to cover. Let me tell it: there is a story here.

When Isaya was king, he ordained the *eluma mabina* to be the sound of his people's unity, for the message of their breath to be borne on the air in minutes from ridge to ridge along the length and girdle of the range. Likewise his son Charles Wesley after him. Father and son said: Konzo homes shall be round, for it is well known no spirit enters a Konzo hut except it be round. The other day, with Charles' return to his people, the word of the eluma was everywhere, even at the airfields.

ix

The Still Point

We went on south. We pushed ourselves with scant relent: spur and gully, spur and gully; each gully with its tumble of water, each spur with its cluster of huts around a swept compound. Nobody had previously traversed thus, nobody black, nobody white... out of highland Bwamba into highland Burahya, out of highland Bunyangabo into highland Busongora. We were braiding this people as none before us ever had. We stayed high, never far from the perimeter of the forest – that was my wish and part of our common purpose for in the higher tiers of habitation Konzo integrity was at its most intact and definable and the inner fastnesses were intimately ours. To stay high served whatever penetration into primal Africa might be accorded me; it was also serving the budding purpose of Isaya Mukirane, which budding has now become the theme of this account.

Isaya and I were indispensable to one another. He was the bellows of my forge and I the bellows of his. I was the initiator and the motivator and the articulator; Isaya delved and conjured and thus raised to visibility the secretive, *within* – the embitha – of his people for the rounding out of the vision of which he would be exemplar, and as exemplar, King. All that, within about eight mere years of this moment we have reached in our gruelling journey, and within thirteen years of his death. There was no such bead yet, cupped in the hand.

Our fame flowed ahead of us: the mystique of my whiteness, betokening mastery, yet Konzo-honouring, Konzo-obeisant, Konzo-guided in all but the drive of it. This was all unprecedented, not hitherto imaginable. Insofar as there were white men, Wazungu, they governed and issued regulations which others, black men, largely carried through; moreover, they governed from below the mountains. But here on his way was a Muzungu with his Konzo comrade, a right hand man, along and high against the forest edge. The Bakonzo's spurs rose as ribs out of the Toro plain. The greater number of fellow tribesmen were ensconced in compounds that lay lower than our route. The big boys and young men would shout up at us and our companions on our higher spurs to learn of our presence and progress, bouncing the sound of their querying off the hard earth wherever the scoop of it might sharpen resonance. By the same trick, they would herald our coming spur-to-spur laterally, across the tight little valleys that divided spurs. Naturally, the fame of us had by now flowed out all around us in that sector of Ruwenzori. We were a moving nucleus of wonderment. Problems, grievances, disputes, ailments were drawn to us as by a magnet. Things possible were expected of me, and things impossible. We would shirk nothing possible. I used to say to Isaya, as a spur to action, 'The best way of getting something done is to do it,' and he took up this fatuous axiom with an amused delight. We patched a little here, ameliorated a little there, at times declared ourselves of no use, at times failed. A clan chief, a certain Biteyo, had a daughter Biira who had a sickness the symptoms of which I forget except that they were grave, and this Biteyo whom we honoured for his age and authority seemed minded to trust the curative powers of white men's medicine over the spells of the local omutahwa and interventions of ancestral spirits. So at one point it was resolved that I would conduct Viira and her father down, out of the mountains, to the mission hospital at Fort Portal. We set off; but within a day, father and daughter had disappeared, defectors from our little mercy excursion for fear of the unknown.

About this time Isaya and I had an interesting conversation. We had been in the presence of a Konzo *omutahwa*, a diviner and

105

counter-charmer, an old one, monkeyish, with hooded eyes that gave him an air of permanent disdain. For one reason or another I had been away from the compound and had returned in the evening to see a note from Isaya left in a cleft stick planted where my path entered the compound, directing me to a certain hut. There I found Isaya with several fellow tribesmen in the medicine man's presence, seated on logs and stools with many species of mammal pelts and reptile skins and fibre bags of bones and desiccated offal dangling from the roof. We were occupying a reliquary of the animal kingdom which was also the smoky dwelling of man, who is chief of the beasts. At our centre, the omutahwa who lived here was caparisoned in a leopard skin and other fur, and leaned forward on the *ekithumbi kyasukulhu*, the grandfather's [ancestral] stool. He was engaged upon a heap of cassava flour in a grass-woven platter.

In this community I was by now accepted, and in any case Isaya must have warned them of my probable entry into this hut. I settled on an unfinished stool to one side. It has since occurred to me that this stool had been left vacant for the spirit to be invoked, as Jews leave a place for Elijah at Passover, since within a few feet of it, against the hut's wall, a pot containing food had been put out as an offering. I have subsequently learned of spirits occupying stools in the intimacy of Bantu rituals, and of empty stools being tilted in ordinary domestic gatherings to prevent occupancy by unwanted spirits. Yet the fact of its being unfinished, and Isaya's care in protecting me from blunders of desecration, help to reassure me across this half-century. The medicine man did shoot me glances from under the hairless lids; yet the rest paid me little heed.

Isaya moved beside me. He murmured, 'The old man is explaining future things by the flour.' The omutahwa was shaking the flour off the edge of the platter on the bare earth, and peering to see how it had fallen. In so old a body all that remained perfect were his fingernails. After each attempted divination, he would sweep the fallen flour into the fire, muttering that it 'spoke' nothing. At length, bending low over a flour pile, he made a slow pronouncement that elicited a sombre, *'E-e-e-ay'* from the assembled group, succeeded by troubled mumbles. Isaya told me, 'The flour says there shall be another death. He sees a hole in it which is the grave.'

The hood-eyed one got to his feet, taking the grass platter with him, and went behind a reed partition. He re-emerged with his carved walking stick, and passed between us all to go outside where darkness had already descended. The group remained. 'They say,' Isaya said, 'he is going up to speak with the spirits.' The territory of the spirits is invariably *up*.

I stayed where I was, Isaya beside me. Among those remaining, in the firelight, I was witnessing the presence of alarm. There was an intensified anxiety also in Isaya's eyes, and the vertical lines of his forehead. I asked in a low voice: 'What do you think about all this?'

'It is what we must believe, Mr Musabuli. 'The 'must' rose out of a layer of being which he and I could not share. My notes record his admission of this. 'You are European.' I waited. 'God made the Europeans better than the Africans in all things. They shall always be so.' 'You think *better*?' 'Yhes, Mr Musabuli. Because we Africans are to be punished he has made us not clever people, and we must have the spirits.' I shook my head. 'Yhes. It is true. I know it.'

I reproduce this fragment from my notes, across the intervening forty-eight years, to pin on the page that sense of irredeemable insufficiency accompanying the so-called Fatal Impact in a world contracting at an accelerating pace. The contraction may be said to have begun with Columbus, or Captain Cook or Van Riebeek, or here in central Africa with H M Stanley and when my grandfathers were going up to university. I myself in Ruwenzori was a participator of that contraction, a part-perpetrator in the eyes of those who insist on laying blame. But let not anyone be too quick to lay blame on Man for this despair – neither on Man nor men, be they good or bad (it is not the point), nor colonisation nor colonialism nor even slavery. Blame – if you must blame – the history of Man, and that is as daft as blaming life for the pain of it. The poignancy I heard that night from Isaya I had already heard from various throats in Africa in 1954 – since when, naturally, I have come to know less than I did then, in the proper meaning of 'knowledge'. Albeit, I can tell you what history subsequently unfolded in the Ruwenzori mountains, and can review the broader narrative of empire and evolving of a three-world world, and Man.

First, as to the mountains. I can remind you what you half-know already, namely that that moment's dialogue, lifted out of the murk and musk of the high hut in the middle of the last century, was uttered by one who within eight years was to become the King of this place; how within the same eight years the colonial protectorate of which he was nominally a citizen would be an independent 'nation'; how within nine years I would be back in the mountains pleading for the reconciliation of Isaya's fledgling kingdom of Rwenzururu with the fledgling State of Uganda; how the mountain kingdom of Rwenzururu would survive another nineteen years; how in forty-five years I would have returned to Isaya's people – by now vastly more numerous – and in the company of his royal son would attend upon the ritual slaughter of sheep and fatted calf sacrificed in honour of him, Isaya, thus to invoke his influence as ancestral spirit, in unhindered reach of the essence of things, in favour of the son's restoration as the repository of the unity and identity of his people.

Next, as to the generality of the opinion Isaya had given voice to. I have reflections which, in the service of boldness in a weasel world, I wish to offer and points I wish to assert. Isaya's was an opinion shared by countless numbers of his fellow Africans at that colonial time of earnest endeavour to redeem the so-called Fatal Impact. I heard it myself from various throats in various formulations, such that, flowing directly from that very journey in the mountains and the months which had preceded it in the company of the Cambridge graduate Erisa, I was impelled to write *The Brothers M*. That fictional narrative was half drawn from life. In it I juxtaposed what was deemed primitive with what was deemed civilized. My story humbled the 'civilized'. It sought to express the point that the truly civilized must be also primitive – just as to be truly experienced is to have remained innocent.

Outside the hut in the dark compound there had been light rain. A thin moon was now up. The clouds had a negative precision to them, white out of black. On this tilting spur certain huts were scattered above us: women moved between them from time to time. I could glimpse the darker lines of certain of the paths weaving through the grasses. I saw the solitary figure of the omutahwa in his many skins and with his stave standing on a knoll a hundred feet away. The outline of his bat ears against the night skyline told me he was staring up towards the mountain heights. In that place, the central peaks were more or less in front, and above, where we were. I had no acquaintance with them yet, other than as a seat of cloud, and of thunder, lightning and hail.

After that, I withdrew to whichever hut it was Isaya and I would be sharing, together with – as a rule – Ibrahimu and Kigoma. There would be a meal to eat; notes to write up, by our paraffin lamp, and then sleep, often taut and thin, and Isaya waking in anxiety to say, 'I was in dreams.' Come up to me, then, by the sunless tributary gullies, to our mountainside, cold, savage and scarcely yet explored by you or me: six or maybe seven huts of bamboo base-leaves sheathing their sprung reed frames and four upright poles, for men bare-footed and bare-legged to keep their fire between three stones – fire which they have carried here as embers with them in pots coiled by their fingers out of their own clay their feet have trod. We crouch about that fire, in the ring of its warmth, shrouded by sheets of cloth beaten by our hands with serrated mallets out of bark flayed from the sacred omuthoma tree such as also shrouds the dead, and further comforted by the dense fur stripped from the corpses of cousin-primates which occupy the forest that lies between us and the towering peaks, and which never learned that they were naked. It is night, and October, 1954. There is always thunder, somewhere; always lightning. There is hail often. One of us, black, short-statured as the rest, wears 'tennis' shoes (already scuffed and torn) and has forced a parting through the dense frizz of his hair as a vain route to other men's supposed salvation. But we have no salvation, not of our own. We are all the same. We have reached as far as this remote high spur of Ruwenzori (having stripped ourselves of all that we cannot carry, which is to say, of all that is not within, at the hour of our need) to discover that we have but a single cry and the same cry, *Lord, have mercy; Kayingo, atsunge.* Thy will be done, what the flour says and the bones say.

Let me stress my point. We white branch of *homo sapiens* came upon the black branch of *homo sapiens* in Africa with our presumptions full blown – as I have fragmentarily sketched already in this piece of writing. We had the Maxim gun, and they had not. We had the written word, and they had not. We had the Church's one foundation and they had not. In all our northern history we were never so sure or so narrow, while they – they clung to survival amid the limitless mysteries of their mountains, lakes, snow and sky. Where the two branches of the forked species touched, however, each recognised the other, and to this day recognises. Where we whites have dared to strip off all that we have pretended to, we have found their *sapientia*, and where they have forgiven they have found ours: we are one *homo*. Learning our devices they become writers, composers, saints; learning theirs, we assume the music and the dance, the primal vision, Eden nakedness. For us, they remember our common roots, such as are of our past *and* of our souls. In the days of our invasion and occupation, we made imperially impossible constructs – states, functional abstracts, methodologies of governance, lifelessness on the grander scale in the name of light and order. Here is and was the fatal impact... Strip, reader, let us pause together, here on Ruwenzori, evolutionary crucible, and enter into what we at times acknowledge, seeking forgiveness, in that we are all crumbs,

> fallen from the Master's table,
> such Mastery as made this rock
> and water made
> and wind, sun, dust, detritus, silt.
> These were his gifts
> indifferently surveyed
> and we, we covert motions
> creviced and murked and damp,
> we swellings in the mud, we
> glomerates, we gave back buds
> and flowers, mosses, love.
> Yea, love we showed him,
> brandished love to Him preoccupied
> with universal things,
> knelt, bowed, on our provincial planet
> demanding mercy.

Are you here in that medicine hut, below the peaks? or four days later in a hunched straw church on Bunyangabo, where with my fellow Konzo we learned that

> One of us
> within our sedimentary nests
> claimed him not Master but
> Abba, Father, claimed and proclaimed
> and so proclaiming died and rose
> sealing at the wood crux
> (where dimensions touch, eternity and time)
> a pact of blood and water
> between the fluke of Him and us.

> We are his crumbs, we diamonds are
> from his terranean carbon ranges,
> tiny and rare, tears for his cheek.
> And of his million million fires

we ring the smoke about the iris of our eyes
his love to recognise.

Isaya beside me on those terranean carbon ranges, in our dark hut smoke, did recognise and ring that love. He himself was 'born again' (his own term, in Lukonzo) at the age of ten, when he was baptised in Bundibugyo's mission church. And he always – when he was King of those mountains arriving at any new headquarters site, confirming his realm – would have not only a barkcloth omutomha tree planted but a church built. Moreover, on behalf of his next son after Charles to survive infancy, Christopher Tabaan, who was born up there in his rebel Kingdom, he sent below for an ordained Mukonzo priest, Anglican, to ascend secretly by night through the high-grassed no-man's-land, and then openly and in the presence of all his people have him baptise that infant with the water of life, together with every other scrap of humanity born to his royal highland entourage beyond the diocesan reach of the comfortable plains. His last offspring, Williams Sibibuka, was also to be christened thus... but fatherless: that was the double thing, baptism and obsequy. We shall come to that.

x

Salt and Heritage

By this levelling to equal crumbs and tears, I mean to remind my reader (not customarily dressed in barkcloth and monkey skins) that those of whom I chiefly write are not apart, not ontologically other; that though you, my non-Mukonzo reader, know nothing of Ruwenzori but what I have told you in these pages, you will find in that remote and savage place, both of that time and of now, an identity of soul, drawing equal water from the common well, heirs to the equal light and equal music. These are neighbours you shall love as yourself. Would I choose to spend these many words troubling you with quaint exotics, turning such tribesmen into objects worthy of condescending wazungu interest through sleight of literary hand? I am not at work to make a crystal cage for an anthropological exhibit.

We made a looping excursion, and have come south, as mentioned. We dipped to the plain – Uganda-side, naturally – and to the murram road that some weeks earlier had brought Erisa and me out of Congo to the west, and on a rackety bus northwards below the eastern heave of the range to Fort Portal. (Aboard that very bus, a few years later, the young conductor was a certain Fanehasi – Phineas. Lodge the name in the memory, for it will return to haunt us)... On this present plainland excursion, we four – Isaya, Ibrahimu, Kigoma and I – intent on marching the borders of the linguistic and ethnic union of Uganda's Konzo-dom, reached the lakes, George and Edward, sleeping at times in the open and in earshot of the throaty commentary of lions. Our lakes, as the map reminds, are linked by a channel, Kazinga, so broad and lazy that grandpa's atlas lumped them as one water, 'Albert Edward Nyanza'. More or less annexed to Edward, between where Kazinga merged with that great lake and the mouth of the Nyamugasani river tumbling out of Ruwenzori's highlands, a dead volcano's

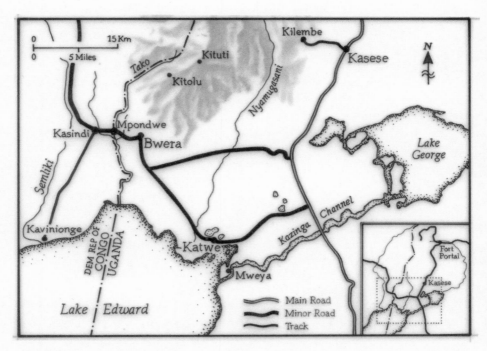

caldera several hundred yards across made a natural saline sump under a hot sky and gave Katwe its ancient industry of salt, traded as much by water as by land.

At Kazinga's outflow into Edward, hippos congregated, their pagan eyes knuckling the surface. Boarding a 25-foot Konzo dug-out, an *eriato*, to which planks were stitched by banana-fibre twine to double the vessel's freeboard, we slid by among the hippos cautiously. Our lake-dwelling companions carried the ingenious hippo spear, *eritumo*, designed to unravel once the steel head was mortally embedded in the beast's life-source – an artery or the heart. For the spearhead was attached to a fibrous float at the other end of the shaft, by twine that tripled or quadrupled the length of the shaft. As the beast plunged, the shaft rode free in the water, to be re-gathered by the hunters. As to the float, the hunters would follow it around the lake while the victim dived and surfaced and dived again, until it grew weak enough for the hunters to risk assaulting it with other spears. A single kill would consume many hours – even days and nights. No man closed on a wounded hippo until he was sure.

Isaya had me gather up on that lakeside such a Konzo hippo-

spear as a further item of Konzo craft, of which I was forming a collection as we progressed: I have the contraption here beside me in Kensington as I write. It was, however, to be nine years before I personally sampled Lake Edward hippo meat – a joint sampling, to be precise, of hippo liver, with a certain Captain Idi Amin who was then engaged in the army's campaign to flush Isaya's secessionists from the mountains.

Hippos then and now were a hazard – the topmost cause of human death by wild animals in Uganda: they capsize man's dug-outs, lazily dunk and drown him since man has no rightful purpose in their water-world. Nor indeed in their land-world. For by night hippos leave the water and browse the lake-shore and its hinterland. Hippos are edgy on *terra firma*, not least for their young, succulent to the big cats. Water is always their safety. Thus if ever man is to be so careless as to camp between a browsing hippo and its nearest water, he and his resting place are asking for hippo-devastation... Our Konzo know their hippo land-lore. See, here was a hippo snare, *kigembi*, which trips the beast so that it drops onto a hippo spear, deadly sharp and already equipped with its float for when the pierced victim lumbers on into the lake.

We ourselves killed nothing, though less out of fear of hippo than of a game warden, since this was National Park territory, newly named after our young Queen, Elizabeth. It encompassed all the north-eastern third of Lake Edward, and the mazy hinterland of savannah, salt-marsh, salt lake, and volcanic crater north and east of the water. Above us, and northwestward, the mountains remained a massive presence under banking cloud. Sometimes with, sometimes without local escort we four moved through this territory behind Katwe. We were sly of foot, since no one lived there and it was populous with animal danger – buffalo, elephant, hippo near (or in) the water. As for the big cats – lion and leopard – these we mostly smelt the tang of, or heard the voice of. Men are not their customary prey; and lesser cat-quarry abounded: gazelle, impala, klipspringer, duiker, reedbuck, warthog. Hyenas dragged at their victims' bones. Delinquent baboons made raids. While elephants are by and large unthreatening, buffs are stroppy. All *we* have are our brains and, at my insistence, my elephant rifle, which was out of its case and assembled for the first time since I came out of the Gabon forest four months previously. I had no mind to fire it unless in defence.

How sooty-dark elephants are – darker in the wild than in the

circus. Is this not well known? And how lumbrous are the pot-
bellied buffalo: downwind of men they turn and weigh the
options, amorality written all over them. We too weigh options,
reading the ears. (The tails meanwhile flick at the rufous flies that
suck their blood.) Big beasts, I know well, when they are not
frightened or ravenous or separated from their young, are
indolent. For instance: who has ever heard of an elephant or
buffalo, unprovoked, charging a man *uphill* from a standing start?
I cannot recall a time when I was not aware of these things – and
cannot but presume that in a matter of but a few hours after
entering a primal scene, any one of us settlers, townees,
sophisticates, boulevardiers, letting ourselves go, would be
regathered by an atavic faculty, instinctual and untrammelled.
Letting go in the wild, we re-enter Eden, naked (so to speak) and
vulnerable, yet *knowing* this place from a former time, preceding
our birth by aeons, wary, wise and unafraid. I was first aware of
this faculty aged nineteen, as a soldier (of sorts) in the Malayan
jungle, and more deeply penetrating that jungle aged 20 to be with
the Temiar hunter-gatherers: how swiftly and surely I came to read
scents, calls, spoor and faeces, and read the caution and curiosity
of fellow mammals. The faculty had been recalled to me in Gabon's
territoire inexploré earlier that present year, 1954, and was never far
from me here in Ruwenzori. Let us be a little the beasts we are.
They neither sow nor reap. They neither sin nor are saved.

Tommy gazelles leaping ahead of us – they stitch the savannah
with geometry. A chameleon is here on a reed beside me where I
have called a rest. I nudge it off on to my hand, and it tries to re-
invent for itself the colour of my skin. When it wishes to escape one
hand I offer it the other. '*O you old devil*,' it says, rolling one eye at
me; yet clings to me purposefully with tiny feet... As evening falls,
vast marabou storks, pantomime necrophiles, rise from whichever
carcase they have been gorging on, and weighted with rotting flesh
fly with whistling wings to their collective eyries in the mountains.

Fear has touched one of us. It turns him kind of sulky, as if I am
wilfully leading him into an ignorant death to which he has no
choice but to abandon himself. His lightness of spirits has
vanished, and his management of English has as good as melted
away. For weeks he had been proudly extending it. But what is the
purpose of small talk in a foreign tongue when lions will shortly
eat you? The place is steamy-hot and with no better sanctuary than
high grass. Moreover the food for us to eat is wrong. No millet

grows here, so we are deprived of our daily *ovundo* (to my relief), and subsist for a staple on omakamata – boiled plantain mash – *matoke* to all old Uganda-hands. Moreover moreover, whereas on the mountainside northwards Ibrahimu arrived in shirt and shorts and sometimes shoes, befitting his status among those usually without any such accoutrements, here every fellow we meet is shirted, trousered and often shod. The salt has made them rich and modern. Ibrahimu is indistinguishable, unless a little threadbare. On reaching Katwe village, I dash him a shirt. I try to cheer him up. 'They're nice people around here,' I comment. 'Yes,' he answers heavily, 'Saturdays and Sundays.' He is making English noises: it is the best he can muster just now. 'Look!' I say: 'We shall be safe. See the stone?' And I point to the heavy stone tied to the thatch of the hut we are to sleep in, by which talisman Bakonzo ensure the security of their homes against raiding beasts. But in his eye, I can see that the stone has confirmed not our safety but the danger we are in.

As for Kigoma, he is Endurance Come What May.

The big lake Mwita Njike makes no boundaries for our Konzo. Families and clans straddle the invisible frontier, which English and Belgian civil servants half a century earlier had drawn in a straight line virtually due north from the mouth of the meandering Ishasha river to the mouth of the Tako, whose waters raced out of inner Ruwenzori. Fifteen miles west of the Tako, at the Semliki's outflow, H M Stanley, wracked and defiant, had emerged from the forest in his river flotilla with his unwilling ward, Emin Pasha; from there, at Kavinyonge, where the Semliki leaves Edward, it is a mere two or three days' paddling to where we were now, at Katwe. Here Stanley torched the village to comply with the scorched-earch policy of the island chief 'Kakuri'. The chief's purpose was to deny the salt industry to the Banyoro. Look to the horizon now, to the low islands from which this Kakuri and his entourage and drummers emerged in a fleet of *eriato* to greet the Breaker of Rocks. Green and sleepy on the horizon rest Katako, Rusuku, Kabazimu, little Izinga *aka* Akatwa Kabalimo, the spirit island, where evil people were executed by drowning with a stone strapped to the back. Old Johannis Mpanya of Katwe remembers Stanley's chief Kakuri as Kakule, first omukama of the islands. Mpanya remembers a lot. If old Maate of Ebupomboli was pedigree, this Mpanya was history.

He is seated on half a stool, on a level below Isaya and me,

118

beside a jumble of drums, his eyes grown smoky. Goatskins and cat pelts dangle from the roof of his hut where we lodge. He has brought out to drape on my broken chair what I take to be a swan skin. But it is not: it is the downy skin of an *ekisohe*. 'The *ekisohe* cannot have a skin,' I protest, having already encountered the word. 'An ekisohe is a fish-trap!' I have only that day drawn the thing in my big notebook. Ah, but the *ekisohe* in my notebook is named after the *pelican*, for they both catch fish... Now this Kakule, Mpanya says, whom Stanley recorded as Kakuri, was a prince of Eisale, the mythic site of Konzo provenance, with Bukobi as its central kraal of which we have heard tell repeatedly on our journey. Eisale, says Mpanya, lies on the western rim of the lake, in what was now Belgian territory. Kakule devised and led the original migration to the islands in order to escape the terrible recurrent visitation of dragged-out death by a coma- or sleep-inducing sickness of whole populations of folk and cattle. White man's science was later to trace this nagana to the tsetse fly and name it *trypanosomiasis*. Though ignorant of the tsetse's role, the cattle-herders were aware of contagion. Kakule resolved to foil it by the four or five miles of water that divided the nearest of the islands from the lakeshore. Thus he transported to his tiny lacustrine archipelago not only his people but all that they required to re-root their culture: beasts, granaries, forges... For this there were no adaptable boats. So he built rafts. Why, old Mpanya still possessed one such *obuato* right here at the back of his house... as an *emboho*, a memento of the heroic days of Konzo-dom. Kakule's migration was at first effective: the next epidemic of nagana passed his islands by. And from that same bastion of islands, as we have seen in chapter i, Kakule defied Kabalega's Runyoro 'and his thieves', in 1889.

It was there on the islands that Mpanya grew up: a thriving Konzo community then – grazing cattle, smithing, weaving fish-traps, building boats, trading salt... Then the tsetse they had escaped so long must have made the crossing from the eastern bank. Tryps devastated them: the British moved the survivors out to Katwe. At that same period what was once all-Konzo territory and Konzo industry became infiltrated by Batoro. The place was no

119

longer their own, least of all their ancient salt monopoly. Mpanya clutched his hands together in his crutch and waggled his knee to shuck the restless sorrow of it.

Lugard had built a jeriba, Fort George, at Katwe, on the strait of land between the fresh water and the cratered salt water. In 1897, when the Battatela tribe far to the west rose in rage against the tyranny of the Belgian settler Baron Dhanis and rampaged through eastern Congo, King Leopold's administrator fled across the lake to take refuge there. I rather doubt he deserved the Union Jack's protection; but one white in half-explored Africa in 1897 can hardly slam a door on another.

From that Battatela tribe, just about the year this narrative has reached, there was emerging a certain Patrice Lumumba. That's a later story.

Meanwhile, despite colonial disappoval, Konzo intercourse across the waters of Lake Edward proved unpoliceable. They ghosted to and fro, using the dark. Here, on Uganda-side, lake-dwelling Bakonzo had learned to be wary of obnoxious Belgians in uniform across the lake, forever demanding their *fiches*, meaningless documents. In Congo, the Belgians called their Konzo people *Banande*. It was an 'invented' word, Mpanya insisted, not authentic, offered to the colonialists, I fancied at the time, as a kind of veil against penetration of the truth of them. (People as *a* people need no name for themselves except in relation to those other than themselves.) The Catholic fathers in Beni were translating the Gospel into 'Lunande' – so I heard. The language was identical to that of Bakonzo residing in the mountains. Among themselves an esoteric communal term that straddled Konzo, Nande, Bindi and other related strains was to enter political currency and acquire the ring of *volk*. We shall encounter it soon in the saga of the coming struggle: *Bayira*.

xi

The Southern Heartland

We left this place where H M Stanley had encountered the island Konzo lord Kakuri/Kakule, and re-entered the mountains and Kitasamba's territory by the spirit's foothills at Isango to lodge awhile with Abraham Lincoln whose picture of him here in 1954 may be placed beside the same fine-chiselled features forty-two years later (p.389) or on his eighty-seventh birthday in 2000. Is there

not Nilotic blood, by the cut of him? Yet he himself rejects such a notion. That physiognomy and the adopted name allowed him to blur his Konzo origins when he so chose. Yet he was a Konzo well enough, descendant of a regional chief from across the border in Congo, where he was born and raised Bahamba Kaleba. He was to marry one of Samwiri Mulwahali's daughters, another grand-daughter of the great northern chief Ruhandika, a sibling of Isaya Mukirane's wife Christine. The two men were thus brothers-in-law.

Linkoni/Lincoln had come south as a young man in the service of the Anglo-Belgian team formed in 1938 to inspect the concrete frontier markers erected in 1911 by the two administrations at the source of the Lamia river in the north-west of the mountains and at the head of the Tako valley in the south-west. Any who has ever tried to trace rivers to ultimate sources will know them as teasingly imprecise highland bogs. (True river sources are the rainclouds, and if rainclouds, seas, by which creation merges seas and mountains.) Yet in our white way we colonialists planted our two trigonometrical pillars which, triangulating with the summit of Margherita, determined the political identity of the race of Man dwelling on either side of the entire course of the Tako.

Out of all his fellows who knew the mountains, Linkoni was chosen by the British administration as a member of that 1938 expedition. He had secured a diploma in surveying in Entebbe, the colonial capital, at the age of 16, in 1929. He was manifestly a precocious one, with a mission-school rearing at Nyakasura in Fort Portal, and then High School in the Ankole capital at Mbarara. He had all the languages – English, Swahili, Lutoro, Lukonzo, Lunyankole. French was not truly needed for the expedition since it had proved invariably easier for British colonial servants to converse in Swahili with their Belgian counterparts in Congo than in the Latinate tongue the British customarily spent ten school-years failing to form an intelligible sentence in. The Mukonzo lad had already taken the name of one of the wider world's all-purpose heroes who had fought to free black men from servitude. Our Ruwenzori Linkoni found his adopted name effortlessly distinguished him in the eyes of Mr Tasker and his fellow administrators redefining that hidden frontier with the eucalyptus markers and stone cairns. Linkoni was a card – he still is. On my first encounter with him, Isaya his brother-in-law sharply objected to his readiness to disguise his ethnic provenance. He had already climbed to the position of gombolola (sub-county) chief at Bwera.

Late in 1954 we set out from Linkoni's house, accompanied by our host and a quantity of not instantly explainable others, including a young Mukonzo teacher of capability named Blasio Maate, destined for a prominent role in our story. We rose by the usual steep ascents and delving gullies bound by a meandering route for the highland village of Kitolu. On the way we spent a boozy night as guests of an elderly brother-in-law of the hanged rebel Tibamwenda, named Kigheri. It upset Linkoni that I should choose to sleep in the same hut as common Konzo tribesmen because, I think, it devalued the implied honour of my having resided with him. Isaya ribbed him: 'I do not think Mister Linkoni would like to be with us in the hut of Kigheri.' Isaya's disdain of Linkoni's airs was to have a macabre consequence in a later phase of history.

Here around me, I came to perceive, was a deeper region of Konzo territory than the configuration of the Ruwenzori's terrain elsewhere allowed. In these southerly reaches, Ruwenzori subsided towards the plain from the upper forest perimeter not with the challenging abruptness of the massif's eastern flank but with a region of clefts and spur-villages in more measured, verdant descent. This was, as to the Alps, Carinthia; as to the *tempestuoso* of the heights, an *allargando* of foothills.

We had fallen in with a bridal party, ascending in order to 'give away' a twelve-year-old to a certain chieftain presiding on a high spur – one already much married, whose name kept cropping up in a variety of contexts. Meanwhile, climbing from the plains through several settlements, we had spontaneously accumulated panoply – I in my slung colobus-skin and bearing a double-headed ceremonial spear with which I had been presented; and Isaya carrying a more practical regular hunting spear. Each of our rods of office was ferruled at the other end and useful as support on steepest clambers. Ibrahimu had cheered up; dour Kigoma's indefatigability had attained a glow of servile pride. Our fame washed on ahead of us and I had a part to play as the Musabuli, 'Redeemer' (as in the Lunande Testament), Isaya had cast me. So far I was self-assigned to recollect to the Bakonzo their inner if not yet their outer rights, and I was thus subject to the surge of enthusiasm which my vicarious 'recollecting' was arousing under Isaya's style of summoning. It was honour and obligation: what might ever be the end of it? I wondered even then. One answer is that after a lifetime of everything else, I am writing this very book. Another is that very destiny being loaded upon Isaya... such that he would die his early death for the sake of it, thirteen years on, a few miles of where we were now here mounting to Kitolu, and lie buried there in bark-cloth under his bark-cloth tree, his only marker.

The compounds on that ascending route were numerous and the excitement persistent: and I was weary. Here in my pocket notebook for those days I have written out in Lukonzo the full conjugation of the verb 'to climb', and in Isaya's own hand are the entries *tukahetuka,* we climb; *tukendesiahetuki,* we will climb. Climb we did and would; yet since our excursion into the plains and commerce with the outer world, I knew I was weary. I felt the bite of my own home, the sweets and softness of my own hearth; my children and

123

my darling. Completing, just then, the last pages of my jotting notebook, I entered a self-accusatory aside: ' Tired and sentimental. Thought of crying, coming to the end of this green [note] book, companion for 3 months.' Yet I had come to the end of nothing.

How could I dare go home? Whatever would I take home now? A deception. 'He who is lifting them out who are sinking down into swamps,' accepting the honorific *Musabuli*, would have proved to be a *voyeur*, one who came to this place – why? – for its exoticism, remoteness, to be the first among these neglected, prognathous little people, presuming to pummel them with questions, rousing their expectations, filling his grubby notebooks, snapping them with his camera, affecting concern, setting out tinsel manifestations of *love* (coming as he did from the heartland of the civilisation that claimed to worship a god called Love), so as to *go home* and write a book (one of thousands coming out that year) and on the cocktail circuit hear them say, *'How quaint your woolly-headed folk! The mountains of the moon? O, daring that. Where will you be off to next? But listen – did you read how Thesiger, no – the other one – in Borneo...'*

'"A certain man went down from Jerusalem to Jericho, and fell among thieves, which stripped him of his raiment, and wounded him, and departed, leaving him half dead." And by chance there came down that way a traveller, and when he saw him he asked him many questions and inspected his injuries and took many notes, and said what a shame several times, and continued on his way, and wrote a travel book, and got on with the next thing that might earn him an advance and give a shine and glint to his reputation.'

There had entered at this phase, on this new ascent, the requirement of a further mode of hope such as that which expects nothing, other than to be true in and to one's inwardness. By a little test, a man may grow. All that we engage upon would end in failure of one kind or another, and every promise contains the seeds of its own betrayal. I would go on, in my slipping, clumsy boots, and would not physically waver. But I perceived no book I might write would 'do justice' to this happenstance journey, in these mountains among these people; there would be no end to the journey but the excuse of death; and no thankfulness for death except at last by having learned to live aright. Already since I had left my home and family that year, a great unfinished business had occurred: that with Erisa Kironde. And now this in Rwenzururu.

What could I ever write?

See, I am writing now, still expiating, failing to do justice.

Kayingo, atsunge. *Kyrie eleison.*

Certainly there was to be no wavering now, on account of the reason burning in our very progression. The first purpose of this journey had been usurped by a subsequent purpose: a cause out-caused as a result of this union with Isaya Mukirane, in unforeseeable enduring function, superseding any travel-book, but entering dreams, entering history, making fate. My publisher was never to get that book he had commissioned because what there was to tell would not be for telling yet: it would be for living, inwardly unfolding, covert motion, giving back flowers, mosses, love; 'doing justice' *inwardly.*

Around us was a broad mazed landscape, a clutter of hills, each with its quilting of tiny farms, and wonderfully beautiful in the southerly panorama glimpsed as we had risen in single file by paths made by immemorial naked feet, out of each dark and tree-crowded gully to the next steep open height. The lesser hills tumbled below us to the plain where they hid the larger trading villages – Mpondwe, Bwera and Isango – which the road from Congo linked with Toro's Fort Portal in the north and Ankole's Mbarara far to the east. Beyond those hidden villages, a broad strath of savannah spun away between the mountains and the lake, Mwita Njike Edward; and the lake itself was to us as good as infinite since its horizon met the sky indistinguishably. To the immediate west of us, erratically perceived, ran the valley of the Tako (*aka* Chako), the border proper with Congo. To the east of us hill upon hill was Konzo-populated and Konzo-tilled, watered by the Nyamugasani with its freight of patriot souls and its numberless tributary rivulets: this was the provenance of Tibamwenda, whose martyrdom (first told here in chapter *v*) in the cause of Bakonzo defiance thirty-three years earlier there were several in the region to remember. Here we were penetrating the southern heartland of dense, mounting landscape so exclusively Konzo that Kampala under a later regime (that of Obote) was to award it the administrative district title of *Bukonzo*, which it still holds. Ahead of us and *up* – up and in towards the massif's dark and snowy heights – was situated that sanctuary thought of by Bakonzo as inviolable. That was Kyatenga, populated exclusively by Baswagha folk, Isaya's mother's clan – highest and furthest

125

cluster of spurs of southern Ruwenzori's inhabited uplands, backed by the citadel of the gods, that ultimacy from which these people derived their right to feel themselves unique and imperishable. Kitolu was Kyatenga's ramparts.

As we were mounting that last league to Kitolu spur, the dark massif long looming ahead was suddenly gone. Storm and hail broke on the instant, battering us, bouncing marbles down the footpath, rapping our faces and our hands. We scuttled to the gully's half-shelter of trees. Thunder amid the invisible Olympus applauded the mischief. This was the way of Ruwenzori, Kitasamba's baiting of us; we might as well have tramped on upwards through his japes. For just as suddenly he whipped storm away, revealing vistas. We resumed; and there, far ahead and in, north-northwestwards, surmounting that washed clarity, momentarily a tilted whiteness of some southern peak dusted by snow, this side of Luigi di Savoia summitland of this universe that nobody so much as considered daring to approach. We gained the brow of Kitolu spur and the level earth of its compound as men purged. We and our volunteer porters eased off our loads. Isaya exclaimed our choice fatuity, lifted from Ibrahimu's English-Lutoro primer, 'Hooray the pig is dead!'

The trainee church teacher at Kitolu here, Isaleri Kambere, was Tibamwenda's kinsman. He had served the rebel as a boy. We lodged with him. As had become my practice, I planted my ceremonial spear beside the jamb of his doorway to indicate residence. Now, all of that Tibamwenda ruckus of 1919-21 began with church. Put another way, it was a war of the gods. Here is what happened. The missionaries were nosing the southern lowlands already, and unwittingly affording to converted Batoro the opportunity for colonisation of their own under the banner of Yesu Kristo. A mud church had been built in the Konzo village of Kanyatsi, with a Mutoro church teacher in charge. Nyamutswa, the patriot-medium from the north of the range and of the same clan as our Isaya, had come to the place to mobilise support with a spirit-singing session. Tibamwenda had his mates strut across the Mutoro's consecrated church forecourt with outsize calabashes of plantain juice and fermenting sorghum on their way to the vat sunk into the ground beyond the compound. There the liquor would become booze, in readiness for the séance invoking the spirits to the Konzo cause. The Mutoro attempted to prevent this insolence with force. In the momentary fracas, Tibamwenda speared the fellow, killing him. The fuse was lit: the Konzo hills took fire – the humiliated flaring proud again in the fastness of their hills. Hanging Tibamwenda and Nyamutswa and their standard bearer Kapoli 1921, we British snuffed the fire not only in the hills but in the heart.

Thirty-three years on, in 1954, here was another sort of Briton and his Konzo team, guests of Tibamwenda's boyhood groupie, and this Briton wondering: how did Isaleri now regard his martyred kinsman? Did I not read in Isaleri an equivocation concerning Tibamwenda – at an ignobleness in the spark of it, perhaps: Kitasamba *vs* Kristo? Or was it that the flaring of the heart of his people, the rejoicing of the hills, did not bear recollection? The remote, indifferent, white tribunal; the 'squeezing to death', as Isaya put the public hanging in the sight of witnesses; the common pit for the three corpses right there at Kagando on their own soil; the puffed up satisfaction of the Batoro: was not that snuffing all a monstrous ignominy? No wonder the cairn which marked the low pit had got overgrown and hard to locate. When in 1420 the English snuffed Owen Glendower's rebellion, the Welsh let their hero vanish; when in 1892 they snuffed Lobengula's and killed him, the Matabele buried him and 'lost' his grave. Losers choose forgetfulness.

Was this, then, what ran counter in Isaleri, clouding my reading of him? For I had arrived at his place, the sanctuary's ramparts, with Isaya the literate, raking the past, *Isaleri's* past, raising it, emboldening it, for some *future* purpose – a book, no less. The only book he had yet encountered was his Lunyoro Bible...

Isaleri was a timeless man. You could not gauge his years, and so already thought of him as ageless. I was to know him another forty-two years. It takes sheer time to unfold another's soul; and if wisdom's in the other, one's own space for that. Wisdom adhered to Isaleri. Well ahead of the written word's arrival at Kitolu, wisdom had come to reside in this one, Israel. His was bone-wisdom. It rested on no external aids. It was nowhere in a book, could be taken down from no shelf, could not be put aside for later reference, to prompt, to prop the mind. It was in the marrow of man, or not at all. It was in the marrow of this man. Such of course is the vital perquisite of pre-literacy. But now he was living on the cusp of literacy.

And also on another cusp: the idea of the shrined word – the pre-existing Word unspoken and unwritten that other words could circle and indicate; light shining in the darkness. Such an idea had only recently come up to Kitolu. It had been brought by a Munyoro preacher, one of the tribe of King Kabalega of former times. This black evangelist had settled upon Isaleri Kambere, figure of natural authority, an 'old soul' as the phrase goes, as the one with whom and in whom to entrust it.

In this role Isaleri must now learn reading, in another's language, for the absorption and the transmission of this Word and this Light. When qualified, the Church of England would pay him 65 shillings per half year, which, since there were 20/- to the £, would amount to six pounds, ten bob per annum. Hence, with Isaleri here in his square hut was a Lunyoro bible, innumerable sounds on Indian paper, foxed, legible to scarcely anyone present, wrapped in a cloth and resting under the eaves, awaiting literacy, promising such light as the darkness would never overcome. Fixed to the vertical inner walls of this hut were already two other writings, endorsed by pictures, demonstrating the trick of twisting intricate marks on flat surfaces to determine sound and speech. One was a pictorial advertisement for Sloane's Liniment. The benefits of rubbing such stuff into the skin were proven by the vitality of the lilywhite lady in the picture and at least six accompanying *words*. The other was an illustrated summary, in folding paper panels, of the life and panoply of King George V of England. In this king's name Isaleri's kinsman and boyhood hero had been 'squeezed to death' over the hill to the east of us. King George V had been Caesar, and we may suppose Isaleri to be about as close to literacy as those Galilee lake-fishermen of Rome's east Mediterranean colony, John, James and Peter, confronted by the absolute requirement to hold on to that light which had entered among them to astonish. Isaleri's infant son Tembo Yesse – Jesse, –

my friend today, would grow up to be ordained a minister in the Church of Uganda, member of the Anglican Communion, within which his father was to teach. At this minute that I write these words, the Reverend Yesse is charged with the care of those Konzo refugees from the highland farms in flight from the armed guerrillas currently scourging the mountains.

Isaleri, then, on our little party's arrival at Kitolu, was half Christian and half literate. There was to him that air of complex sorrow I have spoken of, his hair long and woolly, and a medicine fibre tied across his forehead as a prophylactic against whatever pervasive sickness was in the wind. His tribal feet, the vegetable extension of the body, had lost toes to the jiggers of the mountain. The banana and sorghum beer he gave us tasted of the scent that savoured the lives of all Bakonzo – of hut-smoke, of the plantain-leaves between which the fruit had been crushed by the feet of his family. (Bakonzo sought the savour of the smoke.) Pelts of animals, domestic and wild, and spears, drums and calabashes, hung from the underside of his thatch. Yet this hut, in contrast with its circular neighbours (clad in sprung reeds and grasses), was of mud bricks and straight lines. It had angles of 90 degrees, and three chambers to it. As we have observed, Konzo spirits do not enter squared mud houses. Yesu Kristo surely could so enter: His own house was commonly squared, likewise his cross, an everted square. Meanwhile, colonial-Toro officialdom had crept up here and made Kitolu a parish or sub-parish headquarters. Poll tax was being demanded, and Isaleri was a responsible elder of this place: a *natural* elder. So he was cusped again.

It would prove to be a testing life. He gave twenty years of it to Rwenzururu, Isaya's kingdom, and Charles's. Let us mourn him with recollected love. Please regard the photographs I took of him nine years on, in 1963 (page 251), and again in 1996. He died in 1997, a mere eighteen months before he would have witnessed Charles's triumphant return..

Isaya took from his hands the bible the Munyoro preacher had left, and unwrapped it. On his stool Isaleri waited upon the sound of the words the thing contained. The book was rendered in the language of the oppressor, Lunyoro and Lutoro being one and the tribes cousins: Isaya had command of the tongue: he had been required to teach in it, and read the bye-laws in it. That it was a book at all spoke its wonder. A book was a very *thing* from a world of mystery. No indigenous words for 'book' or 'write' existed in any Bantu language: Arabic was poached for them, via Swahili. As for this book, what it said transcended division among men. It was a strange book. Buganda's children, some dozens of them, in the year the first of my grandfathers I wrote of at the start of Chapter 3 entered Eton, 1886, had been hacked or burned to death on the Kabaka's orders for their ability and willingness to read it; and those burned alive on the pyre of Namagongo – twenty-four of them – had died singing and shouting the praise of the God it told of. Moreover, it was colonising whites, *Wazungu*, this mastering species, esoterically favoured, who had vouchsafed the God, the pantocratic *One*. Thus was intruded this notion of the unspoken and unwritten Word that compelled all these other, *written* words.

I observed the disassociation of the Word – in its purity – from race and tribe, by right of its floating upwards. If in our dark there enters light, none of us can cavil at how we came by it. As crumbs all, there is no distinction among us.

I further report that the manufactures of what passed as civilization had penetrated these southern Ruwenzori hills. The strange book in Isaya's hand housed a razor blade, presumably for safekeeping. The little church further up the spur had a tin roof. I was provided my banana and sorghum beer in a baby's enamel chamber pot. Men and boys had got themselves shirts and shorts, made in Bombay, and most women a printed shift or a frock that made breasts a poor secret. Shoes were often owned, if rarely actually worn – not least because shoe-manufacturers beg to differ from the Manufacturer of man as to what the shape of feet should be. Various pairs were to be taken down from beneath hut roofs and to have feet stuffed into them for the gatherings of elders that the deepening of Isaya's and my researches at Kitolu gave rise to.

We had a method now with our informants. Their seriousness spoke to our seriousness. A rolling group gathered from surrounding spurs, small trusting sagacities assembled at Isaleri's hearth that could bring to mind Snow White's dwarves – Anxious, Eager, Puzzled, Wary, Haughty, Smiley, Ruminant and Dour (alternatively knob-nose, pop-eyes, ape-face, hung-jaw, grizzle-head, square-tache, tweedles dum and dee) – and a lean, desiccated woman smoking an eight-and-a-half inch wooden pipe which she held in her left hand by the stem, with the first and second finger curled over, thus supporting it in the crook of her thumb and on the first joint of the third finger, leaving the right hand free repeatedly to tamp the tobacco in the bowl and re-kindle with an ember from the fire. All these – and Isaleri, with the patience and toleration of the wise, more of silence than any other present.

First, they unloaded fears and fancies. What was the white men up to, dividing Konzo territory with their frontiers between one white tribe and another? Streams were no dividers; they were unifiers where spur dwellers each side fetched their water. And what interest had these whites in the further highlands? Why, it was obvious. Wazungu stemmed from cold climates, and were crowded out in Europe – everyone knew. They were planning to settle up there in the high Rwenzururu, staking their claims. Why else did they make a line above which it was prohibited for Bakonzo to cut trees? It was known the whites were planning to get to the moon to colonise it; meanwhile, Rwenzururu. Why not?

I listened, and demurred. No whites would want to live up there in the mountains. The weather was wicked. There was not enough air.

They retorted: whites kept on going up – they had heard so: from Bugoye, in northern Busongora – what were they seeking? They must be after *something*.

I said, whites like to climb mountains, *erehetuka*, I said, for climbing's sake.

Isaya relayed this. (I wondered how 'for climbing's sake' came out in Lukonzo.)

They were not convinced. There were many whites up high not long ago, for weeks, they said.

I asked how many wazungu.

Twenty, they said. Some of them went up the Nyamugasani valley and on up above the forest. The Nyamugasani, twenty miles to our east, was the largest river tumbling out of the mountains southwards into the lakes. The early Konzo martyrs were drowned in its waters. I was shortly to learn of the Anglo-Belgian expedition of two years previously, composed of geologists, botanists, and zoologists: it had ended in sullen acrimony between the white tribes.

Wazungu have built houses there already, they insisted.

Not houses, I said, not to live in, but huts to shelter climbers – two climbers' huts, one higher than the other on the route up. I repeated: wherever there were mountains, white men liked to get to the top of them, to prove to themselves they *can* get to the top of them. It was in the muzungu's nature.

My interlocutors furrowed fiercely. White designs were not

fathomable. They were digging the copper out of the mountain at Kilembe: this was Konzo copper. They had given the salt industry at Katwe to the Batoro. They had stopped Bakonzo fishing the Semliki, their immemorial site of fish-traps, because of the invisible frontier they had conjured between one white tribe and another...

I glanced at Isaya as he strained manfully to straddle the mutual incomprehensibility of two readings of our single planet and man's predicament upon it. Of course we whites were settling in here. We had colonized the imagination. We were populating the sanctuaries with white socks and topees. The whiting of inner Africa – it was irreversible. A little elder – knob-nose? pop-eyes? – had heard the Wazungu had an atomic bomb to drop on Africa that was going to wipe it out completely.

Now they watched me as Isaya translated.

I said there was no bomb as mighty and no such wish. Isaya added his own self-comforting aside to me, as a Mzungu, in English: 'I think you have new medicine to put on the atomic bomb after it has come down to stop it going burst.'

Outside a very small boy knelt at right angles to the entrance, with his head turned to peer over his shoulder, transfixed by my activity of note-taking... An old man at a hopping run pursued across the compound an escaping kid goat which on being caught cried with the voice of an old man... As proof of Konzo antiquity on these mountains, I was brought a gift of the two brass beads I have already referred to, *esyomberi*, like double-coned nuts, precious as ancestral testes, forged and moulded by Konzo smithies in the old days, they told me, for the adornment of women. Here is a drawing of one of them, on its rag lanyard.

In the course of days, old Kasira emerged as our best historian here at Kitolu. Here he is, in his bush jacket, a physically formidable one – command in the flesh of his emphatic mouth, his hands and thumbs notably powerful, and head recently shaven on the death of one of his offspring, a daughter. He owned one bull and two cows. He had at his fingertips all the generations since the Konzo came to these parts – twenty-one generations in all. Their first mountain landfall was Muramba, across the Tako westwards. They were led by Lumango and his son Muhanya. These two were spirits now; goats were sacrificed to their memory. There were only a few pygmies when the Konzo arrived: they were no trouble.

'What about the gods?' I asked. 'The mountain gods.'

Kasira tapped the end of the Crescent Star cigarette I had given him. (The tobacco's compactness was novel to him, and the heat of its tip unexpected.)

'They were always here,' he answered, in a closed-up manner.

I wanted to ask: how did the Konzo come to know of them? From the pygmies? Or did they bring them and they became mountain-ized – all but Nzururu of the snows? But I feared such questions would seem impertinent. The manner of Isaya's translation from the Lukonzo touched me with caution. To enquire about the origin of that which precedes origins is implicitly disrespectful of the subject of the enquiry.

However, what about the Konzo pioneers of Bwamba? – Kibiniro and Kibunduka?

They were known of here – Kibiniro, they said 'King of Karangura [the northerly peak] and a chief of Buswagha.' (I noted in the clan name Buswagha a connotation of power, and territorial authority.)

And Ruhandika, hero of the war with Kabalega?

Him too they knew of, well enough. The Lamia river and Bwamba were only two or three brisk days away by the lowland forest routes in Congo. Ruhandika had quarrelled with Nyamutswa, Tibamwenda's spirit-invoker.

They reminded me: here in the south they also suffered their invasions. They remembered Kaboyo here, the very first Batoro prince (who split from the Banyoro to carve out his own kingdom, in the 1840s), and his general Kanyakora, raiding their Konzo forebears for their cattle, stealing their territory.

I put it to the group: 'But here in the true highlands you cannot be reached by enemies?'

A communal 'E-e-e-e,' as Isaya relayed it. Smiley grinned his fan of pegs. Yet at once they clouded. It was as if a stinking carrion bird of monstrous size had settled on the apex of the roof.

Isaleri now spoke and others prompted. 'The enemies of the Bakonzo reach us here,' they said. 'The parish (miruka) chief is a Mutoro, the sub-county (gombolola) chief is a Mutoro. We pay poll tax to Kabarole. What benefit reaches us? There is no road to get our cash-crops to market: what are we to Kabarole? We have no schools in which our language may be taught. Our language is being squeezed. What language will our grandchildren dare to speak? Even Nyamuhanga, in what language will he hear us?'

O my people.
They draw me into their dismay. I feel: have I not been with you from the beginning of my days? Or else, what deception am I pulling upon you?

A flute was being played across the compound, the long flute, *enyamulera,* cut at a contour above the high forest from a species of bamboo with two- or three-foot uninterrupted sections. I know which old man had the gift for the *enyamwulera:* the one who caught the kid.

Was that thunder?

I have already written here of Kitolu as the 'ramparts' of the higher inhabited uplands, of Kyatenga under upper forest's edge. Indeed, it was Rampart; it was Gateway; it was Crossing Point – outwardly and, for my intense mentor Isaya, inwardly so; that point from which there was to be for him no turning back. We were touching the hem of history here, past and future, though I was not yet to know.

See, first, how sweet the place seemed; it fecundity, its seclusion. How its crops flourished: plantains and cassava to this level, but not much higher; from here on up, where the frost could reach, millet and mountain yams. Cabbages, tomatoes; Cape gooseberries, look! – and cash-crops of coffee (to be humped down to Bwera market), scattering the spurs' shambas, stabbing the eastward green with their own green. The long peace of the land. So it might seem. All the husbandry and industry; the goats, the hens and, more rarely, tethered cows.

Note, next, the *vigour* of the folk, their highland hardiness, comparative longevity, a common confidence of stocky physique. Sleeping sickness seldom reached them (the tsetse and its evil kept below); they were spared much of the shaking fever (the malarial mosquito abominated hail); yaws was seldom to be seen; epidemic dysentery less of a threat and cholera seldom so; the contagions of anthrax and syphilis of the plains' promiscuities of beasts and of men frustrated here. Yet there *was* talk of a certain sickness on the prowl. We were Rampart, Shadowed Rampart.

Also we were part rampart, part gateway here to literacy: no more than necessary to keep the outer world intelligently *outer;* at arm's length the blear and smear, man's smudge and smell from lower ground. From where I came, below, I recognised that the literacy for which children of the Baganda had been martyred had become the existential blight. To be lettered, of course, need not be so, and was not so when the written word and the trick of reading were rare and treasured, as a source of light, in the same way as a pot contained a smouldering source of fire. Jesus read, for sure; though we have no record of the Master writing except with his finger, unintelligibly, in the dust. Old Socrates read, but likewise only *spoke* his wisdom. Gautama was an educated prince in a region where priests had writing, yet only *spoke*, in a low voice, under a bodhi-tree, to his few....

Homer was blind and sang, his memory made secure by music.

Yet at Kitolu, here, I was aware of the literacy of my civilisation to have become largely blight, a thief of innocence, flouting the right to innocence; the inducer of excess, of a plethora of choice; a tool of power, of vanity and swank, humiliating those without it (however wise) and subjecting too many of those who had it to the ordeal of Tantalus for whom all that tempted him was perpetually in reach yet unattainable. Even now as I write this, forty-five years on, the truth perceived there at Kitolu – with Isaya, with Isaleri – is borne upon me. These pages – how much better narrated to my grandchildren on long evenings at my own hearth, with them presuming to carry within them what was worth remembering, and nothing on the shelf, out there, apart.

Do I not now know how the babble and roar of written words drowns out the word unwritten? In telling about Africa I have twice already invoked Plato's term *anamnesis*: that half-conscious half-recollection of pre-existent treasury-truth that could not survive in time as possession, manifesto, claim, syllabus or written right: that Eurydicean beauty. I am doing my apophatic best with written words. But think of light, please, or music, elusive of worded definition. We shall come to music.

Moreover, this Isaleri had been touched meanwhile by imported Light – he and Isaya. While we were there at Rampart Kitolu, the Munyoro church teacher came back to the place, having heard of our arrival. He wore a black clerical jacket over a long white galabiyya, and held a service in the squat, squared church. He – and we – murdered melody and sang a long hymn in the language of the oppressor (*his* language) to the tune of *Clementine*, number 130 in the Lunyoro-Rutooro book published by the Society for the Promotion of Christian Knowledge. Isaleri was prominent at our altar end of the edifice.

It was a crammed congregation this Sunday because it included the bridal party that had accompanied us from the lower slopes. The same bride and her entourage of child relatives and aunts were fixed upon coming on with us up to the farther settlements of Kyatenga in order to make a bigger show of giving away the 12-year-old to her chieftainly and pagan betrothed. Her awaiting mate could hardly be other than a pagan since – so I learned – he had already 'several' wives. Moreover he was no spring chicken: my companions spoke of his married offspring and a scattering of grandchildren. (In the hurried reproductive cycle of primal Africa, grandparenthood by one's mid-thirties was no rarity.) Kitolu's tiny church was therefore the last geographic point at which the child-bride Khyawatawali might seek the smile of Jesus upon her union-to-come.

The girl had been duly paid for with no less than twelve goats, a demonstration of the highland chief's wealth. Her father, whom I had met below, was a rough bargainer and, being without sons to fortify the economy of his household and secure his status, needed every billy and nanny he could get his big hands on. (He had swallowed down his plantain beer with pursed ferocity and peered angrily into the lees at the bottom of his calabash as if questioning the vessel's emptiness. His world was full of short-changing villains. At least this child had earned him back her upkeep)... Now in Kitolu's church she was mild and docile, as empty a vessel as her father's calabash. Her hair had been neatly topiaried into a V above her forehead. She wore a faded shift which just betrayed the immature pressure of breasts. She squatted on a log beside an eldery female relative deputed to see her safely delivered to her purchaser; being beyond the age of child-bearing, this dame-companion was immune from the spirit-mischief of Ndyoka and thus an influence conducive to fertility.

Being unaccustomed to the construction of squared mud buildings, the men of this place had forgotten to allow for windows. Two ragged apertures had been forced, post-construction, into opposite walls. These and the doorway behind us gave the chamber its only light. Isaya and I had been provided stools, sideways on to the altar, which was built of reeds. I could see how mud had been flung at the inner walls of the church to seal the mud bricks. Across from us, a fire-blackened board was fixed to an upright supporting the tin roof. On the board the church teacher had written in chalk *Matayo 000000239567*, though why, who knows? If teaching numbers, why parade the nought? If the gospel of Matayo/Matthew, was the evangelist accounting the long worthlessness of his life as a tax-collector?

Isaya read the lesson, which was the whole of chapter two of St Paul's first letter to the Thessalonians. He gave it in full earnest, negotiating the strained composites – *nkokukisemerire* ('worthy of God', as his readers had been exhorted to live their lives) – but stumbling at *mutakihabwe* in the next verse, in which those brave and pioneering Macedonians of nineteen hundred years previously were commended for 'receiving' the message as the word *not* of man but of God. Such was the theme of the church teacher's address to a congregation bred to a tradition of spirit-possession by another route. The God-word was a Batoro deity, Ruhanga. Uganda-side Bakonzo were not dignified by any Anglican missionary with their own Lukonzo sound for this chieftain Paternoster God. Not yet. They – the missionaries, Fort-Portal based of Kabarole diocese – knew nothing of the Konzo pantheon, nothing of Nzururu, or Kitasamba, or Nyabibuya, nothing of Ndyoka, or Nyabingi, nothing of... one to whom a special hut, an *engorwe*, would be erected, by ancient tradition, above a spur-village where all could see it, one who was in principle benificent, who was the mate of Nyabibuya and Nyabahasa and Ndyoka, one to whom a fine billy goat or a ram would be dedicated (not a female – since whose would be the offspring?), such an animal wearing its badge of dedication, a neck-bell-omukingi, a clapper in a metal cube. Would this Konzo one or One suffice for the Christian's trinitarian *God*? Was he powerful *enough*? Not even he, entering the house of Nyabebe (malign spirit and 'neglected' wife), could prevent her blight of still-births and infant deaths...

The highland forest tongued down the frontier valley of the

137

Tako, westwards. I could glimpse it through the window aperture from where I was seated, comprehending nothing (at that moment) of the preacher's grinding sermon. I whispered to Isaya, 'What is he saying?'

'He is talking,' Isaya returned.

He surely was. Had my presence prompted him to multiply by 000000239567 the length of it? I could hear excited calls coming distantly from the tongue of the forest. A monkey hunt was in full cry – they have a view. *Wah! Eriah! Wah! Wah! Wah!* They must be closing for a kill. The bride turned her head towards the bright window. These would be people from her destination; pagan people.

Alleruya, said the church teacher.

Alleruya, we rejoined, to invoke the Banyoro God-word.

When some weeks earlier, on Ruwenzori's eastern spurs, in conclave with certain elders, Isaya and I had touched upon Konzo mysteries of Godhead, Isaya had been obliged to slip out of our conclave's hut for the inviolability of an uncultivated place. Only on such ground might the name of this further One be spoken in murmured interchange...

Wah! Eriah! Wah! come the cries from across the valley of that other community from higher up, the pagan lot, tonguing down the forested valley alongside Kitolu's sunny uplands, on their savage Sunday hunt. Savage it invariably was, monkey hunting, as I had already learned on this journey; for we fellow primates can read them, playing upon their panic and despair. From the forest floor, with stones and weak arrows, we people separate a single monkey from the troupe, a hundred feet above in its arboreal world; once isolated thus, the wild-eyed thing, half-souled and piteous, we know we have it. All we must do is pile on the terror from below until, in riven will, it launches for a branch it misses, and plummets to earth, to our clubs and dogs, and *finis*.

Alleruya, invoked the church teacher, the Munyoro.

Where were our thoughts? Where our voices and our prayers? With the hunters from Kyatenga and a feast of colobus-flesh? With our redeeming Lord, lashed, derided, crucified, and for us to be *nkokukisemerire*, worthy of Him?

Here was our packed chapel of squared mud, a light set upon a hill. And there, above and ahead, some peak this side of Luigi di Savoia-Nzururu, crowning the visible world with its tilted glory glistening. Whose temple were these terrestial carbon ranges to be?

The great Pope Gregory would advise his missionaries: *use the pagans' shrine but switch the rituals.*

Today, all but half a century on, that at least is settled. Isaya's very rebellion was itself to provoke that settlement, and the twelve-year rule of Omusinga Charles, his son. Rwenzori has its own diocese now headquartered at Kasese; it has its Konzo scriptures and two Bakonzo bishops, one Protestant, one Adventist; and Konzo *Nyamuhanga* enthroned Almighty.

As for that spur then, my first visit (for I would be coming back here in unforeseeable circumstances), its lonely church and the cries of the monkey-hunters across the valley, I report of Isaya, King-to-be, that he worshipped with conviction, Lutoro text notwithstanding. And when that very evening we spoke of the sickness stalking these the people of his hills, and their taking to medicine fibres on the forehead and spells to counter the *obuttulle-ttulle,* Isaya leaned towards me to say, 'We have to *pray* to let this thing jump to one side,' meaning pray to Yesu Kristo, to intervene, if not with cure as such, at least with counter-charm of infallible love.

We were to climb higher now, to Kyatenga and its dark chief.

xii

Musabuli and the Dark Chief

Climb up higher.

We were rising to the primitive and thus to an inwardness, a version of our truth, however shrouded, to the dread commitment to pull away those shrouds, to hold to our glimpses of the heights: we four – Isaya, Ibrahimu, Kigoma, and I, which names recall poet-prophet (Isaiah), patriarch (Abraham), and any child 'born under a full moon' (Kigoma); and I, ordained Musabuli, hung with the destiny of others – under a vow or holy curse of loyalty such that in this year, my seventieth, of my writing down the present account of it, I endeavour still to fulfil it, and have in this very month hastened back to Ruwenzori in the cause of assuring the people of the mountains the restoration of their rightful king, Isaya's son.

The bridal party preceded us on the narrow track. Khyawatawali had exchanged her shift for a white goatskin; her immature arms were ringed above the elbow with many circlets of yellow olutegha fibre, and her neck was hung with a string of black castor oil seeds.

I had our possessions divided into four quite heavy loads, comprising two packs which contained grey blankets, sleeping bags, clothes, medicines, notebooks, maps, paraffin, cooker, oil lamp, cassava flour, plantains, beans, cooked pork, cameras, light meter, films, torch, washing kit, matches, mess tins, various Bakonzo artefacts such as knives, beads, cultivators, neckrings, pots; items for barter, salt, tea, sugar, tobacco, cigarettes; then the bundles of my companions, which were combined with tripod, elephant rifle and ammunition, groundsheet, and canvas bed. On my person I wore the pistol, waterbottle and map case. I had taken on a porter or two. (Was I getting soft?) My boots slipped. As usual, the rain caught us. My boots slipped worse.

We came upon an odd device erected beside a hut – I had not

seen such a thing before: a stick half as long again as the height of the hut, with a short fat stick bisecting it near the top and a fragment of rag tied up there. What was it? – I required to know from Isaya.

'It is for the wind,' he said.

'A weather-vane?'

'Yhes. A – um – wind vane.'

'What does the man want with a weather-vane?' (Can you hear the bully in me? *I* can. So could Isaya.)

'I *think* he wished one,' Isaya offered, with caution.

'Why d'you think he wished a weather-vane?' (Oh Stacey, for pity's sake!)

Isaya turned to our companions. This required the entire caravan halting as two minutes of enthusiastic interchange ensued, during which it was raining heavily.

'Well, Isaya? What is the answer?'

The porters were in full scurry of discussion. One minute, two minutes.... In my intestines I blamed the lot of them the ridiculous stick device and its rag, and the rain, the mountain, my boots, my temperament. Some days previously Ibrahimu had turned to me in pity, saying, 'You struggle so much, Sir.' The last thing one learns about is oneself. I broke the chatter, jabbing for an answer.

'They say it is a weather-vane,' said a flustered Isaya.

'Oh, for heaven's sake, Isaya – *why* did this man need a weather-vane?'

Isaya turned to look at me hopelessly.

'That is a question should be asked of the man,' he said. 'Do you not think?'

Whatever the rag said, the weather had thickened and darkened.

We went on, in our own dudgeon, of my making. I led. That was to set the pace. Isaya came behind me, then Kigoma. Ibrahimu would trail, arriving always last, usually with a merry smile. Today was no day for smiles. By a series of spur and gully, spur and gully, we were entering fog and gloom, yet progressively mounting. Habitation on the spurs was thin. The foot-worn track would hold to the contour of each spur above the forest of each cleft, then plunge down through the trees precipitously to each stream bed, fifty or eighty feet in vertical measurement, to rise as abruptly the other side to another spur that would have gained us, spur upon spur, a mere twenty or thirty feet. Sometimes the spur's spine was so narrow that man's dwellings clung for their space. It was unwise to build below a ridge-top. Here was a narrow spur, Kabunanwa, where one recent night of storm a landslide had buried and killed, as they slept together, Erikana Mukirania and his wife, leaving a great brown precipitous scar on the earth's moulded face. R.i.p: the mountain earth, that made and nurtured them, remarried them.

We were entering the highest inhabited territory under the southern mountains – Watamagugu, Khighutu – and their uncharted lakes – Kinyamulina and others scarcely worthy of names.

The entry of the child bride ahead of us into her new cold home troubled me. We had learned at Kitolu of the avaloï – those purveying evil, wittingly or unwittingly – stemming from Kituti, our destination. The Munyoro church teacher at Kitolu had insisted on lending me his tall cane walking stick which was his single badge of Christian office like the 'staff' that Jesus himself enjoined upon those seventy missionaries that he sent out, two by two, as the sole piece of equipment for their assignment to Samaria and Tyre. He seemed to see it as a talisman against the devices of the abaloyi. The children accompanying Kyawatawali would surely return it to him, when I was safely through what lay ahead. For they had not yet sourced the evil. They were 'testing', he had heard, as to who was the omuloyi, who was the pre-destined purveyor of the evil. How did they test? 'If a bead, rolled in certain substances and dropped into the suspect's eye, stuck there,' he was the guilty one. 'If the suspect's hand, scooping a piece of metal out of a boiling pot, was scalded,' he was the guilty one. 'If a certain piece of metal heated in the fire and pressed onto the suspect's leg, burned the skin,' he was guilty. 'If a strip of barkcloth, stretched vertically, caused the suspect to trip jumping it,' he was the guilty one. Or she. And then? Ah, there was no Jesus-exorcism up under the mountains. Only the omutahwa-medicine man could divine the penalty. And who was Omutahwa? None but the chief himself, Nyamutswa's own protégé.

As we rose, we closed in upon the eastern flank of the Tako river's steeply descending ravine, all forested. Rain swept us still. An oldish man took up with us, an amiable-faced fellow, relieving us of the burden of our kerosene lamp. Next we encountered a boy who had captured a land crab, which he held live by a string. The old one proposed to the boy that he join us, proffering him the lamp as a symbol of appointment, but the young one rejected the proposal, with insolence, saying that on no account would he go up there – as if the place were blighted. He was afraid: I saw Ibrahimu perceive that.

The weather swung about us but did not relent. We were out of habitation again, without sign of human life except the path itself, and in the gullies the light had gone. At one dark stream where I wished to pause to let Ibrahimu catch up with us, our porters said No, we were not to tarry there: that stream held the spirit of a dead child at the point where it turned in gloom out of sight. The next spur was all forest, never cleared; and descending again were heard – from across the broader valley, the Tako, Congo-side – shouting and drum-burst, and whistles blown. Our old man said they were scaring elephants off the amalima, the cultivation plots. On account of the trees and rain we could see nothing; and thus it still was when we entered on what I learned was the final ascent. I noted, 'Only the lightning gave us sight of the terrain ahead, suddenly revealing the middle distance and involving us in an extraordinary movement as if all our foreground and immediate surroundings had run off and was caught escaping.' The rain fled on ahead of us, and as we emerged from the cover of the trees we were clear of it: the black weather hung like a curtain beyond the ridge, making black what was visible of the flank of Kighutu mountain. It was near nightfall.

From the point of our emergence into tree-free ascent we heard rippling music. Three huts were visible to us on the spur's horizon, two hundred yards ahead and up; and two more to the side. The brilliance and intricacy of the music drew us forward, the improvisation was of a skill and conviction such as we had never previously encountered. All of Kituti's inhabitants were gathered about the monstrous endara-xylophone and its flooding epithalamium.

As, of a sudden, we were observed approaching, the music faltered and stopped. A figure tall for a Mukonzo in some pale mountain cat's skin, standing outside a hut's entrance, turned towards us. I could see his beard. I, in the lead, knew him as the man of our destination, the dark chief, Khavaïru, purchaser and spouse of the child Kyawatawali; medicine man, musician, medium and thus mediator – through music – of Kitasamba, cosmic power; penetrator of heights, pioneer of human settlement, thane of the frontier, thane and disdainer of frontier whether it be political (between what an intervening race of white men chose to designate *Uganda* and *Congo*) or territorial (between where people may risk settlement and cultivation and where the ferocity of cold and height forbid them), or between the provinces proper to Spirits and to Man. This much I as good as knew already.

I met his haughty eye and took his hand, the first white to set foot in the place. In the face I read command, cruelty and a cunning humour. Isaya followed me, exchanging with him the full Lukonzo rocking greeting, taking his time. Thus one measures another, rocking the greeting – *Oneyo?/Ee, nganeyo...* in grave research, mutual, one of another, by voice and eye and sustained handclasp... *Wahinowundi?/Nimirembe... eeeay...*defining the recognisable, the parameters of authority. This highland chief, Ebuswagha bastion-holder, measured us; we him.

At Khavaïru's signal the endara-log xylophone resumed. In a short while he himself rejoined the performers, his kin, and squatting at the treble-end, mastered them.

So indeed that evening at Kituti and into the dark we were embraced by the epithalamium for Kyawatawali upon the endara. It streamed forth late into the night, this music, tributary and

tribute, a snow-fed tributary of power and – tumbling like a snow-fed stream – tribute to Kitasamba, mediating with the god. Khavaïru was the prime exponent of this endara, his chosen instrument, his gift. What we had heard of endara thus far on the mountains was nothing to this. It was not so much instrument as ensemble, gamelan, losing the distinction between what was of sound and of the earth; or what of men and what of spirit; or of one man and of several. Fourteen wooden keys of that same resonant hard wood that drums were dug from, omalumongulu, of some five feet in the bass to two feet in the treble, spanning an octave and a half, lay ranged parallel in ascending and descending order on two fat, juicy plantain stems, parallel on the earth, and each wood bar kept in its place by thin hard reeds stuck upright in the soft plantain. This was the primal xylophone, for up to half a dozen performers at a time, squatted equally on either side, each with a hardwood hammer-stick, omuhumbo, in either hand to caress or tease or bludgeon forth the myriad improvisation. One *marimbero* dominated, naturally: were Khavaïru himself at it, whether at treble or bass, he would lead by intimation; a stream in steep territory led by its banks, to gush or glide, leap or loiter; yet any performer – and they were all his kin and male offspring – could and would feed in a notion of rhythm or pattern; likewise also any drummer to one side. It took its inspiration, this thing, out of the wood bars that the players had chiselled and tuned by their own honing: crouched thus opposite, woven there by eye and movement and sound, they were steeped in their own antiphony, and became one in the symmetry of endara as a body is symmetrically one unit, arms, legs, breasts and buttocks; and unified by rhythm of heartbeat, breath, and gait. Here at Kituti, Khavaïru's outpost of habitation, art in its primality: liquid melody out of raw wood hacked and wrought from pygmies' rainforest; a message drawn from water, rhythm teased out of thunder, chimes taken from the wind and flung to the wind, a function – naturally – found for the endless cycle of birth and decay, a function of evanescence. Here on this compound that first night was the forked animal stating his right to a name in the ears of his creator.

This boulevardier at the bared steep had not bargained for such music in a savage place. After the day's wild rain the night was still and open-skied. One of the three central huts was given over to us. Our lamp was lit, plantain beer in gourds circulated from mouth to mouth. A perfect hen of pale gold was submitted to us, feet tied, inquisitive and doomed, half gift, half sacrifice; and in acknowledgement we stripped her neck of her warm fur-feathers to cut her throat with our Konzo-smithied knife which squeaked on her naked skin. This offering we returned (by Kule, Khavaïru's already married son) to the women across the compound to pluck, eviscerate and stew for our own supper, interminably later; she was rubbery and salty and as unbeautiful in death as she was exquisite in life. Only then, at last, were we permitted the reward of sleep amid the ruminations of the sheep and goats stalled under our own hut's thatch. In the valley steeply beneath gushed the young, snow-swelled, thunder-fed Tako.

We woke to the resumed endara. Festivities anywhere are episodes of defiance – temporality defying timelessness, lamps swinging under a night sky; man making declaration of the meetness of his thanksgiving which the listening ear of God or gods can no more refuse to hear than I, Musabuli, could have refused the ruined flesh and ovaries of that golden hen. As we brandish love to Him, we brandish joy; we have him see and bless our fragmentary precarious order. O Kitasamba, *listen;* listen to the ripple and the reach of your endara, weaving these southern spurs under your southern peaks as the ulema reeds wove the eastern slopes of Konzo Bunyangabo. Observe our complicity, and honour it. Look, here beside this path over Kituti's summit by which I returned in the dawn light from the morning's private function, are elephant's teeth buried grinding side upwards in the mud to request you, weather-god, whose consideration we acknowledge and thus honour, to spare us your lightning; ward us from capricious disaster. By such means of music and charm we rightly plead and trick to render our moment coherent, do we not, Isaya?

Where are *you*, Isaya, this rather glowing morning? Ah, here, returning to the three huts of our Kituti ridge-top by another route. Let us settle quietly here by our hut's entrance, and watch and talk and take our notes. When you come to make your kingdom here its capital will be within half a day's march of where we now are and it will last for twenty years; and the *endara* shall become first your and then young *omusinga* Charles's statutory declaration of royal residence.

What now of the bride, Kyawatawali, in her new firmament? Several others – women, children, young men – were assembled there already that morning, jiggling and shaking to the beat of the

146

endara and an accompanying drum; but not yet she for whose union and fertility they were seeking to make their rhythmed invocation. Already that day, however, with the sun not yet over the high ridges to the east but its rays striking the top of the twin-peaked breast-mountain that hid the peaks from us north and northeastward, the girl-bride had taken her brand new hoe from out of her bundle and laid it out on the floor of the hut Khavaïru had constructed for her on a little buttress of the western slope, Tako-side, of our spur-spine. This Konzo-smithied eisuka-hoe had been a gift to her from Khavaïru himself, delivered to the child in her lowland compound weeks earlier by the chief's male emissary at the time of their betrothal: a gift and a command, *this shall be your diurnal function*. The eisuka had been smithied by the chief's eldest son, Kule, in his own forge, here on Kituti. Now Kule's mother, senior wife – senior to several, three times the child bride's age and already a grandmother through Kule, her eldest – had on the newcomer's arrival the previous evening presented her with a large clay pot. For the senior wife, beyond childbearing, remained chatelaine of her chief's household, and also guardian of the fertility of his amalima-cultivation patches no less than of his loins.

Till now, Kyawatawali had cooked no meal in her new home. The previous evening, Khavaïru had joined her briefly to partake with her and her entourage of a bowl of yam leaves and cassava – a ritual consumption of vegetable produce, binding his bride to her marital function as cultivator of the abalema. Then he had withdrawn to a goat-feast with his menfolk, leaving the bride to settle in for the night in her new, strange place yet amid the reassurance of her own familiars. Now in the morning she would stew up her own first meal, as little mistress for her family companions, in water she would carry up to this new hut from the Tako. The senior wife, whom Kyawatawali addressed as *maama*, had also presented the child with a piece of *broken* pot. This shard she had ritually carried with her to the stream on that first excursion, and on returning by the steep path with the water on her head, she dropped the shard on the path's edge as a talisman against breaking her master's pots henceforward.

It was about 10 a.m. The same senior wife with her now had returned to our upper compound. She had draped herself in a piece of clean calico and already was jigging to the endara's liquid rhythm. Khavaïru had not yet shared the bed-mat of his child bride. I now saw the chief, mounting towards the compound through the plantain grove which draped the spur's upper slope on the western side. He had the cut of magistery in the curve of his nose and the delineation of his shining lips. Against the sharpness of this early morning he was clothed what the female fashion trade of Europe knows as a camelhair coat, whose biography would have included transportation to the colonies in a mission bundle. Moreover, he had on shoes, sockless and laceless: this was surely regalia. He wore a bracelet of brass wire. Following him, wearing her bright goatskins on top of her stained and faded cotton shift, came Kyawatawali, plus her female entourage, and two sturdy adolescent sons of Khavaïru . All were privy to the plot of their patriarch's fertility, that his women should beget him sons. He would give this bride her visits, three or so a week until the seed took hold, and then allocate his nights equitably among the child-bearing spouses. In the woman's later pregnancy he would abstain from intercourse; and likewise during the first flood of lactation following birth. But it would not do for this young one to withhold herself from him long, after each parturition. As for her identifiable rewards, so Isaya forecast, the chief would see to it that more cotton clothing manufactured as for white men was provided her after her first harvest, and after her first son's birth some garment that would distinguish her, and beads.

Khavaïru shortly resumed his place at the endara. The camelhair coat was put away; so were the shoes: instead there were ankle rattles. Kyawatawali shyly joined the dancers, jiggling there, the motion minimal: a shuffled rhythm, each strut no more than half the length of her tiny foot, the body turning five degrees this

way, five degrees the other, with each minuscule advancement adding nothing of dancing and yet in full compliance with the mastery of the mate-woven music in its own entirety, its giftedness, its soothing collectivity and limited stimulation, just as she was in submission to the unfolding rhythm of her ordained role as daughter, chattel-bride, cultivator and prospective womb in the steep, cold Konzo cosmos. Her master here, at work with emihumbo sticks, spared her not so much as a glance. For it would not be so much as Khavaïru and Kyawatawali who would shortly couple; it would be the elemental maleness and femaleness in the communal blood and in all created order that would collide in their own secrecy and dark and unregarded instinct.

I, this white phenomenon, with a Konzo honorific, rising out of the plains from an upper world, was by contrast a *single* one, self-contained and self-directed, among a people who were vessels and purveyors of joint instinctual forces. To them my life was existentially meaningless. Maybe from the bosom of their wholeness they would be obscurely pitying of my isolation, my non-being – me with my questions, my pencil movements on white sheets, my clicking and whirring picture-machines, my clock-tyranny (time tethered to my very wrist); womanless, month upon month, by all the evidence. I was robotic, other, larger than *life*... and yet somehow human, responsive to dogs, infants. I was part-redeemed and brought to the edge of comprehensibility by this teacher-comrade Isaya Mukirane, offspring of a Muswagha mother. Yet Isaya himself was half-single, his solitariness in oscillation with his wholing Konzo identity. I perceived this through a dark glass then, but today more lucidly – how this oscillation gave the neurotic drive to his vision and later achievement... And here was Ibrahimu, another half-single, lately emerged from sleep, beside us on the compound, frowzy, forcing a lank-haired Caucasian parting through the African frizz of his head with a home-made bamboo rake. I ribbed him for it – this was years before the Afros reminded themselves that Black was Beautiful. Ibrahimu good-naturedly defended his parting: 'It is what happens when you are combing your hair, please.'

Symptoms of a mastering culture are swiftly imperative. We had arrived contaminators into paganism. There is no travelling without contaminating. The little bride herself, ascending from 4,000 feet to 7,500 on (albeit) her own mountain, had arrived here already brushed by Yesu Kristo, by his mesmerizing topsy-turvy message, by the prestige of school learning, by Ibrahimu Linkoni's *alias* and all. If she bore this pagan a son, might she not grow wistful for a baptism for him, take a name out of the Book... Matayo, Yesse... for a mud-walled classroom? It is a truism among social anthropologists that their very presence among their theme-folk has pre-distorted normality irreparably the instant of their arrival, so that what any objective 'scientist' moves on to study is in the event never *available* for study.

As for myself, I had advantages, being at least young, and scooping ovundo-porridge into my mouth in my fingers. Nor was I a scientist, nor – precisely – studying: I was delving and spinning in my own way. I was no colonial muzungu, making rules, forming regiments, collecting tribute, bagging game, beating bibles, patting heads: I was matrixed to no distant powers...

Nor, if there was contamination here at Kituti, were we contaminating the pure. There was a *marring somewhere*, in this paganism, an obscure and sinister blight. Isaya and I had wind of it even at Kitolu. Remember the talk of the *avaloï*, a seep of evil. Looking back now, I wonder whether Isaya knew of the origins of the spirit-blight – *otuli-tuli* – some while before it was revealed to me; for an ethnic shame adhered to it. Yet he knew me well enough that I would not easily be diverted from scent of its trail – that, 'slowly by slowly' as he used to say, it must be tracked to its source.

In and around that high compound were several children. Even that first night, two or three boys had crept into the hut we occupied, after our retirement, to curl up in their familiar straw. Over on my side, a rude goat gnawed the end of my wood-framed camp bed or – more precisely – the camp bed the District Commissioner at Fort Portal had pressed upon me so that I might be raised above the nocturnal run of rats. Across the compound, in Khavaïru's hut, among more children, there resided girl twins about three years of age. In the course of days I came to be aware that these twins had no mother present. She had not died, I understood. Nevertheless, she was not to be seen.

Isaya would say to me, 'These people think too much about spirits.'

A seemingly unfinished hut stood further up the spur's spine – unfinished, yet not newly built. It was Khavaïru's spirit hut. Maybe it was not unfinished so much as intentionally without an outer skin of mud or bamboo leaves or grass; it seemed to me that it comprised a little maze of reed and split bamboo partitions whose outer and inner walls did not reach its canopy of plantain leaves and thus allowed light to filter. There spirits might come and go and find repositories for their things.

By means of the things, the spirits made their encounters with us, men. The things prefigured the promises of God such as we of the Semitic faiths have inscribed in our holy books – mercy, promised on our behalf to our forefather Abraham; the second promised coming of the Lord; promised propitiation of our worthlessness; reconciliation promised for mortality; the dangled hope. But let us not jump so far. Let us rather ask: The old Hebraic ark (2.5 x 1.5 x 1.5 cubits) containing *covenant* – was it not a portable engorwe-hut? This engorwe contained certain covenented *things*, as I privily learned, invested by the spirits... a long-dead eagle in a parcel of leaves whose talons were pledged to scratch a wasting child well; a spotted mountain cat's skin, sharply aromatic. When this fur was burned it yielded an ash. That ash, sanctified by incantation, and applied as a tattooing agent to cuts ritually scored with a dedicated Konzo razor, was security against misfortune. Herein also were the pegs that stretched the skins of Ndyoka's chosen creatures of sacred, secret properties of mercy – such hollow pegs as, when blown across by the breath of Khavaïru in his archpriest role, quelled Kitasamba's storms.

Isaya quietly said, of these Kituti people, 'They are expertive with spirits.'

He did not reject their right to seek and beseech propitiation. What Yesu Kristo did was invert the quality of fear, making fear the motive of trust, *Thy* will; he invoked the polarity, so that in our weakness we found our *strength*, and we meek alone inherited the earth. When in eight short years Isaya would return here as incipient omusinga, king, and Khavaïru still as hale and puissant, Isaya would take nothing away from the authority of the dark chief in all that melded Konzo man into the hermetic growth, fauna and weather of his native mountains. What he would do would be to overlay that authority with his own further interpretation such as admitted light. Isaya would elevate the context. To Isaya, Khavaïru was primal Konzodom indeed. Yet Isaya was to be more than such primality incarnate: his was not to be Tibamwenda's and Nyamutswa's rebellion, but to make a place for his people under a Christian sun; a people lettered and bibled; Nyamuhanga-in-majesty; a Konzo pantheon mediated by Yesu Kristo and ancestral spirituality codified by Love at work in ethnic freedom. There's words! Yet such was the rightful flower of his half-mad vision: whether it could bloom we shall in due course come to know.

Meanwhile, let us be aware of the context – how for the better part of seventy years pale, lean missionaries in long shorts and topees had been penetrating tropical Africa with the hot certainties

151

of their conviction. Moneyed, machined and medicined, they were Prometheans of the life force. In the eyes of their charges, what answers did they not have? Or powers? Had not I arrived in this primal place and in weeks was *Musabuli*?

Let not us with the passing wisdom of another age hold their certainties against them, those righteous braves, our white grandfathers, so quick to die of fever, mischance and occasionally martyrdom, giving their all – they and, soon enough among the Protestants, their lady wives – for the benighted heathen, savages, cannibals... a people who provoked the God of righteousness continually to his face, such as Isaiah of old had raged against, 'offering sacrifice in gardens, burning incense on brick altars, crouching among graves, keeping vigil all night long, eating swine's flesh, the broth of abomination in their cauldrons'. Was it not written, that the incompatibility was inherent and wholesale? – that such people were a smouldering fire, smoking in the nostrils of the Lord all day long; that He would not keep silent, the God of Abraham and Isaac and Jesus and Bishop Hannington, but he would repay their iniquities, all at once, 'because they burnt galbanum in the mountains and defied him in the hills'? How could there be compromise? Sweep away, scour out what was. Three months previously, on Moyen Congo (Congo-Brazzaville of today), at the start of this journey that had found its purpose in Ruwenzori, a French trader had made an acute observation to me concerning the natives, namely that when you encountered one with a stammer, you could be certain he was a Christian.

Yet wait. White Christians of a subtler bent, listening, letting go inwardly, surely they heard something different, even in the earliest colonial days. When they groped for the vernacular abstracts of their Testament – for the translation of *God*, the *Word, Righteous, Evil, Justice, Wrong* – in one Bantu language after another was the vocabulary not, with adaptive humility, available? Mercy, Pity, Peace and Love. Were there not those among these ardent Christian minds who located, beyond, an embracing systematized ontology that revealed creation as a plurality of coordinated forces bespeaking a wholeness recognisable to Man and derived from Divinity and demanding of reverence? It took half a century of missionary endeavour to be voiced. A monograph written in Dutch by a Roman Catholic missionary working among the Baluba of Katanga received momentary exposure in 1945 in a French translation, run off a little press in Elisabethville (today's Lubumbashi). It waited another seven years for the Vicar Apostolic's *imprimatur* to sanction formal publication. Two years later, in Ruwenzori, I still knew nothing of *La Philosophie Bantoue* by Father Placide Tempels. Rather, any church teacher that I might encounter, in penetrating the higher habitable spurs of Ruwenzori, would be borne upon by another book, by the evangelist Luke, wherein Jesus was quoted: 'No man putteth new wine into old bottles.' Supposedly the black man's groping ethic had no function in the white man's Good News. There was to be no osmosis. Moreover, the missions and the mission schools were in a race, a race against time and against the evangelizing zealotry of rival denominations, to issue new souls, starched and ironed, in readiness for salvation, attested by baptism and attendance in square-cornered, tin-roofed churches. Whatever was there before was not soul but unspeakable shadow. Bantu vocabulary had no term to distinguish this soul thing from 'mind' and 'being'.

Isaya, meanwhile, was no pastiche white. His soul was to be no one else's mission-issue. He was a Konzo patriot. So not a Christian?

'I came that they might have life, and that they might have it more abundantly,' the new-wine Saviour was quoted in the book by the evangelist John. Had I not witnessed the holy vitality, the inward growing, of benign *ekilimu* won with drum and dance? Had I not met an ardency for a wholing Christ among men amid their 'plurality' and with medicine fibres on their foreheads?

'They are expertive with the spirits,' Isaya had commented to me of these Kitutians, these insiders of his own clan. Spirits or Holy

Spirit, the dividing line was far from clear. Did I have a superior right to nose the dark chief's engorwe-hut when he was absent from his central spur touring his promised lands? Was I in the end any less of a spirits' toy? What ultimate immunity had this lank mzungu from punishment for indecipherable sins?

We crossed to the forge, Isaya and I, where Khavaïru's eldest, Kule, was hammering out a knife blade. Kule was an easy young fellow, not the haughty cut of his father, but swift to smile and please. He plunged the glowing knife into the water pot. We spoke to him of the spirit-hut. I touched upon the twins, the absence of their mother. A stupid fear entered his eyes and spread to his mouth.

The mother had gone away, he said. He did not know where. Neither where, nor why. He gave the knife its haft, finishing it.

Returning up, we encountered both pot-bellied twins on the path. Malaria and the consequent swelling of the spleen had given them their pots. They scuttled off the steep path, rattling. All they wore were ankle-rattles, amulets; protective. I enticed them back with a decorated wrapping of Crawford's Delightful Biscuits. They followed us nervously. One had difficulty hobbling, with her jiggered, suppurating foot.

When we reached the spur's ridge, there was Khavaïru back in the medicine hut, in his Merlin coat and his low hat. The guilt of my intrusion was upon me. He was unaware of our approach. He had calabashes down from under the open-sided canopy. He seemed to be making potions, as was his right and duty. He was priest and he was chief; he was diviner-ruler of these spurs. He was pioneer at every level – the first man to establish human presence this far up the Tako valley. He propitiated the numina. He was a man of metal. No bigger chief was known on the spurs and ridges of the region east or west or south. He was a descendent of the prince Wemera, famous in ancient Eisale. The blood of the chiefs Mubinjya, Ndengwa, Kyavoia, Nzobole and Mutsumbiri ran in his veins. He was chosen chief in preference to his elder brother. As he emerged I saw: he had his rattles on his ankles.

Now that there was sickness about, it was his *obligation* to delve it and placate. There was an epidemic of 'squeezing to death', reported from as far afield as Bunyangabo. I read it as pleurisy or cardiac asthma. In a hut on the descent to the Tunge stream, north, I had found a sick man, an mbandua-medicine man himself, lying twisted in his own filth on the floor, fighting for his breath, whose eyes crawled up to regard me with a haunted, whitish stare. His wife crouched away from him against the opposite wall, in sustained shock. Petero Muhasa of Kitolu had been killed thus. There was the girl Mbambu whose mind was snatched on Kabunanwa spur, where Erikana and his wife were buried in an avalanche of earth. One of the twins – observe – had a rotting foot. Was there not a weaving of evil – and if so, a weaver?

Khavaïru moved down towards the three huts. It lay to him to make them whole. A child was at the endara. The chief settled opposite the child and entered upon his improvisation. Kule rose from the forge below and joined him. The bubbling flood of the music washed over the fear and drew us in towards its fountainhead. It made its circle of safety. Wherever she was, the twin's mother was not within the circle. 'It is not lucky to bring twins,' Isaya told me heavily.

It was hunting colobus I was to come across her. They would rather I had not got to know. Isaya himself would have preferred me not to. He would have preferred 'this thing' to 'jump to one side'. Yet there was no chance of that. We were in the presence of our mortality. There was life; there was death; un-wholeness dogged us; we had entered the vista of disquiet. Life, death; light, dark; good, evil; 'This thing' would not, could not, jump to one side.

Our hunt that day had taken us into the high forest across the Tako into Congo. We swiftly found our troupe of colobus monkeys in their tree-top world above us. Khavaïru had ensured a kill before we set out, emerging from the engorwe wearing his genet skin, and clasping a bunch of twigs once used as pegs to stretch a newly flayed leopardskin. Facing the forested mountain flank where we were to seek our game, he had held three pegs before his mouth to blow across their ends... Our quarry drew us southwards,

downstream, along the Tako valley wall, and then east, deeper into Congo territory. Agitated, they swung above us noiselessly, but we were rowdy, shouting to induce panic, loosing arrows from our weak bows, and flinging up stones and clods of earth which never reached them. Our hunt leader loosed an arrow at one large colobus, to alarm it. Alarm he achieved, and we intensified our efforts to detach it from the troupe. Once detached, no monkey would hold out long. We were at it mercilessly, yet from so far below that only its own loss of nerve – in its isolation – ensured its end: it could have stayed high up, in almost any tree-top, without moving, and defied us. But, alone, the creature's will would go: I knew this already. It made a leap and missed its hold, plummeting to earth: the dogs reached it first. We dispatched it with a spear. Yet it was not our spear killed it, not the dogs, not the deadening thump of its hitting the forest floor, not the misjudged leap. What had done for this black-white aerial beauty, one of a band, was its isolation.

Returning from there towards Buswagha where the land was dropping towards the Tako, we came out of primal forest unexpectedly into an open area of recent cultivation but now evidently abandoned. One newly assembled hut stood about three hundred yards below us – more of a makeshift shelter than a hut. It was occupied. One of our party perceived this at the same moment as I. He made at once to veer our party away, in avoidance. Then I saw the occupant was a woman: she had emerged at the hut's entrance to regard us with gravity, standing quite still, with a cloth of some kind pulled across her.

I guessed at once. I said to Isaya, 'That is Kunihira' – the name of the twins' mother, the 'neglected' wife. It roughly translates as *Hope*.

'Yhes.'

'Then we must go to speak with her.'

None came down and across with me. When I realized that, I was obliged to retrace my steps and try to insist, 'Isaya, I shall need you to translate.'

He followed in silence. I was idiotic white authority. We went down through overgrown millet and abandoned plantains without speaking. She had come to lodge here for the plaintains. Yet I could see no smoke. The hunting party waited with their colobus, our meat. The woman remained in the mouth of her hut. This was violation of a violation: I was at least aware of that.

I halted some feet away from her, greeting her in Lukonzo, and crouched as was my custom, to diminish alarm. I spoke her name. For an instant I had – as it were – touched her, with the name. Isaya was silent, beside me, standing. He had his right: what possible purpose was served by my presence here? What on earth was there to say? Was this a demonstration of pity? In which case, where was to be the alleviation? Was it prurience? I wished to take a photograph of this one, my first witch; and so I did, employing my usual trick such as was possible with my Rolleiflex, pretending to be directing the device at the scene at right angles to my true subject. Through Isaya I asked if she had fire.

She had. (She had carried it in a pot.)

Had she anything to eat?

She had something.

What?

Amakamata, plantains.

How long had she been here?

Three days.

Isaya interrupted this futile dialogue. 'We must leave this lady.'

I stood up. The hunters were not waiting for us and were already moving away.

'*Watyage,*' I said. She did not respond.

We soon caught up the hunters. Little was spoken among us on our return to Kituti spur. We were in the shadow of this mischance of our route, and of my wilful white outsider's exploitation of it.

The recent history and prospects of the woman Kunihira were as follows. After her explusion she had until lately been living close to Kituti. One day she was gone; they did not know where. They were, of course, in fear of her, after her confession. This had been given at a spirit-song session. Khavaïru had been present, presumably in his spirit-medium role. There had been no coercion upon her, no trial by torture. For she herself would have sought the purgation of the evil of which the spirit Kaliamakindi had fixed upon her to be the agent. She herself bore no blame. That confessed recognition of her role, which could not but result in her expulsion, re-united her to the common weal. It made way for the community's re-wholing. She had had three earlier children by her husband, Mubunga, who had returned to his own compound, Bulandera on Kavunanwa ridge. Only the last to be born, the twin girls, Nguru and Ndobya, remained here, to grow up under the guardianship of this omukulu-chieftain of Buswagha, Khavaïru.

'She cannot survive long, I suppose, on her own,' I said.

'She cannot,' Isaya said.

'There is nowhere else for her to go?'

'To her mother and her father, if it is possible.' I suspected Isaya of wishing to mollify me.

The literal meaning of *obuttulle-ttulle* was 'that which cannot be delved', implying that it 'should not be delved'.

Nearly half a century later I have discussed these events with Syahuka-Muhindo, scholar and teacher, who was yet to be born and reared in a village a short day's walk from Kituti: he assures me that among his people, the Konzo, only in the rarest instance would a multiple birth be open to an interpretation of malignity.

Isaya said, 'We are told in the bible that before Jesus comes many wonderful things will happen.'

That night at Kituti we flayed and eviscerated the colobus, and the women chopped it up and stewed the limbs and ribs. Though our meal did not come to us until deep into the night, after hours of stewing, that colobus was excessively tough. Such is the posthumous revenge of any quarry for the pot that has been chased to death. The children ate the offal, except for the unclean parts, which the dogs had, together with the hands and feet. It is characteristically the hands – the slenderness of the fingers, the black skin, the vestigial lifelines of the palm – that, in butchering monkey for the pot, touch a man with the awareness: this is of my *genus*, a fellow primate. Cannibalism is a venial sin.

xiii

The BLHRS Seed is Sown

The neglected wife haunted the ensuing days and nights in Buswagha. Impotence dragged at me. For the offence of her womb, a mother was condemned to slow death by ostracization; yet were I to have the authority of kings I could not save her. I learned that that first mbandua to finger the mother of the twins was a scraggy and tormented fellow, Kavundwi, from Congo-side. Chief Khavaïru endorsed the divination. Frailly she had protested, hapless soul, from the depth of her innocence. Yet neither innocence nor guilt were hers to plead. She was but the vessel of Kaliamakindi, in turn exercising the will of Nyabibuya who was herself but the 'helper' of Nyabingi – as Isaya (so it was put to me) was the helper of myself. (I heard say the two last-named spirits were sisters.) From the moment of her twins' birth the mother would have known of the prowling accusation. All sickness was attributable to the intervention of spirits, and spirits picked their agents to threaten the sacred force of life. To permit the restoration of wholeness to her own people became at once the twin-bearer's function. As I have indicated, she made no complaint at her expulsion. She would be readmitted nowhere among them on these ridges. In the extirpation of evil, pity for a single blighted soul had no role. God was not love *thus*. To force a paraphrase: the principle divine was wholing, healing life. There could be no personal expiating a cursed womb. The twin girls were permitted to survive; Kunihira would not see any of her children again.

She had quit her original place of exile since she did not want her fellows to be aware of her death. Were I to have obliged her to return to her community, such as I might have attempted by a colonial assertion of my whiteness, she would have re-expelled

159

herself instantly. Were I to have attempted to lead her out, down, to begin life anew, she would not have accompanied me. These were her community; she was their sacrifice: it was for her to restore their vital order, on which her own children were dependent. Her own voluntary annihiliation was required of her and by her, before the witness of her ancestors.

She was to haunt too the plot of *The Brothers M*, which eventually became the written product of this first journey into Ruwenzori. It was the uncovering of the plight of such a witch that brought to crisis the relationship of the joint protagonists of that fiction, one black, one white, Mukasa and McNair. The fate of that tragic figure, in counterpart, was my chosen fulcrum for hammering out the eternal curse, or honour, of the species which is not God yet made in the image of God. In my story the black died, and the white survived, humbled (one supposes) for life. The black, Mukasa, was not Isaya but a sophisticate, graduated from Makerere University in Kampala and then from Oxford. I had his late mother born of this tribe, a Mukonzo, and his father a mission-educated Muganda of high attainment in those early colonial days. I led my black protagonist into entering the tribal community of his long-dead mother for the first time, penetrating to the primal pre-Christian heartland at this very place, Kituti spur in high Buswagha, where I had 'penetrated' with Isaya. Accompanying Mukasa was a Scots Canadian, a fellow Oxonian for whom I had decreasing sympathy as the writing of my book proceeded. Novelists should not do that. Readers seek to identify, be it ever so lightly. Only in the last paragraph, after 500 pages, did I slip an arm around Bob McNair and say, 'Well, now you know. Don't do that kind of thing again.' If a man can learn anything of worth, it is confidence to accept humility.

Bob McNair was not I, Daudi Mukasa was assuredly not Isaya (I gave to my fictional figure Kigoma many things taken from the real-life Isaya). Mukasa owed a lot to my companion of the previous months, Erisa Kironde. But Kituti and that high Tako river region of Buswagha were drawn with precision from life as the inner sanctum, and ultimate sanctuary, of the Bakonzo people. As to its chief Khavaïru, his son Kule, and the rest of them, I did not even trouble to change the names – except that, for the tragic witch, who was to be a Konzo aunt of 'Mukasa', I gave a name *Njike* signifying 'locust' in the Lukonzo tongue.

The character I loved was 'Kigoma' – Isaya. I had re-named him in the novel inspirationally. *Kigoma* means 'pertaining to the drum' in Lukonzo; and when Isaya became King, he was to adopt the title *Irema-ngoma*, Master of the Drum.

We remained at Kituti, and those neighbouring hills, spurs and valleys, for some while. We never saw the neglected wife again, or allowed ourselves to come near her place again, although we freely invaded Congo territory. We hunted, we set snares, for birds (the *omughuli* trap), for monkeys (the *olwango*), and the *omukosa* for scampering ground game. We baited an *obulindi* trap with castor-oil seeds and sweet bananas which crushed our quarry (of bush pig) under a weight of stones when it triggered their fall. (Baited with a live goat, a *obulindi* could catch a leopard.) We spent day upon day in the forest. It was hiding bounty. We found honey there; in the tree tops, pomegranates All my jungle sureness came back, such as I

had learned in Malaya at nineteen. I could readily lead the way. We invoked the forest spirits – Kalissia and Kahiyi – refurbishing their track-side shrines, leaving them offerings. We were the frontiersmen of their illimitable territory. And all the while, I was at work with Isaya, building the inventory, making a Konzo record of his recordable universe. Later, I was to make an index of the topics our researches had covered: it ran to one hundred and twenty.

Isaya said, 'We must make a society for continuing this study.'

We were on our stools in front of the entrance of the old hut allocated to us by Khavaïru, across the compound from his own, newer hut. Our entrance opened southwards, down the valley, towards Kitolu and the foothills and plains and lake. The chief's looked out northwestwards, across the upper Tako valley to the forested Congo and the secret ancestral route by the eastern flank of the mountains that linked this people with their fellow Baswagha clansmen beyond the Lamia river border of Bwamba, where our journey had begun.

'How shall it be known? The Bakonjo Research Society?'

'The Bakonjo Life History Research Society,' Isaya replied.

It seemed to me a bit of a mouthful. So I queried the need for 'life history'. I said, 'I can't see "research" avoiding "life" or "history".'

'"Life history" explains to people what it is,' Isaya said. He was intent on this rendition. Later I came to grasp that in the Lukonzo language 'history' and 'life' (as in 'way of life') were inextricable when attached to the notion of 'research'.

'I will write my book,' I said. 'But back in England or Canada I will not be much use.' (I had a journalistic appointment in Canada to take up in the New Year.)

'You will be president, Mr Musabuli.'

I offered myself as Patron. Isaya had not encountered the word.

He was to be Secretary. But prospectively the office would fill the executive function, and therefore carried an air of chairmanship.

I suppose I have remained Patron, ever since, of the Bakonzo Life History Research Society, in all its transmogrifications.

Khavaïru was with us, out there on the compound. He was Konzo Life and History embodied. We told him what we had conjured. He was smoking his wooden pipe. He did not have to be literate, we said, to be the Society's first and foundational initiate.

Would there be meetings and minutes? Would there be members and colours?

There would be constitutions and Kingdoms! There would be citizens and arms! Destiny waited upon the Bakonzo Life History Research Society. Hens pecked among the straw of our compound.

This was the favoured spot to sit and write my notes. It was also the place where folk of all these spurs and valleys knew they could find us, Isaya and me; where they brought us their *cultura*, their lineages and legends, their sagas of hunting and migration, these Buswagha folk of Kahimba, Kanyatsi, Kassekabuhura, Kabunanwa, Kambasa, Kasabo, Burangwa, Kabira and Kinone. They also brought minor ailments. I had aspirin and iodine.

The hens scoured and pecked, the cock crowed and he and his hens mounted the thatch of our hut, which was ancient and full of its own life and growth, a kind of hanging garden on the sag, half-humus, home to rats. The chickens found a rats' nest there in the thatch and pecked the young to death amid a wild commotion. One of Kule's totos scrambled on to the thatch to report the massacre. We congratulated the chickens since we too were at war with the rat-world. Moreover, a rat had just previously outsmarted me. Lying on my back one night on the hut's floor, on the point of sleep, I felt him creep on to my sleeping bag

and find himself an unexpectedly warm place to nestle for the night between my feet in the angle they made with my legs. I let him settle there, and devised a stratagem. With maximum caution I began to draw up my knees, inch by inch, so as not to disturb the snug crook of my ankles. With my knees drawn to my chest I was a human spring and the unwitting rat a loaded missile. With violence triumphant I kicked my legs, projecting into vertical flight the astonished creature. He slammed the underside of the hut's thatch...and descended *splatt* on my face.

When nine years later I was back on the self-same compound, in changed and dramatic circumstances, Khavaïru re-told the story of that flying rat. And of the subsequent massacre of innocents in the thatch. Of course, the two rat-events were linked, both particles of the higher will, which Khavaïru himself by virtue of his chieftainship was forever mediating. Rats, chickens and goats of our compound all partook of the simple procreative energy and balance, deriving from Nyamuhanga's pantocratic authority and accorded point and purpose by Konzo man's chosen habitance here on this high ridge where Khavaïru presided. Of the goats corralled into our hut at night, Khavaïru would pick the white nanny at the appropriate moment in the year and make a sacrifice of her to Kitasamba, who out of the heights there beyond – the unseen white heights beyond the black heave of Kirembe – watched over us, alerted by our chief's intercessions.

All things living were incorporate, as also all things inanimate that contributed to life. Past and future were likewise incorporate; ancestors and descendants, born and unborn. So also were the spurs and ridges woven, family with family and clan with clan, their cultivations likewise interwoven, wherever Konzo had their being beneath the same heights. Man pinnacled creation, and in the ordering of his society held his claim to his pre-eminence within creation. Amid that ever shifting order of life lived now, the chief spoke for it, exemplar and repository of its collectivity. Here was Khavaïru of our forest-bordered ridges, *omukulu w'obulambo*, chieftain of the *ffrydd*, for so long as his strength of body and mind would hold. But we had come among him, Isaya and I, uninvited and unprecedented. Suddenly the scale was altered.

Yet how? And by which of us? Musabuli, or Isaya? I was an emissary from another order, a further cosmos, known of up here but not comprehensible. Khavaïru and I, both then and later, were to remain in mutual awe. Somehow, in combination, the chief's visitors had generated the daring or the gall to dream a dream; three-quarters ringing the mountains in their journey, touching the spurs and gullies, the foothills and the lakes, they had cast a rainbow, a Konzo-wide Society, ekhithinga, bent over the known world, horizon to horizon.

What did Khavaïru at that time read in this Isaya? Not a king in embryo, surely. The 'Bakonzo Life History Research Society'. Well, now. What did that sound like in his language? What pretension! What did it all amount to? An unwritten book. (There was no term for 'book' in Khavaïru's language.) An inventory of scattered testimony and custom. An unmembered network of names and voices. I was returning any minute to another world: my diary makes record of Isaya's 'anguish' at my abandoning him. Rainbows come and go.

I would have to penetrate the heights before I left: that much was assumed. Northwards now, the massif confronted us as always, to challenge and beckon. I would have to climb into the presence of the snows, the justification of Konzodom, the right of the race to its place, deified by the snows, and I not so much to conquer as go up in homage to this people's geo-climatic esotericism. Very early on the morning of my departure, Isaya would have Khavaïru bind me to them in blood, submitting me into the common care of the Konzo snow-crowned pantheon. The little ceremony of *erisakana* took place in the mouth of our hut, with the chief's eldest son, Kule, in attendance. The stars were still visible.

A Konzo razor and ash wrapped in a leaf were fetched down from the engorwe-hut. In the low light I bared my chest. Either side of my breastbone, in a line with the nipples, Kule made three cuts, directed by his father. Into those minuscule wound-wickets, each no wider than a finger, Khavaïru himself etched the dark ash of burned leopard fur, invoking the protection of Kitasamba. This was on the morning of my last day before my quitting Kituti to head for the heights by another route. Khavaïru's talismanic authority was to be called upon within a matter of days. A trace of those cicatrices has endured these intervening aeons.

The chief, our host, accompanied us a few hundred yards, as custom required for departing visitors. The ripple of the *endara* followed our descending party, loaded with artefacts, until the Tako's brisk cascade drowned that music. We halted and shook hands. *E nau bukyaghe, Khavaïru.* Fare thee well.Who would dare suppose I would one day be back in his place to treat with a Konzo monarch?

xiv

Descent into Ague

However tired my bones, and head and heart wrung with remote places, the concluding and culminating assignment was surely to enter up and in. Where was my little study taking place? Ruwenzori-rwenzururu: snow-presence. The heights of Ruwenzori were and are approached by the valley of the Mubuku which assembles its waters from the glaciers and gorges, the coombs and drumlins of the heights, a score of tributaries, east of the range's watershed, and taming those waters in the Toro plain empties them in Lake George. This was the route first probed and pioneered by those English administrators, missionaries and soldiers half a century earlier and established once and for all by Prince Luigi's expedition that claimed the summits in 1906, as we have told. Many had since gone up by that way in the intervening years, including a good few natural scientists; and two generations of Bakonzo porters or guides from the Mubuku valley's upper villages of Bugoye and Ibanda had served them. Many had also died in the mountains, not so much from falls as from pulmonary oedema. Men could not afford to fall ill up there. For climate was strange and the diurnal variations of temperature precipitous, plunging at nightfall from tropic heat to arctic cold, and no quick way out if the lungs began to clog. Inner and upper Ruwenzori was like no other place on earth: its own world, its own vegetation; its own community of creatures; its own climatic eccentricity. No man lived there: man only ventured there; it took the lives of the weak, the unwary, the unlucky, the cursed. To the snowline, it was not less than four days' scrambling climb through as many strange environmental zones.

For the Bakonzo, I knew by now, the sanctity of their inner place was defined by where barefoot man could not tread, which is to say the permanent snowland. It was empty; emptiness. It was the only place they knew in all creation where nothing lived: the identifiable, life-eliminating void. My companions had no names for features of the white heights: no peaks or cols or glaciers. The whiteness was its own presence: place and deity one. Up in the heights that presence, Nzururu, had vouchsafed names only for those pinnacles too sheer or narrow-topped for snow to settle. I had learned that those pinnacles most prominently higher than the snowline, yet themselves snowless, were Nzururu's second generation descendants Kitasamaba the Konzo Thor and his angel-of-healing twin sister, Nyabibuya, senior wife of many-wived Nyamuhanga. He, Nyamuhanga, of whom I have already written in this book, was the everywhere-God, simultaneously of *being* and *making*, simultaneously *progenitor* and *heir*. Thus of all our mountain pantheon he was raised by the Christian proselytizers as the Trinitarian Almighty, the Father-Son-Spirit whose authority Christians would have obliterate or at least dim all other gods. And since he was ubiquitous and ranging, he had no location for his exclusive presence. Nevertheless, all snowless features of the heights – peak, pinnacle, bluff, cliff-face, gully, morass, stream and lake, rock overhang and cave – carried a Konzo name, invariably

implying *numen*, tutelary spirit. And there was ever fog: at this season also much storm, thunder, deluge and katabatic winds. It was Kitasamba's disgruntled season.

I suppose I was going in to do honour to the upper sacrosanctity. I remember having no ambition to summit and violate:

I was too beholden to my Bakonzo mentors. What I sought was only proximity. I had a book to shape: it could not be other than a mountain-site book. Yet I was bone-tired.

I left Isaya to rest at the village of Bugoye, where I recruited three porter-guides. Was my start, that day of constant rain, delayed? For on the evening of this first day's ascent in deep forest, we had not reached our night's rock shelter when I lost my porter-guides. I was mounting third in our file of four, bearing a share of what load there was. It was steep and still raining, and the forest in murk under the dense upper canopy of leaf and fronds, rampant climbers and parasitic clusters. Such daylight as there was had begun to go. I was used to such forest and rain and ascents, battening down and pushing on. Yet we were well above the level of habitation; and the next moment's fragmentary event was something new. On an instant, my two leading Konzo turned wordlessly about and brushed past me so swift and silent they might have been flitting shadows. They shadow-snatched my third companion, behind me, with them.

So they were all gone by the way we had come, swallowed by the forest. My feet took me three or four steps more, from where I saw the large cause of this mute scuttle: an elephant browsing obliviously half a clod's throw up the track above and off to the side. A big beast in sudden proximity jolts a man. Yet here was my chance (I thought) to film old Noah's largest mammal at intimate range in honest nature. I concealed myself behind a leaf or two and a drop or three of rain. I was grateful to the rain for its benefits of sound and scent suppression. I unslung and unzipped my Bell and Howell, parted my leaf, took aim and ran the reel, despite the rotten light. Mine was a carefree jumbo, foraging his or maybe her Eden so as to do it the maximum damage for one lazy supper. I gave him a good eight minutes of my nervous lens in disappearing light: one careless move, one unforseen click, and a great head could turn, ears fan, eyes grow small, and in twenty lumbering paces this mammoth could be upon me and with one insouciant swipe make mulch of me. This beast was no Babar in spats.

It behoved me to withdraw and be re-united with my companions. In the near-darkness now, within a minute I knew I had lost the trail. There was no question of calling out. A man thus placed is best advised to limit his wanderings. I was by nature and experience a jungle-truster, more Tarzan than Mowgli but either way at home in forest and content to share it. I transferred a packet of biscuits from my pack to my stomach and finding a hollow amid the buttress trunks of pudocarpus, curled up in my army-issue poncho-groundsheet to sleep the sleep of a cold damp pupa. There was, I knew, a local species of leopard unique to these mountains. Yet in my heavy sheath I was making little scent. I woke to the arguments of blue monkeys in the canopy. The rain had stopped. When soon enough I located my companions, I noticed Maseraka wore a blue monkeyskin bag, slung by its sewn-up back legs around his neck. 'We are thinking you are dead, sir,' he said. They had found the rock overhang and made a fire, and worried for me or their wages more than I for them.

On our ascending higher, the high forest gave way to bamboos, and at the bamboos' upper contour began the bearded lichen. This trailing relative of the Mississippi delta's Spanish moss lent to this band of highland Ruwenzori an unearthly eeriness. I had encountered it before. But here it dressed the bamboos and giant heathers – the next higher swathe of vegetation – as wraiths and blighted all. Glaucous beards of lichen fidgeted in fog with which they shared a ghastly conspiracy. Any man is ill-advised to wander off into Ruwenzori's giant *philippiae*. I had a false familiarity with these heathers:  they were identical to what I had grown up with in the Grampians but magnified twenty times – that is, not two or two-and-a-half feet but forty or fifty. The density and slipperiness of their surface roots, half buried by moss, comprised the surface for our scrambling feet.

My all but studless leather boots were grossly clumsy. Repeatedly one foot or another slipped through the surface roots into a sort of dark void where, two or three feet beneath, evil water and black mud formed a lower base. A man must not lose the known route here. We attained an overhanging rock named Nyamuleju, Old Man's Beard, at eleven thousand feet, and made a gloomy camp. Let me pause here, feeling odd and dislocated. From here the fantasia was beginning to change anew. Everything grew on everything else – the usnea lichen, the club mosses, ferns, and liverworts all aerial and in mutual grapple for space and light; but now the heathers began to give way to other giantized hosts – hypericums and lobelias and groundsels never less than twenty or thirty feet in height when fully grown.

I was in a place of monstrous beauty; unearthly in that there was no comparable surreality on any such scale on earth. I guessed that fragments of similar phenomena occurred on Kilimanjaro and Mount Kenya. Yet here on Ruwenzori was a world entire that had minted its own many species of mammal, reptile, bird and insect, and its own spirits evoking awe, invoking divinity and provoking vision and rebellion. This was infinite redoubt for this race of man that honoured it by trust and intimacy. Every now and then from here, when the cloud cleared, from out of this fecund inventiveness I could glimpse the sharp white of a peak of glacier two days ahead.

Let us pause for geography. The crust of eastern Africa began to take shape at the start of the Tertiary era. The tectonic faulting that was to give our world its line of lakes from north to south, of Albert, George, Edward, Kivu and Tanganyika, pushed back the rim of the western shield upon itself. This ruckled Cambrian rim had nowhere to go but up, and did so over aeons by millimetres annually. It carried with it plant and animals into the unprecedented biosphere, translatable in European climatic terms to summer by day and winter by night, with massive precipitation of rain or hail or snow – and, so close to heaven, its erratic sunlight imperfectly filtered. The extraordinary demands, infinitesimally encroaching, evolved their mutational solutions. Giantism became the route to survival for those plant species I have already mentioned which, like Jurassic Saurians, dominated and still dominate the savage terrain. Giantism protected the groundsels – *senecio johnsonii advinalis* – by a thick layering of cork, and pantaloons of dying leaves around main stem. The lobelias – *lobelia bequaertii* – shot forth their phallic obelisks, similarly girt, which Konzo, venturing into this Lilliput-in-reverse, strip to the hard hollow core to fashion the *enyamwulera* flute.

By contrast, the solution for the fungi became miniaturisation. Above where I had reached, and I was yet to see for myself, where the altitude breaks 13,500 feet or so and the night's snow lingers well into the day, other plants solved the problem of frozen stems by doing without a stem: the flower nestles into the soil amid a wad of leaves which close like mother's shawl around it as night falls. The last flowering plant to hold out against the cold, a kind of everlasting, crouches to a carpet, as crisp underfoot as frost itself. Do you recall Dr Franz Stuhlmann at nearly such a height leaving proof of his achievement in a bottle among those immortelles, in 1891? That was across the peaks, Congo side, at the head of the Kamusoso valley. This pretty dark-leaved crawler with its pale yellow flowerets is known to us as *helichrysum Stuhlmannii*. It blooms as high as 15,000 feet. Up there it grows to eight centimetres; two thousand feet below, it grows to eight feet. (Dr Franz has a high pass named after him, too. It is in the wrong place for a Stuhlmann Pass, between the two peak clusters of Stanley and Speke and miles to the north of his bottle and where he actually went. Yet let a fellow pocket his immortality where he can.)

Let me not presume. I write of what I know now, not then. I was only at 11,500 feet on the edge of a bogland disappearing into the fog. For myself, I did not hang about so close to gods. I sensed an encroaching weakness. I could not tell if it was gross loneliness that had got me or a marasmus caught from the spooky lichen. I had not had a day's illness in five months. But I was not myself. I turned

my little party round, and with a sense of being pursued hurried down to the overhang at Nyamuleju, re-entering the towering heathers. At my left the four Portal Peaks – a range of undecipherable *stele* within the greater range – seemed to my troubled brain to have shifted, to confound my passage of complex descent. My men built their fire of hollow groundsel logs and cooked our millet porridge. I had no will to eat. We nestled into the flooring of the dead groundsel pantaloon leaves. The rain came back by night. I watched it in half sleep, heady and confused. Rising early, I had an urgency on me, not so much a monkeyskin across my back as the live creature clinging there: I knew we must reach Konzo habitation by nightfall. Indeed, at about 5 p.m. we encountered our first fellow men when we crossed by a fallen tree the swollen Mobuku. Two men were butchering the cadaver of a buffalo that had snapped a leg attempting the crossing. It stank. What use, I wondered, could anyone have for such meat? At about 6.30 p.m. and into dusk we broke from the forest into the first plantations of Ibanda. Stuck into the midst of the track was a stave. A message on a scrap of paper was in its cleft. It read,
'Well come Mr Musabule. I am at omutaka Bwambale's house 50 yards to-right. I am waiting you with pleasure. Isaya Mukirane.'
I did love that fellow for his note, his sweet readiness to greet me here on his own ground, wrap me in his trust.

Entering Omutaka Bwambale's hut, its woodsmoke, its throng and scent of folk and animals, its half dark, its impedimenta – dangling from inner thatch – of calabashes and tools on boarskin lanyards and banana fibres, its Konzo clay tureen on the three-stone hob, and the black sheen of pocked shins ringing the fire and feet that knew the intricate paths as hands knew and loved the clay, was I not at home and safe? I settled on a circular stool Isaya had reserved for me, wrung out, half fugitive come back to the primal group. As I recall it, I was slumped there scarcely five minutes when the whole world rolled over on me, the hut's floor rising to thump me in the face. Somehow the others had kept their balance in this seismic disaster. Lifting me from where I had sprawled, they carried me through some partition where a dark bed was laid.

There the world came to rest, in a manner, but not I. A fever had begun to march through my body, making it tremble in recurring bouts. Quite rapidly the frequency of the bouts accelerated so that the demand of their rigour became all but impossible to withstand.

I watched this acceleration with alarm; the poor heart was challenged beyond its function. As the shaking bouts ran together, I reasoned, 'Nobody can withstand this for long. It is as if I am being required to run one four-minute mile after another.' I was just aware from time to time of Konzo faces, lantern-lit, peering down on me as one done for and about to die, which was the logic of my condition.

When consciousness returned it was daylight, and the quaking crisis passing. Six months earlier, in England, the manufacturers of a brand new malarial wonder prophylactic (Daraprim) had provided me with tablets to test their effectiveness. I was to swallow one per week. I supposed I had done so, even in the mountains, above the mosquito line. Yet what had got me was of course malaria. And if I had been let off the hook of death this time, it was attributable, naturally, by Isaya and all else present, to Kitasamba and chief Khavaïru's medicine cuts, not to any mzungu chemist and his pills. In a day I was strong enough to walk to the road.

Letters awaited me at Fort Portal's *poste restante*, and a telegram from my darling which told me that my first book had won a prize awarded annually by representatives of good judgment to a young writer for a book of any sort. I had not been aware that *The Hostile Sun*, written at 20 and tidied up at 22, had been entered for it. It seemed to me just then, at 24, that such juvenilia hardly warranted a prize. The award seemed to increase the burden of the task ahead, namely to write worthily on Ruwenzori and its own humanity. I was no 'travel writer': that was obvious. Yet my publisher needed to feed *his* children and awaited a fresh 'Tom Stacey' in the genre of exploratory journeying; and before I had so much as entered Africa he had slapped me with a writ to 'do' such a book, paying me a cautious advance against royalties which my infant daughters had already eaten as rusks. Meanwhile, I was aware of an impediment. To enter on my new literary task seemed to me at once to discredit the motive for writing the book. It would mean that the Bakonzo of Ruwenzori had been beguiled by Isaya Mukirane to open their hearts to an intruder from another world for the sake of his writing a book about another exotic people in a remote place. What fraudulence! What sort of Musabuli was this, whose concern for them began and ended with this contribution to his literary fortune?

It seemed to me that only if some further truth had been borne upon me in the course of my journeying and sojourn here in

Ruwenzori, for whatever obligation, and only if that truth called for literary expression by virtue of its truthfulness might a book justly be wrestled out of me. In sum: only if Isaya's people were to add by my creative exercise to the font of human knowledge would mine become a rightful, undeniable task, *on their behalf.*

Already there in the undulating lanes and leafy grace of Fort Portal that last night was I foreseeing the impossibility of taking stock, and giving proper literary voice to any such 'further truth' as perhaps lay amid all that had been unfolded to me these previous months? In a matter of weeks hence I was to take up a post in Montreal and prepare on thin funds a new home for my young family. How could any such book struggle forth from its own latency to *demand the writing of it* out of a jungle of notes in such a span amid such distraction? Was life to prove willy-nilly a procession, a *marche macabre,* of one loyalty biting the tail of another?

Kayingo, atsunge.

And how shall one atone?

My diary falters at this point, my last day in the Kingdom of Toro. Ibrahimu had taken Kigoma with him on a bus, back by the northern road to Bundibugyo. As for Isaya, memory holds the door on our single night spent at the Mountains of the Moon hotel. Isaya was my guest in the next room. I could scarcely afford it. He was ill at ease in the hushed decorum of that rambling exclusivity, its floorboards creaking and its menus typewritten; Windsor soup and crisp linen – ill at ease and out of place, this Zerubbabel-in-waiting of the Konzo Zion... not that he or I could have foretold such destiny. Fort Portal was no place for any Mukonzo of the heartland, least of all our old colonial hostelry. Eucalyptus garrisoned the hotel's grounds; the same great trees lined the few broad murram ways of the town. Eucalyptus spoke colonial power, a British import from Britain's Australia. British eucalyptus were deployed in Ruwenzori as seedlings by Batoro of the Forestry Department along the lower limits of the mountain's forest to indicate the line beyond which Bakonzo, by Government of Toro edict, may not fell.

See him there, our short hero, Rwenzururu brother, once again in his Hindi-cobbled black shoes (17.50 Uganda shillings) and his baggy dark blue shorts cut down from someone else's suit; see him anguished (Syahuka-Muhindo's word) and subdued, furrowed in the brow, suddenly not knowing if he and I had anything to show for our intense endeavour – anything but a reticule of words for the *embitha* of a forgotten nation: the 'Bakonzo Life History Research Society'. An abstract within an abstract of a forgottenness. Watch me as I settle my simple monetary obligations with him with a loop or two of strung shillings, on the verandah there, under the frangipane, under the eucalyptus.

The Kampala bus – the 'Pepsi', in west Ugandan argot of the time – is to leave this early morning from the market place. Isaya walks down with me. He has his Bombay-manufactured suitcase, a mean thing which Kigoma has mostly carried all these weeks; I, a whole clutter of things. We are the embers of a spent fire. How remote the mountains are from Fort Portal: nothing gives them away but a sullen concentrate of cloud over the south-west horizon. The hotel's name was but a hotelier's *Sea-View* fancy.

We vow this and that.

Boarding the Pepsi with three spears, one rucksack, and a coffee-bean bag of Konzo artefacts, I am bound for another planet, by way of Mbarara, capital of Ankole, and Entebbe airport on Lake Victoria. I land the following morning at Northolt, London, to be photographed by the *Daily Express* on the tarmac, wearing my colobus-pelt and in a demure embrace with her who had weaved and waited for me month upon month raising our children. As for Isaya – Isaya of the former planet – this story cannot leave you there, alone with your shabby suitcase and those few looped bunches of Ugandan shillings, vexed in your bones, in the presence of the oppressor, and dreams we have begun to dream pressed between the leaves of an unwritten book...

END OF PART I

PART II

A KINGDOM COMES : 1954-82

The BLHRS Takes Off

After that, Isaya went back to his wife Christine and his two infants, Charles 'Kisembo' ('gift of God') and Kunihira, at Kasulenge in Bwamba. I do not know if he took the bus or walked over the mountains below Karongura by the old route – the way taken by the young Mwamba we had buried. Presumably he got to work again on his new squared-up house set back from the murram road between Bundibugyo and Bubandi. But there was going to be no peace, now, for Isaya, in the new dispensation: no peace, in truth, henceforth, for the rest of his life. His horizons had spun outwards. He had climbed into the mountains – his own – and had entered upon his extended transfiguration, seeing great distances from where he had come to stand, and himself lit there.

Almost at once he was sharply at odds with the authorities: Toro authorities, naturally. I know of this since, within three weeks of my return to London, I received by post a letter in the familiar cautious hand at our basement flat in South Kensington. It was a desperate missive. He had been arrested, he wrote, following some defiance on his part of Toro authority. Strong words and handcuffs had ensued, and though he was released for the time being, pending a hearing of his case, I wrote back to him at once, care of the Post Office in Fort Portal. There must have been an appeal for money – something to do with the charge against him: I forget just what, but have not forgotten the £5 in notes I enclosed which would have comprised a full week's provisions for two babies, a wife, and my unsalaried self.

It was not that I ceased to care, five thousand miles away. I was urgently scribbling about Isaya's mountains and their people, and the small fraught figure was right there in my mind's eye, buffeted and tossed in his sea of troubles from the dual authority of imperial Britain and imperious Toro. The mountains (as I saw it) were his literal and symbolic refuge. The spurs havened him by their height, weather, steepness and secret complexity of folds and gullies. As a visionary refuge, there was our Bakonzo Life History Research

Society, vessel of Konzo brotherhood in their place, Rwenzururu, the esoteric *embitha*. His letter had referred to it. My £5 was ostensibly a founding contribution. I sensed that whatever had befallen Isaya so swiftly after my departure was a sort of willed mini-martyrdom on behalf of his fellow Konzo. Everyone would soon hear of it throughout Bwamba and across the mountains' spine in Burahya and Bunyangabo, and even in the southern heartlands of Busongora, where we had carried word of our purpose: the enshrining of the mountain race in their own fastness. They knew him now, or knew *of* him, and in some manner looked to him. As for me, I would hear nothing of Isaya for more than eight years. Yet for much of that period he remained at my side. For I had re-embarked on a second journey in Ruwenzori, inwardly, a literary journey and a very different one from what I first intended.

I had entered Ruwenzori in the first place to write a book of venturesome travel – my second such book. A mere six weeks separated my return to London from Africa and the start of a challenging role on a newspaper in North America: I set myself the task of completing the commissioned book in that paltry gap. But the prospective book was confronted by a problem deriving from before I had entered the mountains, namely the disintegration before my eyes of my companion, Erisa Kironde, with whom I crossed the continent west to east over a period of months on the long and tortuous route we chose to take to his homeland of Uganda after his completing his BA in anthropology at Cambridge. This was the narrative I was chiefly moved to put down first. Yet it was forbidden me, unless I was to ravage an already riven figure. Thus distracted, I meanwhile had no choice but to confine the prospective book to Ruwenzori and indeed, in those few weeks wrote some three hundred pages of pencilled freehand. It was the wrong book *then.* I was learning what writers soon come to know: that any writing that succeeds is the outcome of a conviction that *this* and only *this* is what must be written *now.* Certainly *in addition* I wanted to tell of Ruwenzori – but as the first exploration I needed to retail the continent-wide grief of Erisa. I felt the travel book running out of conviction as it came off the point of my pencil. I do not recall showing it even to my agent, Anthony Blond, let alone my prospective publisher. In the end I declared that what I would write instead was a novel, set in Oxford and in Africa's mountain heartland of Ruwenzori, playing out a drama between the two protagonists, one black and one white, juxtaposing the unbearable lightness of mid 20th century white civilisation with the unbearable darkness of primal Africa. On hearing of this intention, those with faith in me as a writer of best-sellers sighed.

My young family was nudging penury. Its rusks would be paid for only by my becoming, if anything, an employable newspaperman. In this I was to fare well enough, attaining within about five years a reputation as a foreign correspondent of style and resource, first for Beaverbrook's *Daily Express* (a broadsheet, selling 4.3 million copies daily), and then for the *Sunday Times*. Such heady presence at the centre of events propelled me for a while into national politics. A third daughter had joined the family and I was standing for Parliament.

Meanwhile I had been writing the novel by night. Like Nicodemus, I grubbed for the deeper truths when most others were abed. We all live more lives than one. In its third draft, *The Brothers M* was done as I supposed I wanted it. In 1959 Secker and Warburg took it for Britain, Pantheon for the US, and others for translation. Thus for some four years and five hundred polished pages I had been on my nocturnal pilgrimage to and through Ruwenzori, in the company of my conjured protagonists, the black and the white: Daudi Mukasa, a high flyer of Makerere University, Kampala, and Bob McNair, a Canadian Rhodes Scholar. This contrasting pair of favoured young subjects of imperial Britain, brought together at Oxford, were riven asunder by primal Africa. On their reaching Ruwenzori, they were shepherded by a man called *Drum*, Kigoma, a Konzo *un*sophisticate. It was he who, in a touching verbal gesture, dubbed them 'the brothers M'. This Kigoma, however, was not conjured. 'Kigoma' was Isaya Mukirane, borrowed from life in many fragments.

All that while, therefore, from 1955 to 1959, and broken in upon by long and challenging assignments as a roving correspondent, Isaya was present to me. I used of him what my story needed. My 'Kigoma' borrowed from Isaya Mukirane, but he was not Isaya *whole*. Novelists take these liberties. A reader today of *The Brothers M* will not find Isaya's Philoctetan wound in my Kigoma. Yet the clues were lying there in my notes. Only now am I re-conjuring the fictitious Sambo, who was to be Prophet; King; exemplar of race and place, creature and carrier of first principle; the voice crying with the tongue of Nzururu, 'Comfort ye, my people.'

181

In 1954 I had left behind me, as you will recall, a man of nearly 29 on whom certain modest colonial hopes had been based but whose prospects now seemed shattered. I have gleaned a little of what followed. His arrest swiftly after my departure is evidence enough that the smouldering rage we had warmed ourselves with on our journey was fatally candescent in him. Isaya had at once got up Batoro noses and the kingdom of Toro's establishment was quick to finger him.

Thus boxed in, or boxed out, with no delay he made known to his chosen ones the foundation of the Bakonzo Life History Research Society, whose name I give in Lukonzo for the flavour of its sound in the ears of ordinary Ruwenzori folk: Ekithúnga Ekyérisondekánia Ebíkahabangána OkwaBakónzo. Isaya himself used the English title wherever it would be understood; and in all subsequent records of the movement and of the Kingdom itself, even documents written in the vernacular (as by Yolamu Mulima, Charles' surviving ex-Prime Minister and present keeper of archives) it was the English title, or its abbreviation, BLHRS, which was used. Isaya made his father-in-law Samwiri's rectangular home on Bukangama spur, the pivot of the Society and the idea – that very structure whose building I had intruded upon the day of my arrival in the mountains. Bukangama means a 'site of prominence'. Isaya's own highland home at Kasulenge was close at hand.

Isaya himself was a tireless writer of letters and despatcher of messengers, one of whom was the indefatigable Kigoma of real life. Literacy was everywhere honoured among the spurs. Meanwhile Samwiri himself set about putting down on paper his own ancestral story as he knew it. He too was a Mukonzo of accredited literacy – one of that tiny *élite* of Bakonzo who on colonial insistence had received schooling to secondary level, and who included also Timothy Bazarrabusa, Ezironi Bwambale, Blasio Maate, Henry Bwambale, Ibrahimu Linkoni, and Isaya himself. Of the two Bwambales we shall soon tell.

Word skittered along the spurs and into the huts of the headmen, wherever Lukonzo was the breast-language, of this live repository of Konzo tribal identity. The 'Life' in the History was in its very re-statement: the past at once bursting its cyst to become the root of the present, a pulsing Konzo pride amid the repressive present; for ancestry *lives* in the here and now and the impending future. Moreover, the *erisondekania ebikahabangana*, which we may render 'delving and revealing', was not only in the cause of history but of all of the custom and tradition that defined the Konzo. Such was the higher concept, as Isaya's scripture told him, in which 'all things come alive'. Meanwhile in Isaya himself was combined (as we have seen) not only kinship by marriage with the warrior-hero Ruhandika and his line, but the blood of his fellow-clansman Nyamutswa, sorcerer-patriot, co-leader and ideologue with Tibamwenda of the rebellion of a generation earlier. A mantle was half on him. And since Isaya and his small clan, Hira, were residents of Bwamba with whose eponymous people the Bakonzo shared the gods and history and a way of life, the Baamba were in it too. Indeed, the Baamba were a living repository of spiritual knowledge. They were prior people: it was to the Baamba that the gods of the mountains and the forests first revealed themselves. When Konzo from any region of the mountains required to be re-acquainted with the tutelars of this place, they betook themselves to Bwamba, and Bwamba's shamans. To the Baamba they brought their boys for circumcision at puberty. It was of significance that the Konzo Nyamutswa had been of Bwamba provenance.

Isaya, then, was aptly placed for the regeneration of the *idea*. His mission – that of the BLHRS – while in its founding expression carrying the name of the Konzo, was always to be for and of *Banya*rwenzururu, all the folk of Rwenzururu, *collectively*, which is to say of the mountains and that territory the mountains rose out of, be they Bakonzo, Baamba, the Bambuti, Bambuva or Banyagwaki pygmies of the lowland forests north and west, and even Banyabindi, who entered the Rwenzururu community in the south as slightly haughty refugees from Bunyoro. Bwamba's Bakonzo, meanwhile, stood in relation to their tribal kinsman of Buswagha in the southern heartland in some such way as Galilean Jews stood to the men of Judaea.

The north and south of the range communicated most conveniently not by the interminable switchback of spur and gully followed by Isaya and me but by the secret, forested track through Congolese territory, across the Lamia tributary of the Semliki and on southwards, keeping low, dark and leafy. It skirted the Belgian roadhead of Mutwanga and from that point only began the ascent towards the Tako's headwaters. Compounds of Konzo folk dot that lowland route, where ancestors have cleared higher ground of the prevailing forest, including Buhira, birthplace of Nyamutswa, whose rebellion took fire in British Uganda across the Europeans' false frontier. After Mutwanga, the secret traveller, mounting on a south-easterly trail mostly in forest, will pass through four Konzo communities before delving into the border ravine of the Tako river, on its tumbling course towards Lake Edward, for the final climb into Uganda's Buswagha and the demesne of Khavaïru. For an unburdened man it was a foot journey of some three days; for one hurrying, not sleeping, in flight or on a mission of life and death, half that.

To Isaya, weaving Konzo allegiance into the fabric of the Bakonzo Life History Research Society, it was one territory, one people, Rwenzururian Konzo. Branches began to emerge, with listed adherents, in Burahya, Bunyangabo, and in Busongora which at that time included all the southern foothills, and Kyatenga. All were one with their territorial and linguistic brothers across the invisible frontier. Bwamba-based, the Society was drawing in accredited adherents to the notion of a unified identity wherever the mountains stretched their shadow.

At first, then, Isaya issued the word mostly by mouth, through miruka-parish chiefs and spur headmen. Literacy was not common nor was it necessary for true authority. The 'aims' were as much implicit as spelt out, to uphold the integrity of the Konzo people; their way of life and language; their crafts and music; their home-building and practices of cultivation; the inner authority of ancestry,

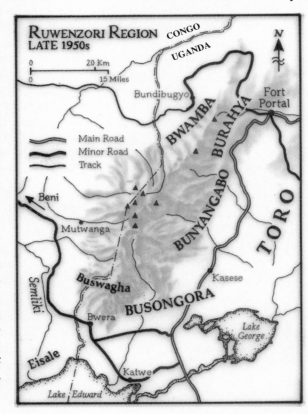

184

and outer authority of their own kind in present-day administration, the use of Lukonzo in any schools and churches
attended by Bakonzo; and the spread of such schools and
churches in their territories. Congo-side adherents had no
confrontational imperative comparable to Uganda-side where
the Batoro and their language, endorsed by the colonial power,
had all-but-universally usurped Konzo authority on their
mountain ground. On Congo-side, by contrast, the blood and
language of the mountain race spread west and south-west
among two or three million of peasant folk to Beni, Eisale, and
Butembo; and though the Belgian colonial hand was dumb and
heavy there was no indigenous challenge to tribal identity.

Isaya resumed teaching. In the foothills south of Bubandi, a
primary school had opened in the parish of Mutunda, drawing its
pupils from the Konzo spur villages of Butama, Bundimbuga and
Bunyamwera, and lowland Bwamba settlements. There he
presided as dominie. The frontier river Lamia ran two miles to the
west. His own home of Kasulenge lay several miles to the
northeast – two or three hours' walk away, by a track running just
beneath the steep ascents. When, in 1958, there arrived in
Bundibugyo two young Norwegian anthropologists, the married
partnership of Kirsten Alnaes and Axel Somerfelt, they found
Isaya based to the south of them in the sub-county around his
school and already a figure of controversy, a 'village Hampden',
Bakonzo and Baamba glancing towards him daringly, Batoro
authority eyeing him suspiciously. He paid a call upon the white
anthropologists and left them in little doubt as to his resentment
of their intended researches into Konzo custom, society and spirit
world. Such research was the preserve and function of the
BLHRS. That same year Isaya summoned a general meeting of
the Society at Kasese, the 'central' village of Busongora adjacent
to the English-managed copper mine at Kilembe. Kasese was
more or less the site of Nyamutswa's mud palace, Nyamisule, at
the height of the rebellion thirty-eight years earlier. Isaya,
naturally, set the agenda and the pace. The experience and
sagacity of Timothy Bazarrabusa, driving down from Fort Portal,
was drawn upon. Their cause would go unheeded, they decided,
no less by the British than the Batoro, so long as they remained
without representation in the parliament, the Rukurato, of the
Toro Omukama, King George. So they would demand that

representation. Fast upon the emergence of this decision, leading figures of the Baamba community applied for the BLHRS to be open to Baamba membership. To this request, Isaya and his trustees readily acceded.

The British District Officer in Fort Portal and his Provincial Commissioner were swift to acknowledge the justice of the Bakonzo-Baamba application for membership of the Rukurato. Here was a necessary and overdue measure of colonial house-tidying. For suddenly and startlingly independence for Britain's East African possessions was in prospect. The previous winter of 1957, Harold Macmillan, Britain's new Prime Minister after Eden's ignominy at Suez, announced his government's decision to loose virtually the entirety of the remaining British empire into independence as fast as could be done, consonant with local decorum and metropolitan dignity. The various processes would take place, of course, on what purported to be a democratic basis, which is to say, one-adult-one-vote for one or another implausible set of expectations and their spokesmen.

Up to that late 1957 few servants of the British colonial structure in East Africa had imagined that their charges would be released from metropolitan care *before the end of the century*. No less was true of the Belgian, Portuguese, French and Spanish administrations in most of sub-Saharan Africa. Readers today, in the 21st century, will find this hard to credit. I write with the assurance of one who knew it on the ground. Northwards, indeed, in 1956, the Sudan had already been let go into a wobbly independence – under military rule and its south rising instantly in rebellion. In Britain's relatively sophisticated and economically advanced colonies of West Africa, a measured pace to self-rule had been set. For central and east Africa there was a different yardstick. At that latitude, like Britain's, France's *mission civilisatrice* surely had half a century to run. (The French had put down a rebellion in Madagascar in the late 1940s in which 78,000 Malagasies had died without Paris or the world raising an eyebrow.) To the Belgians, independence for the Congo – with not a single Congolese African at university in 1957 – was *absurdité*. In Kenya in the mid 1950s Britain had eliminated Mau Mau's dark menace to the white-settled highlands with unequivocal thoroughness. Any notion of Mau Mau's imprisoned leader – 'the leader of darkness and death' in the colonial Governor's Jeremiac phrase – becoming first President of an independent Kenya by the early 1960s, was beyond imagination.

Yet in the context of Black Africa, Macmillan had not so much identified the 'wind of change' as blown it. His over-riding intention was to forestall 'world Communism's' exploitation of indigenous movements of independence. Such a threat was no fantasy. His Colonial Secretary of State, Iain MacLeod, likewise a Scottish crofter's grandson, had set to work with the relish of a Thomas Cromwell of imperial dissolution. By 1958, a stunned Uganda was on a four-year count-down to full independence.

Those in Ruwenzori with regional injustices were not oblivious of such *realpolitik*. They could see it would be far harder to right those injustices with an independent native government in Kampala than to treat at once with the colonial whites in Fort Portal and Entebbe. Such was Isaya's assessment, and it was borne out. The British authorities indeed put their weight behind the call from the BLHRS for representation in the Toro Rukurato with a 'recommendation' to King George of Toro that to his 80-strong Rukurato he add 21 members elected from and by the Bakonzo and Baamba communities. Such a reform, the Provincial Commissioner stressed, was in line with the democratic mood of the times and could only serve the survival of the Toro kingdom within a popularly governed independent Uganda.

With no visible enthusiasm, the Omukama of Toro – by now a Knight of the vanishing empire – accepted the recommendation. Given that his Bakonzo-Baamba subjects numbered in aggregate more than half his Batoro subjects, a twenty per cent representation in the Kingdom's parliament seemed possible to swallow. Preparations for the election of 21 candidates by adult males of villages designated as either Konzo or Amba were duly put in hand for the date of the next renewal of Rukurato members, in 1961. The organisation of the raft of candidates fell to the BLHRS, under the leadership of Isaya Mukirane. The candidates included Timothy Bazarrabusa, who had already entered national politics as a cross-bench member of Uganda's Legislative Council,  the country's own parliament-in-embryo. Bazarrabusa's qualities had been proven by his performance as supervisor of schools for the Western Province. Education had come late to the mountain region, but now was burgeoning. He had seen to the opening of several schools serving Bakonzo and Baamba communities. He was widely liked among all tribes and races, and allowed his name to go forward for a chieftainship of one of the four Saza divisions incorporating the Ruwenzori area. The Batoro selection committee passed him over on the grounds that, as a Saza chief *and* member of the Rukurato, in the case of a vacancy he could come to serve as Toro's acting *omuhikirwa* (prime minister) and occupy the King's chair at parliamentary sessions. Such would be racially intolerable.

Preparations for that 1961 election under Isaya's management galvanised the Bakonzo Life History Research Society. The group campaigned on a platform of Lukonzo and Lwamba becoming the medium of instruction at all primary schools, present and future, in those peoples' tribal areas; the opening up of opportunities in further education to Bakonzo and Baamba; and the provision of dispensaries and health services in the tribes' areas. The group's further demands were more controversial: first, a revision of the original Toro treaties, making due reference to the minority peoples; next, an equitable taxation system; next, the right for Bakonzo and Baamba members to speak in their own languages when addressing the Rukurato. Lastly, for good measure, it demanded an increase in the minority peoples' representation in the Rukurato proportionate to the two tribes' numbers in the Toro Kingdom.

This was brave stuff. The Batoro majority of the Rukurato were themselves unelected: they were members *ex officio* of the Kingdom's structure and appointees of the King. Once in the chamber, they drew themselves up and disdained even so much as to discuss the issues raised by this rump and rattle of baboons and bark-cloth beaters foisted on their conclave by a colonial power grown tired and weak, scuttling its *imperium*. Their omukama - king had been persuaded to appoint a 'constitutional committee'. But did the Kingdom need such a body? Scarcely so. At least he saw to it that this committee included no Bakonzo or Baamba. Yet the baboons were objecting, their furrowed Mukirane banging and ranting at the committee's door, and the District Commissioner in Fort Portal (where life's purpose was running out like the sand of an hour-glass) presuming to hear him. King George Rukidi shrugged his vast shoulders. He had two of them let in, to speak for their savages; whereupon the delegated two dared to propose that their tribes should be *named* in the document of colonial surrender about to be drawn up in London, as recognition of their 'rights' within Toro in an independent Uganda. And more than that: the royal ears heard them insisting that in the forthcoming dispensation of independence, official roles in the Toro 'kingdom' should be shared among the three main constituent peoples of the place: Batoro, Bakonzo, Baamba... involving a rotation among the tribes for the role of Toro's *omuhikirwa*, Premier. This was more than could be stomached. By virtue of their citizenship of this Kingdom, the Mukama responded, all his subjects were 'Batoro'. And as for the premiership, only a 'proper Mutoro' could ever take the role. A proper Mutoro required no definition.

At this the two representatives of the mountain tribes quit the constitutional committee. The committee that thus attended upon the British governor, Sir Walter Coutts, to work out the precise position of Toro within an independent Uganda included neither Mukonzo nor Mwamba. Lobbied by Isaya Mukirane, however, Fort Portal's District Commissioner, Ray Cordery, arranged for Isaya and two colleagues to see the Governor in Entebbe on their own. One colleague was the Mwamba spokesman, Kawamara, and the other an articulate and flamboyant fellow, Mupalya, of mostly Baamba allegiance and provenance; both were recently elected members of the Rukurato. It was Isaya who handed Sir Walter a demand for a separate mountain District, such as would decisively free the bulk of the minorities from Toro governance. The demand, Isaya dared Luther-like to inform the Governor, was 'irreversible', as if they were not in Entebbe in 1961 but at Worms in 1521 – Hier stehe ich, *Here I stand*. Ich kann nicht anders. *I can do naught else.* Gott helfe mir. *So help me God.* Yet at such a point in the Empire's disbandment, separate District status was no longer in the Governor's gift. It may be said to have been in God's, and God – as Isaya would be the last to doubt – did nothing by halves.

Back in Toro's Rukurato-parliament, the Bakonzo-Baamba members challenged the Batoro majority – unelected as they were – as to their very right of representation, and, next, as to the rights of Toro over any of the peoples of the mountains, the Banyarwenzururu. Seventeen of the twenty-one Bakonzo-Baamba members drew up a Memorandum to this effect, prepared by Kawamara the Mwamba, and signed it. This was already March of 1962; independence for the entire country was a bare seven months ahead. If their proposals were rejected, they warned, they would walk out.

The Rukurato majority were in no mood to compromise: the *omuhikirwa* Rusoke was adamant: what Toro had, Toro would keep. The right of a King was other than the rights of any peasant mob: the Mukama George Rukidi III would *nominate* new members of his chamber to fill any spaces the Bakonzo-Baamba left. On March 13, 1962, the seventeen signatories quit. As the scholar Syahuka-Mohindu has recorded it, 'the politics of hope were running out for the Bakonzo-Baamba leaders and were giving way to the politics of desperation.' Isaya and other firebrands were seized in the law's name, imprisoned on a charge of disturbing the peace... and then released. A nominal bail was pledged.

Disturbing the peace? What peace? This was a heady hour. Nerves were everywhere taut, facial muscles tremulous. The old order was giving way. No one knew to what.

Throughout colonial Africa there had always been the two elemental layerings, white on black. In the fast evolving schemata shadows lay on shadows, black on black on black, black national political movements on black races on black tribes, current on current, race on race, race on tribe, tribe on tribe, cultivator on pastoralist, Cain on Abel, steppe on forest, plain on mountain, black Christian on black Muslim on pagan black, Protestant on Catholic, Protestant this on Protestant that, black electoral on black monarchic, black haves on black have-nots, black many on black few and sometimes vice versa... The white armature of this fabrication *Uganda* was all of a sudden gone. What remained were the spaces it had occupied, the serried eucalyptus, the gateways, porticos, aisles, vestiges of a *polis* of which neither the motives nor the styles were indigenous; constitutions, agreements (with riders); arcane methodologies; promises, hopes, vows, declarations, an anthem. In such hot air, a recent Colonial Secretary in London, Oliver Lyttelton, loftily humorous amid the betrayal of the vision splendid, had speculated aloud as to whether indeed the inclusion of 'God is Love' in the baptismal documents added anything of value to a colony collecting its independence? Words should if possible be worth the vellum they were typed upon.

The relevant issue would swiftly prove to be: Who *now* had the Maxim gun, and who had not? In neighbouring Congo, independent since the middle of 1960, whatever the Belgians and the Congolese had actually signed up to had meant bugger-all within 96 hours of the ceremony: the entire vast place had pitched into primordial chaos, governed by gun-muzzle and illiterate trigger-fingers. The colonial period in Congo having endured no longer than my grandfather's adult life-span, the last state was worse than the first. That history I witnessed in the making – the inherent catastrophe of colonisation made manifest in decolonisation. Yet of Uganda, in my old territory, I knew no detail whatsover.

There in Ruwenzori, June 1962, sprung from jail in Fort Portal, Isaya flit to Busongora and the southern foothills. At a rally at Bwera, the BLHRS became transmogrified as the Rwenzururu Secessionist Movement. Isaya was acclaimed its president. The mask of propriety was torn away. Spear points were sharpened everywhere; the spurs rang with the hammers of smithies. Cadres were formed, or formed themselves spontaneously. Voices urged the leadership *at once* to disappear into the high forest. Yet the whole place – Isaya knew – the mountains end to end, had to be held together: the Baamba with the Bakonzo, the broader Banyarwenzururu, the foothills and the high scarps, the educated and the unlettered... Let there be one further grasp at a peaceful way through. Returning to Fort Portal in eschatalogical temper Isaya, with Kawamara and Mupalya, drew up for the two minority tribes their final irreducible demand: separation from the rule of Toro by the creation *there and then* of their own District.

This demand, if heard, went unheeded, either in Kabarole/Fort Portal or in Entebbe. Isaya therefore picked up his pen and wrote in his round hand to King George of Toro: '*If you cannot co-operate with the Bakonzo and Baamba, you have to realize what the Bible says: "The Most High ruleth in the Kingdom of man and giveth it to whoever he will."*' Our President of the Rwenzururu Secessionist Movement had been inspired by the Book of Daniel, Chapter 4. Having thus transferred Kabarole to Babylon, Isaya ratcheted up the menace by going on to paraphrase Chapter 5's sinister graffiti at King Balshazzar's last feast: '*God has weighed the Kingdom of Toro in the balance and found it wanting.*' This fragment of weird Mesopotamian vernacular ends with the word PERES which Daniel translated, 'Your Kingdom is divided'. King George may have known that according to holy scripture King Belshazzar's bloody death followed *that very night* – and the captive people liberated. Isaya was not unreasonably re-arrested instantly, along with Kawamara and Mupalya. His violation was of a local (Toro) law against

191

threatening the Mukama. In Christian Africa, the Bible's truth was, and is, not so much literary as literal.

This time the three were held in separate jails well distant from the region of ferment. For six weeks they languished, treated as Isaya later wrote 'like Roman gladiators', by which he meant 'Christian captives facing gladiators in a Roman arena': Mupalya in Kyaka prison in Kyegegwa, Kawamara in Muhoti prison, and Isaya in Kamwenge prison in the forest county of Kibale. There Isaya was heavily beaten, day after day, by a certain gaoler named Sabastian Rubalita Omukiga. Then all three were peremptorily tried and sentenced to eight months in custody. The sentence proved to be a formula for combustion. More or less there and then, secession became the reality throughout the whole territory within the arc of the lowland road. From that moment no Toro chief dared enter the hills and no Toro or colonial official risked leaving his vehicle without armed escort. The highland spurs and groves had readied for war. Kapoli's ancient ivory horn, stained by the hut's smoke of forty years, was brought down from the thatch and sounded. Balshazzar might still be on his throne, on Kabarole tump, but the captivity of his subject people of Rwenzururu was at an end.

As the reality swiftly dawned, the faltering colonial hand relaxed its grip. Within a fortnight of the sentencing, the three were let out on bail, pending an appeal. Isaya did now run into the mountains, via Bwamba and the secret route through to Congo, to take up his Presidency. He now donned a colobus pelt, such as I had worn myself throughout those hills eight years earlier. On August 15th, 1962, in the hills above Bwera, under a flag in horizontal panels, of blue (Love), green (Fecundity) surrounding a snow-white disk, and yellow (brother Sun), he declared Rwenzururu free not only of Toro but also (if equivocally) of Uganda of which Toro was a constituent part.

The spurs were now alive with the bustle of war. Ridge to ridge, anvils rang. Spearmen mobilized. Headmen and miruka-parish chiefs became captains. Messengers scurried. Paths became secrets, gullies became fosses, slopes became ramparts. Women at the stream pools, fetching water in pitchers, exchanged rumours of war. The word went out, Thuli baghuma – *we are all one. Whoever is not with us is against us.* Ruwenzori cold, Ruwenzori fog, Ruwenzori downpours, Ruwenzori hail, became arsenal. The voice of Kitasamba, spoken in thunder, was the voice of the warden of that arsenal. Lives were lost almost at once. Four Bakonzo at the leper colony at Kagando in the south were shot dead by a panicky Mutoro chief. Batoro officials and teachers in Konzo-Amba communities everywhere ran for cover. Schools shut down from one end of the territory to the other; so did dispensaries, since all the medical staff were Batoro except for one – a Mukonzo dresser. Half of the seventy-odd Bakonzo teachers made idle by the school closures declined to take posts elsewhere. Most of them would soon become teachers in Rwenzururu schools. Scarcely a shilling of poll tax was collected by the Toro administration from either minority tribe. A distracted government in Kampala set up a Commission of Enquiry headed by a worthy Muganda, Dr Ssembeguya, to investigate the causes of the 'disturbances'. Kawamara and Mupalya, themselves standing ever so slightly aside from the armed rebellion, hurried to Kampala to submit to the Commission a 24-page handwritten account of their grievances. They issued this document on September 16th, from the Mengo Social Centre, the dissident leaders' favourite place of cheap lodging in the capital area, ostensibly on behalf of both tribes, signing themselves, 'Your Obedient Servants 1. Yeremiya S. Kawamara 2. Peter Kamba Mupalya BAMBA BAKONZO SECESSION MOVEMENT LEADERS **RWENZURURU'**. Isaya the *de facto* secessionist leader got no more than two passing references, on pages 13 and 15. It was a sophisticated composition, cleanly laid out, and beautifully penned in Kawamara's hand, and naturally carrying a bias towards the Baamba who were 'me-too-ers' in a dominantly Bakonzo affair. Were the Baamba seeking to steal a march upon the Bakonzo? To protect themselves from retribution? There was high urgency: independence was a handful of weeks away and Isaya out of reach. Yet somehow he got wind of the submission, for within eleven days, with the Baamba gone, he himself was at the Mengo Social Centre, writing out in a more fevered hand, on seven very large sheets, a further submission 'in addition to the Rwenzururu memorandum of 15 Aug 1962' – that is, the 'Open Letter' issued on Isaya's installation as President of the already 'seceded' territory of Rwenzururu immediately preceding his Babylonian warning to King George. This new document made no reference to Kawamara's and Mupalya's of less than a fortnight earlier. It complained of mounting outrages against the men, women and children of Rwenzururu and of the murderous intent of Isaya's own treatment in prison. It somewhat incoherently if justifiably stressed the lack of consistency in the signing of a new Agreement in Entebbe between the Government of Uganda and the Kingdom of Toro precisely five days earlier (September 22) which endorsed all of Toro's existing boundaries, ignored Rwenzururu's declaration of its independence let alone the reality of it, and implicitly pre-judged the conclusions of the same Government's Commission of Enquiry yet to report. Isaya signed alone, in his cloud-locked capacity, after a tortuous warning of trouble to come:

Uganda Government failing to grant Bakonjo/Bamba an entirely separate state - we will indicate that the Uganda Central Government has found it costly to protect Rwenzururians who have determined to stand as a nation in Uganda.

Uhuru Rwenzururu, Uhuru Uganda.

President Isaya M. Mukirane Rwenzururu.

Copies to :

His Excellency the Governor Entebbe - Uganda.
The Prime Minister Uganda Entebbe.
" District Commissioner F.P. Rwenzururu.
" Colonial Secretary London.
" Rwenzururu Secession Movement Supporters.

xvi

The Second Rebellion

Of all these goings-on I was unaware. My nightly journey to and through Ruwenzori had been completed; in 1959 the last draft of the novel's typescript had gone to its publishers, and a year later – September 1960 – was offered to the reading public. The plot of my 'Brothers M' – the title of the book – in those mountains and among that folk was personal and cosmic. Yet the story was set at that cusp time of global history: the colonial period giving way to indigenous rule of which none could foretell the outcome.

The new dispensation was a bastard thing, and has so remained. Tribal peoples across the continent, half-Christianized and half-literate, were being bundled into independent statehood, amid an almighty clamour of their own, on a basis of sham nationhoods conjured between boundaries sketched on conjectural maps of half-explored territory scarcely three generations earlier by exalted statesmen and freebooting pioneers belonging, the lot of them, to a remote and alien civilisation. That same white civilisation, after two dreadful internecine wars, was now locked in a third contest of implacable hostility. Such a period had sapped its inner will to carry through the project of enlightenment and tutelage it had grandly embarked on scarcely three-quarters of a century earlier. Riven with self-doubt, bereft of the springs of faith and daring that had sustained its imperial pioneers, it was now bequeathing its former wards the methods and constructs devised to manage populist whim and grievance-mongering in urban, post-industrial, European electorates. The tropical wards themselves could scarcely be blamed if much of this inheritance was unworkable. Admittedly, their demagogues *insisted* on the multi-party, 'democratic' formulae of the so-called Westminster model. Most of them were seduced by the collectivist shibboleths of the anti-imperial European Left. The leaders of emerging Africa found themselves managing states with no viable sense of nationhood, by means of political systems of at most a few years' operative

195

duration, and all but stripped of the presiding bureaucratic *raj*.

I have written of the 'catastrophe' of colonisation. Its bequest was benison-cum-blight, the blight embedded in the benison. In Anglophone territories the benison was the rule of law; an administrative incorruptibility; a structure of education aimed at universal literacy; accessibility of medical care; good roads and working phones; self-sustaining economies and trade; police and defence forces obedient to command; and Christian light. The blight lay embedded in the provenance of these good things, in that it was, by definition, white, that they were dependent for effective operation on white presence, and that the whites had come in the working out of their own destiny not the blacks'. Paternalism was instinctive and explicit. The apparent indispensability of the benison implied a disregard, if not disdain, of the indigenous civilisation, still essentially intact and the marrow of the vast majority. The working of osmosis had hardly begun, so little time or opportunity for genuine *Africation*. In the disbanding of colonial Africa *circa* 1960, the Picts (so to speak) had had no reasonable chance to become Celts. The dismantling of dependence was abrupt, and guilt, shame and feelings of hatred for the traitrous ex-protector at their abandonment were inescapable. Independent statehood as fellow adults in a white-led world postulated equality amid a persisting sense of inequality demanding to be justified. Thus the whites remaining in East Africa found themselves overtly reviled and baited to provoke a hostility where none had previously been in evidence. Covertly, which is to say unconsciously, the whites were *blamed* for having quit the imperial role. The implication of white *imperium* was that it knew its own answers; that what it was offering and purporting to deliver in independence was a human fulfilment on the manifestly grander and superior premise of the colonisers. Yet of course, in the event, that *imperium* did not know its own answers, it was only working them out or, rather, struggling and mostly failing to work them out; it had far from provided 'human fulfilment' in the generality to the white world of *imperium's* provenance. In the event – as those of the black world in a position to inspect and assess the white discerned – it did not even believe in its own God, nor even know how to fulfil the promise of its vaunted literacy. What the newly independent Third World had inherited (at its own incoherent demanding) was a half understood mechanism for operating an alien civilisation enmeshed in its own self-betrayal. What the leaders of Africa had taken up and held aloft was what the indigenous being knew to be deceiving and destructive. To this day such duality has persisted in black Africa, and indeed in most of the world's tropical and sub-tropical ex-dependencies.

Amid all this, what was there as a viable allegiance for the majority of folk? The tribe. This was retrogressive in that innocence is retrogressive from experience, or the oral from the written, or the country from the city. It is as retrogressive as that requirement for entry into the Kingdom of heaven to 'become as little children' as offered by the provider of the light I have written of in the previous paragraph. Any reader reaching this far in the present record will have come to discern indispensable sanctity to ethnic allegiance, irrespective of potential 'downside'. The tribe met the requirement for meaning among so much which, whatever the prating, was devoid of true significance and, whatever the expectation, devoid of true satisfaction. Tribe was a refuge, yes, but as a church is refuge, in that it is a roof of ultimate validity: of strength, truth and intuitive communion.

I learned this in my own 'overt' role as a roving newspaper correspondent coming on top of *The Brothers M*. With the novel completed, I had switched newspapers and joined the *Sunday Times*. The biggest international events of the day became the stuff of my professional life. Much of it sprang from the end of empire, whether that was taking place by force of arms and insurrection, as in Indo-China or Algeria, or by bluff, chicanery and bargaining, as in much of Britain's empire. Sometimes it descended into confusion and barbarity as in the Congo. Off stage or on stage was the spectre of Communist ambition, whether Russian or Chinese. I had got to know the world in the throes of its crises, in the riot of its pain and fear. Year upon year I was witnessing man off-guard, stripped to raw instinct-truth. There were the standard dialectics – have-nots versus haves, left versus right, the weak versus the powerful, the oppressed versus the oppressor, black versus white. Yet everywhere was another force, with no dialectical frame, namely the force of the right to be where we belong: the clamour for meaningful identity, the force of race and place, the claim of belongingness in rightful and indestructible ultimacy. This was not in the first place a political thing, nor an economic thing. It was a soul thing.

I flew in and out between one theatre of news and the other – Washington and Moscow, the Middle East, South Asia, East Asia, Latin America, the Caribbean, South Africa, East, Central and West Africa... in due course, more than one hundred and fifteen countries attended upon, 'weighed in the balance' as Isaya might have put it; and discussion entered upon with so-called 'world' leaders, national leaders, opposition leaders, leaders on the run, fugitives, heroes, rebel commanders. In this role at that period (the late 1950s, and 1960s) Africa kept calling me back repeatedly: the prolonged ructions and birth pangs of some thirty so-called nation states of black Africa had required my reports and analysis for the British reader still caught up in the affairs of that continent. Britain was still a power of global authority; and everywhere the flag had flown, people of British stock were still involved.

As chance had it, one of the few countries which up to that time – late 1962 – had not called for the peripatetic media corps in the run-up to independent statehood and its aftermath was Uganda. Concerning the 'state of emergency' in the Ruwenzori mountains, less than half a dozen paragraphs had appeared, and these only in the *Daily Telegraph* and *The Times*. Being mostly abroad on assignment, I had failed to spot them. As to Uganda in general, the capital was seemingly peaceful; the official opposition was relatively docile; the Kabaka of Buganda had long been back on his stool; the economy was quite bonny, coffee and tea fetching respectable prices. Meanwhile the Ugandan battalion (under British senior officers) of the King's African Rifles had become the Uganda Rifles, the national army. A certain Lieutenant Idi Amin Dada had been promoted Captain, and got his first bank account.

In October 1962, the young Duke of Kent had flown out from London to Entebbe on behalf of his cousin, HM Queen Elizabeth, head of the Commonwealth. He would preside over the lowering of the Union Jack and the raising of Uganda's orange, yellow and black tricolor, after 73 years of British rule. The Hon Milton Obote, a Langi from the north, once a petrol pump attendant and now leader of the Uganda People's Congress party, had ridden to power as Premier with Baganda support by proposing the Kabaka as titular head of state. This the Kabaka, 'King Freddie' Mutesa, now became. As an ex-Grenadier, he had persuaded some of his regimental bandsmen to add their brass, woodwind, drums and cymbals to the panoply of the handover. The news agencies and stringers covered the event adequately enough, with descriptive little stories and a photograph or two. Milton Obote was never a photogenic man. In contrast with the Congo westwards, or Kenya eastwards, little Uganda looked set fair. The outgoing colonial Governor, Sir David Hunt, was to stay on as Britain's first High Commissioner. Meanwhile, a respected cross-bencher out of the new Parliament was appointed Uganda's first High Commissioner in London. It is with him that our story proceeds.

In January 1963, on a return to London, I happened to attend a lunch-time lecture on an African theme at the Royal Commonwealth Institute on Northumberland Avenue. As I left the building I found myself sheltering from the rain beside an African of middle age and evident eminence. 'Are you not Tom Stacey?'

I declared myself, and in so doing recognised to my astonishment none other than Timothy Bazarrabusa. We had last met in Fort Portal as I was setting out for the Ruwenzori mountains a little over eight years previously. Then he was Toro's Inspector of Schools.

'I am Uganda's High Commissioner here.'

The cheerful teeth fanned me a broad smile. For a Mukonzo in the Uganda of that time, this was indeed a wondrous elevation. I congratulated him.

'You know what has happened to our poor Bakonjo?'

'No.'

'They have rebelled against the Government.'

'*Rebelled*'? I had heard nothing of it.

'Oh yes,' he said. 'They took to their spears in September. Now they have got everyone against them – the government of Toro, the central Government. Nobody can do anything with them.'

It was cold and pelting. Good Timothy Bazarrabusa, His Excellency, got into his ambassadorial car to cover the two hundred yards to Uganda House, now the High Commission, at the south-west corner of Trafalgar Square. As to 'our poor Bakonjo' I was infected by that guilt of disloyalty, as when one hears of a dear but neglected friend having fallen gravely sick.

I returned sombre to my office in the gold glass *Sunday Times* building in Gray's Inn Road and went to the cuttings library to seek what might have been published on this 'rebellion'. There I found the few paragraphs I have referred to: snippets from the wire service – Reuters or Associated Press or possibly Agence France Presse –

originating from whoever was their stringer in Kampala, most likely an English desk-man working for the *Uganda Herald*. 'Rebel tribesmen,' the reports ran, had taken up arms 'in the remote Ruwenzori mountains' demanding secession from Toro, one of the constituent kingdoms of newly independent Uganda. Villages had been set ablaze. It was the first internal crisis to be faced by the fledgling government. A reference was made to a 'Commission of Enquiry'.

There was nothing I could do; even if I had known more facts, there was nothing for me to do. There was nothing anybody could do – Bazarrabusa had said so – for 'our Bakonjo'... not even he, who was of these people and their mountains in his childhood and his ancestry, and who had included me in the possessive 'our' on the strength of my long tramp and of *The Brothers M*. We had moved on and out, he and I; the barkcloth and monkey-pelts, the smokey huts and the communal pipe. In my office the telephone rang. It was the High Commissioner of Uganda, asking me to lunch with him, two days ahead.

So then I learned much of what the reader of this account already knows.

And now the past folded in upon the present: at that moment of interchange, when we had just sat down for the meal together, and nothing more as yet revealed beyond the mountain people being all up in arms against the Kingdom of Toro and by spear and torch sealing themselves into their highland citadels. They declared themselves to have seceded (in a way) from Uganda.

'We can't get through to them,' Bazarrabusa said, 'to reach any sort of settlement. They're up there – we don't know how to find them. Perhaps you could.'

I? 'Who is leading it?'

'Isaya Mukirane.'

I had been ready for that. *Isaya Mukirane*. My Kigoma, in his 'tennis', with me through all the long gestation of the novel, tramping on ahead, just a few paces, through the rain, up the steep paths, down to the stream-bed crossings, up again to the next spur; furrowed, earnest, unwavering in all loyalty, all commitment to the purpose; and in that long writing, the nocturnal task of years, the single sustained companion the author had drawn from life even if, in the confines of his fictional role, I had jettisoned half the truth of my man.

Bazarrabusa pressed, 'You could find him and talk to him,'

'Yes.'

'What I'm afraid of is that the Prime Minister will feel the need to send in the army, to try to suppress it. But that would prove very difficult, because of the mountains and the border.'

I heard what he was saying. Popularly elected Prime Ministers are required to be seen to be doing something. Yet how could any army find a rebel headquarters in those mountains? Up which of the hundred valleys or the thousand gullies should their units set off? And having reached the forests, or the hidden lakes and lost ravines, what then? There was the high border into another country, already crumbled into disorder, each bit of it a law to itself. On Congo-side, Uganda's Bakonzo were among their own kind, highlanders and lowlanders, with the lingo, the pathways, the *embitha*. Ruwenzori was Tom Tiddler's Ground. It was a hopeless task for any army. But soldiery could cause much devastation, much suffering.

I asked Bazarrabusa about the army.

It was a single battalion, but a full one, with a support company. It was doubtless keen, only too ready to show its paces for the independent nation. It was commanded by an Englishman, seconded from the British army as were most of the officers except for junior ranks. Bazarrabusa wanted to forestall the false solution of Obote calling in the army. I was familiar with armies in 'low intensity' domestic warfare: how the unsubtlety of armed men in uniform could double the problem, whatever the intention of high command. At nineteen I had been a one-pip ensign in the Malayan jungle, commanding my platoon, to kill those who would seize the place by force. The military was a blunt instrument.

As for Uganda finding its own indigenous emissary to treat for peace, I could see at once: *who would ever dare?* – in that maze of vast mountains, searching for the kernel of the rebellion. There were no means of secret liaison.

Meanwhile, as to the seeds and germination of this revolt, I was to learn from Timothy Bazarrabusa how it had all come about – how the Bakonjo Life History Research Society in its innocence and innocuity had come to be *politics*, had grown hairy and muscular, the standard-bearer of Bakonjo-Baamba nationalism, committed to ridding the people of Batoro domination. In its early days of the mid 1950s, Bazarrabusa himself had been the chairman of the

Society; he had known of my role in its initiation. Even then Isaya, the prime mover, was giving the Society a political and defiant slant. Bazarrabusa continued to lend his patronage to the BLHRS right up to the walk-out from Toro's parliament, the Rukurato, of the seventeen Bakonzo and Baamba members, that March. He could not but acknowledge their grievance. In his very own field, education, he had seen the country go headlong into independence with fourteen students from Toro at East African universities of whom but one was a Mukonzo (Justus Nzenze Bwambale), and none a Mwamba. Of the 115 Higher School certificate bursaries awarded that year in Toro, a mere 19 were from those minority tribes which constituted over a third of the Kingdom's population.

In just such a cause the old Society had thrown aside its bark cloth cloak and put on the paint of war. It was of course the doing of Isaya, his own protégé: Isaya had never been predictable, from the very start, and never containable after our journey together. What had he, Timothy Bazarrabusa, helped to sire? I saw them somewhat like the Elector of Saxony, securing academic preferment for a restive monk, only to find Dr Martin Luther challenging the integrity of the entire Holy Empire. Meanwhile Bazarrabusa had been making a name for himself in the federal capital, Kampala, for competence and balance and grace. When the moment arose for the selection of a figure at ease in a white world who was neither Ganda (as was Uganda's titular President, King Freddie), nor a northern Nilotic (as was the Prime Minister, Milton Obote), Bazarrabusa's name came up for the new State's first plenipotentiary to the Court of St James, the old imperial fountainhead. It was an extraordinary translation.

Way back in time, in the ancestral mountains, a primal responsibility lurked and irked. We who surely shared such responsibility, Bazarrabusa and Musabuli, were lunching in the Haymarket, SW1, ruminatively. He brought me up to the present moment, as best as anybody knew – for it was already months since anyone in charge in Fort Portal or Kampala had had any interchange with Isaya. The mountain tribesmen had formed themselves into cadres of spearmen, manifestly all loyal to their leader, Isaya having formally declared – by proclamation that August 15, 1962, and by his grand, typewritten public missives directed to Obote and everyone he could thing of – the 'secession' of 'Rwenzururu' as a *fait accompli*. Meanwhile his spear-carrying askaris were striking terror into the Batoro and the police, and burning Batoro settlements that had come to encroach on traditionally Bakonzo territory, which is to say, wherever the rumpled land and mountains began to leave the plain.

When in November 1962 the Court appeal against the three ringleaders' conviction was heard in Kampala and dismissed, Isaya stayed doggo and defiant where he was. Kawamara and Mupalya had gone back to prison to serve their second four months. A cordon of depopulated territory now ringed the mountains. The Commission of Enquiry had duly reported: there were justifiable grievances, yes, and misbehaviour on both sides, and no doubt solutions – albeit nothing that would upset the thoroughly 'checked and balanced' constitution of newly independent Uganda with its five Bantu kingdoms and Nilotic north, and nothing to re-arouse the suspicion that Obote's UPC government was at heart 'anti-Kingdom'. The problem of the mountains was: how could the Government go forward from here? There was no one even so much as to carry a note.

No one, that is – my host pressed, as we started on the fruit salad – besides myself. I knew Isaya, he insisted, better than any other outsider. I was in on it from the start ... those first delvings into what it was to be *Konzo*, all through the foothill spurs; I was known and seen to be working with and through Isaya. And lastly, I was unattached to government, a free arbiter. Might he not put the proposal to Milton Obote when the Prime Minister visited London the following week?

Such a proposal was out of the question. In the three weeks immediately ahead, my role on the *Sunday Times* was taking me to the Middle East and Russia: the commitments were not revocable. Thereafter, an assignment in the Far East was assuming urgency. My paper looked to me to cover the major international events. Moreover, it had recently become the first of Britain's national newspapers to launch a colour magazine: if they had a writer with any kind of a following they sought his by-line in the magazine... I had other duties: family; political – I was nursing a Parliamentary seat. My little world was full of this and that. To walk off the map into the heart of Africa for several weeks would be what right-minded people call impossible.

I am seldom good at saying No, a Faustian flaw which would have made me a liability in Eden. I waited in vain to hear myself saying No. I returned to my office and to whatever needed to be written for next Sunday's paper with the expectation that Obote, on his coming visit to London, would scotch his High Commissioner's whimsical idea; and aware of a current of an old dream flowing under the sea.

I was already abroad – in Israel – when Obote arrived in London, and he was gone by my return to my desk. Lying there was a letter bearing a coat of arms of crossed spears, an impala rampant and crested heron bespeaking Uganda. This letter contained a solemn invitation to take up the role of mediator in the Ruwenzori mountains with the least delay. Things were deteriorating: if I was to accept, I must leave within two weeks at the outside. The better part of one week was already gone.

I took the letter along the passage to the editor.

That was a Tuesday – February 5th, 1963. On the Friday I flew to Moscow, and on Saturday I spent two and a quarter hours with Nikita Khrushchev in the Kremlin, in an interview, conducted on behalf of my proprietor Roy Thompson who sat beside me. I was home by midnight on the Monday, with my despatch published the previous day, and the rest of the world's press following it up that day. On the Tuesday night I was addressing the Cambridge Union in defence of President de Gaulle and his cast for our continent as a *Europe des Patries*. (We Gaullists prevailed – as, in the end, tribalists will.) On the Wednesday I was with my wife and three daughters at home in Sussex. On the Thursday my attendance was required at a Governors' meeting of Christopher Wren School, in my prospective constituency. On the Friday I was on a plane bound for Entebbe, on the north shore of Victoria Nyanza, carrying the double-headed ceremonial Konzo spear I had been presented with in 1954, and in my bag the black-and-white colobus-skin, already a little tatty, which I had habitually worn among the Bakonzo. I had secured from my editor six weeks' leave of absence to do whatever was to be done. The current of a prior reality flowing from beneath my sea was flooding me.

xvii

I am Re-admitted

What *was* to be done? After the sortie, I wrote a short, brisk book –
Summons to Ruwenzori in which I summarized the purpose of the
mission as 'threefold – first to find poor Isaya, second to secure a
state of peace, third to obtain a settlement worthy of the lasting
approval of the Bakonjo.' I wonder at myself across this span of
years, hot with my certainties in shouldering my bit of the white
man's post-colonial burden. I was hot enough, to be fair, to pull off
the first two objectives with alacrity. How much did I grasp of the
third?

I had draped a patronal arm around 'poor Isaya'. It was not apt.
A deeper history was unfolding – and still unfolds as I write this
passage thirty-seven years on. It was no longer *my* show, the
Bakonzo's tribal *raison d'être* – if it ever was. The young colonial
Prospero was not returning to the same mountain island of his own
presumption that he had left eight and a quarter years before. Isaya
was no disaffected ex-school master kicking against the ignominies
and petty grievances of quasi-vassaldom to tribal neighbours in
the haughty plains. He was forging a nation in the God-made
mountains of his forefathers which straddled the frontiers of the
phoney constructs of a colonial episode. Four months after the end
of my attempted intervention he would be elevated beyond mere
'presiding' to be crowned King of the entire mountain territory,
Rwenzururu, by representatives of its constituent peoples. Isaya's
had become a reality of quite another order than that of 'Uganda'
or 'Congo'. It was a reality of palpable allegiance, virtually total, by
men and women and children occupying vividly definable
territory, sealed within themselves linguistically and culturally by
common ancestry and common destiny, and with recourse to
common Olympian protection.

What did I suppose when I touched down at Entebbe airport at
noontide on that mid-February Saturday, in 1963? Why, that I had
it in my reach to put it all to rights, a nice little settlement, the
misunderstandings dissolved, legitimate grievances dutifully met

by a chastened Kampala and a curtailed Toro, and an Isaya mollified by some sort of recognition of his authority among the good people to whom he had spontaneously emerged as champion. Urgency spurred me. A formal 'State of Emergency' had been declared *the day before* by the Uganda Government throughout the Ruwenzori area, and that which Bazarrabusa and I most feared had instantly ensued: the whole operational force of the Ugandan army had been sent into action to bring under control all the southern half of the mountains, Busongora. I was sharply aware that by the day, if not the hour, conditions would be deteriorating under which anyone could hope to reach the rebel leadership and enter the process of mediation.

The army's dramatic assignment had been forced on Obote by a sequence of outrages of which the latest, that very week, had been the kidnapping and calculated brutality meted out to the member of Parliament for the region, Ezironi Bwambale. This Ezironi (a Lukonzo corruption of Harrison) was one of that tiny Bakonzo élite, like Isaya himself, to receive education at secondary level under the scheme fostered by the colonial authorities in Toro. He had gone on to study theology at Bishop Tucker College in Mukono. Only weeks previously had he quit the Democratic Party opposition to join the Government (Uganda People's Congress) party. He had dared to speak out publicly against the secession of Rwenzururu at the village of Kinyamaseke in his own constituency. It was a courageous act – not to say foolhardy. I knew the place: the southern heartland's cotton depot on the road to the Congo border. Ezironi was dragged off his platform and bodily borne away by Rwenzururu die-hards. In wild country above a steep ravine, at a place called Kahanga, they speared him in the chest, slashed his right ankle with a panga, speared him behind the joint of his right knee, and again in his upper thigh, all with wicked deliberation. A careless spear-thrust clipped his right eye. Thus mauled and mutilated, he had been flung into the ravine and left to die. He did not die, but crawled away through the undergrowth and reached his own home village of Kasesa, four spurs distant. Even then he was six miles from the nearest road and from any vehicle for the 50-minute drive to the copper mine's hospital at Kilembe, where he would recover, maimed.

Later Ezironi would become Deputy Minister for Culture and Community Development in Obote's first government. He had a prison built in Kasese, the main Konzo town – near to Kilembe –

which was never under Rwenzururu control. The prison took in captured Rwenzururu askaris. I mocked him a little in *Summons to Ruwenzori*. That was unjust. Ezironi was on the other side to my lot, but he was a good man doing for his people what seemed to him wisest. In the ledger of human suffering since those days, who can read  the tally? One day in Kampala, in the year 2000, hearing I was in town, Ezironi came to find me, a man of my own age. I had never met him before. He showed me the scars that bad day left him with, in February 1963 – the spear-thrusts to his chest. My pictures show him now, and then in hospital. After Idi Amin toppled Obote, he was on the run: in escaping the tyrant's executioners he lost an eye. It has not been an easy life. His comment to me was, 'In Africa, for an ex-politican, you expect – ' counting off the expectations on his fingers – 'a bullet, poverty, or life imprisonment.' Something prompted me to offer to pay his taxi home – all of £3. He accepted with undisguised relief.

The day of my arrival in 1963, the Kampala newspapers were leading with dramatic accounts of the opening of the Ruwenzori campaign of which the assault on Ezironi had been the trigger. I read them gloomily in the lounge of the Grand Imperial Hotel to which I had been assigned by a young trainee in the protocol department while awaiting my briefing from Obote. A reporter from the *Uganda Nation* had filed the day before from Fort Portal, a dispatch thick with adjectives.

'The self-styled "King" of the fanatic Bakonjo and Bamba secessionists, Isaya Mukirane, has been declared the main target of the Uganda Rifles, whose troops arrived here tonight. This Dedan Kimathi-like leader of the seccessionists is reported to have retreated high into the green impassable mountains of the Bwera area.'

Dedan Kimathi had been the most notorious of the Mau Mau killers in neighbouring Kenya.

'This afternoon from Government sources in Fort Portal I learned that early tomorrow morning a "very cunning" action by the army is to take place. Uganda's army, led by shrewd Col. W.W. Cheyne, has already closed the area to all strangers. Tonight, with more troops due from Jinja, the whole Alp-like area will be cordoned off. Mukirane is expected to be cornered in the sweep.

'Early tomorrow will be D-day for "Operation Mukirane", and the tough soldiers of the Uganda Rifles will start climbing the mountains. However, some unconfirmed reports reaching Fort Portal suggest that "King" Mukirane might have crossed the border into the troubled Congo.'

I was aware of it being already 'D-day' and I was 280 miles away in Kampala with a young smoothie from Protocol presenting me with a leisurely 'Programme of Engagements' which scheduled my departure for Fort Portal on *Wednesday* – four days ahead. My meeting with Obote was to take place that next morning, the Sunday, at State House, Nakasero.

Obote and I talked for an hour. As so often with those accustomed to high authority, there was no telling where the heart lay. Yet I noted his apparent readiness to settle, rather than hammer Isaya and the Bakonzo into the ground – if I could but establish what Isaya would settle for.

My Prime Ministerial appointment ended at 1 p.m. By 1.30 I had collected my things from the Imperial and told my driver, a Somali, to head for Fort Portal. It was a murram road. We were there by 6.15, about half an hour from nightfall. I told him to drive straight to Bundibugyo – the twisting, bucking road I had last travelled in the King of Toro's Land Rover. We were in the village by eight o'clock or so. A little group of men were standing in the darkness outside an Indian bar: tall ones, northerner 'Nubians', in the Ugandan argot – evidently traders. Then one short fellow, young, detached himself and said he was a Mukonzo.

'What is your name?' I asked.

'Seylversta Mukirane.'

The appellation 'Mukirane' is given to any child born after the death of a sibling.

'Do you remember me?'

'I cannot see you, sir,'

'Come and talk to me.' I opened the car door for the light to come on. He regarded me silently. Then he smiled diffidently.

'You are Musabuli, sir.'

I stepped out and we shook hands. He was fourteen when I was last here – now he was 23, a half-trained church teacher. But the rebellion had shut churches and schools alike. He had a job as nightwatchman at the coffee-drying plant immediately behind us. He said,

'We thought you would never come, sir.'

'Am I too late, Seylversta?'

'I cannot tell, sir.'

'I am looking for Ibrahimu Ndyanabaïsi.'

A few paces ahead we entered the earth-walled dispensary. A single oil lantern illuminated four filthy beds. Lying unattended on one of them, moaning, was the wife of George Kahigwa, Ibrahimu's senior brother and sibling of Isaya Mukirane's wife Christine. I had known her as a girl in 1954. Her womb was 'poisoned', they said, which is to say she was afflicted with puerperal fever. The rebellion had scared away the dispensary's only qualified employee, a Mutoro dresser. We found George himself sitting disconsolately in the darkness of a friend's bare house along the road. We greeted. I at once urged him to get his wife to hospital in Fort Portal. He replied that he could not entrust her to the nurses there: they were all Batoro. Meanwhile, his half-brother Ibrahimu – he said – had been transferred to a clerkship of a *gombolola* some twenty miles away, and several hours from the road. There was a chance that he was visiting the old house of their father at Bukangama. We could reach there in half an hour, once dawn had broken.

I slept that night under the stars in the grasses beside the stockaded county lock-up there at Bundibugyo, knowing that I was in the presence of the mountains which lay back, another world, not visible, yet ruling us in everything we did or did not do, the *mastering* presence. We were hunched against them, in our grasses, our polyp villages, wattle and mud and thatch, our pathetic nests. There was a little thunder, south east; the high places. I did not suppose it would rain that night. It was better to be in the open, better for complicity, for the placing of trust. If the dresser was fled from the dispensary, let George Kahigwa carry his sick wife out of that fetid place back to the cleanliness of his own compound, *up*; lay her before the mountain's Nyabibuya and, indeed, put aside thought of hospital in the capital of the enemy. In the highlands south of us Isaya and his patriots were at work in their own montane complicity, working their *embitha*, self-entrusted to their inner mountains, choosing freedom by means of service, as the Book of Common Prayer enjoins. Isaya would surely not be 'cornered' in any 'sweep' however cunningly devised by shrewd Colonel W. W. Cheyne. Yet would *I* find him? Soon after midnight I was awoken by a lorry-load of drunken police demanding the gaoler to open the lock-up. They had with them, bound by the wrists and ankles, the latest intake of Bakonzo prisoners, arrested for supporting Rwenzururu by their carrying, or hiding, sharpened spears or because their names appeared on captured cadre lists. Soon they would be scattered among other prisons throughout Uganda with the several hundred other Bakonzo already taken in since the previous August.

Seylversta woke me again at dawn in the wet grass. There was the great bulk of the massif leaning over us, clamped in cloud, an implicit darkness, blocking the sunrise; and, below, the forest of Ituri, without visible limit. George Kahigwa joined us. His father Samwiri – Samwiri Mulwahali ('he who comes from afar'), the first of my Ruwenzori hosts – had died, he said. I enquired of what, and good George (a strong one he, whom I know to this day) gave an answer that suggested the slings and arrows of life. So it had been: born to an elderly, superannuated hero of a father whom the rebel-martyr Nyamutswa had made appear a Toro collaborator, and then himself inheriting (from Batoro hands) the *gombolola* chieftainship only to have it snatched away by Toro's *mukama* King. His son-in-law Isaya, comparably humiliated, sucked on Samwiri's gall. George was heir to what remained of the chieftainship.

He and I rose by the old path I had upped and downed before ever I got to meet Isaya all those years earlier. Now as then the heavy cellular plantain leaves of the groves bumped each other in however slight a motion of air, and the sun risen enough to X-ray the live ribbing. As before, the children, warned of our approach, moved ever so slightly off the pathway – part shadow and light, part movement, barely children; and beneath these layers of translucence and insubstantiality, the chequered surfaces and under-surfaces of earth. The reel had run back eight and a bit years. Two highland Konzo women ahead of us, beyond the last grove, in goatskins, great calabash pitchers on their heads, scuttled into the grasses, jogging momentarily awake the babies on their backs.

Ibrahimu stepped out on to the edge of the little bluff and cried out in astonishment. We clasped hands, he shaking his head and clicking his tongue to shake and click away his disbelief. He was married now, and had his *gombolola* clerkship, but the rebellion had put paid to the norms of government.

I gave him no choice: 'We must leave at once for Busongora, and find Isaya. You and I. Every minute counts.'

After eight years, every minute was counting.

'Seylversta will come with us,' I told him. 'Shall we not also take Kigoma?'

'Kigoma? He is dead.'

'Why did he die?' Kigoma was the last sort to go and die.

'He got sick. Then he died.'

I could see Ibrahimu's wife peeling yams and preparing a pot. I said, 'We have no time for a meal. I am sorry.'

He was ready in fifteen minutes. It took me a further hour to secure for him and Seylversta a temporary release from their jobs. To persuade the acting *Saza* (county) chief – a Mutoro, whom I met on the road, with his bodyguards – it was necesary to produce the letter I carried in a lordly type and signed by the P.M.

Within two and a half hours of daybreak my little expeditionary team was mustered and free to leave.

By 3.20 that afternoon the three of us – with my driver at the wheel – entered Bwera village, on the edge of the southern foothills. From here the military campaign was being launched. Our prospects seemed thin. Army operations were already well into their second day. Suspicion could not but attach to me, tramping up in the wake of the military.

The scene confronting us at Bwera's *gombolola* headquarters was thus. Thwacked about the head and shoulders by Uganda Rifle askaris with frayed-ended sticks like switches, some forty Bakonzo prisoners scurried to and fro with armfuls of grass. Another thirty were lying flat on their faces, a black sergeant twice their size standing guard. Across the compound, a young British officer was clearing up a trestle table at which the sad assembly of Bakonzo had just been handed out their six-month prison sentences for spear-carrying and curfew-breaking.

No one was being much hurt. It is the profession of soldiers to strike terror. Yet the sight, and the *noise* of the blows, dried my throat... Ibrahimu and Syelversta sat motionless in the car, watching through narrowed eyes out of faces in which grey had entered the black. The young British officer led me up through the dispensary wards to the commandeered house of the dispenser, another absent Mutoro.

Colonel Bill Cheyne, independent Uganda's first army commander, was a brisk and compact figure who radiated vigour and good humour. 'Ah,' he said, 'you're the man from the *Observer*. You probably think it very narrow-minded of me, but I gave up reading the *Observer* at Suez.'

I said I thought it probably was narrow-minded, but that my employment by the press – currently suspended – was with the *Sunday Times*.

Bessie Braddock, he said, would be disappointed if she came here searching for outrageous things done by the wild and licentious soldiery against the defenceless natives. 'My askaris are the gentlest people in the world.'

By 'Bessie Braddock' he meant to refer to another prominent virago of the current Parliamentary Opposition, one with a more evident avidity for the end of empire – Edith Summerskill. As to his askaris' gentleness, it had been tested right then by one of their number having been killed by Bakonzo spearmen the day before. The man happened to have been the only Mutoro in the entire operational force, which no Mukonzo could have known. A fanciful mind would detect the arm of Kitasamba behind that fatal spear.

Cheyne and I walked over to the Ops Room. I did not look my part, except for the Commando boots which I had hurriedly picked up from an Army surplus store in Oxford Street. My fawn trousers were for a garden party, my shirt for a boardroom. The Colonel gave me a full briefing on the current sorties and intentions of his soldiery, with the object of my steering clear of them. There was an obvious danger of the three of us being shot by the military as we ascended. I was provided with a code name, Grey Plover.

When I returned to my car to tell my companions to get ready to leave, they were still sitting bolt upright staring emptily ahead on a line of vision which avoided sight of a newly arrived group of Konzo prisoners who were sitting on the compound's earth in a doom-laden circle as if awaiting execution. The urge to walk over to the prisoners and say something reassuring was not resistible. It would be tactless to fraternize, in the presence of the army. Yet I knew that none of Cheyne's men would have any Lukonzo. I fumbled in the memory for the Konzo vernacular for Good Luck. It was not to be retrieved. How about a simple greeting – 'Good afternoon' – in their own tongue, to provide that drop of solace that someone, some independent *mzungu* in fawn pants of possible influence, had knowledge of them enough to care? I walked across. My throat was dry again.

'*Bukyaghe*,' I said.

There was no response – unless, perhaps, a fractional intensification of despair?

'*Bukyaghe*,' again.

Nothing. I had to go.

I had no sooner turned my back than I realized I had pulled a quite inappropriate word from my meagre vocabulary, and given them no greeting but a *vale*, a lapidary *Goodbye* – *adieu*, – a confirmation of severance and doom. They were off in the trucks that very night, as they knew, to distant prisons in an alien world of infinite hostility ... and here was this voice, out of the mouth of a long white, confirming with slimy intimacy their expulsion from their Eden. This carelessness clouded my departure: I smart as I tell it now. As Colonel Cheyne drove me out of Bwera camp, two United Nations vehicles from the Malayan detachment across in Congo entered it. Malaya – independent from Britain in 1957, and yet to form the broader, uneasy federation of Malaysia – was among the several nations providing contingents for the (hopeless) UN endeavour to shore up the Congo republic. Much as in Uganda, British officers continued to serve with them. We paused for a brief exchange. Here was a Welsh Commanding Officer, evidently willing to co-ordinate his own troop movements to frustrate Isaya's rebels from establishing Congo-side bases. Yours is wishful thinking, thought I. You can lose an army up there quicker than you can pin a Konzo cadre. You will learn so soon enough. But I kept my counsel.

The vehicle track into the foothills got us half a dozen miles north of Bwera to the footbridge across the Nyamurusega stream, flowing westwards into the Tako, the border river. Just across was Isango – half a dozen tin roofs and a shop. We were less than a mile from the Congo border, here.

I slung my rucksack, still with its BOAC bagage label. Ibrahimu and Seylversta each had their blanket rolls. Ibrahimu wore my colobus skin, I my Bakonzo knife in its engraved scabbard, *olhwuba*, at my belt, and on my wrist the two brass beads, *esyomberi*, forged by ancient Konzo smithies, given me at Kitolu in 1954. My artifacts were talismans, bespeaking old acquaintance. I left the double-headed spear in my car, to obviate any misreading of my non-combatant role.

I said nothing about the direction I would take.

'All right, Grey Plover,' Cheyne said, wry and English. 'This is where we part. Don't get lost.'

He and I had entered on a friendship which lasted all his remaining life. In fealty to the Queen of a dying empire, Cheyne was assigned by his calling to kill or capture the man with whom I, in honour of a prior friendship and a prior cause, had come to treat. He would not have been blind to Isaya's obsessive vision of exclusive group-destiny, for he told me later that he was brought up by parents who were both actively committed British Israelites. Anyway, a year later he would be promoted Brigadier, to command Britain's forces in Borneo protecting Brunei, Sabah and Sarawak from the *konfrontasi* brought about by the ambitious Sukarno of Indonesia. That battle won, and Cheyne designated for further promotion, in 1967 motor neurone disease began to lock him in; and month by month, until death spared him, my little role in London was to bring to Bill Cheyne, speechless and immobile, soliloquies of this and that and a comradeship speaking silently for itself. He was uncommunicant except for the humour responding in his eye. Humour was courage, and courage hope. But it was as if he was entombed alive in clear glass. Writing this brief memorial now, it occurs to me that his quarry of those days, Isaya Mukirane, familiar with scripture, would know of risen Jesus how he entered the inner room by locked doors... Rest his soul. *Kayingo atsunge.*

As Ibrahimu, Seylversta and I began our climb, it was a quarter to four. I knew where I was heading.

So, also, I suspect, does my patient reader. But this world of Ruwenzori's southern foothills had critically altered since 1954: there were no people – or almost none. Isango itself proved to be entirely deserted. On the track ascending northwards from the abandoned village we encountered but a single man: a Mukonzo, fearful and suspicious. He declined to lead us on even as far as Kitolu, we being doubtful of the route, since Ibrahimu and I (with, of course, Isaya) had approached previously from spurs and valleys further east. I guessed the fellow we met was Isango's shopkeeper. The shop itself had been shuttered up against the coming of soldiers and their Batoro porters. Thereafter on the foot trail we came across the occasional dotard, too far gone in mind or body to have run for highland safety when the news broke of the army's coming in.

As to the army, the bulk of the Riflemen were sweeping the eastern ranges of Busongora, to drive any rebel hard core there – like grouse – westwards. By the following day, Cheyne had told me, he would expect them to reach Kitolu. Yet it was dense and difficult country, eastwards, tens or scores of miles of it, spur and gully and forest tongue, and I guessed that whatever span of time had been calculated for it this 'drive' would take longer. Meanwhile, Cheyne had sent five picked men, under a resourceful officer named Keefe, up through the forest northwards along the eastern flank of the Tako valley, the international frontier. The purpose here was, by moving undetected, to cut off Isaya's exit from Uganda at the Tako's valley head where the young river plunges out of precipitous forest from a ravine running, not north-south, like all its lower course, but east-west. This high corner was, Cheyne judged, the natural escape route into Congo by retreating rebels. The maps on pages 39 and 115 may help the reader.

Now, the region he had spoken of was known to me as Kyatenga and upper Buswagha; and precisely such was *my* destination. I felt pretty sure that up to now either it was a still occupied heartland linked to wherever Isaya was headquartered, or at the very least it would be well patrolled by Rwenzururians reporting to Isaya. It seemed imperative that I made it to there before Keefe's commando. If Keefe stuck to the forested ravine, to escape detection, his going would be slow.

From the heights up-Tako, how sweet and mazy a landscape it is, and wondrous the beauty of the place. How it came flowing back to me; and how grievous the exodus of men, women, children, goats and hens, fled from this upland paradise. In all this glory of the natural order, touched up by man, gravity played its part, and the dumb weight of my rucksack grew no lighter with the spreading of the panorama. My companions had their bundles, which were looking to me a lot easier than they deserved. Ibrahimu and I were none too fit, and the sun was on us for three hours. We were carrying almost no rations, expecting to feed – as was my custom – off the locals. But of locals there being virtually none, all we had prospect of was a tin of fruit salad and half a packet of biscuits bought that morning at Bundibugyo.

After an hour of steepish ascents, I exchanged burdens with Seylversta in his proud Christian boots. He carried my heavy rucksack with that diffident geniality that was (and is to this day) the mark of the man. Ibrahimu had begun to plead that we should rest as soon as we reached Kitolu. I ribbed him as a soft plain-lubber of a Mutoro, which set Seylversta cackling. We made it to Kitolu by 6.30.

What had I hoped for here? Isaleri with a Testament, and a chicken stew and obundu? The place and its surrounds were deserted except for two crones and a young man mildly deranged who slurred his speech so that we could make nothing of the torment that gripped him. It was opaque fear, inventing its own precisions, as such fear does. Yet we had spotted other figures ducking out into the grasses. Therefore I called out – Ibrahimu translating – warning hidden ears that all weapons should be concealed where no scouring would find them, and that the approaching military should not be provoked by attack. I guessed that Isaleri, my newly-Christian host of eight years previously and the leader of the community, had already withdrawn northwards and up, taking Jesus with him, or was accompanying Isaya's rebel command group. Both were to prove correct; but he had indeed posted scouts here... The idiot clung to us. We seemed to have got across to him our wish to stay on the path up to Kituti. He went on up, ahead. In normal times this highland heartland was thickly populated: paths, none wider than a pair of walking feet, webbed out into numberless enticements. In holding to a main path it is best not to over-calculate: let instinct run ahead and the feet decide at each questionable fork. Every now and then a memory was stirred by a twist in the track, a tree bridge, or a bald rock at a stream crossing, and I knew I had trodden this way before. There was no telling here which side 'held' the territory we were in: for all I knew, Keefe's men could have already been through or skirted it; they could be camped nearby for the night, or were lying up in ambush. At each cluster of huts atop spurs or hillocks I called out the military password 'Fort Portal'.

And then, in rapidly assembling dusk, just as I noticed the deranged young man was no longer with us, we spotted two figures watching from across a gully, 200 yards ahead on our own path. We stopped. We called. They did not move, or reply. We advanced. We descended to the water, then up towards where they were.

I recognised one of them at once; and he me – with an absence of surprise that told of fate's authority and the enduringness of trust (as Seylversta had exclaimed the previous night: *We thought you would never come, sir.*) He was a wide-shouldered, high-browed Mukonzo whose quiet confidence contrasted with the wild fearfulness of his tattered companion. Soon afterwards I took a picture of him in his same pale blue pullover: Daneeri, Daniel – that same Prophet who told Belshazzar the awful truth of the encrypted *Mene mene tekel upharsin* quoted by Isaya to put the wind up King George. These two were unarmed, save for iron-pointed walking staves. They led us on for two hours into the dark until I was tottering like a losing heavyweight. There on a bone-shaped spur, we turned towards three huts, pale in the moon like the underbellies of three furred creatures. My written record preserves that night:

'We are still several hours from Kituti; but I tacitly capitulate for today. The huts are deserted, and we have no light. But my new companions find with their noses some banana beer in a calabash, and swallowing it too fast after violent exercise I am almost nauseated. After several minutes they return with an ember found in another hut and after we have made a small fire we can see about us. The ember means that the inhabitants have not been gone long – not more than thirty-six hours. But at once our two guides have disappeared. All I want is to sleep, to enter oblivion – I am ferociously exhausted; but Ibrahimu says I must wait: the guides have gone to bring me something. It is cold. I am wet through with sweat, and search for my woollen sweater.

'Seylversta with his favourite-pupil eagerness, says, "This is a second England, sir, because we are cold."

'We are sitting on home-made chairs beside a little table. The hut has evidently been used by Isaya's Rwenzururians as a tiny school – perhaps by Isaya himself. (Keefe, I reflect, may already have got him: it is conceivable. They may be coming back now, towards this same high bluff.) There is a piece of board stuck up on the earth wall with chalk writing on it - UHURU RWENZURURU IPANDISI MUBAKONJO NABAAMBA D.S.R – meaning "Freedom for an independent Rwenzururu for the Bakonzo and the Bamba. Separate District Status." And on the table is an exercise book in which someone has been writing out sentences for translation between English and Lukonzo: "The wart-hog has eight children." "They walk quietly and quietly in the forest because they are afraid of the lions."

'They have found in my pack my old Bakonzo warhorn, made of ivory stained a deep, shining brown by generations of smoke in hut roofs. Seylversta tries to sound it and fails. Ibrahimu chaffs him: "You cannot do it: you have not fought yet." Ibrahimu can sound it, I remember (though he too has not fought) – but I dissuade him: I am in no mood for battle, only sleep. I lean back on the earth wall in my sodden Jermyn Street shirt and Fifth Avenue trousers, anxious about the wart-hog. The others are finishing the biscuits, and they eat half the tin of fruit. Why is there a lion in the forest? It is rare. The wall crumbles against my back and the draughts flow through and knuckle my back. There is a picture stuck on the wall beside me of a "Chief Minister B. Kiwanuka" torn from a Lunyoro newspaper two years old. There is politics here, even if the year before last's. "Rwenzururu ipandisi!" – and watch the lion doesn't get the wart-hog! Put a picture of a defeated Chief Minister on the mud wall – already a half-forgotten man in the rest of Uganda, who is no longer even leader of the Opposition – sharpen your spear, drive it into the heart of a Uganda Rifleman, and his companion will machine-gun you to death and four innocents besides, scuttling out of the compound. That is what happened yesterday, and these Bakonzo companions of mine are calling it a victory for Rwenzururu. Two more Bakonzo actually did meet lions, fleeing through the lowland grasses to the Congo yesterday, and they were eaten too. That was a Bakonzo defeat, my companions say.

'Better put up King George VI's (of Britain) picture on the wall, I suggest, such as they have at the Bundibugyo saza headquarters: he is a stronger spirit than this "B. Kiwanuka". After all, the King is dead and carries a lot of ancestral weight.

'Then we hear a clattering and grunting outside in the darkness. Then talking. Daneeri, in his pale blue pullover, pushes open the door barrier and starts pulling some monstrous thing after him. It is a large home-made bed-frame, with string across it. They have spent an hour and a half fetching it for me from another ridge – down and up a few hundred feet in the pitch darkness.'

As I dozed off, the weak and trailing voices seemed to point up the absence of others, particularly women and animals. There was no cock to crow us awake: the cocks and their dames have been called to war in the guerilla heights. Seylversta the nightwatchman woke me in the last of the darkness, and the night sounds of the stream's gurgle and the tap-tapping of the plantain fronds. I could eat now: a couple of handy bananas. I rubbed out the chalk words to deprive the troops of an excuse for burning this hut.

It was deep darkness still when we set off again. I put on the colobus pelt by which I was known (as Kambalangeya) when last in these places. We were all a little tense, conscious of the rigorous Keefe somewhere west of us, a thousand or two yards towards the Tako or already ahead, preparing his own trap for our quarry on the flanks of the castellated ridge I remembered well, that seals off the valleyhead. We three had sticks now, and Daneeri and his mate as guides. A third additional figure joined us at first light, silently, without comment or introduction. I was soon sweating heavily, and required to drink repeatedly. I began early (and secretly) to weaken. We were overtaken by a squat fellow in rags and a monkey-bag, and welling with delight at the Rwenzururu foray he had participated in below. He pricked his finger with his lance-point, to boast its lethalness. He kept with us for a spur or two, then released himself from our dragging pace.

My boots were my asset on this gargantuan switchback. Sometimes I was pulling myself up with my hands, with my ankles and feet grown numb to the chafing – but the feet never slithered. The path was closing in on the Tako ravine. I was recalling my last ascent this way, following the bridal party of Khyawatawali and being lured by the rippling *endara* in the last ascent. But I had soon lost reckoning of what further distance there was to cover. We rested at a stream, in shade. As we set off again – I in the middle of our little column – I found myself requiring momentarily to pause every five or ten paces. As on a twist the path emerged from a tongue of forest, I saw the reception committee on the rim of the ridge a hundred feet above me, motionless against the skyline: thirty spearmen and

bowmen. Cypresses flanked them. I was too spent to be alarmed. They did not have their weapons raised. They were silent.

And there in the middle of them was a face instantly recognisable.

'Wabukire, Kule!' I called up to him.

'Musabuli!' It was Kule, Khavaïru's smithy son.

At this exchange, all present on that remote hillside were caught up and reconciled by a burst of memory. At that moment I knew that I had been arrow-accurate in my choice of ascent into these mountains.

I struggled to the top, panting and sweaty, in corporeal ignominy. There immediately ahead was Kituti. A large rectangular mud construction had been added: a church, as it proved to be, as yet unconsecrated, built at Isaleri's behest.

Spearmen clustered round. Prolonged exchange of greetings established that Khavaïru was alive and well and in the company of Isaya, their 'king', who was evidently not at hand. The clownishness of his face seemed even more marked: it drew nothing from his father's imperiousness. 'We would have killed you,' he said delightedly, 'if you had come by night.' The snub nose yanked at his upper lip.

'That is what I would have done,' I answered, 'if the spirits hadn't intervened to make us tired and late.'

'God works in a mysterious way,' Seylversta said in William Cowper English, adding his girlish laugh.

I was recognising several of the Rwenzururu askaris. They were drawn from the spurs to the south and east of us. Various wore monkey-bags – one, in an overcoat, had a transistor raided from a Batoro hut below, at this moment relaying a Test Match commentary from Australia. This band of men, it grew evident, were the Praetorian Guard, and between them they had taken part in many of the recent forays into the plainlands – burning, beating, sometimes killing. It seemed that all they wanted just now was to lead me on in triumph to Isaya, their king – *omusangania*, they spoke of, 'disposer and reconciler'. I gathered he was across the valley, which would have put him on Congo-side Rwenzururu, together with more askaris and the rebellion's elders including Isaleri and Khavaïru. Now it was I who opted for a little caution. This was assuredly another state of affairs from that of 1954. In my own eyes at 33 I was a plausible evolution of the self of 24. Isaya had however entered another mode of being; President or King, or 'Dedan Kimathi-like secessionist', he had acquired the attitudes of majesty, a power of life and death, the right to spare or execute.

This was something other than my 'Kigoma' of *The Brothers M*, dogged aide and delver of tribal roots, touchingly grateful for the Mzungu's enthusiasm. There was to be no picking up where we left off at the bus terminal in Fort Portal.

I sat there on my cap-inverted mushroom stool, leafing through my own big notebook of the former era, looking up the names of other inhabitants of Kituti. I came across the note left for me at Ibanda on my descent from the heights. *Well come Mr Musabule. I am at omutaka Bwambale's house. Please turn 50 yards to-right. I am waiting you with pleasure.* Within an hour or so of receiving that note, I had been delirious with malaria. Let me not presume; let me not seem to presume. On the back of that very scrap of paper I now wrote out a petition of humble access.

My dear Isaya,
    I have come back. I have come back to try to help you and your Bakonjo [sic] in their time of trouble. I heard in England of the great things you have struggled to achieve for the beloved Bakonjo, and of the suffering of the Bakonjo people.
    I look forward to greeting my dear friend again, who taught me to love and to respect the Bakonjo people.
        Tom Stacey
        Musabuli

It was tranquil here in the full morning under the cypresses at seven thousand feet. Here in the earth of the path's edge were the same half-buried elephants' teeth, warding off Kitasamba's lighting. While I was carefully writing, several men came up and, stamping bare feet, saluted me with vigour. I returned them the most insouciant of my Brigade of Guards officerly salutes. 'Thule baghuma', I said; *we are one.* I put the message just written (with the old one *verso*) into a little leather cigar case made for two fat cheroots and given me by my wife as a twenty-second birthday present, and handed it to Kule for delivery to Isaya *omusangania* across the valley. Kule picked a sturdy young Rwenzururian who marched stiffly up and stamped his feet before me like, more or less, a guardsman. I asked him in Lukonzo for his name. He answered me in English.

'I am forest.'

This was a phrase evidently learned from Isaya himself. His name proved to be the Lukonzo word for forest – *Omusitu*. Under the adopted Kinyamusitu – 'man of the forest' – he would be spoken of in future years with awe and trembling and we should mark the name. This Kinyamusitu set off with Daneeri who, I noticed, picked up my pack to carry it across to Congo. I was not to see that cigar case again.

Kule urged me to follow behind my own note. But my instinctive preference was to give Isaya time to accustom himself to my proximity. In the present context, for me to have returned to these remote kingdoms – to have returned after seemingly having left for always – was an intrusion more disturbing and penetrative than to have arrived for the first time. In this space of gratuitous waiting I wrote up my record. My new companions regaled me with their people's exploits in various theatres of this mountain war. They told of the spearing of the Uganda Rifleman on patrol in the Nyamugasani area two days earlier. When I let on that the man they had killed was the army's only Mutoro, they clasped one another wide-eyed with astonishment and glee. Some of them flung their spears in re-enactment. I reminded them that three Bakonzo were machine-gunned to death in that incident. This sobered them not at all. Seylversta declared, 'God is our leader. He is with us in all things.'

At length I proceeded on the two or three hundred yards through the plantains to Kituti proper and Khavaïru's compound, the very site of germination of the Bakonjo Life History Research Society of which my present companion, Ibrahimu, was a witness. We entered beneath the great spreading tree, shrouding the settlement, in whose lower branches the endara keys used to be stored between the bouts of sustained performance. Now I saw lying there the same beams of half-sacred omulumongulu wood in their chromatic lengths, all higgledy-piggledy and penetrated by moss and fungal spoor, amid the rotting plantain stems that once helped to give them lease of their liquid music, symbol and paraphernalia of this furthest place of permanent habitation; now victims of our war. Would not Kitasamba, inspirer of music, avenge himself?

The huts of the compound were, for the present, not occupied. I was guessing at Isaya's tactic: to melt with his followers to the forest and the heights, into Congo and the inaccessibilities, emptying the upland villages for Uganda soldiery to burn or not to burn, and leaving an eerie void across much intricate territory which this enemy could never garrison and would always render them exposed to lethal, darting attack, even if only with spears against guns. Enough crops would escape wilful spoliation; further up and in, or across in Congo, new and hidden shambas would be cleared, dug and planted. Meanwhile, my old lodging in whose thatch the hens killed the rat was so sagged and heavy with weed and creeper that the earth was visibly reclaiming it. There were the three firestones of my old hearth: young archaeology in the dark and dank. Ahead and up, the engorwe-medicine hut had got a tin roof – protecting what? Not Khavaïru's charms and potions, surely, for they were portable and with him.

I and my companions began an unhurried descent towards the Tako valley, by that northwestward-tending path which would bring us on towards wherever Isaya had his base and held his court. I was daring to commend ourselves at having out-marched Keefe. Scouts had just joined to report the presence of his party still half a day behind us, down-valley in the forest edge. Now I saw the messenger, Kinyamusitu, forest-man, returning by the path ahead. Behind him was the pale blue of the pullover of Daneeri, still carrying my pack. They seemed to be hurrying. Kinyamusitu came up first, and stamped his feet, but gave me no salute. He produced a buff envelope. Daneeri joined him, sweating. The envelope bore a rubber stamp reading *Rwenzururu* Bakonjo-Bamba,* making an oval frame, and within the oval the word *Date*, against which was handwritten 19 Feb 1963. Inside was a small sheet of laboured ballpoint penmanship, in English, thus:

Dear Mr T. Stacey, Kiraro Rwenzururu.
Sir. We are so glad to hear that the President Rwenzururu's great friend is at home which pleases the President Isaya M. Mukiane Rwenzururu whom you are so unfortunate to see at this critical time.
The President Isaya M. Mukirane will be very glad and hopeful if you write to him and inform him all what you have come for and all that you want to advise him which may be of great value to the people of this disturbed country Rwenzururu.
(Signed) Yostasi Kule
President's Private Secretary Rwenzururu.

All my companions, new and old, had fallen mute.
I sat down on the steep bank there, beside the traverse path, to

write a prompt reply to this weird missive. It was necessary to betray no dismay to my companions, let alone alarm. Naturally they recognised a setback: Omusitu and Daneeri had set off from Kituti as heralds of a somewhat supernal reinforcement. I could hardly expect to efface the obvious fact that their king-president had reacted with a 'Not so fast!' I lightly commented to Ibrahimu, an able interpreter of purposes as well as words, that naturally Isaya had prior need to have it explained how I came to be here at this particular juncture. Ibrahimu had seen me first enter the territory of the mountains in King George's Land Rover.

I noted the edginess of the half-dozen or so Rwenzururians who had been descending with me. Now they began to drift away singly or in pairs – going on down the hill where I could not go. Meanwhile, on a fresh piece of paper, I was writing:

The Private Secretary
The President of Rwenzururu. February 19th, 1963.
Sir, I am pleased and honoured to receive your letter of today, bringing me the good wishes and welcome of President Isaya M. Mukirane, Rwenzururu. I am happy to have this opportunity of explaining more fully the reasons which have brought me back to Rwenzururu, the homeland of the Bakonjo-Bamba people, at this time of crisis and anxiety.

I have come by my own wish and my own decision. Reports have appeared in the newspapers of England that the Bakonjo-Bamba people were having to fight to preserve their rights in their own land, and to throw off the domination of Toro. During my work and journeys among the Bakonjo people eight years ago, I had been taught by the President of Rwenzururu to regard the Bakonjo as the finest people in Africa, people whose qualities were ignored by the authorities of Uganda.

Knowing that there were few – if any – others who could plead for the cause of the Bakonjo-Bamba among those who were oppressing them, and believing too that my love and concern for the Bakonjo-Bamba could be put at the service of the President of Rwenzururu, I came on an aeroplane from London, and made my way at once to Rwenzururu. I have already been able to warn many Bakonjo, as we have mounted to Kituti, of the coming of the Uganda askaris. For it is my deep wish to bring to an end the killing of loyal Rwenzururians, and to assist the President to find a way of securing the rights of the Bakonjo-Bamba in Rwenzururu by a means that will bring honour and peace to the President and his people.

I have many things to put before the President, and he must judge if any advice I may have to offer him now in these threatening times will truly be of assistance to his people.

I am, Sir,
Your Obedient Servant,
T. Stacey

Some of that would strain Isaya's modest sweep of English, let alone his Private Secretary's. Well and good, I thought. A little counter-pomp was in keeping with whatever I might have to contribute kept well up my sleeve. All I had to write on was a block of jotting-paper, and no envelopes. Isaya's letter – signed in the name of this Yostasi Kule and written in a square and primary hand peculiarly similar to Isaya's own – was on a page neatly torn from an exercise book. So there was not much disparity of materials. I improvised an envelope out of another sheet, addressed it to *The Private Secretary, The President of Rwenzururu*, and handed it to Kinyamusitu who went off with it briskly, unsmiling and unsaluting.

If one is in the role of self-appointed ruler, one cannot play it by halves. I had often thought of Napoleon – Corsican nobody to Emperor, all in eleven years. The chutzpah! Yet all the grandees of France were soon lining up for appointments and offices, and marched and fought and died, crying *mon Empereur, mon Empereur.*

There were now only three Bakonzo left – my chosen two, and Daneeri, with my pack. Seylversta was looking a little Sambo-eyed and exposed here, half way up and half way down the path to wherever. He said, 'We are now praying that God will guide the President to see Musabuli.' God usually did what Seylversta asked.

Ibrahimu gave a chortle. 'The President of Rwenzururu!' he declaimed like an official greeter. Was it less than an honour for this student-teacher Isaya Mukirane to have taken for wife his father's daughter?

We could not reasonably wait there on the track for God and his mysterious ways to resolve the impasse. A path led off northwards towards a spur where it seemed Isaya had built a camp for his askaris. We made for that. It was thatched and walled with dried plaintain leaves, and divided into two – one end sleeping quarters, with bunks for twelve, the other end a classroom for military and scholastic instruction. There was a blackboard with Isaya's writing on it; two wooden model rifles, a few bows hanging from the roof. It was similar to the camps for adolescents I had seen on my earlier journey built by Bakonzo in hidden corners of the mountains for the rites of circumcision and initiation into manhood. As we entered it seemed entirely deserted – if only very recently so. Then from a pair of kitchen huts just below there crept out furtively a boy of eight or nine. All at once he recognised Ibrahimu, scampered up and greeted him with glee. For Ibrahimu was none other than his uncle, and this was Isaya's eldest boy, Kisembo – Charles Wesley Mumbere – whom I had last seen in Kasulenge in Bwamba as an infant of two. Next, the boy's mother appeared, ducking out from the kitchen's entrance: Ibrahimu's sister Christine, Isaya's wife. Brother and sister now reunited with astonished delight: they had not seen each other since Isaya fled to the hills last September, and she followed her husband here with the five children by the forest route through Congo.

She was hardy, this one: not a sign of strain from the harrying uncertainties of her life. The youngest child, Alice, still suckling, was on her back.

Mama Christine and Ibrahimu settled down in the classroom to regale one another with news.

I went to lie down on one of the bamboo bunks. My feet and lower legs stuck out over the edge. Sleep evaded me: hunger, not tension, kept sleep away. From time to time faces of Rwenzururu askaris peered in quizzically. I could hear voices outside. Surely this delay would have Keefe upon us: we were on the vulnerable side of the river, which I knew Keefe to have been instructed not to cross: a bulleted body left on Congo-side could spell international trouble. This side, Keefe was free to engage in any plausible gunning down or rounding up.

Ibrahimu roused me: a messenger had arrived.

It was another buff envelope, stamped and dated the same day.

Within I found a six-page 20-point 'open letter' in English dated August 15th, 1962, the day of the formal establishment of Rwenzururu following the Declaration of Independence six and a half weeks earlier, on June 30th. It was a gruesome catalogue, much of which I was familiar with. 'Bakonjo and Bamba natural refused to pay taxes to a new unwelcome foreign yoke of the Batooro dynasty. Leaders in 1919-21 e.g. Tibamwenda, Nyamutswa, Nakapooli, Nkwirakaghu, Kalikura, and Kindongi etc were hanged, shot, and slaughtered as if they were goats.

'Other had their eyes removed and they were then wrapped in dry banana leaves. The leaves were then set on fire and the "blind" people in them were thrown into Lake Kaitaborogo which is near the Toro Government Central Priso Muhoti!!!'

There followed an elaboration of the tax argument, on much the same basis as that of an American colonist complaining to Lord North's government of 1776 – i.e. the injustice of taxation without representation; next, the education argument (no vernacular schools, few scholarships. Bakonzo wilfully held back); the religious argument (no ordained Bakonzo); the territorial and natural wealth argument (Konzo salt and Konzo copper expropriated and exploited to the exclusive benefit of others); and then the long lead-up to the final break of seven months earlier.

'After Batooro had been made rulers in our country, they kept Govt. posts in their hands. Even if a Mukonjo/Mwamba has a post, Batooro undermine him until he is dismissed.' In this pungent fragment I heard the personal voice of Isaya. 'But we should make it clear we are not fighting for posts now. What we want is to take over the Government in our own Country Rwenzururu which will be under protection of Uganda Central Government.'

A cadenza is headed *Declaration of Independence of Rwenzururu on June 20th, 1962:*

Right from the beginning our ancestors refused to have the Omukama of Batooro as the head of their Rwenzururu Government. After the Bamba and Bakonjo had handed their petition of 18th Feb, 1962 demanding Secession from Toro, to the Central Government announced how they would declare and install their Complete Independence from Batooro on June 30th 1962.

This announcement is contained in the Telegrames and the letter sent to the Premier on 21st May, 1962, with Copies to

His Excellency the Governor and the Colonial Secretary London.

After this announcement Bakonjo/Bamba celebrated their Independence. At these celebrations, we made a bonfire at Kasulenge and hoisted Rwenzururu flag. Batooro, however arrested some of us at this happy hour . . .

The Prime Minister was again told of Rwenzururu Independence in the letter of 20th July, 1962 . . .

And a coda

FINAL

In view of all these reasons Bamba/Bakonjo, the true inhabitants of Rwenzuru have agreed to united and throw of the hoke of Batooro rule. These is no doubt that after their 70 years rule, Batooro have failed to solve our problems. Our fore-fathers were forced to accept Batooro Superiority but they and their Abakama [kings] failed to administer our Country Rwenzururu sincerely. This lack of sincerity of Batooro has made us resume our grandfathers struggle to throw off Batooro and their Omukama...

To all these sentimental grievances which are presented before the Officials. The Central Government is carefully asked from to day, to arrange any quick means of removing Batooro Officials with their Omukama from our Country Rwenzururu to Bunyoro their Original ancestors withen afortunight.

With the same effect we are requesting the Central Government to make an Imprompty organisation in Co-operation with Rwenzururu leaders, how the deserted Headquarters will be organised until Government is re-formed. Failure to put this into operation would certainly mean re-Cival war against Batooro, by which, we as the true inhabitants of the Country, are not aware nor afraid in fight for defence of our milch Rwenzururu.

Now, let us all be in wait no brutality nor torture *Shall* make us ever plead for mercy, for we prefer peace and freedom of speech in an Independent Uganda to malicous Batooro Government.

Long Live Rwenzururu, Long Live Uganda.
Uhuru.

It was now about 4.15. The last message came about an hour and a half ago. I judged Isaya's headquarters was no more than half an hour by fast messenger. I went outside into the afternoon heat. Isaya had been up in these mountains now for some five months. What I had seen so far might seem a ragtag and bobtail operation. But this was deceptive. I knew by now that he had the entire highland population of the tribe as his militia, from one end of 'our milch Rwenzururu' to the other, and that virtually all the Bakonzo and most of the Baamba were in sympathy of the rebellion, whether they were lowlanders or highlanders. There was going to be no military solution.

I joined Ibrahimu and Seylversta over by the bamboo platform where the camp's pots were dried after washing up. The only one of Isaya's askaris to have stayed with us was Daneeri, sitting stolidly to one side, pulling at the grass. Isaya's Christine and young Charles Wesley Kisembo and the toddler Alice had slipped away, presumably to rejoin their master. Ibrahimu said, 'I think you should write another letter.'

So I did: brief, courteous, no pleading. I addressed it to the private secretary and handed it to Daneeri.

Forty minutes later I saw Daneeri returning by the traverse path with three spearmen I had not seen previously. He had a third buff envelope. The communication was handwritten. It read:

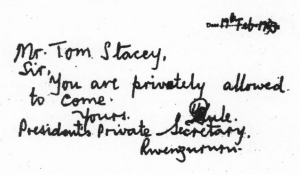

I privately went at once, with my two, and Daneeri, and the three spearmen.

xviii

President Isaya of Rwenzururu

The spearmen led off a spanking pace. Unsteady, I used my long stick like a third leg. We crossed the swift dark Tako into the Congo by the trunk of a tree, felled and trimmed for the purpose. Where it rose steeply at the further bank it had been nicked for footholds. I remembered the tree trunk: I had crossed it previously for the hunt. It was jungle here. The spearman immediately ahead stopped abruptly and began to beat with his stick at the path's edge. On the end of the stick he raised a long, bright green and extremely slender snake. It was dead. He draped it over the branch of a sapling.

The ascent proved demanding: it was excessively steep and so much coming and going had made a morass of mud underfoot. The spearmen went on at their own pace and waited for me, like dogs on a ramble. I was pulling myself up and on, foot by foot, with both hands on the stick as the old men did. A monkey in the trees to our left gave a cough-bark and Ibrahimu said it was singing.

I had no wish to arrive breathless and disorderly. I saw lightness ahead through the trees: a clearing of sorts. It was nobody's headquarters. Then we broke out of the forest line and had entered patched cultivation. I could not recall a settlement here, from 1954. The tone of the spearmen's chatter had changed to expectancy. I seemed to hear drumming, only to suppose it was the inner sound of my heart: but I was mistaken twice, since it was the sound of cassava being beaten in a mortar. I looked above to glimpse the women at it, through the plantation; and they stopped to watch me. We passed huts: women and old men had gathered at the entrances to scrutinise me silently. Then the growth opened. In sweat and fluster I followed towards a tiny hut, and round the back of it, and Isaya rising stiffly to greet me. I said,

'Greetings and love.'

I had that ready.

'Oh yes,' Isaya replied. 'And love. It ees.' He had uttered no

231

English for months.

We embraced, unequally, he so short, I long.

As we unfolded I noticed he had slightly filed his teeth, serrating them into shallow Vs. A brief, uncertain beard had joined his chin.

'So you have come back, Mistah Tom.'

At once he caught sight of Ibrahimu, his brother-in-law, and his kinsman Seylversta Manyumba. The eyes gleamed damp and a smile broke forth. Yet I was aware of a severe control, a stiffness and *hauteur* pinning him. We are here beside him, I thought, yet he could be gesturing to us from the battlements of his fortress. He has bastioned himself into his own kingship. To Ibrahimu he said, in Lukonzo, 'I thought we were to be parted for ever!'

Someone brought for me an egg-cup stool. I leaned back against the outer earth wall of the squared hut, suddenly cool in my new sweat. For that minute we were without words, I 'so unfortunate' to see him 'at this critical time.' The kingdom circled us with its valleys and steeps and spurs which paltry man could make habitable wherever he chose to clear the trees and make a compound for hunched huts, roughly ringed, holding to one another in frail community among their patchwork plantings; and every compound webbed in frail community by the thread of pathways by naked feet with each neighbouring spur. It was so tenuous, so close to non-being, this kingdom, and simultaneously of such grandeur. I gazed across and up at the black castellated mountain guarding the great heights, Kitasamba's dwelling place, not truly penetrable or measurable. This kingdom was insubstantial even to the degree of evanescence, utterly vulnerable as habitation to the torches of its enemy yet by that same token of frailty *strong* by virtue of the pact between these folk and the gods of their inner forest, steeps, storms and snows. Of this frailty and strength our Isaya here was exemplar, a seven month emperor, his jacket shabby and his canvas-and-rubber Bata lace-ups part practical, part ceremonial, enthroned by the reflexion upon his own person of his own vision among his fellows. We sighed. At length he said,

'When I had this your lettah, how hard did I jump! How hard.'

I was to learn almost at once of what he termed 'certain advisers' urging him not to let me cross to him: not only lest there should be a trick, as some chose to suspect, but also for the sheer violation of the sanctum. These 'advisers' (soon I would get to know who) did not know me as co-architect of the dream. The Private Secretary was squatting on a log beside Isaya: Yostasi Kule, callow and furtive, with a monkey-bag round his neck, full of exercise books.

I began to describe what had led to my journey here, exaggerating the minuscule coverage of Ruwenzururu's secession in the international press and fuzzing the directness of Obote's invitation. In truth, I was my own man, a mediator to the very root. Yet I had to begin from the premise that in the world as it is, so stubborn as to national frontiers, the unilateral secession of Shangri-La was not in the longer term a goer. 'Rwenzururu' would have to come to terms with Uganda sooner or later; and the sooner probably, the less misery. At this reunion, restoring innocence, I trampled no tulip dreams and made it seem no more than that I was sure I could persuade 'Prime Minister Obote, Uganda' (that other state) to give heed to whatever proposal I would bring to him out of the mountains from President Isaya Mukirane, Ruwenzururu. Isaya listened to me with one hand and sometimes both resting on the curved butt of his polished walking stick – that very stick he had cut from a tree near Kasulenge in Bwamba prior to our setting off on our trek through the mountains. I had with me a photograph of Isaya with the same stick.

Then I was brought a basin of warm water. I withdrew a little distance for a wash. Returning after my first cleansing in three days, I was offered a bowl of boiled plantains, entirely bland. I could not stomach more than a few fingerfuls.

Isaya returned to my side. We talked on till nightfall; and in this resumed interchange I began to detect two things. One was an awe at his own authority within his mountain people and the trust they reposed in him. This contained a factor of intoxication. The other was a readiness, indeed an eagerness, to be martyred in the cause. I studiously avoided turning to the Rwenzururu situation as such, but whenever it was skirted in our conversation he was quick to pop forth with expectations of sacrificial heroism – 'We shall die, if we must', and so on. I recognised a striking inflation of his self-view such as I feared made the prospect of its abandonment unbearable. A Mosaic if not Messianic syndrome had entered him. It had perhaps never been absent far, although in 1954 he had been inclined to project the role on me. Isaya now suckled on the dream of Rwenzururians a nation among other nations and he their elective monarch. This very morning of the 19th of February 1963 he had written personally to the Secretary General of the United Nations from which Rwenzururu was not reasonably to be excluded.

The Hon'ble Mr. U. Thant.
General Secretary of United Nations.
Sir,
    With reference to the Uganda Prime Minister Government declaration of sending Uganda army to fight "the innocent people of Rwenzururu Govt. Central Africa" which was heard on the Radio Uganda on the 16th Feb. 1963.
    The Uganda Government Army started invading Bakonjo-Bamba of Rwenzururu since last year and so many people have been wounded and shot dead using coarsive actions which has very much disturbed the man's freedom as far as Uganda Govt. Report is concerned!
    On the behalf of my people of Rwenzururu Government – I have the honour to apply for the United Nations Protection against Uganda disturbers Govt. which failed to protect us properly as a result we decided not to be protected by the Uganda Govt. referring to the letter dated 17th Nov. 1962 addressed to the Uganda Prime Minister Obote – a copy to you.
    I hope your quick assistance will soon stop Uganda Govt. Army before destroying Rwenzururians who have no weapons to defend themselves.

Yours faithfully
President Isaya M. Mukirane
Rwenzururu.

Copies to :
Rwenzururu Government supporters
Rwenzururu Government Police Force
The Prime Minister Obote and Uganda Govt.
    "   "   "   Foreign Countries.
This missive was already on its ways to the UN Secretariat in New York, having been despatched earlier in the day by 'Rwenzururu runner' via the descending forest north-westwards for posting in Mutwanga, Congo, where a tottering mail service perhaps survived.
    Between Rwenzururu and other 'Foreign Countries' he may have perceived a difference of scale – that his military arm was but spearmen, his territory Bundibugyo to Bwera in the longitude and

Kasese to Mutwanga in the latitude, his seal of office a rubber stamp, and his state papers in a monkey bag; yet beyond that difference of scale there was no difference in kind from his fellow Heads of State and *their* statehoods. For a people were a people, a language a language, a homeland as much a homeland in Rwenzururu as anywhere else. Indeed, what other nation on earth could claim an inaccessible, not to say unexplored, interior, with all the national sanctity thus implied?

I was personally well versed in regional secessions and instant nation-claimings. For my newspaper I had reported from the scene the sudden flowering and just as sudden de-flowering of Moise Tshombe's Katanga, and the even more momentary blooming of Albert Kalonji's South Kasai. Both fragmentary entities calved from the Congo had had just time enough to issue their own postage stamps, and Tshombe's Katanga its own currency and aircraft livery. Yet both were so swiftly scythed and furnaced. I told Isaya of these harsh lessons of recent African history. (We were neither of us to know that Tshombe would bounce back to be Premier for a while of all Congo, from its capital Leopoldville.) My accounts left Isaya subdued. That very week his people were sensing the hot breath of the Ugandan Army in pursuit of them, in their supposed inaccessibilities. I told him of the collusion between the two commanders, both British, of the respective forces of the Ugandan government on one side of the frontier (unrecognised by him) and the forces seconded to the United Nations – the very troops of The Hon'ble Mr U. Thant – on the other.

Yet Isaya had another shot in his locker, a shot I had allowed myself to overlook. He reminded me of it by means of an earlier letter, despatched the previous month to Mr M Obote, Prime Minister, Uganda, but copied to 'Rwenzururu Government Police Force; Rwenzururu Government supporters; Uganda Minister of Regions; Uganda Minister of Home Affairs; Uganda General Governor, Entebbe; Uganda Police Force, Fort Portal, Rwenzururu; Uganda Information Newspaper; General Secretary United Nations; the Foreign Countries'.

Sir,
With reference to the information collected from Mwebingwa, Wamanya Newspapers of 29th De. 1962-22nd Jan. 1963 and from the deserted Toro Government document

of 7th Jan. 1963.

The Batooro Government Officials have come to understand how ignorant and unworthy living in our lovely Country Rwenzururu.

You are strongly advised not to waste Uganda Government Officials, Rifles, Money, and time visiting and supporting Batooro in my Independent Country Rwenzururu – which is no long a part of your "disturbed country Uganda", referring to the letter dated 17th Nov. 1962, addressed to you Obote-Uganda Government – copies to the Foreign Countries.

By this Copy, the Rwenzururians are advised to stand firmly in their homes – the God, King of Rwenzururu is sending down the Rwenzururu heavenly spirits with sharp swords which will slash down those who are disturbing and invading the innocent Country Rwenzururu!

Yours faithfully
President Isaya M. Mukirane.
Rwenzururu.

The secret weapon lay there in the last paragraph. Virtually by definition, Rwenzururu was invincible. He was changing the negative strength referred to already to a positive one. The deity *and* the place of snows were invoked as one, Nzururu. Whether through the agency of the half-Christianized Nyamuhanga or of Kitasamba, the Konzo Thor, the divinity and his cohorts (Snow and Hail, Fog and Cold, Thunder and Lightning) would do for the enemy no less ruthlessly and finally than the Russians' winter-god had done for Bonaparte. Isaya narrowly avoided identifying himself with pure divinity by the comma after 'God' in the last paragraph. Yet there was no call for precision here. The dual point was that Isaya sensed himself and Rwenzururu to be exempted from defeat by means of the combined impenetrability and sanctity of their mountain *patria*. This Omusangania knew himself to be in collusion with that divinity before which men have trembled since man began, in such a manner – as Elihu reminded Job – as made the heart of a man 'leap out of its place', and constrained a man to 'listen, listen, to the thunder of his voice and the rumbling that comes from his mouth. Under the whole heaven he lets it loose, and his lightnings to the corners of the earth.' Holy Scripture coursed through this fellow and spoke to him and for him and Rwenzururu out of the book of Job, specifically enough in Chapter 37. 'After it his voice roars; he thunders with his majestic voice and he does not restrain the lightnings when his voice is heard. God thunders wondrously with his voice; he does great things we cannot comprehend. For to the snow he says, "Fall on the earth"; and the shower of rain, his heavy shower of rain, serves as a sign... Then the animals go to their lairs and remain in their dens. From its chambers comes the whirlwind, and cold from the scattering winds. By the breath of God is ice given,' whether that God be named Nyamuhanga or Kitasamba: he resided and presided here in Ruwenzori and Isaya could call him up on his people's behalf. This was a sacred war, and its leader under divine guidance and protection. In the terms of my assignment I was dealing with no Cincinnatus, summoned from the plough for a given assignment and longing to turn his sword back into a ploughshare just as soon as the job was done, but a Jeanne d'Arc with a double-headed spear in darkest Africa and tragi-comic pleas in half-babu English to the powers of an indifferent world. A Toytown, black Jeanne d'Arc. Yet in its marrow truth this revolt was not Toytown: it was elemental to man on earth, the eruption of a pact of race with place, *hier stehe ich – ich kann nicht anders*. Out of his ignorance he had snatched a certain truth; and I, moreover, was half with him. Had I not already let on to him that the single Uganda Rifleman so far killed by his askaris had been the battalion's only Mutoro? Of course I had ... and gave him just the evidence he expected that the numina of the mountains were active in the Konzo cause. It was my assignment to tease and cajole him out of his reality into my *un*reality. I promised him how, as soon as we had concluded a favourable settlement, he would come with me to England as my guest. He frowned at such incredibility.

'Mis-tah Tom: I don't know.'

'I will pay your fare by aeroplane. You will meet my wife – she has heard me speak so much about you. And my children.'

'Can I?' I expanded the notion. 'Can I?' he repeated, yet beginning to smile. 'Is eet?' – meaning, Would you really have me believe such rubbish?

Our exchange was infused with delight at our unforeseeable reunion. My diary of that day reads, 'All the time I am talking to him, I have the sensation that he is not really believing that I am here.' His heart had readmitted me, but his mind was resisting.

When I recalled for him the detail of the trust of our former journey, he said, "In those times we were very happy.' 'Those times' were not these times. He was loaded now with limitless authority and limitless responsibility. I confirmed to him that the entire army of Uganda was engaged in looking for him, and suppressing his movement. This included the Aztec spotter aircraft we could now see circling the lower Tako valley to the south-east of us. 'All for me?' he said.

Was I feeding his delusion? And did I not doubt the superiority of my reality?

In our old companionship we had known serenity, delving and devilling out the truth of his people on their steep ancestral compounds. Then after I left him, the pain had come back on him with a rush – from the open wound of the fatal impact, the colonial presence endorsing the authority of Toro, endorsing the negligibility of his Konzo. Together, in our first journey, we *had* recovered something of the long peace of the land, the quilted cultivation, we had heard laughter in the plantain groves, had tapped into the old wisdom, cradled by the antiquity of the people in their immemorial fastness. The canopy of cloud had opened for us, and there unmistakably were the peaks in all their brilliance and strength. He had caught sight of it all, in such a manner as to alleviate if not to dissolve his pain. To repeat what I have written in this book: one could live below these mountains for years and never see them, never suppose that they were there. Yet Isaya *had* seen; what he saw was no illusion. On the contrary: Nzururu's heights were the true, permanent, redeeming reality, his and his people's companions and dwelling place; and to escape his own pain and meaninglessness, he had vowed to reclaim the authority of his people among them.

I had not noticed the arrival towards nightfall of the figure whom for months I had laboured to build into a work of fiction as the exemplar of pagan Africa. Here now, kneeling before me, shaven-headed (since there had been a death in the family), was Khavaïru, as Merlinesque as ever I recollected; and the cunning, humour and command present in him still, but not quite the mercurial savagery I had earlier ascribed him. He took my hand, and thus mutually attached we ran out the long elaborated Lukonzo greeting. Had he been in the immediate vicinity of Isaya and me all these hours we had already talked? Surely so. He would have been one of those inner courtiers warning Isaya to be wary of this muzungu bearing his blandishments.

I was quick now to produce a roll of photographs taken in Kituti, his village, in 1954. The chief clutched them greedily, and off he went with a private grin at sight and possession – for the first time in his life – of his own image in reproduction. My forerunner H M Stanley, with whatever cascade of coloured beads, could not have outdone me for aptness of gift.

Next to rejoin me was the Christian presence of Isaleri. How fine a face and broad a head! Surely some fuller cohesion of spirit had entered him these intervening years. I remembered the shadow in the face of former times, the jumbled hair, and the medicine fibre: the inner rivalries of spiritual authority, at Kitolu then. Now he too took and held my hand, and I let him scrutinise me with a deep gaze: at the same time I heard the note of pride in Isaya's voice that this one, this Isaleri, collateral descendant of Tibamwenda, a seer born to the role, whose authority reached from Kitolu northwards to Bulemba (then known as Bulimdengwa), southwards to Isango, eastwards to Bubotyo and westwards to the Tako in the valley below us, should be a counsellor of his royal  train. They came to me now, the women and various of the elders, singly or in pairs, from the side, to kneel before me – in no servility, but courtesy only – offering greeting, and then a constant flow of Rwenzururu askaris with their spears and bows, reassembling at this new headquarters, to step up and salute their King-President beside his visitor. I caught in Isaya a wisp of self-deprecation at my witnessing this elevation to sublimity since we were last together.

At length little Kisembo – Isaya's Charles Wesley, his eldest and his heir – brought me a yellow hen, with its feet tied. I took her, as the sacrificial gift she was, and passed her across for execution somewhere off-stage, presumably at the hands of his mother Christine, the King-President's consort, who had crossed here from Uganda-side with her children ahead of me. I heard the sharp protest of the bird at death behind the hut. Night had abruptly fallen. Lightning persisted over the castellated mountain northwards, between us and the high peaks. Low thunder pursued the lightning, light-speed and sound-speed in their old Ruwenzori dance and measure.

I too was a mere forty-eight hours back into an earlier world, a primal one. I had no appetite, yet in my sweater now, with a sleeping bag as a shawl, I squatted on a log beside the glow of the hut fire, waiting for the meal. Isaya had withdrawn with his wife and his offspring to some cave he spoke of. I ate with no relish, chewing on the thin rubbery flesh. But Seylversta had said grace: the salty juice and gristled ovary were ritually partaken. I crawled into my corner beyond the fire where plaintain leaves had been spread for my sleeping space. The hut filled slowly with spearmen. Only the fire illuminated this interior. Thus far it was a rebellion without paraffin. It was as well to show no lights up here. If Keefe was across the valley, let us not tempt him with lights.

In our frailty our strength lay. It was the familiar doctrinal paradox. In having nothing we had all. In these mountains, along this forest edge, we will-o'-the-wisp rebels were beyond expectation of capture or defeat. In the lowlands they might encircle villages and round up those with weapons or Rwenzururu documents: this they had done, according to a Lutoro news broadcast we picked up that very evening – two hundred taken prisoner in southern Busongora and five hundred in Bwamba . Also by radio we were told of a lofty message of gratitude from King George of Toro to the Government in Kampala for its decisive action. But up here the mountains were ours, the forest was ours, the 'God, King of Rwenzururu' was ours; we had only to melt into what was ours. If they found a hastily abandoned camp or a loyalist settlement of huts and torched it, in one day or at most two we could re-create it out of the natural product of our birth-right territory and this time sited *in* the forest and so protected even from the vicious prying of a spotter plane. Such would come to be the proven strategy.

Our weapons were pathetic. These spears and these bows – what could they avail against Brens and rifles? Look at our bows! They were for agitation of monkeys in the forest canopy. Look at our spears! They were for scuttling pigs. In these two days since the Enemy had committed itself with trained men, uniformed, and the sure-fire of guns, and Wazungu officers, our spears had gotten but one, against all our casualties, slain and captured.

240

Up to two days ago, certainly, we had brought terror through the mountains. Kabarole-appointed headmen no longer dared to suck tax out of our people to enrich the Toro kingdom, or otherwise exert their mean domination in the name of the Mukama George Rukidi and his backers in Kampala. Our spearmen saw to that. We had mutilated a few of our own blood-kind who, like Ezironi the parliamentarian, had sought to rebut the sacred ideology of Rwenzururu self-determination. We had eliminated, by execution, those few Konzo quislings who were minded to give us away to the foe. Such had been the extent of our external, martial assertion. It was – if one has to say it – pathetic. And yet...

And yet, it was enough to have rendered *ours* the entire region of the mountains south to north, east to west, the habitable and the uninhabitable, the hospitable and the inhospitable, the accessible and the inaccessible, a region irrespective of frontiers or of anachronistic colonial history; and *ours* (whether covertly or openly) that entire swathe of quilted Konzo lowlands from Bwera to Nyabirongo and beyond, southeast, to the hippo lakes and the saltworks. All of that ancient *Rwenzururu*, the promised land, was ours, acknowledging *our* aegis, compliant to the will and the vision of this very court where I lay curled, half awake, uncertain of my bodily efficiency, in virtual darkness amid the odour of goats and smouldering logs. It was enough to have provoked the committing of the entire army of the fledgling State of Uganda, and its spotter aircraft, to presume to deny us what we rendered irrefutably *ours*.

We here, on this ledge in Congo, lanternless, were the knot of the vital threads of Rwenzururu, Isaya's kingdom: the Kingdom of the Mountains of the Moon, already seven months into its defiant *regnum*. What absurd defiance! What negligible threads! This, on Bukuke spur, the capital of a unique civic culture? – subliterate, a stamping in bare feet, panto-saluting, uniformed in tatters and monkey-skins, weaponed with mock guns, sanctioned by a rubber stamp 'Bakonjo-Bamba', a pastiche of a pastiche of a defunct empire. What were we but threads of threads, Khavaïru the pagan thread, Isaleri

the Christian thread, Kule the metalwork thread, Fanehasi the administrative thread, Kinyamusitu the martial thread; and Isaya himself, thread-gatherer, flag-weaver, bannerman, ideologue and seer, ruling by fiat (and his rubber stamp)... *What on earth was I engaged in*? Where was the substance? Just what might this *Rwenzururu* comprise, either now or ever? A montagnard, Banyarwenzururu *politeia*? Here, on this scarp? At the upper forest's edge, scarcely explored, habitance affirmed by the scattered emanation of hearth-smoke, by a web of pathways, a random collage of millet patches, plantains, yams? A scurry into the grasses? A movement of specific shadow? A polity of evanescent humankind made anew from the crumbs of other tables, half-grasped, half-known; sans forge, sans quarry, sans scripture, in this place, at this height?

Was this how anything began, out of Eden?

When you put away metaphor, and go again to the beginning, there is only the Word, which is neither written nor spoken. It was, and is, I say again, the silent pact of race and place: a divine surety of immemorial origin to which the mountains and the ancestors bore witness. The claim, therefore, is upon immemoriality; and the fight is for the right to straddle what is of this life and this world, measurable and creaturely, and what is not of this life and world, not measurable or creaturely, and yet of our suetude, our privy interpretability, our *embitha*. Therein is the 'straddling', therein the rope bridge and, I fear, the requirement to fight.

Sleep creeps up on a man. As to the realm of Rwenzururu itself, conjured by Isaya Mukirane, what assured its substance was indeed its unsubtantiality. It melted before the forces that came to confront it, and, and, and seeped and swarmed around them. From time to time its territory would be invaded, its encampments burned, its askaris gunned from the ground and from the air. It would lose its King-President, first by capture, later by death. It was not to be immune from inner dissension. Yet it was never defeated. Its sway was over a mountain nation of some hundred thousand citizens, solid in their allegiance. The head of every family would come to pay annually to the Government of Rwenzururu a receipted poll tax. That Government maintained an army, soon enough to be drilled and uniformed, of several thousand, and half that number of police. It divided its territory into defined counties and sub-counties, each with its chiefs, sub-chiefs, headmen and the rest. It maintained a central exchequer (hidden in the forest). A cabinet of eight members, each with his ministerial portfolio, served successively Isaya, the regents, and Omusinga Charles. Thus the Kingdom of Rwenzururu would build schools throughout the mountains, train its teachers, import its classroom materials, establish its courts of law, and carry out their judgments. Likewise it would build its churches, at which and through which faith in Jesus was taught according to the tenets and style of the Church of Uganda, beholden to Canterbury. In its formal existence it was to endure for twenty years almost to the hour until, on August 15, 1982, Isaya's son Charles Wesley (our eleven-year old 'Kisembo' here), at the age of thirty, signed terms of reconciliation, not surrender, with the President of Uganda, this same Milton Obote after an entire turn of the wheel of his own destiny. Twenty years further on, the year of completion of this book, the *embitha* and expression of Rwenzururu remain the paramount issue in that part of Africa. Last year, 2001, the forty-nine-year-old Charles declared (from a most unsatisfactory distance) his operative Omusingaship. This followed the findings of a study, commissioned in the year 2000 of dispassionate academics of Makerere University by the Government of Uganda, that eighty-six per cent of the people of that mountain region and of those languages, Lukonzo and Lwamba, supported formal recognition of the titular monarchy of Rwenzururu in the person of Isaya's son Charles.

That next morning out on the sunlit compound, one could hardly have guessed the actual consequences for the history of Rwenzururu of my intervention. The meeting between Isaya and me seemed full of the promise of a tranquil, negotiated re-integration into Uganda of a Konzo tribal community and territory defined, recognised and rewarded with rights. If it had all turned out thus, all I need do here would be to re-tell the story of what I have already put down in that 'short brisk' book, *Summons to Ruwenzori*, written at the time. Since it did not so transpire, the story warrants re-telling in the light of what *did* come about, and continues to unfold to this day. So with hindsight's benefit, let those weeks of my own engagement be sketched.

That dawn the sun rising on Bukuke spur of Isaya's kingdom took care to wake me. I supervised its progress across the plain where I had set out, from 3,000 feet above it. The length of the Tako valley dropped before me southwards. Layers of white mist islanded innumerable lesser hills and spurs that cluttered the divide between the valley's flanks. The strengthening sun dissolved that white density until the only mist to remain was over Lake Edward, Mwita-Njike, Locust Drowner, whose nearer shore was twenty miles distant. Gradually the lake's lucent, green-blue sheen attained visibility. The surface of the waters was light not substance, and the landscape between was of light in a perpetual variegation of greens, sliding and shifting in this restless season of rains. This light was art, the Maker's *ebullitio*, bubbling forth, for Him or us to regard and to note that it was good.

I had drafted a letter to the Prime Minister, Mr Obote, by 8.15 a.m. when Isaya rejoined me, accompanied by three spearmen and the Private Secretary, now attired in a dark blue pinstripe jacket made by Montagu Burton, the Fifty Shilling Tailors. The President of Rwenzururu and I sat out there in the middle of the little ledge of flat earth. The spur had become a hive of spearmen. The dreaded Keefe, we learned, had now recently passed Bulimera, the bone-shaped knoll where I had sheltered the previous night but one. He was coming on up by furtive marches along the forest edge, possibly imagining he and his élite troop were not being watched all the way. The truth of it was that this intrusive Keefe was flushing large numbers of Bakonzo from where they had taken refuge in the Uganda-side tongues of forest. All morning, women

and children and men too old for Rwenzururu service were streaming past our spur, escaping by the hunters' routes I had grown familiar with eight years before, to scatter themselves among the settlements of relatives Congo-side. Kinyamusitu, Mr Forest, moved from group to group with the transistor radio nestling against his monkey-bag and going full blast with the Test Match. The refugees paused on the rim of the compound, gazing with hanging lips at Kinyamusitu's voicey-box, then to me and back again to the disembodied voice. They were loaded with everything they could carry – the women turned beasts of burden with huge Konzo baskets on their backs, four feet in depth and two-and-a-half across, crammed with earthenware pots, cassava flour, plantains, black beans, and as often as not topped by a pair of cuffed chickens – the whole caboodle supported by fibrous straps passing under the basket and across the top of the head. Before them, herded by the children, their sheep and goats were being shunted along, cropping at what they could, while they could. The men – all but the old – were gone to war.

War. This was war. It was like this along the length of the mountains under the precise inspiration and imprecise direction of Isaya Mukirane, Omusinga, King-President, Irema-Ngoma, whatever. His agents were already collecting Rwenzururu poll tax, tiny sums or tribute in hens or yams per family head, passed across to mukungu collectors in exchange for a primitive receipt two inches square, kept as secret talisman of brotherhood and faith. The perimeter of the inner kingdom was defined by the lowest of those compounds where only Rwenzururu poll tax was paid; the perimeter of the outer kingdom was defined by those settlements where Toro poll tax was paid alongside the secret Rwenzururu tithe. In some regions – as across the valley in southern Busongora – a territorial no-man's-land had opened between the inner realm and the outer realm, which messengers and scouts and smugglers crossed by night or just before dawn armed with passwords or a murmured slogan – *tuli baghuma* : We are all One – and absolute intimacy with every delving pathway: delving down and delving up.

And yet here was I on Bukuke compound going through and re-revising the draft of a letter designed to take the first big step towards peace and reconciliation: *i.e.* a proposal that in exchange for the withdrawal of the military to their bases in the foothills, Isaya would call off hostilities from his askaris and himself come out on a promise of safe conduct to discuss a full settlement in privacy. I had delivered a longish verbal prologue before unveiling my little draft, which I then went through with him. Isaya was all assent, and at a certain point of comprehensive harmony I retired to 'take a rest', while he set about briefing the Private Secretary on the preparation of the fair copy. When I re-emerged to scan the perfected offer I could not but notice that a couple of extra demands had been popped in: the release of the several hundred prisoners, and the withdrawal of the Uganda Rifles not merely to the foothills but to the plains. It had come to read as from one Prime Minister to another – Rwenzururu seeking 'friendly relations with the Government of Uganda'. I surreptitiously edited out some of the lordliness from the final *final* version although I could not block 'Uhuru Rwenzururu!' after the signature, nor entirely wished to.

An envelope was found – indeed, a batch of envelopes. Two were addressed to Obote, as Prime Minister, of which the second contained a note from me to the (other) PM, endorsing Isaya's good intentions concerning the cease-fire. I sent a further message to 'shrewd' Col. W. W. Cheyne, which ended, 'When this messenger arrives, wd you pse give him some aspirins, multi-vitamin tablets, and antiseptic.' All three envelopes went into a fourth, rubber stamped *Rwenzururu Bakonjo-Bamba*. The messenger was to be Isaleri's half-brother Batulomayu Kisiraho, a visionary-looking fellow of about thirty-five, not so young for a Mukonzo – scraggy, wonder-eyed, intensely committed to the cause and of proven stamina and resource. He was already established as Isaya's chief courier and more than courier: as go-between – since many of the messages he carried were not written but word-of-mouth. This Batulomayu – which is to say, Bartholomew (adapting Hebraicized Greek, Bar-Ptolemy, to the Bantu tongue) – was to stay in our story down to the very present. A matter of mere weeks before writing this passage, thirty-seven years later, I was conversing with him on a spur just below Kitolu, still scraggy, wonder-eyed and close to my heart.

I wrote out for younger Batulomayu an explanatory *laissez-passer*, in English and Swahili, and urged him to carry no stick in case some dumb soldier chose to mistake it for a spear and shoot him. He stood solemnly in front of Isaya, seated on his stool in the compound, and as he took his leave, saluted. Isaya bade him well, assuring of the protection of the spirits of Rwenzururu; at which Batulomayu saluted once more with such vigour that he needed to restore his balance before turning about to go.

Of course, Batulomayu got safely down the mountain and delivered his peace-package into, near enough, the hands of Bill Cheyne personally. There at Isango he was given a good meal, and requested to wait a few days so that he could carry back a reply, and was treated with courtesy and respect, which surprised him. We in our heights knew nothing about this, nor all the promise it held for Obote, Bill Cheyne, Bazarrabusa and the rest of us pacifiers ... though little of that promise would be fulfilled. There would be no settlement – not, at least, for another 19 years; perhaps, indeed, never yet. There would be no real attempt at negotiation. There was to be a temporary cessation of hostilities – such alone was attributable to me. The actual omen of these interchanges was altogether other. It was anamnesiac vision; paradise deferred; earthly intransigeance; sacrificial death. The gods of the mountains were never not involved. I was about to lead this other world into this-worldly charade.

It was not that Isaya intended to fool me or those I was lining up to treat with him. It was that his rebellion had been conceived and was driven by a collective dream of ethereal psycho-territorial liberty, while I had come to mediate a settlement which at best would offer, for a while, administration of the Bakonzo-Baamba region separately from Toro, and with perhaps a few economic and educational inducements thrown in. Isaya was already engaged in the realization of his people's fantasy. He was borne upon its wings. That fantasy was something quite other than 'separate district status' and the rest of it. He was wholly identified with Rwenzururu. In such settlement that my intervention might lead to, where was there a role for the rebellion's exemplar, its king, its martyr-in-waiting? He had to die for this thing. He was not to be cheated out of this right. He absolutely needed martyrdom. Moreover, the prospective martyrdom was on behalf of all of primal Africa, albeit Christian-tinctured and reaching out for literacy and articulacy. To be fair to myself, I had perceived this already and had raised it in *The Brothers M* in terms of the Platonic concept of the recollection of prior existence and prior innocence – in the present instance Konzo and mountain-girt, wherein incontrovertible meaning rested in truth-to-themselves and, by such a state of being, opened the door upon all-being. This paradise regained was not negotiable, not subject to compromise, settlement, district boundary lines, international frontiers, economic inducements or opportunities for classroom learning. Nor was it eradicable.

So why, if he was going to play-act, had he consented to see me at all? And having let me back in, how came he to authorize and sign a letter to the principal figure of alien authority and current instigator of war against his kingdom, namely Prime Minister Milton Obote, declaring that he would come out of the mountains to talk peace? Might this have been a cynical gambit to give himself a little breathing space to re-assemble his tribal forces and devise a strategy to combat the intrusion of Uganda's standing army?

My answer is that Isaya was not play-acting, either now or at any time over the coming weeks of my to-ing and fro-ing between the mountains and Kampala. He could hardly have refused me admission to his presence since I was, after all, the fellow seedsman of the Idea. The Idea had been germinated in our trust one of another, here in this place in the Konzo cause, a deep mute commitment between two men. On the skin of my white chest were visible the six dark cicatrices of a Konzo razor and the pigment of fur ash sanctified by Konzo invocation. Truly, I had sown the courage for this thing he had made. He could not deny the reunion.

Next, I had come bringing him credibility and flattery in terms of the outer world's constructs of power. By my presence Isaya's pretensions of kingship or presidency of his mountain tribesmen and their Shangri-la were rendered plausible. Suddenly his voice was being heard, his grandiloquent letter-writing was getting a response. In this interchange was an implicit endorsement of his own reality. It was almost shocking.

But that was as far as he could dare to take it. For he would be asked: *What do you really want?* – just as Bazarrabusa had said to me, We can't find out what he really wants. Isaya could not have said. A man cannot easily march the borders of his own madness (although it has been occasionally attempted). What Isaya really wanted was to live an idea, Rwenzururu, by ruling it; and because it could never prove truly liveable on the ground, any more than the Kingdom of God is liveable on earth, he would die for it, for the acolytes of his dream. I have uttered the word 'madness' spontaneously but not inappropriately. Of course, Rwenzururu was and is the product of paranoia, but no more so – in the limited vision of those pioneer 'psychologists' who coined that word in the latter half of the 19th century – than Christianity or, for that matter, any revealed faith. What would we expect Jesus Christ to have answered if, as is perfectly possible, Pilate had leaned across to him in all earnestness and asked, 'My dear fellow, what exactly do you want?'

248

While we were waiting for the messages to be sent by the hand of
Batulomayu to bear fruit or for fiercer realities to impinge, we spun
away a day or two on Bukuke spur practising spear-throwing and
archery, and as a former officer of the English monarch's protective
forces I rehearsed assembled Rwenzururu askaris in parade drill,

young Charles Welsey 'Kisembo' lining up with the big fellows.
Some carried wooden dummy rifles. They were magnificently
enthusiastic. The salute was an act of quivering loyalty. Under the
flag we rendered and perfected the Rwenzururu National Anthem.
This comprised the best available descriptive vocalisation of
embitha, and is sung (to this day) to an admirably singable melody
in the *Ancient and Modern* tradition.

Rwenzururu wethu!	Our Rwenzururu!
Rwenzururu wethu!	Our Rwenzururu!
Rwenzururu wethu Mulighighirwa,	Our revered Rwenzururu
Wayire-hi?	What became of you?

Tukabia twamalengekania ngokuwabya	Whenever we think of how you fare,
Emiisoni iyatsububuka!	Tears flow!
Omubughe wethu!	Our own language!
Omubughe wethu!	Our own language!
Omubughe wethu w/Olhukobi,	Our own language of old,
Ayiire-hi?	What has happened to it?
Hatia abirihinduka mwa Lhuhyana,	Now it has been corrupted into Lhuhyana,
Omwatsi abere makuru!	News is now called *makuru!* [i.e. the Lutoro word for *omwatsi*, news']

I signed the Visitor's Book, which had an elephant on the cover. My predecessors as visitors appeared all to be Bakonzo, from various parts of the mountains, and included some who had arrived here as Isaya's prisoners and who may or may not have survived. I proposed to Isaya the establishment in peace-to-come of a centre for Bakonzo crafts, for the spending by foreign visitors of their money, and for a Land Rover track to be built up to these heights and a Government Rest House to be established here. (Such an idea, in truth, repelled me.) We took pictures of each other, sometimes with me propping up the flag, sometimes cast as a spearman and Charles gripping father's ceremonial stick with Isaleri behind him for ecclesiastic endorsement. Kinyamusitu, his future C-in-C, stood at my left elbow. By the afternoon our leader was swept by headier transports. 'We have made an independent country!' he exclaimed to me, in the presence of a motley of

his askaris. In their pelts and rags, and armed with spears. 'We are free! *Now* we are free!' My notes tell of his mind shifting unaware between the planes – between as it were the visionary heights and the *realpolitik* of the steppe, the snow-bound Kitasamba-fortressed inner citadel and the contested lowlands. The landscape lent itself to the mindscape: it floated and shifted below us, in and out of substance, by reason of light and weather – below us and indeed above us. As my low fever began to return in the afternoon I myself could not but half surrender to the idea of this place as magnificent refuge, of one's living and dying here enclosed on three sides by the heave of forested mountains, whose imperceptible hunters' routes were known only to us, and half-barred to the enemy by a Tom Tiddler's frontier ... and on the fourth side, southwards and beneath us the labyrinthine spurs and mist-gathering gullies of upper Busongora dropping to the shining plain and the sheen of the illimitable lake. This *was* the kingdom and the liberty, this veritable exiguous patch of flattened earth and crouched huts of sprung wattle and plantain fronds or bamboo sheaths, this and all its lacery of habitance on the mountains, Uganda-side, Congo-side. We *were* the gossamer kingdom.

I had gone into my squalid corner, in flushed torpor, to sleep off whatever was afflicting me. From time to time they brought the

251

news of Keefe's laborious progress up through the valley's forest. Khavaïru came to me with a ratskin bag 'to keep my money in'. He marvelled at a tiny photograph of my ten-year-old daughter, and congratulated me on the fine dowry I would be receiving for such a little beauty when, very shortly, I would be marrying her off. The day thickened into restless nightfall. Kinyamusitu joined us with the transistor, and at 7.15 p.m. the news in Lutoro told us of the announcement by Toro's *omuhikirwa* (first minister) that the piling in of more soldiers and policemen was the only way to peace in the mountains. They kept the transmitter on as they chatted around me, and when I suggested they should not waste the battery Kinyamusitu declared that everything must die and the hour of death was chosen by the spirits. This opinion tickled the sophisticate Ibrahimu. More and more seemed to crowd into my hut, and with them the fog. The talk and the fog alike drifted and circled.

In the morning all was bright, and gazing across the deep valley and a little below us, at about two miles distance we saw Keefe's troop at the Rwenzururu camp I had paused at while awaiting Isaya's invitation to cross to him. We watched the enemy file out of the camp, to ascend towards where Kituti's compound lay above. A thread of smoke, most precise, rose into the still air from a corner of the camp. It curled, and thickened into a skein. Orange flames rose where the smoke had been, and then blazed like a flower out of the green valley-side. An hour or so later I crossed with a group of spearmen to the camp which Isaya had built with such pride. Amid the smouldering embers we found a knife and several pangas with their hafts burned off. Nothing else remained – the bunks, the blackboard, the beans in their plantain-leaf wrappings, all gone to char and cinder. An ekhinanga-harp, companion and teaser of song and of melodic invocation, was boot-stamped into the ground; and beside it lay a ratskin purse, like that just given me by Khavaïru, its pink feet curled like fern buds, the only surviving thing.

On and up at Kituti, nailed to the door frame of Khavaïru's new edifice, the unconsecrated church, was a message in English and Swahili:

WE ARE ASKARIS FROM UGANDA RIFLES. WE HAVE BEEN HERE FOR AN HOUR BUT I TELL YOU THAT IT IS YOUR CHANCE TO COME DURING YOUR ABSENCE HAD WE TO FIND YOU HERE YOU COULD DIE STRAIGHT... IF YOU DO NOT LEAVE YOUR PARTIES YOU ARE TO DIE.

This was not Keefe-speak, white-at-black. It was African-speak, black-at-black, Nubian-on-Bantu. Seylversta speculated with alarmed titters on the fusillade we would have met with if I had not spent so long labouring up from the smouldering camp. I guessed that the Keefe patrol had not been gone for more than half an hour. Here we would abide, awaiting Batulomayu. We tried to tidy the place up. It was after all the nearest thing to our capital city, these five huts and the new squared-up mud-brick worship-site, halfway dedicated to the alternative truth. (Our genuine capital was wherever Isaya chose to plant his stave.) Later we cautiously toured the spur's broader boundaries. We were approaching a red-flowered Kaffir-boom tree when round a bend in the path ahead appeared a tattered angular figure carrying a haversack. It was Batulomayu!

Telephone: Entebbe 441.

PM/PERSONAL

OFFICE OF THE PRIME MINISTER,
P.O. BOX 5,
ENTEBBE, UGANDA.

21st February, 1963.

SECRET AND PERSONAL

Dear Mr. Stacey

Thank you for your letter of the 20th February.

I have given instructions to Colonel Cheyne that the troops deployed in Busongora shall forthwith cease active operations and will remain in their present positions. I am not prepared to order their withdrawal to Bwera and Nyabrongo, and of course they will resist if they are subjected to any attacks.

I am sending Onama, the Minister of Works & Labour, as my personal representative to Kasese tomorrow. I hope that in view of the standstill order on operations which I have given, Mukirane will be prepared to set out his proposals. I will arrange for an officer to be at the footbridge at Isango from 1400 hours tomorrow, Friday, and very much hope that you will be able to come down with Mukirane's proposals to meet him there. If Mukirane himself would like to come with you, I hereby guarantee that he will receive safe conduct, and will not in any way be detained or molested.

At your first meeting at Isango, I hope that you will be able to arrange a meeting with Onama which Mukirane would attend under safe conduct at some place (possibly Isango) convenient to all sides. At this second meeting discussions could be opened on Mukirane's proposals.

If these discussions prove fruitful, I could myself arrange to come up to Busongora on Tuesday to continue the negotiations with Mukirane.

You should assure Mukirane that no-one regrets the present violence in Toro more than I do. I well know that the Bakonjo and Baamba have grievances, and my Government is most anxious to consider them. But the first requirement before any negotiation or discussion on these matters can proceed is a return to peace in the area, and I hope that Mukirane will be prepared to enter discussions which I now propose in this spirit.

I need hardly say that the contents of this letter - which you may show to Mukirane - are most strictly secret.

Yours Sincerely,

Milton Obote
PRIME MINISTER

xix

'Try again to come back...'

We embraced, he puffed and perspiring, beaming all over his Christian face. He had been ascending with all speed since daybreak, taking circuitous paths to avoid the military. From a pocket of the ruin of his jacket he produced two envelopes, one which had 'OHMS' blackened out, Her Majesty having quit the Ugandan scene, and 'On Uganda Government Service' overprinted. Its contents were electrifying. In it, the Prime Minister (Obote) told me he had given instructions to Cheyne for an immediate halt to operations, though troops would retaliate if attacked. He was sending his Minister of Internal Affairs, Felix Onama, to Kasese at once, and an officer would be waiting for me at the footbridge where my ascent had begun 'at 14.00 tomorrow' to take me, furnished with Isaya's 'proposals' to talk with the Minister. 'Tomorrow' was today, and it was already just about  14.00 hours. (They were underestimating these foothills.) If I could get Isaya to accompany me, the letter said, his safe conduct was guaranteed. And if discussion with Onama were to be fruitful, Obote himself would come to Busongora two days later to conclude a lasting settlement of Bakonzo grievances.

Well, well, well. On the instant I wrote to Isaya with all my exhortationary skills, that without a minute's delay he should meet me at the Tako border river crossing, and descend with me to conclude a triumphant settlement with the seat of constituted power. There was a tide, I more or less said, in the affairs of men which taken at the flood leads on to fortune. Brave Batulomayu would not wait for food, and pocketing my letter with that copy of

Obote's to me addressed courteously to Isaya, off he went across and up to Isaya in the company of (at my bidding) Ibrahimu, the Rwenzururu President's brother-in-law who would be hard put to keep up with the fleet Bat. I sat down under the scarlet flowers at the bend in the track to read Cheyne's letter. This of course was white-to-white.

I congratulate you – it is good to know you and I wish you well. I got your letter at 0755 and I had it in the hands of the P.M. at 1130 hrs; now here I am back at Bwera writing to you at 1630 hrs. [So he had flown in himself with the letter] – I say this not only to show you that I am taking this all very seriously but also so that you can tell Mukirane that the Uganda Rifles are fairly efficient!

I hope very much that you and Isaya Mukirane will come to the R/V at Isango tomorrow. I will have an Officer there w.e.f. 1400 hrs. at the footbridge and he will stay there all night. As soon as you arrive he will let me know and I will come and see you and discuss the next move. I give you my assurance Mukirane is completely safe in my hands and in those of the Uganda Rifles. It will be best if he can come; it will save time and I believe in the long run will make liaison etc. much easier, and I am convinced he will benefit by coming.

As regards the army and its ops. I am ordering all ops to cease NOW. This will take time to get around but should be effective by midnight. Anyway I am sending your messenger back with a safe conduct pass and he can use it for you on the return journey. I will *not* follow him!

May I add some caution about underestimating my askaris? It wd be a mistake if this happened as Mukirane might overplay his hand. At present we are playing in accordance with the British Book of rules. We will continue to do so but this is Africa and do you not think the rules might not change? This Bn – 4th K.A.R. – had the highest MAU MAU heads to its name in the Kenya emergency and they are as tough as hell. It has a name in E.A. which noone can rival and it has many men in it with first class jungle experience. I do not want to suggest that we wd be bound to be successful in the end but we could make life unbearable for the poor Bakonjo and virtually prevent Isaya M. from exercising much control or influence. Even on this op. they have been to places which I doubt if you will credit. Still I do not want to brag but things are never straightforward in Africa and it would be an error to underestimate Uganda Askaris.

Your comforts box is with your messenger; please return the haversack in due course.

My askaris will fight back if attacked BUT NOT OTHERWISE. If you get into a scrape shout 'MIMI BWANA MKUBWA RAFICKI'.

Look after yourself and remember I'm here to help and here to provide all the facilities for you and I. Mukirane to meet the 'right people'. Rest assured the matter has the highest priority. Beware of security; please ensure you do not let on to anyone outside I.M. what is happening: if you do, all will be to naught.

Yours ever
Bill Cheyne.

'Things are never straightforward in Africa'. Indeed, not by the British Book of Straightforwardness. A *PS* adjusted the rendezvous expectation to a time beginning the following morning at 10 a.m. I dashed off a couple of letters each to Cheyne and to Felix Onama, the Interior Minister, to say that it would be Saturday at the earliest before I could make the rendezvous. This I entrusted to the stalwart Doogulas. The wait began. It would last Isaya's lifetime.

I descended to the Tako. It had rained and gotten slippery. 'It is a second England,' reiterated Seylversta, who knew England to be a rainy place, and cold, and wanted me to feel at home. I knew no English dell like this high tropical ravine. Across the stream it was a haunted grove, to judge from the leaf-swathed pots put out for hungry spirits. I came to see this was no grove to hang around in. I re-ascended to Kituti to make a fire and brew tea. Khavaïru's son Kule the smith had joined us. Towards nightfall a dishevelled Ibrahimu appeared among us, to report that he had reached the cave which Isaya had been using the past four days only to find he had retreated higher into the mountains with his family, Isaleri, Khavaïru and Fanehasi Kisokeronio. Batulomayu had continued undaunted to deliver his letters. Minutes later another messenger entered. This was young Masereka, a Rwenzururu askari and member of Isaya's personal guard. He had a letter in the presidential hand.

This was black-to-white.

My dear Tom.
Rwenzururu visitor.
I am glad to inform you that we are
still on the way to the Rwenzururu
Farthest Private Cave.
It will be taking time to pass
Message from the Uganda Prime Minister
Mr. Stacey to the President Isaya M. Mukirane
Rwenzururu Uhuru.
President Isaya M. Mukirane
Rwenzururu.

When I was sleeping in this hut eight-and-a-half years previously I had used that same word, Cave. Now it was more vault than cave. I crawled in. The creepered thatch impenetrable and earth walls had been drawn by the ground beneath to its bosom. The thatch had itself become a stratum of life, seeding its own garden of flowering weeds, cryptogamia, climbers, creepers, and turning to soil by the deposits of lizards and rats, now re-aroused by human presence after five or six days' abandonment. The skins, cobs, fascicles, gourds, potions, pots and implements, shelved or dangling, were within our hands' reach, should we have been corpses buried there in a crouching position. On chief Khavaïru's bamboo bedframe, like a catafalque, I stretched in the damp smoke of our cooking fire and dreamt dead-ends and lost causes.

He was 'glad to inform' me, he had written, so I would be glad to wait, here in this second England. He was glad to be going up, and inwards, into his very own, inaccessible, Private, Konzo mode of being, having been momentarily tempted down, and outwards – if only by means of messages, couriers, proposals, protests, and apparent intentions – into the deceptively accessible, public world of Babylonial post-colonial *realpolitik* and statecraft. So at dawn I rose and perfunctorily washed and brewed, sensing but not seeing the sun rise beyond the cold fog that clamped us; and the first true signal of human reassertion among our minute cluster of habitance was the limpid notes of a flute coming from behind the vault-hut. A lanky spastic boy emerged into the compound with his fashioned reed that was part of himself, his fist-eloquence, handling and stroking his world beyond the reach of his fingers or the powers of his rheumy eyes or his crippled tongue. Since the flight of his fellows, days earlier, he had been hiding up with his flute in a nearby clump of trees. I guessed it was our smoke that had drawn him out of hiding, since any soldiers' open fire would have risen otherwise than ours, filtering through the warm slopes of damp thatch. The flute of this simpleton Krishna restored our hearts. One of the young askaris, Yofesi, had set about repairing the shattered ekhinanga-harp.

Of course I did what was required of me – despatching young Masereka down to Isango with letters to the Minister and Cheyne explaining the predicament. Masereka was all muscle and energy, and moreover in love – with one of Khavaïru's daughters, for whose dowry he was thieving Batoro goats whenever the opportunity arose, rather as young David thieved Palestinian foreskins to win King Saul's daughter Michal. Masereka would be gone a full day or more. Gradually our presence here – specifically, I supposed, that of myself, making for a kind of communal protection on account of the colour of my skin and my secret pass-cry – drew back members of the old community: an older wife of Khavaïru, coming to kneel in greeting after my years of absence, the chief's elder brother, striken with a cavernous ulcer to the very bone of his thigh, which I attempt to disinfect and bandage; Masereka's young bride, jut-breasted, callipygian, stumping to and fro between the huts, putting everything back in its proper place, fetching faggots, water, plantains, winding and re-winding the cloth around her loins as she passed. And likewise the sounds multiplied, of the women sweeping, cracking firewood, peeling plantains, mortaring cassava. The cock was back on the old hut's sagged thatch, and had got a lizard; the covetous hen had joined him, but flapped back to earth when she realized her chicks could not follow her. Men came in from neighbouring spurs. They had encountered the Uganda Riflemen, Keefe's patrol, but were spared by providing a goat for slaughter. I tested their view as to the citizenship of Uganda or of Rwenzururu and learned what I already knew: they had *never* supposed themselves citizens of Uganda... Quite late, some hours into darkness, a flurry of fresh voices outside in the compound told of the return of Masereka, in the company of Doogulas. I was invited by Cheyne in a note to descend as soon as I could, to see the Minister and review the options.

This, then, I did, the day following, in the company of my Bakonzo gang. Strength was returning to my legs, and breath to my lungs. At Isango I confabulated earnestly with that big warm bear from West Nile, the Honourable Felix Onama, Home Secretary, as we would say in England. We worked out all that the Konzo could in all reason constitutionally wish for, removing the yoke of Toro, to all intents and purposes; opening opportunities for Konzo advancement; enhancing the tribe's cash-crop farmers' economic prospects; the spreading of schools and medical care; the release of prisoners – all of this contingent upon Isaya's full co-operation with this prospective 'agreement'. The Prime Minister must, naturally ratify it, and the tribe be sounded...

For two more days I heard nothing more from Isaya. I spent the days building links with the lowland Konzo in and around Bwera and Isango, northwards into the foothills and westwards to Mpondwe and the populous Congo border along the lower Tako, where as near as nothing I was snatched as a 'spy' by the appalling Tonton Macoutes of the Congolese gendarmerie – Bangala thugs in dark glasses and sideburns. I had innocently stumbled on the smuggling racket in Ugandan coffee and Congo beer the gendarmes were operating at the road border. I began to build up a

Konzo base of co-operative members of the tribe's intelligentsia. These included my old friend, the teacher Blasio Maate; Ibrahimu Linkoni/Abraham Lincoln; and Samwiri Mutoro, yet another schoolmaster, of fully Konzo provenance, his name notwithstanding, a figure of diffident solidity who grasped at once the significance for his tribal fellows of what was in the offing and what could be forfeited if Isaya played intransigent. This Samwiri had earlier been kidnapped by Isaya's chosen raiders, including our Masereka, carried to the mountains, made to 'recant' as Isaya's trembling guest, and then re-deposited at his lowland school on a pledge of future unwavering loyalty. Ibrahimu and Seylversta were full of quips that any sign of less than 100 per cent devotion to Rwenzururu and Samwiri would be re-kidnapped by this same Masereka here with us and submitted to some fresh ordeal of terror.

They were life-and-death quips. Samwiri's diffidence was justifiable fear. Here in the lowlands, those Konzo who held positions of trust and authority where the writ of the Toro police still ran or the army held sway lived between a rock and a hard place. Rwenzururu loyalists (our Masereka among them) had half-killed Ezironi Bwambale, MP. Bakonzo or Banyabindi collaborators, albeit a rare breed, were coldly executed: Fanehasi would see to that. When Samwiri had returned to Bwera from his abduction and attended the next Rwenzururu gathering at a neighbour's house, Toro police placed on him a home curfew from which I was obliged to obtain for him a formal release. Such a dilemma dogged certain lowland Konzo. A year later, my old friend Ibrahimu Linkoni was appointed chief for the Bwera sub-county by the District Officer, Ray Cordery (a survivor from the Colonial era). It was not difficult for voices to persuade his brother-in-law Isaya Mukirane to suspect him of acknowledging the authority of Toro of which his office was a part. A Rwenzururu hit squad was despatched from the hills to visit him in his home where, quelling his struggles, they severed the tendons of his right hand with a Konzo razor to immobilize it permanently. In behaving thus, Isaya's Rwenzururu was betraying itself; doubting its own authority.

Meanwhile I took my message of reconciliation back to the Tako border, upstream from the frontier post on the road. I was now joined by Blasio Maate, my comrade to this very day, and two further fellow schoolteachers of his. I called through the vegetation in Lukonzo: *Rwenzururu shall be won by peace!* I would glimpse my hearers, mouths agape, interrupting their chewing of sugar cane, uncertain whether to run or approach. At length a great throng of lowland refugees assembled beyond the Tako's busy waters – thirty feet of river – to hear what word this Mzungu was carrying. My Konzo companions billed me with the honorific Isaya had bestowed on me, musabuli, saviour (or, more comfortably 'rescuer'), who had reappeared more or less miraculously at this fraught juncture. These were nearly all strangers to me, though some had rumours of my association with Isaya. A big crowd – several hundred – had assembled across the stream to hear me, and Seylversta likened the scene to Jesus putting out into the Galilean Lake in a boat to address the shore-bound multitude. At first my own little band of loyalists would cajole them to advance and listen, since here was Musabuli come from across the seas. As I was translated phrase by phrase, disputes concerning my message broke out along the rim of the throng. I grew fearful we would ruin our simple cause. Some of the men were making gestures of contempt, shoving off our words with their hands. (Thirty-five years later, within a few hundred yards of that place, my audience was greater – perhaps 20,000. Then it was easier: no shooing of hands, no rim disputes. A different enemy sat in the front row of easy chairs.)

Then the next day we had gone up to the Kitolu again, the frontier of the sanctuary. We were a party of six or seven then. Folk had begun cautiously to return to their homesteads. Word of peace was trickling out: if it was a man we met, we would be loaded with gratitude. This peace was our new gift. I would respond, *Nai ngwete evitsange* – 'I am happy too'... All this time it was Batulomayu Kasiraho I was awaiting – the bearer of Obote's letter to Isaya to which as yet there was no answer. Surely he could not descend without passing this way?

Yet he could! Here was the flash of Daneeri's sky-blue pullover: once again we had touched the rebel core. Batolumayu had indeed passed on down that very morning, Daneeri told us, carrying two letters: one for me, one for Obote. There was nothing for it but to skelter back to Isango. This time I ran, colobus-skin flying, stickwork inspired. I was in canvas shoes now. I outstripped my Konzo. What had taken a day in the ascent took three hours in the descent. At the army's base I learned that Cheyne had just left for Fort Portal: Battalion headquarters had been pulled back that day. As to our messenger Batulomayu, no one in Isango had seen or heard of him. At Bwera I burst in upon the Mutoro saza-county chief who had returned to his office in a premature move to reclaim, if not his power, at least the seat of it. He had heard of me: that was unavoidable – I was the angel of this little peace, brokered on the presumption of reducing Toro authority. So I had to play down the purport of my intrusion: I was just locating a certain Mukonzo carrying a message from one chap to another. I withdrew with as much decorum as the situation permitted, and by now realizing Batulomayu could not be in Bwera, walked back north the few miles towards an Isango occupied by no more than a company of (potentially) hostile troops, under the command of an English major, a fellow old Etonian, and his formidably built Second-in-Command, the former King's African Rifles heavyweight boxing champion, Captain Idi Amin Dada. It was on the way to Isango, with the unexpectedness we had come to expect, that we ran into Batulomayu!

'Dear Batulomayu,' my diary tells, 'he was almost weeping with relief. For three days he had been carrying the letters from the Leader. Having at last reached the foot of the mountains he had become convinced that we had gone off to Fort Portal with the army, and had been in despair. I could see he had hardly washed since I last saw him. Forest mud caked his trousers.'

I sat down there beside the track while the others found food for our courier. The buff envelopes, stamped 'Rwenzururu* Bakonjo-Bamba' were respectively inscribed 'Mr Tom Stacey, Rwenzururu' and 'The Prime Minister Mr Obote Uganda Government'. The letters were identical, both directed to me, and not even signed by the man himself but by the slavish 'President's Private Secretary Rwenzururu' whose Christian name Yostasi (Eustace) shared the same root as my own family name. The mean missive read:

Mr. Tom Stacey,   Rwenzururu * Bakonjo-Bamba
                                        19th February, 1963.

Sir,

With reference to the Prime Minister's letter of 17th Feb. 1963. You are advised to go back and tell Mr. M. Obote-Prime Minister Uganda to remove his Military and all his Government officers from Rwenzururu Government which has no relationship with Uganda Government that has disturbed the country Rwenzururu referring to the letter 17th Nov 1962 addressed to Obote-Prime Minister Uganda.

Before you go back to England try again to come back and inform the President Isaya M. Mukirane Rwenzururu after removal of the Uganda Govt. Army which is now disturbing my country Rwenzururu!
Yours sincerely,
Yostasi Kule
President's Private Secretary Rwenzururu
Copy to: The Prime Minister-Uganda
My name and Obote's were each followed by a tick in red ink on our respective copies. The date was wrong. It was all *wrong*.

Stand back. Stand back these intervening decades. Had I forgotten where I had begun? Did I not *begin* in the mountains (on perusing Grandpa's atlas, with its rivers of dots), and from there descended by these raw rock nullahs, and farthest private caves, upon the quilted landscape, the habitance, laughter in the orchards, and the gurgle of streams? Had not I, explorer, entered on a boundless act of faith? Had not I sealed that self-same commitment, through the devotion of our legs and backs, in every weather, with this self-same Isaya on these very mountains?

Yet who was this now arriving back here out of the mapped lands, every yard of them ordnanced and surveyed, he so busy a body, on leave of absence from the proper world of affairs, of planned economies, white governance and the rest of it, impervious powers; a younger man of Milner's young men, Buchanesque, resourceful, in collusion with the self-appointed Good and statutory Great of the international scene? In less than nine brief years, what betrayal.

Before you go back to England try again to come back and inform the President Isaya M. Mukirane Rwenzururu... Rwenzururu, the mountain core-land, the impenetrable site of home, the sleeping Lord grown restive, the place of being, inner truth, the unnameable half-named, Brahma, Himalaya, Nzururu-snow, snow-deity, of which its people were keepers of behalf of all creation. This was *shrine*, in its own sweet right, the right of beauty and splendour and majesty and mystery, these carbon ranges, set mid-Africa, mid-universe, phenomenal, warranting priesthood, even these insignificant tribal folk, with their toytown political pretensions, who were covenanted to the place, whose authority in it was prior to any others', as guardians, interpreters, initiates, bound in fealty to the sanctity and the liberation thereof. This Isaya M. Mukirane, the ordained and temporary coherer of the territorial kingdom, was their *omusinga*, anointed head, *irema-ngoma*, throne-occupier, exemplar, putative definer of the indefinable, whom I – it could be said – had put up to the vision of it. I had begun here as *musabuli*, redeemer-figure; now it was he. I had first worn the colobus skin; now it was *his* fleece and the kingdom's. *Come back and inform...*

Today I read those words with such poignancy. *'Come back again and speak to me, hold my hand, the hand of Rwenzururu. Have you forgotten what we dreamed? Can you not see our country Rwenzururu?'* I see the blackened stubs of a smoking camp. I hear the liquid melisma of an idiot's flute...

I drove at once to Fort Portal, in a military vehicle. I conferred with Onama and Cheyne. A light plane, the Aztec, awaited me at the airstrip. It carried me to Jinja, beyond Kampala, on Lake Victoria, where I conferred with Obote. I flew back to Fort Portal, conferred further with Onama, flew back to Entebbe to see Obote for the third time, and gathered up a new, masterly letter, black to black... It was not in the end to be of much avail what I did or where I flew.

Back in Isango, I was reunited with my Konzo companions. I was fired anew, and fooled, not just by my own persuasiveness but that of Obote's second letter, in which the Premier had repeatedly referred to his own sensibility of Bakonzo grievances and to Isaya's 'great perseverance and undoubted love for the people affected'. It had opened the door upon the disassociation of the mountain people from Toro.

In a field above Isango my little team and I were to be fed for our next ascent by Captain Idi Amin. To provision his own men, the Major, Iain Grahame, had purchased the carcase of a hippo recently culled from Lake Edward by the Game Department. The beast had been flayed and butchered into bloody steaks which were roasting on open fires, one for each platoon, among the assembled men. Most of the men came from the savannah and bush of far northwestern Uganda where the hippo is not known, except as a half-mythic leviathan of the remote river. They were unwilling to touch this admirable source of protein. As a small price for feeding Ibrahimu, Seylversta, Masereka, Doogulas and myself, I agreed with Idi to accompany him on a short stroll through the seated rows of glum Other Ranks, each of us with a hunk of hippo liver in the hand, which we masticated with relish, congratulating one another on the excellence of this chop-chop. Our manoeuvre had little effect on the men, but it seeded a comradeship with Idi Amin whom I visit in exile to this day.

Isaya – so I picked up – had shifted his base to a village in Congo above the western Ruwenzori roadhead of Mutwanga. One option was to plunge into the Congo-side forest and seek him there. However, I knew there to be much agitation at the influx of tens of thousands of Ugandan Bakonzo among the villages of their Congolese tribal brothers, and months of witnessed horror in 1960 had left me wary of confronting Congolese in uniform. Moreover, I hoped to lure Isaya to a further meeting at a point as near as possible to the lowland Uganda borders of his domain, where he might dare or deign to descend for talk with Onama, or Onama might perhaps risk ascending to.

Isaya had already designated Fanehasi Bwambale to be my host on my return, and Fanehasi's spur, Ekobero, just south of Kitolu, to be my base. Or maybe Fanehasi had proposed himself, to keep watch on me. For Ekoberu we now set out. My acquaintance with this Phineas-Fanehasi had begun in 1954. He was then a strongly-built fellow of nineteen. My camera had caught him standing proudly aside from Khavaïru's endara, which was flooding the place with its sounds, as if there were better things to occupy young men than prattling music. He was a cold fellow, capable and ambitious. He was, moreover, a kinsman of Isaya's wife, Christine, through her father, Ruhandika's son. To that extent he began as an insider. A little schooling in the lowlands had led to a job on the Toro-Ankole bus-route, which gave him Swahili and a scrap of English. Now he had become Isaya's choice as Rwenzururu Chairman for the whole of Busongora, a formidable role, and he not yet thirty. He had a wife, of course, dearly bought, still childless after four years, and such lack of offspring made for a metaphysical voiding in any Bantu. Yet this Fanehasi had power. It had fallen to him to maintain the Konzo of this southern heartland in ideological conformity. He presided over, had perhaps been the instigator of, the duffing up of Ezironi Bwambale, MP, which outrage had precipitated the wrath of Uganda Rifles which had seen to the shattering of his territorial authority in a matter of days, his spearmen captured in droves, and his fellow uplanders become a rabble of refugees. Into this disaster I had entered – a bewildering irruption – brokering peace. Fanehasi was with his master, Irema-Ngoma Isaya Mukirane, at that moment of the arrival of the message in my cigar case. Surely his first response would have been intense suspicion, that this was a trap to lead the armed enemy into the very nest of the kingdom. Later, at my arrival at Bukuke, he may have seen a glint of truce, a space to re-group and reassess, and so had not demurred at Isaya's first letter, though he was not present at its drafting and final composition. What was a *letter*? What anyway was writing but abstraction? It was a bus-ticket. The vital thing now was for the Irema-Ngoma to be spirited out of my immediate reach and well distanced from any temptation to negotiate, and meanwhile to exploit the peace...

Yet even so Isaya had *personally* entreated me to return to him again. Fanehasi could not stop that.

Young still, narrow in the look and manner of him, giving away little under the cloak of studied courtesy, Fanehasi was always his own man. He would sometimes laugh, yet with no mirth. The smile was dry. His symbols of status were a pair of ochrous corduroys, and also George, bigger than he, a species of *aide-de-camp* and, in the manner of Isaya's Yostasi Kule, bearer of this Chairman's monkey-bag of papers, exercise books and ball points. He gave his George the run-around. He fed me well; I cured his diarrhoea. He never trusted me. Why should he? If ever I was to broker a deal between Isaya and Kampala, it would shatter the dream of Rwenzururu and evaporate on the instant his own remarkable authority throughout this vast territory. He was nothing much without Isaya's Rwenzururu. He had so lately come into his own. Already a nick-name had come to be attached to him, a kind of *nom-de-guerre*, 'Kisokeronio'. It described his mysterious ubiquity, which would indeed become legendary – a 'Pimpernel' reputation, which had the enemy ever guessing where he might materialize next. He began to adopt the sobriquet as his own – his 'Kisokeronio' to Isaya's Irema-Ngoma as Dugashvili's Stalin was to Ulyanov's Lenin. Fanehasi Bwambale Kisokeronio would see to it that I brokered nothing: Rwenzururu would stay.

So it was, for twenty years. By his own lights, he could not but block me: I concede him that. Yet before the first six or seven years were up, Fanehasi himself would become an outcast of the kingdom. Moreover, *to this day* he is a guerilla commander in the mountains, abductor and killer of many of his own Konzo, a brigand feared and abhorred by his fellow tribesmen and an indifferent violator of the mountains' sanctities. We shall return to him.

So, then: back to 1963. I brought Fanehasi into my confidence. With Ibrahimu translating, I sought to persuade him of the full and generous letter from Obote, proposing a lasting solution of which the pair of them could settle the details. I ran through with him the contents of my letter to Isaya. As soon as Batulomayu was on his way – he said it would be at least four days before he could be back, with or without Isaya – I proposed to Fanehasi that he escort Seylversta down to Isango with a note for delivery to Cheyne summarising the present situation. He complied.

All around us, the countryside was being peopled once again, families filing home from their refuge in the forested highlands and the Congo with vast panniers, driving their animals. We could tell which paths were in use again from the chewed cane fibres scattered on them. Each day I took a new arc of country, to tell forth our message of peace and compromise on favourable terms. Sometimes I slept as a guest of influential figures on their spurs. One of my hosts was Gerisoni Ndambireki, later to become the Kingdom's Minister for Natural Resources. A record from my diary recalls the mood. 'Everywhere our message is well received and understood. We are accompanied from compound to compound by fresh proselytes. My team is working superbly. Ibrahimu, the chief interpreter, is supported by Seylversta, and Doogulas and Masereka as porters, guides, messengers or heralds.

We mount to Bulemera, Masereka's home, and stumble on a group of Rwenzururu askaris in a misty glade engaged in a massive brew-up of banana beer to celebrate the return of their families. M[asereka] cannot bear to be separated from his fellows any longer; and when I send him on to Kituti with a small gift to Khavaïru (who I hear has also returned), he does not come back to me. Seylversta comments that he was like the disciple "who ran away when Jesus was being tried". I counter that neither I nor our views are on the way to crucifixion.' Yet in a manner of speaking, I was mistaken. It was easy, then, for a white man in Africa to presume that his admirable good sense was grasped and his practical advice would be followed; to this day he deludes himself.

At Ekoberu, Fanehasi plied us with the good things of his cultivation plots and orchards. His little wife killed, plucked and boiled for us the best of his chickens. From Ekobera I was going forth daily to preach a gospel of compromise. We were joined by an emissary of the Rwenzururu Chairman of Bunyangabo, a certain Twalibu, who had walked sixty miles through the foothills to reach us. I supposed myself to be making headway. Obote's second letter was snug in my pocket. Then one midday at a solemn gathering in a sunlit compound I caught sight of an untidy head over the top of the grasses, approaching at a fast walk. Half-caked in mud, from Ebulema, deep in Congo, through mile upon mile of game-haunted forest, wonder-eyed and pent in anticipation of this very reunion, Batulomayu was among us, bringing a letter, dated March 3rd. It read:

Mr. Tom Stacey,
England U.K.   3rd March, 1963.
My dear Tom,

Referring to the letter dated 23rd February 1963 addressed to Mr. Obote-Batooro Uganda Government, a copy to you Mr. Stacey.

I haven't understood why you didn't send the Obote's document to my through Mr. Batulomayu Kasirahwa Rwenzururu runner.

If the document was not addressed to me you are advised to take it back to Mr. Obote-Batooro Uganda Government which has no right to discuss with me privately. The matter is put into the hands of the United Nations Organisation referring to my document of 19th Feb. 1963, addressed to Mr. Uthant – Secretary General of the United Nations, a copy to you too.

Batooro Uganda Government officials have different plans which you are advised to be aware of, if not they may turn you into Judas that may destroy your friendship between Rwenzururu Kingdom, referring to your letter of 1st March 1963.
Yours sincerely,
President Isaya M. Mukirane.
Rwenzururu.

Copies to:
Rwenzurururu Government Supporters
       "   "   Police Force
Mr. Obote-Batooro Uganda Government.

Lest I grow to be Judas, whose end was sticky, I should set off without delay to whatever remote reach of the Congo Isaya had set up his court, to deliver my letter with all the privacy it deserved, eschewing megaphones and U Thant and all that. I consulted with my present rump of *élite:* They agreed. We set off at daybreak the next morning, and Fanehasi presented me with four eggs, a dozen oranges and limes and two paw-paws. Seylversta commented, 'God says we should love one another. So is Mr Fanehasi following the words.' I guess Fanehasi knew I would fail. He accompanied me for half a mile along the track, mounting northwards, as Konzo custom says.

We were the same few plus Batulomayu and a firm-footed, thick-thighed yokel who gamely stood there to be loaded with whatever we chose to heap on him. It was my intention to cut straight across to Isaya's new Congo camp, or his Farthest Private Cave, wherever it was, up there, over there, north-westwards. All our while at Ekobero and Kitolu, the 'God, King' weather-spirit Kitasamba had been playing up in that direction; glowering. I knew that this would have affected Isaya's mood. In Rwenzururu proper, church and state were instinctually indivisible.

Our route took us anyway through Kituti. I saw at once that the little compound was busy with life. Naked totos were outlined against the fire through the entrance to the first hut. The old women were back, smoking and chewing. Calabashes of banana beer from the Great Bulemera Brew-up were stacked against Khavaïru's own hut. Smoke seeped through my old rat-hut's slumped thatch. Only the endara key-beams lay neglected, scattered and slimy under their tree. The place was, as ever, gloomy and tree-locked; only the irrepressible physique of Masereka's betrothed, emerging from the vault-cave of the rat-hut, defied subjection to her father's sullen magic.

Khavaïru himself was all at once at our side. He looked bleary and hung-over. The two of us settled down by his hut wall while I described all that had taken place since I had last seen him. I invited him to accompany me on to the presence of Isaya. He left the proposal hanging, and sent Kule, his eldest, to fetch an ember from one of the women's fires in the other huts to light his long-stemmed pipe. He did not want me to go on to Ebulema, he said.

I said, Why?

Because I was too valuable to the Bakonzo people, he answered. I should not be casually lost. The Congolese were a law to themselves. If it was necessary for someone to go to persuade Isaya back to this side of the frontier, then he, Khavaïru, would go himself.

I allowed a silence. Which of us would have the better chance? The chief, certainly, if he was convinced of the rightness of it. This was Buswagha clan country; this was the seminal site of the idea and the movement. Isaya could hardly deny Khavaïru.

I said, Kituti would not be Kituti until I heard the endara again.

In the remaining daylight we cut fresh plantain stems on which to lay the regathered keys, cleansed and hard-edged again. The place trembled with music anew. Next day he set off, at dawn, in his prehistoric hat and camel hair coat. I entrusted to him a letter for Isaya. *'This is the last letter I shall write to you until I see you.'* I sent Seylversta to accompany him, so that I might know what transpired if Isaya did not come. Thank heaven, Seylversta had abandoned his snobby boots. He had in his bundle a copy of *Three Men in a Boat* which he had found in my pack – a novel to which he had become attached. He was convinced he had met in Kampala the character, William Samuel Harris, mentioned on the first page.

I stayed for a while in Kituti because of the sick who came, or I was led to, sometimes infants whose skin was so loose over the tiny bones that if displaced it did not readily return but merely slithered back. All I had was codeine, iodine and malarial prophylactics. I was too old a hand to make as to cure what I could not cure. In normal times there was a dispensary at Bwera, operated by a Mutoro. I was striving for that kind of normality. After a day or so I went back to Kitolu so that, if Isaya were to come, it would be a little lower. And there at Kitolu now was Isaleri. He took me in like a son. Here is my record of him then:

'He is a man of endowed wisdom who seems never to have been young. I feel him to be no older than when I was his guest 8 years ago. He is different from all the others, in his deep and monkish voice, his huge, patient eyes, and his unkempt hair, woolly, not frizzy like the others. His hair and low brow above those ox eyes give him the air of an ancient icon: one of the elect of God.'

Our days began and ended with prayers, Isaleri presiding, Batulomayu the half-brother reciting. We prayed for the good estate of all men, and for Rwenzururu, the principle. Jesus was a Rwenzururian from ages past. The strength of the hills was His also. In the evenings, we also sang hymns, led by Batulomayu in his thin rattle of a voice. They were plodding, Lutherish hymns, first written out, surely, in square breves in four-line staves. Sometimes we sang similar, Rwenzururu anthems – of the reach of our land, the height of it, its fastness, its industry, its foison, its forges and manufactures, its victories.

> Now we can see (here) Musabuli who caused to be withdrawn
> Uganda Rifles askaris from our land, Rwenzururu.
> Mukirane summons all the people of Rwenzururu.

I was the *musabuli* referred to. I and Isaya were likewise pantheoned. Yet there was discord in Olympus.

Deputations paid court. Fanehasi flitted by, re-weaving his web as the spurs re-populated. Primitives came from the forest perimeter and Congo-side, to see their first white. A blind flautist was led across through the fog from three spurs away, seeing me with all his other senses, and let me search out a mzungu melody on his reed. I advanced my Lukonzo grammar that crowded my notebook. On the third evening I crossed the compound and walked down through the scent of the cypresses.

It was a superb outlook, the smoke of bush fires twenty miles southward and below, on the plainland dividing the massifs, our Ruwenzori and Rwanda's Rutshuru. All was luminous in the low sun, the entire green plain aglow, as also the surface of the boundless lake disappearing southeast. Where the hippos dipped, circles of ripples went out and made water bailiwicks. For the benefit of any watcher, the brazen mass of the sun dipped into dense black cloud-mountains, piled on Rutshuru's earth-mountains.

On the fourth morning, very soon after dawn, an arrival and a voice. 'Mr Isaya has come.' Through the hut's entrance, I glimpse the ochrous corduoys.

'Ah, Fanehasi. Good. He is here?'

'He is at Kituti.'

I emerged to take Fanehasi Kisokeronio by the arm. 'We shall all go to Kituti together.'

271

XX

The Dark Side of Love

'Things are never straightforward in Africa,' Bill Cheyne had written to me. On that same skyline on the ridge below Kituti where I was first confronted by the Praetorian Guard stood another group, among whom I spotted Khavaïru and Seylversta. Once more in his snobby boots, Seylversta was looking as if about to be called up by the headmaster in front of the whole school to receive the prize for having come top of everything.

I congratulated them both briskly. It was then that I learned Isaya was not at Kituti after all, but across the Tako valley – and the frontier – at Bukuke. And *there*, said a wiry fellow in Wellington boots and a pink windcheater stolen on a raid, he was awaiting me.

I said what I thought in five words, and marched on up past the flowering tree to Kituti compound. Reading anger in my step, the idiot boy started up and came weaving towards me to pacify. I found a stool. I had Seylversta find me a 'reading book' from my pack. I would stay there content with my book, and with the Prime Minister's letter, until the Emperor Isaya chose to cross the valley. Various of them came to me in consternation. They included those of distinction – Blasio Maate, school teacher; Samwiri Mutoro; Emilio Kibingo, ex-member of the Rukurato, Kabarole's Parliament; Johnny Bisika, school teacher. All in their shoes, ties, jackets-over-the-arm, briefcases. I was brought to speech.

'What sort of a leader is this, who does not approach to within a full day's march from the enemy?' An enemy which had in any case declared a truce.

A while passed. A two-man deputation approached from across the valley. From the edge of the compound they delivered their verbal message. The Kibanzanga welcomed my return. He requested me very kindly to join him at Bukuke to read the letter I am carrying for him.

I reminded the messengers that Rwenzururu was to be built on this side of the border: I regarded myself as a servant of the Konzo people, not of Isaya Mukirane. If Mukirane considered it his task to serve the Bakonzo, that service would presumably take place on their own territory. The two departed with sounds in their ear of approval of my quaint counter-stubborness.

Time passed. The next to reappear was Wellingtons and pink windcheater. This Yeremiah stamped up and saluted. From his pocket he extracted a piece of paper. On it was careful pencilling.

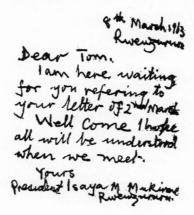

8th March 1963
Rwenzururu

Dear Tom,
I am here waiting for you refering to your letter of 2nd March. Well Come I hope all will be understood when we meet.
Yours
President Isaya M Mukirane
Rwenzururu.

This fragment caught me unawares. It echoed so poignantly the last note addressed to me, eight years previously stuck in a stick at Ibanda on my descent from the heights, minutes ahead of my collapse from malaria –*Well come Mr Musabuli. I am in omutaka Bwambale's house 50 yards to right. I am waiting you with pleasure.* Even now as I re-tell this moment nearly 38 years later I pause bare-headed for such a friend, such friendship.

'Where is he now?' I was beyond bluff and bombast.

Yeremiah said he was descending to the Tako where the log bridged the busy water.

I took Daneeri and Khavaïru and Yeremiah. I led – it was an old descent for me, half a mile, through the cassava, through the plantains, into the tongue of primal forest, the relative darkness and secrecy. At the straddling tree there was no Isaya. I said to myself, it was further for him to come down from Bukuke; I would wait. Part of me was weeping. I sat on the log, Uganda side, away from the haunted glade on the Congo side where the snake had died. I filled my water bottle. The tail of my colobus pelt trailed in the current. The water tumbling here, secret crossing point between two countries – one colonized from the Atlantic, one from the Indian ocean – would flow eventually into the Mediterranean. At this dark place the continent pivoted.

I waited. The pink Yeremiah had long gone on up, Seylversta with him. By mid-afternoon uncertain weather was breaking northwards, lightning flicked, Kitasamba rattled drums. I called Khavaïru and Daneeri to their feet, and entered on the ignominious ascent. Since a couple of roast maize cobs at breakfast I had eaten nothing that day. It was wickedly steep. Northwards, this forest tongue spread into greater forest and ranged eighty miles to circle the peaks; and to the west it ran all the way down the flank of Ruwenzori to merge into the Ituri, the greatest forest in all Africa. At some point, still in forest, here was Syelversta bouncing down the track, to spur me into this last...futility. 'He is now waiting for you in all hopes!'

Oh, good Seylversta, Sylvester Mukirane Manyumba, you Christian man, where did you gather up your villainish Victorian name? I do not recall a Sylvester (for you have regularized the spelling now) in biblical writ. Yet you surely are, and always were, a biblical man. (You are widowed now, and three sons not yet through their education, and have found a good widow to assuage your loneliness.) You would always seek the will of God in this vale of woe, even the dark steep forest cleft of the valley of the Tako. What was the will of God? What is it still? Was it that I half-smeared in outer mud and inner sweat, short on dignity and stripped of racial presence, should emerge from the dark and inwardness of the border canyon into the light of cultivated land, patches of yams and millet, plantains and cassava and lower hutments, and wilfully refrain from raising my gaze to the clear summit of the ridge? Out of the top of my eyes I could not but be aware of the outlined huts and a squat figure standing on the edge of the compound for my arrival. All chatter had stopped. When at the last instant I did look up at Isaya, there on his mouth was the beginning of a mischievous-apologetic smile. Five weeks earlier, I would have it recalled, Nikita Krushchev had awaited me in the Kremlin for mankind to be suitably informed as to what answers he might have to my questions on the future of the world.

I shook his hand. 'Isaya, I do not do this for you, I do it for the Bakonjo.'

I would release his hand, but he would not let mine go.

'We are glad.' There was a play of nerves in the surface of his face – on brow and upper lip; and the hard weight of the lids. 'I wait and wait for Musabuli.'

Let me now be brief. I have described in moderate detail elsewhere (though I was a little blind, then) what ensued in the following

274

three to four hours – the two stools out in the compound, Isaya from time to time reaching for his stick to fold both hands over the horizontal handle, the gang of adherents to one side (Fanehasi Kisokeronio, his heavy George, Khavaïru, Kinyamusitu, Masereka, Yeremiah, Daneeri, certain other askaris); my view of the mood of Uganda's government; of the relative goldenness of the opportunity to receive favourable terms for the Bakonzo-Baamba; how I had declined to deliver Isaya's last letter to Obote because of its irrational incompatibility with the previous letter; the unveiling of Obote's present letter; the exegesis of its content; its magnanimity; how he, Isaya, must accompany me this very day on the descent for Isango so as to reach there on the morrow; how his attendance there would secure the release of hundreds of Bakonzo prisoners; how his own safe passage there *and back* would be guaranteed; how I was brought a meal, quite early in the proceedings, of a basket of boiled plantains and was left to eat alone, according to Konzo custom; how within the impenetrable cloud upon the heights behind us, lightning persistently darted. When at times he put the stick aside I sensed a marginally increased readiness to listen. Now he reached for it again.

Fanehasi, in his corduroys, sat ever so slightly detached from the rest.

Isaya stood. The phase of intimacy and English, was done. The little assembly gathered. Isaya addressed them. Seylversta rendered for me in English whatever I feared I might not be following. In his address I received compliments for my work for the Bakonzo-Baamba. The origins of the proposal for talks with Kampala were outlined. I waited for his relaying of the offer indicated in Obote's careful letter. It did not come. I heard him veering: what would all the local leaders of Rwenzururu throughout the mountains think of his entering negotations? What would be the view of Kawamara and Mupalya (both of them still in prison)? I saw the conclusion looming: that before he entered *any* talks, he must first engage in what would prove scarcely possible, namely protracted consultations with his own side.

'How can we tell if a meeting [as proposed by Obote, and me] would help Rwenzururu? Unless we have discussed it with all our leaders everywhere? First, we ourselves shall talk. Then we will say if we shall talk with Uganda Batoro Government!'

A collective *eeay* confirmed him in his circular sagacity. The heavy head of the old one with the deep ulcer in his thigh, Khavaïru's elder half-brother, rocked stupidly back and forth.

If a cudgel might convince, I would have taken to it. In the event, I laid out my stall of reason and narrative. The old one crept up to squat at my feet; someone gave a push to a plantain stem for his rump to rest on. He looked up to me with sagged eyes like a dying hound. Fanehasi, to my left, remained at one side, very still, and cold about the eyes.

I said I could probably arrange for Kawamara and Mupalya to be brought to any negotiations. If anyone needed firmer assurance of Isaya's own safe conduct to a conference in Isango, then they could hold me here as hostage against his return. You have to go and learn for yourself what can be obtained for the acceptance of Rwenzururu before you have anything for the other leaders to decide upon, I said.

Isaya jumped up. 'We cannot agree!'

How one's heart can become lead in the chest.

'Can we agree?' He turned to his dumb claque.

I tried to explain anew. Then –

'Shall we crawl before them?'

He was so quickly hot; buckled by the strain.

I said, 'You will be making your last mistake.'

'I am not making a mistake,' he returned in English. 'I did not make a mistake going to Ebulema [his Congo hide-out].'

We were spiralling into verbal brawl; the downward spiral. At a petty *impasse*, I resumed my stool. He too sat. The option of drawing a revolver, such as I had worn hidden at my crutch on various previous assignments, and of cutting short this entire fantasy by blowing out his brains, flickered at me speculatively. Oh yes: it flickered. Kampala would have thanked me, perhaps postumously. I took his hand in mine. 'Politics,' I reminded him in the old adage which once used to tickle him so, 'is the art of the possible.' I was telling myself the same thing. Maybe if he would give his word that he would see Onama this week and came with me as far as Kitolu, we could each perhaps arrange preliminary conferences with the deputation – the sixth form – already waiting just across the ravine.

'We prefer to die,' he said.

Nothing remained this side of reason. There was only the ancient comradeship wrung dry. The light was beginning to go. Protruding from the thatch of a hut below, atop a little pole, I noticed a device of wood comprised of a flattened stick bisected by a shorter, fat stick. Eight years before I had seen such a thing, and when I had bullied Isaya with questions if it was a weather vane had found him evasive. Look back at page 141. Now, from above, I could see it was the simulacrum of an airplane, and that what had troubled him then was that a grown Konzo householder might seem to have been childish...

He was sitting bolt upright, the presidential beardlet yanked down by finger and thumb its inch and his obsessed eyes thrusting from his head. When ever so lightly I pressed him for a response to my suggestion he began to rave, 'We cannot fear them! They cannot hurt us,' the neck clenched, voice falsetto. 'We do not recognise them! We shall rule them!... We shall send them from Kampala. They [may] come to crush us with atomic bombs. These bombs, we do not have them yet.' The irritation of reality was brushed aside.

It was almost dark now. Khavaïru and Daneeri had quit for the other side of the valley. But Isaya's raised voice had brought others from neighbouring huts. He turned to confront me. There was no holding him.'They have atomic bombs in their aeroplanes!' (He meant the spotter plane, that little Aztec that ran me to and fro.) 'We shall die. Bomb them! We cannot speak to them!' He was addressing anyone and everyone in earshot. An oil lantern joined us on the compound, and he went on raving. (Where was his Jesus now?) 'Why should we meet at Isango?... We shall make them climb.' A chuckle came from Fanehasi.

'Let us not restrict the borders of Rwenzururu,' I said. 'Isango is Rwenzururu.'

I reached for his arm, which went stiff, but he did not throw off my light grip. I drew him back to sit on the stool alongside. The stream of fantasy resumed – Obote crawling up the mountains, U Thant blitzing Kampala. The pupils of his eyes had dilated to obliterate the whites. I had no choice but to challenge the absurdity of his notions, to show him deranged in the presence of his devotees. I would isolate him now, as best I could, so as still to be of some service to his people. I found the Lukonzo for mad – *omusire* – 'dotty'; yet *alikwebirimu*, 'possessed', would have been more apt. It was a risk to myself, that insult. I sensed the shock of

277

its use, and my own encircling of alienation.

It was cold now. He had disappeared into the hut which had been my sleeping quarters here. I called after him that I would spend the night in Kituti, and that he could still join me on the morrow. I heard a voice from the other side of the wall: 'I cannot think to write,' misunderstanding me. I picked up a staff – not the one I brought but the first that came to hand – and was off into the descending path.

Seylversta was beside me, afraid. I had no light – nothing but the stars. I could not presume to take with me any others.

The two of us had just entered the pitch blackness of the forest, where the land began to fall away steeply, when I heard a clatter beind me, and – accosting me – was Masereka, and with him Fanehasi's George. Did they suppose I would not have found my way? Even with Masereka's instinct and intimacy with the forest route tracks, we crossed the Tako, elsewhere than the straddling tree-trunk, wading.

The danger of forests at night is to a walker's eyes. The danger of arriving by night at a sleeping place where war is in the offing is to be mistaken for enemy. Was I enemy now – this busted Prospero?

xxi

From Presidency to Kingship

Close upon midnight at Kituti top. A chorus of dogs; light was visible through the walls of Khavaïru's main hut. Figures emerged from it because of the dogs, before we ourselves called. What met us was not hostility but alcohol, not spearheads but Kule's absurd nose gone more bonkers and uptilted by banana booze. The whole sixth form of southern Busongora, plus Twalibu from Bunyangabo, had sat up awaiting us, warned by Khavaïru of the auguries of the Bukuke confrontation, warmed by his beer. A calabash of liquor was in my hand almost at once, hot yams were before me in a leaf on a basket; baked plantains in a clay bowl. Khavaïru himself materialized from his own dark to squat on a tiny antique of a stool not six inches off the earth.

I retailed it all. I made us, ourselves, the flagship of reason, still with an opportunity for the Konzo to gain by accepting the proposed concession on a promise of peace. I made Isaya half-fugitive in another country, pursued by the Furies his vision had unleashed. My listeners were mostly compliant, the pragmatic Blasio Maate thoughtfully supportive. His fellow schoolmaster, Kibingo, was 'hectoring', I noted – no doubt through the impossibility of squaring the old dream with reality, yet it seemed that by the time we all turned in amid a stew of grog, fumes, smoke, blather and exhaustion, I had pulled him around into a mushy solidarity with the rest of us. Kule, assigning me my bedspace, required to check on the durability of the protective cuts his very own hand-forged razor had made either side of my chestbone eight years earlier, and half a dozen of them peered in solemn honour by low lanternlight, with *ehs* and *tsks* and noddings, at the one-ness of Konzodom. Seylversta said, 'We are also praying Jesus is in these cuttings.' My codeine from Bill Cheyne brought comfort to a girl wracked with bronchitis in the partition beside me, yet another of Khavaïru's offspring.

In those next few days I descended in a progress, or egress, of peace, repeating my parting Kituti speech at all the settlements on the route and to all the groups of young and old who had come down the hills or across from other spurs to meet us. I would do

279

my best, I promised, to persuade Central Government to implement the solutions the abandoned agreement had foreshadowed – which would free Bakonzo from Batoro control, at least for the present. Peace would bring schooling and medicine further into the mountains, and peace meant laying spears aside. If they wished it, I would press for a road – a jeep-track – to be built up to Kitolu to bring down the peasants' cash crops to Bwera's market. Certainly, they would see again the presence of soldiery, but in no mood of belligerence unless there were Bakonzo assaults on them or on Batoro presence in the fringe community.

Somewhere around Bulemera, pink-sweater Yeremiah joined us – come from Bukuke, Congo-side. He it was who had told Isaya

that my advice to him to descend and settle a deal was a 'trick'. Now he was sullen. From him I learned that Isaya was on the point of returning to Ebulema, and taking Fanehasi and the rest with him. Early next morning I was bidding adieu to Isaleri and Batulomayu on the track beyond their huts. And here Twalibu left us, for his long trek back to Bunyangabo. Honoured Doogulas had a bruised heel, and we had to leave him there. Whatever I might attempt further to secure for them in Kampala, I would not now be able to re-ascend to Kitolu to tell them of it. There was trust and love in these improbable friendships and these peculiar commitments. I went on down, with Ibrahimu, Seylversta, Masereka, the dogged George – Fanehasi's stooge – and the distinguished schoolmasters. Linkoni joined us at Bwera. Ibrahimu, his wife's young brother, would stay on with him.

A Land Rover and driver awaited me. My immediate task was to return Seylversta to his home at Bundibugyo, round the north end of the mountains. Young Masereka wished to accompany him, so he came too. There I stayed the night with Ray Cordery, the Government's administrator and former District Commissioner at Fort Portal. He and I drew up lists of those 'agents' from among the Konzo community who would replace Batoro officials in the Rwenzururu regions. We pondered the route and the means of constructing a road linking Isango to Kitolu. Thus rehearsed, I flew in the Aztec to Entebbe to firm up the settlement, such as it was, with Milton Obote, the Prime Minister, and Felix Onama, his Minister of the Interior, in Kampala. I sensed their earnest intentions, but could not estimate their will or ability to carry things through. So various were their political and constitutional obligations, there was no persuading them to make the administrative 'settlement' other than temporary. I knew, of course, that any encroachment by central Government on the authority of any one of the five constituent Kingdoms of southern and western Uganda, with whose complicity Obote had sneaked to power, would be seen by the rest as an encroachment on the authority of them all. The Government was to reassess the settlement six months on.

While I was in Kampala, all at once Somalia – next but one country north-east, more or less – vortexed into crisis. Because of the Cold War we of the West lived in dread of the Marxist bacillus whenever the amenable government of a Third World country was threatened with overthrow. The generic term 'Third World' had not yet been coined: we knew such ex-colonial territories then as Under-developed, a term which the next year in Britain the newly-elected Wilson government would deem to be condescending, and so was politically corrected to 'Developing'. Whatever post-colonial 'developing' might be taking place, it was our common hope that it would not be in the direction of, say, Cuba or North Vietnam, since such developments tended to rend the globe. So to soothe my patient editor in London and inform the readers of the *Sunday Times*, I slipped aboard planes via Nairobi to Mogadishu to review the crisis. I interviewed the President, Ali Shermarke, in due course to be murdered, who was courteous to me and expansive, partly because he had been honoured by being received in London recently by our own Prime Minister, although Mr Macmillan, the President recalled, had dropped asleep during their *entrétien* at Downing Street. After so many weeks among my stubby Rwenzururians, it seemed to me that Divine Invention had crafted no woman superior in comeliness to the Somali; and to this day I remain of the view that she who had inspired the writer of the biblical *Song of Songs* could not have been other than a Somali.

Within – what? – three days of the Mogadishu interlude, I had returned to Ruwenzori, or at least to the central villages at the base of the mountains, to report to such leaders of the Konzo community I could find on what had been promised me in Kampala. Time was running out for me, and I could not reascend into the hill villages. I returned first to Bundibugyo in the north-west, in search of George Kahigwa and in order temporarily to reassemble my translating team. The agreements were to be announced two days ahead, and I wished to bring personal word of them to my trusted friends. But there in Bwamba I found that the cessation of Bakonzo hostilities had been followed instantly by a reassertion of Toro authority by the Mutoro saza-county chief. This apparatchik, learning that there had arrived in their midst two men who had been with Isaya Mukirane, namely Seylversta and Masereka, had them both arrested on invented poll-tax charges and thrown into the Bundibugyo lock-up beside which I had slept the first night of my return to the mountains a few weeks earlier. Their wrists were handcuffed to their ankles. Thus hobbled they had lain without blankets on the concrete floor until now, two days later. Masereka, in his criminal innocence, had been found to have been carrying in his tattered pocket a document belonging to a Mutoro at whose murder he had assisted several weeks earlier. The situation did not look promising from the outside, let alone the inside.

I found the saza chief. I described to him the critical role played by these two, his prisoners, in the achievement of the peace which, with me acting at the behest of the Prime Minister, had been brought to the mountains and allowed him to resume his functions. The fellow was unmoved. At length I had no choice but to tell him, gently, that I could not advise the tribe not to molest him if he persecuted my principal aides thus. The double negative has its uses. I was taken past the great eucalyptus opposite the county headquarters building, under which was Seylversta's grieving mother. I could feel her following me with her eyes as I continued with the saza chief's clerk down the track and across to where the mean little prison stood. I was let into the compound by the door in the high stockade. Only the trusties were out in the compound, sweeping: my two were in the cells, on their concrete floor. They were brought out, now, handcuffed together, as if being led forth to execution, and thus I photographed them before they had any notion as to what was happening. I ordered their uncuffing, and was obeyed without demur. Together the three of us emerged into freedom. 'We are all trusting you as Jesus, Sir,' opined Seylversta. And there was his mother. Our Good Lord would have pulled it off without having to threaten the stubborn chief. It did not pass me by that in my role as a novelist, in the penultimate episode of *The Brothers M* I had secured a far from dissimilar jail-break from the lock-up in Mutwanga for my main African characters, including Kigoma/Isaya, by means of white-man's bluff.

Thus re-teamed, and heady with freedom, we dropped in upon such Konzo leaders as I could find in the larger villages of the tribal fringe, where the hills met the plains, in Burahya and Bunyangabo counties, to spread our report. Thence to Linkoni's house in Bwera, where re-united with Ibrahimu, we engaged upon what surely Seylversta would entitle the Last Supper; and he did. I sent gifts into the mountains – something for Khavaïru, something for Isaleri – to be carried by Masereka, that fine untamed young man who would soon marry the dark chief's daughter, and would rejoin Isaya, Irema-Ngoma, and see Rwenzururu through to the peace of 1982, only to be murdered by that rebellion's successor, the National Army for the Liberation of Uganda, NALU, in the late 1980s, under the generalship of Fanehasi.

I was in London later that week, and my colleagues on the Arts section or Sport glanced up lazily to note that Stacey had returned from wherever it might have been. Issues of illusorily greater moment at once swept down upon me in their customary cascade. I circled the world. Six months later I heard from Ray Cordery, shortly to retire from the infinite spaces and unrealizable hopes of central Africa which had borne up him and his civilisation since his early manhood. He wrote to say that the Bakonjo 'agents', replacing Batoro chiefs and collectors in the mountains, had worked well enough, gathering in a good pile of poll tax. After some faltering, Kampala had prolonged rather than renewed these arrangements, but then had made the grave mistake of attempting to recruit these same Bakonzo into the unreformed Toro structure. This had alarmed the mountain people, and who could foretell the outcome?

At the very start of the following year, 1964, a virulent epidemic of insurrection swept eastern and interlacustrine Africa. It began on January 12 in Zanzibar, with the violent overthrow of the elected government of that island, three weeks into its independence. Eight days later, at ten to two in the morning in the capital of neighbouring Tanganyika, Dar es Salaam, mutineers of the army seized power. On the evening of January 24, four days later, President Nyerere requested the British, whose commando carrier *Centaur* had steamed up from Aden with a battalion of marines aboard, to intervene and depose the mutineers. This was done the next morning by 7.50 a.m. Meanwhile, the virus had flit both to Kenya and to Uganda. The previous day (January 23) British troops had been called in respectively by Prime Minister Kenyatta of Kenya to quell the mutiny at his army hq at Lanet barracks, and by Prime Minister Obote of Uganda for the overthrow of mutineers at Jinja barracks. That same fortnight, the Hutu of Rwanda had risen against the Tutsi, in the first of the post-colonial massacres with which the world was to grow numb with disbelieving familiarity. As for me, after slipping into and out of Zanzibar under its triumphant and bloodthirsty revolutionaries, I rented a light plane from Nairobi to Kigali, Rwanda, to report the aftermath of the massacres. I poked among mass graves. Tens of thousands of Batutsi had fled for their lives into southwestern Uganda. There I found them, thirty-two thousand in all, in four vast camps presided over with calm competence by a nineteen-year-old from Sheffield recruited by the recently devised organisation VSO, Voluntary Service Overseas. This was Gordon Taylor, less than a year out of grammar school. His intention after this interlude was to return home to train for service as a policeman. Other currents evidently came to lift and swirl him, for, thirty-six years later, while organising a band of pilgrims originating in Lindisfarne and Whitby, on their way by foot to Canterbury to greet the dawn of the third *soi-disant* Christian Millennium on January 1st, 2000, I found him as the Rev. Canon Gordon Taylor in whose care and cure lay the souls of the residents of Goole, East Yorkshire. Young Gordon's charges in Uganda that January 1964 had meanwhile come to provide what would become the core of the Rwanda Patriotic Front, which amid various ignorant armies clashing by night, entailing the death of hundreds of thousands by massacre, disease and starvation, has effectively provided the Rwanda of today its present, once again Tutsi, government.

From Gordon Taylor's headquarters camp it was a mere half day's drive to the southern edge of Ruwenzori. Seizing the opportunity I made a dash to Busongora in order that, in the hours I had to spare, I might learn what had befallen 'my' Bakonzo and 'our' Rwenzururu. My momentary destination was the Bwera home of Ibrahimu Linkoni. My old friend Linkoni was now *gombolola* (sub-county) chief. In this difficult role he was soon to endure the mutiliation of his hand as an alleged *omukolikoli*, collaborator, with the Toro kingdom's administrative structure – a cold cruelty endorsed by his brother-in-law Isaya and carried out by Fanehasi Kisokeronio's team of hit-men, as I have already narrated.

A visitor in a hurry amid the measured courtesies of the tropical world will be told what is thought comfortable for him to hear. Thus at Bwera they told me how in those intervening nine months Isaya had remained holed up in Congo with his posse of diehards, and how life in these southern uplands had shaken back into something akin to the customary benign pattern: Isaleri back at Kitolu, with the surrounding folk; Khavaïru at Kituti. It was true (they said) that when from time to time a detachment of Uganda Rifles based at Isango patrolled up into the highlands, Khavaïru and his fellows would vanish into the Congo; and also true that a few weeks earlier the road gang – virtually all of them Bakonzo – building the vehicle track I had proposed from Isango to highland Kitolu, had been attacked by spearmen despatched by Isaya and led by Masereka, who burned their huts and scattered them, ending the work on the road... I took Linkoni in my Land Rover up the few miles of new track, and found – at Ekobero – a half-brother of Isaleri Kambere to whom I entrusted a gift of a shirt for delivery to my old friend. There I heard of Isaya's askaris having raided the shambas growing ideologically incorrect crops of coffee and cotton, uprooting the plants... I was a man in a hurry – too hurried to put two and two together. That same night I was in Kampala and the next in Lagos, Nigeria. The Ruwenzori mountains were back on the moon.

For eighteen years I was to know almost nothing, until in the late summer of 1982 – as I shall come to tell – my wife and I were to find ourselves welcoming at our house in Kensington a recently abdicated king. This was, indeed, the King of Rwenzururu up to some eighteen days previously and none other than Charles Wesley 'Kisembo' Mumbere, then aged 30, son of the late Isaya Mukirane, first King. Ex-King Charles' visit to London had been arranged by the Government of Uganda in celebration of the deal by which the territory of the mountains and the generality of the mountain people were formally reconciled with the rest of Uganda after the defiance of precisely twenty years of declared secession. It falls to me now to sketch in the story of that sustained defiance from the day Isaya and I parted in dissension. The truth is that whatever the verifiable expression of its *regnum,* the Rwenzururu kingdom never ceased to exist in the minds of nearly all the mountain people, the Banyarwenzururu. It was always reigned over, if not always in full polity *ruled*, by Isaya Mukirane until his death on September 2, 1966, and thereafter – following his crowning on October 19 of that year – by his son, Charles Wesley ('Kisembo'), in whose name and by whose consent a regent conducted the affairs of government in his stead for most of the period until in 1970, at the age of 18, Charles formally assumed his full authority as King.

Let us now piece the sequence of events and the structure of this phenomenon with what fragments we can find. Pick the memories of old men, sift childhood recollections of those who grew up under Rwenzururu rule, draw upon the writings of the scholars of the tribe such as Syahuka-Mohindu and Yona Balyage, gather in the scraps of physical evidence of the workings of the cloudy state – snapshots of military parades, receipts of tax payments, cuttings from newspapers published beyond the borders – and talk it through with Charles himself. Then join the dots and lineate something strange and rare.

The little group which left Bukuke the day after I had brought to Isaya the last letter from Obote, arrived at Ebulema spur, deeper in Congo, comprising intact the royal court of Rwenzururu. If this episode of 'negotiation' with Kampala left him fazed, he did not show it. His mind had made a contest of phantasms; his conduct instinctively determined the winner. Either he was to have *genuinely* negotiated with Kampala, and so let the Kingdom of Rwenzururu slip away into the realm of dreams; or he would engage in make-believe dealings with Kampala and thus not only preserve but reinforce the palpability of his Kingdom. What he dreamed he now proceeded to realize with renewed doggedness. From this supposed sanctuary in what he termed Kyatenga saza of Rwenzururu amid his 'Banande' tribal brothers, Isaya now set about establishing schools, a centre for training teachers, and further centres for the training of a gendarmerie and what was termed 'advance leadership'. This pattern of training came to be repeated during the coming two years in all seven of the sazas that comprised the kingdom. Each saza had its chief, approved and confirmed by Isaya. The man chosen to be Kyatenga chief was a certain Yolamu Mulima, a man of 25 or so, of a natural authority and high ability.

Isaya sought to vitalize his precarious unitive eminence. Up to the time that I was with him that March, he had assumed the title of President of his people and his territory. Yet already in response to the collective ache for a governance that is in the last resort unchallengeable, Isaya was already spoken of as 'King' – *Omusinga*. This hovering sceptre of kingship received on June 29th that year, 1963, a shaft of endorsement from three venerated clan leaders and scions of the ancient mountain settlers, themselves once ritually installed *bami be mbitha* according to Konzo tradition and now mandated to perform the ritual of kingmaking – Rupande of Mangirisipa, Basikania of Kikura, and Baundeli of Mbaghu – laying their hands on my old companion and so bestowing the title of *Omusinga wa Rwenzururu*. Is there not in the gift of man that by which, in the speaking of the word, he is bridged to the immemorial? Once the title was bequeathed by those three, clan leaders from the length of the mountains gathered at a site named accordingly Buhumbania, 'assembly point', which I have not located, that mid-year, for formal installation of Isaya as Omusinga. The style he took was Isaya Mukirania Kibanzanga 1

Musabuli. This name, now royal, evoked, in Isaya, the Hebraic-Christian allegiance; in 'Mukirania', the assuagement of Konzo spirits on behalf of any child born following a sibling's death; in 'Kibanzanga', the fixity of the role; in 'Musabuli', the regenerative honorific such as, for a while, was lent to me. The figure 1 envisaged male lineage. This first King of the line, then, at Buhumbania, was seated on a finely carved and ancient stool, draped with the skins of leopard, lion and colobus. Both hands of each of the clan leaders were laid upon him. Such is the common manner of fealty: hands laid on or hands linked in the presence of spirit, making vow. The negligibility of individual lives – the aches, pains, envies, weaknesses and fear; the petty rights, grievances, vauntings and vices – was subsumed by the collective embitha of language, lineage, territory, myth and hero. They sang – these people: Bakonzo and Baamba alike are indefatigable singers; all significance goes into song, spirit-voice and man-voice antiphonal and mingled – they sang at Isaya's enthronement camp,

Sitwendihula!	We cannot give up our struggle!
Sitwagalhula!	We can never give up the struggle!
Kand sitwendisyalhuha	We shall never give up the struggle
Kithe kiabererera!	Until we win our goal!
Nali twanasyakwa	Though we may die in the course of the struggle
Abana bethu n'abitsikulhu	Our children and children's children
Bakendisyahathikana erithabalha	Will persevere with the struggle we have begun
Erihika kyabibererera.	Until we reach our goal.

Had I not myself been brought to recognise that the compulsion to art in these people found its release in music? – the *eluma's* collective respiration, the *endara's* funnelled stream, the *enyamwulera's* fluting meditation, the plucked *enzenze's* secret improvisation, half-prayer; the song as medium, offered and received, art in its primal sophianic function opening beauty to men and men to beauty: to their own transcendence and thus, simultaneously, to their frailty and accursed creatureliness. To our Bakonzo, Isaya's Rwenzururu was an astonishment, like a love that takes the breath away and gives a man such breath as he never dared believe he had. Our *Kingdom*! *Our* Kingdom! It was a visceral revelation, in the sheer idea of it: the wild surmise; their own inner mountains, snow-crowned, in the sudden view – Kitasamba's pink on Nzururu's unassailable sheen – of what incredibly was revealed as theirs.

Thus now was released – through this political glimpse – the sprung creative coil in man. Among these Konzo what it found was *voice*. They made words and music of it. They sang it. They have sung it ever since (their opponents ought by now to have learned they cannot bludgeon song). Certain songs of those days took form, and spread as repertoire among the mountains. In 1966 and 1967, at Mutiti village in lowland Bwamba, down by Bubandi on the Congo border, where there was no front line – no rack of spears – yet a prevailing Rwenzururu patriotism, a duo of musical ethnologists, Peter Cooke and Martin Doornbos, were to record on tape several of the songs of highland patriots, at a special recital, *konsati*-concert, singing their tribal history, their yearning and despair, from the highland repertoire of those days, of which a good thirty years on I would pick up many an echo in the sung greetings for Isaya's returning heir.

We shan't again sit and eat with a Mutoro/Be off with him!
Goodbyee!/We have utterly declined his company.
This is the third war to have taken the lives of many./The first was Nyamutswa's, the second Kabalega's.

Folk memory had muddled the historical sequence.

Long ago we had Nyamutswa and Tibamwenda/who refused to pay Batoro taxes. The Batoro killed them, dumped them in a single grave.
Then came Isaya to delve the story of how these men died/and from his research he wrote down the truth in exercise books.

Indeed, he did. We both did. I still have my exercise books. I wonder what became of Isaya's.

Many another balladed the Bakonzo-Baamba membership of the Toro Rukurato, the election of their champions, the walk-out from that assembly, the raising of the flag of rebellion, the Commission of Enquiry, the whole story. Even I turned up, as the 'colobus-wearer'. Several songs were little paeans for Isaya, like the narrative song with the refrain *Mister Isaya, so very intelligent, threw off the yoke of the Batoro* and another celebrating Isaya's semi-magic articulacy which supposedly carried his message to the corners of the earth and had the refrain *Isaya speaks like a radio*. They gloried in song Isaya's intransigence and his defiant honorific Kibanzanga. *Then Isaya told the people they had taken the wrong path and left the true one./Kibanzanga alone did not change his mind up to this very day./Friends, be not deceived again as we were before./Only Kibanzanga, the saviour-musabuli, did not change his mind.*

Our Rwenzururu colobus, ngeya, with its snow-white streak, had become the emblem of their territory's inner inviolability swinging free and high. The creature nourished them too. *Colobus, colobus of Rwenzururu/has a white band./It is truly benificent.*

When the short flutes, the long flute, the little harp, the endara-xylophone, were joined by the drummer, *da-da-da,* in stabbing triplets, song leapt spontaneously forth, as virtual improvisation, and on the high slopes the voice of women, men and children, sometimes loosened by a slurp or two of beer, took form and rose, tiny and rare, from out of the high slopes. They sang: *The day when the horns will sound/and the dead will rise/and the mountains begin to tumble,/my love – where will you take me?/Weep, weep, weep and shed tears, tears./Weep, weep. The land will return to us.* A formidable earthquake that shook the entire range in 1966 seems to have inspired those eschatological lines. They were a refrain. The solo voice, maybe, echoed the Jericho of Exodus: *When the earth quaked, we people, we were asleep./We awoke thinking the Son of God was back./When the soldiers heard it/they thought the banyambulya* [high forest fugitives]/ *had descended among us./We loaded our guns,/then realized it was in the ground itself.* Laments rose against the mountain flanks like the curl of smoke from hearths, no less negligible and evanescent. *Mount Rwenzururu, with its beauty,/how we suffer.* It was sung prayer; art being prayer, each vital gesture so infinitely puny upon the actual face of creation … as puny, one may say, as Isaya's rebellion on the political face of the globe. *Rwenzururu has its own King/*

Bakonzo, Baamba, Rwenzururu!
  Surely, friends, let's fight like men.
Bakonzo, Baamba, Rwenzururu!
  Kilembe's, Muhokya's, Katwe's riches [ie copper, crops, salt] *all are ours.*
Bakonzo, Baamba, Rwenzururu!

Erihika kyabibwera, until we reach our goal!

The goal, of course, was not reachable. The government in Kampala, having been misled by me, were at their wits' end as to how to treat with such rebels, who would settle for nothing. The constitution with which Obote was obliged to operate (with a small but naturally inhibiting rump of Colonial Service whites working on in his Secretariat) prevented his chopping the whole of the mountain region out of Toro and rolling it to the Konzo-Amba patriot-fanatics... The very nature of the thing, Rwenzururu, was not in the end political; it was scarcely terrestrial; it was sacred *struggle*, an elevation of suffering, and as such the essence of human existence in the Christian interpretation – the caprice, hollowness, ephemerality, and pretension challenged by the grandeur of spirit (Isaya's own), and the splendour, power and majesty of snow, peaks and territory impenetrable and uninhabitable by men but only by gods, or Nyamuhanga-Trinity. Isaya was at work for Him, at an altitude as high as people could reasonably live, invariably founding a church wherever he planted his stave at each successive capital-camp.

By this same token, the Kingdom itself oscillated between the

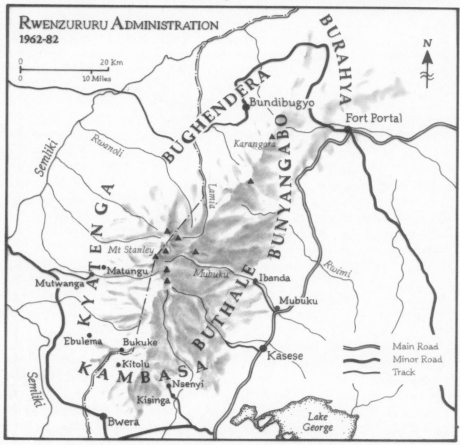

realities: that of the idea, and that of the *actualité*. The very first abithunga – departments – of Rwenzururian government were of spontaneous *montagnard* communal expression: Defence, Culture, and Churches – *Churches*, be it noted: the Word of Jesus in and as Lukonzo. Structure as such came with the addition of a department of Local Administration. For his Kingdom, Isaya created six sazas (counties) out of territory divided by the government of Uganda among four sazas, plus a piece of the Congo. Rwenzururu saza were named as Kambasa (southern Busongora), Buthale (northern Busongora), Bunyagabo, Burahya, Bughendara, and Kyatenga. Burahya and Bughendara straddled the local northern end of the mountains to take in Bwamba; Kyatenga, as we have seen, comprised the western, Congo-side flanks of inhabited Ruwenzori. Isaya operated his command by messages carried by trusted runners despatched from his 'farthest private' base in Kyatenga county to his saza chiefs. Some of these chiefs were formerly Bakonzo Life History Research Society chairmen of the same saza, others were new appointees. In Bunyangabo, the new man was John Basinghirenda; in Kambasa, the cold and alarming Fanehasi. The first function of the saza chief was to establish Rwenzururu control of the subdivisional tiers of gombolola-subcounty, parish and spur, and the second to collect annual poll tax of 25 Uganda shillings, or one billy-goat, from every adult male, each payment to be officially receipted. Revenue thus generated was shared in ordained proportions by each level of administration, including at the pinnacle the Kingdom's central exchequer. With the tax, each saza was to establish and maintain its own centres for the training of teachers and police, schools, and of course its own askaris.

Not trusting the security of his own Uganda-side provinces, Isaya stayed in Congo, except for occasional appearances on the eastern bank of the Tako river such as I have cited. His memoranda and letters fluttering out through the mountains as if from an ethereal dovecote were copied out by hand, each bearing the imprimatur of the mystic rubber stamp. Later, in 1965, a typewriter was provided by supporters in the Congo. Notwithstanding Isaya's personal evanescence, when ukases arrived on the high spurs of the cantons obedience was presumed. From time to time emissaries came to him, wherever he held court. King Isaya was an indefatigable copier. If U Thant, Secretary-General of the United Nations, got a letter, the Rwenzururu saza chiefs got a copy of it. If Milton Obote got a letter, so – up to 1963 – did Sir Walter Coutts, Governor-General.

By that year of 1963, all along the Kingdom's edge long-suffering Bakonzo and Baamba were paying two whacks of poll tax: one to Toro, one to Rwenzururu. If Toro caught them with a Rwenzururu receipt they would be up in front of the court; if Isaya's men caught them without one, they were not safe in their beds. On the other hand, most of the tribesmen were paying Rwenzururu willingly and proudly. I had not been vouchsafed this fact on my flying return visit in 1964. A mutually sullen stand-off persisted between Bakonzo and Batoro whenever the communities touched. The Baamba had no comparable territorial frontier with Batoro; but no love was lost between the communities. Meanwhile, the activities of detachments of Uganda Rifles, Obote's army, inflamed tribal hostility between Bakonzo and Batoro and drove the Bakonzo in upon themselves and their own high kingdom. A report survives by a former British Assistant District Commissioner of Toro, David Pasteur, then working as Under-secretary at the Ministry of Regional Administrations in Kampala, on a series of incidents up the valley of the Mubuku river and its main village of Bugoye, where I had come down with malaria within minutes of my arrival there from the inner mountains in 1954. Pasteur, already an experienced Ruwenzori mountaineer and noted geographer of those highlands, was tipped off by the Mukonzo serving as Agent for the Mountain Club at Ibanda, a few miles further up the valley from Bugoye. On November 16 and 17 he was able to investigate the incidents since October himself and establish the facts. A detachment of Uganda Rifles was posted in the valley. Soldiers on foot, out to intimidate, thirsty for action, let off their guns into the air, alarming a 13-year-old goatherd and his friend, who together scampered for cover. Idly, soldiers shot the 13-year-old dead, and brushed aside the protest of the police who were to recover the body. In nearby Kyanya village, soldiers were led to the home of a certain Mulembero, against whom a Mutoro, accompanying the troops, had a grievance. Witnessed by his wife and his brother from the shelter of long grass, the man was intercepted as he carried two of his small children. He was commanded to put the children down and walk from the askaris, who promptly shot him in the back. As for Aberi Bagenyi, also of Kyanya, a group of four Uganda Rifles askaris rounded up his 30 goats and moved them to their camp, on the pretext that a Mutoro claimed the goats. On the local head of police security in Bugoye, a Munyankole, taking up Bagenyi's case, a group of twelve Uganda

Riflemen returned to the victim's house, stripped it of valuables, and set it alight, and after raping three of his daughters returned to base where they continued to hold all but eleven of his goats. Such incidents, covering a single month in a single lowland valley, multiplied by the eight (or so) Uganda Rifles detachments ringing the mountain area, amounted to no mean cascade of atrocity over the year, mostly unrecorded, mutely suffered, but all embedding the fact and intransigeance of Rwenzururu.

As for Kampala, it knew not which way to turn. Obote's Ministers and their remaining handful of British civil servants twisted and turned for a constitutional means of obliging the Toro kingdom to devolve authority among the minority tribes to those own tribes' representatives. They were responding in part to a fresh and persuasive, if doomed, plea in a 14-point memorandum submitted (as from a Post Box in Bwera) by the Baamba, Kawamara and Mupalya, now free, as signatories, and supported by eight Bakonzo of distinction including my own former allies in reconciliation, Samwiri Mutoro and Emilio Kibingo. That memo, dated a mere ten weeks after my departure, called for the reconstitution of Toro as a three-tribe territory to be known as Rwenzururu District, to be governed by a rotating Secretary-General and its parliament to be reconstituted as Rwenzururu Rukurato. The existing Toro monarchy would be effectively abolished. It was entirely reasonable and had not a chance. It made no reference to Isaya. It was in large measure the work of the highly literate Mupalya, who was soon to tire of the whole endeavour. It served to demonstrate, however, the emergence of a lowland Bakonzo-Baamba axis that, while it stood for radical reform, saw no future in the outright defiance of Isaya's Rwenzururu.

Next year, 1964, Kampala leaned upon Toro and divided Busongora into two, entitling the western half 'Bukonjo'. In August, the Minister of Regional Administrations, J W. Lwamafa, signed an agreement with King George and his Omuhikirwa to the effect that no more Batoro chiefs should be appointed to Bakonzo or Baamba areas, and that those already nominally serving there should be transferred or retired. Toro ignored the agreement, on the grounds that its implementation was to take place in the light of new county council elections – which were not practicable. The issue was as much financial as political: paying for chiefs who dared to collect no money or perform any functions was running the Toro government into bankcruptcy. Meanwhile, the new District Commissioner in

Fort Portal, a Teso named J K Inyoin, arranged for the parallel appointment of 94 new chiefs from the minority tribes in their lowland areas – with the approval of the Toro Public Service Commission, which had to foot the bill. In the mountains, nobody of Rwenzururu fell for that particular rearrangement of the Toro-region nomenklatura. Rwenzururu persisted willy-nilly.

Parliament in Kampala came dancing onto stage like an elephant. In a debate in March the Minister of Animal Industry, Game and Fisheries, a certain J K Babiiha, came forth with a prediction. If things went on as they were, he declared, the Bakonzo and Baamba faced 'extinction' within two years, 'and there will be nothing but to declare the area a national park.' The Member for Ankole South-east proposed clearing out the entire Bakonzo tribe from the mountains. When the issue returned to the Chamber in August, Batoro MPs had grown markedly more restive and stroppy. Parliament heard that Batoro teachers were living 'in terror', and Toro chiefs in Bakonzo-Baamba areas (though still drawing their salaries) were skulking at home, not daring to administer anything. The official death toll of Batoro and of Ugandan soldiery had risen to 116, with 'two missing'. Minister John Lwamafa declared that the 'question of a separate District must not be entertained by any person in Bwamba or Busongora'. Such a change would need a two-thirds majority in Toro's *rukurato and* in the national Parliament. He confessed that 'at the moment it seems that the law as it should be is not really being administered because of conditions prevailing in those areas.' I should say so! The Minister for Justice, Cuthbert Obwangor, assured his fellow parliamentarians that the extension of the Powers of Emergency would enable the Government to 'stop this nonsense once and for all'. Statesmanship and diplomacy had failed, he said, and the Government intended to come out with all the forces of Law and Order, blah blah. Basil Bataringaya, Leader of the Opposition, gave his (Democratic) party's consent to the continuing Emergency powers on the understanding the Government took 'resolute action' to 'wipe out lawlessness within two to three months'. Isaya Mukirane, said the Member for Toro East, 'should be arrested as soon as possible and brought to justice.' *But of course.* Kampala's elephant dance had become a reel. The imagination may substitute George II's Parliament of 1745 hotly debating in Westminster the administration of the Scottish Highlands.

Meanwhile, Bonnie Prince Isaya, ensconced uneasily in Congo, was spawning his own administration in the mountains. He had his fledgling army of young spearmen-patriots organized county-by-county, weapons hidden in the forest, and paid for out of county-collected taxes or not paid for at all; he had his administrative chiefs, at all four levels; he had his churches, schools, and courts. This governmental *bricolage* of the fledgling state not only endured the leader's absence: it evolved spontaneously its own forms, procedures and disciplines, with Isaya personally approving senior Rwenzuru appointments. Yet his holing up among Bakonzo/Banande on the Congo side in the wild country by no means guaranteed his safety. It was never advisable for him to stay long in the same place. From his base at Ebulema he moved north to Matungu, beyond the valley of the Lhume river cascading out of the southerly high peaks into the upper Semliki. For a while thereafter he moved south to Eisale, to the home of Koroneri Maate, father-in-law of his henchman and chairman of Kambasa saza, Fanehasi Kisokeronio, who had taken a second wife across in Congo. Eisale was the Bakonzo's seminal provenance in the hilly woodlands north-west of Lake Edward.

Somehow Isaya must have misjudged the factions competing for local supremacy in the chaotic Congo where central government had long ago imploded. In June 1964 he was seized and locked up in the prison of the regional centre of Beni. There was even a court hearing, on a charge of his causing dissension. Yet what else was there but dissension, with all the smuggling and armed gangs, and the Mulelist guerillas roaming and raiding in the name of the murdered Congolese President, Patrice Lumumba? It was these very Mulelists' sympathies with Rwenzururu that told against Isaya. By some fluke, Kampala got no wind of the arrest of their quarry, and a month later Rwenzururu's King was half-released into house arrest at Butembo, the next big village south – by twenty miles – of Beni, in the charge of one Kaligha Mulere, who had made his name giving trouble to the Belgians pre-independence. I may mention in passing that I had been in Butembo ten years earlier, searching for survivors of the clapper-lip people who inhabited that and surrounding villages in the earlier years of the century. The clapper-lip cult of facial mutilation was a response to the maraudings of Arab slaving gangs operating out of Zanzibar when that region of Western Congo became the furthest point of penetration by the slave-raiders. The local people, notably the women – almost certainly Konzo speakers – sought to make themselves unsaleable as slaves by grotesquely distending their lips with the insertion of wooden plates in childhood. The ploy largely worked.

Here at Butembo Isaya now had his young son, Charles Wesley 'Kisembo', aged twelve, reunited with him. He was fixedly grooming Charles as his heir and successor. Did he sense his own days to be numbered? He was obsessively intent upon educating Charles, to acquaint him with the functioning of statecraft even of such a Cheshire Cat state as Rwenzururu still was, and to pass to him the ethos of the Kingdom. The ordeal of sustaining belief in its reality at this period must have been formidable. Charles' mother Christine had remained behind in the mountains where, incidentally, she had given birth in February, 1965, at Buhumbania to Christopher Tabaan – with whom she had had to flee for both their lives the very next day. Times were not easy. At Kaligha's house, Isaya and young Charles were assigned three guards of which two, I notice, bore Konzo names. That gives the clue, perhaps, as to how Isaya managed to slip the leash and make a dash with Charles for freedom. He was re-arrested with his Rwenzururu escorts while crossing the Kisalala river. His escape landed him briefly back in prison. But Masereka spirited young Charles away in a Land Rover put at Rwenzururu's disposal by Congolese Bakonzo/Banande supporters. Soon to be released – perhaps as a greater source of disruption inside than out – Isaya was to be reunited with young Charles; and the two fugitives at last got to their former west-side mountain base of Matungu. The masterly hand behind these successive reprieves from extinction was that of Isaya's chairman of the vast Kyatenga county (comprising all of Congo-side Ruwenzori), Yolamu Mulima.

At Matungu, Isaya at once gathered up his wife Christine and little Christopher and headed for Kiribata on the Congo flank of the upper Tako. That high borderland proved to be the best option while the royal group was being harried alike by both Obote's Uganda and Mobutu's Congo. Bukuke on the forest edge became the favoured base. After the August showdown in Kampala's parliament, September and October 1964 were to prove dire for Rwenzururu. The military, now shed of its British officers, swept through the highland ridges burning, looting and shooting at anyone in flight and at any ordered male formations with or without spears. To Isaya, did all this not resemble the persecution of the early Christians under the tyranny of Nero? Did not it serve to harden *faith*? The Uganda Rifles came, killing, scattering the believing flock, pillaging, and went. Yet the surviving flock instantly re-assembled, in quiet determination. Isaya ordered no retaliation.

By February 1965 he felt able to return to Buswagha territory on Ugandan soil, establishing himself at Ihandero, near Kitolu, and resuming – as his companions of that time remember it – his 'full rule'. He expanded his cabinet to ten portfolios, under his own premiership: Finance, Justice, Security, Education, Natural Resources, Health, plus the original Regions, Defence, Culture and Community Development, and Churches. The Minister of Finance, Yolana Mwambalha, was soon to double as Speaker of the National Assembly, and for this Assembly, *ekhyaghanda,* was erected a substantial, circular thatched edifice – a single chamber – in the forest above and beyond the inhabited heartland of the Bakonzo uplands. They would call the place *Kahindangoma* – the Drum Centre. Across a deep-forest gully just beyond, the royal residence was built. Under the spreading *omutamba* tree, Isaya established his Buhikira (Palace) Primary School. Young Charles, now 14, at last resumed his formal schooling, which had broken off in 1963. Tembo Christopher was the school's first headmaster, and to him was entrusted the scholastic advance of Rwenzururu's prince and heir. Soon the school got its own thatched premises. Also in attendance at the Buhikira was the kingdom's own Mukonzo chaplain, the Rev. Liminya, of the Church of Uganda, one of only three Bakonzo yet to be ordained priest. This Liminya had been evangelising among the pygmies of Ituri. Now he had been assigned to the heart of Rwenzururu by a bishop determined to ensure that the core of the rebel kingdom lay in Canterbury's bosom not Rome's. This same chaplain baptized the infant prince Christopher Tabaan, and consecrated the new churches initiated by Isaya. He conducted Holy Communion, kept the links with the Church below in the plains, and blessed the organisation of Rwenzururu Boy Scouts established by Isaya. Sensing a subcurrent of sympathy in the mother Church, Isaya sent a deputation to the Archbishop at Namirembe Cathedral in Kampala, pleading for a separate diocese for the mountain peoples and for the use and publication of a Konzo liturgy. Simultaneously, and most properly, he despatched Bakonzo emissaries of the respective persuasions to the Roman Catholics at Rubaga Cathedral, and the Seventh Day Adventists, and to the Muslims at Kibuli. It was surely the deputation to the Anglican Archbishop that sowed the seed. Nineteen years later would come the Konzo diocese of Kasese, preaching the gospel from a Lukonzo bible, worshippping with a Lukonzo liturgy, and presided over by a Mukonzo bishop; that Anglican initiative in turn would hasten the creation a couple of years later (1986) of a co-terminous Roman Catholic diocese, also using the Lukonzo medium, with its bishop drawn from the tiny Banyarughuru tribal group from beside the Kazinga channel between Lakes George and Edward; at that same future period, not to be ethnically upstaged, the fervent Seventh Day Adventists would headquarter their own vast diocesan 'Field' at the Konzo town of Kasese. The garnering of souls in Africa was never not a race.

In Kampala, meanwhile, in 1965, the political climate was altering. With post-colonial tutelage finally shucked off, and allured by the substance of his power, Obote hankered for a freer rein and to be done with the constraints of the Kingdoms. He had noted with what contempt Nehru had treated the rights of the Princely states which Britain had so fastidiously and futilely written into the constitution of independent India. The particular insult to the totality of Obote's authority was obstructive Buganda. Yet Toro by its very existence was also an impediment. A significant and potentially rich and productive section of the kingdom was outside its control – and thus outside anyone's. Toro was fast running out of money, paying for unutilized chiefs, and unable to finance services in areas it did control. The Toro government from the Mukama down was disinclined to face the reality, or incapable of doing so. Their maladministration was notorious. Several of their officials had pocketed Toro advances on motorcars, and quit office with the proceeds. 'There is no point,' Regional Minister Lwamafa told cabinet, 'in seeking the co-operation of the Toro Government. Neither the present Government nor a new one will officially co-operate in what is required, but it is possible that once a solution is imposed they will not object but will be glad to be relieved of the problem.'

All of this was reported by Lwamafa to the Prime Minister and fellow ministers in Entebbe on June 26, 1965. He also told them that Isaya Mukirane and Rwenzururu had a 'strong grip' on all of upland Ruwenzori. Kawamara for the Baamba had meanwhile split with Mupalya, for whom support had withered, and was working surreptitiously to back Rwenzururian defiance. The present security situation had eased, but the confrontational lull might be deceptive. Following the kidnap of an officious Mutoro in Katwe, a pitched battle involving some five hundred Batoro and numerous Bakonzo took place in the little salt town on July 3, in which several were killed and maimed. Any attempt at holding local elections in August would result in massive boycotts. Few if any would vote, and maybe no one would dare to stand, in the Bakonzo-Baamba counties. The Minister, just returned from a tour of the lowland Ruwenzori areas, recommended Central Government taking over administration of the Bakonzo-Baamba region, the appointment of an Administrator – with the powers of a District Commissioner, but headquartered elsewhere than Fort Portal, for all those areas, and, under him, a rack of 'advisory councils' in each county. To cover the cost of all this, Central Government could draw down all royalties over and above £25,000 payable by Kilembe copper mine, which was just then doing rather well. Lukonzo could be used as the 'official language' by the advisory council in Bukonzo, but not anywhere else. The Toro government naturally objected to all this, and refused to disband its own chiefly structures. Nonetheless, the Central Government's Ministry of Local Administration held barazas at which they could let the people know what was proposed, with a view to holding new County Council elections. Obote came to Bwera and made a speech. 'I understand that there are some Bakonjo who go around saying they are ministers. These people are not ministers at all. If they are anything they are thieves. Who elected them? Why is it they are making you pay money to them?... What do they do with this money you pay them? They fill their own pocket while all of you live in fear.' He was listened to politely, in African silence. Next month, October 1965, he was back in the region, addressing a baraza in Bundibugyo. 'I am told,' he said, 'a man called Mukirane is now in the forest. He calls himself the King. Is there any king in the world that cannot meet his people? Now, I am Prime Minister of Uganda. I am meeting you in the open. I don't meet you in the forest. I discuss in the open. I see you in the open. When you smile, I think you are happy. When you are unhappy, I am also unhappy. But if you run away like animals, I must lose interest in you.' He announced the coming of a 100-bed hospital in Bundibugyo. (It was never built.) Leaflets were printed in Lukonzo, a rare gesture of translation, bearing a youthful picture of Obote, who half-promised a role for a Mukonzo or a Mwamba as a Minister in his 'Kafumente' if the tribes co-operated with the offered structure. Since no one would dare distribute them by hand, they were scattered from the air over lowlands and highlands alike from the loading bay of the Police Air Wing's Caribou by the same English Under-secretary of the Ministry of Regional Administrations, David Pasteur, lying on his stomach with a heavy policeman sitting on his legs.

Whose, then, was the reality? Almost immediately a grand operation was planned to capture Isaya 'and as many of his ministers and close adherents as possible' (to quote from the minutes of the police conference held at Fort Portal on January 3, 1966). The participants included the Army, the Special Forces, the Police and CID. The Congo government was to be alerted. The men would comb every dwelling of the entire highland area of Buswagha for suspects, arms, and documents, and cut off the guilty fugitives' retreat with the Congo. They had the help, so they supposed, of an exceptionally valuable Rwenzururu renegade. This was Fanehasi Kisokeronio. Right up to Isaya's return to Uganda territory Fanehasi had been seen to be the right hand man of the Omusinga, and the hit-man too, toughest of the breed. Yet he had been passed over in the distribution of Rwenzururu cabinet posts, and indeed as army commander. It is said that Isaya had ceased to trust his judgement and was wary of his thirst for, and abuse of, power. That autumn of 1965, early one morning, Fanehasi led a band of his cronies in an assault on the Buhikira, in an attempt at a *putsch*. The attack was foiled. Fanehasi was overpowered by Isaya's guards, trussed, threatened with execution, spared by Isaya, but thrown out of the Kingdom. At Bwera, the police picked him up, treating him as a prize captive. For the price of his release he offered to work with Government forces. Yet evidently as they neared their D-day, doubts crept in as to Fanehasi's dependability.

The great sweep was to begin on February 9th with the army moving up to 'seal the border' and the Special Force securing the highlands from 'villages west of the border', presumably in Congo itself. The operation had been preceded by three days of reconnaissance, including from the air. It would take three weeks and was bound to succeed. It would 'raise the morale of the people in the area, show them that the Government [of Uganda] was taking action, and start to re-establish normal administration of the area.' On February 8th it was called off. That part of the kingdom of Rwenzururu to be honoured by the attention of invading forces had melted away in anticipation. The would-be invaders had entertained a notion of establishing a permanent administrative base at Kitojo, south of Kitolu, but that idea too was abandoned: nobody was there to be administered. If the morale of the people was raised, it was on behalf of their allegiance to Rwenzururu.

Bakonzo children growing up in upland Busongora and elsewhere remember it as a time of sweet order and tranquillity and a high, sustaining patriotism. Even to study at school an all-Lukonzo syllabus was an act of fervency; everyone had a role and function in the scheme of things. Such a child of the time was the young Arthur Syahuka Mohindu, the future Makerere political scientist, in his village a few miles south-west of Kitolu. There across the gully the black-clad soldiers trained, under their officers

 designated by a red stripe down the trousers. The rising star of the defence force, Kinyamusitu, came from Syahuka's spur; Syahuka's uncle was Isaya's Minister of Natural Resources, Gerisoni Ndambireki, with whom I had lodged in 1963, and who just the other day, in 2000, when I climbed back to his pretty spur after an absence of thirty-seven years, recalled for me the range of his functions – protecting the forests, preventing erosion, distributing seed grain, guarding known mineral deposits. His given name, Gerisoni, like that of Abraham Lincoln at Bwera, marked him with the promise and ideals of his namesake, William Lloyd Garrison, associate of the slave-releasing American President. Syahuka and his childhood contemporaries all joined the Boy Scouts, and moved around with their Scout staves, coiled rope on their belts, barefoot or in wooden sandals, 'helping society, building houses for widows' – round houses, naturally. Rwenzururu courts heard the disputes and tried the criminal cases (Gerisoni was later to become a magistrate). High courts – as at Ihandero – adjudicated on the most serious offences. On a Sunday all this high world, bathed, tidy and devout, filed to the nearest thatched church and sang and sang. Messengers flitted to and fro across all the Kingdom, Bughendera and Burahya, Bunyangabo and Obuthale, Kambasa and Kyatenga.

Trade was done covertly between the Uganda-controlled lowlands and Rwenzururu-controlled highlands, not only in crops

and animals for market, but in the counter-purchases of clothes, school books, scout kit, uniforms for the army (black) and police (khaki), and the modest paraphernalia of state. The main paths might have their army checkpoints, but no power on earth could police the grass tunnels between the lower and the upper worlds. Rwenzururu policy was to avoid confrontation, eschew provocation.

Those were the days. There was a sense of youth, a sense of the pristine, of golddust in the crevices and lapis lazuli among the pebbles. Real money, in innumerable threaded bunches of shillings, was stored under permanent guard in the national treasury in a forest cache of the utmost secrecy. Peace lay across the mountains tremulously. It was all at a cost of unrelenting vigilance, periodic dispersal, and frequent movement. For Isaya, to meet influential Rwenzururu supporters from lowland Uganda, Congo was the safer rendezvous. We know that in April 1966 he was back at Eisale, deepest Congo, to confer with friends from Kasese, Uganda. This same Isaya, conjuring all, ordaining all, seemed to hold it as if by an intense personal sorcery. The effort killed him. He was only 41.

xxii

The Succession of King Charles Wesley

Charles Wesley Kisembo, not quite 14, heard of his father's death at 6.25 p.m. on September 2nd, 1966. Isaya's actual passing, at his house on Bulemba spur, Uganda-side, had taken place at 5 p.m. He had fallen suddenly and mysteriously ill on the last day of August, and on September 1st was in a coma. The next day his spirit left his body – *erisohoka*, he 'let go the shield'. It took half a day for the cortege bearing the coffin to reach the site of burial, at the seat of government and the forum of the people, ekhyaghanda, in deep forest Uganda-side. Beside the grave grew the half-sacred bark cloth tree, in the pelt of which the corpse was wrapped. It was a military burial, conducted by the Reverend Liminya. *Eh*, men, women, children were in shock, dazed; the very gods bereaved.

The Premier-omulerembera of the time was Samwiri Mukirane, and he continued in his role; but the Council appointed as regent Yohana Mwambalha, already an effective Speaker of the National Assembly and Rwenzururu's Minister of Finance. Word of Isaya's death was issued to the regional leaders among the mountains the very next day, September 3rd by a letter signed by Samwiri as Prime Minister and addressed to the Secretary-General of the Organisation of African Unity in Addis Ababa, the Secretary-General of the United Nations in New York, and to me. My copy arrived from Kilembe weeks later in its airmail envelope but by sea because of 'insufficient' stamp values. It was addressed to 'Mr Tom Stacey – Englanda – UK' which was, miraculously, enough for the Royal Mail to forward it to the Party headquarters of the constituency where I had recently fought a parliamentary election and which in turn sent it on to my newspaper office off Fleet Street. From my desk I looked out into the well of the building. My Isaya, my Kigoma, my small King. The paragraph of Samwiri's collective epistle which said to 'the Outhorities who are being written in this letter'... 'if you are able to come and comfort the Outhorities of the

THE PRIME MINISTER'S OFFICE.
BUHIKIRA CENTRAL OFFICE.
RWENZURURU KINGDOM GOVERNMENT.

The Secretary, General,
O.A.U. Addisabbaba - Africa.

The Secretary General,
U.N.O. New York - Europe.

Mr. Tom Stacey,
England - U.K. ✔

Sirs,
Re:" To reshow the death of the Omukama Kibanzangha Rwenzururu Kingdom
Government"!!!.
You are informed the death of the Omukama Kibanzangha Rwenzururu Kingdom
Government, who was atacked the sickness on 28th August.1966; and dead on
2nd September.1966; at thirty Six thirty P.M.!!! who was forty two years of
age and left awiddow - Six Children, two boys and four girls.
He has been Educated man and wise one, who was teaching in Uganda Gover-
nment Schools in few years ago, from ninenteen hundred fifty one (1951)
up to ninenteen hundred Sixty two, and being a President of Bakonjo life
History Research, which took him seven years working as a President and he
was elected in ninenteen hundred Sixty one (1961) to be acouncilar in Tooro
Government, after that he rebuilder and formed the Rwenzururu Kingdom Government from ninenteen hundred Sixty two (1962) up to ninenteen hundred Sixty
Six (1966) Ruling as a King of Rwenzururu Kingdom Government, and having
apointed the Ministers and Civil servants among the Rwenzururians of the
Rwenzururu Kingdom Government.
The Rwenzururians - Ministers - Civil servants - Military and Police
of the Rwenzururu Kingdom Government, their are in Much Sorrow because of the
death of their King Mukirania M.Isaya Musabuli Kibanzangha Rwenzururu Kingdom
Government - Africa!!!.
In the name of the Rwenzururu Kingdom Government Powers, You are asked
to forbid the Outhorities of the Uganda Republic Government not to disturb
the Outhorities of the Rwenzururu Kingdom Government, those who are still
finding any derection of Scating - distroying the Peace of the Rwenzururians
of the Rwenzururu Kingdom Government - Africa.
The Outhorities who are being written this letter and informed the death
of their King Kibanzangha Rwenzururu Kingdom Government, if you are able to
Come and COnfort the Outhorities of the Rwenzururu Kingdom Government who are
in Much Sorrow, because of the death of their King, You can show yourself
in Clerkship to the Outhorities of Rwenzururu Kingdom Government - Africa.
May God blease you Peacefuly.

Mukiraniasi S
PRIME MINISTER.
RWENZURURU KINGDOM GOVERNMENT.

Emitahula:-(Copies).
Kabaka Mutesa II Bughanda Kingdom Government.
The President Nyerere Tanzania Republic Government.
"   "   Jumo Kinyata Kenya   "   "
Rwenzururu Kingdom Government Officials.
"   "   "   "   Ministry Of Security.
"   "   "   "   "   Immigration.
"   "   "   "   "   Finance.
"   "   "   "   "   Justice.
"   "   "   "   "   Education.
"   "   "   "   "   Regions.
                                State.
                                   /D m.O.
Rwenzururu Kingdom Government National Assembly.
"   "   "   Ministry Of Churches.
Abanyakiaghanda ky'Embita y'Obukama bwa Rwen—

Rwenzururu Kingdom Government because they are in Much Sorrow', was spoken, I know, to *me*, none other. And what might I do? I sat at my desk amid my deadlines and self-multiplying obligations The final obsequies were to take place at the grove of the Buhikira on October 25, to be followed by the crowning of young Charles. How suddenly a true function for that beater of the bark – in which all chief mourners would be caparisoned – lying in a cabinet at my home in Sussex, an ethnic artefact, a thing of the past.

Well ahead of that date, on September 13, eleven days after Isaya died, a ferocious memorandum was issued from Rwenzururu's 'Ministry of Security', immaculately typewritten, demanding of every department of the Kingdom maximum vigilance against attacks, house-burnings and encroachments by Ugandan and Toro forces. The same memorandum required that all 'foreigners' were to remove themselves from Rwenzururu territory or face the consequences. It was a purposeful call to solidarity at this critical juncture. It was despatched not only to all Rwenzururu administrators, from Bwamba to Busongora, but copied, in effect, to the world.

To the world beyond it was saying, Ruwenzururu is still in business. And the world beyond, which is to say Uganda itself, was distracted. Some four months earlier, in May, Milton Obote had summoned his recently appointed army commander, Major-General Idi Amin, and instructed him to bombard the Kabaka of Buganda, King Freddie Mutesa, Uganda's President, out of his palace at Mengo, Kampala. The assault took place by night. Failing to kill him, it sent the Kabaka scuttling *incognito* for the Rwandan border and temporary escape to London. Obote was now on course for the formal abolition of not only Buganda but all five of the Bantu Kingdoms and their monarchs woven into the painstaking tapestry of Uganda's constitution at independence – Toro included. A fell swoop. With the same constitutional ripping-out, Uganda was to sever its allegiance to the Queen of England. Milton Obote was to be no longer Prime Minister of Uganda but President of a republic, perhaps for life (or death), since it was not long thereafter that he was to declare Uganda to be a 'one party state'. All that was to come in 1967. Meanwhile, in late 1966, whatever phantom kingship might still linger on in the Mountains of the Moon, with its little king who Obote had pronounced fitted no definition of a king, was nowhere near the forefront of the minds of the internal *putsch*-maker of the distant capital.

However, Kampala had had wind of Isaya's death within two or three weeks of its occurrence. By October 5th, 1966, the Deputy Minister of Regional Administrations, S E Isiaga, was in Fort Portal, attempting to persuade the Toro government – the Omuhikirwa and old King George – to get rid of their chiefs appointed for the Bakonzo-Baamba areas, who were sitting in idleness and fear, and to approve a new raft of Bakonzo and Baamba chiefs supposedly acceptable to the populace. The Omuhikirwa of course prevaricated. The 1965 establishment of 'advisory' county councils independent of Toro had proved pointless since they were bereft of any executive arm. Later that October 1966, Uganda's Cabinet got a full report on 'the present situation since the death of Mukirane'. Reviewing the background, it was obliged to say that 'following the Prime Minister's visit' (in September 1965) 'there was a considerable swing towards sympathy with the Central Government, particularly in the lower areas.' But that little waft of flattery was forgotten by the next but one paragraph:

> 5.   There is no doubt whatever that the Rwenzururu administration has been for some time, and still is, extremely effective in the mountain areas. There is a de facto boundary beyond which Government Administrators and Agents are at present powerless to penetrate. There is a full organization of chiefs, a considerable number of so-called ministers, an assembly of Rwenzururu organization representatives, courts, prisons, a pseudo-military organization, schools are run and taxes are collected for which type-written tickets are issued. Unwritten laws which are, nevertheless, extremely effective are promulgated by the regime. The whole organization copies the Central Government, and the chiefly hierarchy of the Toro Government. Official correspondence is sent out and the organization behaves as though it were the legal government of the area. The regime is accepted by the people living in the areas and on the boundaries because they have no alternative but to do so. This fact is an embarrassment to the Central Government.

The paper acknowledged that Isaya's death 'will not kill the movement', but stressed that it gave the (Ugandan) Government 'an opportunity to step in if action is taken promptly'. Just how might Government 'step in'? Why, by appointing *miruka* (parish) chiefs in the Rwenzururu areas – all except Bunyangabo county, which was too vast and geographically impenetrable – and give them armed protection for a few months. And who would come forward as candidate for such *miruka* chieftainships? Ah-ha! There would be none with such a death-wish.

Meanwhile, in the mountains, the fear was of a usurpation of the slender line of hereditary authority. The Court had been warned by the reckless disloyalty of Fanehasi Kisokeronio. Yet power allures the ambitious, even in Shangri-la. The successor to the omusingaship was yet a mere boy, and the kingdom itself so young. Nor was there an obvious explanation of that early death of the Founder-King for the far-flung community of Rwenzururu patriots. Poisoning would be suspected; even if there was little cause to postulate foul motive, the whisper would be, *Poison?* Poison is ever a dark option in Africa. The widowed Queen was pregnant again, presumably by Isaya. A second fear was of Kampala taking advantage of a moment of headlessness.

Swiftly, that October the student king Charles was promoted to Grade 3 at school at the Buhikira, and on November 1st, now just 14, he was crowned 'King Kibanzanga II', the boy-King taking the appellation of his father which declared him adamantine, Hier stehe ich, *Here I stand.* The coronal adornment, Charles 'Kibanzanga' has told me, was of cloth. But he must hasten to his majority, and wisdom. In his private journal he wrote: '4 December [1966] God helped me. Promoted to Primary 4.' In the event, Isaya's yielding of the shield to God appeared to stimulate Rwenzururu to fiercer patriotism, more implacable determination, a yet keener self-reliance of the individual Rwenzururu sazas. Soon after that death the earthquake referred to on page 290 shook the mountain region. Several brick or breeze-block buildings in Bundibugyo and Bubandi crumpled irreparably, including the two main lowland schools outside Rwenzururu's jurisdiction. Harugali and the Rwenzururu hill region felt the tremor: the hill men read it as a portent. In the Ugandan capital a new Cabinet paper that next March, 1967, confessed to the strengthening of the rebel kingdom. 'In general,' it reported, 'it seems that Rwenzururu has suffered no setback following the death of Mukirane.' In Bwamba 'the morale of the pro-

Government elements is low... Dissatisfaction with Central Government is also stronger than before.' In Bakonjo country 'a substantial part of the hills [is] totally under Rwenzururu control.' In Bunyangabo, the entire hill area was under Rwenzururu, with a no-man's-land below separating Batoro and Bakonzo regions; so also in Burahya, in Rwenzururu's north-east. In April 1967 Charles joined the Scout movement, becoming a patrol leader. Meanwhile, fresh disaffection was brewing: a figure of influence at the old Court, bodyguard to the dead King, now close to the late King's widow, sought to succeed to the all-but-vacant kingship. His own brother, Rwenzururu Chairman of Bunyangabo, could guarantee the backing of that rambling saza. The would-be usurper staged his coup – and failed. With their local champion captured and detained, Bunyangabo pulled out – seceded from the kingdom, striking a deal with lowland administration for a high level of Konzo control of Konzo territory. It was a sickening blow. Back in the thatched capital the usurper was tried and sentenced to death.

Just then Uganda struck. On September 24, 1967, government troops swept up into the southern heartland and put the entire community to flight. They found the seat of government, ekhyaghanda – palace, parliament and the ministerial headquarters – at Ihandero, a spur or two to the east of Kitolu, and torched the lot. The condemned man made his escape and fled to Bunyangabo. Charles too evaded capture, and took refuge in the house of a certain Muleghuli. Even now the enemy did not find the deep-forest treasury. Yet the disruption had been grievous. Family by family the people crept back; the ekyaghanda was rebuilt; the Government of Rwenzururu gathered up its threads of many colours and the weave resumed. Yet now it seems they were never long without harassment. Next year Charles was advised to shift his personal headquarters back across the Tako river to Bukuke, resuming his studies there. His dead father never ceased to peer over his shoulder. 'December 4' (1968), his diary records, 'raised to Primary 6.' The year 1969 began more tranquil, and the administration returned to Ihandiro. Mwambalha's regency cabinet, with Charles' assent, even considered a permanent reconciliation with Kampala. They despatched a bright young Mukonzo, Masereka Bonefasi, to the Ugandan capital with a brief to find a suitably dispassionate lawyer to represent Rwenzururu's case in anticipated negotiations with President Obote. Bonfasi was indeed directed to an amenable legal partnership, but when the

head of the chosen firm returned to his native England and then *his* partner was deported, the initiative ran into the sand. The year ended with an entry in Charles' diary which tells of his priorities. 'December 4, 1969. Primary 7. I came top.'

On February 8th, 1970, the Commander-in-Chief of Milton Obote's armed forces, who was still Idi Amin, brought into play in the mountains his new secret weapon, a wondrous toy. A helicopter gunship, crewed by Israelis, flying low, swept over the horizon of each spur and valley of the forest perimeter of northern Bukonzo, instantly located Rwenzururu's re-established governmental headquarters. If any reader wonders how Israel came to be pursuing Uganda's dissidents, the answer is that it was gathering support at the United Nations Assembly in New York among the newly independent Third World states to frustrate Muslim support for the Palestinians: such are the workings of global democracy. A column of troops swiftly sped up from the foothills – Nubians, mostly; pagans – and once again torched the sanctum. Rwenzururu reeled; the old gods crouched, the gods of the *inner* sanctum and Rwenzururu held – the old communion of race and place, *thuli baghuma*, one-ness, the collective of blood and suffering, embitha-secret – endowed by nature; and the cabinet, omulerembera-premier Samwiri Mukirane and his nine ministers, and the awaiting Prince, son of the martyred founder, formulator of the vision, likewise *held*. Even when the Regent Yolana Mwambalha was killed in an internal feud, Rwenzururu *held*. The hour of start of Charles Wesley's reign proper was fast approaching. He was 18.

In March 1970, he personally began to master the typewriter. In June that year, he enrolled in a correspondence course offered by a British tutorial college with a branch in Nairobi. Rwenzururu had its privy Post Box numbers at Bwera and Kasese, not unconnected with the Church of Uganda. In October that year, still 18, at the Buhikira, Charles was formally ceded his full authority as Omusinga – King of Rwenzururu – by the assembled elders and cabinet. He was accorded the further title of Irema-Ngoma, Keeper of the Drum. His mother Christine was endowed with the title of Nyamukama, Queen-mother, albeit herself reaching for a share of drum-authority. This 'drum' was not so much object as quality; it was neither *a* drum nor *the* drum but *Drum*, the quality of *drumming*, a rhythm in the inward ear, in the blood, a wordless command which unified folk, combining three sanctities of Beat,

Beast and Tree or, alternatively, Dedicated Sound, Dedicated Dance and Dedication itself, drawing all as by a magnet into a circle of fealty, willing the feet into vow. Charles' accession to full kingly authority was further sanctified by the church of Jesus, through the endorsement of the preacher Bawalana Timiseho, a Mukonzo who had lately emerged as one endowed by the Holy Spirit, a Christian, fundamentalist in doctrinal matters. With Omusinga Charles' backing that same October this evangelizing Timothy launched a 'Gospel Mission' at the Buhikira, the royal precinct, re-established at Ihandero.

Soon enough, so Charles' own diary records, the fledged young king and his entourage toured eastwards, to the Rwenzururu subcounty of Obuthale. This was the site of the ancient copper diggings and my speculated site of the lost foundry, first spoken of in this book on page 89. The significance of this peregrination lay in the centrality of Obuthale amid the tribal territory Uganda-side, overlooking the main lowland settlement of Kasese and the adjacent modern copper mine of Kilembe which employed many hundred Bakonzo (including, at that time, as a foreman, Seylversta Mukirane, my beloved companion of 1963). It so happened that global copper prices had lately been sliding. A result of that was the British company which extracted copper at Kilembe deciding to pull out. Milton Obote, being a child of Britain's post-war ideology of paternal socialism, nationalized the site. Under Government management, the defunct mine re-engaged men to manufacture rods from the residue of copper stock, and telephone and electricity poles out of the conifers planted on the old mine's slag, and to keep in repair the murram roads of Uganda's western region with the graders jettisoned by the mine. As for Charles, from his temporary base in Obuthale, and in the company of his visionary Timiseho, he ventured down as far as Kyalema spur where a Church of Uganda church already stood, and where he lodged at the house of Masereka James. All this was assertion afresh of the reality of Rwenzururian authority among at least the Bakonzo, wherever their territory. Setting forth from there on Thursday, December 17, 1970, the young King engaged on a new mountain tour. In southern Bukonzo he descended to the road at Bwera, to be hosted by Erisa Mukirane. Thence he returned to his formal capital at the Kahindangoma, in heavily wooded country, not more than a few hours' ascent from the roadhead and mission station at Nsenyi. *Hier stehe ich.* Does not this boldness of his itinerary demonstrate the indifference of Kampala just then as to what was going on in Puck's mountain realm? Where were you, Obote?

And what were you doing in Singapore in January 1971? Why, you were attending the Commonwealth Prime Ministers' Conference and your former army commander General Idi Amin, a popular figure with whom you had been careless enough to fall out, took the opportunity to seize power. Or – as Idi himself urged me to believe when years later in his place of exile we talked through the entire happening hour by hour – to have power unexpectedly thrust upon him by the disaffected military and a disillusioned citizenry.

Idi's tempestuous dictatorship was to endure until 1979. Being in charge of a country is no piece of cake, especially if reading and writing do not come easily to one, but General Idi – quite soon to swell to Field-Marshal – trusted his instinct which was often remarkably sound, albeit a somewhat blunt gauge. He was for instance an uncanny tracker of beast or man, of quarry or enemy; and also an uncanny cross-tribal communicator, being able to speak on a good day anything up to seventeen of Uganda's languages, simply discovering himself to have acquired them by overhearing speech in the barrackroom or cookhouse. These did not include Lukonzo, since there were no Konzo in his army; yet he was familiar with Ruwenzori as we have seen and was perhaps touched by sympathy for the quaint little hardy people. He was anyway reminded of their cause by a persuasive memorandum submitted to him in Kampala from a group of Bakonzo elders on May 10th, 1971. These sages, headed by Daudi Kibatsi Isibiira, were acting on their own without the support or even the direct knowledge of the leadership of Rwenzururu. They represented a continuing divergence of Bakonzo-Bamba opinion, or at least an equivocation much as I had encountered on the ground in 1963 and had myself striven to exploit in favour of a peaceful compromise isolating the intransigent. Isibiira's initiative was intended not as a betrayal of Rwenzururu but rather as another route to the same end, in the name of the practicable and in the spirit of peace. (When Isibiira died in 2001,

Rwenzururians honoured his memory.) But he knew the temper of the Konzo visionaries, and that he and his fellows would be forbidden – were they to have asked Charles – to put their plea to the new President in the name of the secessionists. Idi resolved to act. Instinct prompted a route to rid himself and Uganda of an open sore in the Ruwenzori mountains by deciding upon a 'Separate District' of some description exclusively for the Bakonzo. Freed as he was from any restraints by Toro's dissolved kingdom he ordained the creation of *Kasese* District, incorporating the whole of the two southern counties of Busongora and Bukonzo. To a substantial degree, the new Kasese, with considerable autonomy as to its own management, was indeed Bakonzo (though including lowland Basongora cattle people); but it was far from being inclusive of *all* the Bakonzo Rwenzururu tribe. On its promulgation, Charles and his new cabinet surely felt wind had been taken from their sails...

What could they do but repudiate it? *Their* kingdom was essentially other, territory of dream re-entered upon waking, spirit-medium-mbandua's voices having taken flesh; an already self-governing kingdom exclusively Bakonzo-Baamba to the full extent that Nzururu's mountainland would permit allegiance, overt or covert. Idi's was a relatively simple, stroke-of-the-pen regional enactment. To do more – to have incorporated additionally into that single entity the entire Bakonzo- and Bamba-inhabited regions of the Uganda-side lowlands would have opened a whole row of cans of worms. Yet *all* that territory, plus Kyatenga on the Congo side, could not but be the *ne plus ultra* which the Rwenzururu leadership would settle for. So while Kasese District came into being, under largely Konzo management, in the lowland regions, Rwenzururu remained intact in the upland regions. Rwenzururu proper had long ceased asking anything of political Kampala unless to be left alone. Only to the extent that Idi's move divided the tribe did it bear upon the Buhikira in the mountains. A sort of hiatus between Konzo militants and moderates had been enunciated; but on the tribal Konzo 'net' the two entities of governance settled for a workable symbiosis without a desire for confrontation. The Kasese District officials drew their wages and performed their functions in the plainland community, which paid to Kasese its poll tax. Quite a large proportion of the community living at the base of the mountains and among the foothills and jumbly lowlands of

Nyabirongo also paid covertly (mostly willingly) a second 'graduated tax' to Rwenzururu. In the hills and upland communities, Kasese collectors never ventured: the tax was all Rwenzururu's, as was the administration. Idi's Ugandan army, mostly his fellow northern Muslims known imprecisely as Nubians, manned so-called 'roadblocks' on such footpaths they were aware of emerging from the hill country and maintained at least a nominal presence in each Ugandan subcounty. As for the young Konzo patriots, proving one's manhood was getting down and up dodging these pathblocks. If indeed you encountered a pathblock you could expect to be searched. Anyone found with a Rwenzururu tax receipt or other document indicating compliance with Rwenzururu would be handcuffed and liable to summary imprisonment. Naturally everyone soon got the hang of editing their pockets before they approached the unofficial frontier. Whenever goods of a suspicious nature or in a suspicious quantity required to be brought up into Rwenzururu – such as the police uniforms already mentioned, schoolbooks, school uniforms (shirt and shorts for boys, blouse and skirt for girls), and medical dressings – cover of darkness and the web of secret tracks were the smugglers' allies. Smuggling always has its joys. Yet all the while, common trade in, say, animals or crops for the twice weekly lowland markets at the roadheads, or in regular household purchases at the lowland shops or markets, proceeded along the acknowledged routes with practised insouciance. Under Idi's regime, it was a rare event for the troops to bestir themselves for a foray into the mountains. The Konzo came to look upon the new President in Kampala as rather less vicious than his predecessor.

As to which regimes – that of Uganda or Rwenzururu – had the deeper claim on the hearts of the people, there was no contest. Rwenzururu was life and liberty of a kind the tribal people had only dreamed of: their own governance with their own young

314

monarch and commander-in-chief, and his Konzo cabinet of mostly respected officers of state. Constitutionally, the clan system within the Bakonzo and the Bamba was given emphatic authority, with the Kingdom obliging the election by each clan of its leader, and clan leaders becoming the kingdom's legislators on clan issues under the headship of the King. In what way were such figures 'elected'? Why, by the people's scrutiny of their trustworthiness and their loyalty to the ideals of Rwenzururu, such figures emerging by palaver, spur by spur. Thus headed, each clan was to be served by its own committee, with functions to assist the authority of the family, to oblige enactment of ancestral ceremony concerned with birth, marriage and death, and to give succour to orphans, widows, widowers and the poor. Likewise, the authority of village elders was upraised: their inherited commitment to that particular spur or locality, their cultural function, and their bridging role between King and populace.

The king, in the person of Charles, was vested with the power to make the senior appointments at the centre: the Speaker of the national assembly, the saza chiefs, the police commissioner, the army commander, the premier and ministers. He was served by his own inner committee, drawn from these senior figures, and that committee became the prime policy-making and administrative organ, yet ever sensitive to the views of the parliamentary assembly. He presided separately over bodies concerned with clan affairs, with women, youth, culture, and over the village headman's council. Oh, it was brave structuring; and it functioned. Charles reconstructed his cabinet to comprise nine portfolios. He selected as his new Premier – omulerembera – the hard and canny Yolamu Mulima, who had performed so resourcefully as chairman of Kyatenga county, Congo-side, during the dark days of the mid-1960s and whose authority was still visible in this picture I took of him 28 years later. Charles himself took the Defence portfolio with Kinyamusitu as his right arm. The other eight were Finance, Internal Affairs, Regions, Justice, Education, Works, Labour and Foreign Affairs (for Rwenzururu was nothing if not an independent state of the global community). Four further senior roles were recognised at the centre of affairs: that of the Speaker of the National Assembly, the Chief Judge, the Deputy Minister of Defence, and the Deputy Minister of Finance. Four portfolios of the previous government had been dropped: Health – perhaps because there was little that could be achieved beyond invoking Nyabibuya, without a doctor in the kingdom or the possibility of manning so much as a dispensary; Natural Resources – since the conservational rules were in place; 'Culture and Community Development' – since the re-assertion of much that was Konzo in language, artefact, song, instrumental music, ritual, and in the weft of society, role and inner style had already wondrously transpired; and Churches – since, given the ubiquity of the places of Christian worship in the mountains, God could be left to be His own interpreter. The King-founder of Rwenzururu, Isaya, had stitched Jesus into the primal weft of the kingdom. It had never been less than a holy and a Christian struggle, its creation (if not its execution) never less than the working of God's justice; and he himself – Isaya – of the line of prophets, biblical, directed by the Absolute, barred from compromise, a Nehemiah albeit of the New Testament. In all this Charles had grown up, from his early childhood fashioned and honed as his father's successor, revering the universal *ecclesia* of Christ which in the gospel of the Church of Uganda (beholden to Canterbury) was careful to keep its links with Rwenzururu from below the mountains and at last to provide scripture and liturgy in the Lukonzo tongue and train and ordain ministers from the Konzo community. Thus Christian Rwenzururu clung on to its orthodoxy and its commerce in the Word of God with the outside world. An ordained Konzo priest had been intruded into the mountains of Bukonzo to baptize, in 1967, the infant prince, Williams Sibibuka, born to Isaya posthumously by his wife Christine Mukirania: her third son. Thus also, four years on, succeeding to the full powers of his Omusingaship, Charles was accompanied and guided by the Mukonzo evengelist Timiseho.

A Pauline discipline was applied by Charles to the conduct of his people. When it came to excesses and frivolities of lowland modernity, there was censorship. For example, the immoral temptations of the mini-skirt, sweeping Africa in the mid 1970s, reached the shops of Bwera and Kasese. Omusinga Charles decreed a ban. Any young Mukonzo hussy caught wearing the thing would be brought in her shameless apparel before a drumhead *miruka* court. The culprit found guilty as seen, two horizontal slashes were made by the judicial knife, sufficient to scar for life, the upper one on the thigh marking the level of naughtiness the mini left exposed, and the lower on the calf marking the approved skirt level for any decent young Rwenzururu citizeness. Beautified or macho hair-dos becoming the fashion in the barbering salons of the plainland villages – what we would call today the 'Afro' style – were also disallowed, and returning Rwenzururu citizens thus Absalomed would be judicially shaven. A strain of the Roundhead had pierced the national ethic under the eye of the exclusively Protestant leadership. While eluma festivities were permitted, drunkenness was frowned on, and alcohol as a route to spirituality was no practice of the Court.

Yet spirit-singing and the role of the medium-mbandua certainly persisted, and no region of the inhabited mountains was without its *omwaliro*, spirit hall, of mud walls and lofty thatch: in the presence of sudden death in war you did not cease to invoke, through the agency of an mbandua, the tutelars of the mountains, Nyabibuya or Kitasamba, for martial preservation or success in pursuit of the enemy; and the spirits responded, indeed, at the privy sessions with their shudderings of the premises, the hissing and the clickings of their unearthly proximity: you could hardly afford to pass up their endorsement, risk their wrath. Up there it might be said not only Rwenzururians but Jesus too needed all the help they could get. The mountains' Jesus lost little by being less exclusive than he was in the lowlands and gained the earth, that is to say the mountains themselves, the creative event. He gained the feminine principle, Gaia, of which the all-male Protestant Father, Son and Spirit were so inordinately stripped. As I have hinted, the vestigial litany of these forgotten people was beginning to name, as Almighty God, *Nyamuhanga* – the Konzo generator of creation. The church below permitted this Nyamuhanga neither his chief consort Nyabibuya, sister of Kitasamba, nor any of his lesser wives. Moreover that further ground of all that was and is, which was neither on the one hand all that was temporal and spatial, and of life and death, nor on the other hand of eternity and infinity, but both, each reflecting the other through the presence of the inner mountains and their peaks, had no place in the cosmology of the imported God. Here in Rwenzururu, however, the frail citizenry lived hard by the very rock on which divinity rested, on which the 'church' of man's perception, be it pagan or Christian, was founded. This was what I venture to

317

describe *gaia-ecclesia*, genetrix, against whose bosom they sheltered, whose snow-melt watered them, whose storms awed them, and peace nursed them. Into what they already had, they admitted the light and the dark of a supposedly Christian Nyamuhanga with a powerful wife.

About this time they hewed out into written words what guided and inspired them. This remarkable document entitled *Aims, Objectives and Organisation of the Rwenzururu Kingdom* was produced under King Charles's presidency and Mulima's premiership, as a constitutional thesis, by a body of wise men known as the Central Research Committee of the Bakonzo Life History Society. The committee was composed of 'representatives of all Counties or Regions of the Ruwenzori Mountains': it was thus the direct product of the vision of Isaya himself. It breathed his passion, his touched grandeur and purity of intent. Since it was framed, explicitly, not only for the guidance of all those of the Bakonzo and Baamba who could read but also for the enlightenment of the world beyond, it was produced in immaculate typewritten form in Lukonzo and in English, all thirty-one sections of it on twenty pages of foolscap, closing with a list of credits to those who had contributed to the Founder's vision, thus:

ACKNOWLEDGEMENT

Special tribute go to the Chairman and Chief researcher, King Isaya Mukirania Kibanzanga together with his family and those he consulted during his research work during the years 1954 – 1962.

Others are:

1. Mr. Maathe Bulasio	-	Busongora Branch currently Kasese District.
2. Mr. Obadia Munakenya	-	Bunyangabo branch
3. Mr. Balyananzighu Yosamu	-	Burahya branch
4. Mr. Kahiwa George	-	Bwamba branch currently Bundibugyo District
5. Mr. Stanley Tom (Isemusoki)	-	United Kingdom England.

The first-named is Blasio Maate, the teacher (and future administrator) from Bwera, and the penultimate is George Kahigwa, of Bwamba, brother-in-law of Isaya himself, both of whom we have already encountered in this text. By God's Grace, these two fine men survive to this day in good health. The last named is myself, mythologized a little, in that, as so frequently occurs among the mountains, my name is merged with that of the Breaker of Rocks, H M Stanley, who first put Ruwenzori into the atlases of the world. In the same manner the title *Isemusoki* credits me with fatherhood of the son Musoke born in 1960 in Fort Portal to the anthropologist Kirsten Alnaes who, originally in the company of her husband Axel Somerfeldt, came in 1958 to Bwamba to make her remarkable study of Konzo spirit-singing, as has been referred to. Kirsten and I have long been friends, but not lovers.

This treatise of Aims, *Ebilhubirirwa*, is unmistakably the work of civilized men. It is embued with generosity; it is premised on lasting ideals of mankind with an insistent urgency – freedom, peace, unity, tolerance, the collective weal, the sanctity of culture and heritage, and the essential rightness of creation. Of the headings of those 21 sections, give ear to some: 3. The Creation of Peace, Unity and Freedom in the Kingdom; 6. Equality, and Respect for the Disabled; 7. Protection and Respect for the Elderly; 10. The Role of the People in Development; 14. The Role of Youth in Development; 15. The Role of Women in Development; 22. Personal Development in the Kingdom; 24. Family Management; 28. The Environment, and Management of Natural Disasters...

There among its cardinal aims was 'the truth and clean leadership among [the Kingdom's] mountains and plainland people', and that the Kingdom 'shall uphold, preserve, protect, and defend the cultural values, norms, and practices of the people of Rwenzururu, e.g. burning cultural fire on the mountain, giving offerings, and hoisting the flag, for the maintenance of a firm foundation.' Such 'offerings' and the 'cultural fire' were indeed to the tutelary spirits of their place. It was insistent on equal respect being given to 'all people', and that positions of authority should be open 'to every person in Rwenzururu on individual merit' provided they were of 'high moral character and proven integrity.' And, interestingly, 'The Kingdom of Rwenzururu aims at stamping out tribalism and sectarianism, especially in the awarding of jobs.' The same note of inclusiveness and tolerance carried through to Section 3: 'The Kingdom shall put in place ways and means of ... respecting people's views on matters of religion, culture and language' – a principle detailed in Section 21 (on 'Religions'): 'The Kingdom shall accord all right and freedom of worship without any political intervention./When need be, the Kingdom shall liaise with religous leaders to elect Bishops and Chief Qadis', thus explicitly accepting the presence and rights of Islamic converts. 'The Kingdom,' Section 3 continued, 'aims at establishing ways and means of protecting *and* respecting culture and environment and ensuring that they work for the good of all' – a theme expanded on in the section devoted to Culture itself, committing the Kingdom to 'developing, protecting and upholding cultural practices for the dignity and honour of the Banyarwenzururu' among whom Bakonzo, Baamba, Basongora, Batuku and Banyabindi were specifically named; and the protection and promotion of their languages. Education was, likewise, a recurring theme – first as a 'cornerstone of the Kingdom's development process' (under that Section – 4 – devoted to Rwenzururu's independence), and later, as several obligations listed under Education (20): compulsory schooling, penalized truancy, combating illiteracy, the freedom to establish church schools or private schools, and the welcoming of educational NGOs (Non Governmental Organizations). A function of the clan chiefs was, indeed, the establishment of funds to provide scholarships in the outer world for the brightest sons. It was formally insisted that 'the Kingdom shall accord respect and dignity for those who are not natives of Rwenzururu and for their property. These people shall include, but not be limited to, those employed, traders, businessmen, and seekers of asylum for whatever reason'...

So it rolled out, Rwenzururu embued with ideals worthy of the Greeks, blessable by Christ, a very proper expression of the sanctity of race and place, admitting no retrogression, nothing shut and dark and turned upon itself. And yet, what else moved in the swirl of Kitasamba's mists? – Isaya's storm-troopers frustrating the building of the road that I had proposed, the instinctual razing of the cash-crop of coffee and cotton laboriously planted under the aegis of the colonial power, the insistence on the circular dwelling that allowed for no expansion by addition... Rwenzururu's exercise in collective, tribal anamnesis was surely the reliving of an archaic ideal, tinctured by the Grace and Gospel of late imperial England, yet essentially African, affronted by the abstract conceits of deferred rewards, of capital and labour, of mass-market commodity agriculture which every drought, flood and crop blight would make a ruin of, of personal aggrandisement by the display of riches, of the rights of man over the whims of gods.There was no politics to fit the life Isaya's Konzo were inspired to live; and slow by slow the alien dislocations of modernity crept from the polluted plain by spoor and seepage to infect the upland compounds. The tin roof, the squared hut, middle-men and greed, crept and seeped. Charles clung to his ignorance of the outside world. He strove to hold his subjects by whatever of their own tradition made them aware of the uniqueness of their own kingdom in the comity of kingly nations. We boulevardiers may smirk at the copies of his promulgations and protests posted off to the Secretary-General of United Nations or the Queen of the Commonwealth, who never replied. Were they not but declaration of the indestructibility of Rwenzururu's rights amid the babel of humanity, to advance under its own banner towards some sort of Rwenzururian light? Rwenzururu would plead its cause, would have its say, oblivious of absurdity. Was it known at the Buhikira, the palace compound on the slopes of Rwenzururu, that by that date a fair score of so-called nation states with populations or territory less than that of Rwenzururu had their voting powers and their representatives at the UN in New York, determining the shift and tilt of the affairs of Man – from Tonga to Qatar, from Monaco to Bermuda? Very likely not. They did not ruminate on scale and knew nothing of the streets, satanic mills and ideologies of other men. What had Israel of tented old needed to declare nationhood? Nothing but twelve sons of a single father and a strip of Canaan – and loyalty. Wherever Rwenzururu's leadership perceived a slipping away of patriotic ardour, it presumed to oblige it, if necessary by the threat of terror or terror itself. A sense of continuing 'struggle' had to be maintained, demanding inner no less than outer commitment. '*Tuli baghuma*' – 'we are all one' – was the cry we have heard already; yet notwithstanding the collective vision, one-ness was not the day-to-day reality. Those *down*, somewhere between one-third and half the Lukonzo-speaking people, operated their lives within the Uganda government system. Almost all the Baamba lived *down*, even Kawamara himself, however committed to the Rwenzururu purpose. In due course the secret imposition, not to say criminal hazard, of paying a second 'graduated' tax to Rwenzururu had come to irk many. In certain lowland market villages of Busongora and Bukonzo and possibly elsewhere the market traders – Bakonzo themselves – lived in fear of being raided by Rwenzururu askaris. The highland spearmen would descend (for example) on a central village like Kisinga at the start of a market day, ring the area, close in upon the market, and oblige the women to load the fish and other produce into baskets and carry it by their hidden routes up into the hills. Such raids would be undertaken on Rwenzururu government orders. Charles himself was titular Commander-in-Chief, and seen as such.

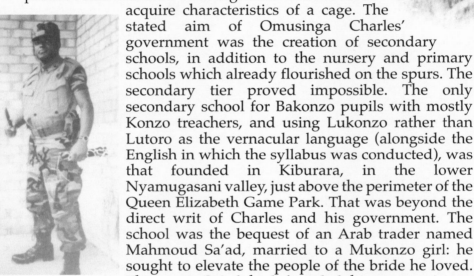

Parallel to all of this, for Rwenzururians of promise and ambition their highland redoubt could acquire characteristics of a cage. The stated aim of Omusinga Charles' government was the creation of secondary schools, in addition to the nursery and primary schools which already flourished on the spurs. The secondary tier proved impossible. The only secondary school for Bakonzo pupils with mostly Konzo treachers, and using Lukonzo rather than Lutoro as the vernacular language (alongside the English in which the syllabus was conducted), was that founded in Kiburara, in the lower Nyamugasani valley, just above the perimeter of the Queen Elizabeth Game Park. That was beyond the direct writ of Charles and his government. The school was the bequest of an Arab trader named Mahmoud Sa'ad, married to a Mukonzo girl: he sought to elevate the people of the bride he loved.

The same Sa'ad had founded his own primary school for Bakonzo in Bwera, close to the mosque he also built there – a school with an Islamic ambiance. The Rwenzururu leadership welcomed the opening up of these opportunities, notwithstanding their Muslim base and the consequent emergence of Bakonzo converts to Islam... and notwithstanding they were *down*. Elsewhere than Kiburara highland Bakonzo seeking secondary schooling had no choice but to live with relatives below, off the mountains, and changing their names to disguise their provenance, enter schools in which Rutoro was the prevailing vernacular and the teachers largely Batoro.

So as Omusinga Charles' gallant eyes ranged his provinces he was aware of the strains and divisions of his people. He could not but wonder where it might all lead. He was a handsome young man – small-statured, as Konzo are, but the head well chiselled, strong in the chin and nose, and marked grace in the expression. He bore himself with unfaltering dignity, spoke quietly and slowly, commanded with a look. He knew the authority of silence. The role for which his father had moulded him was natural to him now. He dressed either in his military uniform as in this rare snapshot where, flanked by Kinyamusitu, he took the salute at a

Rwenzururu passing out parade at the Kahindangoma School of Infantry, or in long fine smocks and a domed *qubbah*, smuggled into his court by the trader Hassan Katigiti (who also obtained – in Kampala – the uniforms for his police and Scouts and askaris). He married tiny Zeuliah, a girl of the right blood from the Buswagha clan, approved by the elders of the Bakonzo and strengthening the dynastic potential. She became his Queen, and Rwenzururu waited for a kingly heir. Charles was no puppet. He promoted those he had learned to trust, for their skills and loyalty – Yolamu Mulima as his *omulerembera*, Prime Minister, and Kinyamusitu–forest as his Commander-in-Chief, both gritty men. He could be magnanimous. For example, he accepted back into the fold the renegade Fanehasi Kisokeronio: contrite for the time being, the fellow was too effective a guerilla to do without. With Bunyangabo he maintained cautious, respectful links. Alternatively, he could be draconian. His askaris under Kinyamusitu swept down upon those suspected of siding with central government, the quisling *esyondaghangali*, spearing those in flight; trussing those caught, they frog-marched them back into the inner mountains for judicial assessment, torture and detention until deemed chastened, cleansed and compliant enough to risk release. In June 1977, a sharpening of Rwenzururu's frontiers was decreed: all Batoro occupying what was deemed Bakonzo-Baamba territory were given fourteen days to move out. And how those Batoro moved! By what means was such notice given? Why, in cleft reeds, with written warnings (in Lukonzo) planted in the vicinity of the homes of the unwanted.

Charles himself maintained control over issues of policy. He presided over Rwenzururu's national ekikali-assembly, which was convened regularly, clandestinely, to hear out the worries and wishes of its delegates – spur chiefs and clan elders, *abatahwa* and *ababandua* – with gravity and calm. He held court in style, in his hidden grove, performing his kingly role with his young Queen at his side in their regalia, their gowns and headdresses and sometimes shades as the occasion demanded, their seven royal drums, nine spears, four carved stools; leopardskins, lionskins,

and the pelts of the colobus monkey; and the finest woven bags and baskets. He maintained his Court musicians and his dancers, stilt walkers and contortionists, flautists and drummers, and performers on the great endara xylophone. His entourage bore their titles. The Kingdom throughout its length flew its flag (where it was safe) and sang its anthem: the Buhikira-court showed the way things should be done. As we know, every now and then the entire cast of Court players with whatever props they could carry found it necessary to disperse at haste into the surrounding forest. Field-Marshal Dr Idi Amin Dada, President of Uganda throughout most of the seventies, the 'last King of Scotland' as the writer Giles Foden has wittily enthroned him, being familiar with those mountains, was surely aware of how exasperatingly elusive was any all-military solution to this relatively innocuous if stubborn secession. His local commanders knew well enough that any mass burning of huts was a game two could play, especially where the other side had infinite recourse to refuge. From time to time, operating on supposed information, a patrol of footsoldiers would move out from the encampments (each of a few dozen, stationed in each Uganda-defined sub-county comprising the Rwenzururu area), and snake into the hills to seek out a particular Rwenzururu miscreant. Failing to find him they would torch his house. Sometimes co-ordinated with these ground operations, sometimes independently, Idi's helicopter gunships – no longer crewed

and supplied by Israelis but by his new military collaborators, the Libyans – would sweep the populated ridges and send the Konzo peasantry scurrying for cover; or likewise scour the perimeter of the upper forest, to nose around for the demon king's ekyaghanda, focal point of government: the Buhikira-palace, and – if they knew of such a thing – the ekikali, the national Konzo assembly house. However, the Ugandan enemy never did locate the new government headquarters established after the catastrophe of 1970: the Kahindangoma, the 'drum-site' as that *embitha* grove was privily known, vigilantly sentried at every approach, couched in forest and preserved in this rare photograph of a political rally in train. For the enemy it was a vast region to scour, so complex, clefted, erratic, strange and switching between squall and shroud of fog and katabatic draught. Kitasamba was nothing if not Rwenzururian patriot.

So King Charles and Queen Zeuliah's royal bamboo thatch was never violated in those subsequent Seventies. No heir was vouchsafed to the couple, not so much as a daughter. Charles convinced as King, was never less than kingly, emerging from behind the split bamboo portière of his royal hut. Yet kingship craves dynasty. Where there is nothing in stone, and all but nothing in writing let alone print, lineage was the natural embodiment of durability. Moreover Charles deserved a son to dislodge, with a function of fatherhood, the fixation of his own sonship of the founder-father . The elders conferred. Substitution by a sister for a barren wife has always been acceptable in Bantu practice: Zeuliah had a sister.

xxiii

Obote Reenters

Idi fell: in April 1979 the army of Tanzania, where Obote had been holing up under the shelter of President Julius Nyerere for eight years, pushed into Kampala amid a surge of looting. In alliance with them were various rival factions of armed Ugandan exiles or dissidents. The largest group was led by a spirited ideologue, a 36-year-old Muhima from the Ankole, Yoweri Museveni. The next largest group – albeit far fewer than Museveni's – bore allegiance to Obote and his Uganda People's Congress party. An amiable academic, Professor Yusufu Lule, chairman of a coalition of half a dozen factions united by little beyond contempt for Amin, found himself on the steps of the Parliament of the charming, ravaged capital being elected President of his country. Beyond the suburbs a befuddled Idi hung about in the bush for a month or so longer with a bunch of his men, on the off-chance of landing a blow that would switch the course of the contest in the eleventh round. At one point he blundered into a unit of the Tanzanian 'liberators' whose commander, so Idi has told me himself, was so delighted to encounter this old comrade-in-arms from the colonial Kenya African Rifles that he quite omitted to apprehend let alone kill his tyrant-quarry. In the end Idi retreated north into his West Nile tribal bailiwick before skipping the country. His first place of refuge was Libya, and his next, after six months, Saudi Arabia where cushioned by the mercy of Allah he still awaits the apt moment for a fêted homecoming. In Kampala, meanwhile, in 1979, Yoweri Museveni was appointed Minister of Defence. But the put-upon professor could not hold the coalition. After sixty-eight days of ineffectual Presidency Lule gave way to Godfrey Binaisa, a Muganda lawyer, who would readjust the coalition, the Uganda National Liberation Front, and survive in office seven months, likewise achieving negligibly. Milton Obote personally returned to Uganda on May 27,

1980, to reactivate his Uganda People's Congress. Political parties were back in business. Obote's placeman Paulo Muwanga snatched interim power in May 1980. Elections were to be held that December: a measure of rigging and gerrymandering ensured Obote's UPC and their (momentary) allies the victory. Yoweri Museveni soon withdrew into the bush of his native Ankole and south-west Buganda with some forty of his stalwarts, to begin a guerilla campaign which in the style of Fidel Castro in Cuba in the later 1950s would win him more and more territory until finally, five years later at the start of 1986, the supreme power in Uganda which he holds to this day would be his.

Bear in mind this future frame as we return to our mountains after the fall and flight of Idi Amin. There – consider: peace proposed herself. The flown tyrant's soldiery had all but vanished with his vanishing. The strife of confrontation and battle was quite elsewhere and was, moreover, vicariously engaged upon by Tanzanian troops and a largely foreign occupying administration, pushing on from the distant capital northward into Uganda's Nilotic hinterland. The kingdom of the Mountains of the Moon was half forgot. The Rwenzururu leadership seized the opportunity presented by the collapse of central administration. An attempt by Kampala's new regime to appoint or re-appoint in Kasese a raft of their own chiefs had Rwenzururu chasing out the lot of them, in an operation known as 'Liberating Kasese'. The fugitive chiefs went to ground in the District Headquarters on the edge of Kasese town, behind the frail shield of a fledgling government's alarmed and underpaid police. Scenting something new in the air, the saza of Bunyangabo applied to rejoin the rebel kingdom.

A fresh figure emerges. He is a certain Amon Bazira, a Mukonzo of Nyabindi stock, which is to say of heritage admixed with non-Konzo blood, in the usual instance Batoro. This mix accorded the Banyabindi a reputation among the common run of Bakonzo for sophistication and physical authority, being as a rule taller, and for a distancing *hauteur*. Young Amon, of vigour and ambition, had grown up in the southern foothills, attending school at Kitolu and Bwera, and getting his first university degree in Political Science and Philosophy at Makerere, and a

second degree in International Law by correspondence with a British institution. He entered President Lule's government as Director-General of Intelligence. In this role, one of his earliest tasks was to organise a national census. There would be no census among the Bakonzo without the consent and participation of the Rwenzururu leadership. The first response to Bazira's request from Omusinga Charles, Irema-Ngoma, keeper of the mystic drum, was a cheeky question as to whether the Uganda government was also considering carrying out a census in Kenya or Zaïre.

A story hung by Bazira and Rwenzururu. As a schoolboy, he had daringly visited Isaya Mukirane, Kawamara and Mupalya in prison. He had grown up in the surreality of a Kingdom whose frontier was a mountain contour. He had run to school with his fellows across the highland gullies; he had been watched by them from their fastness with vicarious pride as he made his way in the other world below. When he was a Makerere undergraduate the regency government of Rwenzururu had sent to him young Bonifasi Masereka to seek in Kampala a team of lawyers capable of representing Rwenzururu in negotiations with Obote – an initiative which as we have seen came to naught. After his graduation, during the later years of the Amin tyranny, he moved easily in Dar es-Salaam among the self-exiled *bien pensants* of Uganda's socialists and liberals. His fellows perceived his ability, his single-mindedness. By virtue of his not belonging to a major tribe, he was a natural enough choice for the Intelligence role under the governments of Lule, Binaisa and Muwanga.

Now at the prospect of coherent rule, a national census: but how might the people of Rwenzururu be counted? Being of these people's provenance and blood, Amon could enter among them freely where no census officers dared to tread, which now included Kasese town itself. This census issue – counting the heads of the Bakonzo and Baamba – became the context of dialogue between the fumbling administration in Kampala and Charles Wesley Irema-Ngoma's government of Rwenzururu, of whose credibility Amon needed no convincing. Negotiations on the conduct of the census evolved naturally into talk of reconciliation between Rwenzururu and Uganda. Meanwhile, with the fall of Amin a vacancy had arisen for the role of District Commissioner for Kasese District, comprising the whole of the southern reaches of Ruwenzori. For this post the name was advanced of a Mukonzo of rare credentials. This was none other than Blasio Maate, who first entered these pages in 1954 as a young school teacher, and although always a voice for conciliation had gone to jail after my visit of 1963 for his mere complicity with the Rwenzururu movement in an episode which I have reported here. On his release he had been exiled to northern Uganda where he had entered local government. Amon Bazira now saw to it, at the start of 1980, that Blasio should become the first ever Mukonzo District Commissioner – of his native south Ruwenzori region. Finally a third figure steps from the wings, to flank Bazira: a young Mukonzo patriot, articulate, energetic and capable, springing from Kyarumba, just east of the Nyamugasani river in which the first patriots were martyred. He was winning respect as a school teacher in Kigezi by the shore of Lake Edward. He was Amos Kambere.

Thus was a frame forming that harbingered an historic shift. In the mountains, in the Kahindangoma, in the Buhikira, was there not a new scent in the air? The Amin soldiery, the uniformed detachments of Nubians, lazy and dangerous in each of their subcounty encampments, had vanished. The outer challenge to Rwenzururu had in this present interregnum evaporated. What ensued was an inner threat – that, with Toro cast aside as a political entity and Kampala docile, this kingdom itself was somehow to be swindled of *raison d'être*. Was not the highland poll-tax imposed on lowland Konzo seeming to some otiose, even extorsive? Was not the division of authority by slope and contour coming to seem a needless barrier to brotherly cohesion? The flowering of apparently benign if weak government in Kampala after years of misrule was opening the petals of the mind: ethnicity, yes, let it bloom if it would – yet what now shall be done with this bloom in the African garden? Konzo and Ganda, were they not ancestral siblings? Did not spear-pointed defiance and invited siege lock the Rwenzururians out of further education and senior roles in Ugandan life? The right to 'self-determination' was enshrined in the charters of the fora of international man – the United Nations, of which the missives of Isaya's foundational patriots had no right to be ignorant; and prior to the UN, the League of Nations, if anyone were to delve their history. What then shall be done with that 'self', once determined? For these vigorous Bakonzo and Baamba, for all their thrust and high intention, once

330

confirmed and acknowledged in their quilted habitation, their lingo, collective lilt, their lines of hills, their snowy deity, what next?

The tree sure of its rootedness in its own soil and growing in its own space spreads its limbs and shelter, shares its fruit and scatters its seeds. At the end of 1979 the Omulerembera Mulima, mastering premier of Rwenzururu for nearly eight years, stood aside for Muhongya Yeremiya. The interchanges with the new Uganda National Liberation Front government engendered by Amon Bazira gathered a certain momentum. They drew in Blasio Maate, the new District Commissioner. Young Amos Kambere flit between the lowland base and the royal eyrie much as I had done seventeen years earlier. They drew in the Church of Uganda: Archbishop Wani, a convert from Idi Amin's small northern Kakua tribe, who had succeeded to the Archepiscopate after the murder of his predecessor, Archbishop Luwum, by Idi's savage henchmen, had not overlooked the rights of the Lukonzo-speaking people nor the Rwenzururu 'movement's' Church of Uganda. Wani was talking of a new diocese of Ruwenzori South, based in Kasese, calved by the existing inflated Toro-dominated Diocese of Ruwenzori, based in Fort Portal. Were not now Bakonzo-Baamba rights implicitly acknowledged in most matters of governance in their mountains, folds and gullies? Alongside the government of Rwenzururu there was now taking shape under Omusinga Charles' direction an Elders' Forum, comprising those from both plain and mountain: a unifying sagacity.

On the return to Ugandan soil of Milton Obote that May of 1980 and the certainty of a multi-party general election in a matter of months, an extra factor of divisiveness entered the Bakonzo. The caretaker administration of Paulo Muwanga was fixed upon ensuring the return to power of Obote's UPC, of which Bazira was an adherent. That mid-year 1980, Omusinga Charles of Rwenzururu declared for peace, which Bazira was all set to broker: Rwenzururu, said Charles, would henceforth pursue its aims in Uganda by diplomacy and negotiation rather than spearpoint or gun muzzle. Those 'aims' were implicitly in relation to Uganda (as distinct from Uganda plus Congo/Zäire of which Rwenzururu was also composed); and such 'aims' – Bakonzo-Baamba authority on their own ground, equal standing among the constituent peoples of Uganda, rightful share of Ugandan funds for the exploitation of Ruwenzori's resources – implied on their

331

attainment an approaching day on which the dreamtime of Rwenzururu's independence would be formally ended and the mountain Kingdom dissolved into the only country from which it had felt the necessity to declare its 'secession'. Highland Bunyangabo was now back in the Kingdom, lined up for prospective Konzo rewards.

This made wings. If Rwenzururu were to reintegrate, so thought the plainland Bakonzo harried from both sides, then *get on with it*: make this deal on our equal status, free up the economics of our rich territory, and join the brave new Phoenix-Uganda that Obote II promised. By contrast, certain mountain Bakonzo sensed the betrayal of their waking dream, their Camelot, their Lyonesse. An ache, as of love obscurely forfeited, stole upon the highland spirit. It would take two full years from Charles' declaration of peace in 1980 to resolution, and dissolution... a species of dissolution. As Bill Cheyne had observed, 'Things are never straightforward in Africa.' Yet the same may be said of the human heart.

Not everyone in Uganda welcomed the prospect of the return of Obote and his UPC: far from it. Many remembered the fellow for his contempt for the constitution he had put his signature to on independence, for the dead hand of his State collectivism, for the allure of the groceries that political power put in reach of his protégés. But Amon Bazira, Director-General of Intelligence, was Obote's man, and Bazira would deliver Rwenzururu to his master-in-waiting. Integral to any prospective deal was that Omusinga Charles' citizens should not stand aloof from the approaching Ugandan elections. They should vote – and they should, the Omusinga opined, vote UPC.

The Rwenzururu Bakonzo southern heartland comprised three constituencies under the revised boundaries: Kasese South, Kasese West, and Kasese North. Bazira himself was to contest Kasese West, centred upon Bwera and its neighbouring border township of Mpondwe. As his constituency agent and Mr Fixit he took on none other than the restless and ubiquitous Fanehasi Kisokeronio. Young Amos Kambere became the UPC's front-runner for Kasese South, comprising all the lowlands from the lake edge north into the densely populated Nyamugasani foothills. Kasese North presented a difficulty. This constituency incorporated the little township and railhead that gave the District its name, and the neighbouring mining site of Kilembe. An attractive candidate had emerged for this parliamentary division who stood outside the inner circle of the Rwenzururian, Church-of-Uganda, pro-UPC hierarchy. This was the youthful and ambitious agricultural officer Vito Muhindo, then the Assistant District Commissioner in neighbouring Kigezi. Vito was set to stand under the colours of Uganda's prevailingly Roman Catholic Democratic Party, the principal country-wide opponent of the UPC. As the date of the General Election neared and Omusinga Charles voiced open support for the UPC, a group of Rwenzururu zealots in Kasese North concocted a plan to disqualify Vito Muhindo by preventing him registering his candidature by the stipulated date. On the eve of his deadline they abducted him and tied him up in a hut in Bunyangabo's central foothill village of Kitswamba. Vito was of daring and resource. He contrived to escape and to make a dash across country northwards towards Fort Portal, the regional capital and the venue for registration of candidature. He made ground swiftly, but he had not reached the relative safety of the road before he was challenged in half darkness by a band of Bunyangabo Rwenzururu Youth Wingers. They were ignorant of Vito's escape and had no idea who he was. He, likewise unaware as to who his challengers were, and supposing himself to be in territory populated by Batoro, replied to the challenge in Lutoro. This misjudgment cost him his life: a Youth Winger's spear flew and got him in the chest.

Such a killing was no part of Bazira's or Charles' strategy. It was (I have been often assured) a mistake, and a consequence of *trop de zèle*. In overall charge of the Youth Wing of Bunyangabo at that time was Bonifasi Baluku , whom I was to come to know later for his spontaneous and infectious Konzo patriotism. Bonnë's *trop de zèle* had involved him in the abduction of Vito, and he was already seeking the escapee's recapture when the spear dealt its blow. In the end, the consequences of that spear were fatal not only for Vito but also for Bonnë. Sixteen years later, when managing the parliamentary campaign of Charles' brother Christopher Tabaan in the 1996 general election in a very different political era, a single bullet flew through the evening dark in a Kasese street and Bonnë fell dead. No assailant was ever apprehended, and no one much doubts that this was an ancient score avenged. As to the further consequences of Vito's mortal spear, they are to this day incalculable. In the sequence of the narrative, we trace them next to the 1980 election in Vito's stead not of the Rwenzururu UPC candidate but of a Konzo figure of a rare stamp and unexpected provenance: a certain medical doctor, Crispus Kiyonga.

Politically, Dr Kiyonga represented a loose federation of Ugandan intellectuals and idealists who sought to overlay the factionalism of the past with a structure of national unity. This *coterie* took the name of the Uganda Patriotic Movement (UPM). It had the support of several of Kampala's leading lights, including my trans-African companion of twenty-six years before, Erisa Kironde, who in the unrolling of time had become head of the Red Cross in East and Central Africa. This UPM was endorsed by Fronasa, the armed Front for National Salvation which, under the command of its creator, Yoweri Museveni, had provided the largest contingent of armed Ugandans – some 9,000 at its peak – to join with the invading Tanzanians in the overthrow of Amin. The UPM proved too shallow in the root to flower electorally, and swiftly withered after the charade of the vote was done. Its only candidate to be elected to that Parliament of 1980 was indeed Crispus Kiyonga at Kasese North. This was to be the unpromising start of a political career of no mean brilliance, and gore. And at once we must strike a contrast and a parallel. For this Crispus Kiyonga was one of a kind with Amon Bazira – each of the same bean row and from adjacent pods; and to grow to be mortal rivals. Surely these two young men, whose courses had interwoven repeatedly since childhood, read one another with a searing mutual perception. Let us recall how Bazira was of the Konzo sub-group the Banyabindi, a distinction that accorded him a membrane of élitehood. Kiyonga likewise sprang from a sub-group of the broader Bakonzo community, namely the Batalingi, long settled in the region of the Tako valley along the frontier with Congo and whose native dialect of Lukonzo indicated past admixture with non-Konzo blood. Each, then, was entering the limelight of public affairs among a people swept up in the dramatic assertion of their unique ethnicity from a point ever so slightly to one side of the core ethnicity. Bright son of a thrusting Mutalingi mother, Crispus Kiyonga had distinguished himself swiftly at school at Bwera, won himself a place at Makerere university, studied medicine, and came to the notice of the daring Museveni as a competent, dependable organiser of fellow-students on behalf of Fronasa. Young Kiyonga, by contrast with Bazira, held himself *déraciné*, aloof from dramatized ethnicity. He took for wife a bright young Munyankole, which is to say, of Museveni's people. Had not life and ambition brought him *down* the valley and *out* across the plains? What was Nzururu now to him, let alone

Rwenzururu, which was *up*, and *in*, with its spears and skins and *embitha*? In Kasese North he had benefited from popular disgust at the jape that brutishly ended the life of Vito Muhindo and manifested Rwenzururu at its worst. He befriended Vito's devastated widow, Christine. Yet once in parliament in Kampala, Kiyonga could see there was nothing he could do, a lone voice, and Obote back with the old habit of submitting all other considerations to the preserving of his power. Was he even safe from arrest or elimination? Within three or four months of that flawed 1980 election his own mentor, Museveni, slipped away into the bush with his gang of armed stalwarts to fight for his own version of unity, justice and the rest of it for however many years it might take (it would take six). At the same time Crispus Kiyonga, MP, removed himself and young family to Nairobi to earn his living in gynaecological practice.

Meanwhile in the mountains the Omusinga Charles was listening to new siren voices. These voices spoke of the consolidation of Rwenzururu's achievements within the 'new' Uganda. What, say, were the 'Bayira' now to be raised to equivalence with the other ethnic constituents of Uganda? What if their own administrative authority on their territory were to be guaranteed by the orderly, negotiated dissolving of the Kingdom of Ugandan Rwenzururu into Uganda itself, which would unite the tribe Uganda-side? What, say, were they to win their own diocese, and their bibles and liturgy were to be in their own language? What, say, if Lukonzo was to become the language of learning in all their primary schools? Had not Archbishop Wani himself, hearkening personally to the voice of Nyamuhanga-creator whose representative on earth in Uganda he was, awoken to the right of these people of the mountains and lapping plains to their own ecclesial authority, their own bishop, cathedral liturgy, vernacular Common Book of Prayer and the rest?

The sirens were, of course, Amon Bazira, who had now entered Obote's government as Deputy Minister for Lands, Minerals and Water Resources; and young Amos Kambere, now Member of Parliament for Kasese South. Both were proven Bayira patriots; both looked to shape political careers within a structure headed by a figure of authenticated slipperiness whose soldiery, an African generation earlier, had gunned down the Kingdom's founder's askaris, taken Bakonzo in their thousands into captivity, and hunted that founder and father through the mountains like a bestial trophy. A *bona fides* of the sirens' intentions was the appointment of the Mukonzo Blasio Maate as District Commissioner for Kasese. Such an appointment was unprecedented in itself and doubly remarkable in that the figure chosen was the early Rwenzururu loyalist. Blasio was already proving his effectiveness on 'Bayira' territory on the plain's edge where the roads ran. The offer of scattering roles amid the Ugandan administration of the *volk's* territory to those who had helped build and sustain Rwenzururu was therefore carrying plausibility. In all, three sazas, ten gombololas, and thirty-two parish-mirukas were thus designated for Bakonzo-Baamba. If we look back upon those defined swathes of administrative territory and the infinite interior they ringed, we may today perceive the true dimensions of Rwenzururu acknowledged no less by Kampala than by Charles's citizens themselves. Meanwhile the Archbishop was at work – or, put another way, the spirit of the Anglican Lord was at work, that Lord which looped and interwove all those mountain chapels founded by Isaya, and further spawned by Charles, with Namirembe Cathedral in far Kampala.

In late 1981, flitting priests plus Amon and Amos arranged a meeting between the Omusinga Charles Irema-Ngoma and Archbishop Wani himself. Charles would, unprecedently, descend from the fortress hills by way of Busyangwa and Ibimbo and the valley of the Rwempya, the westward tributary of the Nyamugasani, to the mission church at Nsenyi. For his part, the Archbishop would walk up from the roadhead of Kisinga, a mile to the south, having passed through several Rwenzururu checkpoints since leaving the main road at Kinyamaseki. So indeed his Grace did walk, escorted by the politicos Amon and Amos, together with Bishop Kamanyire of Fort Portal and the existing Diocese of Ruwenzori, to meet Charles there, at Nsenyi, where the two were caught on camera. The entire bush around rustling with Rwenzururu weaponry. There the group cut a deal on a prospective new *Diocese of South Ruwenzori* whose flock would be for the most part

336

Charles's citizenry and whose funds would come from their pockets and their national treasury. All this, not quite yet but foreseeably soon.

So much for souls. As for soldiers, Rwenzururu's army of askaris, they were to be assured training in Dr Obote's forces, the Uganda National Liberation Army. Theoretically they would have the chance of winning promotion in spite of the senior ranks being already filled by Nilotics of the President's Langi or their Acholi confrères. As for Charles himself, on ceasing to be King, rather than be offered one of the (worthless) honorary Doctorates such as were habitually confettied by black American universities on African leaders as a badge of prominence, he would be granted genuine further schooling in any part of the world he chose, together with a piece of land at Kasese, and a shop, a bus, a private car and a holiday in London, England.

A car, a bus, a shop...? A mess of pottage? What were the spurs to make of this, those widowed by the struggle, those who sacrificed their sons? Who among the mountain people had not been obliged not once but many times to flee their compounds in the ultimate cause of Rwenzururu and to watch, from some inner refuge *up*, the curl of the smoke as their homes were torched by the former troops of the self-same silky republican back in Kampala? What of Charles's scattered army, its units of askaris and armed 'youth wings' semi-autonomous under their several commands such as the mountainous terrain dictated? Could the King, Keeper of their Drum, their own General who had signed their Certificate of Qualification, disband them at a stroke on the pretext that the day was won and that the people of the mountains were acknowledged masters of their territory within the greater entity of Uganda? Long were the consultations and palavers among the *ekikali*-deputies of core Rwenzururu, the privy

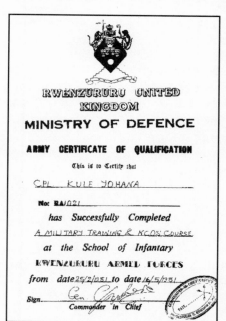

RWENZURURU UNITED KINGDOM

MINISTRY OF DEFENCE

ARMY CERTIFICATE OF QUALIFICATION

This is to Certify that

CPL   KULE JOHANA

No: RA/021

has Successfully Completed

A MILITARY TRAINING & NCOS COURSE

at the School of Infantry

RWENZURURU ARMED FORCES

from date 25/2/1981 *to* date 16/5/1981

Sign.

Commander 'in Chief

council of elders drawn from plain and mountainland alike, Charles's own tight cabinet, and the warriors... Can we not overhear those warriors: Kinyamusitu-Forest, commander-in-chief, and his men; the chain of his command; the mythic raiders; Beowulf and Glendower; legionnaire and *legendarius*; the men of the spear and now of the bullet, of the blood of death (and also of life); guardians of the mythic freedom, the inner, upper, foggy and forest freedom, the dark-trusters, *embitha*-guarantors, whom no pact or written deal could trap and truss? What would their blandished Omusinga have them forfeit for a bus, a car, a shop, a patch of lowland realty, realty-for-royalty, proffered and nudged at them by that snake-eyed Nilotic now crept back to power and pomp in Kampala, him whom they had once rejoiced to see downed by the bruiser Amin? What trust could you place in him, Obote, and these upward-thrusting intermediaries with their book-learning and governmental simony? This was Africa. Pacts were made and meant in blood, open wound to open wound, cicatrice to cicatrice, not on sheets of post-colonial paper. Had not Rwenzurururians lived the true Africa, for the better part of two decades, and *lived* as in living memory in these mountains none had dared to live life? Kinyamusitu sulked in his tents. He was not alone.

Bazira overheard and knew this, of course; young Amos Kambere knew it. They could play a long hand, yet not interminable. The two were patriots, surely, but they were modern men. Their patriotism said, Unify the people. The greater fact was Uganda, in and through Uganda would they and their fellow Konzo rise. They had the arguments, but not the gods. Had I not personally once known this very situation here? They would let Charles do the persuading among his people, but not for ever. A date began to loom, a decimal digit, twenty, all the digits that Nyamuhanga provided for the extremities of Man: twenty years since Isaya Mukirane, in August 1962, had re-sounded Kapoli's horn and declared Rwenzururu born into freedom: the fifteenth of that month. The very roundness of the figure, twenty, would endorse the thesis: this was to be no surrender but a sort of triumphal evolution, a metamorphosis, a melding, the sacred river's lake-estuary, Rwenzururu embosomed by Uganda. Yet who could trust whom? Could the sirens underwrite the good faith of Dr Obote or the proper behaviour of his troops? Could Charles indeed yield his Kingdom, dependably and intact? Was not

Kinyamusitu still unmoved, sulking in his tents? There required to be a preparatory foregathering of both sides if ever there was to be a public sealing of what was being brokered.

So in June 1982 Nsenyi was again to be the site of a grave *baraza*. This meeting was to be attended not only by Amon Bazira, Amos Kambere and Archbishop Wani but by the Ugandan Chief-of-Staff, Brigadier Oyite-Ojok. With the party from below came Blasio Maate, whom all sides commended as a 'safe pair of hands' wherever Bakonzo were concerned. Once more this distinguished array reached Kisinga in elaborate cavalcade by the murram vehicle track between high grasses through a series of Rwenzururu roadblocks, at the first of which Chief-of-Staff Ojok and his escort were ceremonially disarmed. Once again, they walked the final mile to settle down at the old mission house, more or less under the cross of Jesus, to shape with Charles and his inner council the approaching historic entente and the method of its popular endorsement, nay, celebration, two months ahead. There would be a mighty concourse of Konzo folk, panoply and rejoicing at tribal reunion, mutual forgiveness between Rwenzururu and Kampala, everyone the victor and the future golden... Kinyamusitu sulked in his tents and won awe by saying little.

Word was put around as mid-August neared. On the spurs, as in the picture, the military and civilian population gathered to learn of the looming reconciliation. From all over the Bakonzo-Baamba regions children were to be bus-ed into Kasese's two-street township that was masquerading as the mountains' capital. Military trucks and charabancs were mobilized. Crammed

with folk and flagged and streamered they carried in the celebrants from wherever they had clustered at the murram roadside that ringed the mountains. One such vehicle rolled off the road and fourteen children died. This was mass festivity, tribal to its roots, Batoro and Basongora keeping low, security very very tight. The army was sharply briefed and readied against those who might try a spoiling – since this was, in part, a fudge; and whomsoever Charles would persuade to descend with him, civilian or soldiery, would not be representatives of all, not quite all, with Kinyamusitu no longer merely sulking in his tents but hostile... Yet, come! Fanehasi Kisokeronio, that hardened toughie, blood on his hands, he was already down, having been promised by Bazira chairmanship of the Kasese Land Board; and Charles was King – *he* was coming down, melting Rwenzururu into Uganda. *Eryandangala*, the 'descend' (as Syahuka translates it, nouning the verb) was policy. Was ever there a Kingless Kingdom?

So the morning broke, the fifteenth of the month, August 1982, and the mountain monarch was to gather his retinue and ministers at his ever-hidden, ever-secret forest capital, and descend caparisoned and shod to greet the world of other men and there upon a daïs set amid the great boma of Kasese, the open site of spontaneous assembly, unskein his realm. It was a Sunday, a heady and astounding time. Fore-gathering there were vast quantities of Konzo man, from down, from up; those of his subjects who never yet had seen him yet honoured him for all he was to them – Irema-Ngoma, interweaver of their spurs and cols, keeper of ancestry that threaded their story in and out of gods of the inner heights, son of a father who had taken back the authority they had lost or (in this world) never had; and those of the plainland villages beyond his aegis, beyond the rattle of his drum and the long call of Kapoli's horn, to whom he was scarcely more than myth and exactor of tribute for their mythic right of unity. This day that unity was to be attained and in the attainment spent. The lowland drummers were there without number, and dancers, *eluma*-flautists and *endara*-xylophonists turning the whole air milky for the concourse; song-groups of children by the score, balladists, panegyricists. Opposite the canopied daïs and its microphones was erected a tented pavilion of tiered seats with a front row of easy chairs for dignatories and their flowered ladies. Amplifiers were set up all around the boma on poles to disseminate the message. A Minister of State was rumoured to be attending, Chris Rwakasisi, closest of all to President Obote in Kampala, panjandrum of the President's Office; plus the Chief-of-Staff of the Ugandan Defence Forces on hand to confirm the formality of peace out of the formality of war. Military vehicles were massively thronged and soldiery and police in benign if watchful mood, for this was to be a *tour de force* of welcome and reconciliation, a petty triumph in a mighty place, the Mountains of the Moon's descent to planet earth, the horizontal taking the vertical by the hand and saying, Lie with me.

Would he truly materialize, this king, from out of the fastness? – out of twenty years of whisper, wonder, caught breath – from beyond an entire generation of mystery, father-to-son, founder-martyr to chosen heir, and heir not only to Isaya but to Tibamwenda, Nyamutswa, Kapoli, Ruhandika, Ngununu, Nyavinji, Ndyoka, Kitasamba, Nyabibuya, Nzururu, heir to the snows, heights, cold impenetrabilities, bridging from that antiquity and unknowability to this *present*, this empty awaiting daïs... was he truly to materialize and unsceptre himself?

xxiv

Eryandaghala

And now descend, sir...

The truth is, Charles had quit his Buhikira the previous day, August 14. His mother, two brothers and two sisters, his wife Zeuliah, his several ministers in shoes, his quorum of three or four dozen askaris, his Rwenzururian ordained clerics, his soothsayer, and the armed royal bodyguards, male and female, came down by various routes somewhat surreptitiously to the Nsenyi rendezvous. Charles remained in combat gear, camouflaged against the possibility of assault from Kinyamusitu and his merry forest men – just how many that might be, God knew, but the merriest, the hardest and merriest for sure – and remained in combat gear right up to the moment of encounter with Amon and Amos at Nsenyi's mission compound. From there, soon after dawn on the 15th, the Omusinga party walked through high grasses to the Kisinga roadhead where they entered their serious limousines and assorted other cars, jeeps and trucks in which the lowland greeters were to conduct and escort the Rwenzururians out. Charles's uniformed men climbed aboard the UNLA lorries carrying their rebel spears and rifles – a token group, it must be said, since every able-bodied male citizen of Rwenzururu was more or less a soldier. They drove in convoy by the lanes of those jumbly lowlands to the graded murram road running eastwards from the Congo border through the Queen Elizabeth II Game Park to the junction with the north-south road to Kasese.

Those too old to get to Kasese, or who dared not leave their flocks, clustered at the roadside to glimpse the fleeting wonder: the eldritch king in a limo on the plain at 40 mph. From Muhokya five miles south of Kasese township the scene was all but stripped of inhabitants: everyone was gone on ahead to Kasese. At the boma there, by courtesy of short-wave army radio, word flurried among the vast concourse of the royal progress on the road: bearded fife and *omulungulu* drum fevered up the multitude. The dignitaries from below nudged through the throng in their dark cars to take their seats: Minister of State Rwakasisi, Minister of Local Government Rurangarana, Deputy Minister of Lands, Minerals and Water Resources Amon Bazira, Chief-of-Staff Ojok, Bishop Kamanyire, other lofty clerics (Roman Catholics, Adventists, Muslims) such as dared look Rwenzururu in the face; Yeremiya Kawamara, representing the Baamba; and therefore no Batoro, scarcely a Musongora, and no Crispus Kiyonga, MP. The drums quickened and crescendoed and amid his own men (still armed) King Rwenzururu Charles, Irema-Ngoma, now in braided caftan with flared sleeves, shirt, tie, dark *caudillo* glasses, and a stove-pipe toque whose layered stripes combined Rwenzururu's colours with Uganda's, was – *eh!* – in their midst.

What thunder of drumming, rumble of male exclamation, swell of female ululation, bellowsing of *eluma* reeds, what ascent from descent! What morning götterdämmerung! The Rwenzururu askaris, cheered as heroes, were de-bused and corralled tactfully, to be badged, bountied and re-engaged by emollient recruiters. One such was that very corporal Kule Yohana, who came with his certificate of graduation in Rwenzururu's Armed Forces (pictured on page 337) as proof of his military capacity and who serves in Uganda's army to this day... And speeches. What speeches! Rwakasisi, Ojok, Bazira... How they did tell it forth. Each was translated, exhortation by exhortation, truism by truism, pious hope by pious hope... Rwakasisi, speaking for the President, declared that all was reconciliation, there was to be no revenge, the prospect for the region was brilliant, and would those left sulking in their tents come out (handing over their weapons) while the mood was on, to receive 'honour and prestige' for their smart action? Oyite-Ojok declared that this ex-king, Irema-Ngoma (the drum-title remaining valid, albeit the drum diffused) would not be swayed by any doubters, for surely his armed followers were at this very moment fulfilling their military vocations by joining the UNLA in the further cause of Uganda. Rurangarana declared that ex-Rwenzururu administrators were assuredly to continue in their roles at county, sub-county and parish levels, but under the fatherly authority henceforth of the government of Uganda. Amon Bazira, architect of this mystic coming together and mastermind of the entire *coup de théâtre* at Kasese, declared that the Rwenzururu 'movement' had spearheaded a 'struggle for human rights and human dignity', which was why *et cetera*.

And finally Charles, Irema-Ngoma.

Except for the first few sentences of greeting in the English language, he spoke in Lukonzo and was translated (into English) phrase by phrase. The whole thing took two hours. He delivered it all with sustained conviction: a noble and commanding figure. Significant parts of the peroration had been drafted, understandably, by Bazira and, equally understandably, were festooned in those passages with sub-Marxist rhetoric which if not intelligible to his listeners in either language could have hardly failed to impress them with what a Primary 7 level education plus an English correspondence course could aspire to in the way of impenetrable sagacity. Charles referred to his co-tribal hearers not as Bakonzo nor even as fellow-Rwenzururians (for that was only up to midnight the day before) but as 'Bayira', since this Konzo-coined heterogeny comfortably included Bazira's own Banyabindi sub-group and perhaps at a stretch the Baamba. He spoke of the long 'oppression and inequality' inflicted by the Batoro as the 'colonial legacy'. The Rwenzururu rebellion had become a 'revolution'; the bands of raiders and torchers had become 'cadres'; and the barkcloth-and-monkeyskin peasants of Rwenzururu who grew only such millet, plantains, yams or cassava as their families needed to survive on had become 'the masses'. These 'masses' of the audience were told they had become 'much more aware of their rights and civic duties than ever before. The masses here [they also learned] 'are politically educated. Their struggle has educated them. To educate the masses politically means that the totality of the nation of Uganda is a reality to them as citizens.' *Up to a point, Charles Kisembo*, Fanehasi Kisokeronio might well be thinking, wherever he was in that audience, since that Chairman of the Kasese Land Board's citizenship of Uganda was not to prove a sufficient reality to prevent him pretty soon going back into the forest to take up arms again against Uganda. 'The political struggle here,' Charles was telling his audience, at any rate in the English script, 'has enlightened the people, and they are fully educated about the politics of Uganda. By going through the fires of Rwenzururu, the cadres come out as tempered steel, and conscious of the prevailing politics of this country.' The assembled *proletarier* must have listened with awe to this commendation of their maturity in the underrunning dialectic of historical necessity.

As Charles now re-told the history of the 'struggle', even the BLHRS had become infected by the worm of political correctness. 'In 1954,' he told his audience, 'Isaya Mukirane, the founder of the Rwenzururu movement, began the *Bayira* Life History Research'... the organisation which 'set in motion the consciousness of the Bayira of their identity.' My notes of the October morning in 1954 to which he referred do not endorse such a title. Yet as Charles waxed upon the history told in these pages his voice rang out with an Isaian outrage and poetry – of how twenty-four years previously, at this very site of Kasese, the Life History Research Society convened its delegates alike from the mountains and the lowlands to bring forth a Bayira (Bakonzo) political manifesto. 'At that meeting the Bayira swore that if they were to wake up one day to find themselves confronted with the stark choice between war and slavery, they would choose war and fight. They were resolved to fight with everything they had, if need be with sticks and stones and with their fingernails...

'For a long time the Bayira were subjects of the now defunct Toro kingdom. All down the years we were treated as the gentiles of that Kingdom. Our people were subjected to and endured actual cruelty. But just as cruel were the invisible walls which existed between us and the Batoro under Batoro rule. How regrettable that the Batoro evolved a caste-like system to emphasize their social distance from us. They acted with a puffed up arrogance... [Our people] did not accept Toro rule because it followed a route of exclusive self-interest, vanity, envy and hostility to us... The Toro kingdom was a vessel that would carry us into dishonour. This was a grave matter and my people had a duty to resist. We knew that the outcome of submission to Toro rule would be our destruction spiritually and intellectually...'

He acknowledged the caprice of history and implicitly of geography. 'The Bayira were aware that before they were annexed to the Toro Kingdom, the people in that Kingdom had seen the white man first. The Batoro arguably were in contact with Western

345

civilisation and benefited from it before us. By virtue of this they might have become more politically conscious, commercially competent and educationally more advanced than us. One cannot blame anybody for having been "blessed" by historical accidents of white culture reaching them first. [The inverted commas around "blessed" appeared in the official translation.] But what we were ready to condemn vigorously as utterly evil has been the attempt to perpetuate that position arising from their good fortune by unjust means on the presumption that their community was a "chosen tribe".' British rule, Charles argued, endorsed the notion of the superiority of certain tribes. The Bakonzo ['Bayira'] under Kibanzanga Isaya Mukirane refused to accept subservience. 'This is the principle that has guided the Rwenzururu movement. The movement has had one motto: "Better to perish than live in slavery".... On our part, we were awakening to a sense of our historical identity by launching the Rwenzururu movement, and there was a rapid growth towards our awareness.

'For us, we are Bakonzo ["Bayira"] and we want to remain so for ever. We are not tribalists simply because we belong to a tribe. We are Bakonzo for the simple reason that we can no more avoid belonging to our tribe than any of the rest of you can avoid belonging to your various tribes. We are against any deliberate attempt to obliterate tribal distinctions. We hate any attempts intended to make any of our tribes in Uganda disappear. We are also against any tribe thinking that it is above others, and against the incitement of tribal sentiments such as can result in this or that tribe becoming elevated at the expense of others....'

And yet, 'The Bakonzo have had a sense of special unity which marks off those who share in that unity from the rest of Ugandans. Strong Rwenzururu sentiment has been the outcome of a shared history of suffering and of a tradition of corporate endeavour. This has evolved a kinship which has bound the Bayira into a one-ness. They recognise all they have in common, but do not stand away from those of other provenance. Their heritage has become distinctively their own, in the same way as a man lends his character to his own household. The Bakonzo have evolved an art of approach to things. They have a rich culture recognizably distinct from that of others.

'The solidarity of the Rwenzururu movement tells of its high survival value, given that our people here have had no modern means of politicising their struggle... The movement has acted as a trustee for all Bakonzo wherever they are... Our own zeal and determination have always been enough to create our own fighting force...

'To us the fight for freedom and human dignity has been an overwhelmingly important mission. Only those who know not what freedom and human dignity are can underestimate their authority within us here. If you were to be deprived of these you would fight for them with bare hands if you had no weapons. For Bakonzo who had lived in freedom and dignity before the whites decided to annexe their territory to Toro, the determination to gain that freedom was formidable.

'The Bakonzo were ready to defend their rights. They never backed away inwardly, thinking that sacrifice could wait till the morrow. They knew that by postponing hard decisions until the eleventh hour would be too late. They had to accept risks. We were determined; and we have shown time and again that what we had to do we could do, once we recognised the necessity of doing it.

'There have been some beyond our boundaries and timid pessimists within the region who supposed our struggle could not endure for even three months. Again and again courageous men proved them wrong. We are convinced that if we did not fall captive to our own fears and – more specifically – to the fears of the vocal minority, we would surely continue our struggle to the end. We knew that freedom would not come of its own accord. We were entering a phase of Uganda's history when we had to work to ensure that freedom. We were prepared to sacrifice other priorities in the name of the supreme goal...'

It reads well, and no doubt it sounded well. It was a persuasive apologia as to why Charles was where he was, doing what he was doing. It was an exercise in the secularization of Rwenzururu. The theme was quasi-political: human rights, something called freedom. He went on to complain of the absence of Bakonzo in virtually any office of significance in the administration of Uganda. The speech had made Rwenzururu into a 'movement' that was decidedly linear, headed for a 'supreme goal' which was presumably the present moment, in that he was apparently disbanding Rwenzururu and personally abdicating, willingly and more less triumphantly. The Mukonzo scholar and dedicatee of this book, Syahuka-Muhindo, has commented, 'The disbandment of the Rwenzururu Kingdom, hitherto a hindrance to the unity of the people, brought new hope to the people – namely that peace

347

would return to them.' Yet had not my error of judgment nineteen years earlier been to attempt to interpret Rwenzururu secularly? It was not linear and political and secular: it was round and theological. It was not in the first place about achieving things, progressing things, but about *being* something. Ruwenzori was and is an inner place, penetrable from within by obeisance, letting-go, and to all intents inaccessible from without; and the tribe encircled it, Congo-side and Uganda-side alike. Rwenzururu was never about putting its placemen in power in Kampala or, for that matter, Kinshasa: it was about its own inner being, its astounding territory, its *embitha*, Kitasamba's mystic brume.

Charles half knew that. His speech sounded warnings about all that could still go wrong if it turned out that, with Rwenzururu gone into voluntary liquidation or apotheosized, according to one's reading of the matter, the Bakonzo and Baamba still found themselves or felt themselves to be second class citizens in the brave new Uganda of Obote II. That is to say: he had his doubts as to the very premise of this grand durbar. And surely he half knew his whole endeavour was serving Amon Bazira's political ambition. The speech veered off into a panegyric on Obote. 'We have come because there is an era of understanding, under the able leadership of Dr Apollo Milton Obote. He leads a government in which we have full confidence. He leads a progressive government determined to revive Uganda... Dr Obote came back to Uganda with a great mission: to rehabilitate and reconstruct this nation... Our political wealth, if exploited, our manpower, the splendid policies pronounced, the creative powers of Dr Apollo Milton Obote, are ample material to build a truly mighty and abundant Uganda...' Obote had been in power a second time for over two and a half years, operating a regime characterized by avidity for power; corrupt, incompetent and collectivising. It had three more years to survive. Museveni's guerilla group, the National Resistance Army, was already denying him slices of the country quite close to Kampala. He was soon to lose his most effective commander, Ojok, in a helicopter crash... 'So today,' Charles concluded, 'I am handing over my soldiers to the government of Uganda and I am handing over the guns as well, so that the security of my people will from today be vested in the government of the Republic of Uganda. We have come down prepared to contribute to the concept of one

Government, one Nation, and one Parliament.'

Thus King Charles, Irema-Ngoma, Omusinga of Rwenzururu, twirled and flung his Excalibur back into the lake.

That night he spent with his family as guest of Yofesi 'Richman' Mutanywana, Mukonzo owner of a palm oil factory in Kasese. Yofesi had charge of Charles' shop, car, bus, and patch of Kasese real estate. And then to Kampala with little Zeuliah and his mother, to the Parliamentary Building, to be pictured there flanking the Ugandan President he
and his father had fought so long. Before that August was done the ex-King of Rwenzururu was on a British Airways flight to London, Heathrow, accompanied by Amos Kambere, MP for Kasese South. Timothy Bazarrabusa, Obote's first High Commissioner in London had long since returned to Uganda, to be murdered one evening on the streets of Kampala by persons unknown and for reasons unknown. In the mother-city of what most still knew as the British Commonwealth, the party of two had the name of one long known to the Bakonzo, the function of whose hand was perhaps to have risen from the lake and caught the sword by the hilt and drawn it beneath the surface of the mere.

End of Part II

PART III

KING OVER THE WATER : 1982-200?

xxv

Roll-Call in 2001

So, was this the end of it?

Twenty further years are gone – and the mountains remain, the high rock, the snouted glaciers, the swirled fog, wild declivities, sudden lakes, gulches, bogs, the standing giants – lobelias, groundsels, ramping helichrysums, and bearded lichen trailing from precipitous heathers ten times the height of a man. What men? Armed men, men at war, guerillas. Fanehasi Kisokeronio, old Phineas – you are *still there*, fighting? It cannot be...

Yet it is. You have fathered sixteen offspring by your several wives. You were slow to quicken wombs at first, but then the children came. Of those sixteen souls all are dead but a handful, many of their young lives ended violently, by bullet or spear, in the heights or in the forest; others of sickness, cold, deprivation or mischance. Is it for Rwenzururu still that you have struggled on? Have you a notion, old Phineas-Fanehasi, what you struggle for? For Charles's restoration? Charles *did* return for a dramatic week – you know that, Fanehasi – after more than fourteen years of self-exile in America, with me beside him, to address the multitude again at the same boma at Kasese. Were you there then, in late November 1998, skulking among those 'masses' – not any fewer than 30,000, maybe 50,000? No: you surely could not have risked recognition, so very much blood on your hands, capricious murder, raids, abductions... so much vengeance earned. So where *were* you on that phenomenal reappearance of Charles after fourteen years' sanctuary in America? At which high forest edge with your desperadoes, waiting upon reports of the tumult below, the concourse and the tumult, the delirium and the drumming? – and you all the while, the true keeper of the flame, guardian of the embitha, excommunicated as the enemy of peace? Can you read their motives and their expectations? They were gathered there to greet Charles in the name of *peace*, Fanehasi, and Konzo peace

353

moreover, such as once the people had tasted in the days of Rwenzururu. Is it that you have long despaired of such peace, Fanehasi – that Konzo integrity is impossible within the frame of any country called Uganda? You fancy, Fanehasi Kisokeronio, do you not, that a proper peace and proper integrity belonged only to this proper dark, in your mountains and forests, where you alone of the founder-figures remain in loyal championship. You are loyal to your despair.

I do not suppose that either Fanehasi or Charles could give expression as to their motives. That is for us outsiders, sophisticates and for the most part white, boulvardiers who have learned the hard practice of getting by without our childhood, be it the childhood of our race or of our single selves. As for the issue of Rwenzururu and its kingship, the people and their place, outer and inner, such as is alive to this day twenty years after the formal dissolution of the formal kingdom, there shall be no end of it until the *raison d'être* of being African has come to an end. Such a double ending will come about in the course of the working-through of human suffering, and black Africa has become no more than a region of the world's map not so much of *being* as of temperamental and stylistic hue. Its core contribution of living primality will have come to be as irretrievable as his own childhood to any of us. In most of tropical peasantry the occurrence of weaning is as a rule delayed many, many months beyond the average that has evolved in the smart, globalized world, and delayed with it are the onset of cerebralized existence and the penalties thereof. In old black Africa, primal innocence at the core of communal and individual life is thus prolonged, seeking and finding its role in compound life and clan and tribe. Therein lies its remnant claim to be a version of paradise, therein lay its vulnerability to the fatal impact such as came so late to the long-'dark' continent, and late of all to such as the Bakonzo and Baamba of Ruwenzori. *Their* grief had always been two-faceted: that of their felt humiliation at the hands of their plainland neighbours the Batoro, and that derived from what I have called their anamnesis: their living recollection of a former, primal innocence. Each face of grief reflects the other. The first may seek and secure a measure of alleviation by secular means, and in many marked ways has done so; but the other grief being of its nature not readily definable has not been readily ameliorated in definable ways. It has been a grief endemic and subliminal, and it spoke, and speaks – it knew and knows not why – out of the muzzles of the Kalashnikovs in the hands of Fanehasi and his coterie of factional guerillas in the mountains, and in the unquenchable clamour for Charles's reinstatement as someone entitled Omusinga and fit for honour in a thatched Buhikira on a tump above Kasese.

As for me, Tom Stacey, *mzee*, I succour that reinstatement as I succour my own vanished innocence in every prayer I utter for all sorts and conditions of men. For although I am justified in casting sub-Saharan Africa as entrapped anachronistically, I in the context of the societal evolution of man in his global village am convinced of the universality of the spiritual yearning that 'entrapment' so vividly throws up. The spiritual vision is always *primal* and always *innocent*: a vision, a faculty of seeing, that has as its sacred and vital function the countering of the secularization of man which would for ever entrap him in himself.

I tell an unfolding story. Where shall that story have brought Charles by the date this book goes to press? As I put these words on paper, our Charles is back in America once more, a king-over-the-water, waiting for what he supposes might be a formal summons to constitutional reinstatement as Omusinga waRwenzururu, King of the people and territory of those mountains. He knows quite well that the people crave for him and that the rulers of Uganda are now aware of this. Were that reinstatement to occur, will you, Fanehasi, be at hand as Charles receives his constitutional crown and the noise of drumming rolls among the mountains? Or will your rivenness and guilt oblige you to slink away on Congo-side and die in double exile among the shards of your boyhood imaginings at Kitolu?

There are few of us left, we founder-members. Here is the roll of those we knew who are no more.
Kinyamusitu, army commander, shot in 1991 in the mountains by his younger brother who had promised to persuade the old warrior to lay down his spear and could not so persuade him;
Timothy Bazarrabusa, teacher and diplomat, snipered in the street of a Kampala suburb, in 1966;
Henry Bwambale, PhD, the Bakonzo's treasured academic and one of their earliest graduates of Makerere, mysteriously and fatally injured on a visit to a lover;
Isaleri Kambere, the sage of Kitolu, called quietly to his Christian

Father- Creator, Nyamuhanga, at great age, in 1997;
Chief Khavaïru, claimed by Nyabibuya at ripe age in the late 1980s;
Kule his son, smith, with his clown face, too young, of fever;
Bonnë Baluku, political activist, assassinated by single bullet in a Kasese street in the parliamentary campaign of 1996;
My *Masereka* – lusty, daring Masereka – gunned down by latter-day mountain rebels for denying their will – around 1990;
Amon Bazira, patriot and mediator, ex-Minister and rebel leader, as shall be told: abducted and assassinated in Kenya in 1993;
Yaramiya Kawamara, leader of the Baamba, of age and sickness, in Bundibugyo;
Isaya Mukirane, founder-king of Rwenzururu, my long companion, long gone.

And who in our story lives on besides you, Fanehasi, prowling your forests, and me? Blasio Maate, elder statesman; Batulomayu, great runner, quondam judge in Rwenzururu; George Kahigwa. Ruhandika's grandson in Bwamba, senior elder, Isaya's brother-in-law; Ibrahimu Ndyanabaïsi, George's younger brother, who accompanied me in the mountains in 1954 and 1963; Seylversta the good, widowed, with three strong sons; Amos Kambere, Member of Obote's Parliament in exile in Vancouver; Yolamu Mulima, ex-Omulerembera, guarding the Rwenzururu archives, in retirement in Kamughobe; Ezironi Bwambale, ex-Minister of Obote's government, pierced by Isaya's hit-men, half-blinded by Amin's; Gerisone Ndambireki, ex-Rwenzururu minister and judge; Abraham Lincoln, ex-administrator and teacher, in his mid-eighties, and his wife; Christine Mukirania, Mrs Lincoln's sibling and indestructible Queen Mother; Christopher Tabaan, MP, her second son, the new Kibanzanga, serving a second term in Parliament; Sibibuka Williams, her third son, born fatherless; Charles Wesley Mumbere himself, Irema Ngoma, in resumed self-exile in fabled America, 'constitutional' Omusinga-in-waiting, so he would have us believe; Dr Crispus Kiyonga, Charles's avowed adversary, ' Commissar' of Museveni's National Resistance Movement and Africa-wide administrator of the World Health Organisation's assault upon the scourge of AIDS.

All this cast of Bakonzo are of the current of my life to this day, and one more, one of the few non-Bakonzo players on the bloody stage of former years whom I see in his sanctuary in Jeddah, Saudi Arabia, a figure of much religious devotion, yet hale and muscular and quite recently the father of his thirty-eighth child, namely Field

Marshal Dr Idi Amin Dada; aching for home and an impossible absolution. Beyond my personal span of continuing acquaintance is his old adversary, Milton Obote, hoary and shaggy now, holed up in Lusaka, Zambia. The unrolling story of the Bakonzo people of Ruwenzori flows through my office in Kensington by mail, e-mail, fax and phone. One of Fanehasi Kisokeronio's few surviving offspring has until recently been my guest at home throughout his year-long course on 'information technology' at the City of London College: Zostine (Justin) Kiongozi and I at breakfast weigh the odds on Charles's return as titular monarch of a once and future realm.

Was Charles to go back, come back, to stay? For certain: that was, and is, the consensus. If so, what as? Not as before – king of an independent mountain kingdom, gathering his own taxes, manning his own borders, ordaining all. He had personally laid to rest *that* Rwenzururu two decades earlier at the boma at Kasese: August 15, 1982. Neither he nor his people would have stomach for any fresh rebellion – no stomach nor achievable purpose. How he would return would be as the embodied sceptre of the Banyarwenzururu on their mountain ground re-caparisoned as Irema Ngoma, King-Guardian of the Drum, in the received role of 'Cultural Leader' of all the Bakonzo and their hill-related fellows. Clause 246 of Uganda's present constitution explicitly allows the re-introduction of such titular kingships if the local people want it, together with the panoplies and councils – all politically gelded. By this Clause, the 37-year-old Ronald Mutebi was installed as Kabaka of Buganda in 1993, with President Museveni's patronage. Such a restoration of the Buganda line took place after a hiatus of twenty-seven years since the deposition of his father. 'King Freddie' Mutesa, as has been told before in this book, was bombarded out of his palace in 1966 by Idi Amin on the orders of Obote, and three years later was murdered by poison in his lodgings in the East End of London. Under the same constitutional provision since 1993 have been restored the royal dynasties of Toro, Ankole and Bunyoro, roles of pomp and ethnic symbolism not of power or tribute-gathering. Ronnie Mutebi's Kabakaship in Buganda can be traced through six centuries and thirty-six reigns. The other three restored royalties lay claim to much briefer dynastic spans; yet set alongside any of them the one-and-a-half generations of active Kingship in Rwenzururu is a slight thing. Museveni has understandably prevaricated. His own early ethic was socialist and republican. He sees the evolution of nationhood in Bantu Africa as impeded by the rivalry of tribes, of which Uganda has a jostling twenty-seven of no mean size (and several lesser tribes). He has voiced his approval of the British having abolished the essentially feudal structures of the former tribal lordships in 1928: thereafter, only Central Government was enabled to permit the levying of tax or tribute. And yet this very President has made constitutional space for certain kingly restorations: the consequence of his cool appraisal of mute force of ethnic allegiance. Even the mass deportations Stalin, he may have observed, did not eliminate the folk-memory of the Crimean Tatars and other minorities; after two full generations of brutalized dispersal amid vast Asian spaces, they came back. Museveni is a pragmatist. He privatizes. He likes to get things done, is exasperated by the incompetence that hobbles Africa everywhere. Having grown out of his own ideological clutter he is scornful of others'. If multi-ethnicity is an indissoluble fact of Uganda, he will make merit of it. The Bakonzo are not an 'ethnicity' Museveni can overlook. For, consider, they occupy the best guerilla country in all of Africa. That country straddles Uganda's frontier with a vast and endemically chaotic neighbour. The Bakonzo through forty years have shown themselves to be of positively Luther-like intractability when their aspirations are overlooked and the stubbornest of fighters on their own steep ground; in brief a damn nuisance if not handled with finesse. And, further, their territory offers to Uganda substantial sources of wealth in minerals, oil, hydro-power, agriculture and tourism, all of which have been put in peril or forfeited by conflict for forty years.

Let us now see what has happened these past two decades. For the story we tell of one place and one people at one time is a parable for all men everywhere at any time.

xxvi

1982-93: Omusinga at Large

In early September 1982 my wife took a telephone call at our house in Kensington. It was a personage from the Uganda High Commission seeking me. The voice said that he had with him in his office in Trafalgar Square a certain Charles Wesley Mumbere, who knew me, and with him Amos Kambere, Member of Parliament. The two men had flown in that day from Entebbe. Amos came on the line. His companion Charles Welsey, he explained, son of Isaya Mukirane, was in London for a visit of some ten days paid for by the government of Uganda following the formal reconciliation of the Kingdom of Rwenzururu with the government of President Milton Obote. The trip to London was part of the peace price. He, Amos Kambere, was the local MP.

That afternoon there they were, settled in our Kensington drawing room. I had last seen Charles nineteen years earlier. He was eleven then, and I thirty-three. I had heard little of Rwenzururu meanwhile besides of the death of Isaya in 1966, and the stubborn survival of the secessionist state. A trickle of lowland Bakonzo reaching London or passing through had made contact with me, all of them on educational grants of one kind or another. Notable among these, because of his later political role, was Barnabas Bamusede who had come to Britain in the late 1970s for instruction in journalism. A brief report in *The Times* in the mid 1970s had told of the continuing secession of the mountain kingdom notwithstanding the granting of separate District status to the Bakonzo-inhabited southern half of the mountains as *Kasese* district. In July 1980, a correspondent for the *Daily Telegraph*,

Christabel King, made contact with the Rwenzururu leadership through Amon Bazira and a meeting was arranged on a spur in Bukonzo with Charles, 'a magnificent figure in a white uniform covered in badges of rank... accompanied by his young Queen, Zeuliah and ten members of his cabinet. He was guarded by his chief of police and a number of soldiers carrying automatic rifles.' Charles had recently sent a deputation to President Binaïsa. That was the start of interchanges of which I was to learn the conclusion here in my drawing room these two years later. Meanwhile in Jeddah, Saudi Arabia, in 1981 I had chanced upon Idi Amin, in a well-pressed tailored suit and gleaming hand-made shoes, accompanied by what appeared to be an ADC just as smart as he. It was eighteen years since we had eaten hippo together in the Ruwenzori foothills and there was a lot of ground to cover. But we had time to talk of the Bakonzo. An avuncular fondness for them was touchingly evident for those who would appreciate Idi as uncle, and I had sensed the old monster admired them for their guts in standing up for their tribal recognition. I told Charles of this, and he *was* touched. After all, it was under Idi's rule that Bukonzo country had been designated, and Kasese District had been sliced out of old Toro – these Kampala-revised structures awaiting Charles, so to speak, on his descent and reconciliation.

A natural grace attached to Charles as he sat there with a cup of tea, with Amos Kambere at his side. His manners were exquisite, his voice pitched high, and airy. Amos did most of the talking, for Charles Wesley's English had been little exercised since he had learned it as a boy at his father's knee and through his correspondence course as a teenager. We honoured the memory of his father Isaya; I learned what one is permitted to know of that strange death, and then of Charles's own accession to the kingship. I learned that upon his descent from the hills, Charles had at once become the Bakonzo's senior elder, albeit only thirty; and at once the most significant figure in the urban community of Kasese. His visit to London was part of his reward for reconciliation. During the coming few days I showed the pair something of London, and booked them into a cheap and cheerful hotel in Pimlico, fitting the purse of the Ugandan High Commission which was picking up their expenses. Neither confessed to me that the military leadership of Rwenzururu, in the persons of Kinyamusitu and his ultras, had rebuffed Charles' and the elders' decision to descend, or indeed that there were any recalcitrants still *up* with their weapons, in a lowering primal commitment to the old vision. Shall we presume that my visitors were banking on Kinyamusitu and the rest coming to see their irrelevance in this new Uganda and having the decency to fade away? Let us presume nothing. In Africa, in Ruwenzori, layer rests upon layer: light plays with darkness, darkness with light, forest with savannah, fog with sunshine, lightning with thunder; as an unnamed psalmist – not David: a Hebrew voice more primitive than David's – chanted antiphonally of the Lord's Kingship, *Clouds and darkness are round about him: righteousness and judgement are the habitation of his seat... His lightnings give shine unto the world: the earth saw it, and was afraid. The hills melted like wax at the presence of the Lord: at the presence of the Lord of the whole earth.* Kitasamba of the high places might have prompted such a psalmist. Charles and Amos said nothing of Kinyamusitu, kept mum about Charles being obliged to come down to Nsenyi that last time in camouflaged gear for fear of ambush by his erstwhile followers, gave no hint that certain regions of those uplands were now denied to him. Here was an altogether discontinuous reality, Nelson's Column and the Houses of Parliament commentaried by the earliest and very perishable 'Musabuli' of his relinquished Kingdom, and he, Charles, informing his host of his intention to enroll in this or that educational course in the United States once he got himself established in Kasese with his car, his bus, his shop.

In the way one does, I half promised to pay a return visit to him in Kasese, ensconced in legality as senior Elder. Would I ever find the time? After Charles was gone a week or two later, I began to watch Uganda more closely. The Obote regime held on, autocratic and corrupt, armed by Colonel Gaddafi of Libya and weakened by Museveni's spreading insurrection. A couple of years later, at 6.30 p.m. on September 23 1984, I was at work in my London office when the telephone rang and it was Charles Wesley. He had flown into London that morning from Uganda, he said, bound for Washington DC to start the educational course long promised him. Reaching Heathrow awakened him to the fact that he had left behind in Uganda his connecting air ticket to Washington. Stranded in London, he awaited the the missing ticket's arrival in London by the first available plane from Entebbe. Meanwhile, the High Commission had parked him in an hotel room in the unpropitious *quartier* of St Pancras where he was bored half to death watching meaningless television. I at once drove across

Town to gather him up. How could I entertain him for the evening? A cinema? Surely too similar to the television screen his eyes had been strapped to these past six hours. A stage play? Incomprehensible. A musical? The dazzling revival of that season was set in the wonderland republic for which Charles was headed, albeit a generation or two earlier. This was *42nd Street*, starring the compelling Clare Leach. I bundled him into the car and set off for Drury Lane, where, though otherwise sold out, two central stalls in the third row had become vacant that very moment, ten minutes before curtain-up. My guest and I settled into our places for this most sophisticated of American spectaculars, next to Valerie Hobson, herself a former star of West End musicals, and her husband, the Right Honourable, but lucklessly defrocked, Jack Profumo to whom (recognizing me on slight acquaintance) I introduced the ex-King of Rwenzururu. Uganda was a country Profumo knew from an official visit twenty years previously when Secretary of State for War. The show had its Afro-American elements, not least in its 1920s' jazz, albeit a far cry from the *eluma* and *endara* of Ruwenzori. Charles offered no comment whatsoever on this theatrical experience. Where was he? Between two worlds, hunched into a cyst.

Charles was to leave for Dulles Airport, Washington, next morning on what was intended as a one-year course in English and business administration, chosen for him by Uganda's embassy there and designed for students of what was coming just then to be known as the Third World. This was to be followed by a further three-year College course in this or that, whereafter he would return to his Banyarwenzururu as a yet more effective elder statesman... Let not men dictate to destiny. By early the next year, 1985, Obote was on the ropes. Museveni's guerillas controlled a vast swathe of the country with the capture of three key garrisons. In March Museveni initiated a new front in the Ruwenzori mountains which, as ever, served as unbeatable territory for a rebel army to operate from. The Bakonzo as a tribe kept themselves detached from the conflict, suffering mutely from the suspension of commerce and development. I heard that work on the building of the 'Tom Stacey Primary Boarding School' near to Kyarumba, initiated by Amos Kambere in his own constituency, had had to be stopped before that worthy mudbrick project got its roof. Ruwenzori's UPC politicians could no longer fulfil their functions. Throughout all the southern half of Uganda, Obote's dispirited army was now reading the writing on the Babylonian wall. Two Okello brothers, Tito and Basilio, emerged as leaders of the dominantly Acholi element of the Ugandan army. They secured the expulsion of Obote, and themselves clung to power for exactly six months. In January 1986 Kampala fell to Museveni's 20,000-strong National Resistance Army, a blunt and capricious instrument. On the 29th of the month Museveni was sworn in as President of a Uganda in fine disorder. Yet set among the post-colonial leaders of tropical Africa this Museveni was to prove himself a figure of a different water. He had observed the catastrophic decline of Tanzania under Julius Nyerere's collectivist fantasy, and the corruption devastating the Congo and corroding Kenya. He noted the sustained political fever induced by supposedly 'democratic' multipartyism. And though admiring the independent idealism and guerilla prowess of the quasi-Marxist Eduardo Mondlane in Mozambique, he courted Western aid. So he set out to establish a system of governance stable in its structure which permitted the people, at least in theory, to elect those from whom he would be obliged to pick his ministers and to govern local councils. His National Resistance Movement's decade-and-a-half of rule to date has critically depended on his leadership. First Britain, then America, chose to take this new man at his own valuation, as the best bet among a clutch of thoroughly bad bets; they gave him the benefit of doubts, and disgorged aid, most of it distortive and corrupting, and all of it fostering a mentality of dependence which perpetuates the dependence it is designed to end.

Now, this Museveni won power at the end of a long guerilla campaign. Thus, force comes to him naturally enough – if not necessarily *personally* at least enacted for him by those on whom he chiefly depends. Articulate opponents had no place in the early years of Museveni's Uganda. Many ducked abroad, mostly to London, others to America, others to neighbouring African capitals. Amon Bazira, former Obote minister, and young Amos Kambere, ex-MP, remained in Uganda. In June 1986 Amos was arrested on a fabricated charge of fraud. In August Amon Bazira was seized, initially without charge, until Museveni's Internal Security Organisation, ISO – a kind of Tonton Macoute – staged a weird charade in an attempt to frame him. Some five hundred Nilotics from the north, arrested for other reasons, were trucked to Luzira Prison and assembled in the outer compound. Bazira was then extracted from his cell, placed on a dais among them, and photographed by the Kampala press who were issued with a statement to the effect that this was Bazira addressing subversives he had personally recruited. Such a story was duly published, but when it was ridiculed he was freshly charged with the abduction of Vito Muhindo during the election campaign of 1981, which I have already described. All of Obote's UPC Members of Parliament and senior Party officials were likewise locked up in Luzira jail while charges were sought against them. Some were tortured by the ISO in Basima House, the principal interrogation centre of the ISO, until they confessed or incriminated others or died. In the prisons, however, families could visit and prisoners had access to lawyers.

In Washington DC, Charles Irema-Ngoma had been observing the ructions of his parent state. With his graduation from the Smith Business School, and a mortar-boarded photograph to prove it, in February/March 1986 he had flown back home for a few days by way of Brussels, Kinshasa (Leopoldville) and Kigali, capital of Rwanda, and then slipping across the border for the 150-mile road run to Kasese. There he saw his daughter, Furaha, his sole offspring, recently born to his wife Zeuliah's sister. Zeuliah herself remained his wife and Queen, and he prevailed upon the elders to arrange for her to visit him in the States. This was fixed for June, on a return airticket bought by the American political scientist Nelson Kasfir, then working up a monograph on the Rwenzururu rebellion (on which he had called to see me in London). I was on standby to shepherd Zeuliah through Heathrow for her change of flight, since Charles' Queen had never previously travelled except to flee into Congo through the forest, and as a mere four-foot-three was, as Isaya put it to me in his letter, 'a bit small'. In the way of Africa, obstacles emerged to frustrate the visit, due perhaps in the first place to the drying up of his source of funds, or to the Ugandan embassy in Washington. Or perhaps little Zeuliah with her barren womb and formally cuckolded by her sister lost the heart to be uprooted?

Dr Crispus Kiyonga will be remembered by followers of this story as the parliamentary candidate elected for Kasese North in 1980 after Vito's murder. At once perceiving the futility not to say hazard of attempting a political career in opposition to Obote, he had decamped to Nairobi – as I have told – to make his living in gynaecology. When his former paragon Museveni won control of most of western Uganda including his own tribal territory of the lowland Bakonzo, Kiyonga got himself to Rwanda to offer his services to the coming man, in the first instance as a doctor. On Museveni's accession to the presidency of the country a few months later, Kiyonga at once entered the cabinet as Minister of Co-operatives and Marketing. He was swift to prove his competence and loyalty. Kiyonga had a further advantage: wedded exogamously (to a Munyankole) and a long away from home, he was conveniently *déraciné*, unencumbered by that half-hidden multiplicity of family and ethnic obligations which compromises the integrity of so many in authority throughout all of Africa and much of the Third World. Within a year Kiyonga had taken the central portfolio as Minister of Finance. In such a role he could hardly be expected to countenance the spending of public funds on a protégé of the former regime who also happened to be an early political opponent. When Charles's student's allowances abruptly stopped, our ex-King still required to eat. He got himself a menial job in a Washington hospital. He had no longer any legal right to remain in America, yet was clearly in danger of capricious arrest were he to return to Uganda. He applied for political asylum in the US and asked me to support his application. I submitted my grounds for so doing and in September 1987 swore the document as an affidavit for his lawyer.

Meanwhile, Amos Kambere languished in jail in Kampala without a sign of legal resolution, a forgotten political prisoner ripe for doom. That autumn I raised the issue of his detention for the second time with the British High Commissioner in Kampala, and he in turn raised it with Museveni, by then a recipient of substantial British aid. In November Amos was released, and returned to his wife, Edith, and their children in Kasese. A few weeks later he received secret word of his imminent re-arrest or covert elimination by the ISO. It was a ploy of the regime at that period to be seen to respond to international pressure on matters of human rights, and at a later point in time, when attention had lapsed, for the former victim of persecution to be spirited back into custody or to suffer a fatal accident. Without so much as a night's delay Amos decamped with his family across the border to his ethnic brothers in eastern Congo, and shortly settled for a while in Goma, that exquisite colonial resort sited beside Lake Kivu with whose people Amos shared the vernacular.

As for the more prominent figure of Amon Bazira, his lawyer had appealed to the High Court for his release on bail, pending his trial. In January 1988, after 18 months in Luzira prison, bail was indeed granted. Amon had not held the security brief under Obote

for nothing: he knew the tricks... or most of them. Without qualm he jumped bail, flit Uganda, resumed links with Amos Kambere, with whom he posed for a party-political photograph in front of a suitably sylvan mountainous backdrop in a Kinshasa sudio. He set about forming an armed movement for the renewed 'liberation' of Uganda, already the fourth or the fifth liberation since liberation from the paternal rule of Britain. Such has been *la ronde* of post-colonial Africa; and to freeze any smirk of condescension on the faces of my non-African readers, I suppose I could invite them to re-read in sequence the Party rhetoric of each successive victor proposing to displace the government of their own democracies (or alternatively recall to the mind of serial lovers their sequential declarations of the eternal commitment of their hearts). The difference is that in Africa, what you cannot argue out or vote out you shoot out. When I in England heard of Amon's intentions for his NALU, the National Army for the Liberation of Uganda, as I soon did during 1988, I sang a song of caution. It seemed to me that notwithstanding the campaign of abuse of power, Museveni was winning a fair measure of acceptance among the long tormented citizens of Uganda. After some twenty years of governmental degeneracy, there was a fresh coherence to the place, however imperfect. Among the serious Western purveyors of international authority, Britain was setting the mood for America and securing international approval for this Museveni: the two big donors were set to go on giving him the benefit of any doubt for some while to come. I offered these generalisations courteously by phone and letters, as Amon busied himself obtaining funds and weaponry from neighbouring states who might themselves take comfort from the discomfiture of Museveni. Such states at the time were, first, Rwanda under a Hutu government threatened by a Tutsi rebel army of Ugandan-reared refugees who were ethnic Hima brothers of Museveni and of whom I have told in this book on page 27. Many of these Rwandans fought with Museveni in his push towards Kampala from Uganda's west and south-west; some, like Paul Kagame – at the time of writing the Rwandan President – held key posts in Museveni's administration. The Tutsi rebel army in Rwanda was the beneficiary of Ugandan supplies and weaponry, mostly provided by the United States – *matériel* intended for the so-called Christian rebels of the south Sudan, headed by an old comrade of Museveni in his university days in the 1960s in Dar es Salaam who is now engaged in unending war with the fundamentalist Islamic government in Khartoum. With Museveni's younger brother as his principal general, and Kagame then responsible for his Internal Security Organisation, such diversion of weaponry was easily managed. Khartoum, naturally, was affronted by Uganda serving as a conduit of weapons and a sanctuary for its internal enemies: they too would not be averse to priming Amon Bazira's NALU with a little cash and a few guns. As for Zaïre (as Congo then was), the then dictator, President Mobutu, perceived the threat of Museveni's Nilotic destabilisations of Bantu Rwanda and Burundi, and was content for NALU to operate from his nominal territory.

And what was to be the nucleus of Bazira's very own Maoist, Castroist, Mondlanist or, for that matter, Musevenist territorial roll-up rebellion? Why, that rump of Rwenzururu recalcitrants Charles and we had left up the mountains in August 1982. Bazira's NALU was to be a *national* movement, or rather army. He scarcely needed the evidence of his exemplars – Mao, Castro and the rest – of the advantage of beginning in relatively inaccessible territory, preferably highlands such as the remote hills of Shensi or the Sierra Maestra. For Amon Bazira Ruwenzori was home ground. Folk there had known him from boyhood: his feet knew the very tracks, even on Congo-side; he spoke the lingo. He neither needed nor expected Kinyamusitu and his gang of unrepentants to grasp his broader vision; all *they* required was the sniff of a cause once again, up there in the hills, some anti-Kampala function at last for their hoarded firearms besides colobus monkeys and forest hogs for the pot. There were not more than about a hundred of the seasoned die-hards up there. Yet now, with new rebellion in the offing and his old mentor on the run with anger in his bones, Fanehasi Kisokeronio threw in his hand as chairman of the tedious lowland Land Board and rejoined the mountain *banditti* if not for national Ugandan salvation at least to restore the *raison d'être* of Ruwenzori, namely to fight from a fastness. Whispers spread of what was afoot. Other dissidents and victims of Museveni's personal interpretation of 'freedom and democracy' (his own slogan) found their way to the steep forests, including an ex-colonel of the National Resistance Army, until the rump had doubled to some two hundred. In 1989 Bazira announced his NALU to be in business, that is, the business of civil war.

My instincts were other. From time to time I said as much, when my counsel was sought in London. It was not my affair, yet I was concerned for my friends and more than my friends. Uganda had endured enough rapine from its rival claimants to power. The scale of massacre in the so-called Luwero Triangle on the perimeter of Buganda north of Kampala perpetrated by soldiery during later months of Obote's rule and under Tito Okello was beginning to emerge in the grisly form of vast pyramids of skulls, which survivors were starting to use as tourist attractions. Museveni had come to power by no caprice of opportunism but with calculated ideas of how to reconcile popular consent with coherent governance. Multi-party democracy on the 'Westminster' model, so fixedly espoused, had proved unworkable in Africa as in much of the Third World: for simple folk to live life in perpetual proximity with an alternative patronal regime supposedly available made for collective unrest, if not psychosis. Museveni knew and knows the unsophisticated to be most comfortable with Pharaohs – their authority indisputable, for better, for worse, for justice, for cruelty: usually both. By and large his subjects (in the south, at any rate) have slept easier at night with any foundational political option closed off but the lesser, local ones kept ajar. The National Resistance Movement's constitution is 'It' so far as Uganda's political frame is concerned: no party structures permitted at the various levels of elective consent, from Parliament to local councillorship. So far – since 1986 – periodic electoral choice at the Presidential pinnacle has been more theoretical than actual, since the NRM governmental machine in one way or another hogs the mechanisms of national publicity, the logistics of campaigning, and the methodology of the vote. The NRM regime, taking over chaos, started ruthlessly, with too much of the army for too long a law to itself, and an ugly secret police. Slowly the largely tribalist persecutions of the soldiery were curbed and the caprice and viciousness of the Internal Security Organisation became more circumspect. Yet even if Museveni himself might have wished for probity, financial corruption is widely perceived to be thriving among his ministers and generals, and Uganda has lately (2001) been ranked third on the shame-list of the world's most corrupt countries.

Indigenous government in Africa is a lot more difficult than ever colonial government was. A sensible outsider regards Museveni's Uganda in the context of its neighours and in the context of its past. I, for one, am not going to cavil at lesser evil. Nor did I when Amon Bazira was mounting his NALU: I thought the insurrection to be misjudged. Out of the rump of Rwenzururu veteran die-hards clustered around Kinyamusitu and newly defected Fanehasi Kisokeronio, Bazira built up a force of his ethnic fellows on Congo-side of several hundred, perhaps as many as a thousand. It was not difficult, with a modest stash of foreign money. The recruiting sleight-of-hand among the young Banande illiterates involved the circulation of a fistful of American dollars – say $200, a dazzling sum, flashed before the eyes as future rewards for the prospective oath-of-allegiance swearer at the point of his being issued with his uniform, plus a guaranteed replenishable messtin and a weapon representing virility. They joined up lustily enough, with but the vaguest notion of the cause. They were based at Buhira village, north of Mutwanga between the mountains and the Semliki, birthplace of Nyamutswa and core site of the Hira clan. The name of the exiled King of old Rwenzururu was inescapably invoked.

That use of Charles' name was not so fine, in my view. In early 1990 I dropped in to see him in his little flat in Hyattsville, a black precinct of Washington DC. He had held on to his job in the hospital. He was gracious and orderly and ex-kingly, subsisting on paltry funds in a world utterly remote from the one he innerly belonged to. Among the largely white hospital managers who employed him and the largely unqualified Afro-American staff he worked with, the provenance of this 'Charles W. Mumbere' would have been unimaginable. Conversely, here was the former King of the semi-explored Mountains of the Moon of Central Africa in daily attendance at a megalopolitan North American masque of medicine among irredeemable strangers. I wondered with alarm at his loneliness, and hoped that in the downtown Washington mélange of coloured immigrants he had found a woman. He had assumed a double persona: Prince Charles Wesley Irema-Ngoma (in the rendering of his letterhead) and Charles W. Mumbere, a Washington black struggling to pay his rent and phone bills on the wages of a hospital porter. He had none within reach to speak so much as a sentence of his own language. What havoc might that not play on a man's sense of identity? I had encountered African migrants to the Western world or the Communist bloc whom such strains had reduced to paranoia. I could not in all fairness dissuade him from aligning himself with Amon Bazira's NALU since an ex-African king pushing trolleys in a North American hospital has to align himself with something. There is surely a condition familiar to the psychiatrists of the free world's major capitals classifiable as 'exilitis', such as afflicts those living a life of sustained abeyance, hanging upon the overthrow in their own time of the hateful regime that has usurped power in their own now forbidden home. Sufferers are condemned to clinging to the prospect of home with a desperation that mounts in inverse ratio to its dwindling likelihood. Museveni was at work consolidating his power and acceptability, if not exactly popularity. Charles aligned himself with Bazira's NALU, more or less publicly, as a sort of airy sponsor. I felt myself a dog telling him that although I endorsed NALU's principles of fair and honest government, I considered it would get nowhere militarily. His response was to send me a photo, montaged in a Washington studio, of himself in combat gear looking like a panther ready to pounce – an image evidently calculated to inspire that very gang of unreconstructed diehards who had pledged themselves to oppose his descent in 1982 if necessary by eliminating him, and who now comprised whatever hard core NALU's fighting force could claim to have.

Shortly before my visit, the US Immigration and Naturalisation Service had turned down Charles' application for asylum. His lawyers renewed his request, and I and Nelson Kasfir, now a Professor of Government studies at Dartmouth College in New Hampshire, together with two other academic specialists of the African scene, polished up our arguments, citing the latest violations of human rights in the Uganda of the day. At the appeal hearing in May the US authorities relented: Charles Wesley Mumbere (ex-king, Keeper of the Drum, symbol of the identity of a race of men in the remote heart of primal Africa) won his right to survive as a medical skivvy in the Afro-American downtown of the administrative capital of what was generally taken to be the most advanced nation on earth. To alleviate this conflated meaninglessness, so I was glad to learn, Charles had gathered up a lady companion, a nurse from Sierra Leone and fellow recipient of asylum, each of them samples of the flotsam of the Age of Empire which the United States of America had worked so assiduously to bring to an end. Matters were taking on a semblance of a narrow permanency. He moved his flat to the ever so slightly more salubrious Washington precinct of Silver Spring.

I stayed in touch with Amos Kambere by letter-writing, in his various places of refuge in Zaïre, urging gently that he should detach himself from the armed movement against the Museveni regime and seek a lasting exile of stability and opportunity for his wife and young family. This urging had come to convince Amon Bazira that I was 'against' NALU. Well, in so far as I had a view, I was against the guns if not the policies. Bazira needed Kambere's ability. Yet I was glad when, in 1992, the Kambere family was granted formal refuge in Canada. They settled in Vancouver where Amos got a job with British Columbia's postal service. With characteristic swiftness, his competence and dependability were recognised, and he was rewarded by promotion. A year or so later, on a visit to Vancouver to give a paper to a seminar on penology, I found him there, his heart in Uganda and Ruwenzori, his children growing up black Canadians. The Konzo presence in Vancouver was soon to be increased in tragic circumstances.

In July of that year, 1993, the thirty-three-year-old Ronald Mutebi, heir to Buganda, was to be installed as the new Kabaka of his people in accordance with the provisions of the freshly-minted constitution of Uganda. Ronnie had lived in exile in England since the flight of his father, the last Kabaka, in 1967, when he was seven; and since his father's death had been brought up by English guardians. I was to cover the forthcoming coronation for *The Independent*, and planned to drop in on Nairobi to talk with Amon Bazira, on my way to Entebbe. It was a fact generally known that Bazira had made the Kenyan capital his home in exile. By this date, the activities of his so-called 'National Army' for the 'Liberation of Uganda' had shrunk to almost nothing. NALU was little more than a dark presence in the high forest edge; mean, hutted encampments haunting the upper villages of certain valleys.

Amon's political following had likewise dwindled. The spectre of the name remained, however – his and NALU's; – and for me Amon was never less than a penetrating observer of the Ugandan scene on which I proposed to report in the context of the coronation. He had already sought my guidance on the further education in the West for his promising son, Daniel Kashagama. Bazira's actual whereabouts in Nairobi were a secret tightly kept, including from me; but I telephoned him from London in advance and we arranged a rendezvous at a location in the Kenyan capital known to us both, intending a few hours' ruminative discussion. I was there on time. He failed to show up; I rang his number to be told by his wife Dorothy that he had left the previous day for Addis Ababa, capital of Ethiopia. I flew on to Entebbe puzzled.

xxvii

An International Assassination

I had been absent from Uganda as long as Ronnie Mutebi himself, that is to say, a long generation. Word of my presence in Kampala spread among the tiny community of Bakonzo residents there, as if I had been one of the Seven Sleepers returned to the streets of Ephesus. My hotel, the Sheraton, became a locus of magnetic visitation. Since two of those coming to see me will re-enter our story, let me identify them: one, Charles' youngest brother, Wiliams Sibibuka, a young fellow of slack charm then aged 27, and another kinsman of the exiled Irema-Ngoma, a cousin, in middle age, one Ibrahim Muhonjya, a Muslim, a man of wit and warmth and a trader in telephones, and suffering just then – as many another Ugandan African in business was suffering – from the flooding back of Indians whom Idi Amin had so hectically ejected, every man jack of them, two decades earlier. They attended upon me, these Konzo, sipping tea or taking a cake in the foyer where there was a bad pianist, as if I was not entirely real like other men enmeshed in history but a sort of simurgh, harbingering the return of their own King; an elder swallow of an unimaginable summer.

As to Kampala's upper class Baganda, I was one of the international corps of guests or press which touched tribal pride with an extra spot of gilt at this restoration of their ancient line of kings. Ronnie Mutebi, Kabaka-to-be, flanked by Presidential minders, held a press conference under a tree where I conveyed to him the congratulations of Idi Amin, which the ex-President had charged me to deliver in a telephone call before I left London. A shudder passed through those present. It was the same Idi Amin who (on Obote's orders) had shelled Ronnie's father out of his palace on a nearby hill one night twenty-six years earlier, sending him in flight and in disguise across the border to Rwanda, never to return. Messages from the retired monster were rare. But it was not for me to inhibit the expression of another man's remorse. Thereafter I re-entered my old newspaperman's skin, neither emissary of an exiled *caudillo* nor champion of a forgotten tribe, but sinking myself into the rituals and panoplies of bringing back, in gelded form, the royal line of Buganda: the mock victories over symbolic foes on Buddo hill; the investitures of their new King with spears and shields and a sword of justice, with great swathes of barkcloth, a calf-skin and leopard-skin; the libations and secret pledges of allegiance to each of the clans (the leopard, lion, colobus, otter, locust, civet, elephant, lung-fish, mushroom, sheep, buffalo, grey-monkey, antelope, edible rat, yam, bean, bushbuck, dog, jackal, roebuck, hippopotamus, genet, cow, hornbill, rain, grass, crested crane and red ant); the dancing and the singing; the sworn commitment to rule with truth and justice; the climactic sounding of the Mujaguzo drum and the consequent voicing of every drum, male and female, through the surrounding landscape; the entire pagan paraphernalia, brilliantly executed over three days, then capped and sanctified by a Christian God with second coronation on that self-same pagan ground by the Archbishop of the Church of Uganda and a fistful of attendant bishops. In all this ritual and panoply, display and secrecy, vow and invocation, something of profound significance was going on. Man in a single burst of inventiveness was expressing the unity of such evocation as he could apprehend, of all things living that bore upon him, of place and race, of time now and time ever, vitality and death, obedience and deity. I was aware of there being voices among the Baganda that took exception to the restoration of this Kabakaship, the usual mock-superior republican voices with easy arguments dismissive of symbol, and I was aware of those arguments dying in the presence of this living expression of identity that twenty-seven years after the abolition of the office of the Kabakaship and all that went with it the thing was spontaneously restored out of the collective *soul*. It was an issue and issuance of soul. I scrutinized in particular President Museveni, a secular figure, during his quite brief, subdued attendance, wondering what demons he may have feared himself to have uncorked by this remarkable 'cultural' concession. He had given an interview to the man from the *New York Times*, in which he told his interviewer, Russian by origin, that contemporary states 'grew out of the feudal state. Russia was created by the Tsars, not by the Communists; England by the kings. We [Ugandans] should not give the impression that we did not have centralized government until the British came... It is important to commemorate that our ancestors had attained this level of integration. The same task that our ancestors were grappling with faces us today. We are seeking wider unity to command access to more human and natural resources... In the end, there is no difference between the traditionalist, the Pan-Africanist and the nationalist. As a nationalist, I say to the cultural revivalist, your cause serves my cause.' And the President found occasion to remind his interlocutor that through his mother he was descended from that specialist clan which kept the sacred drums of the Kings of Ankole.

I pondered all this on behalf of my Konzo. Unlike these Baganda, with whom their myths claimed common descent, they had no early form of 'centralized government', even though they might say the mountains themselves, Nzururu and his fellow Olympians, had presided centrally ever since man inhabited the hills. Yet a more palpable King-led government had happened between 1962 and 1982 than anything Buganda had known for a century. The precedence of Baganda was shortly to be followed by a clutch of tribal others as the 'royal' guests from Ankole, Toro, Bunyoro and Busoga suggested. Omusinga Charles Wesley Mumbere of Rwenzururu had sent a message of congratulations to the new Kabaka (copy to me) from his flat in the Maryland suburb of Washington. Yet I knew Kabaka Ronnie to be hard put to place Rwenzururu on the map, let alone in history; and in truth, along with my Bakonzo visitors to the Kampala Sheraton I could detect no gleam of a constitutional crown for Charles in the coming era of Museveni.

I was in Kampala, yearning to go back to the mountains to seek out my surviving friends. Yet I had not the time to spare to do justice to any such re-visitation. So I flew directly back to England.

There struck an unexpected blow, two and a half weeks later. On August 17, 1993, a Tuesday, at 7 a.m. the telephone rang and I heard an African voice saying what I mistook as 'This is Amon' to which I instantly responded, 'I was so sorry not to see you at breakfast in Nairobi.' But my caller corrected me, identifying himself as *Amos* (Kambere) ringing late at night from Vancouver. '*Amos!*' said I – 'what is the news?' 'The news is very terrible. Museveni has murdered Amon.' Amos Kambere had that very hour received a distraught phone call from Amon's wife Dorothy, in Kenya. A body identified as Amon's had been found beside the road to Naivasha, on the route to Uganda. Amon had evidently been entrapped the previous Saturday, lured away from his home by a telephone call purportedly inviting him to a meeting with Arap Moi, the Kenyan President, only to be seized on the way to or at the proposed

375

rendezvous, and abducted. Amos and I deduced that his abductors were intending to deliver him alive into the hands of the security apparatus of Uganda, and that, aware of this, Amon had attempted to leap from the car, only to be shot in the endeavour. Amon would have been wary of such a trap. Suspicion at once arose of collusion between the Kenyan and Ugandan security services. Almost certainly the operation had been partly bungled. Beyond doubt the hand of the Uganda government was in it. I at once telephoned Amon's son Daniel in Nairobi and his widow Dorothy; and in the immediate hours and days was able to advise the surviving family of five on seeking asylum in generous-hearted Canada, where they too were soon to settle in Vancouver. (There, Dorothy would shortly suffer a crippling stroke.) Meanwhile, I alerted the British and Ugandan press to the fact of this murder, since it seemed right to me that such political assassinations should be brought to light for the sake of future potential victims. Yoweri Museveni himself was well known to be protective of his reputation among the aid-providing international community in matters of 'human rights'.

Bakonzo patriots were swift to attribute the abduction of Bazira to their own stock quisling, Crispus Kiyonga. No evidence of Kiyonga's involvement emerged at the time or has emerged since. And in fairness to the true perpetrators we should remember that Bazira was in the business of armed rebellion on the soil of Uganda. Kiyonga himself had lately left Museveni's cabinet as Minister of Finance, yet he remained an insider at the court of the President and was soon to return with the portfolio of Internal Affairs. The Bakonzo as a whole had not identified with NALU, as I would come to discover personally. Yet in Amon Bazira they felt they had lost a hero who for a while had played the national stage and latterly – if ineffectually – the international stage; and they remained unreconciled to Museveni's 'National Resistance Movement' government. Charles Wesley's response was assertive. He wrote to me about ways and means of brushing up his military skills. He issued a sheet in bold sans-serif summarizing the 'military career of General Charles M. Wesley, son of Isaya Mukirania Kibanzanga, the First King of Bayira/Bamba'. 'General Charles,' it began, 'started his Military Training at the age of fourteen as a Combat soldier and then he attended the Military Officers' Academy as an Officer Cadet where he learned Military Administration. After successfully finishing his military training at [the] School of Infantry, Kahindangoma, General Charles became an Instructor of Army

Recruits and Officer Cadets at the same school. In May 1981, Charles was promoted to the rank of full General by the Defence Council... The ceremony of pinning the rank badges on General Charles was conducted by Major Richard Kinyamusitu...' He was soon writing to me with requests for an instruction manual and videos on British military training. He circulated the photograph of himself in combat gear and panther-like attitude among his loyalists at home in Rwenzururu.

These martial pretensions troubled me. Was loneliness flaming the imagination? In the latter half of 1993 he issued a lordly statement, containing a threat of war upon the Batoro, should Patrick Kaboyo, the newly reinstated Mukama of Toro, 'claim even an inch of any property or land that is within the current jurisdiction of Bundibugyo and Kasese districts' (the northwestern county of Bwamba having been re-titled Bundibugyo). This document was despatched to all five royal heads of the restored Bantu kingdoms, and to Museveni himself. Was there something I did not know? Indeed there was. With the assassination of Bazira, and the killing of Kinyamusitu shortly thereafter by his brother after a misjudged attempt to persuade the veteran Rwenzururu commander to give up the guerrilla struggle, the ragged Konzo rump of NALU in the mountains had turned back to Charles, the Drum-Keeper, to assume titular command of the movement, such as it was. A letter had been sent under collective signature, which certainly included that of Fanehasi Kisokeronio, to the exiled Omusinga in Washington offering him this dubious honour. Charles had accepted, and kept it dark. Yet soon enough, in November 1993, an 'Open Letter to all Bamba/Bayira in the Rwenzururu Kingdom' in the same bold sans-serif type, was disseminated declaring that 'Our Kingdom has been restored'. Perhaps with the sense of a secret stage to play upon,

Charles called upon both tribes – 'Academicians, Artists, Businessmen, Peasants, Students and all the Religious leaders' – to treble their efforts to rebuild 'our Kingdom'. He urged his people to remain on guard 'day and night' against 'discrimination, oppression and segregation' by the Batoro, yet fervently declared, 'If Rwenzururu Kingdom is to prosper, we should refrain from Tribalism, regionalism, sectarianism, conservatism and any other such isms.' This plea was genuine. By 'tribalism' Charles meant looking inward, refusing to work with non-Konzo talent and energy, wherever it might bring benefit to his people. Next, it called on the government of Uganda to release land for peasant farms in both the Ruwenzori highland National Park and the Ntoroko game reserve, between the mountains' northern foothills and Lake Albert. 'We cannot allow our kingdom to be a zoo, or our people to be a museum piece,' the document declared. It concluded ominously, 'It has come to my attention that some Bayira, Bamba and our friends are... betraying our people, sometimes leading to death. Those people shall be held responsible for their actions. Posterity will never fogive them... God Bless You All, OMUSINGA CHARLES WESLEY IREMANGOMA, RWENZURURU KINGDOM.'

Reports of this 'threat of war' appeared in the Uganda press. There were popular calls for his return from the mountain people. Charles was assumed at the time to have made his home-in-exile in

10 The NEW VISION, Thursday, June 23, 1994

Rwenzururu want leader back

By John B.B. Nzinjah
in Kasese

Kitswamba sub-county. in their re-

the Bakonzo in Kasese to ac- cent the creation of a

absence of the observance of al norm

them that the NRM govern- ment free-

England, a misapprehension possibly due to my occasionally issuing press statements on his behalf from my London office. There were safeguards in Charles seeming will-o-the-wispish. Most of his pronouncements were issued from the 'Buhikira Royal Palace', occasionally adding a Kasese Post Box number. But in truth it was a palace-in-the-sky, of his imagination and wan expectation. The Presidential office in Kampala surely knew at least approximately where and how he was living. Uganda's Washington embassy had this awkward exile's Post Office box number. Charles was to insist later that at this time he privily despatched first one letter to Museveni, seeking to open discussion on the issue of NALU and then, on receiving no reply, another which likewise evoked no answer. Soon we shall come to Charles' motive for accepting the 'leadership' of NALU. Meanwhile, it must be said, NALU's soldiery remained purposeless and ineffectual.

In the middle of 1995 came a new blow to Konzo pride, and a personal catastrophe. On July 11 the economist, Dr Henry Bwambale, most distinguished of the Bakonzo's academics, teaching International Finance in the faculty of economics at Makerere University, died mysteriously in the house of a lady friend in Kampala. The body had been spirited instantly to the mortuary; no autopsy was held; and the police put it out that the unlucky Dr Bwambale had slipped in the bath and cracked his skull. Foul play was widely presumed; accusations of a cover-up were voiced. Dr Kiyonga was then Minister of Internal Affairs; during Kiyonga's previous tenure at the Finance portfolio, Bwambale had served on the state's budgetary committee; and he had subsequently stood against Kiyonga in the Parliamentary elections in Bukonzo West. One effect of this calamity was to make Charles fear more sharply for his own life. He took even greater pains to ensure that his actual place of residence was not revealed. In November 1995 he was injured in a car accident. Even so, greeting me at the New Year, 1996, he wrote that he continually thought of visiting his family in Kasese: 'I just pray to God to let it happen.' It was surely a remote prospect. Museveni seemed entrenched for life, succoured by Western aid; and with the one in, the other was out.

That April, 1996, the Geographical Faculty of Makerere University was to stage in Kampala an international conference on Ruwenzori, under the chairmanship of Dr Joy Tukahirwa and the presiding figure of Dr Henry Osmaston. I, in London, locked into diurnal functions as a publisher, and immersed (with any time and energy to spare) in researching and writing a work on quantum mechanics and the mystical experience, surely had no right to break away to central Africa to discuss the ecological fate of the Mountains of the Moon. Yet here was Henry Osmaston, doyen of the world's specialists in the tropical highlands, urging me to drop everything and attend. He is a hard man to gainsay. I suppose him to have a more comprehensive scientific knowledge than anyone on earth of highland Ruwenzori, and know his commitment to its preservation to be on the same scale as his knowledge. Nine years my senior, Osmaston entered the Colonial Service after soldiering in the Second

World War, and his first posting was to the Forestry Department of Uganda. Thus Ruwenzori-the-place entered his blood-memory as early in life as Ruwenzori-the-people entered mine. Earlier still in the shared blood-memory of each of us lie the same rigours and rewards of the same house of our common public school. I dropped all, and caught the flight. When a space emerged in the planned proceedings, I walked to the rostrum and ad-libbed a speech. A miasma of political correctness had been drifting over the conference scene, blurring the realities and vitiating effective conclusions. No African speaker had dared to mention the word 'tribe', and while the term 'Bakonjo' (*sic*) was occasionally breathed, the people were otherwise invariably anonymized as the 'mountain communities' or 'the local population'; or reduced to statistical fodder as 'human resources'. Various recommendations put forward on 'conservation', 'land use, 'sustainable growth', 'prevention of erosion', and so on, blandly gutted the people of their right to be. That the mountain *volk's* identity as *Bakonzo* might be brought into play in the attainment of these scientific goals was inconceivable. The effect was an infinitely lofty condescension on the part of the conference's African eggheads towards the tribe. Insofar as the people of Ruwenzori entered these discussions on the environmental fate of their homeland, they were a mush of peasantry whose methods of survival and age-honoured usages needed to be stopped, improved, or otherwise farthingaled. When my chance at the rostrum came, I raised the theme of Bakonzo identity as the key 'spiritual factor' in the future preservation of Ruwenzori. I tried to explain how no plans and programmes for the 'management' of the mountains would succeed unless they carried with them the hearts of the Bakonzo *as a people*; yet at present the Bakonzo were virtually unrepresented on the lordly Uganda National Park's Management Advisory Committees for Highland Ruwenzori and comparable bodies. I conjured a new and, hopefully, critically influential body: an exclusively Konzo 'environmental forum', comprised of a score or so of highland elders, literate or illiterate (it mattered not) combining with those few Bakonzo well educated in environmental science who were now emerging as specialists in conservation, park management and eco-tourism. I proposed that this 'forum' should face both ways – outwardly, to guide the Uganda Wildlife Authority, National Parks, government Ministries and official bodies concerned and, inwardly, to the tribe itself whose children they should be charged with educating from the earliest age in the treasure of creation of which they, the Bakonzo, were the guardians and the gatekeepers. Thus would we seal and sanctify place with race, in accordance with the genesis of man on earth, obedient to his creator and thankful too. Implicit in what I proposed was a vibrant pride in tribe, tribe looking – legitimately – both ways, yet from a confidence and sense of unity bearing its unifying symbols, not least its king, *omusinga*, or 'cultural leader' in Musevenspeak of the day. The true highlanders who alone comprised the community concerned with the issues raised by the eggheads of the conference were exclusively Bakonzo. Yet that highland Konzo territory was administratively and politically parcelled out among at least three and possibly four tribes – Bakonzo, Batoro, Baamba, and Basongora. Since only one tribe was engaged on the territory we were so devotedly seeking to protect, Ruwenzori surely ached for a tribal figurehead. Who better but Charles himself? Who else at all? My little paper sought to be non-political in intent, and to arouse no extraneous passions. It brought in Charles only in the historical preamble; but anyone who had any real dealings with the mountains knew of Rwenzururu, the kingdom, and that there was a controversial king over the water.

I had resolved that, this time, as distinct from my 1993 attendance at the Kabaka of Buganda's restoration, I would make a dash for the mountains, if only for a few days. I had reached out to Charles before I left London for Entebbe, and he had issued me with a brief in his careful, favourite-pupil handwriting, as follows:

> This is my message you should kindly deliver to my people in Kasese:
>
> (1) I miss them, (2) I Love them
>
> (3) In order to achieve their goal, they should co-operate and work hand to hand with the Government of Uganda.
>
> I wish you safe journey in East-Africa
>
> Yrs.
> Omus. Charles Wesley Irema-Ngoma

He also asked me to visit on his behalf various of the key people in Kasese, which had come to be accepted as the Konzo capital: the Church of Uganda's (i.e. Anglican communion) Bishop Zebedee; the custodian of whatever remained of his property, Yofesi Mutanywana; the elected L.C. ('Local Chairman') 5, Barnabas Bamusede, who was in effect the representative of Museveni's no-party Party, the National Resistance Movement, resident in Kasese District; and Charles' own immediate family: his mother Mukirania Christine, and his brothers Christopher and Williams.

The long fortitude of the diminutive hospital attendant in Washington DC, in keeping alight in him the frail flame of his kingship in territory way beyond the compass of his fellow Washingtonians' fancy, impressed me. His need for his subjects told of proof of their need for him. Such is the nourishment of faith. The justification of kingship is in the subjects' instinctual craving for the office of kingship in their midst – an office beyond dispute, beyond hierarchy, the office itself sceptring its incumbent. The justification of the claimant is in the right of his claim and the daring of his presumption. Charles had never wavered. However menial his daily tasks, however pushed to find the rent for his cramped apartment, Charles was never less than or other than Omusinga waRwenzururu.

xxviii

'This Is My Message...'

I rented a low-slung Japanese car in Kampala and drove west with three of the five native Bakonzo who had attended the Makerere conference. Of these the lady, Millie Nzirambe, was employed by the World Wildlife Fund in its Fort Portal headquarters, one good man worked for the Natural Resources Programme in Bundibugyo, and the other – of high ability – broadcast weekly a persuasive feature on conservation for those in the hills with radios. I had – what? – four days or five to fulfil my brief from Charles before my flight booking and home duties demanded my return to London. It was thirty-two years since I had dropped in on the mountains; thirty-three years, half my lifetime, since I had quit the presence of Isaya Mukirane's tattered court on Bukuke spur in Congo with Ibrahimu his brother-in-law and righteous Seylversta, and stumbled in darkness across the highland Tako stream to Kituti and the awaiting elders. Yet I was what I was: a white nerve-fibre in this black tribal body transmitting a vivific signal out of the past and across the intercontinental space. I remained the sole link between the father of the nation scarcely nation-born in the early 1950s and early '60s, and today; and between that father's Omusinga-son, holed up in faraway America, and his subjects. I was a Mercury of tribal validity. Only that previous evening in Kampala I had been reminded of the existential imperative at work. I had taken supper with a distracted Kabaka of Buganda who that day had been physically prevented from leaving the building of his parliament, the Lukiko, which he was politically obliged to dissolve at the present onset of Museveni's re-election campaign as national President. A group of inflamed young citizens had blocked his way, in misplaced fear of the elimination of a tribal right. For King Ronnie it had been an unnerving experience. In the matter of tribe, one is handling *ntu*, being, and dynamite.

We took the northern, murram, road to the mountains, by way of Fort Portal, that eucalyptus-shaded administrative centre adjacent to Toro's capital-kraal of Kabarole. It was where I had

383

spent my first night in Uganda, with Erisa Kironde, in 1954. We pulled up at the Good Time Bar in the main street, opposite Quick Electrical Works, for a late lunch of goat stew. The old colonial shipshapeness of the place had given way to an easygoing tropical patch-and-make-do. Order was vested nowadays in the 'NGO', Non-Governmental Organisation, which took shape as a scattering of initiatives by the 'First' world in the 'Third' with varying degrees of high intention and political window-dressing. Westerners in twos or threes came and went on drop-in, drop-out contracts, each NGO with its packet of aid, in cash or equipment or provisions or skills. When the sweets ran out, the foreigners went home and that was that. A poster above us spoke of Man's inherent goodness amid what he must suffer, *My friend with AIDS* (the writing ran) *is still my friend.* At Fort Portal we said cheerio to Nkayarwa Justus, who would hitch a lift to Bundibugyo and carry with him a message from me to George Kahigwa, now the senior elder of the place, that he and his brother Ibrahimu Ndyanabaïsi should know I hoped to make it to Bundibugyo to greet them before this Ruwenzori visit ended.

We set off south. Remember how, from Fort Portal, you cannot see the mountains. Remember how it is that a man can so very rarely view the mountains from afar, or from aside. He is informed of their presence by his map. But here are men who are of the mountains; short, dark men, staved, suspicious, sinewed in calf and thigh, whose bodies tell of the steep slopes, with lines of strength about the mouth, whose skin bears the shine of woodsmoke. Yet you scarcely see foothills, nothing excrescent. For the mountains, though very great, are set back, suggested only by a diminution of light along the south-western and western horizon. There is no knowing the mountains until you are on them and consequently *of* them, possessed by them. We were driving south now to celebrate the surrender of a man's matter into the body of the earth, which is to say, a death.

John Matte had died on the Friday. His body was interred at the foothill village of Ibanda on the Sunday. Today was Wednesday, the first of three days of funeral. Matte had died in his early fifties, he the doyen of the Konzo's mountain men as guide and prober, balancing obeisance and daring. He would have been a boy when I went up in 1954 into the bearded lichen at Nyamuleju and had had to descend, disordered, by the hurrying-on of malaria. Matte had grown up with the assurance that mountains bred; he fathered

Rwenzori Mountaineering Services, RMS, and also forty or so children by various wives until the prostate gland got the crab.

We had turned right, off tarmac, at Bugoye, on the gorge of the Mubuku torrent that brings down glacier-melt from within and up. On the potholed murram we were twisting up among plantain groves, passion fruit, cassava, a steepening of mud and rock, then the ganglion of mud edifices of Ibanda village and a throng of a hundred and fifty assembled under awnings of bright blue flour bags, originating as Aid for the refugees of Rwanda sixty or seventy miles to the south of us. I pulled into the compound of a hut beyond the assembly, and disembarking with my companions walked the hundred paces back to the gathered mourners. They were crowded behind a central Chesterfield opposite which were placed a bench and several chairs, sitting places for the senior mourners. I exchanged the Lukonzo greeting, and space was made on the Chesterfield for me and Millie Nzirambe and Agostino the broadcaster. A silence had opened for me to make my address. I introduced myself and they remembered how it had been, what their fathers said: that very *mzungu*, last here in this village 42 years gone, with Isaya Mukirane when he too was a young man, and Charles Wesley Iremangoma their ex-king of Ruwenzururu was a child of two. I compressed the tale. 'Musabuli,' some murmured, others 'Kambalangeya' (colobus-wearer), and others, 'Isemusoki.' Into the last appellation had entered the fuzz of legend, for it was then that I found I had assumed the mantle of fatherhood of Kirsten Alnaes' child. It did not and does not matter whether Adam or Noah, I was the earliest Konzo-committed white, come back. 'I have been to visit Charles Irema Ngoma in Washington, America,' said I, Millie translating. For such Lukonzo as I once had was all but gone. 'I told him I was to attend the Rwenzori Scientific Conference in Kampala and that I hoped to make a short visit to Rwenzururu. He wrote down a message for me to bring to his people.'

Applause. *Eh-eh. Iremangoma.* They were tremendously alert.

I opened out Charles' letter, and spoke it. Dignitaries approached to grasp my hand. An elder asked, 'Has Charles Iremangoma finished his studies?' An old one, Zebediah, recalled portering for me to Nyamuleju rock shelter, through the past's mists. He was grizzled now, yet muscular and stubborn in the body. He withdrew and returned in a pale criss-crossed jacket for our photograph. I made my contribution of several thousand shillings, about \$20, to the expenses of the funeral, and behind the huts paid homage beside the grave, on which the cross of Jesus was formed in full relief on a concrete slab.

That evening in Kasese, fifteen miles to the south, were the three I was commissioned by the old young king to visit: the bishop, the big-shot administrator, the businessman. On the top of his holy hill, Bishop Zebedee, Mukonzo, emerged from his bungalow to greet me in early darkness, filling out his tee-shirt's slogan 'Movement for Christian Democracy' with a body built short and thick befitting one born and bred in a highland village. Two of the tee-shirt's words had me depressed and wishing to recall to these latter-day Christians, subscribing to 'movements' rather than to truth, that the same *demos* that was calling out 'Hosanna!' to Jesus when on a donkey he entered Jerusalem on the first Palm Sunday was chanting 'Crucify him!' by the Friday. Bishop Zebedee owed his office to Rwenzururu, yet was not one of us. I knew that he knew that I knew *that*, as I drank up his Fanta orange-soda. The Church of Uganda would go along with the powers-that-be, not with an exiled menial in an American hospital with a fancy title on his note-paper who could disturb the status quo. One of his 39 ordained Konzo clergy was Isaleri's son Jesse Tembo. I showed him a 42-year-old photograph of Isaleri, already wise (page 127). The bungalow palace was crammed with Jesus gewgaws, stickers, caps, jars, basketry, and pennants, and among them in an ecumenical frame a message from the Pope. Ecclesiastic ambition hung in the air. That same first evening, delivering Charles' formal greetings to secular authority in the person of Barnabas Bamusede, the 'LC5', at his official home within the confines of the Kilembe mine site, I got a similar response: deep wariness at the pagan force comprising Charles, Omusinga, the idea of Rwenzururu kingship. I had not spoken with this Barnabas since 1980 when under the Binaïsa government after the fall of Idi Amin he had come to London on a grant to 'study' journalism. Now he called to the lady over by the cooker and the fridge, stickered with a reminder that 'Jesus Saves', and presented the tall and graceful Violla. 'My wife,' said he, 'is a Mutoro. You see: I married the enemy.' Barnabas, sharply alert, was himself *déraciné* in this mixed Bakonzo, Batoro, Basongora and Banyankole capital of an overwhelmingly Konzo District. He wore a West Africa collar-less smock. Political ambition hung in the air. I knew that he knew that I knew that this Barnabas Bamusede was the creature and chief functionary of Dr Crispus Kiyonga, former Minister of Finance and currently Minister of Internal Affairs; and that the recent death of Dr Henry Bwambale, Kiyonga's opponent at the last Parliamentary election, remained without credible explanation.

'So you are continuing the Ruwenzori story,' he said. 'But you are not young any more. You've grown bald. You could not get up the mountains these days.'

'I would be up there faster than you, Barnabas.'

'I don't climb the mountains any more. Now, what is there that you can find to write about us?'

Do I constitute a little threat? I wondered. 'Very likely I shan't write anything at all. Even if I do come to write something, writing is not the purpose of my visit.'

'But it will not be a visit of no purpose.'

'Your people are part of my life. A piece of my being. When a young man has a vivid experience, as I did among your people and your mountains, it makes an impression which remains. The Bakonzo gave me affection and trust. That makes for obligations.'

'So exactly why have you come back?'

'To see old friends, if I can find them.'

He was combative and wary together. I laid before him my ideas for a 'Bakonzo environmental forum', simultaneously to raise Bakonzo self-esteem and protect the highlands' pristine creation.

Whether or not married to 'the enemy', Barnabas himself was a Mukonzo, just as his master had to be whenever he came to Kasese District, the site of his constituency. 'You should meet our Mukonjo minister,' he was saying as I prepared to leave, 'and tell him your ideas.' *Mukonjo*, he had said.

As for the businessman, Mzee Yofesi Mutanywana, he owned a maize meal factory, a cotton-seed oil factory, a rambling bungalow, two large farms producing maize, millet, plantains, pineapples and cotton, and a substantial piece of property at the very start of the trekkers' route to the inner mountain peaks, at a site called Nyakalingija above Ibanda. He was the richest man in Kasese by a long head. He stood scarcely more than four foot in height and was illiterate. He was married to Betty, an iron butterfly. Because of his known competence in matters of business, when Charles found himself stranded in the US in 1986 he had passed into Yofesi's care the quite substantial property conceded to him on his descent from the mountains in 1982. In Charles' absence, Yofesi put it to me, given the complexion and complexity of that absence, one could hardly have expected that property to have stayed intact, could one...? It was apparent that Charles' return would be, well, awkward. Was indeed Charles to return? Would he dare? Amid these unusual deaths – Bazira, Bwambale?

It was clear to me already, beyond any doubt, that the Konzo *demos*, the people in their instinctual mass, craved his return. Yet two things about my brief from Charles were interesting: first, that the three figures he had commissioned me to pay his earnest respects to constituted current power in this Ruwenzori region (in the three big overlapping spheres of church, politics and money); and next that none of the three wanted Charles back. Charles would wake the Sleeping Lord of tribe. He was trouble. His light would outshine theirs. He was better off where he was, far away and insubstantial, a Cheshire cat up a foreign tree. They knew Charles still looked to a future for himself, a tribal future. It was up to me if I wished to weave a basket for private Ruwenzori dreams out of such withies of the past as I could still gather up: they could tolerate that. As to the fate of the mountains and their people...

I went at once to call upon Christina Mukirania, Isaya's widow and Queen Mother, at the family villa above the town. It was set in half an acre of land, trim and to all appearances deserted. I wandered behind. Out of the smokey gloom of an open-faced improvised hut where hens pecked and a pot sat on three stones in a log fire, emerged an old lady. She was instantly recognisable. Word of my presence in the country had already reached her, and she knew, naturally, of my continuing role in Charles' life. She was less astonished than

dismayed that I had caught her early in her work-a-day shift, not finery, at the ancestral hearth. To this mother of the nation, herself a legend of indesructibility, I was not so much a source of news as a function of ceremony. I was to be done the honour of an immediate meal of stew of chicken whose neck, naturally, had first to be wrung and its feathers plucked. On the veranda with her youngest, Williams, now twenty-nine and out of work, we turned the pages of my album of photographs from forty-two and thirty-three years previously. Williams' infant offspring spilled around the place. This site, to the local folk, was the 'royal residence' of Charles, the Kasese buhikira. My picture record of her own remote past, of figures clad in skins and barkcloth, amid their beehive huts of bamboo sheath leaves, left the old lady unmoved. It was not for her to grow excited. In a life of extreme vicissitude and perpetual uncertainty, her function was to maintain the thatch, the fire, the stew-pot, the umbilical principle; to be immovable and unmoved. I told her of Charles in America and her question was, *Who did his cooking?* God knows what she had witnessed, been privy, party to.

When occasion arose, Mama could declare and augur like a sybil.

I had three mere days and a low-bellied Corolla to do what I came for, to weave my basket out of the past, out of the old fierce commitment to the race and place. I drove south and west to Bwera. I was seeking Blasio Maate who as a young teacher in 1954, had joined Isaya and me in discipleship in our research and climbed with us by degrees with the bridal party to Kitolu, where Isaleri Kambere the wise presided. I was also hoping to find Isaleri himself, whom I knew to be living still, well into his eighties, yet whom I would have no time to reach on my feet, as would be necessary. I had no four-wheel-drive machine for the steep road to Kitolu which I myself had caused to be built in 1963. Next, Batolumayu Kisiraho, our runner, carrier of all the messages that came mightily to nought. There was also Linkoni – Abraham Lincoln, outliving all.

All of these four were of the southern heartland and in so far as that heartland had an earthly capital it was the lowland townlet of Bwera. Blasio lived there and also Lincoln. Rather as Kasese had grown up at the mountains' base half way along the eastern flank as a consequence of the mining enterprise, so Bwera at mountains' southern base had grown as the entrepôt of the agricultural produce of those favoured foothills, particularly coffee. It too had a Post Office, three (rival) churches and a mosque. Its little warren of lanes and earthen homes for – what? – seven or eight thousand folk, lay on the potholed east-west highway, was the first port of call for all goods vehicles crossing into East Africa from the Congo. It had shops and bars and a mechanical repair shop or two, and venereal diseases and Aids in higher incidence than elsewhere among these people.

My little entourage was young: 'Prince' Williams, and Millie Nzirambe of the World Wildlife Fund, and Hellen (*sic*) the daughter of the unlettered tycoon Mzee Yofesi and his iron butterfly. They argued with unquenchable energy about how and whether and when the absent Omusinga Charles should return to his people, which was proving to be the issue underlying all the politics of the region and was lent an immediacy by the Presidential election campaign which Museveni had unleashed upon the country. It struck me with clarity how, on the one hand, the forces of secular power in Ruwenzori, namely ecclesiastical, financial and political, were hostile to or fearful of the restoration of Konzo identity such as the return of Charles would entail while, on the other hand, the hearts of the ordinary people, young and old alike, were with Charles and what he and his office meant to them as Konzo. The powerful few all but belonged to the ethos of the white, the masses to the ethos of the black, old Africa; the few to the world of time and money and possessions and deferred rewards, the many to the world of no time, no money, steep earth and the drum. The President was a man in a suit and the people, the true people, had no need of shoes: only their own space to plant their yams and fish their fish and speak their tongue. The Presidential election was in large measure a charade in that there was no question of any result being permitted other than Museveni's re-election – which might have happened in any case: one would never know. Yet a 'democratic' contest of a sort gave grievances an airing, it brought opponents of the regime out into the open, it identified which pockets of the country most hated Museveni's no-party One-Party, and it provided the US and Britain, who liked to have Museveni there, a correct political pretext for backing him with aid for various hidden agendas. Crispus Kiyonga, Minister of the Interior, arch-foe of the omusingaship, conduit of guidance to Museveni on all matters touching this region, was out campaigning with characteristic tenacity on behalf of his master's re-election. A further election lay in the immediate future, for the national parliament. I had chanced to return to Ruwenzori at the hot season for politics; I kept on nearly bumping into this Dr Kiyonga and his team as I whipped around the handful of very local initiatives of collective good intentions in the southern lowlands to which I had contributed small sums of money from London in recent years in response to their beautifully phrased and hand-written appeals.

At Bwera, I found Abraham Lincoln at home with his wife, the sibling sister of Charles' mama, whom she so strikingly resembled. Now at eighty, this Linkoni maintained all his faculties of mind and dignity of bearing. It was then I learned of the judicial maiming of his hand that he had endured at his brother-in-law Isaya's behest, when he was struggling to fulfil his role as sub-county chief for central Government during the early days of Rwenzururu. I have told of this on page 121. Linkoni showed me the scar; he demonstrated the incapacity of his  hand. I noted the absolute absence of bitterness. Such was the way life was. The proud enduring cast of the white head declared an ultimate self-command by his surrender to *che sarà sarà*. When I produced the folio of my photographs of 1954, and we reached the picture of himself aged 38, he made no comment and scarcely paused to scrutinise it. So I prompted him: 'Who is this?' He replied 'Abraham Lincoln' as if the one in the picture was of someone else; as indeed it was, in a Heraclitan truthfulness. Yet when I next produced a copy of my little book (of 1965) entitled *Summons to Ruwenzori*, he was suddenly violent, grabbing at it furiously with his good hand and not letting it go. I told him I had only four copies in the world, and that

391

this one was for Blasio Maate. He was adamant. He would only release it on the promise that as soon as I returned to London I would send him one of my remaining three (which I did). The book was treasure here: it comprised the only enduring record theoretically available to the world at large of the reality of Rwenzururu. To possess a copy bestowed *noblesse*.

It was little Mbambu Yolicy (=Alice), Isaleri's granddaughter, at the lowland secondary school at Karambi, as far as my car would reach, who volunteered to run up the hills – a four or five hour scramble – to tell her grandfather of the intended presence the following afternoon at Blasio Maate's lowland house of Tom Stacey Musabuli. I had called in on the school of 470 pupils to offer to speak to the children of the importance to the world of their mountains. And when by courtesy of the Head I did, they were amazed. They were taught nothing about their mountains, nothing about their own history, nothing about Tibamwenda, or Isaya Mukirane, or Rwenzururu. Behind where I spoke the dedicated principal had hung a verse in embroidery, in a frame: *Better to strive and climb/And never reach the goal/Rather than drift along with time/An aimless; worthless soul.* Yolicy was a weekly boarder. On this, a weekday, she strove and climbed. And thus it turned out there at Blasio's on the afternoon of the morrow, all we four, four quite old men – our host Blasio Maate around 70, Isaleri at over 80, and Batulomayu around my own age of 66 – had homed in upon the little bungalow in a snug, leafy dell just below the road that led from Bwera to the Congo border. Blasio had been absent in Kampala the previous day, and on his return that night had been told by his daughter Maria, of striking grace, to expect me to come back from Kasese to see him this following p.m., and how I had sent a message into the hills proposing his home as this rendezvous.

It was of course amazing: the amazement was amazing. For although I guess that Blasio himself – former District Commissioner under Obote's last regime, domiciled *down* and with a motorcar, Post Box, and sometimes a telephone – was probably aware that not only was I still alive but also alert to Bakonzo affairs and their mountains and their King, to his two veteran Rwenzururu comrades I was a figure of pure history and, if by any chance technically alive, meetable only in heaven.

Blasio in a brown suit and striped tie met me outside the house on his sward of muscular grass, and there we embraced like old lovers as Charles's brother Williams recorded the moment on camera. The other two were evidently awaiting me in his front room; and indeed, in the gloom, Isaleri was now rising to greet me immediately on the left of the doorway as I entered. One at a time, I thought. Isaleri and I held one another's right hands in the African manner of greeting that lets old acquaintance flow back cutaneously, fingers around fingers, in dumb immobilisation, *wawukïre/kutë?/eyeho!/wynoandi?/nimerembi*, rocking, a lilt, a pulse discernible across – what? – forty-two years since my first entry into his highland ground of Kitolu where the word of a single God had just begun to displace the several voices of Tibamwenda's and Nyamutswa's coven. Instead of the medicine fibre of those lost days I saw that above the front pocket of his cornflower blue jacket he wore the red badge declaring him to be a CHURCH OF UGANDA SENIOR CHURCH ELDER. I turned to greet Batolumayu, who instantly transmitted to me that same limpid urgency of hope-against-hope which he invariably brought to all his message-carrying thirty-three years previously. Blasio stood beside, beaming amid the joy of it, we four all sealed by ancient trust and blood. Such instant intimacy was contaminated by the presence of a government official, a Local Chairman 2. I perceived that my attendance here at Blasio's house among this gathering of oldies could be construed as a political event and that, playing safe, Blasio had notified governmental (NRM) authority. This creepy apparatchik in our midst, or on the edge of us, intruded caution into our interchange, the pith of which would be reported (I supposed) to Barnabas Bamusede, the LC5, in Kasese. I knew already that Blasio, appointed to his former District Commissionership at Amon Bazira's behest under the Obote government of some fourteen years earlier, had endured his share of threats and persecution under the incoming regime. I knew too of NALU and Bazira's murder. Yet settling down now into one of the chairs that ringed the walls of the small dark lime-washed chamber, festooned with printed cards of mutual celebration of this or that Christian festival on looping strings, I opened with a bold delivery of Omusinga Charles' message of 'I love you, I miss you, and obey the Government' (such as, of course, I had already dutifully retailed to Bamusede). I told them of my sustained contact with Charles; of his intention to return at the right time; of the Ruwenzori Scientific Conference which provided the context of my visit; and of my proposals for a Bakonzo Environmental Forum. The complexity of this was relayed in Lukonzo sentence by sentence by Hellen, a lusty wench who flirted with my left hand so determinedly during the proceedings, removing my signet ring, that I wondered whether she had been instructed by her mother to seduce me.

I sensed the senior guests from the hills were waiting for me to stop. As soon as I did, Isaleri rose to his feet, and gazing straight ahead gave voice to prayer of thanksgiving for the gift of this extraordinary reunion – a prayer which then flowered into a grace for the meal they were evidently about to receive. Blasio conducted his senior mountain guests, plus Batulomayu's carpenter son who had escorted them down, plus the local political panjandrum, into the back room, for a meal which Blasio's wife and their lovely Maria had been preparing. This repast I and my Kasese companions – Hellen and Williams – were spared; but in half an hour the diners had rejoined us. Speeches followed, each speaker standing. First was to be Batulomayu, who retailed his own story of devoted service to the Kingdom of Rwenzururu first as a messenger and later as a judge, and then to NALU from which he had defected less than a year previously. He recalled my own role as one who shared their food, and slept in their houses, and how I had come back to find 'a people which had suffered long.' He himself had lived in rebellion most of his life, and so had fathered only seven children, not the dozen he would have wished for, and when he finally took advantage of an amnesty, he had no home to go to – nothing but a letter from the LC5 (Barnabas Bamusede Bwambale), which he produced for me to read. It was in English.

District Resistance Council
Kasese District Administration.
To whom it may concern.   10 July 1995

Batulomao Kasiraho

    The above-named person has returned to Uganda from exile in Zaïre where he has been for several years.
    He has already reported to the office of CGP District of Kasese and of course to this office.
    The purpose of this letter therefore is to request whoever to ensure Mr Kasiraho is helped to settle in society without any interference.
    Solidarity
    B Bwambale
    Chairman
    District Resistance Council

'This letter has produced me no benefits,' good Batulomayu concluded. 'But you have written many books which many people have bought. So you have money to help me build a house to live in.'

In reply I reasserted my undying loyalty to the Bakonzo people, my support for justice towards them now. I promised not to stay away from them for any long spell again. Though I could not be a one-man aid agency, I would try to contribute to his tin roof. I doubted he was sleeping in the open, with Isaleri his half-brother, and every second man up there his cousin. Next was Isaleri to rise, for a considered speech. 'When I heard it was Tom Stacey,' he said, 'I thought it was a dream. My wife, when she heard that he had returned to us, she was so full of joy. How could we ever imagine he would come again? When he came the last time, he warned us of the army approaching. He saved us from being shot. We had to hurry away that same day. We left a goat for them [i.e. Bill Cheyne's Uganda Rifles, of February 1963. Isaleri was referring, I think, to my shouted warning in the midst of an apparently deserted Kitolu, on my return there in the company of Ibrahimu and Seylversta, before I had encountered Isaya's Praetorian Guard.]

'So we give thanks to God for that time and this time. Since you left, our troubles have resumed and continue to this day. For many years it was very hard for us. There was a time, not long ago, when we all had to come down and stay down. That was for one and a half years, beginning in 1990.' That was during NALU's offensive. To Isaleri, while Rwenzururu had always a touch of paradise, etherial freedom, NALU was a scourge. It brought the weight and viciousness of the UPDF upon them in response to an insurrection they had no sympathy with. They were punished for the shelter their terrain provided. NALU thankfully was inactive just now, the rump of its adherents back in Congo from where Batulomayu had recently slipped across to collect his bounty-less pardon.

Then Blasio rose, in his striped tie. Blasio began with Idi Amin, responding to Rwenzururu by giving the Bakonzo Kasese

District... and then turned to his own appointment as District Commissioner, originally under the caretaker government of Binaisa. He had been in charge of the place at the coming-down, *eriandanghala*, of Charles in 1982. When Museveni got power in 1986 he continued for a while as 'District Superintendent'... until the system was radically changed. He glanced at the LC2, that upstart. As for the present, ten years on, at this moment of my return, he was Chairman of the Boards of Governors of this school or that. He sat, that grand man.

So wherein lay the persisting injustice, this gnaw of incompletion, something inner unresolved or unresolvable, such as I had found everywhere I had been among these people in the few brief days since I had come back again? – among that little community of the mountain people in Kampala, quietly captained by the political economist at Makerere, Syahuka-Muhindo; at John Matte's obsequies; at each of the communal self-help projects I had been supporting with small sums hidden in envelopes from England which comprised a woman's agricultural group at Kinyamaseke by the Queen Elizabeth National Park boundary, a model farm a few miles in towards the hills, an orphanage for 20 infants run with a bubbling overflow of Christian love beside the cottage hospital at Kigando by Millie Nzirambe's sister Dorothy; and lastly this flawed reunion at Blasio Maate's? We are no longer at ease here, they seemed to say, in this new dispensation. We shall vote, yes, if we have to, in the way in which we are told by those who manifestly have the power (since it is too dangerous for the body and too hazardous for the spirit to vote for those who do not already have power), yet we do not trust those with power over us, either locally or nationally, do not trust them nor suppose they care for what we are, *Konzo*, as a people. We do not know where we are going, whether we or our young are going anywhere, or whether always we shall be covering up, ashamed of what we are as soon as we go beyond our own borders...

Only when I bring them Charles's message, opening it out in front of them, does some flame seem to kindle in them, the lost king of the legendary kingdom: *tell us, you who say you are in reach of him, will he not come back again?*

Naturally I was aware of the inhibiting factor of miscellaneous ears at Blasio's house – the LC2's and Hellen Kabugho's, and the tongues of the prattling young. Then quick fortune smiled upon us perversely. Returning to my long-suffering car which I had left on the road above Blasio's house, beyond a hundred yards or so of high growth, I found that it had yet another flat tyre. As Williams and the rest set about changing the wheel the opportunity was there for me to be wholly alone with my ancient friends amid the shrouding wild pampas grasses. There I learned that the obstacle to the return of Charles and the proper, consequent reconciliation of the Bakonzo people in the new Uganda was Dr Kiyonga. The name was spoken in an undertone, rather as Isaya once murmured to me the name of that most chancy of female spirits, Nyabingi. That too had been vouchsafed on uncultivated ground. Yet this present 'obstacle' was no spirit but their own local boy, a Mutalingi-Mukonzo from a spur above the Tako not more than half an hour's walk from where we stood, the most capable, variously influential and wealthy Minister in the President's inner cabinet, currently of Internal Affairs. Was all this more and other than the anguish of being black and African in a continent now well and truly robbed of innocence, delicacy and instinctual wisdom by a predator outer-world that was white, brutish, and meaningless? I did not know and do not know as I write now. Were the Baganda, say, with their tribal eminence, their dynastic history and their restored Kabaka, of another heart than these Bakonzo? To a degree the answer was Yes. And I had and have further rumination, implicit in this whole tale: that all which Africa knows as *tribe* is integral to the species man in all creation and all history, past, present and future; and that in the evolution of the soul – by definition a genial current – 'tribe' in a broad sense and narrow will always play a part within creation's One, just as humankind's instinctual forces (embodied most vividly today in Africa) will always nourish man as Spirit. Be it termed, therefore, prejudice or philosophy, my allegiance on the omusinga issue among the Bakonzo of the Mountains of the Moon had and has its marked directional tilt, whatever destiny would have in store.

Our wheel was changed, and I and my motley of young guides and facilitators were off again in imminently closing darkness for another night at Kasese, which I would spend at the little town's only hotel worthy of that term, the Margherita, named after the cousin of Prince Luigi of Savoy who was Italy's Queen when the Prince was the first to summit Ruwenzori. This hospice, prettily set a mile or two behind the shanty-town of Kasese, on the foothill between Kasese and the mine site of Kilembe, had recently been acquired from the dead hand of State ownership by a Mukonzo entrepreneur, a species of rarity, working with State-borrowed money, to provide the basic amenities. From its long, covered veranda a guest could gaze on higher foothills, cleared and cultivated, tiered exquisitely two or three thousand feet further up, and – beyond – to blue ridges, uninhabited, twice as high again which for ever tantalisingly barred the gaze from the further, inner citadels of peaks and snows. What, by night, gave away the presence of further, mightier summits was lightning – lightning and the perpetual restlessness and threat of the heavens.

Near to, below the veranda, the land fell away to an extended valley floor of dense reeds and grasses that concealed low springs of bubbling mud almost too hot for an omutahwa to submerge the body of a sickly client seeking Nyabibuya's mystic cures. For this place Kasese and its mine were sited on creational unease, what geographic science calls a 'fault', where the maker of the world in his primitive mode offers quailing men a hint of his latent force.

My tasks yet were innumerable, and of course multiplying as word spread of my re-emergence from half-forgotten time; and my remaining days absurdly numbered to two or three. Wherever I went, gatherings spontaneously coalesced. Folk from this compound were swiftly joined by folk from the immediate circle of compounds: old men came forth to wring my hand; grins opened around beaming gums, 'Stacaye...Stacaye..' or sometimes 'Musabuli' or 'Isemusoki' – it was the same, I was the resurrected presence of archaic white allegiance from earliest Rwenzururu and before; and I would issue Charles's message and speak of the meaning to the world of the mountains of which they, the Bakonzo, were gatekeepers. Thus a throng spontaneously materialized when, north of Kasese the following day I passed up the road towards the foothill village of Maliba, and having made my speech enquired of the half-a-hundred gathered there which of them knew of Seylversta Manyumba Mukirane, for I had picked up word that he had retired from Kilembe with his family to farm in this vicinity. As is the infallible rule of Africa, someone knew, and slipped away, and within an hour beside a certain open pathside, beaming in flustered disbelief, stood Seylversta. *Eh*, in the the eye of Jesus, what is thirty-three years? A twinkling. And in my eye, who could this be but Seylversta, the child's goodness preserved by time and misfortune in the eyes and lines of the old man for as long as body breathed. Afloat upon our bubble of reunion, he led me home through dense moist plantain groves and cassava patches, amid which we passed a lump of rock as vast as a house, concerning which he commented. 'This one is made by God: He Himself. He lettus usey this rock for drying our clothies.' At his neat home of dark mud, half-roofed with tin and half with reeds, Seylversta had reared his family of four boys with his wife until her death two years previously. That bereavement  lay upon him. We partook of a meal of the best of all his produce – pineapple, bread, millet and chunks of impenetrably muscular goat – all of which was of course thanksgiving and preceded by a grace launched into by Seylversta and lasting several minutes, drawing from a text I could not precisely locate in my memory concerning Abraham and certain angels, and concluding, in English, 'our lovely Father, I thank you for this well-wish to bring to us back this very dear friend and helper.' Dearly beloved and deeply consistent Seylversta.

This same 'friend and helper' could not make the road journey to Bundibugyo, as I had hoped, to find once again my and Seylversta's brave companion of 1963 and mine alone of 1954, Ibrahimu Ndyanabaïsi: the road had so deteriorated as to be impossible for any but four-wheel-drive vehicles. Thus my last night was to be in the Margherita Hotel, and here I was found by Barnabas Bamusede, LC5, hot from the campaign trail for the Presidential election, or more precisely re-election, which was to take place countrywide two days ahead. Barnabas said, 'Each place I have been to they are talking about you. You seem to have been everywhere.' We were joined by Mzee Yofesi, our local plutocrat, and his Iron Butterfly, Betty, parents of Hellen. By obtaining political asylum in America, this couple now put it to me unequivocally, Charles had made himself an alien in Uganda. And since he was an alien it had been impossible for them to prevent the bulk of the property he had received on his descent from the mountains from reverting to the Government, which had sold it to an Indian and pocketed the proceeds. So now I knew. This was Kasese, West Uganda, not Kensington and Chelsea.

What if Charles came back, I asked.

'It would be quite difficult for him,' said the Iron Butterfly.

A little later, on the veranda writing up my diary and the darkness beyond, there was a certain commotion outside at the Margherita's entrance as of someone of consequence arriving, and there sure enough below the steps – as I crossed the little lobby to return to my room for my pencil sharpener – two formidable Range Rovers were pulled up below the steps. Two powerful followers, not conceivably Bakonzo, were right there by the reception desk, in flowered shirts. These were foreigners on my territory and warranted a greeting suited to the hospice's camaraderie and the Lion Special beer brew and piped rock music emanating from the bar and garden-side veranda beyond it. I laid a hand on the belly of one of these late arrivals, recommending a watch on the waistline, which the fellow took in jocular part yet I spotted a lurking menace to him. Returning by the same route within the minute I saw there between the toughies a shortish Mukonzo-looking fellow with wide-awake eyes such as I recognise from photographs of Museveni's cabinet team. Our eyes met.

'You are Tom Stacey. I am Kiyonga.' Here, then, suddenly, our Buonaparte, the ethnically off-centre *arriviste*, the political shooting star, with his bodyguards. 'I heard you had come back.'

I told him what brought me – the Ruwenzori Scientific Conference. He said,

'Let us have breakfast together tomorrow morning.'

So we did, I with my long spoon, in a corner of the dining room, taking him through my own knowledge of the mountains before he was born, through to Amos Kambere – 'He jumped bail' snapped Crispus Kiyonga – to Amon Bazira whom I would counsel, Crispus, with two questions: What hope has your NALU of success? *and* Should not Museveni be given a chance? The international community has given him a chance, said I (echoing my counsel), to make a go of what passes as a democracy here in Uganda. A quick smile touched Kiyonga's lips. I tried to imagine what he made of me, what he supposed I was truly here for, what advantage or benefit I expected. He would think in terms of something personally gained, which was the way the white world, the outer world, had taught this child of the Tako valley to think. I might have said to him, Old men ought to be explorers, and dream dreams. That would have had him more sharply puzzled. Yet he knew that I read *him* and that I didn't condemn him out of hand; he knew what they would have all told me of him, his enemies – those he had chosen as his enemies – and yet here I was, spending the time of day with him. I told him I too had been in politics, so he knew I knew about the necessary deceptions... yet would be unlikely to condone murder which had slid out of fashion in English politics in recent centuries though not, of course, in Russia a mere generation ago; or Germany, two generations. I told him of Charles's message, stressing how sound and sensible it was. He said the fellow was free to return any time, as an ordinary citizen. 'But they venerate him,' I said, and he at once returned, 'There is no tradition of Kingship among the Bakonzo.' Not quite yet, I thought to say. I wanted him to feel at ease. I told him of my proposal: the Bakonzo Environmental Forum. That caught his fancy, so much so that I feared he might espouse it and make it his political concubine for commercial purposes. I already knew of his attempt to raise money for a touristic enterprise of his own in the sacred mountains. So we parted in mutual wary comradeship, exchanging phone numbers. He left for Kampala there and then straight from the breakfast table. I too was due back in Kampala that evening, and on the night plane to London...

He was no Beelzebub, this Crispus Kiyonga, but a politico on the make, having a high old time in a dangerous place – high status and, if it goes wrong, high penalties, not excluding death. He was a mortal man who had first struggled to make his way amid the churning mud and muddle of an 'emerging' Africa by the remarkable route of White Man's medicine, Galen not Nyabibuya, committing himself to curing the sick and bringing into the world healthy babies from mothers he spared from infection or fatal haemorrhage; and who, with such a discipline of doing good by the sober exercise of diagnosis, analysis and holding fast to effect's descent from cause, had turned that self-same discipline to politics and the acquisition of power: power nationally, in the White Man's mode, within territorial boundaries and governmental forms made by whites not blacks, Ugandan not Rwenzururian. Did he not deserve the power he had so assiduously, so solitarily acquired? Was he not a man of the future, the only possible future in the world as it was; while I, maudlin white, was choosing for whatever imperfect motives – literary vanity, even – to give credence to a superseded Africa, tribal, of the past, and of darkness? – and I engaged thus right here, on his own native territory with which he would for ever be measurelessly more intimate than I, in all its murk, ignorance, fear and superstition.

And maudlin I, also sophisticate, boulevardier, would sadly say, I see your point: yet what use the future or the past without the present? What use this third or fourth Five Year Plan or Nyamuhanga and all his angels without prayer? What use the power and the glory, the splendour and the majesty, the steep plantations, these tectonic rifts, the Mountains of the Moon, without love? Yet I see your point, Crispus Kiyonga, man of power, as you sweep off in your Range Rovers, flanked by bodyguards. And your Museveni will have won another Presidential term, plausibly enough, by 76 per cent of the votes supposedly cast. For two minutes on the veranda, I watched his little convoy curl down the road below me until it disappeared behind the shoulder of the foothill.

'Psst,' said somebody on the veranda.

It was Williams Sibibuka, Charles's younger brother. He jerked his head.

I followed him out of the hotel and over rising ground. Beyond a knoll in a hollow under a wide sky, six young men sat in a circle. This circle admitted me, fresh from the presence of the enemy. Beyond the sunlight the mountains hung above us like an impossibly vast sea poised to break and devastate all men and all men's measureless insignificance. The six young men were the core of a Kasese youth organisation bearing a more elaborate title expressing an allegiance to the place and their own derivation from its soil and patrimony. All six were of thrust and attainment and included Charles's next brother along the line, Christopher Tabaan, some nine years the Omusinga's junior; a son of Fanehasi Kisokeronio named Zostine, already mentioned in these pages, who (thanks to Bishop Zebedee) had stayed down away from the forests and rebels, to acquire a further education; a Muslim Mukonzo of flair and force of personality; and a non-Mukonzo born and bred in the locality of fervent adopted commitment. This eclectic young élite had waited out of sight to snatch me from tentacles such as got Laocoön, just as soon as the fellow left the breakfast table and set off for Kampala. Here under the sun, under the overhang of the mountains beyond the valley bed and its hot springs, we were free-spirited – free as the yellow birds, the weavers and the lemon doves that flit and swept our own eastward- and inward-orientated vicinity, up to the very limits of human habitatance and cultivation and no doubt into the forests beyond, the hunting ground and hiding ground. I shed contamination by pointing out at once that corner breakfast table was open for all to see – specifically, the observing eye of Williams Sibibuka – and the conversation open for anyone that wished to share it. But now of course we were in secret conclave, our old gods listening in, to figure out the restoration of the Kingship and, ah-ha, the springing of Chris Tabaan as challenger to Kiyonga's current placement MP for this very constituency in the approaching Ugandan Parliamentary elections. We talked for an hour.

I flew off home that very night to London. This was late April. I reported to Charles of my faithful delivery of his tri-partite message and of his people's warm reception of it, often with applause. I listed those fifty or more Bakonzo and the dozen or so other senior figures with whom I had discussed the political situation, the future of the region, and the prospect of his own return for which the people yearned; I added my personal counsel that he should, and indeed could relatively danger-free, return as a 'venerated private citizen' who would naturally be consulted on regional issues, and possibly also stand for Parliament in due course, rather than as one seeking re-installation as Omusinga of Rwenzururu at this juncture. I wrote of NALU as a spent force that had disturbed and in no way uplifted the mountain people; and I sent him my own ideas for a Bakonzo Environmental Forum, stressing the value to him of an environmental stage on which to play a role of leadership among his people. I spoke of Kiyonga as a fixture on the power-scene in Uganda and that we were best advised not to cast him as a permanent Enemy Number One. I sent him photographs, including of his former principal bodyguard. He wrote back emphasising the significance of 'Rwenzururu' not as 'a political thing but a cultural and spiritual thing by God and other local spirits.' As to Kiyonga, he could not see him as other than an implacable and perhaps mortal foe to him, for ever up to 'dirty tricks' and one who would 'always want to kill his political opponents' so as to secure his role as 'dictator of the area'.

In June, two months on, Charles' brother Christopher Tabaan threw his hat into the parliamentary ring for Kasese town's constituency – at the last minute, for his physical safety – to contest the seat with the sitting member, a Kiyonga man. The 'cultural and

spiritual thing by God and other local spirits' stirred in the grasses, snouting and butting against secular power. Christopher soon found his hustings voice and humour, adopting his father's 'Lutheran' honorific Kibanzanga, Unbudgeable, *Hier stehe ich*. He caught up the entire hill vote above the town to the very man and woman, and won the seat. I wondered if this was to be the morning star of Charles's coming home... as Chief Citizen Charles, Charles the Voice of the Mountains, King Charles of Rwenzururu.

xxix

The Mountains are Invaded

Suddenly, in mid-November that year, 1996, war erupted. I was in the Persian Gulf engaged in business when my London office came on the line to report that they had received by fax a *cri de coeur* from Syahuka-Muhindo at Makerere that dreadful events were in train, and that I must speak with him at once by telephone. With the aid, no doubt, of various satellites, I did indeed reach my friend Syahuka-Muhindo on a bad line, and from that moment began to piece together the following extraordinary train of events. Syahuka-Muhindo was in grief and alarm for reasons that will become clear as the story unfolds, though much was still unclear at the time of our first imperfect long-distance conversation.

On the night of November 12, an invasion force of several hundred men from Congo (Zaïre as it was then known) swarmed across the Ugandan border at Mpondwe, just west of Bwera. Uniformed, armed with modern guns, including rocket-propelled grenades (RPGs), and evidently at least partly trained and operating to plan, this wild corps seized the trucks and vans clustered as usual at the border post, and thus equpped with wheels and fuel, occupied first Mpondwe and then Bwera, overrunning the police posts and the small Ugandan army detachment just north of Bwera towards the hills. Shooting as they went, they swept eastwards to the big market village of Kisinga. There they captured the jail, releasing the prisoners, and obtaining a store of prison uniforms in which they dressed units of their soldiery who infiltrated the neighbourhood masquerading as convict cotton-picking parties. Their further objective in this initial push was apparently Kasese town and its airfield. By the afternoon, the UPDF (Ugandan army) garrison at Kasese, rudely awoken, had roared down the road southwards and westwards to confront the invaders. Fierce combat had ensued: the UPDF vehicles were detroyed by rebel RPGs. However, UPDF reinforcements from Mbarara, capital of Ankole, sixty miles to the east, had been summoned to join the counter-attack, with tanks.

Who on earth were these marauders, self-conjured out of nowhere? At that first phone exchange the only certainty was of some kind of Islamic motive. In a short while we were able to piece the answer together a plausible answer. For the most part they were disaffected Ugandan Muslims, from the more southerly, Bantu region of the country. Many were militant young, from Buganda and – further east still – Busoga, where the Muslim minorities supposed themselves to have become a side-lined element of the population under a regime of prevailingly Christian allegiance. For several years Museveni's Uganda had been engaged in war-at-one-remove against Sudan, along their common border. Sudan was then enduring the fundamentalist Muslim rule of General Bashir. Guided by the subversive ideology of the academic Turabi and bankrolled by Iran, Bashir's Sudan sought to Islamicise all of sub-Saharan Christian or pagan Africa. Such a stance and activity had naturally alerted the US which deemed its function as one of providing the Christianised Nilotic tribes of southern Sudan with weaponry, supplies and cash in their generation-long revolt against Khartoum. The conduit was Musveni's Uganda. Khartoum responded by suppplying the voodoo Kony rebellion of northern Uganda with mines and weapons and by subverting Uganda's disaffected Muslims. Amon Bazira had established links with Khartoum and NALU. On Bazira's murder, NALU's remnant soldiery, holed up in camp at Buhira in the Congo, lost their *raison d'être*. The agents of Khartoum seized the opportunity to develop links with NALU on the ground. NALU's spokesman was a certain Rogers Kabanda, by blood half Mukonzo and half Muganda. With him was the old warrior diehard, Fanehasi Kisokeronio. First they met in Goma, the lakeside capital of Kivu province; they reconvened in Beni, near to Ruwenzori. Ruwenzori's old links with Islam, forged by the Arab trader Mahmoud Sa'ad whose wife was Mukonzo, which I told of on page 321, assumed new form through the proselytizing enthusiasm of certain of Sa'ad's Muslim offspring. Young Muslim recruits for warfare against Museveni's Uganda began to be smuggled in Sa'ad buses from Uganda's central cities into Congo, and to enter training in their hundreds alongside the rump of NALU. Thus was created the ADF – the Alliance for (implausibly) Democratic Freedom. Equipment was smuggled in by air through Kisangani (formerly Stanleyville) with a nod and a wink from the authorities. Mobutu, dictator of Zaïre since the early 1960s, had smiled upon these goings-on. With American arms diverted from the South Sudan's Christian rebels, Museveni was now openly supporting the rebellion against Mobutu which was gaining momentum further south in western Zaïre under the banner of Laurent Kabila. Directed by Khartoum, the ADF was hoping to build up their now essentially Islamic rebel force formidably enough to be launched upon the very centre of Ugandan authority. Astonishingly enough, nothing of this jiggery-pokery appears to have come to the attention of Museveni and his government. Nor do I believe it was known to Charles in America; and certainly not to me in London.

The grander plot was overtaken by the unexpected advance of Kabila's rebellion. Though no Tutsi himself, Kabila's fighting force was largely Tutsi, much of it reared in Uganda following the 1964 massacres in Rwanda, and supported on the ground by ethnic brothers in the Ugandan army (UPDF). The prospect loomed of the ADF's presence in Zaïre being overrun by Kabila's Museveni-backed surge northwards. Thus in a manner familiar enough in the high tropics, the ADF invasion of November 12 went off half-cock – the rebels in mere hundreds not thousands. When the UPDF, reinforced from Mbarara, hit them hard at Kisinga and Nyabirongo on the 14th, those that were not killed fled into the mountains, taking refuge in the forest edge where they were entirely dependent on the mountain-wise Bakonzo contingent and notably on a guide of the invading forces, a son of Yolama Mulimu, ex-premier of Rwenzururu.

Crispus Kiyonga, Minister of the Interior, was alerted at dawn of the previous day, November 13th, 1996 to the fact of the invasion. He summoned his Land Rovers and bodyguards and sped off for the zone of war, seven hours away, reaching the little town of Bwera by mid-afternoon. He intended to rescue his Mama. Indifferent to danger, he drove into ADF territory until, at the edge of the town, his little convoy of civilian cars came under fire. The cars swerved into a plantain grove; their occupants leapt for cover, the Minister himself sprawled beneath a bodyguard. Fire was returned, the coast made clear, and the gallant mission successfully carried through. He was in and out with Mother before the big battle and big carnage had begun. But this was his territory, and his blood was up.

The invading *tabliqs*, as the ADF were characterized, appear to have dreamed of riding into Kasese, securing the airfield, inviting assistance by air from Sudan. From such a base they would ride eastwards to be welcomed in Kampala as saviours of Uganda from tyranny. A dream it was. As tyrannies go, Uganda scarcely rated. Its government was well entrenched and, if not greatly loved, was generally accepted. Yet Museveni had received a fearful jolt; he himself descended upon the Ruwenzori area while his Interior Minister, Kiyonga, entered upon an exercise of officially endorsed cleansing of any Bakonzo of southern Ruwenzori perceived as hostile to himself or the NRM government. The victims included not only Konzo Muslims but activists in the cause of the return of Charles and restoration of the Omusingaship. Many were capriciously arrested, held in darkness in bunkers too low to stand upright, and questioned under varying degrees of torture. Homes of the innocent were raided by police or army and ransacked for evidence of complicity. It was in the frenzy of this vicious and gratuitous pogrom that old Blasio Maate was arrested and beaten: he reached out by telephone to Syahuka-Muhindo who reached out to me.

From Al-Khobar, Saudi Arabia, the best I could do was write a swift letter to the editor of *The Independent*, the only British newspaper to have reported the *tabliqs'* invasion. Kiyonga's purpose by inference if not evidence, was to identify 'Rwenzururu' – the loyalists, the sentiment, most particularly the king – with the marauding villains: to identify it thus in the public eye and, especially, in the eyes of his President. In the generality it was the commonplace of a bad situation being made worse by the response to it: yet it was more. A regime of terror was now instituted among all those Bakonzo perceived as opposing the consolidation of Kiyonga's authority, most especially those likely to stand for office in the looming council elections.

Simultaneously a new terror descended from the high forest against the mountains' peasantry – from one end of the Ruwenzori range to the other.

In the compilation of this book, I have occasionally remarked on the acts of evil in and upon Ruwenzori that have accompanied its writing. That is only natural for one who has claimed love and loyalty to the people of that place and to have seen love and loyalty reciprocated. In such a case, I could not presume to overlook their present suffering, and sometimes agony, while bringing back to life their past. I have been speaking all this while *to* them as much as *of* them : to have overlooked the *now* entirely, for the sake of the *then* would have been to have sat beside the sickbed of a grievously suffering old friend recalling our common childhood yet refraining from taking his hand in comfort when a paroxysm of present pain seized him. At times an ejaculation of prayer has broken from me, Kayingo atsunge, *Lord have mercy.*

The suffering began from the perimeter of the higher forest, above the cultivation line and from across on Congo-side, almost at once: the few hundred – not more – armed invaders and marauders propelled by a burning hatred and a depraved Islamicism who had regrouped under the name and command of their 'Allied Democratic Forces', ADF. These *tabliqs*, oathtakers.

Those 'allied' were, as we have seen, the rump of NALU and disaffected Muslims of Uganda's Bantu peoples reinforced by weaponry, cash and ideology intruded by and from the Sudan by way of Congo. Sudan's motive was to de-stabilize Uganda whose President, Museveni, had so readily accepted the backing of the USA in the cause of its international campaign against Islamic fundamentalism. In this cause, America sought to spur the Christian and pagan rebels of South Sudan in their rebellion against Khartoum, which had already persisted with scarcely a pause for some four decades. Once, twenty-eight years earlier, walking in illegally from Ethiopia, I had briefly joined that rebellion. If Khartoum now sought to open a 'second front' against Uganda, no better geographic base could possibly be found than the Ruwenzori Mountains, as perhaps Amon Bazira had originally drawn to their attention. Khartoum could hardly have supposed that the motley of soldiery bursting across the Uganda frontier at Mpondwe that night of November 12, 1996, could have rolled on to Kampala. But if the remnant force were to be flung back into the mountains and persuaded to regroup and terrorize Uganda's western region, a malign political purpose would still have been served.

Precisely that occurred; and in the survival of the ADF in their chosen territory the participation of the rump of NALU's mountain men was essential. This element was Bakonzo born and bred on Ruwenzori, and those Banande of identical language, culture and blood but of lowland Congo-side provenance, originally recruited by Bazira. Their forest commander was Fanehasi Kisokeronio, now some 60 years of age, and irredeemably brigand. Under parallel military command, so far as I can ascertain, came the bulk of the rest, yet if they were to survive and move and operate in and from the forest of the mountains at seven and eight thousand feet, their reliance upon the veteran highlanders amid the densities and cold and declivities, and for the tracks, caves and impenetrable sanctuaries, was total. Moreover, if havoc was to be the only possible attainment of these brigands – havoc and desolation – it was in the interest of the Sudan to have them here where they were virtually uncapturable, demanding unrelentingly the presence of the UPDF around the entire perimeter of the massif, consuming in quantity Museveni's men, matériel and money, a fair quarter of his cumbrous army. So they were persuaded to evil, dressed up as militant Islam, traducing that Faith, and swiftly compounded evil in the manner that it is uniquely compounded: each act of outrage upon creator-loved creation being expungible in the black heart of the perpetrators only by a further outrage. The tactic of that evil was terror. Konzo-guided, the ADF brigand bands by night burst upon sleeping Konzo spur-villages, burning and looting, slaughtering the adults and seizing the children or youngsters. These young they abducted into their forest camps where, out of obliteration by terror, they 'converted' them as *tabliqs* – branding them with new Islamic names, instructing them in the sophistication of killing by Kalashnikovs and stealth, and conducting them in identical nocturnal raids on their fellow tribesmen and even their own kin, to murder, burn, loot, and abduct the young as recruits to their esoteric devilment. Fear and horror gripped the entire highland community; the raiders struck from Bundibugyo in the north to Bukonzo in the south.

The pattern was established at once – so swiftly that, for certain, there must always have been a double plan in the minds of the high cabal. That cabal had roused the Konzo-Nande element of the fighting force to invade Ugandan territory with the promise of a kingdom of their own if Kasese was taken, an 'Islamic' mountain realm with the former king, Irema-Ngoma, brought back from Britain (where he was supposed to live in exile) and restored to authority, his former Christianity swept away. This promise was part of the common confession of those ADF askaris captured in the Ugandan army's counter-attack. Likely as not, the cabal had no true expectation of their forces' capacity to hold lowland townships and roads and Kasese's airfield: it suited their purpose well enough to infest the mountains and with their modern weapons disrupt the region in such a way as to demand the

410

presence of large units of Museveni's troops. Such would have well suited the purpose of Khartoum, which was providing the funds and most of the weaponry (the rest of the guns having been pillaged from the police posts and UPDF units overrun in the original assault). It probably suited well enough the indigenous high command since it gave to such 'political' leaders as Rogers Kabanda a stage to strut upon, issuing statements and threats against Museveni, and it restored to such 'military' figures as my old companion Fanehasi (Phineas) Kisokeronio the exercise of his old vocation of forest banditry.

So the guns and ammo slipped in by way of Kisangani – Stanleyville as I used to know it – and the vipers made their nest nearer to hand in the prevailingly Nande town of Beni. There the ADF could return with impunity from the rigours of Ruwenzori to sleep and roister, as befits soldiery whether Islamicised or not: an evil-hole in that furthermost east of Congo which was (and is) an endemically evil country, as I had learned young. The Congo cannot help itself. It had an evil birth and the blight has stuck. It is like the blight that grips certain of those *malheureux* whom I befriend in the Vulnerable Prisoners' block of the London penitentiary I visit weekly when at home, who were so unloved and damaged in their infancy that any notion of the inherent goodness of man as created by God is inconceivable: they grow up amid shards of incomprehensible compulsion resulting in crimes that make them 'vulnerable' at the hands of their fellow prisoners who are doing time for respectable crimes like robbery and drugs. The Belgians first 'made' the Congo as an entity, as we have seen, a unit of space on an all-but-blank map bearing little more than Africa's matronly outline; they contained it within speculative frontiers with neighbouring spaces, justifying its 'unity' on the basis partly of sketch-maps and cartographic guesswork dotted on rolls of cartridge paper by the powerful hand of the Breaker of Rocks, H M Stanley, and partly of semi-fantastical compacts secured by the self-same Stanley with painted chieftains via slippery interpreters straddling, as a rule, at least three languages. Those earliest Belgian colonisers, naming it Free, the 'Congo Free State', despised it on the instant, and enslaved it: its countless blackamoors – adult, growing and infants at the breast. So they reared it evil. When I was first there, living *black*, moving through it *black*, in the early 1950s, not sleeping under the same roof as a fellow white for weeks and months on end, the outer world had been persuaded to admire the

Belgians as colonists. Two-colony colonial Belgium was admired for a strictly paternal efficiency and for the mute docility of the natives which surely bore witness to their contentment – while Britain's Africa seemed all a-seethe with home-grown demagogues, student protests and smouldering insurrections.

Since then we have witnessed in Africa horrific eruptions of the post-colonial neuroses in all but a handful of states, yet nowhere on a scale more gruesome and sustained than in the ex-Belgian dependencies. The ADF was Congo-generated and Congo-based, and in its stylistic viciousness Congo-inspired, taking on from its Mulelist precursors and corrupting by precedent, evil breeding evil. Am I seeking to exonerate my mountain Konzo by blaming Congo's history and the *sâle Flamand,* as the blacks had come to characterise the former master? I will say that in the ADF, cruelty won a man his spurs, and that that was very 'Congo'; and I will say of the highland Bakonzo actively engaged with ADF – Kisokeronio and his henchmen – teaching those strangers the mountain lore, that they violated the sanctity of their place, betrayed their gods, and stand accused. The first of those captured by the Ugandan army told of the tribal and religious miscellany of the original ADF rebel cadres – Bakonzo or Banande, Banyankole, Baganda. Of the Konzo-Nande element, some were half-Christianised and lapsed, some pagan, and most Muslim. Virtually all of the non-Konzo/Nande were Muslims from Uganda's Bantu south where Jesus, variously denominated, was Number One and Muslims were obscurely disadvantaged. Several had been recruited by promises of 'courses' awaiting them at the Congo capital of Kinshasa. Mohammad Saad's 'Concord' bus brought them to the border; once across, they got no further than training camps right there at Kasindi and half-an-hour's drive north-westwards at Buhira. The leaders' promises were tailored to the rookies' aspirations – 'democracy', an 'Islamic state', their 'Mukonzo King' for the Bakonzo. Each ethnic group had its own camp. Any man attempting to desert would be pursued, trussed and locked away.

Uganda's principal daily newspaper, *The New Vision,* ran a factual report of the captured rebels' statements but gave it a mischievous headline declaring 'BAKONZO KING PLANNED INVASION'. Nothing in the piece itself bore out this claim; but damage was done. By that mid December 1996, I was back in London from the Middle East, and Charles was urging me to issue for him a denial he had drafted. I refined the prose, and had

Charles solemnly declare, '*I, Charles Wesley Irema-Ngoma, would like to defend my reputation by categorically denying any involvement in the rebel activities against the government. I had no fore-knowledge of the invasion of Kasese District which ended many innocent lives... I know nothing about the creation of so-called 'Allied Democratic Forces' which were allegedly formed by a group of Bakonzo people...unknown to me... On 15 August 1982 I made it clear that, from then on, the Bakonzo people would no longer express their demands through violence. I stand by my word of that time, and the Rwenzururu declaration of "Peace, Reconciliation and No Revenge"... I extend my sincere sympathy to those Ugandans who lost their loved ones in the conflict of Kasese.*' New Vision ran the statement on January 9th, under the heading BAKONZO KING CONDEMNS INVASION.

But the killing had only just begun – the killing, the maiming, and most vile of all, the abductions. The people began to flee from the torn spurs, hurrying down to the relative safety of the plains' edge, the mission precinct, proximity to a unit of the UPDF, out of what had always been their sanctuary. By May some 70,000 in Bundibugyo District alone were reported as displaced, mostly into shabby camps of one-chamber earth-and-wattle huts in narrow rows, quick to catch fire, the refugees prey to dysentery and cholera, struggling to survive on food aid leaking from Rwanda and Kivu in the south, and frequently targeted anew by ADF raiders. The hillmen of Burahya and Bunyangabo came down, as did the hillmen of Busongora and Bukonzo. Kitolu families fled their farms: it was the *quatre cents coups* for the old Isaleri, the latest rupture of the community he had spent all his life making its meaning. Amid the pandemonium that fine man sank swiftly and died. In due time the Bishop would appoint his son, the Rev. Jesse Tembo, a pastor to the refugee community: by then, two years later,

413

an estimated 230,000 highland Bakonzo were cowering in lowland camps where they were still not safe. Ruwenzori was not a fashionable misfortune: no Western camera-crews descended upon the site, scarcely a paragraph crept into the international press. But in Uganda it was a gross, persisting lesion. In this new tragedy ignorant or malicious voices – both – sought to implicate old Rwenzururu and, by association, Charles. In July 1997, President Museveni spent three days in or around Kasese. An elder asked him how he stood on the issue of the return of the Irema-Ngoma, the self-exiled King. According to a published report the President replied he was not opposed to his return, provided he used no violence 'to regain his royal position'. Charles responded with a statement issued from my London office 'sincerely thanking HE the President for being the first President of the nation to recognise the Kingdom of his Bakonzo people.' The President's remark was scarcely recognition – merely, the keeping of a door ajar. Nevertheless, Charles was bucked. When that late August Diana, Princess of Wales, died so grotesquely in a Parisian underpass, Charles Irema-Ngoma of Rwenzururu had me forward his handwritten condolences to Elizabeth, Queen of England, which were duly acknowledged by the bereaved family. That autumn he received via my office in London a letter from Kasese's elders of which I was not privy to the contents except as is indicated by his immaculately word-processed response:

OMUSINGA CHARLES WELSEY IREMA-NGOMA
USA
8th Oct 1997

Hello dear Elders

Thank you very much for the letter you wrote to me expressing great concern over the insecurity in Kasese and Bundibugyo Districts caused by rebels of ADF and NALU, who are seriously terrorising people of our areas.

First, I want to make it clear to you that I am not supporting the rebel activities… You should take it as a fact that I am not collaborating with any political rebel organisation in the country, although some [rebels] are using my name as a tool. They are deceiving people that they are fighting for my return to Uganda.

He went on to deplore the wickedness of the rebels and declare his sorrow at his people's suffering. Elders must be aware that the rebels were intending to impose an Islamic government…

I do not think we can accept a government based on one religion. I want to appeal to and warn neighbouring countries which want to instill their influence on Uganda by supporting and arming Ugandan rebels… I appeal to all Elders to support and work hand in hand with the Uganda Government to bring the rebellion to an end… FOR GOD AND MY COUNTRY.

The document was in English because that is the neutral language, not favouring the Bakonzo over the Baamba or other citizens of Rwenzururu of lesser ethnic groups: English was the customary medium of his public statements. Barnabas Bamusede, Kiyonga's man and Kasese's 'LC5', got his copy: the thing was on record. But so long as Rwenzururu remained a source of inspiration among the people, as it did, and so long as Charles lived on as a mythic hero-King across the water, Crispus Kiyonga and those who clung to his coattails required to isolate Charles, and discredit him and the Rwenzururu vision. A fresh stratagem was taking shape. The District Councils of both ends of the mountains had lately voted for the erection of a monument to the martyrs of the first rebellion, ended in 1921 with the execution of Tibamwenda, Nyamutswa and Kapoli. The Kiyonga faction saw an opportunity for an alternative patriotism, an adjusted reading of Konzo history. We have seen how, from the moment of his entry into national politics, Crispus Kiyonga had enjoyed the allegiance of the widow of Vito Muhindo, prospective candidate for parliament in the 1980 elections which brought Obote back to power. Vito was carelessly speared to death by a bunch of young Rwenzururu zealots who, in that region (Bunyangabo), were beholden to Bonnë Baluku. Kiyonga had slipped in to replace Vito, and with the widowed Christine's endorsement won the seat. That comradeship endured, and now the time approached for Kiyonga to return the favour. For Christine herself intended to enter parliament in the May 1998 election as Kasese District's Member in the Women's Interest, such as the constitution idiosyncratically called for. Now it so happened that Christine's daughter was married to a lawyer, Bob Makoma, grandson of the Konzo martyr, Tibamwenda, and heir to the chieftainship of the dominant Baswagha clan held by his old father,

Cyril, Tibamwenda's surviving son. The ploy was: *If Konzo patriotism is indeed to prove ineradicable, and is to persist in a yearning for a tribal kingship (such as the constitution now allows), let us place our Bob Makoma in the running. Whether or not he himself has any appetite for such an office, at the very least it will muddy the waters for the*

Omusingaship of Charles and cast a fresh doubt on the issue in the Presidential mind. Substantial ceremonial was consequently devised to mark the unveiling of the monument and the plaque to the three heroes at Kagando, where they had been martyred by the judicial colonial noose. Kiyonga the Internal Affairs Minister was there, Bamusede the LC5 chairman of the region's Council was there, Christine Muhindo was there, Bob Makoma was there with his father, Tibamwenda's son, Mzee Cyril. Now, this Mzee Cyril had chosen to

stay aloof from Rwenzururu throughout the entire struggle and life of the Kingdom, continuing his clan role in the Toro and Kampala structures. Cyril's boozy uncle may be recalled from when I lodged with him in 1954 (page 122), how he drooled on... On the present occasion, all these Konzo dignatories were to speak, and did so at length. The significant absentee was of course he upon whom the mantle of those martyrs had fallen, namely Charles himself, and the big hole in the speechifying was any reference to the twenty years of the Kingdom of Rwenzururu which had transformed the standing of the mountain people.

The event received enthusiastic coverage in *The New Vision*. Popular attendance, however, was a lot thinner than the organisers had hoped, and this was because other figures of consequence of the region, loyal to Charles and the heritage of Rwenzururu – such as his brother Christopher, the sitting Women's member, and the sitting parliamentarian for the constituency in which Kagando lay – had sussed out the ploy and put the word around.

When Charles received the newspaper report, he was surely moved by a low rage. What got him most was the report of Mzee Cyril's speech. He sat at his word-processor in Washington DC and wrote his public 'thanks to Kasese District Council for the wise...decision to allow a memorial to be built in remembrance of our three gallant heroes... Those three innocent heroes truly deserve to be respected and remembered for what they died for. Before I left Uganda I proposed that some of our streets should be re-named after those heroes...' Then there crept in a whiff of the sardonic.

'Sir,' *he continued, for the document was formally addressed to his committed opponent Bamusede, the LC5,* 'it is sad that I missed the ceremony... I should have been there, because if I have grown up rough, it was because of those three heroes when we were fighting for their noble cause... Many Government and local politicians in Kasese gave very fine speeches. Unfortunately my father, the late King Isaya, and I, as the people who fought tirelessly for the rights sought by those heroes, were not represented at the ceremony... The most interesting and great speech was the one given by the Chief Clan Leader of the Baswagha clan, Mzee Cyril T Makoma... It was a wonderful speech...' *But, he wrote, he would like to respond to some points in Mzee Cyril's speech.*

'If Omukonzo/Mwamba person is respected anywhere in the world, it is because of the efforts and bravery of my father, the late King Isaya Kibanzanga, who put his life on the line of death for all Bakonzo people... In order to have a strong voice politically, my father created a Kingdom for all Bakonzo people regardless of the clans they belonged to...' *He was warming to his theme.* 'Some Bakonzo people became cowards and left Isaya alone in the battlefield. Instead of helping him, some decided to continue to serve their masters, Batoro, by attending Toro Rukuratu while our boys and girls were being killed on the front line by Batoro who later were joined by the Central Government forces, who also were encouraged by some of our Bakonzo to go and kill their fellow Bakonzo. Now the most shocking thing is that, after the hunting is over, those who did not want to join the hunt are claiming the killed quarry to be theirs. Oh, come on, people, let us use some common sense. We have witnessed so many revolutionary wars in the world, but at the time of victory we don't see those leaders who spearheaded those wars giving power to other people; instead, they become leaders of the countries they fought for.

'If the Bakonjo people vote for a Kingdom in their areas, I am still the King of Bakonzo who fought for their human rights, respect and integrity.

'Mzee Makoma made it clear that he is the Chief of the Baswagha Clan in his area, and that's true; I don't object to that. That doesn't mean that he is the King of all Bakonzo. And that's normal, in the culture and tradition of Bakonjo people we used to have clan chief, "Abakama b'Amalambo", who ruled a very big land. So I believe Mzee Chief Cyril Makoma is one of those Bakama which under my Kingdom represents all the clans of Bayira/Bakonzo.

'My Kingdom is the right one to rule our area because it is not based on any single clan, and it does not cause any discrimination and division among the people. I know my blood belongs to two clans of the two heroes of Nyamutswa, who's Omuhira, and Tibamwenda, Omuswagha. I am Omuhira by clan and my mother, Christina, is Omuswagha. Her grandfather Ruhandika was a chief. So I have never regarded my Kingdom as belong to one clan, "Abahira". I can't do that, because this is a Kingdom which was chosen and supported by all Bakonzo elders, and when my father died, all elders supported me to be crowned as their King. From that time I am still highly respected all over the world as the King of the Bakonzo. Even His Holiness Kitasamba blessed my Kingdom...

'On this point, I certainly recognise the Basongora/Banyabindi as a part of Bayira because of intermarriage between us. I don't discriminate against them; they should respect themselves as Bakonzo people and join other Bakonzo in making decisions on the development of our area.

'I request the Kasese District Council to consider the late King Isaya Mukirania Kibanzanga as one of our heroes. This is the man who started the struggle of remembering our earlier heroes... If our generation decline to remember Isaya, believe me, the next generation will remember him and look for his grave. AKALAGHIRIRE SIKATAMBWA.

'Finally, I would like to suggest that politicians should leave this issue whether Kasese or Bakonzo people should maintain their traditional role or not to the people. Let them have a free vote about it, instead of politicians coming and blocking people's minds. This is not a political issue; it is a people's traditional issue.'

Good on you, Charles; you always were a bonny fighter. You socked it to them, those who would airbrush from history the Kingdom of Rwenzururu and your father's achievements. Posterity won't let you down – and nor will I. Let them be warned: akalaghirire sikatambwa – deny the reality at your peril. On January 29, 1998, *New Vision* published the entire 'response' to Cyril Makoma's speech as their main leader-page article under the headline, '*I am the rightful King of the Bakonjo*' and a photographic portrait of Charles. Once again the other side, by striving to undermine Charles's cause, had bolstered it.

xxx

The Vendetta Darkens

With the usual ten thousand things to occupy me, I in remote London followed the fortunes of Ruwenzori and its people and Charles in America only to the extent that my counsel or intervention were sought and my friends needed me. To Charles I was surrogate uncle. I did not presume to follow every twist and turn. Surely Clause 246 in Uganda's bright new constitution, and the consequent restoration of the Kabakaship in Buganda and of those other Ugandan kingly dynasties, had put verve into Charles's claim to return one day as Omusinga of the Bakonzo and their associates of the mountain community. I could not but be struck how the Kiyonga faction, however small a minority of the popular will it represented, could not let the issue rest, even with Charles so far away, unfunded, and with no structured movement of local support. They kept on returning to it, like Raskolnikov to his crime, and every time they did so they made their situation weaker, made themselves more vulnerable to the truth.

And this 'truth'? That, surely, as Charles chose to put it: 'This is not a political issue, it is a people's traditional issue,' those words 'people' and 'traditional' leading off into what cannot be contained by the here-and-now and the secularity of politics but are of existential being. Secular and existential must of course for ever mix and merge, jostle and clash. State and church, one might put it, do not lie easy (and if they do, they probably oughtn't); neither is a stranger to power, and power does not so much corrupt as seduce in its own cause. Charles once had secular power, in his own mountains. Now Kiyonga had the lion's share of secular power and Charles's authority had floated upwards to the mystical or settled around the soul. Yet Charles had his handful of activists on the ground – his own brother in parliament for instance, with two or three others, including Loice (Lois) Bwambale in the 'Women Seat', and Bonnë (Bonifasi) Baluku who ever since the ending of the formal Kingdom of Rwenzururu had served as prime mover-and-shaker of health centres and the like among the Konzo community. Bonnë served as political agent for all those of the

Rwenzururu inheritance running for elective office locally or nationally. He was vastly popular. In March 1998 Bonnë was preparing the ground for Yokasi Bihande's election as Kasese's District Chairman, having recently stewarded the re-election of the Honourable Loice (to give the lady the honorific customary for Ugandan MPs). Loice had been opposed by Christine Muhindo, widow of Vito, the capricious victim of Bunyangabo's Rwenzururu's 'Youth Wingers' in 1981, as we have told. This Christine had long been a member of the Presidential staff, she being an old friend and shelterer of Museveni in his guerrilla days. Her sibling brother was serving as the President's *chef de protocol* when she sought the Kasese Parliamentary seat. The new – and crucial – campaign was only just under way when one evening in Kasese, in the small street behind the mosque, Bonnë Baluku was walking home. It was at that brief five minutes of swiftly closing equatorial dusk. A bullet flew, and almost at once a second bullet. One round or other got Bonnë in the head. He fell. The moment of his darkness was the moment of that day's darkness. When people dwelling at hand crept out with torches to where lay the body, that of their old hero Bonnë, it seemed it had been mutilated, as if ritually. No killer was apprehended. The police were beholden in their slackness to the Ministry of the Interior.

The stain of Bonnë's blood on that street-side murram stained the entire campaign. Eight weeks later Bihande was elected in a mood of voters' stunned sympathy comparable to that stunned sympathy at Vito's death such as had won Dr Kiyonga his first parliamentary victory some seventeen years earlier.

Not a soul supposed the motive of that death to be other than political, and almost everyone said so, including Charles who issued a two-page closely typed statement of condolences to the people of Kasese District. In his first sentence he declared that the elder Bonifasi Baluku Mbalibula 'was brutally murdered by ambitious politicians', and further on referred to 'a number of important Bakonzo sons who died through mysterious killings whenever elections were expected.' This he addressed to Barnabas Bamusede, 'LC5' – the District Chairman – under whose broad authority the hunt for the perpetrator of the murder was supposedly taking place, and he requested me to issue it to the press, which I did. Copies also went to the President, the Minister of Internal Affairs (Kiyonga), his Chief of Police and various others, in the old Isaya Mukirane style of general post. In the event not much of a hunt, if any, took place, and the real Raskolnikov remained unmasked. Mourning Loice, however, became an even more popular favourite while long-widowed Christine was personally compensated by the President with the post in his own office of 'mobilisation secretary', that is, a secretary with executive authority.

If, however, that murder misfired, serving mostly to strengthen Rwenzururu's Charles and smirch the dark ones, there was shortly to drop into the hands of Charles's adversaries a gift of a weapon. The continuing torment of the ADF raiders which had all but emptied highland Ruwenzori of its inhabitants was being countered with some energy by Uganda's army. This campaign was pursued on both sides of the border, since Mobutu's government in Kinshasa had by now lost control of most of Western Congo. That early August, operating on Congo-side, the UPDF had overrun an ADF encampment and captured documents implicitly associating Charles with the wicked rebellion. The pieces of paper comprised a few letters from Charles to a certain Ngaimoko, in 1994, indicating his – Charles's – acceptance of the titular leadership of NALU following the assassination of Amon Bazira in Kenya in 1993. To ascribe an involvement by Charles in the ADF was perhaps tendentious, in that the camp overrun had long ceased to be a NALU affair, but was distinctly 'ADF'. Yet the shift of allegiance of NALU's senior Bakonzo soldiery, including Ngaimoko, to ADF was well established. One letter warned NALU's leadership against placing trust in Rwanda and Kenya, which had participated in the murder of Bazira. There were, it seemed, at least three letters from Charles bearing his then Washington address, together with one of the photographs of Charles in camouflage gear, from the 'pouncing panther' series for which he had posed in the early 1990s. The Ugandan army commander, Brigadier Kazini, instantly grasped the significance of the find. Kazini himself came from the Ruwenzori region: with a father from elsewhere he had grown up on the plain's edge with his Musongora mother when Rwenzururu ruled the mountains. Presented with a little subtlety, the finds could serve as a bombshell.

Dr Kiyonga got to work. A meeting of Konzo tribal elders was convened at the luxurious Mweya Safari Lodge for August 27 (1998), to be chaired by the vice-chairman of the National Resistance Movement, Moses Kigongo. The Konzo dignitaries were bus-ed in to that exquisite lakeland site and given the full flattery of governmental hospitality. The press were assembled, to record the shocked comments of the delegates. *New Vision*, the principal national daily, quoted one of Isaya's former ministers, Yonasani Kamabu; 'That boy [Charles] has done us bad. He has betrayed us. Now I do not want to hear mention of him. How can he start killing people like that?' A District Councillor chorused: 'This man has ashamed us as Bakonzo and as staunch supporters of the government.' *New Vision* ran the pouncing panther picture across several columns, and flagged the story damagingly:

Bakonzo king attacked for backing ADF

At the time I had no inkling of Charles's dalliance with the rump of NALU. When news of this exposé reached me, I was mostly alarmed at the effect it would all have on the stricken refugees from the mountains. Since November 1996 they had been enduring the violation of their inner, higher places; now came the violation of their guardianship of the highlands, personified by the Keeper of their Drum, Irema-Ngoma, so long the repository of their pride. Had the very exemplar of their collective being treasoned himself? I at once reached Charles by telephone to urge swiftness of response. For several days, all I got was his answer-phone. By September 8 a series of further meetings had been put in train by Dr Kiyonga and NRM *apparatchiks*, first in Kampala and immediately thereafter in the tribal heartland, to expose the 'evidence' and make speculation fact. In Uganda Charles's influential allies, principally the parliamentarians Christopher Tabaan (his brother), Loice Bwambale, Apollinaris Kithende, and Kule Muranga, strove to limit the damage by accepting the fragment of NALU evidence and promising that the Omusinga would shortly issue a statement which would explain all. This promise did little to prevent the Ugandan press implying Charles's involvement in ADF. It was mid-September before I personally had reached Charles and had from him a 'Statement to the Press'. It was a lordly peroration, with little of the urgency called for, and was addressed to the nation – 'Fellow Ugandans'

'First of all,' *he opened,* 'I would like to indicate to you that I love you very much and highly honor your human rights. At the same time, I am proud to tell you that I love my country, Uganda.

'However, you must have heard or read in the newspapers that I have been allegedly accused of backing ADF rebels and that I am actively involved in their active line of terrorizing and murdering innocent Ugandans in the areas of Kasese, Kabarole, and Bundibugyo districts.

'In this Statement I would like to express my strongest denial of these allegations that I am behind the ADF rebels. For God and my country, I am telling the truth, nothing but the truth: I have never at any time supported the rebels of the ADF movement; I have never had any contact with them... I want to inform these people of the affected areas... who have been brutally hurt by those barbaric and faceless anti-government rebels that I have sincere sympathy and sorrow for all their grievances, past and future you are going through at the hands of the ADF rebels... There is no way any leader like me, with a normal brain, could lead such a dangerous organisation and order them to go around torturing and killing innocent people... I simply regard them as bandits, just street thugs... I still am trying to think how I can help the government of Uganda to end that barbaric rebellion in our area.

'Let me say this: the only person Ugandans should blame strongly in all this is the President of Sudan, who is supporting, financing and heavily arming rebels, purposely to install an Islamic government in Uganda...

'I am planning to visit the affected areas of western Uganda very soon in order to express my love and sympathy to my fellow Ugandans who are going through serious suffering by the rebels, and to discuss with them what could be the best solution to end the rebellion.'

He had signed the paper with his habitual flourish. I pushed it out as best I could including to the Africa Service of the BBC. But it failed to confront the hard evidence of Charles's link with NALU on which his mortal enemies were basing their vilification. A few days later I was able to secure Charles's agreement to a further press release in which he came plausibly clean. This included the following paragraphs:

'The documents, letters and photographs produced at the meeting of senior Bakonzo from the tribe at a Rwenzori regional gathering at Mweya Safari Lodge... gave a fundamentally misleading impression. This is because the photograph and letters were captured in a camp abandoned by NALU, not in the ADF camp as was reported.

'Moreover, the letters written by me which were produced at the meeting belong to several years ago, as does the photograph of myself in combat uniform. I have myself been dissociated from NALU for several years. The single recent 'NALU' document produced at the meeting makes no reference to me.

'As is well known, NALU was founded by the late Amon Bazira, a former Minister of the Uganda government, who was a close friend. Because of our political friendship, Bazira introduced me to his movement as a Chief of the region, but not as a movement member. He kept in touch with me until he was brutally killed by Secret Service agents in another country in 1993.

'After Bazira's death, NALU members requested me to command their so-called Liberation forces. At that stage I was in contact with their Chief of Staff, who had obtained a picture of me in combat gear taken several years previously. However, realizing that it was not the right thing to lead a movement against the Uganda government, I made the decision to quit and resigned immediately. From that date I have taken a neutral stance in Uganda policies.

'There was no military operation during the brief period in which I was seen by some as the leader of NALU. NALU has been effectively dead since 1994. Any more recent documents atempting to identify the extinct organisation of NALU with the ADF of today are wholly misleading, and presumably seek to justify the ADF...

'I appeal to any members of the ADF from our area to surrender and give up their arms to the government of Uganda...

'I am planning to visit the affected areas of Western Uganda soon in order to demonstrate my love and sympathy to my fellow Ugandans who are going through serious suffering from the hands of the rebels. And I look forward to discussing with them the best way to end the rebellion in our area.

'For God and my country...'

Planning to visit? But yes. That very month, September 1998, the Presidential amnesty offered to those in former rebellion against the regime who had expressed contrition was publicly extended to Charles Wesley Mumbere. Was not something afoot? Indeed, and it was Norway.

Five years previously, to the month, after prolonged interchange conducted with the utmost secrecy, little Norway had stepped onto the world's stage with the Oslo Declaration of Principles which for the first time since the creation of modern Israel offered a basis of settlement between the Jews and Palestinians. This extraordinary feat so fired the Nordic spirit with the powers of its secret balm that the same spirit sought to penetrate other issues of intractable mutual hatred around the globe. One such was that between the Tutsi and Hutu in Rwanda where by the later 1990s the French-armed Interahamwe militants of the humiliated Hutu had become a vicious regional scourge. The Norwegian peace-maker in the region, Bent Rönson, working for a Christian charity independent of, yet approved by, government, naturally grew aware of the neighbouring conflict sustained by the ADF in the Ruwenzori Mountains. The well-publicised 'exposure' of Charles at the Mweya meeting suddenly brought to his attention this unexpected Irema-Ngoma living in exile as figure who might become the agent of reconciliation. So he put it to Museveni that this Charles Irema-Ngoma should be persuaded to return on a visit home in the interests of peace, at least between the Bakonzo element of ADF and Kampala. Museveni assented. That next month, on October 9th, there flew into Washington DC a delegation comprised of two Uganda parliamentarians – the member for Soroti, Mike Mukula, and Charles's brother, Christopher Tabaan – and the Rev. Kamese, head of the charity 'Give me a Chance', all three escorted by Rönson. Charles, it was agreed, would return to Uganda a few weeks later, on a visit, to be reunited with his people and so far as possible initiate a reconciliation between those die-hard Bakonzo participants in ADF and the government of Uganda. Norway – the tax-payer or the charity-subscriber – was stumping up the air fares. There were to be mass rallies at five sites around the base of the mountains. His personal reward for success was undefined. It was to be a 'visit'. Nothing was presumed as to his re-installation as Omusinga. And how might he perform? For fourteen years he had been tucked away in a strange continent, amid a strange society, his old skills of authority unexercised, his own language asleep in his ear and on his tongue, and he remote from intricacies of power in his native patch of Africa.

Uncle-surrogacy rustled my bosom. To accompany him seemed all but impossible. My mama at nearly 98 was knocking at another door; and moved to put my own and my fellows' stated allegiance to the rude test on the imminent advent of a Christ-dated millennium, I had within the previous fortnight publicly launched 'Pilgrimage 2000' for the following year, 1999. On this pilgrimage the feet of faithful were to be invited countrywide to converge over a period of weeks upon Canterbury for the millennial hour, treading the winter roads by several routes from several holy sites on the perimeter of Britain – Iona; Lindisfarne; Whitby; St David's Head; St Michael's Mount; Holywell; Walsingham; and St Paul's Cathedral – under my overall direction. I questioned Charles as to how much he thought he needed me. He replied with a faxed letter and customary grace by 'cordially inviting' me to acompany him, if I would pay my fare to and from Entebbe, while in Uganda I would be part of his delegation. This was followed by a request that, since his own flight to Uganda was now routed not through Oslo but London, would I kindly arrange for him to broadcast on the Africa Service of the BBC as he passed through London. I travelled to my mother's bedside where my brother was in handy attendance, delegated preparatory tasks on Pilgrimage 2000, engendered enthusiasm in Bush House for the BBC to interview Charles, and awaited him at Heathrow, where I planned to pick him up at breakfast time, bring him into the city for his broadcast interview, and get us both to Gatwick for the late night flight to Africa. Africa intervened by Charles and his 'fiancée' boarding a bus at Heathrow bound for Gatwick without exiting at the Arrivals point where I awaited. After locating him at Gatwick, I brought him to my house in Kensington where I photographed him in the garden. Neat as a button, in a dark suit and with immaculate haircut and gleaming teeth, and spontaneously selecting the flat-slabbed surround of a fountain in the garden as a kind of plinth to stand upon, he faced the camera like a young Mussolini, head held defiant and a hand across his chest. Here was a man rehearsing his

CALENDER - 1999

OMUSINGA
CHARLES WESLEY MUMBERE
IREMANGOMA

destiny. He did well on the broadcast, being articulate, balanced and firm as to the role he hoped to play. And this pleased me, for knowledge of the BBC transmission would soon spread in Uganda, in particular in the circle of the President in whose eyes Charles's 'international' status would be enhanced. He had already spoken with Museveni by telephone from Washington.

Later that evening we were dining at Gatwick. We were four, the other two being Bent, the Norwegian peace-broker, and Henrietta, from Sierra Leone – a descendant, as her Anglicized surname suggested, of one of the freed slaves returned as black colonisers of the West African mainland, at Freetown. This Henrietta was an immigrant nurse in the same Washington hospital which employed, presumably unwittingly, the once and perhaps future king of the Mountains of the Moon. As 'fiancée' she was presumably a prospective queen; and as Charles was instinctively rehearsing a role, so was Henrietta. But what role? Every item of her appearance had been calculated with intense forethought. Her black skin shone. Her purple lips shone. The bejewelled fingers, and their nails, shone. Her hair – a wondrous concoction of tight

Medusa plaits, some naturally black some imaginatively blond, and all constrained and interwoven with rings of brass and wood – shone. The lazy body's upper half was enclosed in a cable-stitched sweater of spangled wool, the lower half – I forget. Insofar as tribal queens are there to reproduce, she undoubtedly convinced. In cubic terms her outer form could have accommodated tiny Zeuliah, Charles's now rejected former Queen of Rwenzururu, twice over. After lights out in the royal four-poster, scented and sleepy, at the end of a hard day for an Omusinga fulfilling functions, let none intrude with judgment. In terms of the daily demands upon a consort of modern kingship in the conduct of his affairs and the management of his household, had she a notion as to the scenario she was about to enter? None at all, I surmised at Gatwick, and that surmise never altered. Henrietta was to proceed through the following days like a doll whose eyes, unconnected to any internal mechanism, opened when she was propped upright and closed when horizontal. She never wore the same outfit twice. I became inwardly aghast at the plastic debt Charles must have amassed to clothe this pupa of his choice. I wonder if the debt is yet cleared.

In our *haute*, or fairly *haute*, *cuisine* airport restaurant, Henrietta ordered, insistently, a hamburger, a dish not featured on the menu. While she awaited this hamburger's arrival she rolled bread in her mouth so slowly that the white doughy lump lingered in view from time to time in the middle of the purple mouth like a hostage pleading for rescue. I began to discern that the blond contributions to her coiffure were not her own rooted hair but clippings of other, presumably Caucasian heads. Such a concoction must have also set back Charles a bit. Meanwhile there was Bent. Bent, a young forty, was in charge. Indicating Henrietta with his head, he muttered, 'She is to stay in the background.' Bent had fathered six children, he said, and lived a daring life. His wife occasionally joined him on his peace-harvesting adventures. I would meet her later. Bent had no deep knowledge of Ruwenzori and all that, and I deemed it tactful not to seem too knowledgeable but to hang back, an attendant lord on this otherwise all-black pageant. I admired his flair, and his phlegmatic Scandanavian style.

xxxi

Charles and Museveni

They three flew first class, I tourist. At Nairobi airport we assembled for breakfast. On my return from a stroll, Charles drew me aside confidentially. 'Your flies are open, ' he said. We embarked on Uganda Airlines' only aircraft, a 50-seater working its only route, Nairobi-Entebbe and back again. On Entebbe's tarmac a deputation awaited Charles; a cabinet minister (Muruli Mukasa, responsible for the nation's security), the Member for Soroti (Makulu), Charles's mama and indestructible Queen Mother Christina in flowered cotton, gathered and ruffed in the bubu fashion; her two other sons: Christopher Tabaan, MP for Busongora South, and young Williams, now a little prince, with a video camera; a crippled Rwenzururu veteran warrior; and the new LC5 of Kasese, Yokasi Bihande. With the deputation was a bodyguard or two in plain clothes, plus a handful of press photographers or cameramen, and a child with a looping garland of tropic blooms.

And here was Charles emerging from the aircraft at the top of the steps. The hospital menial of the day before yesterday (currently on leave of absence) was this morning a king, more or less, kingly enough in the cut of him – steady and commanding of eye, the smile pursed and rationed, firm in the chin and the

Hamitic profile; and behind him now, as he began the descent, the consort lady, resplendent today in purple, on approval from the shop, as it were, for the duration of the party; then Bent the Brave; then after a minute or two (with Charles securely on his native soil and already garlanded), my loose-limbed self, attempting anonymity, slung with a camera and wearing a species of zip jacket with handy inside pockets. I fell in behind the greeted and the greeters, catching with my lens Charles (flanked by Henrietta) being bouquetted by his beloved daughter Furaha dressed in black-and-white, beside his Muslim cousin Ibrahim Muhonjya. The party moved towards the terminal block, built like a catafalque, a veritable jewel of late colonial banality. In 1976 Israeli commandos captured the structure for a full hour, omitting to destroy it, when rescuing their Arab-hijacked airliner. As the rest entered the VIP lounge, I slipped away to secure an entry stamp on my passport and gather up my suitcase, to emerge from the catafalque on the arrivals side ahead of Charles and his welcome deputation. Up a bank opposite I found myself amid a gathering of some two hundred Bakonzo composed of drummers drumming, dancers in grass skirts dancing; children in school uniforms rocking; Bakonzo gentlemen in Sunday suits, ties, and solemn shoes, grinning, and stilt walkers teetering. No sooner was I recognised and placed in the scheme of things than I was extracted from the mêlée by Charles's brother Christopher to join the group in the VIP lounge.

We cavalcaded into Kampala, I in the third dark blue Mercedes with Mike Mukula, MP, urging me (the mission's interplanetary legate) to wave at the Bakonzo throng as we followed Charles, Henrietta and the Minister for Security in Merc number one, and the Queen Mother, her two other sons, suddenly princes, and Bent the Brave in Merc number two. Kampala normally took fifty minutes: we were there in half the time, through the shanty suburbs and three or four dozen versions of Christianity, moving in tight convoy – too tight and too quick for your average sharpshooter to bring rifle butt to shoulder. Kampala is a city of hills and its hill of governance is its most elevated, elegant and leafy – a hill of leisurely space, state edifices laid back, and classy hospices. Here Charles and his lady, and I too, were checked into a three-story colonial villa converted into apartments, property of the National Resistance Movement's Vice-Chairman, as guests of a State taking a gamble on peace, placing its bet on the tribal face of the dice. Charles was narrowly guarded on the level below me, with his shining lady and his old mama, half-confined in his rooms by security heavies at the door. As for myself, once bathed and brushed, I joined the Minister whose brief was Peace, Muruli Mukasa, for a Nile beer on the terrace. The very least courtesy I could do him was to let him discover – by means of a seven or eight minute summary of this story so far – what on earth I was doing here.

No sooner was daylight gone – it jumps over the wall at latitude zero – than we were transported, in spirit no less than body, to – what else? – the Holiday Inn, for a rally that was a taste of things to come.

We sudden dignitaries were shepherded onto a long dais. Some two or three hundred Bakonzo were corralled below us, seated in rows, the venerable, the young, all those, indeed, awaiting Charles at the airport, and more. How had all these mountain people got themselves to the remote, half-alien city, let alone this mid-African implant of ersatz Americana? Ferocious drumming crescendoed as Charles, in clean-cut suit, soul of dignity, took his seat centre-stage. An empurpled Henrietta flanked him, with his aide and cousin, Ibrahim Muhonjya; and next the Minister for Peace, Muruli Mukasa, and the Mukonzo MP for Bukonzo East, Apollinaris Kithende; then Bent the Brave with *his* wife, whom Norway had flown out for the heck of it, and at the other end of the row my own improbable self who received a rumbling cheer when the Minister for Peace presented me to the throng as that very Mzee of the Bakonzo who had known this Charles, their guest of honour, since he was two. Out broke the drums anew and the songs of the ardent young, solo verse and group refrain. In the Holiday Inn edifice behind us, were there not tourists from the USA, filling time between retirement and oblivion with this and that – a 'safari' , say, to the crocodiles of the Nile headwaters, or the gorillas of Bwindi, – who would be questioning their black waiters, S*ay, what the hell's going on in the garden?* And the waiter, if he knew, would say,

'It is to welcome home a King, sir.'

'You don't say! King of where?'

'The Mountains of the Moon.'

'The *Moon*?'

(But no waiter would have named the mountains that.)

'Tell us, waiter, if you know, where's he come home from, this king?'

'Washington DC, it is said.'

'You're kidding! What's he been doing over there?'

Only I could have answered that; or Charles, or his shining consort: a hospital orderly, for the past eleven years.

He was a natural as King, this small, dark mortal man. He went to bed kingly and rose kingly. It struck me that he had never for a moment ceased to suppose himself Omusinga of Rwenzururu, with his trolleys and his mops in his denim uniform on the night

432

shift in the corridors and spacious elevators of his hospital. (Did he wear a name-badge, *Charles*? I had never presumed to enquire.) We were already taking him as king. He had the trick, Charles Mumbere, of making a little ring around him, a measuredness of speech and deportment, not to be ruffled on royal Stool or Scaffold; a little distant from the rest of us, a presumption of loftiness. And why not? 'He's been practising since he was four,' his brother Christopher Tabaan was to remark to me a few days later with an edge of wit and scarcely a trace of rancour. Here was Christopher below us just now, with others of the inner family: mama Christina Mukirania, and Charles's 16-year-old child Furaha Cristabel, and maybe her mother and even her aunt, little Zeuliah the Queen he set aside, now half-Ophelia-ed in her abandonment, so I had heard – I wasn't sure who was who among the faces, just below my place on stage, yet I fear it *was* Zeuliah, indeed no bigger than a cubic half of the one in purple glistening and moist alongside her ex-everything.

So Charles, whatever the inner family's wrack and stress stemming from the fact of kingship, was yet unmistakably king. In his speech, Muruli Mukasa, Minister for Peace, was using no such title as of now; this was Citizen Charles W Mumbere, conjured into trial Omusingaship by Presidential flick of wand, auditioning for the part, conceivably to re-earn the role in, strictly, the national interest not his own. But Charles, look, was already doing the part, the king part: and Museveni, had he been present, would know this part to be that of king not of any common kingdom but, uniquely, an impenetrable kingdom, barriering a frontier.

The rival choirs of schoolchildren sang panegyrics for their returning king in interminable charming lyrics: no pleas however urgent from the master of ceremonies could persuade them to cut so much as a couplet. For they had rehearsed and rehearsed; each stanza accompanied by coy or morose or joyous gestures, their Bonny willed by their longing from over the ocean; the strains of their long orphanage; their need of him in their present predicament; his past heroisms on behalf of their meaning. Charles sat back and lapped that meaning: the handsome head, eyes benign, aristocratic lips half a-smile. He was royal sculpture. Now with a frenzy of drumming, hands and drumsticks flying, on came the dancers with a shimmy and counter-shimmy of kilted grass snatched this way and that around the hips and a syncopation of rattles around the ankles, bare feet stabbing. Was there ever such primal rut proposed on the clipped sward of the Holiday Inn? And now the stilt men and the contortionists, that fellow who by muscular device made his stomach entirely to vanish beneath the rib cage only to roll it back up from his groin, and his buddy who so commanded muscles of his belly that his middle became bellows that drew weirdly open on either side only to contract back violently at the navel. Freaks and dwarves adorn a primitive court.

Mama Christina came to the microphone to thank Nyamuhanga, God, for rewarding her womb anew with the homecoming of her firstborn in his rightful spot. She orated formidably, this one, and naturally employed, so I was to learn, words of the old speech of the tribe, like *sooth* and *dolour*, *fealty* and *liege*, which lent her the seer's authority she has long held. Then it was Charles himself.

I guess he had addressed no gathering since 1984. His Lukonzo had gotten rusty; kinsman Ibrahim Muhonjya in his hajji hat pulled out the vernacular for him. He lauded Museveni, 'the best President Uganda has had.' He had come, he declared, in the cause of peace (what else?), and first he would discuss the route to peace with his President. Meanwhile, he had counter-yearned for his people all these years: now at last this chance for reunion in their time of pain and disruption. He would take his homecoming step by step, moving to each quarter of his home country and listening to the people's voice. The unspoken word was Omusinga. It was a brief and cautious speech and could hardly have been otherwise. None of us knew where these next days would precisely carry us, butting our immaterial into their material, our timelessness into their here-and-now, our kingdom into their republic. It seemed to me that it was as if, suddenly, we were to descend a second time, *Eryandanghala*, to their plateau out of our mountains, into which involuntarily we had withdrawn when Mister Seven's threatening dispensation had taken over some thirteen years earlier; and that the price of our accommodation into this new temporal order was the immobilisation of an ignorant army befouling our very mountains.

In the foyer of the Holiday Inn, here was our prime strategist, Syahuka-Muhindo, political scientist and patriot, and my friend. We greeted. If there was any one man who might guide us amid the present entanglement, clotted with so much blood, it was he. That next morning at our hotel base Charles appointed Syahuka-Muhindo his chief adviser.

Those next few days in Kampala we were waiting upon the summons of the President. They were fully active days. Charles confined himself to his apartment under the protection of his kinsman Kisaija, a senior detective in the Uganda constabulary, who established a rota of guards supervising his ward's premises round the clock. Holed up there with him and Henrietta was Charles's mother, preparing every mouthful he would eat, to save him from deadly poison; she was to continue this function throughout his entire stay in Uganda. The local press was covering the story thoroughly.. That next day I gave a long interview to *The New Vision* which published it in the Sunday edition under the helpful banner, 'Irema Ngoma above Politics.' By then, readers of newspapers in Uganda knew who Irema Ngoma was. I had persuaded the press to write Bakonzo, rather than the (unintentionally) disparaging Bakonjo, and I was beginning to dissuade them from slipping in the patronising 'self-styled' whenever they referred to Charles as 'king' of the Bakonzo or of the mountain people. I played down Charles's involvement in NALU. 'Charles accepted titular leadership of NALU in 1994 on the basis that there would be no more military activity. And he was associated with them for a very brief period... Charles has a unique chance of reconciling past divisions between UPC [Obote] and Rwenzururu and NRM [government] supporters. He is now convinced the Bakonzo should work with the Museveni regime...' Charles evidently saw the article late in the day since he telephoned me from downstairs around midnight to express delight.

Meanwhile he was at work publicly softening the edges of mutual antagonism with Dr Kiyonga, Uganda's Health Minister, who as everyone knew was the spectre at the ball. Even the songs of the welcoming schoolchildren had mocked his wiles, in sly metaphor. Now the antagonists met in the presence of press photographers in that same apartment when mama was ensuring no unseen hand slipped lethal juices into her son's ovundu-porridge. We are agreeing to differ, they announced in jolly manner. Reciprocating hands draped shoulders, gripped a wrist. This issue of kingship – why, if the one says it is divisive and the other says unifiying, surely the democratic process... After a couple of hours of their private conclave, Syahuka-Muhindo slipped out to tell me with a beaming smile, 'I am steering!' Next, Christine Muhindo, widow, mobilising secretary from the President's office, called on Charles to be at last accorded condolences at her bereavement of 17 years previously. Were not the commanding eyelids of the President himself upon these wary overtures? I supposed so.

Then all at once we were up at State House, Nakasero, six

Kiyonga meets with Mumbere

By John Banalya

THE Minister of Health, Dr Crispus Kiyonga, yesterday held talks with the King of the Bakonzo Charles Wesley Mumbere at Mosa Courts in Kampala.

Kiyonga said holding different opinions does not mean that there is a clash.

He said his immediate concern is to bring security to Kasese while others concentrate on discussions about the restoration of the monarchy and other issues like the development of the economy.

The two embraced in front of the chief negotiator for Mumbere's return, Soroti Municipality MP Captain Mike Mukula.

'The issue of the monarchy is not related to security. The ADF question is complex because it also involves the element of Islamic fundamentalism,' Kiyonga said.

Mumbere said he has not forced anybody to call him King. He said kingdoms are naturally created and the followers have spiritual attachment to them.

'I was crowned King upon the death of my father. The problem is that our Kingdom has

ALBERT AYIGA ONDOGA

area has been postponed until further notice.

According to Captain Mike Mu la, one of the organisers Iremangia will not be to we rn Uganda before meeting the President

Mumbe was scheduled to meet President Museveni and Maj. Gen. lim Sa Saturday ut the meeting failed take off.

On Friday Kiyonga and Mumbere agreed o the rest ation of the monarchy

Kiyonga said the monarch will not h to bring jce to Kase But Mun re said poli cians sh ld leave to Bakonzo iern to deci upon he estoration the king n.

The di reement w at a pres conference the Moveme Secretar called on the Me ment V Chairma Mo Kigongo, et Mumber Mumbe said he ca to clear name abo recent n orts that has been acking reb in wester Uganda.

'It is th I took ov leadershi f NALU up the dei of Am Bazira. T was in 19 I wrote letters th were four with the A rebels t they we addresse to the th comman s of NALU

PEACE AT LAST: Dr Kiyonga (left) shares a moment of joy with Wesley Mumbere yesterday.

or seven hundred yards to the top of the hill behind us, to sit with the President in the Cabinet room for what turned out to be two hours and forty-five minutes: Charles, Henrietta (ablaze today in scarlet), Charles's mama Christina; Syahuka-Muhindo; Kasese's members of parliament, Loice Bwambale, Apollinaris Kithende, Kule Muranga, and Charles's brother Christopher Tabaan Kibanzanga, and Dr Crispus Kiyonga; a Mukonzo man of business, Paddy Kabagambe, more or less trusted by both camps; Museveni's Minister for Peace, Muruli Mukasa; the peace brokers Mike Mukula, MP, and Bent and his wife; the Minister for Presidential Affairs; and me. Museveni was, and commonly is, as amiable as a bear: a big fellow, and this morning in a pale grey shirt open at the neck and a T-shirt beneath, he welcomed us individually, circling the table, with a paw-shake and the Lukonzo greeting, where appropriate (for instance, to me). If bears may be said to bowl, the President opened from the head of the table with a long-hop to me, well down the table: How did I come to be involved? *The New Vision* had by now published a second interview with me, and his fancy had been caught. So I told him succinctly – how, crossing Africa in mid-century with a Muganda when most in the room were scarcely born, if at all, and needing a people unknown to the rest of Man to write a book about, I lit off into mountains and was drawn into the life of the people, leaving with them a piece of my heart and as it turned out the seeds of a rebellion. Museveni absorbed this reflectively: the oddity of whites. He remembered Erisa, my old trans-African companion. Then he spoke of the ADF, how peculiarly vicious they were, and how tricksy an enemy – quite unlike, for instance, Tito Okello, he reflected, which entailed straightforward army *vs* army – and how the core of the ADF, dammit, were Bakonzo... What could Charles do?

Charles, composed, soft-spoken and rehearsed, thanking the President for his hospitality and all that, replied that he would urge his people *actively* to support the Government. In so far as they were mountain people, he hoped to be able to reach that ADF 'hard core' with messages to abandon a struggle which was surely futile. He would discuss the present scene with the elders and various other fora of Konzo or Mba opinion... Museveni the bear intervened to draw upon Holy Scripture which, he recalled, invoked the law at two levels, the 'Moses Law' of an eye for an eye, and the 'law of Jesus' who, as they drove the nails through his hands, so the President said, prayed aloud, 'Forgive them, Father, for they know not what they do.' He, Museveni, was minded just now to apply the Jesus law, offering an amnesty to those who gave up and handed in their Kalashnikovs and the rest of it. But for those that did not take advantage of this amnesty, he said, he would be 'sharpening his knife'. For his UPDF was getting to be more and more effective even in those difficult mountains... From where I sat, Charles and Museveni were separated by a bronze kudu in half relief, rather beautiful, on the wall behind. I recalled how it is said of bears, Keep on the right side or beware.

Charles took this opportunity now to straighten the record – as much as was necessary – about NALU. He explained how he was an intimate of Amon Bazira in former days: that was an historical fact, and how on Bazira's 'death' (no reference here to judicial murder, possibly sanctioned within these very walls) he had accepted the leadership of the rump of NALU on the ground that, leaderless, it could cause mayhem among his people. Meanwhile, he might have the chance, he said, from the seat of command, to persuade those NALU rebels out of the mountains, as he succeeded in doing with all but a few of his followers in 1982. Yet he, Charles, despite his repeated attempts to make contact with His Excellency Museveni in order to work out a package of reconciliation, had had no signal of any response whatsoever from up here at State House. (Our side, of course, supposed an intrusive anti-Charles hand close to the President's office had intercepted Charles's urgent propositions.) Thus frustrated, he abandoned NALU as long ago as 1994. Our man now turned to the unvoiced issue, the mystic context of his presence here. He sought Presidential provision for the restoration of the Omusingaship. His people, he said, had recognized the Rwenzururu Kingdom: he believed they wanted their Kingdom back under the new provisions of the constitution. He made his point succinctly and clearly. He graciously thanked his host for listening.

'Why have you stayed away so long?' said Museveni, temporal leader.

'I was told I would be seen as a UPC supporter and either arrested or shot.' Charles paused before adding, 'It seems I was the one and only UPC supporter.' We chuckled at that.

The President turned to the MP for Bukonzo West and his Minister of so very much along the line of recent Ugandan history – of Co-operatives and Marketing, Finance, the Interior, now Health. Such confidentiality, such intimacy – what did they not know about one another, these two smart ones? Had they not conferred and colluded every week of their lives for years, maybe, most *days* of most weeks? How loyally, how sedulously, Dr Kiyonga, have you served your man, I thought, your Mr Seven, the number of plenty, adding to his stature by your occupation of such a clutch of high offices. Who am I to think harshly of you for such loyalty, for seizing your chances in this chancy life? Now you are back as Minister amid your first discipline, medicine, in which you challenged yourself as a lad on your remote, neglected spur beside the Tako, mere yards from the border of another white tribe's colony, walking home one day from school to confide to your mother (she whom you rescued a couple of years ago from the ADF invaders), *'Ma, I've decided I shall become a Doctor.'* And you did. You earned curative medicine's ancient symbol of the poisonous snake set upon a pole, of mortal wisdom harnessed as healing authority, given to the Israelites by African-born Moses whose very bulrushes concealing his cradle were watered by the mountains in our frame, Ruwenzori. Moses surely inherited that symbol of the serpent from his pharaonic master, whose headdress was invariably depicted with the cobra raising its head from the seat of consciousness, the pre-frontal region of the brain. Brainy one, I thought, how quiet you have sat at this meeting, not a peep, good as gold, butter wouldn't melt... you, snake-symbolled, the power to save life or clip it off, you of light and dark – like that seven-starred Bear at the head of the table with his benign side and dangerous side. With what shock must you have learned from your Bear of this imaginative Norwegian notion that bringing back Charles Irema-Ngoma from America to Ruwenzori, subtly flattered as to his national value, might undermine the motivation of the ADF! And moreover that it was your exposure of Charles at Mweya that alerted the Norwegian to Charles's potential usefulness? Was this not the biter bit? How had you responded?

'Now, let us hear from Crispus Kiyonga...' the Bear was saying.

Crispus – up the table and across from me, near to his President, very likely where he often sat in cabinet – was not at all comfortable. He set off into a denial that he had attempted to isolate Charles at the famous Mweya meeting. (It was an unconvincing protest, and not directly relevant.) The context of his 'exposure' of Charles's letters found in the ADF camp, he insisted, was that there were those among the people who would object to any monarchy: there was no precedent to any such monarchy. Were the people to vote, he said, and were they to vote for a King, they would regret it within five years.

That was all he said; yet it was enough to release the tongue of another of us who had remained hitherto silent: young Apollinaris Kithende, MP for Bukonzo East, who swiftly described a series of mysterious deaths in Kasese, or connected with it, which so troubled the hearts of the people – Tom Baluku the ex-UPC MP, Dr Henry Bwambale the distinguished economist, Amon Bazira, Bonifasi Baluku. This intervention was daring stuff, heaven knows, in the Bear's den, and as Kithende had launched into his list I glanced across at Kiyonga and saw the alarm in his eye, and that he was now engaged in furious note-taking. The swift scene and, above all, the look in Crispus's eye brought back to my mind that instant a clip of film shot by a German camera team two decades earlier of a cabinet meeting presided over by Idi Amin, perhaps in this very room, in which that tyrant had verbally fingered his Foreign Minister, Michael Ondoga, for his reported denigration of his person, the camera catching the nakedness of the fear in the Minister's eye – and how a fortnight later the Minister's body was found in the Nile below Murchison Falls among the bloated crocodiles... Museveni's cabinet room was a passably far cry from those days; and now today's President – who saw precisely what the plucky Kithende was implying – intervened with a genial analogy from some other part of the country, of which the drift was that with approaching political maturity this type of 'problem' would cease to occur. He rose to tour the table and as I shook his hand I wished him very good fortune. It was a hard enough job ruling anywhere, I thought, let alone Africa where nothing is quite as you would suppose, nothing is sure, nothing predictable, there is only the sound of the drumming.

xxxii

Ecstasy of the Drums

Early the next morning but one we all assembled in our Kampala hotel forecourt – Charles in a perfect suit, Henrietta in brocaded ivory, Charles's Muslim cousin Ibrahimu Muhonjya visibly Islamicized in white thobe and ghotra – to enter our white Mercedes limousines, and thence to speed to Entebbe airport for a flight in a neat little Yugoslav 4/10 20-seater to the grass airstrip at Kasese, a couple of hundred miles or so westwards. There we descended to the intense muttering of the drums. The drums and the hands that worked them, and all those they thronged, were set back from us behind barriers; and for the first time for these forty-four years my ears picked up the eluma reed-flutes, so many dozen lungs becoming one living thing, exhaling and inhaling, collective shawms circling drums. Charles, garlanded by two four-year-olds as he stepped on Kasese turf, traipsed by a line-up of local dignitaries, escorted by the stalwart Yokasi Bihande, LC5 – Charles with Henrietta, and some of the rest of us. UPDF soldiery packed around us: Charles was to be guarded so sedulously this astonishing week just beginning in which he was to earn (or not earn) his right to be back among his own people by galvanising them into confronting the terror and themselves helping to extinguish it (or not).

The big colonel-in-chief put me beside him to drive at high speed in our ten-vehicle convoy to our quarters at the Margherita Hotel. The present reign of terror, he said, was attributable to a mere few hundred, perhaps not more than *two* hundred ADF brigands. Against this well-armed motley the colonel had the service of seven battalions – which was seven times the number of troops in the service of Bill Cheyne when I walked up through the lines to locate Isaya in 1963. He had a further 1,200 Bakonzo scouts, he added. Despite all this, the ADF had driven or scared at least 230,000 Bakonzo out of their highland homes. Two nights ago and three hundred paces from the hotel where we peace-patriots were to be based throughout the visit, a band of ADF had raided two homes in that area of humpy savannah, killing six and abducting two. This ADF was showing the flag, showing its fangs.

441

The crucial political engagement was upon us almost at once. For Charles was to begin by coming before, as it were, the regional Sanhedrin, the Kasese District Council, in their council chamber at Rukoki, a bare utilitarian hall a mile or two outside town. It was 'crucial' for all the following reasons. These five or six dozen councillors, mostly men, had had their distinction confirmed by voters from all over the District that comprised both the largest concentration of Bakonzo of any of the three Districts incorporating the mountains and their suffering inhabitants, and the commercial hub, Kasese town. They had been assembled to hear their brother's self defence. This was Charles's first swing at publicly stating his case after the great smear of Mweya. His performance would set the tone for all that was to follow. Who could guess his style or foretell his nerve?

The Speaker of this Council, a certain Mbura, was a Kiyonga man, who would wish to make the meeting a kind of Star Chamber convened to 'try' this Charles Mumbere, so-called Irema Ngoma and would-be Omusinga. Yet, the way things were, that could clearly not be so. Instead of burying Charles, Mweya had resurrected him. Incarnated in their very midst, he had to be heard out now. That was in the African tradition, and it was in the quasi-democratic practice of Museveni's Uganda. He could not but be allowed a window to exonerate himself. Moreover, something was massively astir. When word escaped of Charles Wesley Irema-Ngoma's impending re-visitation, popular response was galvanic. By the wish of the President, five rallies in the cause of peace had been planned for the coming days. They threatened to be formidable. From end to end of the mountains every man, woman and child of the Konzo community seemed to have thought of little else. The drums told it: the Keeper of the Drums, of the spirit of the Drums, their mountain Drums, was returning; and he at last was surely to hear again those Drums, with mortal ears, *his* Drums. On every side the would-be opponents surely sensed and saw the symptoms among the common folk – they, the secular voices, the artful machinators, with the levers of supposed power. Play this wrong, they perceived, and they could be swept away. So, caution, caution and wariness amid the demotic swell. Maybe this Mumbere Charles, this ex-exile, would himself play it wrong, unpractised all these years at public appearance, rusty in his native tongue, capable of misjudgment as to all the eddies and counter-currents under the sea.

A prayer was given, that God in His infinite wisdom should,

well, not overlook this occasion. Let not that brief and elemental discipline of spoken prayer be discounted.

Speaker Mbura sat up there centre-stage, solid, square-jawed, satisfied, with an aura of knowing that much more than the rest of us about whatever matter was under consideration. What a gift such an aura is, for whoever has it can never be wrong-footed, never be flustered; and how envious had I been of that aura of others during my own foray into politics in early life. Up there beside the Speaker was Charles himself, and those other dignitaries who were to make up the platform cast of our travelling circus. Each of our original Members of Parliament were accorded the excessively polysyllabic title of 'Honourable', from which the Bantu tongue instinctively edits out the N and its adjacent syllable and dutifully plies the aspirate. The MPs were thus presented to our meeting as the Horrible Muruli Mukasa, Minister of State for Security; the Horrible Mukula, peace-broking member for Soroti; and the Horrible Kibanzanga Christopher, Member of Parliament for this very constituency and, of course, Charles's brother. Up there on the platform were also Yokasi Bihande, the LC (Local Chairman) 5, warm, capable, without airs and one of us; the District (National Resistance) Movement Chairman, one of them; and the Resident District Commissioner (theirs too). To my imprecise relief, Henrietta had been left behind at the hotel, presumably to unpack whole trunkloads of garmenture. Bent and I sat sideways on, just below the stage. We were introduced to the gathering from the platform. It seemed to me that one dark figure was absent. Yet not for long. Muruli Mukasa was scarcely into his verbosities than there arrives, by the door at the far end of the hall, the figure of Crispus Kiyonga. You felt the shiver. He mounted the stage and took a seat at the far end. He must have driven from Kampala, rising no later than 5 a.m.

We had prepared our homework. Muruli waffled grandly on, about peace, development, and what a marvellous government it was that he belonged to. This visitation of Charles Mumbere was all about the defeat of the ADF. That is what he said. Yet of course we all knew it was also about something larger and longer, namely the restoration of the Omusingaship, and thus the very ethos of the People of the Mountains, as a people, legatees of Rwenzururu. The only acknowledgement of this issue by Muruli Mukasa was that, naturally, it would be a matter of dispute. Yet, wait: if this was so disputable, on what premise was Charles here at all? Syahuka-Muhindo, our guru, never for a moment lost sight of the true double agenda. He it was who had drafted this imminent first key-note speech for Charles, to which I had been invited to offer a few refinements; and after Muruli, and Mukula, and the Movement man, Charles himself spoke. It struck me that there was an incompatibility in train. Here Charles was to be tested by the councils of men which presumed to determine the future, but out there he was already quite beyond any testing: he was engaged in the fulfilment of history already written, and these people in the chamber already knew that: *akalaghirire sikatambwa*. None here could buck the *zeitgeist*. They had all heard the drums.

Now then, English was this council chamber's medium – I should have mentioned – because of the variety of local ethnic constitutents: Konzo, Toro, Songora, Mba, Nkole. Listen:

'Mister Speaker, Sir.

'I thank God for having brought me home.

'I wish to thank God for having kept you all alive.

'I am grateful to you Mr Speaker and the whole Council for having allowed me to meet and address these great leaders who have been popularly elected by the masses, and who indeed represent the popular principles of the Movement system of governance.

'Article One of our Constitution says, "power belong to the people". In the decentralised system of governance, I am made to understand, you now run the affairs of Kasese as a District. I wish to submit that I am still internalising the whole concept and studying the Local Government Act. Needless to say, I think it's an excellent innovation which brings services closer to the people.'

Further gratitude, said the text – and that was followed by a dollop of flattery for the President and the 'entire leadership of the National Resistance Movement...' in the areas of the economy and security.

He was 'very happy to be home.'

'Mr Speaker, Sir, you will already be aware that I was the leader of the Rwenzururu Movement and until 1982, the head of the Rwenzururu Kingdom Government as king Iremangoma. I do not intend to tell a long story beyond mentioning to you that in August, 1982, I led the entire government of the Rwenzururu Kingdom out of the deep forests of the Rwenzori Mountains. This followed an understanding which was reached between my government and central government. It was also a result of my personal conviction that by bringing my government down from the Rwenzori mountains, we hoped to eliminate violence in this region. A commitment was made between me and government that I should go to school in the United States as a "special student". Government agreed to support my stay in the USA and pay my tuition fees... However, this support was stopped soon after the National Resistance Movement took over power and firmly established a government. The reasons for the decision to terminate my scholarship were never explained to me. Mr Speaker, I have brought this to the attention of His Excellency in recent correspondence that I suffered a lot in the USA after the abrupt termination of my scholarship.'

He had come back to Uganda now, however, in the interest of security of the territory with which he was deeply associated.

'Mr Speaker, Sir, it does not surprise me that my name comes up in the control of security in the Rwenzori Mountains. For many years I led the Rwenzururu Movement. Moreover, I was and I am still widely esteemed as the Iremangoma of the Bakonzo/Baamba throughout the entire mountain and lowland region.

'In these two capacities I have been involved with the security question in Rwenzori, ever since I was a young boy. One day, my role in it may come to be critically assessed. One thing that will emerge is that I have never chosen to be a rebel; it is the fraught and painful history of the area that makes me look like a rebel born and bred.

'Mr Speaker, I categorically assure you I have no acquaintance or connection with the ADF whatsoever. From time to time I have read reports of their disgraceful activities. I have formally (and repeatedly) disassociated myself from that rebel group.

'I here admit before this august council that I knew something about NALU. I knew about NALU leadership from the late Amon Bazira, who was the founder of that rebel movement. However, I would like to point out to you Mr Speaker that while I had previous acquaintance with those who came to initiate NALU, I knew very little about the activities of that movement and played no part in them at that time.

'I temporarily accepted titular leadership of NALU when Amon Bazira died. This was on the request of Bazira's followers. This may have been a misjudgment on my part.

'At the time, Mr Speaker, I had a reason for getting involved in the manner that I did; it was to use what influence I might have – albeit at a great distance – to affect the nature of the movement and bring its followers out of the bush just as I had earlier brought out the Rwenzururu fighters. I knew too well that it would be a difficult task. When I brought down the Rwenzururu fighters I was in full charge. But here was NALU which looked formless, a movement about which I had little knowledge except that, leaderless, it would become even more problematic, and my people of the Rwenzori region were going to be the ones to suffer most. I worked from my past experience in an attempt to control the excesses of NALU as best I could.'

Instead, he declared, he put his trust in Uganda's new constitution of Uganda, which brought about parliamentary elections from 1994.

'Mr Speaker, the focus of my concern on this visit to my country, Uganda, is security. I believe deep inside by heart that I have come to Uganda at this time with the following potential beneficial consequences:

'(a) to help establish a good sense of active trust between His Excellency and the Government of Uganda on the one hand, and the people of the Rwenzori region on the other...'

Our man had started off calmly if uncertainly, as one dependent on his written brief. But now he began to leave his text and in his veins his own blood moved. 'It is not going to be an easy fight.' He meant the fight, the campaign, for peace. 'What I have heard about ADF makes me almost cry. Because I have been a liberator. I have never ordered my forces to open fire or aim a gun at a baby, a pregnant woman, an old man. Only,' he said, of his own past as commander-in-chief of mountain askaris, 'they would crush someone who wants to stand in their way.' That brought a little splash of laughter, the authentic voice of the once and future king. But what we were all now facing was a self-breeding, self-compounding evil. 'These rebels are not coming from one rebel group.' He meant there was no context of instinctual allegiance. 'They are coming from so many tribes... But *our* tribe, we will try to convince them.'

'We' of royalty: in his own person nothing, in his omusingaship something other. 'I would like to appeal to all of you,' he said to this very audience, which included as we knew at least two of those implacably opposed to him, 'to be behind the government to help in fighting this exercise' – that is, implement the initiative of peace; for even already some of us were afraid that there were those present who wished to see him fail, his authority disproved, and the terror persist. He ducked back into our text:

> 'I am here to make an appeal to all the people who may have joined rebel activities in the Rwenzori mountains on the mistaken assumption that they were following me, or fighting for the Bakonzo/Baamba people. If there is anyone among the ADF or any other rebel group fighting government who claims to be doing it in the name of fighting for Bakonzo/Baamba cause, such persons should come out of the bush immediately to join peace-loving Ugandans in order to establish a peaceful and united society. This is the call I am making now. I shall be repeating it wherever I will go to address the masses.'

Then he was off into a plea for regional government aid, especially for 'the remote areas occupied by the Bakonzo;' and for 'our people to be highly involved with the security personnel (UPDF) in the rebel-affected areas to defeat the enemy. We must isolate rebel elements from outside using Rwenzori terrain as a base to fight Government.'

All of this came across with conviction. I was not yet sure where this local political élite's sympathies lay concerning Charles himself. It would take courage for anyone present to reveal himself as an opponent of Kiyonga's, in the presence of that figure of power and stealth. And it was only now Charles proceeded towards the second of our strategic plans. He did so on tiptoe, coming up behind his stool – behind the presumption of a stool.

'Various positions have been taken up on the issue of the Kingdom of Rwenzururu. There is evidence that my people of Rwenzori have this issue at heart. *My* position, which I stand by very strongly, is this: the kingship issue must not be our primary concern at this moment. We should clear the security problem first before we tackle the kingship issue. I am the Iremangoma and whoever acknowledges in me thus should accept this position.

'I have not read the whole of the new constitution of Uganda which I received from the Vice Chairman, Alhaji Moses Kigongo, after my arrival in the country. Yet I am convinced that the constitution offers a good starting point on this matter. We should all of us loyally follow the constitution as it is and take its provisions as our starting point. Mr Speaker, I hope that I shall clarify this position to my people outside this council when I get the opportunity to address them. I want to assure you that I am not in any hurry on any issue, except the issue of security...

'For God and my Country.'

Charles settled back. He had sat throughout. The applause was, I sensed, good in parts – very likely most parts. Crispus Kiyonga slipped in front to say a few words – below the platform, modestly. He was going to upstage no one. Not at all. He welcomed Charles. He made us laugh. He exuded a Sambo innocence. He sat down. Speaker Mbura rose to ask for contributions from the floor... and accepted one from a councillor of middle age wearing shades with fancy gold arms, who made the point that being killed by the hand of NALU four or five years ago was not so different from being killed by the ADF today. Yet this evoked a low swell of disapproval. The logic of the assertion crumpled against the illogic of the implication that the horrors of the ADF derived from the historic motives of Rwenzururu. That murmur from the belly of the hall, because it was wordless, and because the chair was listening and wary, was all we needed: it was all right, *it was all right*, Charles's account of his actions had been taken in and accepted; we were leaving Mweya behind us now: from this hour on in the playing out of our reunion the head could let the heart take over.

The heart of the populace took over at 2 p.m. that day (Wednesday, November 25, 1998) at the assembly ground beside Kasese town, called Rwenzori Square. There they were gathered to

448

embrace their returning Omusinga, King, in their vast numbers. In rapid convoy from the Margherita, he swept down among them with his party in three black official Mercedes which had arrived that morning from Kampala. Military vehicles crammed with soldiery led the cavalcade. Then Charles and his Queenie dolly, ivory-brocaded, and the Minister for Peace, in Car One; and then Mama Christina, and Bent the Brave and his wife and me and Christopher Tabaan Kibanzanga, in Mercs Two and Three, followed tightly by a mini bus and another truck full of troops. Our vehicles nosed the enormous throng. Estimates of the size of crowds are notoriously subjective. When I was settled in the front row of easy chairs beneath the rim of the great awning which sheltered row upon row of local élite behind us, I put the number of folk present at this first rally at some 30,000. The reporter of *The New Vision*, Uganda's most professional daily, with no pro-Charles axe to grind, ventured an estimate of 50,000, and ran a page 1 picture of Charles, seated beside his supportive LC5 Bihande and

Mumbere blasts ADF

KYOMUHENDO MUHANGA

ROYAL WHISPER: Mumbere (right) is addressed by a guest as Kasese LC5 chairman Yowasi Bwambale looks on.

BY JOHN THAWITE
AND JOHN NZINJAH

CHARLES Wesley Mumbere, king of the Bakonzo, has challenged the Allied Democratic Forces rebel leadership to explain why they are killing, maiming, raping and abducting innocent Ugandans.

"I cannot understand what type of commanders ADF has, who order their fighters to massacre children and slit the bellies of pregnant women, the very people they claim they are fighting to liberate," Mumbere said at the Rwenzori Square in Kasese town Wednesday afternoon.

Mumbere, who was mak-

ing his first public address after arriving in Kasese earlier in the day, told a crowd, estimated at 50,000, that atrocities committed by the ADF "tarnish us Africans internationally" and show the world "we have not understood human rights."

"If the ADF and other forces fighting Governments think they

are liberators, why not attack armed forces and leave innocent people alone?" he asked.

Meanwhile, Mumbere has declared that a Bakonzo kingdom exists and he is the successor to the throne.

"But the Uganda Government has never

Turn to page 2

receiving whispered advice from Syahuka Muhindo. Thirty or fifty, it was a lot. Most had been waiting for days, in the African manner. As Loice Bwambale remarked, 'Kings are always late.' If a people awaits a king, it is indeed for them to keep their lamps trimmed, their drumskins taut.

The drums were nudging ecstasy as we settled, and as Omusinga Charles came to the middle of the row to his sofa, right there in the flesh before all those people beyond twenty or twenty-five places of baked earth, gracious, handsome, winsome, assuredly royal, their own Omusinga Charles Wisley [sic] Iremangoma. It was as if all the banners, placards and plywood arches raised over the heads of this concourse had conjured him. These decorations for the most part featured a certain great-eyed official portrait of their Bonny Prince, dating from before his departure for America and made in fact not by Carlo di Benedetti but by the Live-for-Ever Photo Studio of Kasese, PO Box 41. Immediately facing us as we took our places across the open patch, was erected a podium for the speech-makers, buntinged with the Rwenzuru colours of blue, green and black (with a central circle of snow-white Nzururu), and the yellow, orange and black colours of Uganda. We stood first for prayer, and from that brief Christian invocation entered, still standing, Uganda's national anthem led by some fellow's amplified larynx, and then immediately thereafter the Rwenzururu anthem.

Rwenzururu wethu!

Rwenzururu wethu!

Our Rwenzururu! What has become of you?

It was like, I thought – these tens of thousands of throats – the sound of rollers breaking upon the long line of the home shore as it is picked up by the ears of a mariner who had been away at sea for years on end; and amid those rollers he picks up the sound – surely? – of his own church bells. Oh yes, our Rwenzururu, the Kingdom, had had its churches, if without bells.

Khuatya thwamakulengeka-nia ngoku wabya

When we think of how you used to be

Emiisoni iya tsububuka

Tears flow.

Charles stood there erect in his *Il Duce* pose, right hand diagonally and flat across his chest, chin held high, mouthing the (variable) verses with which he had grown up as a child and which I had last heard nearly 36 years earlier on a spur above the Tako, Congo-side. It always was a great tune, somewhere between the Battle Hymn of

the Republic and She'll be Coming Round the Mountain.
Omubughe wethu!
Omubughe wethu!
Our language!
Omubughe wethu w'olhukonzi 'ayire-hi?
Our very own language, what has become of it?
Hatya abirihinduka mwa lhuhyana
Omwatsi abere makuru.
Now it has been corrupted into another tongue. 'News' has been bastardized as the word 'Makuru' [A Lutoro usage].

Of course, the entire front row of Very Important Persons likewise stood for this pair of anthems: none could possibly demur, even if the NRM Commissar and the Minister for Peace must have furiously wondered what seccessionist canticle they were not endorsing, and in Kiyonga's and Bamusede's and Mbura's gullet it was surely gristle – and they must have heard that everyone knew that anthem, the entire 30,000, 50,000, whatever the number was, united in song in the recollected pain and the yearning right down to the present moment. Song was ever the Konzo genius, and song was ever sacred, drawn from and dedicated to spirit.

Even before we sat I knew that nothing much could go amiss with this meeting, indeed with this entire reunion of Charles Irema Ngoma coming back out of the isolation of exile to his people at the

time of their renewed torment, Charles could not but be a vessel of their martyrdom, historic and now. Ours was the mountain place, Nzururu's place, ours the language, ours the identity, ours the martyrdom. There is none can out-deepen depth. There followed rocking songs by big school children, of mixed genders, wonderfully smart and laundered, the young bosoms riotous with pagan patriotism beneath their church's smocks, the drummers drumming, Charles leaning back in his deep chair, mopping his brow with a neat square of white.

Then Christopher Tabaan, local Member of Parliament, took the podium to introduce us visitors. First to go up to deliver a brief harangue in English, was Michael Mukula, MP, peace-broker, then Bent the Unexpected; then it seemed to be my turn, since Christopher was saying, 'I would like to share this moment with our lo-ong friend' and I was up there with a microphone to give three wabukiri greetings, and then to tell the multitude in my own language how I had been taught to love and honour the Bakonzo people by the father of Charles Irema Ngoma, namely Isaya Mukirane, forty-four years ago [great cheer]. For I had arrived in the mountains as a young man, alone, carrying nothing, and had been taken into Isaya's heart, so I brought him into my heart, and we travelled on our feet the length of the mountains – from Bundibugyo, to Burahya, to Bunyangabo [the cheers mount with the rhythm of the names] to Busongora and Bwera, from where we mounted to Kitolu and Kituti and the land of Khavaïru. There it was, in 1954, that I came to know that this was a people I would support all my life, since they had been neglected for too long and 'marginalised' (a cross-breed coinage familiar to the cognoscenti of the Bakonzo) by history and colonial boundaries, and by the steepness of the mountains, yet these Bakonzo were heirs of the mountains, their guardians of the heights for all mankind, and these mountains were a treasure which would make the Bakonzo famous throughout the earth.

It was a short speech, as befitted the 'moment' Christopher had spoken of. It flit through my mind to end it ' Thule baghuma' – we are all one – which was the early battle-cry of Rwenzururu; but I refrained because I thought it might be perhaps incendiary and that if anyone were to use it, that one should be Charles whom they all awaited. And await they yet must; for after me it was the turn of four captive members of the ADF of Bakonzo blood. These cowed prisoners-of-war had been brought up alongside the podium in a military vehicle. They were not fettered, yet manifestly alarmed in the midst of this sea of odium: two were shuffled on to the podium and related briefly into the microphone in Lukonzo how they had been deceived by the lies and blandishments and terrible threats from their leaders into the killing and rapine of their own people, and terribly lamented their errors.

Immediately upon them, the no-party Party Commissar (such was his title) was at the microphone, using English and Swahili to tell these 'masses' who were assembled not for him but for Charles nothing that they did not know already; and next there came in the stilt-dancers and contortionists, and dancers circling the drummers and *eluma*-players and an old vestal in her colobus-skin; and then at last up steps Mbura Jerome, speaker of Kasese District Council and the former MP of this division, displaced by Charles's brother and thus no friend of Charles but indeed a Kiyongista fellow-traveller, to announce Charles himself.

Charles came up to the covered podium like the local-boy champion of the Fight Game entering the ring to box for the international belt, to massed rhythmic clapping and the pealing of ululation. Mbura was gone and there beside him was the diminutive figure of our sage and academic, Syahuka-Muhindo, with a typescript of the core text of what Charles was due to say. But Charles was to need no prompt. He was off in Lukonzo, quite rid of rust now after a week or more in the circle of his own people, with each phrase or sentence given out by a skilled translator into English, with his own amplification, stationed just below the podium: 'I thank God Almighty who has turned all this planning into reality.' He narrated the manoeuvres that preceded his homecoming, and told of the context of his emanation out of mythic America, and the nature of his present brief. He was at ease up there instantly: compact, fluent and assured. He had of course been here before, at this very spot, on August 15, 1982. His style was factual and without oratorical flourish. Soon he was leaning on the reed balustrades which enclosed three sides of his little bamboo platform. For a while he broke into English, at which his interpreter simply switched to his own Lukonzo tongue. He issued an invitation to the rebels in the upper forests to come to see him here. 'Tell them,' he said, to those who in this assembly we knew must be present with swift access to the armed men up there, hidden and listening at one remove, 'tell them they will not pass to victory.'

My mind wandered to them: Fanehasi, that old devil whom I had glimpsed growing up since his late adolescence, hunched at his cave-mouth, by his camp fire, attended by his wives, his several sons (who had been slow to enter this world at first): and he, Fanehasi Kisokeronio, now formidably weaponed with Russian and Eastern European mechanisms of killing, Kalashnikovs and landmines, products indeed treasures of civilisation, the marque of modern power; and he fiercely wondering what to make of this return of Irema Ngoma, young Charles, who forgave him once for his treachery which was not of course treachery but the true flame of hatred burning in him – hatred of all that lay below the mountains, scum-Batoro and the great conspiracy of Kampala against him and what he fought for. Was not Charles Kisembo traitor? How would he, Fanehasi, have his several score of armed followers respond to such an 'invitation' from this ex-Omusinga – his own Mzee Kirama, Mobina, Charago, Kawaida, Muleristo, Jarino, Winka, Kadingu, Enoch, Justus, Kambasa, Kabanda Jojo... we had roll-calls of their names; we knew them; knew those who knew them... So how now would Fanehasi direct them? Were they not by now too steeped in blood and murder of their fellows to listen to such an 'invitation'. They would perceive it as a trap. He would warn them so. Yet might they not be wistful, some of them, for the rhythms of peace, of crops sown for assured gathering, the clay pot on home hearth's three stones, the rhythm of pregnancies and coming to term, the rhythm of genealogy? Would he risk to brand Charles now as one corrupted, suborned by flattery from Museveni and his crowd, as one for ADF execution? No, he could not risk that. But he would mount raids in the lowland communities during this week of Charles's travelling circus – darting raids to remind them sharply that the mountains were his even if he had emptied them of their people – his and Kitasamba's, to whom he had been loyal and who would surely repopulate his mountains in his good time.

Up on the podium Charles had dealt with the calumny at Mweya. Now he had come back here, with the confidence of the President demonstrated by having had allocated to him, Irema Ngoma, as many Mercedes-Benz motorcars as were allocated to heads of other states. So the oration moved towards the prospect of a resolution of this persisting horror, by the offer in his own name of an amnesty to those coming down, handing over their arms and eschewing violence. Final applause rolled like those waves along an interminable shore, rolling perhaps by faint murmur or murmur imagined into the foothills that reared immediately westward, populated or depopulated. In this manner our mariner came ashore among his people, albeit they in their dislocation. It was I think Bihande who from the podium closed this first and most tremendous of the week's barazas. Among the renewal of the drumming and in the prospect of intoxication the throng swarmed around those Benzes as we nosed out of Rwenzori Square, militarily escorted, and cavalcaded beneath the arches proclaiming Welcome to His Majesty Charles Wisley, portraited above and incarnated below in the Benz ahead, to our hillside Margherita Hotel base. It was about four thirty p.m.

You would think all this endorsement enough for one day, but not so, not for the man of the hour. He had yet to enter under his own roof. Within a half hour Charles had re-emerged, spruced and refreshed, and with his personal entourage of Mama, two brothers, Syahuka-Muhindo, Ibrahim Muhonjya and me. We re-entered two Benzes and made for the Buhikira, the family's residence. I had long been accustomed to whatever edifice graced by Charles and by his late father as his private living quarters being termed his 'palace': now we were headed for the little villa set in its own space of tilted ground above Kasese on the mountainside of the town. Climbing out in front of those same steps where two and a half years earlier I had been greeted by mama Christina, to eat her stewed chicken and study her indifference at the photographs recording the scene of her young motherhood. Here today was in addition an impressively constructed and immaculate single-chamber parliament house of grass, reeds and inner uprights; and opposite it, its own miniature, unmistakably an *engorwe*, a spirit house.

Prayer had preceded both the assemblies already attended. Likewise this coming more intimate assembly in the tribal *ekhyanganda* parley-house would be preceded by devotions. Into the tiny circular chamber of impenetrable thatch which even the Bakonzo had to crouch to enter by the half-tunnelled doorway and dangling screen, I was beckoned to accompany Omusinga Charles, mama, and Syahuka-Muhindo. In the murky interior the priest-*mbandua* of the Baswagha inheritance awaited – without regalia, in the light of a single candle – the returning royal son. In this secrecy Charles donned a bark-cloth toga. He declared his obeisance to the tutelary spirit of the mountains whose name I shall leave unmentioned, was entrusted by the mbandua with a spear resting against the wall of the *engorwe*. Charles gripped it. Its shaft was stained by smoke of generations of mountain hearths. Its pointed metal ferule was firmly in the earth at our feet and leafed spearhead at the level of my own head. Charles repeated a brief vow. Mama presided, which is to say the authority of the inwardness of her eyes and the strength of the shape of her mouth sealed the solemnity of this oath upon the wood fashioned out of the most durable tree of the primary forest and the metal of primal foundry and forge, pledging defence of his community of man, assault upon those who would threaten it, and pursuit of the meat of fertility. We could hear the pounding of drums outside the hut. Certain votive objects lay under a cloth on a high stool or low, narrow altar. Among those objects momentarily revealed was a bible and a pot which contained, I supposed, ash, representing the residual essence of certain animals which in turn spoke of fortitude, self-protection, physical power, connecting men and specifically this near-king with the pervading genius of creation. (At home in Kensington, in the Royal Gardens of that name, permanently open to the public, there is erected on a plinth a 20-foot bronze commissioned from G F Watts in 1903 of a naked rider on a champing mustang and entitled Physical Energy, imparting to our Monarch and maybe to the Monarch's subjects that same mythic endowment, *ntu*.) More was spoken in our *engorwe*, in a low tone, nothing of which I made out; and when I questioned Syahuka-Muhindo a little later he was coy, perhaps supposing there was too much to explain or that words were no good at doing the explanation. And yet it was this little event I have subsequently come to suspect that sparked the writing of this book of many, many words. Why exactly? Because here in this hermetic tabernacle almost as a participant I had been carried beyond the range of my cognisance. Despite the presence of the Holy Bible I sensed myself exploring again in the proper mode of exploration, where no one of one's own kind has been before, entering what may never be fully comprehended; and here being taken back beyond the frontier of the present time to Chief Khavaïru's *engorwe*, his sanctum at Kituti where he worked the spells that brought us monkey meat and whose ingredients hung in a bag – the leopard fur whose ash still perceptibly stained the tiny cicatrices on my breastbone. This *engorwe* and its goings-on were the citadel of our camp – the camp of the entire mountains and the race of man that inhabited them and which stood in confrontation to that other camp of Dr Kiyonga with *his* medicine, and state authority, money, modern soldiery, technology and power temporal.

Emerging by the dangling screen into daylight we were taken

across the compound to the ekhyaganda-parleyhouse, some twenty feet high and forty or fifty feet in diameter of spirally woven reeds, thatched with grasses. Here was a seated gathering of about forty. These were the inner circle – mostly male – of what may be termed the collective regency, the tribal wise, including those of the maternal clan, *Baswagha*, through which the prevailing inheritance flowed in Charles's blood and spirit. I took my seat in the row of deep armchairs facing this gathering, three places along from Charles. A fine young ewe was led in on three legs, bewildered by its sudden and sinister eminence. Mama Christina was there, centre, awaiting it, with a short announcement of dedication and a Konzo knife in a sheath of wood patterned with scorched dots. She unscabbarded the blade and handed it to Charles who at once plunged it into the animal's heart. Blood leapt onto the clean straw spread there on the earth's floor. Charles now returned to his central ceremonial chair, and as he spoke in Lukonzo his counter welcome to their welcome of him, the sacrifice to Ndyoka – at first with a little spasmodic kicking of hind legs – was skinned. For pagan man to be reconfirmed as King, gods must feast.

xxxii

Charles and the Green Snake

The Kasese Cobalt Company is a many-million dollar Canadian operation producing a quarter of the world's supply of cobalt, the metal ingredient of such high-tensile items as the rotor fins of jet-powered aircraft. Such a fin forged from the cobalt in the tailings of the old Kilembe copper mine extinguished by the falling price of copper during Charles's rule in Rwenzururu is I suppose the equivalent of the leaf-like head of that spear ritually bestowed on Charles the previous day and, at least in theory, forged out of iron wrested from Ruwenzori ore at Buthale in immemorial times. At breakfast early that next morning I was conferring with John Aird, Scottish engineer and Chief Executive of the KCC which employed well over one thousand local Africans. So I conducted Aird to talk with Charles in his private quarters; and from that scrupled and discerning man the Irema Ngoma learned of the value placed by the KCC on the dependability and skills of the substantial Konzo element of its workforce. Yet as a consequence of the killings and rapine of the ADF in the immediate vicinity on the previous night but one, no fewer than six of Aird's European senior staff had declared their intention to quit: just about the entire German contingent. This posed the company with an intense recruitment problem, and if the raids persisted they would jeopardise the survival of the entire industry whose value was not only to the local economy but to Uganda's.

I rode to that day's great rally at Kitswamba in the second car with the Queen Mother, Christina. The two of us, approximately of an age, represented continuity and perhaps a measure of indistructibility, having both outlived already by half as much again the average life span in these capricious tropics. She was done up as for church, in a flowered cotton garment to her ankles, loosely gathered, the bodice fitting close, and shoulders puffed in the African fashion. I do believe there were white gloves. Her three sons were all in awe of her. She never referred to Isaya. She never displayed emotion, unless it be obduracy and a presumption of the ultimate penetration of her will.

She had endured everything, extraordinary hardships, carrying her fire as ember in a pot, her baby beneath her bark cloth on her back; sleeping in the open on the cold heights; strangely widowed; losing a child to Ndyoka and to death; mothering this king; witnessing apparent catastrophe, apparent triumph; witnessing executions; privy to the maiming on her husband's orders of the husband of her sibling sister whom she grew up uncannily resembling. She was Ruhandika's granddaughter; and though she had at one point been baptised Christine, or Christina, and was married to an Isaya, and was the daughter of a Samwiri and the sister-in-law of an Ibrahimu, her spiritual allegiance predated Jesus Christ, Isaiah, Samuel and Abraham, and if from time to time she attended church it was to hedge her bets.

Kitswamba was an old Rwenzururu bastion, named not after the mountain deity as its sound suggests, but the ground elder that stifled the plantations of its first settlers. It is situated along the road northwards into Bunyangabo 'old county' and by a trail westwards up a valley that descended from the heights. I had passed by the place, yet further in, and higher, with Isaya Mukirane, in 1954. It was here the hotheads had taken Vito Muhindo hostage during the election of 1980, and from where Vito had escaped only to die by the hands of those of hotter heads yet. Here we now had a mighty rally, twenty or thirty thousand. Henrietta was in peach today. Several of the patriotic young were wearing T-shirts bearing the image of Charles's head. Some ladies carried parasols, as it might have been at the cake-walk hour in New Orleans after the liberation by Abraham Lincoln of the slaves. After the Rwenzururu anthem, massed schoolgirls brought up their hands in a drilled salute for Charles – Charles so much at ease, leaning back with a smile of fine teeth, carven lips and iridescent skin. Crispus Kiyonga was there, all the mountains being his presumed territory also, and this very place his first constituency to represent under a forgotten and discredited regime. He arrived at our rally separately, kept a cheerful mien, and did not open his mouth publicly. He had had his little word at the initial, closed meeting of District Councillors – we have seen that; – and he must assuredly address the crowd when our sequence of great barazas reached his own constituency of Bukonzo West. But that was not to be until the fourth of the series, the last in this southern half of the mountains (leaving only the final rally, planned for Bundibugyo in the north-west). We speculated how he would handle his own rally, since it could be nothing if not a rally *for*

459

Charles. What might now be passing through the complex mind of Crispus here at Kitswamba as he sat through all the songs, all for Charles, rejoicing at Charles's presence, lamenting his absence, narrating in all but explicit fable (which everybody understood) in the lyrics of these schoolchildren and under the coaching of their teachers the sheer mischief, not to say wickedness, done to the patriots of Rwenzururu and to the cause of Charles the present hero, at his, Crispus's, devising and machination? The poison-fanged viper of the songs that lurked green and unobserved in the grasses, Ruwenzori's deadly *atheris viridis*, *enzoka nyarunyatsi*, was none other than Kiyonga himself, and here he was in the front row as if it were all the jolliest of theatre. What choice had he, I supposed, but to be tickled by the blood ascribed to his doorstep? It was their little joke, these kids; he could take a joke... and is it not a fact of life, in times and places where death is commonplace, decreed as much by God as man, that the human device of inurement is to make a joke of it? You cauterize by humour, even if it is you yourself who are the perpetrator. So you sleep at night.

Once again I was a warm-up speaker, this time in a place where English was less known, and so was translated into Lukonzo phrase by phrase. I was given again the honorific Musabuli which Christian liturgy in the vernacular had lifted out of the earthly league, from helper-out-of-bogs to Saviour. Later I was drawn aside for a long interview for television. Charles was presented with a fat goat and a bolt of cloth from a little girl with bows of purple in her hair. Purple was Kitswamba's colour, and Loice Bwambale, parliamentary representative of all south Rwenzori women, stepped out in a wonderful plaid of purple nylon, in formidable oratory on the theme of Charles and peace and the people's will.

Then Charles. He was visibly filling out into the old role, symbol of expectations, harbinger of an active unity. When we were back that mid afternoon at the *ekhyanganda*, the pristine new parleyhouse at the royal family's homestead, Charles presided upon a gathering of some fifty Rwenzururu veterans. Here we were where the blood of the ewe had been spilled the previous day, the straw now cleared away. Our overt purpose was to find among these trusted insiders from the Kahindangoma of yore those whose kin or comrades had gone on to serve the ADF who at the express plea of their old Irema Ngoma might reach them to dissuade them from their aberration. I remembered several faces from 1963, and they inevitably remembered me – their only visitor from the outside world for the better part of a generation, and white-skinned at that; and especially I recalled young Charles Kisembo's personal tutor of that time, Yosifati School Band: the laughter still there in his crumply face, the delight ever brimming at his pupil's advance. How had his boy come on, at nearly 50 now, back from America – *America!* – and arriving here at the Buhikira in presidential Benzes, no rebel now and all but, all but constitutional Omusinga. They were jacketed and necktied almost to a man, scrag-necked, crag-faced, cataract-eyed, rheumy, gnarled and leathery in the hands, acorn-fingernailed. Whoever would venture up into the forests, through that long no-man's land of deserted spurs and abandoned plantains of yams, millet and tapioca, would surely be their sons and grandsons. The talk thrust on in Lukonzo, each man rising from his place upon the bench to make his contribution – since Charles was very much the Omusinga-in-council here. Yet what each man said was compact, emphatic, felt and urgent, spoken out of present pain and ardent expectancy that the route through to justice for the tribe, and to peace, which was for the tribe to find yet was so difficult to chart, would by intervention half-divine descend upon them in this re-conjured Omusingaship. For let us be clear as to the unclarity: here under this thatch were gathered the voices of the previous generation of mountain rebels who had lived and fought for justice and a peace whose elusiveness likewise drove the present generation of Bakonzo mountain rebels, their kin, into deeds of intolerable wickedness. Here were old men risking again to hope... At the end, the gentle dismissal: all those oak hands gripping mine and my nostrils catching the smoke-scent that belonged as much to the pelt of humans as to every other pelt and artefact glowing in the firelight from between three stones in windowless huts.

And what would truly come of this endeavour? No formal method of surrender, of the handing over of arms, had been devised or announced; no deadline for the offer of amnesty. I was concerned that Charles should justify his claim to omusingaship under the famous Clause (246) in the eyes of him whose gift it ultimately was: President Museveni. I said as much privately to

Charles himself, and to Syahuka-Muhindo and Ibrahim Mukonjya, taking supper with the latter two that evening – for Charles continued to eat separately, of food now prepared exclusively by his brother's wife. Yet this was Africa, they reminded me: sharp edges like deadlines and *procedures* of surrender had little place. We were preaching a mood of reconciliation, and if Charles was to be re-stooled with Kampala's full assent in the formality of his Buhikira it would be the consequence of no pat bargain.

At next day's rally at Kisinga we were to repeat the message. Kisinga is that lowland market village close against the maze of southern foothills where the tumbling Nyamugasani river levels to the plains and its final meander into Lake Edward. It was for years the funnelling-point for provisioning old Rwenzururu, capital region for the hills to the immediate north. It lies a mile or two below that mission station where Charles and Archbishop Wani met in conclave to bargain out the new diocese and the ultimate Descent, and it was there that Charles had emerged on August 15, 1982, to be driven more or less in state to Kasese. That entire region was peculiarly vulnerable to ADF assault and there had indeed taken place the abduction by ADF raiders of six children from a Christian boarding seminary, celebrated for the quality of its education, situated on the nearer side of Kisinga, a few months previously. Nothing had been heard of the innocents since. And only yesterday night the evil ones had shown their flag and fangs once more by raiding the village of Ibanda, up the Mobuku valley to the north, on this occasion killing six. God knows if the innocents of 1997 were those killers of 1998. We were therefore wary, and well soldiered. I rode once more in the second Mercedes, with Mama Christina and Charles's daughter Furaha Cristabel, a shy sixteen, single stem of the all-but-royal line, beloved of her father.

Immediately upon turning off from the pot-holed main road at Kinyamuseki, first hamlet west of the Queen Elizabeth Game Reserve, onto the murram vehicle track northwards towards the mountains, the convoy halted. The would-be king was hustled out of his Mercedes into our accompanying minibus. This was to deceive any ambushers or snipers. Two or three miles further along our cruelly rutted track, a tyre of the third of our trio of Benzes blew. Its passengers Muruli Mukasa, Minister for Peace, and the rest of our grandees, were further loaded into our own vehicle so that the Cabinet Minister (with whom

462

earlier that morning I had engaged in solemn discussion about the eventual prospects of Islam in a technological world of global villagehood) was now perched on my knee. Thus heaped we attained the boma of Kisinga and its massed concourse. Once again twenty or thirty thousand tribesfolk were assembled. Arches and banners trumpeting His Majesty Charles Wesley Irema Ngoma, Omusinga wa Rwenzururu, spanned the routes of access. Here we were a few hundred yards from the new monument to the early martyrs of Konzo patriotism, the erection of which today's opponents of Rwenzururu had striven to exploit for their own agenda; a mile or so from the forest orphanage to which I had made modest contributions; and a couple of miles from where the previous member of parliament for this contituency, Bukonzo East, namely Amos Kambere, had been erecting the Tom Stacey Primary Boarding School... until he was thrown into jail in the first weeks of President Museveni's rule.

A parading brass band of late teen-age schoolboys greeted us, executing a slow march derived of course from colonial recollection of British-trained infantry; and I, in my front row seat, and having at their very age been drilled in the movement as a Guardsman to a skill worthy of corps-de-ballet, itched to instruct them. Girls in canary yellow came on to present a song of joyous welcome, which they followed with a lament for those who had died in the (Rwenzururu) struggle and also for Charles's long years of exile – the sorrow mimed by the fingertips of the right hand resting against the cheek, and the head tilted and eyes great with grief. Dr Crispus Kiyonga now arrived, to a respectable cheer, and took his seat. We were involuntarily measuring these cheers. He would not speak at this rally: that would come on the morrow, in his very own parliamentary constituency, Bukonzo West, right against the frontier. Yet while we were weighing his relationship with these 'masses' or, rather, theirs with him, it was perfectly obvious to us that he could have not got here without passing under all those

Charles-adoring arches; and that when the 'national anthem' was called for, he would have been piercingly aware that it was only the vastly resonant *Wethu Rwenzururu* that the crowd chose to launch into – simultanously holding aloft a huge banner WELL-COME TO HIS MAJESTY. The present Member of Parliament was the boyish Apollinaris Kithende, and with characteristic pluck he told them all from the podium, 'We [Bakonzo] want only one cock to do our crowing.' Everyone got the point instantly and gave him a formidable hurrah. Moreover when Minister Muruli Mukasa, no friend of tribal kings, and a junior figure under Dr Kiyonga in the ministerial pecking order, chose to speculate into the microphone that if and when it came to people expressing their views on the 'Omusinga issue' they might well decide against (like the Banyankole), they did not like it at all.

When it came for Charles to speak there could be no escaping the fact that here was a person wholly in role, fulfilling his destiny, at ease and more than at ease; for in these – what? – two and a half days since touching earth once more in Ruwenzori he had come to assume kingship, meeting the people's adoration with his own unaffected recognition of his function for them. They wanted their Omusinga and he indeed was it. There was that blithe purity to this mutuality. Indeed, there was an 'agenda' to what he spoke of – and he covered the ground as to his own passing linkage with NALU and the present requirement to extirpate ADF and all its evils, but what eventually was taking place was his engagement with his people and theirs with him. It was the same under-running purity of the Rwenzururu Omusingaship of former times, irrespective of the ructions, lapses and conflicting ambitions in the handling of state affairs. I remember how I would say to his father half a century earlier, when Isaya was railing at this or that lack of 'development' in the mountains, that 'Poverty is purity', by which I meant there was an absolutely precious accessibility to untrammelled truth in peasant life whereby everyone had nothing more (and seldom anything less) than what was seen to be necessary for life: there was indeed no money, only the elemental barter between one neighbour and another, between one skill and another, between man and his soil, man and forest (all beholden to the spirits) – a barter like love. Such was the unspoken presumption within Rwenzururu when it took form (as one might say perhaps of

Christianity and even Marxism also); and here was the same barter at work in the gift of these people of their loyalty to Charles as king and Charles's trust in them as subjects of his kingship. They were his treasure and he theirs. There was no measurable value to this treasure, it struck me, as I listened to all these speeches and witnessed at these performances of song and dance at Kisinga: indeed, the very nullity of measurable value was the strength of us Rwenzururians. It brought to mind that passage in the apocryphal Book of Wisdom which speaks of God's placing greatest value on Man's possession of the spirit of wisdom, against which all of Nebuchadnezzar's official 'power and glory' is seen in the writer's imagination as so much gold, silver and precious stones and amounting in God's eyes to 'a grain of sand, a puddle' compared with true gnosis. The other side had all the grandeur of state, the authority, money, soldiery, structures of administration and so on, while we could scarcely buy our breakfast. What we had was intuitive and intangible; and lest I might be tempted to credit myself as a sort of conjuror amid these elfin gifts through possession of a unique awareness of them, that very evening back at the Margherita Syahuka-Muhindo passed me a succinct, forensic analysis of the interiority of Konzo identity which he had recently composed on his laptop in a thousand or so words, under the title of Embitha. Their 'Konzo identity', I noted, while fed by inner secrecy, was nonetheless inclusive of those smaller, weaker tribes within the compass of the Bakonzo's mountain-based authority: specifically the Baamba and the two Ituri pygmy groups, Bambuti and Bambuva.

And later that same evening, Syahuka-Muhindo and Ibrahimu Muhonjya and I, having come back once more to our hospice after accompanying Charles to a twilight meeting with the representatives of Bakonzo youth in the parley-building at the Buhikira-palace, were brought up sharply against the third factor, namely the horror that was the context of our presence here. The Rev Jesse Tembo, son of Isaleri Kambere, had come to tell us that at dawn that very morning the ADF had pounced on a homestead near Kitswamba, the previous day's rally venue, snatching four children, injuring the mother, and killing the father. All day at Kisinga we had been regaled by children, just as at Kitswamba: ardent, innocent, the picture of purity in spotless uniforms, each school distinguished by its colours, drilled to word-perfection in each and every stanza. Those snatched innocents of Kitswamba, now fatherless, had surely themselves performed for us the previous day. I went up to bed in furious sorrow at this phenomenon of Evil. Look how it shrieked to be recognised, in its sheer compulsion to confront by its nullity. My small bedroom opened onto a balcony ten feet above the rising slope of ground beneath, a scaleable height. Nothing intervened between that slope of hill and the mountains behind. From the balcony I peered out into the night and in my mind's eye there they were, hidden by the high grasses, waiting their opportunity. Oh, they were alive to their own evil; they fed on it, gloried in it. We are brute nullity, they are calling at us. We are apostles of despair. We are the gargoyles come down off the architraves and cornices of the mountains. We are baboon-faced, cackling, rictus-grinning. We are the *disparates* of Bosch and Goya, we are Satan's other truth, the arse-end of truth, all that's left of truth after what your lowland politicians have done with it, your tongues sticky with lies and your fingers sticky with money, and your lowland churches greasy with heavenly promises for the sake of earthly power. That is how you justify your evil, Fanehasi – do you not? – that it is honest, it pretends nothing. Can I not see you now, Fanehasi, hidden there in the pitch darkness, in the high grasses, squinting up at this little hotel, with the white man silhouetted on his balcony? It's been thirty-seven years, hasn't it, since Isaya Mukirane designated you to provide my shelter on your spur above Kitolu. Even then you knew that at the root of all this pain, this gnaw of hopelessness, was the coming of the white man, Stanley below the mountains, Stacey in the mountains, the white man of such powers and presumptions that stole away whatever it was that once gave the black man meaning, gave meaning to you and your folk in these, your mountains. Even Isaya Mukirane himself was half-sold on the white man's thinking. 'So what have you left me to be loyal to, *mzungu*? My despair. For which I will kill and burn and maim, and abduct children of my tribal blood and tongue, to twist them into the same loyalty, using white man's weapons to enforce this, to make the last blood sacrifice to these gods of the mountains not of any goat, of any fat ewe, but of men, our selves; if it so be, the whole tribe.'

Note then now how near we all were to the heartland of the old rebellion and the present rebellion, as we assembled for this final south-Rwenzururu rally at the open ground by the primary school at Mpondwe, just west of Bwera against the Congo frontier. The spurs began their tiering immediately to the north of us; the foothills mounted beyond, and the mazy landscape rose and rose towards the 'impenetrable forests' and the inaccessible declivities and steeps to the southerly inner peaks, Luigi, Stairs and Baker. The river Tako dropped out of those heights and forests and curled and gurgled two and a half miles to the west of us, making the frontier. Up its valley where cultivation gave way to forest for ever thereafter, at Kituti, and across the deep-bedded stream, was where it had all begun forty-four years before, and where I had myself returned those nine years later. What number of folk were there here now – ten thousand? Fifteen thousand? Surely Dr Kiyonga's electoral machine in his own parliamentary patch would have wished to discourage attendance? Most certainly they had so wished and acted. All our party knew it. With wonderful impudence one of the early groups of *balladiste* school kids, uniformed and rehearsed, actually sang of it, right there in front of Kiyonga himself: 'They came to us by night/They came to threaten us/"Do not go to the rally!"' Perhaps the threats had in some degree succeeded. Kiyonga would have wished no rally here at all, yet understandably had not dared to express to his President the uncomfortable truth that this figure of potential peace in the mountains was a mortal threat to his, Kiyonga's, entire political being, and that any baraza here would be a baraza for Charles as king and a shroud for him. For this was a Charles event: any coming here would come for Charles not Crispus. Yet Crispus Kiyonga must be host.

Henrietta was in black, trimmed with white. She chewed gum.

Muruli Mukasa wore his dago glasses. Kiyonga was darkly suited, Alice his wife in red. Detective Kasaija, Charles's kinsman and bodyguard-in-chief, sat immediately, but *immediately* – an arm's length – behind his charge. I was beside Mama, in her golden bandana, two along from Charles – between her and Christopher Tabaan, MP. Everyone looked worried. Somewhere among the mob before us and around us was drumming, the inner voice, half rejoicing, half warning: you never could tell. At the singing of the Rwenzururu anthem, which of us was not apprehensive? The weather was not settled.

An official in a reddy-brown felt skullcap, the colour of dried blood, listed the raft of dignitaries and petty officials present, several of whom were to speak. The selection and order of the speakers had no doubt been devised by Crispus, host. Thus we were to have his best selection of song-birds, subtly modulating their song, welcoming our 'guest of honour' as anodynely as they might, without title, without if possible much mention of his name. So we had the Minister for Peace, the No-Party Party Commissar, the Resident District gauleiter, the District Movement Chairman (Barnabas Bamusede), all Kiyonga voices, voicing their gratitude that their guest of honour, despite his having been away so long in unnecessary self-exile, despite his misjudgement as to the leadership of NALU, had returned at last in cause of what they called 'security' in the 'District'. They were unloved, the lot of them. The audience showed it. In between came the children's songs: they could not actually deny the children: and the children baited them in verse. The local figure this audience truly loved, Blasio Maate, once their District Commissioner, seated just behind me, was not called to give his speech, though he had come prepared with one. He showed it to me in typescript. It told of the long struggle of the Bakonzo for rightful recognition and indeed of my own early part in that – 'we thank Mr Tom Stacey, a white man who wakened us to realize we were backward and half slaves, that we should pull up our socks for our aid...' and it told of the true achievements of the Rwenzururu kingdom and welcomed Charles in 'rejoining your former strugglists'. But there were those of us whom it was not reasonable or possible to silence, and among them was Loice Bwamable, myself, and Yokasi Bihande, the current 'LC5' whom the voters had chosen to replace Bamusede. Loice Bwambale, the ladies' parliamentary voice, rang out with characteristic lustiness such as might be heard by those listening in the forests beyond the new No Man's Land, 'Let us all support Charles Wesley Irema Ngoma in fulfilling the covenant he has already made with the President in Kampala.' She took the microphone under a multicoloured parasol. But I chose the awning-topped podium, to give them all as sweetly as I knew how, and with reasonable concision, the story of my own and also Isaya Mukirane's first entering, by way of this place Mpondwe-Bwera, of the southern Rwenzururu heartland, and of the shaft of light and prophecy of things to come that we were bestowed with at Kituti in the furthest highlands. Gesturing that way from my perch, I noticed storm clouds mustering and picked up the first diapason of thunder. I secured a cheer or two.

Yet it was Bihande who stirred them all up in a joyful wonderment at his sheer effrontery. For Yokasi Bihande was not only impressively effective as an administrating LC5 but also the essence of straightness. With his robust straightness he had beaten at the polls his corkscrew opponent and predecessor. Bihande mixed an attractive trustfulness of his fellow men with a fearlessnesss of those he found unworthy of his trust. He entered upon a tale – another snaky fable. 'When we were young, do you remember how we went into the forest with our catapults? We felt hungry – we found something to eat. Now there's this bunch of delicious berries. But there's a big snake curled beneath it!' Laughter. 'Yet snakes don't eat berries!' Laughter. 'Why doesn't it just go away? And since it doesn't, why don't we all have done with it?' A cheer. 'If the hungry people want to feed on the berries, why, let the people feed!' A broader cheer. 'The people have the power to get what they want. Is that not the very premise of the authority of the National Resistance Movement?' Oh, they did delight in that. I could not see the big snake from where I sat, but Bihande could: he was looking right at him as he, Bihande, in effect invited the Member's own constituents so to cast their votes at the next opportunity that no amount of threat, inducement, fiddle and faddle would keep the fellow in the seat.

So Crispus came to the podium with a fistful of notes and his vulnerability showing like a preacher with his flies open. He launched off with a Lukonzo axiom about him who takes on an adversary needing to plan each and every move. The adversary he intended to refer to was of course the ADF, and the planned move to the bringing back of 'our brother' Charles to help persuade the rebels of their folly. But pretty well all of us present could not help but read Charles as his chosen adversary. And when he went on to express his appreciation of this 'brother' returning after all these years, we none of us believed a word of it. We all knew that the last thing that he wanted was Charles back here, in this role or any other. This was not an auspicious opening, and he never got his audience with him. He retailed the whole rigmarole of the Mweya exposure, and claimed he had never for a moment supposed that 'our brother' would not have an explanation, and how we should all be grateful to this brother for being so 'open' as to admit to the authorship of those injudicious NALU letters. Thus he sugared his barbs; and thus also he was by way of laying forth how this most contrary situation had come about: that here in the midst of his most intimate ground, where within half an hour's barefoot walk along the Tako valley, he was born and reared on a compound of earth and grass huts, and within half an hour on bare feet of his first school of Bwera (learning in the Lutoro vernacular), in the heart of his native constituency of Bukonzo West which he represented in the far-off national assembly, he was facing a large concourse of his very people gathered to welcome that very figure for whom his antagonism was notorious. No wonder he clutched a fistful of notes. How had he permitted this utterly foolish confrontation to occur? For he was surely no fool. On his appointment as Minister for Health, he had not lost a minute having built right here in his constituency the smartest rural hospital in the land (even if the road by which any patient might reach it was all but impassable). He took endless pains, by every tortuous route, to ensure his placemen held the strings of local authority. This parliamentary base was vital to him, and surely he knew he was not loved – not loved on the same gut grounds that Charles *was* loved. This day he could have no possible doubt that these masses were drawn here by a devotion to Charles and little doubt that here in the presence of Charles his constituents had lost their fear of him, Crispus, who could be so pilloried to his face as

to be likened to a big snake. He must now know the issue before
them was not whether this 'brother' Charles Mumbere bore any
guilt for complicity with the rebels, but whether true peace, lasting,
treasured peace such as, echoing the Psalmist, the mountains
would bring to the people, would not best be installed and
protected by kingship – and specifically *this* kingship, Charles's,
among *this* people, the Bakonzo. He was clever. Now he was
obliged to snake his way out of having been too clever by half.

He could not dodge the 'Omusinga issue'. It must, he declared,
be addressed: we must recognise the role played by Isaya
Mukirane. (That got a little burst of applause.) But no sooner had
he acknowledged the role of Isaya than he turned to the role of
Tibamwenda – and in a trice we were spotting him fabricating out
of Tibamwenda's progeny a pretender to the Konzo royal stool that
otherwise he claimed did not exist. Moreover, if any such
omusinga was to be postulated – he put it to us listeners – why, he
must be omusinga not just to such as us but to the Baamba, the
Basongora, the Banyabindi and any other tribal elements bearing
upon the territory. There would surely have to be a council of
elders of not just Bakonzo but all the small tribes to consider such

a complex matter.

So declared this Mutalingi-Konzo, from just up the valley here,
a fellow that fraction *à côté*: plausible, modern-minded,
'democratic', a word which is to imply, under the present zeitgeist,
by no means a unifying consensus as was the vision of the
Athenian *demos*, but a massed plurality. And we all now sensed the
utter division between this figure up on the podium, Crispus, and
his opponent Charles, who had yet to speak. This Crispus was of
the modern world and Charles of the ancient one: Crispus of the
white man's ethic, Charles of the black man's; white usurpers had

made Crispus, raising him out of his compound of mud and thatch and schooling him in the white man's ethic of personal advancement, wealth, property, the unending paraphernalia of vicarious identity, reinforced by the discipline of white man's diagnostic medicine, of germs and prophylaxis, and the whiteys' politics of economic gain, deferred rewards, individual advancement, each man for himself and in himself, dis-eased by the democratic premise. (Had this not grown to be the self-vaunting, self-deluding metaphysic of my skin colour?) While this Charles, Irema Ngoma, was product of a primal wholeness, *one* people, *one* lingo, *one* heaving territory, *one* scent, us-ness, Konzo, Rwenzururu, embitha, one ground of being, *ntu*; creator and creation undivided.

Thunder. We glanced north, into the immediate hills and the further mountains, where restlessness had been gathering these past two hours. It was black there. 'A council of elders of all the constituent tribal elements,' Dr Kiyonga was saying, should settle whether kingship was desirable and, if so, who might fill it. (The speaker revolved on his podium so that no part of the surrounding assembly should feel themselves overlooked; and we in our chairs and under our VIP canopy watched how that clever head, fed by the fist of notes, was supported by so markedly powerful a neck of which uncommon muscles stood out prominently above the ears.) And might not this issue, the omusingaship, make for divisiveness, eh? (A rumble of disapproval was audible, and an incipient restlessness in the great crowd gathered on the instant.) Would the raising of this issue not arouse the disapproval of central government?

At once a barracking broke out. A boo-ing swelled; the head of the enzoka up there on the little platform swung above his audience in surprised affront. And with that hostile murmuring the sky – we sensed at that moment – had come to gather above our heads, the weather spread from the mountains to sit upon us darkly. In such mood Kiyonga quit the podium; and in such mood the male rattle-dancers stamped, spun and twisted their bodies before us. The colobus-hooded one, marking all man's monkeyness and the Bakonzo's mountain-monkeyness, since this trapezing long-haired species more black and white was unique to these mountains, led the troupe. Then up stepped Muruli Mukasa in his bush jacket and uncalled-for dago shades under the lowering skies, Minister for Peace, who had not peace in his gift, and he was permitted little more than five minutes before a greater power let go the first great drops of rain. All at once the voice of Kitasamba, which is to say thunder, was heard in our midst, taking up as it were from the recent drumming of the ankle- and elbow-dancers, and the rumble of dissent that Kiyonga had evoked. I glanced north; I glanced above; all was black. The powers that belly the clouds let go their waters with a *whump*. Speakers and speech were at an end. The entire concourse skeltered for cover. They were gone. Muruli himself, to escape a soaking, scurried for the shelter of our marquee. We dignitaries alone were shielded in our places. I caught Kisaija's eye: we acknowledged the intervention of mountain deity.

Kitasamba thus emptied our boma for precisely twenty minutes, at which point his deluge abruptly terminated.

A sky of the utmost cerulean opened above us; in a matter of three minutes the entire assembly had regathered, and now – by the conjuring of the genial Bihande, LC5 – into the open space before us and at a distinctly alternative spot to the tainted podium, lo, a beefy macho-American Japanese station wagon, called a Hi-Lux, had nudged its way. The roof slid back, and out of that neat aperture, raised two or three feet above the uncountable heads of his audience, emerged the upper half of Charles Wesley Irema Ngoma, the Omusinga of the lot of them. Immediately alongside him, on the runningboard below the vehicle's open door, Charles's bodyguard, Kasaija, held aloft over his king a multicoloured umbrella, not against Kitasamba changing his mind, nor against the now jocund sunshine, but as a kind of royal canopy, a rainbow dome as a point of reaching focus, and giving him, Kasaija, the justification for his immediate protective presence. 'Oyë, oyë, oyë' Charles sang out the welcome to his masses as they echoed him back. And thus bathed in their adoration he launched off with fluent ease into his speech of which the theme was peace, unity and reconciliation. For the sake of those present who were from the army or Kampala or the non-Konzo administration he was translated sentence by sentence into English: Charles here, now, at this climactic gathering of southern Ruwenzori, his Rwenzururu, could do no wrong. Peace was naturally in his gift because he was by birth, history and inheritance of the mountains which, in fact and symbol, we had been forced to cede to those who had set themselves so cruelly against their fellows.

In Charles conducting his audience through the Mweya exposure, so in the African manner the inference rose among us all that whatever the pretensions and misjudged political agenda of Bazira's NALU, it was a movement engendered by and in the mountains and could not in that mountain factor be categorically disowned by him. He was king of the mountains, the senior mortal, and whatever the mountains were also of him. He did not say it thus: it was for us to remind ourselves. But he chaffed Kiyonga on the matter of kingship. '"What will a king do?"' he echoed his adversary. 'You are a cabinet minister, you make the rules. It is for you to tell us what we and our king may do.' Yet of course it would never be Dr Kiyonga who could tell them. It could be – already was – a mystic brief, descending from the mountains. We all knew that. Had not Kitasamba deluged off the king's opponents, or semi-opponents, plainsmen, the cheese-paring and condescending Kampala toadies, and opened this cerulean heaven for all of us to hear Charles out today? When he was done, after an hour or so, with a Wasinjya, thanks, for their attentive love, a voice from somewhere pitched off into *Rwenzururu wethu,* and from many a thousand of throats there swelled forth the first verse of the mountain kingdom's sacred tutti.

You see how in Africa there are no hard lines; not squares but circles; no finalities; not steel or concrete but clay and thatch; and men are covert motions, creviced and murked and damp, swellings in the mud. That is the manner in which, unbuckling prose, I touched upon the primality of life earlier in this story. Sure enough there are deaths, and disasters, at points in time; and births and fine flowerings. Yet what prevails in black Africa, what is at work in man, are the hidden forces, the within, the compact with fellows and the earth; the tongue, the land, the drum and drumming; the ancestral spirits on whom fate hangs, rather than on the ordinance of governments and the grand exterior functions Cartesian man seeks to prescribe for his destiny and meaning. I could readily end this book here, and let my Western reader dream out the further narrative of the *Tribe*, this race and place; for since that concourse at Mpondwe on the Congo border there have been at this time of writing no seismic rifts or cataclysms to switch or shunt the evolving narrative. I have brought you this far in my own way, partial, erratic, half blind, into their imperfect wholeness, their holiness, to the degree to which I have been myself admitted and capable of recording. All the main players are with us still.

Yet you will want to know:

Has Charles been formally proclaimed Omusinga, king, of all his people?

Have the ADF and the forces of evil been extirpated from the mountains?

Have the Bakonzo people returned to their ancestral slopes?

Could I, maimed explorer, from some high scarp, look now on the long peace of the land, 'upon her hills and hollows, and amid them other hills, myriad, intricately watered, quilted by cultivation, by habitance'?

Whose now are the incredible snows, the glaciers and the clusters of fogged peaks – the old gods? Or have they all gone to the great contaminator, blighted Mammon, the tourist industry?

To all of these I can now provide answers of a sort, and, quite summarily – but I pray not superficially – you shall have them.

xxxiv

The *Disparates* Quelled

That very next morning, Sunday November 29, 1998, I was roused shortly before seven a.m. with a rap on my door at the Margherita. I opened it to the bodyguard of the Honourable Dr Crispus Kiyonga, Minister of Health, whose compliments he presented with a proposal that I join the Minister and his lady at breakfast there and then. For the couple were about to take the road back to Kampala. Kiyonga, his Munyankole wife Alice and I had the mountain-facing verandah of Kasese's only hotel worthy of the name to ourselves.

It was evident, Crispus said, that Charles was to play a role of significance among the people. I was someone, he continued, who it seemed had the ear of Charles. So he urged upon me two things: that when Charles returned to the United States (as it was presumed he very shortly would), he undertook studies of sufficient weight to enable him to fulfil the functions that might come his way as usefully as possible. Next: would I not use my influence in favour of Charles perceiving his future role as figurehead of the Baamba no less than of the Bakonzo?

I could not be but intrigued by this dual injunction, and that I should have been called so early and urgently to receive it. I was on easy terms with Dr Kiyonga. I respected (and respect) his abilities. I knew he had weaned himself from tribal thinking long ago; he had signed up to the prevailing civilisation, which was mine. I understood him, and pre-forgave him half his misdeeds, fictitious or otherwise. He was a senior national functionary at a Tudor court: life expectancy was short. I guess he knew that this was my broad comprehension. Perhaps he perceived me as a post-colonial nostalgist who sought to be reassured that at least something of what we British had got going all those years ago was still of worth: the race-to-race trust, for instance, black to white. Maybe there was some truth to that. Yet what I had helped to start, of course, was nothing colonial or post-colonial: it was the mountain Kingdom Charles inherited.

After he had swept off that morning to Kampala in his official car, with his escort, it seemed to me that Kiyonga's breakfast brief to me was intended to persuade Charles into staying safely off-stage in never-never land – to wit, America – as long as possible. The motive of the second injuction was more complex: that in so far as Charles might seek to frame his claim to 'cultural' leadership under the famous constitutional clause, he did so *multi*-culturally, in a context where tribal divisiveness could be exploited to the discredit of the omusinga premise. Now, at a certain level, a relatively sophisticated level, such a division very likely *could* be exploited. The Baamba of the mountain's north-west (where the rest of us were awaited on the morrow) were a significant ethnic group, maybe some fifty thousand, with their own language and awkward territory in the Rift, occupying a District in which they numbered a majority. Consequently they had their own political aspirants, some of whom Kiyonga surely knew and presumed he could provoke into resisting Konzo domination. And while from its very inception the Kingdom of Rwenzururu had as its declared aim and endeavour to include the Baamba with the Bakonzo, the smaller tribe's allegiance to Rwenzururu was scarcely as urgent as their fellows'.

Yet more privily, more intimately, unspokenly – either aloud or even silently – there is that in the relationship which naturally bonds these two peoples.

The analogy is that between the English and the Welsh, which race supplies a quarter of my own blood. In history, the English have fought the Welsh and, winning, have narrowed the other's territory to a fragment of what it once was. For centuries the English have dominated an island which was once – approximately speaking – all Welsh; English has thus become the prevailing tongue, if not exclusive, and the language of government; those who call themselves English have long comprised the majority. With all this the Welsh have been at first obliged to comply, and after a while, in Man's perpetual nuzzling and foraging for peace of heart, content to comply, and in time and in no small measure proud to comply. For in the name of the English the island grew to greatness and carried the Welsh with it. Moreover the Welsh knew that however obvious and obnoxious the subjections and impositions, however unrelenting the authority (in cultural metaphor) of iron over bronze, the English from the start had drawn so much from the artistic, conceptual and mystic bounty of the Welsh, and had continued to do so, finding among the Welsh the preponderance of their musicians, seers and poets to this very day. And while students from the middle class protested with induced violence and pouter-breasted political arrivistes demanded pastiche authority in a regional Welsh capital, the mass of the folk in their midnight instincts acknowledged the peace and fruits of an ancient symbiosis. Moreover, just as the Baamba provided the Konzo with many of their tribal *ababandwa*-doctors, spirit mediums-*abathawa* and animal and vegetable medicines and bequeathed their cosmology of mountain spirits to the Bakonzo, so did the Bambuti and Bambuva pygmies of Ituri draw from the Baamba their language, their metal tools and sole access to the world beyond the forest, while bringing to the Baamba the same forest's animal and vegetable secret treasures.

This tiered allegiance, I venture, was invisible and true; Kiyonga's tactic, plausible and wrong.

Meanwhile, that Sunday we were to worship God. There is no call to ask which God. St Paul's Cathedral, Kasese, provided space comfortably for a mere 600 souls. A new cathedral, thrice its size, also of mud, was being built on a hill above. The faithful of the Anglican communion, forming the largest Christian following by far among mountain-dwelling Bakonzo, had to make do with their present confined forum of devotion.

On the face of it, ours was a service of thanksgiving for the homecoming – albeit temporary – of Charles. But what was also being offered up to the overarching Nyamuhanga was a tangle of complexity such as only Ruwenzori could contrive. As we have seen, our Mukonzo Bishop Zebedee, the first ever, owed his diocese and by derivation his office to the fact of Rwenzururu's twenty-year defiance. Yet the stance that Zebedee had taken concerning the Omusinga issue was not a lofty detachment but hostility. He customarily took pains to point out that there was no tradition of kingship among the Bakonzo. Such a stance, if ungrateful, was understandable in one who sought to number among his diocesan flock not only its overwhelming Bakonzo but also plainland Batoro and Basongora, whom his competitor, the Roman Catholic bishop, not a true Konzo, was proselytising vigorously. (We had already attended upon the Roman Catholic hierarchy the previous evening.) Very likely our bishop went along with the fashionable disdain of 'tribalism', and sought to reconcile to his altar those minorities which had felt the sting of Rwenzururu's exclusive patriotism. But now that the current of local affairs had taken this unprecedented turn, the Bishop's stance would bar him from bringing much influence on the omusingaship should it become a formal reality. It already was, unmistakably, a reality of formidable allegiance.

Our cathedral was utterly packed. The girls in their laundered dresses in church-school violet, rocked their hymns of open harmony in ardent veneration of this historic moment. What missionary, bringing to Africa north Atlantic Protestant hymnology, could have guessed how the Holy Spirit would come to rock a hymn thus among the converts? Here were pew upon tight pew of schoolgirls in Sunday uniform, effortlessly drilled by the sacred beat required of humanity to breathe, to pump the blood, to walk, to be cradled as long-unweaned infants on mama's back as she treads or works the hoe. Now by implicit extension being rocked in virtual adulthood, melded in worship and holy antiphony: praise, and plea of mercy. The words of the Lukonzo hymns could well have been first written down by Charles Wesley himself – I could not tell.

Our own Charles Wesley Irema Ngoma was seated to the left of the altar, near to the bishop, and we few – his somnambulist consort (in raspberry for God), his mother, brother Tabaan Kibanzanga and I – were placed beside him. After the prayers, confession, canticles, and responses, it was for Kibanzanga, their MP, to place this act of worship in its context, since Charles himself was to confine his address to the bare identity of Omusingaship and peace. When I was unexpectedly signalled to speak to the congregation from the altar step I drew my brief exhortation out of the primal call of the psalmist's heart, 'Come, seek his face,' and its antiphon 'Your face, Lord, do I seek,' which I had been reading that very morning after breakfast with Crispus Kiyonga; and from there I could move at once to the Christian faith of our Charles Wesley's father, which I personally witnessed, and to the naming of that father's son after one of the great revivalists of the Christian message in England. Father and son alike would say today to everyone in and of our mountains (I said) that the times spoken of by the prophet Micah had arrived, to beat swords into plowshares and spears into pruning hooks. I gave my little homily in English, which remained untranslated, doubtless missing most of those present. When, after a hymn and a creed, the bishop rose to preach, they had the Word in their own tongue.

Bishop Zebedee's text was that opening sally of St Paul's letter to his Corinthian flock urging them to cease their bitter disunion. 'I appeal to you brothers and sisters, by the name of our Lord Jesus Christ, that all of you be in agreement and that there be no divisions among you, but that you be united in the same mind and the same purpose... Has Christ been divided?' Perhaps he was speaking to the Omusinga-ites and the Kiyonga-ites, perhaps to the ADF and those countless hill-dwellers who had fled them... That is the very passage of Paul's letter, oddly enough, that makes one of the two references in Holy Scripture to 'Crispus', himself one of the saint's earliest converts and an official of the synagogue at Corinth. In his letter Paul goes on to lay stress on the simplicity of his message 'Christ crucified,' invoking Isaiah as witness to the irrelevance of human wisdom, 'No eye has seen,' Paul quotes from the prophet, 'nor ear heard, nor human heart conceived what God has prepared for those who love him' – a calm solemnity that follows immediately upon Isaiah's outburst to God, 'O that you would tear open the heavens and come down, so that the mountains would quake at your presence... to make your name known to your adversaries, so that the nations might tremble at your presence!' Where there are mountains, dear friends, deity is due.

We were in the quake zone theologically and geographically. Meanwhile, at the altar steps a live heifer was now auctioned enthusiastically on behalf of the new unfinished cathedral, and various other gifts of natural produce, including a tray of forty eggs which the successful bidder presented to me. Immediately after the service we climbed to the site of the new cathedral, cruciform and vast on its hilltop. (Rival Christianities in Africa were building cathedrals in the late 20th century as European navies were building dreadnoughts in the late 19th century.) There was I, still with my forty eggs, when I was reunited with Seylversta Mukirane, *confrère ancien*, for whom earlier that morning I had despatched a resourceful Konzo lad on his motorbike, up the Maliba valley northeastwards. We embraced – what else? If in my life there are good threads in the tapestry, Seylversta is one of them.

As the morning was Christian, the afternoon was Muhammadan. At the parleyhouse in the grounds of the Buhikira, Ibraham Muhonjya had assembled a deputation of thirty or forty delegates from the Islamic community to outpour to their Omusinga the pains of the persecution they had endured since the first assault on the region by the forces of the ADF exactly two years previously. Here was Hajji Muhonjya in his Zanzibari taqia, intimate and cousin of the Omusinga, to ensure that this minority let go the voice of their tribulation. For since that invasion, Muslim Bakonzo had taken the brunt of governmental vengeance. Several of those present were wives of citizens of the District who had been swept up by soldiery or police in response to the assault of November 1996 for no better reason than that they were Muslim. Ever since the menfolk had been held in one remote jail or another without charge or prospect of release.

To march the full borders of his demesne, our small king and his party, heavily guarded, was lastly to head for Bundibugyo. The road journey from Fort Portal to Bundibugyo, which had taken me an easy hour in 1954 and 1963, now demanded an entire and arduous day in either a lorry or a four-by-four, pitted as it was and gashed by water runnels and ever vulnerable to ambush by the dark enemy. Thus, at Kasese airstrip that Monday morning we embarked aboard our Yugoslav 20-seater and rose into high cloud to cross the range diagonally at the northern end somewhere above Karangura into whose forested heights the askaris of this Charles's great-grandfather Ruhandika had spirited the child Kasagama, last thread of the Batoro's royal line. We floated above the spine of the range in wispy cloud at the altitude of its highest peaks, I straining south for the celestial splendour of immaculate desolations, of H M Stanley's organ prose with all his Welsh stops out. Naturally it was all wrapped in leaden mist.

Our dinky plane, making a toy of the world, swooped in a tight arc from 12,000 feet to deposit us in a clearing in teeming woodlands of the lower Lamia valley. The strip had been hacked out by troops some miles below and beyond the marooned provincial centre of Bundibugyo, capital of the District which the Baamba share, a little better than equally, with Bakonzo and a flitting population of forest pygmies. Memory of this place, my own earliest landfall on Ruwenzori, was of openness and light. Yet here all was cramped and murked by growth and wariness and steep dark tracks. Drums greeted us, and ululation, as Charles Irema Ngoma, the Drums' Keeper, stepped out. We were hustled into the military trucks and, by a grossly ill-maintained ribbon of primal road, crawled in convoy to where the townlet lay, half an hour above. Here was all a-jumble. Only when we had been corralled into a council chamber and called to prayer did we touch – for that moment – a kernel of tranquillity. This place Bundibugyo clamped between mountains and forest, between one country's supposed jurisdiction and another's, was not merely marooned by its virtual deprivation of links with the world beyond, but also knew itself to be under siege by the rebel ADF, a siege maintained both from the upper and lower forests and – dreadfully – from *within* this blighted populace. Cowering encampments of refugees from the mountains scabbed this lowland community, with numbers that would soon rise to one hundred thousand souls. Even in their encampments the pitiable refugees were not spared raids, abductions and gratuitous killings at the hands of the rebels. It was a haunted place, of soldiery and spies, nothing of permanence, nothing whatsoever of peace.

The struggling Resident District Commissioner – representative of a government of a country all but severed from this enclave – had issued a typed-up 'Programme' as a frail claim to order amid weltering confusion and despair. 'Subject: ' it ran across the top, 'Welcoming Charles Wesly [sic] Mumbere to Bundibugyo District (Son of the Soil)'. It comprised seventeen items and flagged the speeches of no fewer than eight local dignitaries before the Son of the Soil himself might walk to the podium and do his stuff. Before all this was to occur in open air, here in the council chamber perhaps the crucial encounter for this region of the mountains was already taking place: Konzo elders gathered to examine this so-called Irema Ngoma on whether he really had played a part in the generation of evil that had so terribly befallen them. Chairman of this inquisition was none other than his own uncle, George Kahigwa, sibling of Mama Christina, he who with his father Samwiri had taken me in on my first night in these mountains all but half a century earlier. Good steady George. Now he quizzed this aggrandised nephew, with his load of titles, as to exactly what complicity he might have had with the ADF or its NALU complement. This was to prove the sharpest grilling to which Charles had yet been subjected. Uncle George Kahigwa was the senior elder of the entire community, and given his intimate blood link took upon himself to probe for the truth of it. Charles was in fettle now and answered well. The air was cleared. Our party and the elders next moved in a swarm to the grave of Kawamara, the Baamba's leader in the rebellion, to honour his spirit; thence we swept on to the boma, the crowds, the drumming and our covered stand. Once again the speaker's podium which was decorated with Rwenzururu's colours. As to the unfolding of the programme it need be said only that the speakers dwelt on the severity of tribulation that the guerillas were relentlessly visiting upon the people. Baamba were numbered among speakers and crowd alike, and the issue of Omusingaship was muted. Charles, Son of the Soil, *was* honoured here; spoke cleanly and strongly; was not hero-worshipped. What I have written a few pages earlier concerning the symbiosis of the Baamba with Bakonzo was reflected by what we were witnessing.

For myself, I had already been greeted among the elders, and by none more warmly than by George Kahigwa himself. Yet it was George's younger brother, Ibrahimu Ndyanabaïsi, whom I most urgently sought – he who had been at my side throughout both of the earlier journeys in the mountains. George vouchsafed that Ibrahimu was not at all strong these days and he did not know whether he would have been able to get to the meeting, since he lived a good day's walk from this site. I did ache for Ibrahimu; and felt sure that he would have heard of my return to Ruwenzori two and a half years previously and of my intention to see him then – a hope stubbed by the condition of the road – and of my likely presence now. From my seat under the dignitaries' marquee I scanned faces. Then my gaze drifted to the mountains behind, as I had first seen them and been drawn into them as a young man. They came and went and came again: throughout all the interminable Programme the patrols of mist never rested.

When all was done and with urgent obedience to our UPDF protectors I was pushing through the mob to my vehicle, suddenly a voice said my name. No further than three paces from where I had hesitated, a frail old fellow, half-hoary, was greeting me: the sheer light brimming in his face pleaded recognition. Ibrahimu! The embrace was joined. Under thin cloth (for he wore a jacket, with a tie) I felt the thinner arm, wasted by more than age: two old hearts leaned on one another; and then the shouts of my keepers demanding my immediate embarkation dragged me from him. I had not time even to unhitch my camera or to find the £50 note that I had pocketed for this very encounter. Yet some other fellow there – I know not who – had a camera in hand. I bid him, 'Snap us!' and he did.

At the airstrip, George was bidding us adieu. 'Ibrahimu was there,' I said. 'Take this for him. Please see it is turned into shillings.' When I was first in Bundibugyo a shilling here was silvery coin with a hole in it for string, pockets being rare; it bought five eggs and was equal of an English shilling, twenty to the pound. Paper now, it took two thousand such abstractions to buy five eggs, while my proferred red note, bearing the wigged head of the Bank of England's gatekeeper in 1694, would but lift Ibrahimu's annual cash income by half as much again. Six months later, revisiting, I found him in Kampala, in the household of his nephew Christopher Tabaan, MP, and all at once we were equally young.

That Bundibugyo rally was Charles's last throw as King-that-was and King-to-be on this revisitation to his kingdom. That very evening from Kasese airstrip I flew on to Entebbe in the same aircraft, and thence that night to Gatwick. The next day saw Charles back in Kampala and at once into conclave with the Presidential office on means of following through the initiative and his appeals to fellow Konzo darkening the forests with their Kalashnikovs and self-breeding deeds of hate. A Task Force was formed under Syahuka-Muhindo's guiding hand, supposedly to implement tactful amnesty and resettlement of those Bakonzo of the ADF who might be ready to renounce their life of terror. Charles, for his part, found himself widely perceived in Uganda as heir to tribal leadership in his mountains. I had played my part in this by rolling an article or two into Uganda's principal English language daily, *The New Vision*. Charles was swept off for a courtly visit to Ronnie Mutebi, Kabaka of Buganda, at his palace at Mengo; tribal royalty to tribal royalty. Yet no Presidential endorsement of Charles's role was

forthcoming. He had no money and precious little organisation, nothing but the manifest devotion of hundreds of thousands of his people. Moreover, he was intent on returning to America in renewed pursuit of the chimera of further education on some such contrived discipline as Business Administration, to be financed by the Uganda government. He was still a pupil-to-be at 48. By the time he got aboard his plane, via Europe, for Washington DC, in mid-January 1999, wrangling over the financial support he might receive, once back in the US, from a strapped Ugandan exchequer had cost him much of the prestige he had won in presidential circles by his performance among his people.

The New Vision, Thursday, December 3, 1998   27

PEOPLE

Through Mumbere, the government can get the allegiance of the Bakonzo," Stacey says

An English orator for the Bakonzo

By Kahangi Kabeye

TWENTY-three year-old Tom Stacey wanted to write a book about Africa, so he planned a mission to cross the width on foot. With his good friend from Cambridge, Mike Edwards, they started off on the Alitacia coast in the west and travelled into the interior.

They passed through both Congos, Gabon, Cameroon, the Gold Coast [now Ghana], Ivory Coast, back to the Congo, crossed the border at Kasese, and then onto the Rwenzori Mountains.

Ultimately, he saw was to study the people living in the mountains, because no one had done it before. Then he met James Mukirane, the only leader in the whole region, and Stacey became deeply involved in the affairs of ...

It is three years on as I write these words. The players are still on the stage; the gods still in the mountains. The Bakonzo highlanders have lately returned to their spurs and little farms, where here and there I have visited them. The rebels are seemingly broken and have scuttled away into the shabby towns of eastern Congo, leaving their record of wickedness in and beneath the mountains Uganda-side. Some of their surviving abductees have crept home, dazed and strange. To a few of the ADF's intervening atrocities I have made reference, in mourning, as they occurred during the writing of this book. Sometimes revulsion at their crimes swept the whole Ugandan nation, and even peeked out of the columns of the press of an outside world long numbed to mass suffering in Africa - as when in 1999 raiders from the ADF, seeking to abduct youngsters, set a mixed-tribe school afire in Kabarole district and thus murdered 87 children in a single torching. The Ugandan army's newly designated Mountain Brigade probed the highlands and upper forest edge in missions of search-and-destroy on both sides of the international frontier. Such operations were possible since for the past several years Uganda has effectively made the region of Congo lying north-west of Lake Edward and the Semliki valley its own military colony, in league with compliant political leaders – currrently, in our ethnic territory, a Konzo from Mutwanga named Mbusa Nyamwisi. There is valuable timber to be slipped in from Ituri by and for the senior soldiers and their associates in authority in Kampala. Gold ore is likewise to be got from Bunia, west of Lake Albert, in Hima territory. Uganda's presence across a vast swathe of north-western Congo has enriched Ugandans: Uganda's soldiery has fought Rwanda to hold on to that control. The troops of both countries had originally established themselves in territory comprising half of the vast Congo state, originally in the mid 1990s as allies of Laurent Kabila's rebellion against Joseph Mobutu's thirty-year dictatorship. As presidents of the Congo neither Laurent Kabila nor his son Joseph, who succeeded his murdered father, could assemble the power to dislodge them. Meanwhile, some 11,000 Zimbabwean troops, invited in by Kinshasa, have been holding the Rwandese back from mineral-rich Katanga and also Kasai with its industrial diamonds – to which Zimbabwe has been freely helping itself.

Charles's personal intervention that week of November-December 1998 was indeed followed by a trickle of defections from the rebels but also a series of ferocious assaults ordered by high command as if to defy the Omusinga's intervention. Ten days after our departure from the region a force of some two hundred rebels attacked the technical college at Kichwamba near Fort Portal, killing eighty-seven pupils and abducting fifty. Such terrible depredations, especially of schools, continued throughout 1999. In December of that year the rebels boldly attacked Fort Portal's Katojo prison, killing two and abducting no fewer than 355. By the year's end the depopulation of the highlands was virtually total. Marooned Bundibugyo was worst persecuted. The little town, ringed with its camps, now containing 105,000 refugees in all, was targeted repeatedly, the rebels enjoying ready access through the lowland forest. They raided for food, for fuel, for tools, for weaponry, for sheer lust of killing, burning, slashing flesh, maiming. It was as a ravening plague, a terror virus, linking the ADF with three other rebel groups in that region of the Dark Continent - Mai Mai, Interahamwe and Kony. Cholera slouched back to Bundibugyo, into the camps, a demon of old, Kasinini. The continuing terror had little or nothing to do with the Bakonzo of Ruwenzori, or political Rwenzururu or any restoration of a Konzo kingship. Bakonzo rebels were still operating in the mountains; that we knew. Fanehasi Kisokeronio was still active, yet we had heard imprecise report that he and his immediate following, numbering around ninety, operated independently of the non-Konzo leadership of the ADF and were pillaging separately. With high courage Charles's brother, Christopher Tabaan Kibanzanga, together with Yokasi Bihande, Kasese's LC5, and Zostine Kiongozi, journalist son of Kisokeronio by an early union, had on their own initiative arranged to be secretly spirited into the forest above Mutwanga for a parley, after a five-hour ascent by night, with a rebel delegation acting on Zostine's father's orders. This daring was done in the hope of persuading what remained of the Bakonzo nucleus of the futility of their savagery and of shaping some method of quittance. Overtly it was fruitless, and the UPDF blunderingly shot and killed the two go-betweens of this encounter; yet I suppose such legates of the outer world, penetrating the rebels' forest and in the after-glow of Charles's triumphant lowland visit, could only show up the pointlessness of their campaign. By and large that 'Task Force' of Syahuka-Muhindo was frustrated by those close to the President – those whose chief intent was for Charles to be denied any credit if peace approached.

December 1999 saw two developments which over time would prove decisive. The UPDF's Mountain Brigade, already referred to, was established by Brigadier James Kazini, who (as we have noted had grown up with his Musongora mother in the shadow of Ruwenzori and was familiar with the Lukonzo tongue. The other was the signing in Nairobi of a peace accord between Presidents Museveni of Uganda and Omar Bashir of the Sudan, under the presiding guidance not, this time, of the Norwegians but of ex-President Jimmy Carter of America and his mediating secretariat, the Carter Centre. This blessed act of intervention cut the flow to the rebels of funds and weaponry from Khartoum.

As for myself in London, amid the ten thousand things and the organisation of the looming pilgrimage from all over Britain towards Canterbury for the Millennial hour, the same Ruwenzori hands of old held mine, and mine, as ever, held theirs. The affairs of the mountains, of men and nature, flowed as usual through my office. Charles had returned to Washington with his only offspring, Furaha Joyce Cristobel, 16. Furaha's right to free schooling in the US was jeopardised by her marginal illegitimacy. On Charles's (and Furaha's) behalf I pleaded with the US authorities African traditional practice in the context of his kingly role, and satisfied those lenient folk as to its arcane logic. Charles was shortly to move

households to Harrisburg, Pennsylvania, whose expatriate community included another distinguished Konzo fugitive, the Reverend Nelson Kuule, and his jolly family. To me it seemed desirable in every way that Charles should follow through his role as peace-maker in the mountains, not least to maintain in the President's mind the usefulness of his authority. With this in mind, I dropped in on Charles and his daughter Furaha and partner Henrietta in Harrisburg in early June, 1999. The Uganda government had failed to fulfil its promises to fund Charles's further education. So with an extra mouth to feed - Furaha's - the fragment of family was finding life a struggle and Charles was locked anew into his hospital shifts. In August, briefly back in Uganda to attend the wedding of Ronnie Mutebi, Kabaka of Buganda, I snatched the chance to revisit the mountains and assess the urgency for Charles's return in the cause of peace and the consolidation of his future role. After tapping tribal-wide opinion, and closeting myself with one or two in government, including the Minister for Peace, Muruli Mukasa, I returned to London convinced that Charles should go home to Ruwenzori instantly or risk losing the core of what he had won. I wrote him a detailed report, hoping to persuade him that his notion that one day the President would spontaneously invite him back in his royal role, all expenses paid, was fantasy. Formal acceptance of his Omusingaship under the constitutional provision would come only as a consequence of manifest and sustained popular pressure, and that would require Charles to be there. Such pressure alone would persuade Museveni to override Crispus Kiyonga's Iago role and have the issue put to a decisive test. To forestall Charles's fears of being unable to support himself, I put in train the setting up of an 'Omusinga Trust' to receive contributions from supporters and income from the efficient management of Charles's patch of real estate in Kasese town. Meanwhile, I would personally stump up for the air ticket.

So I mailed him with a 6,500-word report on September 3, 1999. Our king was not responsive. I watched him withdraw into a weary disdain. 'I will think about it,' he wrote to me. Already I am Omusinga, was what I read in his reaction. Who's to say I'm not? Regard my writing paper, my royal crest, lion and colobus, spear and pruning hook. (Who is this ex-colonial Mzungu to tell me what to do and how to play my hand?) I go to my bed a king, I rise a king. I go to work a king. Assiduously I work my shifts, pushing trolleys, swabbing floors, disinfecting flat surfaces. They know they can depend on me, the administrators, the doctors, surgeons, anaesthetists. They are white and I am black, one among the many blacks. Some of these fellow blacks are undependable, get drunk, smoke hash, get this woman and that woman. I am not thus. Among these American whites and American blacks I am one more Third World black, lucky to be here, at the hub of the First World, an adopted black, First Name *Charles*, Middle Initial *W.*, Family Name *Mumbere*, ever grateful for the opportunity of assimilation into the exclusivity of the United States of America. I reveal to them nothing of my further names, Irema Ngoma, Kibanzanga, Omusinga waRwenzururu, which comprise me truly, as I truly comprise my people, on their spurs, beneath their high forests, who wait for me, if need be for ever since I their King, versed in kingship, am their King's son and heir, dependable from earliest childhood, was taught my writing and my grammar by Yosifati School Band, was commended by him and by my father, King and also school teacher, strict in all his standards, shaping me as his successor so that when he died - of a heart attack, of nothing but a heart attack - I could be instantly *King* though I was scarcely fourteen, and from the age of eighteen ruled my people with full authority (a fuller authority of kingship than any such king in Uganda or Congo) for twelve years, whereupon at my own discretion and upon my own provisions I abdicated. Yet they did not hold to those provisions, those republicans and autocrats (who come and who go), so that my people called for their King to return, called and clamoured so that even the autocrats (of a crook Kampala government which disregards its promises) had to call me back. And instantly I was king, visibly so: they saw me - single of mind, undeniable, not truly challengeable, however they may presume to qualify my role with their constitutional niceties, or seek to starve me of money. Did I not grow up to be king, and reign as king, without 'money'? Yet I collect my wages at my hospital here, in this ever alien city, I collect them carefully, every dime and cent, and pool these wages with those of this lady of my fancy from my own continent, who is halfway familiar with the expectations of my people; and when I shed my hospital overalls, and get back by bus and subway to my four-room flat, I am in my Buhikira, Palace: I am, and operate as, Omusinga, King, answering my correspondence, issuing my pronouncements, upholding my royal right which, if you insist upon a word, is divine.

So this long paper from Tom Stacey Musabuli, as my father would say – yes, a loyal-meaning friend, yet white; familiar with our mountains, with a little of our language and a knowledge of our customs yet scarcely subject to our gods; listened to perhaps too readily being the clever writer of books about us and our mountains and other things – I shall, as I have told him, think about it, turn it over, from my uniqueness and godly right as King, and therefore not beholden in the last analysis to our own will but to the will of our Lord Kitasamba or of Christian Nyamuhanga. Are we kings, of the divine authority with which our people (on heaven's behalf) have invested us - or else we would not be taken or accepted as kings at all - are we to be responsible by our own devising for generating money to support us, or for fabricating the structures of our authority? These are ordained - others will see to it...

Now we will sleep in our inexpensive kingly bed beside this lady nurse of ours, who accepts us in our flesh; and in the morning we shall write to Tom Stacey *aka* Kalambalangeya, colobus-pelt wearer, to enquire of him in London the name and address of the company which provides the regalia of the royalty of his own country, England, for us to confer with them as to our own needs in respect of ebitswero, how we shall be caparisoned for the affairs of State.

XXXV

Kitasamba Draws the Line

By early 2000 the rebel forces in the mountains were significantly less active. Starved of funds and recruits and bereft of expectation, they were driven - may we not suppose - by little else but the sullen will of their leaders, and by self-compounding guilt. Once we men are convinced of our irredeemability, we subsist in a vortex of evil and evil's companions, fear and self-revulsion. No fellow man can rescue us from all this; and if God shall work among the lost, it shall be by other works of his creation: by that of tangency which is pure; by the essential beauty in the creative act; mountains, children.

In London in April 2000, hearing by report laughter of children from the repopulated spurs of the southern heartland, and putting aside the other things - the measuring out of my life in coffee spoons, the winding of it in balance sheets - I seized a few days to ascend anew the region of Kitolu, for the first several miles by the very road I myself initiated in 1963 and after that by foot, in the company of Zostine Kiongozi (whose father Fanehasi Kisokeronio, you will recall, had kraaled me in this very region during my frustrated mediation), and Syayipuma Augustine from Ibanda. We were to seek out my other, briefer, host of that distant year, Ndambireki Gerisone (which is to say Garrison) who would become Isaya Mukirane's Minister for Natural Resources, and who I had heard from his cousin, Syahuka-Muhindo, had now recovered his old home. All about us on this and neighbouring spurs there was man's cultivation renewed, fruit – plantain groves, root crops, grain crops. The mud walls were patched, roofs re-thatched, the compounds' earth swept. Did not the very streams between each spur rejoice? Children in their scores had assembled on a slope above the hut Ndambireki and I conferred in, awaiting me to re-emerge and greet them, the first white many had yet clapped eyes on, though most knew my name from their grandparents and some had glimpsed me addressing Charles's Mpondwe rally.

This afternoon, then, after my open-air lecturette to them on the history of their own spurs down to the death three years earlier of their own Israel - Isaleri Kambere, Senior Church Elder, Jacob and Moses of their exile – they clustered and clamoured about me with their exercise books and progress reports on all their subjects of study and qualities of conduct, which were Writing, Reading, Number and Maths, English Oral, English Reading, General Knowledge, Drawing, Rhymes, Games, Cleanliness, Punctuality, Responsibility, Sharing. On the point of my departure the head pupil, or she who was top in Oral English, made a speech of thanks and asked what I might wish from them: she meant, from the produce they were re-growing there. I said, Please bring me Batulomayu Kasiraho. Instantly, in laughter, they fled away like birds to be the first to find him, and twenty minutes later all but bore him to me on their wings to where his lateral path joined my descending path. A tree bearing apricots grew there, where he and I, old men, could sit and share again our recollection and our prophecy. The place the children chose for us was tilted, beautiful, looking out from the myriad hills in sunlight above the valley of the Rubiriha upon the usual infinity of plain and lake 2,000 feet beneath; and from this semi-paradise, this ex-rebel runner-judge and I reviewed the evil lurking still in the forest above us and in the politics below us.

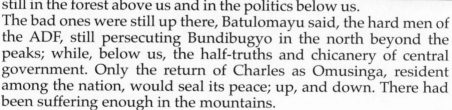

The bad ones were still up there, Batulomayu said, the hard men of the ADF, still persecuting Bundibugyo in the north beyond the peaks; while, below us, the half-truths and chicanery of central government. Only the return of Charles as Omusinga, resident among the nation, would seal its peace; up, and down. There had been suffering enough in the mountains.

In the mountains, suffering enough. Gadfly assaults persisted through that year, 2000, yet dwindling. Spur by spur, protected by their own militia and sometimes by the Mountain Brigade, peasant communities began to re-occupy their highland farms. A poll taken at the President's request by a demographer and social anthropologist of Makerere university, Kabann Kabananukye, found that 86 per cent of the Bakonzo *and* the Baamba favoured the idea of a collective Ruwenzori omusingaship, in the implicit presumption of Charles

Irema Ngoma filling that role. That he had not been installed, and no procedures for it were in place, were perhaps why the local vote for the President that February was shaky. Three weeks later, in mid-March 2001, early one night, three covered trucks entered Kasese town, pulling up sharply at the main street's southern end. Armed men leapt out. They opened fire without discrimination on anyone in sight, gunned down eleven - Bakonzo and Batoro among the dead - and then in blind destructiveness set fire to thirty-seven stationary cars. On a signal, they leapt back aboard their trucks and roared southwards out of town, neither they nor their vehicles ever to be traced. It was the weirdest incident, scarcely explicable. But in Kampala, Dr Kiyonga at once announced it to be the work of the Omusinga movement in league with the ADF, and nudged the President towards the same presumption. Though the ADF possessed no vehicles - being forest men, mountain renegades - and no gain for the Omusinga's cause by such an atrocity being conceivable, it was made the pretext for the Kampala-directed army, police and RDC to arrest key figures from among Charles's civilian supporters in Kasese and hold them without charge and without revealing where. Notable among these was Godfrey Kabbyanga, well known to me, a young man of ability and uprightness, debonair, head of Kasese's Youth Movement and one of the five Trustees-in-waiting of my blocked Omusinga Trust. Godfrey was held for several weeks, without light, in a space too cramped for him to stand, brought out for interrogation, tortured (his left arm broken), and released uncharged but broken like his arm, a shadow of himself. Charles in Harrisburg and I in London were at once in touch to defend him from false witness; to uphold the truth as best we could. Christopher Tabaan, MP, in Kampala held a press conference to rebut Kiyonga's insinuation and the President's misguidance. My friends supposed the entire affray to have been dreamed up and concocted by those same forces that immediately thereafter organised the retribution, which was its purpose. I do not know.

Who was there in Kasese or Kampala to hear the voices of the children of the mountains, the voices of primal innocence, the innocents, the tutelary spirits? There are always those with ears to hear. What have I been writing of, in these many pages? Not politics. Not votes. Not guns. Not speeches; charge and counter-charge. Not even of kings and presidents and constitutions. My trinitarian theme has been the mountains, the people, and what has bound the two of them: these three eternals. The place the race defined, the race of men the place defined, and the exercise of that definition: the mutual knowing and the mutual being. I with you have been exploring where the map stops and another map begins, taking us into the conjectural, into holiness, revelation, containing certainty. Which is to say, when occasion has arisen, out of prose and object into poetry and subject. *And now descend, sir, by these raw rock nullahs that conies have crossed alert for eagles, come down on strong feet into the land's first groves. Listen - the first of their laughter in the orchards, and gurgle of water.*

In June, in Kensington, I picked up word that the next month, July 2001, with Government deeming the eastern flanks of Ruwenzori at last to be free of the scourge of guerilla forces, visitors would be permitted to re-enter, to climb into the heights again, to research (for instance) the upper territory's fifteen unique species of mammals, the twenty-five unique reptiles, the eighteen unique birds, the fantastical giant vegetation and score upon score of strictly Ruwenzori insects, mosses, lichens, for the first time since the rebel invasion of 1996 and the invaders' flight into the highlands. Was the millenarian reign of true peace at last descending on our tormented slopes out of the heights, the immaculate desolations, the First Person of our trinity? And if that might be so, who better to test the matter than the one who for long months had been rising early to re-enter the hills in his Kensington study?

Therefore that very month, the day after the family's celebrating my wife's seventieth birthday, and selecting from the high altitude equipment of our son Sam, a Himalayan mountaineer, I took plane to Entebbe and hot-footed westwards to Kasese. A compulsion had hold of me, perhaps sinister in one of such length of tooth, to climb to the snows of the inner inaccessibilities, source of the mountains' good or evil such as I had circled all my life, as if I would engage in an eternity challenge, sidling up to God in a place appropriate to us both and muttering, 'This is me. You'll take me now?' The peaks rise, as will be recalled, to over 16,000 feet, and determine the very line which the King of Belgium, 'Souverain de l'Etat Indépendent du Congo' (as Leopold styled himself at the time), and the Empress-Queen Victoria of England divided the mid-African territories they had come so capriciously to possess. I took with me my treasured friend Syayipuma Augustine from the village of Ibanda at the foot of the customary

495

climbing route; or, rather, he took me. Though we needed but one experienced guide and three porters - a total complement of five Bakonzo - a posse of thirteen tribesmen in all, from Ibanda and its higher neighbour, Nyakalengija, formed itself spontaneously to set forth with me, come what may. My go-between with these others was Syayipuma himself, experienced from pre-ADF times as an escort to researchers and so-called (so *branded*) eco-tourists. He was not himself a snow-and-ice man, so he chose for me one of the doyens of the Bakonzo summiteers, John Mudenge. Syayipuma is a man swift of mind, of passionate good humour and unflagging vigour: not five feet tall and a face you would suppose its maker had scrunched up in a moment of laughter and slept on. Perhaps he is the best loved fellow in Mobuku valley, and I surely love him too. He does not often stop talking; while Mudenge John - he scarcely ever says a word. I came to love him as well, as one  comes to love whosoever quietly and persistently obviates the probability of one's own extinction. None of my companions was older than half my age, and most not a third of it.

We set off at daybreak of the very first day permitted by the government Ministry (alas, called Tourism) which, only eighteen months previously, had had to face eight American and British visitors murdered by Interahamwe Bahutu in its Bwindi Game Reservation some eighty miles to the south. The victims were members of a group which had paid out several thousands of dollars to watch the mountain gorilla in its natural state in the Rutshuru upland forest. That particular massacre was done in relatively cold blood since the tourists of other nationalities were spared: it was to be death by passport. Americans and Britons represented countries with governments which for some years had been providing weapons or aid to the (Nilotic) Tutsi of Rwanda, immediately across that frontier with Uganda, while casting the then governing (Bantu) Hutu, whose army was supplied and trained by the French, as the exclusive villains of the conflict. Syayipuma himself had been accompanying the tour party as its organising guide and had witnessed the murders. As the

Interahamwe had marched away the survivors of the party as hostages, Syayipuma contrived to escape by virtue of his tiny stature. What was left of the Uganda tourist industry could hardly countenance a comparable event in Ruwenzori. The UPDF's James Kazini, now a General, had staked his reputation - and a plot of land he had bought in a prime site for a hotel in Kasese - on there being no rebel groups operating on the east or south of our Ruwenzoris. Kisokeronio and his gang were still somewhere at large, but the nearest rebel presence was believed to be in the north-west, in Bundibugyo District. That previous week Uganda's Minister of Tourism had organised a motley of East African journalists to ascend to the first night's halt on the long-established climbers' route to the heights, at the overhanging rock called Nyabitaba, scrambling up in the wake of a group of Bakonzo clearing the old track of its undergrowth. One of their number ascended further with a Mukonzo guide, Jerome Bwambale, but was turned back by a damaged ankle. The opportunity was therefore open for an old hand and an old pair of feet, mine, to be the first to return to the glaciers of the highest cluster of peaks, Stanley, after the four preceding years of quarantine.

It would be an ascent of the reclamation of the heartland from Fanehasi Kisokeronio who had forfeited so terribly his right to the mountains. Attaining Nyabitaba's rock shelter and adjacent hut that first night - an ascent of some 2,800 feet from Nyakalengija - as we boiled our tea and stewed our mutton over an open fire, I regaled my thirteen Bakonzo on my ancient acquaintance with him whose very name they had grown up to quail at. I detected unease among some. We were in deep forest here, and had been so throughout the ascent; and through three rebellions Fanehasi had acquired attributes of a forest sprite compounding evil and elusiveness by magic means, which is to say not combatable by merely mortal men. On the territory of bogeymen and sprites it is not tact to bandy names about. There was among us fourteen one who had been abducted by an ADF detachment beholden to Kisokeronio, and the experience had been fearful: he and his fellow captives force-marched through the steep forest under heavy loads until some collapsed, only to have their throats cut (so as not to risk the sound of a shot). Our escapee never laid eyes on the demon leader... But come, said I, I have known the fellow since he was seventeen, have hunted colobus with him, roasted pig with him. (I would demythologise the fellow, deny him rank among the little gods. Yet there was that in me which bled for him.) He was sixty-four now, I said, a foolish old man, with a cause born dead. Why, if he attacked us here, I bragged, I would call out to him by name and tell him, Drop your stupid gun: I'll take you in a plane to London where your own son Zostine, student of Information Technology, has been my family's house guest this past year, and together we will teach you manners!

The laughter flickering from the start escaped in a burst now, the glee of it rocking on their haunches Syayipuma and Senior Private Josiah Makwano of the Ruwenzori Park Rangers, who was equipped with a sub-machine gun and a shortwave radio, having selected himself as my personal protector. (Josi was another who *bred* laughter as certain priests breed peace.) So we exorcised the enemy that first night, and took to ourselves the rightful spirit of this shelter-site of deeply overhanging rock which Konzo hunters had known and used from immemorial times. Nyabitaba, the name, means the place of tobacco – an imported transatlantic linguistic echo here – and the smoker whose aroma human nostrils had detected there was Kalissia, hunting god, who was known to smoke... and also to have but one leg (the left one) and consequently a stave. Later, in the filtered dawn, we made totemic offering to Kalissia of a  small beast formed of a fat plantain's seed-pod with crawly legs. We were entering now our proper dark, and would re-assert the tutelars.

For I would have it that the mountains we were set to penetrate were, and are, the Creator's self-revelation to the people of that region: a sanctity and a sanctuary wholly justified, by any measure meeting and outspanning the stretch of human speech. I shan't make myself an idolater; yet surely will I allow awe, allow homage, a calculated submission, on the part of proximate mankind no less apt than Sinai evoked, or Seir, or YHWH-jireh, being that mountain where Abraham was led for the intended sacrifice of his son; and such awe, homage, and submission here were towards created heights and mystery on an incomparably greater scale and ferocity than those of Judaic experience. In the three nights before this ascent had begun, sleeping at Kasese and Ibanda, I had been violently awoken by two thunderstorms and a seven-second earthquake. The inner heights, the convulsive shield from which they were created, were ever and dramatically present; and I had come back to them in apt obeisance before I left England, re-

498

writing my will and touching base with those I seriously loved, on this or that insouciant pretext.

So far, so good. But I had got up to this contour once before, forty-seven years earlier, as I have told. That next day's hike was graver work and swift to tell on me: an evil passage of vast tree-cluttered boulders, chaotically heaped, taking us out of the sub-alpine forests into the bamboos. I was already at the dangerous margin of physical resource. I made it to that night's shelter by counting my steps in hundreds and refusing to raise my eyes to the precipitous demands of the immediate route: I fixed them on the feet of the fellow in front. We were now above the customary level of the bigger beasts, elephant - whose recent spoor and droppings we had encountered - and giant forest hog and Ruwenzori leopard, and the range's unique colobus which agitated in troupes the topmost foliage above our heads. Here there were many birds - the crimson-breasted turaco, ubiquitous - and at our feet the sudden beauty of Stairs's purple-pink orchid; creeping galaxies of seven-petalled ranunculus rwenzoriensis; and whenever the trees or bamboos allowed, heaving mattresses of helichrysum guilelmii, the petal's pink so intimate. Exquisite ferns abounded; moss cities elaborated into beauty and invention beyond all telling, pleading one's own miniature citizenship; and old man's beard trailed the upper limbs of everything.

I rested here. Syayipuma brought me tea, cold banana fritter, avocado sandwiches. I was not hungry. I was already aware of three of me on this ascent: the will, the body and the observing eye. This eye (or I) was peculiarly dispassionate, watching for which of the other two was liable to crack first. The will showed no cracking symptoms. That in itself was interesting. Yet the body, obviously, would have its laws. The limbs, notably knees, ankles, thigh joints, were admirably efficient. I was beginnng to award them daily stars. The more arcane mechanisms - heart, lungs, and circulating blood - were beyond prediction. Which of them would 'go' - and how? That previous evening, having reached that hut, I supposed that if it had been sited a half hour's climbing further on I would not have 'made it'. What did that *mean*?

After that second night I took a day's sheer leisure. You could glimpse a fragment of snowy peak from the Bujuku stream bed there, at the hut named after that late John Matte whom we had buried at Ibanda five years before. The snow we saw was three days

499

ahead by any measure: it seemed impossibly distant, absurdly high and inviolable... On our setting out on day four afresh, immediately ahead the giant heathers began. I remembered them, and the wicked trail a man must take via stream-beds, root-ladders, and false ground of mossy twigs. Bakonzo call that place Bwina bw'amaganga, which means a place of holes or hollows - for if you misjudge your step you plunge a leg or even most of your self to your armpits to mother earth's true floor, as often as not a liquid floor or sludged mud, from which there emerge the straddling roots of Ruwenzori's fifty-foot heathers. My companions do not like this belt. It occupies - vertically assessed - a thousand feet or so of that entire contour of the mountains to a level of about 11,500 feet. It is wicked going. Frequently the chosen trail of ascent (maybe the only feasible route) is by way of a cascading tributary of the Bujuku river, whose ravine or valley flanks we are following. A rock overhang in the midst of it named Nyamuleju, or Old Man's Beard (or Spanish moss or trailing lichen, in other parlance) tempts the climber to rest. This is as far as I had reached in 1954, turning back at that point on account of what proved to be malaria; but this time I resisted pause. We were soon to emerge into more open ground and the first of the obelisked lobelias, gigantesquely lunar and twenty or thirty feet in height. Around this point of the ascent I was aware of an elemental carnality fuelling the will, as if I were engaged in a terminal rut: a last act of lust, and yet not without a homage beyond gratification to the object of that lust. Before us stretched the Bigo bog, Bog of Bogs (Bigo means Bog in the vernacular), made infamous by the afficionados of Ruwenzori's heights for the inescapability of its mud, requiring as a rule the climber to jump or fail to jump from one tussock of carex to another. Yet because we were the first to be here for

some five years, Bigo's surfaces had stabilized. Moreover, sunbirds abounded, feeding on all that flowered, flittering flowers themselves - blue, yellow, green, and now one here surely scarlet, each one tiny and quick - reminders, emissaries, of a creative court of gratuitous beauty. For me that bog was a blessed easement from ascent. I danced through and photographed my companions under the vegetable grotesques: lobelias and groundsels of the same improbable hugeness.

What makes for this giantism? Have I not yet said? It is the consequence of a climate comprising summer by day and winter by night, fed - or tormented - by vast rainfall and a diurnal dose of infra-red and ultra-violet from a sun immediately overhead whose rays are filtered by negligible atmosphere. No other massif on earth matches this.

From beyond Bigo the clusters of summits now began to loom, ahead and above, sometimes in cloud sometimes in sunlight: ahead and westwards, Stanley; northerly, Speke; southerly, Baker: all three extensively glaciered. Immediately to our right rose Mount Gessi, snowed but not glaciered visibly from where we were. Beyond Speke, the edge of Emin was just visible, with fragments of its glacier surviving the rise in global temperature in this past quarter century. Beyond Baker, southwards, and masked from our sight, there rose Luigi di Savoia. Each of these, as I have told (p 42), comprised a group of tops, as also did the Portal Peaks, now behind us, east and north-east - a range within a range. Thus were we ringed; and thus clamped and claimed by the heights. We made our camp where two huts still stood just beyond the Bujuku's slate-blue source-lake at 4,000 metres: 13,120 feet, at sundown the temperature plummeting. In my hut we had made our fire, having carried up our own charcoal and dried faggots. From here, on the open faces of the slopes, three of the four main cladding species - St John's Wort, the giant groundsels and lobelias - appeared to falter and all but cease to grow from a point some two hundred feet higher than the campsite. Only the everlasting-helichrysums hung on, reducing in stature as they mounted to the cold. Yet I was to discover over the next three days that in sheltered bowls and clefts the giant species continued to occur and flourish at much higher altitude, almost to the snows; as did the highest dwelling sunbird too, the scarlet-tufted malachite, fed by nectar generated nearest to the gods.

I crept into my sleeping bag doubled with a felt lining, wearing a string vest, a long-sleeved denim shirt, a second long-tailed woollen shirt, two pairs of underpants, two pairs of longjohns (silk and cotton), waterproof trousers, leggings, a woollen jacket zipped to the neck, heavy socks, trainer shoes, and a wool hat under the sleeping bag's hood. By day I had not worn, and would not wear, a quarter of all this. We were already getting rancid against the skin, the lot of us. I had quite lost my appetite, was eating almost nothing, but holding to my son's cautioning that I drink as much as I could. At five a.m. I awoke requiring to pass water. My fire was long since dead. Syayipuma who had begun the night in my hut had evidently moved to the adjacent shelter where I found him asleep with all the others. Their fire glowed red and broad and all lay there circling it hugger-mugger in blankets and sacks, warmed as well by one another's bodies as by the throbbing embers. They looked like survivors of a shipwreck on a raft.

In the bitter pre-dawn hour the peaks that rose two to three thousand feet around this bowl were very present: underfoot all was ice-brittle. The surface of the lake, very still, was unearthly. Our bowl was also ringed, close at hand, by a strange sound or, rather, sounds. These sounds came from a multitude of sources. I had never in my life heard such sounds. The sounds were rasping plaints - each one an individual sound, yet each unvaried: a sole expression, a fixed plaint, each from a single rasping throat. I knew what this could only be. The Ruwenzori hyrax, in its numbers, at this darkest hour of night on the slopes around me, in full throat, was foraging the remnant grass, each declaring its presence to its fellows. These were our conies, alert for eagles if they were to venture in the light of day from the rock burrows I had remarked already on the last hours of ascent the previous day. My companions had reported that these creatures can mount vertical rock faces with tiny claws of exceptional prehensility. (Later that day I was to find their dainty prints in the mud.) Meanwhile, this was their nightly agora, and this their hour.

Opposite: Ruwenzori's Mount Stanley: approaches, glaciers and summits

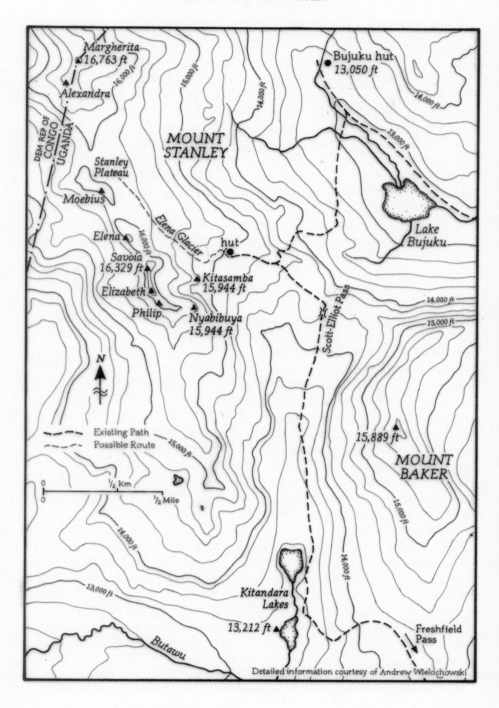

Margherita
16,763 ft
Alexandra
DEM REP OF CONGO
UGANDA
16,000 ft
15,000 ft
14,000 ft

Bujuku hut
13,050 ft
14,000 ft
13,000 ft

MOUNT
STANLEY

Lake
Bujuku

Stanley
Plateau
Moebius
Elena
16,000 ft
Savoia
16,329 ft
Elizabeth
Philip
Elena Glacier
hut
Kitasamba
15,944 ft
Nyabibuya
15,944 ft

Scott-Elliot Pass

14,000 ft
15,000 ft

N

15,889 ft

MOUNT
BAKER

Existing Path
Possible Route
15,000 ft
15,000 ft

½ Km
½ Mile

14,000 ft

14,000 ft

13,000 ft

Kitandara
Lakes
13,212 ft

Butawu

Freshfield
Pass

Detailed information courtesy of Andrew Wielochowski

The sleep I had just woken from was my last for forty hours... Ten of my thirteen Bakonzo were not to ascend with me to the final hut, Elena, from which the assault on Mount Stanley's glaciers and peaks is made at 15,000 feet. Those ten were not equipped for such a height. They would traverse - I use the term loosely - a day's tramp southwards to a pair of other lakes, Kitandara, beneath the precipitous west face of Baker and which drained westwards into the Butawu torrent and Semliki, to await there the remaining three of us: Syayipuma, Mudenge and myself... for Bwambale Henry was to climb with us only to Elena and to dump our load before descending to rejoin the others. This was after all a mzungu thing, this 'conquering' of glaciers and peaks: not a proper Konzo calling: white man's hubris, not to say profanity, to breach the permanent snowlands. Mudenge had learned this craft since he was a boy of fifteen to fulfil the need of these driven whites: a man of silence, in a small green curly-brimmed hat, in compact with the gods, squaring it with them, this white man's compulsion. He will not mention Lord Kitasamba up here, nor Nyabibuya, even though it is Kitasamba's pinnacle that disappears into cloud just here above us at Elena's hut, immediately across the snout of the glacier named by the first mzungu ever to reach this height after one of his own Italian princesses. The identity of the two pinnacles that stand sentinel over the central and highest whiteness were vouchsafed to Mudenge's and Syayipuma's ancestors by the gods themselves, when Man first penetrated this high place for no other purpose but to make sacrifice and venerate: *Kitasamba* and *Nyabibuya*, twins, twinned pinnacles, soaring out of their separate voids three hundred metres apart to a precisely identical 15,354 feet. Each was free of permanent snow: there was no ledge for snow to rest. Nothing further in and up, under permanent snow and ice, had been named by the gods except as *snow*, nzururu, since the territory of snow was Other: a void announced, a presence beyond life or death. Here (at the equatorial girdle of the Earth) native man, stranger to shoes, could not tread. The mountains themselves were the spoken Word of gods: so I have said. The permanent whiteness, then, the godhead, nzururu, featureless: which of us men, whether white or black, had right to presume to define that which by definition was indefinable?

And I, had I reached this point to venerate? To offer myself as sacrifice? - reversing the ancient roles, these young Isaacs conducting their Abraham into the mountains in his seventy-second year, bearing their faggots, for their necessary immolation? To measure my *self*, after all these years, while there was vigour enough still in me? To learn from my adoptive Konzo what they most valuably and secretly had to vouchsafe me?

I am prone to veneration.

I had brought with me here two small books: Martin Buber's *I and Thou* and Dante's *Purgatorio* in Mark Musa's translation; only these two. Buber the Jew was rendered in English (from the German) by the Christian, Ronald Gregor Smith. So my torchlight reading at high altitude straddled cultures, straddled faiths and straddled human epochs. I had intended bringing not *Purgatorio* but *Paradiso*, for I had lately awoken (with joy) to the significance of Dante Alighieri having found himself obliged to laurel woman, Beatrice, as the servant and reposer of Man's soul. In the scramble of departure from Kensington, I had pulled down *Purgatorio* from its shelf in error and was stuck up Ruwenzori with Virgil not Beatrice as my guide. *Tant pis.* This soul of mine was to prove unready for ultimate destination; yet if guide and lover were to be one, might there be discernible here the eternal *Thou* of Buber's *I*? I caught myself reading in Buber's essay: 'At times the man, shuddering at the alienation between the *I* and the world, comes to reflect that something is to be done. As when in the grave night-hour you lie, racked by waking dream – bulwarks have fallen away and the abyss is screaming – and note amid your torment: there is still *life*, if only I get through it, but how, how?; so is this man in his hours of reflection, shuddering, and aimlessly considering this and that...'

Indeed, it was no paradise, at this height, but a taste of Hades, and purgative for sure. At 15,000 feet no men live, have their being; we are in aggregate never more than a handful, at such a height, in whatever high mountain region of the globe.

I presumed nothing for myself, attaining Elena hut that evening after a steeply clambering ascent and across a final passage of naked anticlinal strata - seven steeply tilted rock ramps – we the first to be up here after so long a human absence: I was only dreadfully alert. I had already ceased eating. Nausea had fixed on me: I was subsisting on water, tea, Nurofen and soup – one cupful occupying me for half an hour. I noticed my hands were swollen. I was aware of pressure in the feet. I knew nothing as to my face, having brought no mirror, and shaving by guesswork reluctantly every second day like Yasser Arafat. Later, photos showed my face ballooning. I was undergoing classic mountain sickness, though unaware of it by name. The effort any movement took me was inexplicable. Here I was not exactly short of breath, but for all the breaths I took I perceived that little of the thinnish gruel of oxygen was being recognised by my blood's struggling gills as fuel. Even a trip to the bog (which at Elena demands hands as well as feet to scramble there and back) was ordeal. A few hundred metres to the south-east the god-twins soared out of their abyss into an upper abyss.

All that night in that high hutment I lay awake. Waves of shivering swept my body in its multi-layered coverings. I learned to quell these waves only by 'deep panting' and noting each exaggerated pant. Sleepless nights pertain to endlessness. 'Shuddering at the alienation between the *I* and the world' I 'aimless considered this and that.' How and why had I trapped myself up here on this forsaken bluff? I pondered such as I loved, who seemed still to hold me in regard... not least my Himalayan son: what would *he* say of this wrecked ancestor in his funk and folly? On the morrow I must be in the snows and *up*. What would there be to that, for such as Sam? He would summit Margherita and be down here again in four hours flat. So why was I like this? My legs were good, my heart still beat; the weather had held all that preceding day. So why this Gethsemene night? My Lord was agitated, scripture records, at what he knew must happen. Yet I recalled that when, in early dawn, they came for him at last - Judas and the rest - he was calm, and remained thereafter *calm*.

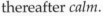

Calm came at about 4 a.m., and thereafter calm remained. It was the calm of reconciliation; *Thy* will; the *It* yielding to the *Thou*.

Calm, yet not much strength. Moreover, weather looked uncertain. It took us some half hour to brew up, half hour to kit up, three quarters of an hour to negotiate the tricky rocks to the glacier's snout: Syayipuma, Mudenge John and I. We cramponed up. There was a snow cave there framed by icicles, with a rock floor. Syayipuma crawled in and wanted me to photograph him, as if this glacier edge was something to chalk up. Innumerable climbers of earlier times had preceded us: this was no place to stop and swank.

We mounted Elena's snout and set off in heavy snow at a steep angle, roped against crevasses. Fog had swirled up from the surrounding voids. Thoughout the previous day we had ascended in brightness and sharp cold; today we had this fog, and the thermometer up, weakening the snow's crust so that I, built half as big again as my companions, broke through the crust at every step - which they did not. I sank to half way up the shins or even to the knees with each pace gained. Within an hour I was taking ten steps - steps not paces - and stopping for twenty breaths. The fog had closed on us. The effort was enormous: I persisted in a counting-house of numbers, leaning into the sightless mountain on Sam's ski-sticks to restore my rationed breath - rationed by the curdled blood's inefficiency. Twenty breaths, ten gruelling steps. By that approximate level at some 16,000 feet where Elena's steeply tilted glacier was flattening into the long level of East Stanley glacier - part of the wholly glaciered Stanley plateau stretching to Moebius and the two crowning peaks pushing five or six hundred feet above the plateau's surface - our visibility in all directions was down to little more than a hundred yards. This was not the purple passage desolation H M Stanley had told us of, from his dugout on the Semliki 14,000 feet beneath. At moments I was just aware of the dark wall of Mount Elena's eastern face two or three hundred paces due west. Southwards, the immediate summits of Savoia, Elizabeth and Philip, peaking a mere three hundred feet higher than where we stood and none more than 600 yards distant in a lateral measurement, were quite lost to us. There was a glacier in their midst, I knew, gazetted as 'Coronation' as recently as the 1950s, tightly encircled by those three western sentinels and Kitasamba and Nyabibuya on the east. I would never see it.

What had induced us to press so far in these conditions? In part, the sheer caprice of upper Ruwenzori's meteorological reputation. Weather will swing in minutes; fog materialising - as often as not from beneath - into a smiling sky, occluding all, or else clearing just as swiftly, revealing all. You place your bets: climb in, and up. (We had brought our little flags to mark our return route in the snow if Kitasamba's fog might seek to claim us utterly.) So, partly to seize any chance on offer, and partly my disbelief that Will was not enough - that, hitherto (for seven decades, give or take an infancy) Body had been compliant to Will's commitment, is my best answer. Where does a man go when the Will is disobeyed? On? I had run absolutely out of gas. If the fog had parted over Margherita and the gates of Paradise had opened there to welcome me in person - St Peter and the full Valhalla - I could not have made it. I had stopped tramping. I said nothing: to breathe was all I sought. Mudenge

said, No, he would not go on. He alone of us was acquainted with this snowland. No one butts the fates here. Syayipuma snapped us, Mudenge and me, in the fog of the god who had drawn the line for me. The truth was - we each knew it - Ruwenzori had killed hundreds, literally so, in its brief century of recorded ascents, or attempts at ascent - the falls, crevasses, and most frequently of all pulmonary oedema gotten at high altitude with no means of descent or medical alleviation. We three hung there, in whelming silence and emptiness. What now?

Two figures loom.

Men? Here? Two other human figures at fifty or sixty paces from us, cresting the plateau from below. Surely not.

They have seen us. They approach - they too are roped. A Mukonzo, a young European; roped.

'Hello. Wawukire.'

We are alongside. A hand is offered.

'Gustave Corti.'

'How do you do?'

'You are Isemusoki. Too much fog.' He was a young Italian. 'We must go down.'

He had a mountaineer's taciturn authority. He had yomped up behind me, starting two days later, with a Konzo guide and a porter. At Bujuku his guide had fallen sick, so he brought up his porter who had never been on the snows before, all the way from Bujuku that very day. His jeans had a tear in the knee. His map was a page torn from a *Rough Guide to Uganda*. He had no compass. I took to the fellow immediately. He had no notion as to what it had cost me to reach this point.

'Indeed, we must go down.'

Corti and his porter descended ahead of us, following our flags. I began to retrace our costly steps. Each step I sank to the knees. I could see Corti's and his porter's tracks parallel to ours: they seldom broke the crust. I could not fathom this injustice. Already in a couple of hundred yards of descending I was floundering. I was mightily exhausted. I caught the anxiety in Syayipuma's voice -

not for himself, of course: for me. Here was Mudenge, only his eyes speaking, and assessing.

'Help me to balance a bit,' I said.

They came alongside me, one under each arm. I gave them my sticks. In the matter of departure from the coil, due in some degree to one's own misjudgment, there is frequently an issue of personal dignity. We all remember Captain Oates precisely for his style, his Englishness, when the game was up... Maybe the day would come when a later Antarctic expedition, pushing on beyond Beardmore, would find his body, as on Everest Mallory's was recently chanced upon. Mallory had taken a bad tumble.

I do not suppose there was much decorum to that further descent of Elena glacier, Mudenge under one arm, Kitasamba-side, Syayipuma under the other, Margherita-side. Orwell's repulsive pig Snowball came to mind, and his all-inclusive commandment, 'Four legs good, two legs bad,' We were six legs good, two legs bad. With six legs my boots seldom went through the crust. So we made it, without style, to snows' snout and good hard rock. Mudenge said he had noted the glaciers retreating these past twenty years.

The fog had remained around us, all the way to Elena hutment. Corti and his Mukonzo had gone on down 1,600 feet to Bujuku. They had brought no rations with them for an extra day up at Elena. There was no fog below us now. In the hut I remained in nausea. This time it took me an hour to swallow a mug of soup. Yet I slept. Next day dawned clear and sharp. Corti got back up to us mid-morning, again with his porter. Neither of them knew anything of the complexity of hazards amid the peaks should the weather switch again, or indeed the right route up Margherita. Readily I lent him John Mudenge, our doyen of the peak men, wishing them both to summit in the exercise of Mudenge's craft and in the fulfilment of Gustavo's determination. I had been brought to obedience and obeisance on the high glacier. I was not here to conquer: to 'embrace a reality we do not control' is the true requirement. Moreover, there was an historic aptness to an Italian taking out the geographic top, named by an Italian after an Italian queen, following this longest ever gap in the climbing of Ruwenzori since Luigi did his conquering in 1906. This Gustave/Gustavo, 29, knew nothing of these mountains' climbing history, yet he was an experienced Alpinist. He had been working in Uganda's north for four years for a Christian charity fitting limbs to children maimed by mines provided to the Kony rebels by a Sudanese government seeking, as they sought here, to weaken and torment a US-backed Uganda. He had first come out as a six-months' volunteer, found a vocation, and stayed. The radio told him Ruwenzori was to re-open, and he vowed to make a dash for it before his contract ended a mere seven days hence. The Alps offered no chance to cap 5,000 metres, and here all this while was Ruwenzori, 5,110, tantalizing him.

I myself descended with Syayipuma, taking the southern route to those paired Arthurian lakes, Kitandara, at 13,200 feet or so, where my assembled eleven greeted us in song led by Senior Private Josi. Corti, with Mudenge, joined us in camp just before sundown: he had got his top and his first 5,000 metres. Next morning the Italian set off to race on down ahead with his team of two, while I, over three days and nights, by way of a snow-flurried Freshfield pass and its bleak tarns at 14,000 feet, and steep descents, by waterfalls, magical landscapes, bogs, ravines, certain excursions not made by any man in years – Mudenge just ahead to give me, repeatedly, a step with the haft of his ice-axe – reached once more the first settlements above Nyakalengija. Out of one lost world, you may say, into another.

In this evocation of the sanctities of the one world to redeem the profanities of the other, there was to be a culminating episode. Throughout all of our nine days together my companions had been telling me of their fears and bewilderment concerning rumours of what distant authority in Kampala had been cooking up for the touristic exploitation of inner Ruwenzori, of which these men of the Mubuku valley were the sole gate-keepers and guardians, now that the place was free of brigandage. All information that had

reached them so far seemed to me to be guile and half truth, and so I promised to devil out the facts and bring back to them the full truth of the matter before I left for England. This indeed I did, returning to Kampala to do the devilling; and coming back to the valley a week later to hold a public meeting on a grass slope at Nyakalengija late one afternoon, flanked by Syayipuma and Jerome Bwambale. What I had to tell the couple of hundred gathered there caused, justly and intendedly, consternation since we were revealing commercial mischief which I and two young Americans of high purpose had uncovered: monopolistic mischief, with high authority's endorsing connivance, which would have resulted in all these good folk of the valley fulfilling their arduous, skilled and ever-dangerous functions at pitiable wages for the sly enrichment of foreign buccaneers and their cronies in government. I had brought with me the full truth of it word-processed out in clear classical Lukonzo, translated by Syahuka-Muhindo himself at Makerere University, and duplicated two hundred times in Kasese the previous night, for the enlightenment of the innocent.

Out there in the open at the top of the inhabited valley, perched on a bench above a craning of heads and a straining of ears, Syayipuma, Jerome and I were Marx and Engels adjuring them - the guides and porters of the only route to the mountains' heights - to unite: they had nothing to lose but their chains! At the climax of this harangue, as we were pushing out my Lukonzo leaflets into clamouring hands, armed authority roared up in a couple of four-by-four eight-seaters, alerted by agents of the Kampala conspirators to an 'illegal gathering' at this most ultimate of roadheads, and arrested the three of us. We were bundled into the vehicles and carried away for interrogation: the Kampala newspapers got wind of it. Yet our mission had been accomplished and my promise kept: we had already done our stuff of public exposure. Within the subsequent ten days, we had succeeded in scuppering the corrupt and tricksy scheme, and had thus helped to open the way to equitable stewardship of our mountains and their inexhaustible treasures.

Of this entire ascent and descent there is no end to what a man could write! I could have told of every leaf of every tree, every frond of every fern, every rhizoid of every moss, every spoor of every lichen, every crystal of every web of frost. I could have told you everything and informed you - formed you innerly – not at all. What need the world know of these heights, except that they are there? This is the truth: that *if my will had its way there would be no entering these inner mountains* unless by Konzo men in monkey furs and barkcloth cloaks, with their spears and arrows, in search of wild meat to rut upon, or to leave a fetish for the one-legged sprite-of-the-hunt Kalissia, or else to be privily inducted by their feral quarry into looking with their dark eyes only out upon creation and never in upon themselves. That is a sacred skill. International grandees manning UNESCO, between petty banquets and intercontinental flights, have decreed the Ruwenzori Mountains a 'World Heritage Site' which classification seeks to stipulate that they should be protected from man the despoiler, the exploiter; this Manichee. How shall any such decree be given force and substance? Kayingo *Lord*, look down on us with mercy.

Now we pray,

Lord, may Your will be reconciliation and the balm of Your mercy be upon us all;

our King in Pennsylvania, handsome yet poor, in civil wedlock now with his lady nurse, yet promising his Konzo elders a more solemn union still with a tribal bride on his inevitable return as Omusinga;

his commited adversary, Dr Crispus Kiyonga, Commissar (that very title) of his President's No-Party Party and now disposer of a budget of no less than one billion US dollars as Africa's chairman (in recognition of his undeniable administrative gifts) of the international committee charged with the combating of Aids;

Fanehasi Kisokeronio, his spear laid down, his Kalashnikov hung up, now that most of his children are dead and his senior wife has scuttled back to her folks in Kasese from the old man's Congo hide-out.

As to Your mountains and Your mountain people, may

they be commended to Your keeping;
as to this boulevardier, not tripled now but unified, may his
song rise to You on behalf of all Your creatures.

Peer, then, out from this story as if through a high window. You
will see a white man writing about black men, and about his
English self in Africa among Africans, across almost half a century.
As your eyes strain for what more may be seen from that window,
so has my own account of events strained beyond its own locus
and narrative – beyond the specificities of what I have been
witnessing in Ruwenzori this past half-century towards what the
study of a tribe may show the student to be generally true of men
at any place in any time: a straining out from multiplicity towards
a certain universality.

You who have been beside me for so long will have grown
familiar with what I claim to be a constant in man's presence on his
planet, namely the holiness of ethnicity. Race and place, I say,
belong to one another not just inexorably but righteously: the
proper sense of his ethnicity feeds Man the conviction of his
identity and a glimpse of his grandeur. No substitute exists for that
food. For a man to be deprived of it in the context of his grandeur
is as for a man to be deprived of his childhood in the eye of his
maturity. He is a man without root: without root he is without leaf.

This ethnicity is a protean reality – an allegiance implied by
every combination of blood and language, territory and history,
culture and inheritance, cosmology and ethic: a reality on the
change by the decade, the year, the month, the day, the hour. It will
be today broad, tomorrow narrow. It will mutate, shift, merge, mix,
be wilfully adopted, or consciously assumed, or parasitical upon
another. It will misrepresent itself, misread itself, dishonour itself;
and it will inspire, uplift, and rally. It will be subject to exploitation
and corruption; it will be conducive to glory and sacrifice. It will be
a source of war and a source of peace.

Whatever its outward face, it will always be subjective. No one
person's sense of what it means to be of this or that ethnic
persuasion will be identical to any other's. It will be for ever
collective yet for ever private. In that privacy and intimacy will
reside its holiness.

For it will be the conduit of any person with the ground he or
she has sprung from, or chooses so to believe: the enwholing
provenance by which any ground – any steppe, delta, island,

peninsula, archipelago, crescent of fecundity, desert, mountainland, jungle or megalopolis – is understood as being of all creation. By token of that link with creation is a person's link to the creator. As it is a conduit thus inwardly, so it is outwardly: in that, from such rootedness a person or a people may flower and fruit in the service of the generality of their fellows and of the generality of ethnicities. Thus the privy sanctity is justified. He whom Christians know as their faith's founder prayed Abba, Father, in Aramaic to a deity defined by his earthly Jewish root: He prayed for, and with, all mankind.

The record in this book of the people self-defined as Bakonzo, resident on the slopes or in the shadow of the Ruwenzori massif, and heirs of the memory of at least two rebellions and of the Rwenzururu Kingdom, is in some measure a record of their holiness. It has both informed and been informed by the neoplatonic and Christian interpretation of the truth of Man's presence on his planet which my own long life has borne upon me. This book speaks of my support not only of the Bakonzo in their self-determination but of the idea of tribe. I have come to perceive that the political and intellectual fashion to decry or deny ethnicity in Africa to be foolish and dangerous: the blood we ascribe to expressions of tribalism we should more accurately ascribe to the fear in the centralising authority of artificial post-colonial states to accommodate the reality of the tribe as the fount of men's right to grow and the spark of their fulness.

This same truth applies no less to the rest of mankind than it does in black Africa. When that ethnicity is denied or neglected so is a vital component of sanctity. Man instinctively delves for it, presses for it – sometimes fights for it – or he diminishes (not least in his own eyes) under the loss or theft of it, whether by conquest or through political collectivity, globalisation or ideology. Ethnicity is a requirement of soul – of man as soul – no less among pale skins than among dark. There is no culture déraciné. The failure to perceive and confess what is instinctually and divinely at work here is the blight-mark of big government in today's world: a wilful obfuscation and cause of un-meaning. Conversely, the first treasure of any people is a living sense of who they are as a people, their embitha, the will to preserve that sense or restore it or celebrate it or establish it in whatever circumstances of purity or admixture, bastardy or flux in which they can acknowledge it. It is never less than sublime; and no exploiting of that energetic will by those of corrupt intent can more than temporarily occlude or distort the essential sublimity.

In such an assertion there is nothing retrogressive, nothing ungenerous or ultimately exclusive. Shall Elgar the Englishman be deaf to Dvorak the Bohemian? Come, come. If Adolf Hitler as political führer was of the Devil, does that render Wagner the musician unsublime? We have noted in this book the endeavour by the framers of the 'Aims' of Rwenzururu to place at the centre of the Kingdom's ethic that which was noble and outreaching. Such an ethic has remained with the Bakonzo leadership with whom I am to this day associated. I do not know how it will fare under the political vicissitudes and communal hazards of contemporary Africa; yet, as I write, it is there.

Black Africa is condemned to much suffering. It suffers already on a gargantuan scale. Pandemics ravage the continent; innocent generations are cursed. None of this will swiftly change. Incapable of preparedness, it is a continent vulnerable to the caprice of climate, to the consequences of drought or flood. For the most part it is a continent incompetently and corruptly governed. The incompetence and corruption and unpreparedness are the whelps of a despair at a presumed, predestined inability – indeed, a mute unwillingness – to compete either as nations or as a folk with a world where white men's values and white men's technocracy masquerade as civilisation. Friends in England ask, frowning, what future has black Africa, and alerted by my hesitancy prattle on about the bases of power in the greater world – the Western capitals, the structures of international funding – having long ago written off Africa as a player in the destiny of the planet, since the subSaharan continent is irredeemably a place of serial disorder and self-compounded misfortune. 'As for this tribe of yours . . . '

In less than a page I shall have fallen silent. Following the path of my own exploration and my own reading of what I have discovered, my dreaming self (that self capable of detachment) shall have once more climbed in and up to the glaciers and snows where no thing mortal dwells, and in dreams or in detachment shall let go my isolation and my silence there. This dreaming self shall have left the rest of us below, my readers of the First World and my creature-self, inhabiting our slack hubristic epoch, fearing no God, seeking and counting our comforts and pleasures as our purposes. Do we not measure and re-measure the standard of what we call our living? We are not at ease. Do not many of us affect to belong nowhere? Are we not vauntingly déraciné, post-modern, without antecedent, each encapsulated in an idiotic, personal democracy ? And what demos? What kratia? In that each of us is a citizen of one state or another, how many of us yet readily know (or much care) who we are or what we stand for, live for, or might ever die for? Outside of the football stadium are we not shy of 'we' … shy, or half-apologetic? Ah, but we are not at ease, at inner peace. In its ridiculous conceit, time present (to which of course we all belong) has or all-but-has the answers. And yet we are not at peace. In Africa man is still tribal (with Kalashnikovs and AIDS and mobile phones), suffering gargantually. And we – do we not suffer? We suffer monumentally, in doomed pursuit of earthly answers to heavenly issues.

The mountains remain, the mountains of the moon, shining there unseen in the heart of the dark continent: Gargantua and Monument, refuge of gods and sometimes men, mountains making around their hems their own race of men. Look out from this window – no, look from this high scarp, on the long peace of the land, look upon the hills and hollows and amid them other hills, myriad, intricately watered, quilted by cultivation, by habitance.

FINIS

A Further Note on the Vernacular

Since little has yet been published about Bakonzo history and ethnology, I have taken the liberty of writing proper nouns or the technical vernacular as I have heard the sounds. Sounds can vary between one region of the mountains and another. Here and there, this liberty may have already introduced a difference between myself and others, mostly Bakonzo themselves, who have more recently come to write about the tribe. My friend, the distinguished anthropolgist Dr Kirsten Alnaes, who has made an important study of Konzo spirit songs, developed her own orthography. Thus, for example, the spirit I record as Ndyoka occurs in Kirsten's text as Endioka – the initial vowel indicating the spirit in her wholeness as distinct from a specific role. I tentatively let my spellings stand.

Where you find African names or words ending in a single *e*, please sound it in the mind's ear.

Not infrequently no true English transcription is possible. I have already mentioned the virtual indistinguishability of the *l* and the *r*, and the *b* and *v* and *w*. (In my original notes I coined the consonant *bv*.) The same problem afflicts a sound which is not quite *Tya* or *Cha*, and can hence go down as *Ta* – as in that important torrent which provides the boundary between Uganda and Congo in southern Ruwenzori, the Tako.

Deep valleys and difficult terrain make for marked variations and three identifiable regional forms of Lukonzo are acknowledged, the speakers of each readily understanding the speech of the other two.

Konzo   –   the root term indicating specific connotation of the tribe with which this book deals. In ordinary Bantu parlance, this 'root' would not be used alone, but in English it is permissible, and can be handy.

*Mu*konzo – a member of the tribe.

*Ba*konzo – the plural form; and thus also the tribe as a whole. But we should note that in Bantu usage, the consonant *b* is often heard, and transliterated, as *w*. Early European references to the people thus often appear as *Wa*konzo (or, to be precise, *Wakonjo* or *Wakonju* - the significance of the substitution of *j* with *z* being discussed in this book). A further wrinkle on the drift of the English *b* into *w* is that it will sometimes reach the English ear as *v* - and thus I have at times transcribed it, in deference to aural precision.

Lukonzo — the language. That's easy, language being nothing if not lingual - tongued. The wrinkle here is that in Bantu parlance the sound *l* becomes interchangeable with *r*, sometimes settling as the half-way house, *lh*. Thus, while one may correctly write the Toro language as Lutoro, it is often given as Rutoro, or (good missionaries striving for the sound of it) *Rutooro*. Recent orthography makes the Konzo tongue *Lhukonzo*. The moral for the reader is: Do not strain for rules, and a Pentecostal ease of understanding will come upon you.

Bukonzo — the, or in the actuality, *a* piece of territory, place or country occupied by Bakonzo.

Ganda — the root (and also a mythic person)
Muganda — a member of the tribe
Baganda — the tribe, or a plurality of that people
Buganda — their territory or country. (Of course, the British gave their name to an entire Protectorate of their own making, which contained and contains at least 27 sizeable tribes.)

Nyoro — the root
Banyoro — the tribe
Munyoro — a member of the tribe

Toro — the root, and also in this instance, the territory, or kingdom
Batoro — the tribe, or members of it
Mutoro — a member of it
Lutoro — the language (often orthographized as Rutooro)

Nkole — the root
Ankole — the place
Banyankole - the tribe
Munyankole - a member of it

Songora   - the root
Busongora   - the place
Basongora   - the tribe
Musongora   - a member of it

Mba   - the root
Bwamba   - the place
Baamba   - the tribe
 (*alt.* Bamba)
Mwamba   - a member of it
Lwamba   - the language

Wazungu   - white men (*from the Swahili*)
Mzungu   - a white man

ntu   - personhood (approximately)
bantu   - people
muntu   - a person

You will have noticed that, in Bantu languages, what precedes a word's root determines its role. Do not therefore be fazed by the sometimes unexpected way in which Lukonzo nouns are pluralized.

Glossary

(Vernacular words used once, and explained in the text, are not included. A final *e* makes for a syllable. The initial *o* preceding certain nouns is omitted where specifity is indicated: for instance, what appears below as *omutahwa* might thus occur in the text as *mutahwa*.)

Abahira	a Bakonzo clan (Lukonzo) (guinea fowl totem)
amawolero	neck-ring (*ebewolero* - multiple neck rings) (Lukonzo)
Bito	a Nilotic racial or social strain, or the bearer of such an hereditary strain (Bantu)
bukyaghe	goodbye (incorporating the wish for the other to live to see the next morning)
buhikira	main royal residence; 'palace' (Lukonzo)
busulu	a peasant's tribute or tax (Rutooro)
buthale see *obuthale*	
ekirimu	vital force (as of 'life'); sometimes hostile energy. An alternative orthography is *ekirimu* (Lukonzo)
ekyaghanda	a tribal assembly house (Lukonzo)
eluma	an ensemble of single-note flutes, ritually beared (Lukonzo)
eluma mabina	a prolonged spirit-honouring dance and festivity accompanied and inspired by *eluma* flautists and drummers (Lukonzo)
embitha	an esoteric vow or idea, usually applicable collectively (Lukonzo)
enanga	a lyre-like instrument, with eight strings, played while resting on the lap (Lukonzo)
endara	the Konzo xylophone, comprised of (usually) 14 keys (*esyonzomboli*) made of hardwood (*omulunongulu*) blocks of gradated lengths, ranging from about 5 feet for the lowest note to 2 feet for the highest, and covering about one and a half octaves. The keys are laid on plantain stems. The *endara* is played by two or three squatting performers on either side rapping the keys with sticks (*emihumbo*) in complex and frequently syncopated 3.4 or 4.4

	time, and may or may not be accompanied by drums (Lukonzo)
engorwe	a spirit hut (Lukonzo), built of reeds and grass only
enyamwulera	a long recorder-like flute, containing stops (Lukonzo)
enzenze	a Bakonzo two-stringed musical instrument (Lukonzo)
enzoka narunyatse	a venomous green snake (*atheris viridis*)
eririma	cultivated plot. Pl. *amarima* (Lukonzo)
eriato	the stitched canoe (Lukonzo)
eribanda	lowland tribal territory (Lukonzo)
eryandaghala	the 'descending', the formal descent from the mountains of the secessionist government
galabiyya	the loose and often seamless garment from the neck to the feet, often embroidered or coloured, commonly worn in the Mahgreb (regional Arabic)
gombolola	an administrative region, or sub-county, part of a *saza* (Rutooro)
Hima	an Hamitic racial or social strain, or the bearer of such an hereditary strain (Bantu)
Hira – see Abahira	
irema ngoma	keeper of the drum (commonly used as the principal royal title for Charles Wesley Mumbere. Frequently elided as *iremangoma*)
jeriba	stockaded fort (Swahili)
Kabaka	the king of the Baganda (Luganda)
kahindangoma	seat of government (literally 'drum h.q.')
Kayingo atsunge	Kyrie eleison; Lord have mercy
kigoma	drum
matoke	plantain mash, the Ugandan staple (Luganda) (Lukonzo - *omakamata*)
mbandua	medium while possessed (see *obubandua*). Pl. *esyombandua* (Lukonzo)
megara	approximately 'soul', or the human spirit in activity (Kinyarwanda)
miruka	a small administrative region, or 'parish', of which many comprise a *gombolola* (Rutooro)
mukungu	headman, as of a spur, or village (Lukonzo)

musabuli	redeemer or rescuer; latterly 'Saviour', as in the New Testament (Lukonzo)
mwita njike	Lake Edward. *lit.* 'killer of locusts' - which is to say, its width is greater than any locust swarm's uninterrupted flying span (Lukonzo)
mzungu	white person
nagana	sleeping sickness - trypanosomiasis
ngeya	the Ruwenzori black-and-white colobus monkey, *colobus angolensis ruwenzorii*
Nyamuhanga	the creator-spirit, and hence the name chosen for God in Christian terminology (Lukonzo)
obubandua	ritualized singing, involving converse with a spirit via a medium (Lukonzo)
obulambu	spur, or ridge, Pl. *amalambo* (Lukonzo)
obundu	a glutinous porridge of boiled millet flour (Lukonzo)
obuthale	1. metal ore (usually iron); 2. the smelting furnace
obuttulle-ttulle	the activity of malevolent spirits - a plural word, in use in the Bakonzo (southern region of Ruwenzori, and one of several such terms current in the highlands (Lukonzo)
olhubugho	bark cloth (Lukonzo)
olutegha	a species of fibre-producing tree (Lukonzo)
Omalemansozi	a title meaning 'ruler of the mountains' (Rutooro)
omoöso	a many-purposed metal tool, with a crescent blade, used as a hoe and a reaper
omuhikirwa	Toro premier (Rutooro)
omukama	lord, or king (of the Batoro); Lord, as in biblical usage (Rutooro)
omulerembera	senior official; the title used for the 'Prime Minister' of the Rwenzururu Kingdom (Lukonzo)
omulimu	soul (Lukonzo)
omuloiyi	a purveyor of an evil spell (pl, *abaloyi*) (Lukonzo)
omusangania	disposer and reconciler, somewhat in the Solomonic sense (Lukonzo)
Omusinga	King (Lukonzo)

(o)mutahwa	a spirit healer (Lukonzo)
omutaka	headman of a compound
omutoma	bark cloth tree (Lukonzo)
saza	an administrative region, approximately the size of a large English county (Rutooro)
wabukire	the first greeting of the day, and thus usable until well into the afternoon (Lukonzo)
wasinjya	a term of gratitude - 'thank you' (Lukonzo)
wassibiri	a greeting appropriate for the afternoon, especially if the person greeted has been encountered earlier in the day (see *wabukire*) (Lukonzo)
watyage	a variant of *bukyaghe*
wazungu	white people (plural of *mzungu*)

Map List. The maps have been drawn by Jennifer Skelley

Picture list. The author, or his companions using his camera, took most of the photographs, and Caroline Stacey made the drawings of artefacts. A few photographs from between 1970 and 1982 were taken by Rwenzururu veterans. (p.u. = photograph unsourced)

his consort, the Minister for Presidential Affairs Muruli Mukasa, and Dr Crispus Kiyonga (*far right*). 1998

457   At the newly built tribal assembly house at Kasese, a ewe is readied for the propitiation of the spirits.

460   Charles takes the rostrum for the first time in 14 years.

463   A banner typifying those which festooned Charles's route.

467   At the Kisinga rally: *left* Charles, with the author, takes a break from the proceedings. *Centre and right* revellers invoke the spirit of Rwenzururu.

469   The author addresses the Mpondwe rally. Yokasi Bihande.

471   At Mpondwe near Bwera, in the heartland of Kiyonga's constituency, he and Charles were to clash head-on.

474   The skies clear for Charles to speak at Mpondwe.

478   Bishop Zebedee greets Charles warily.

485   HH Ronald Mutebi, Kabaka of Buganda, at his Kampala palace, gives an audience to Charles of Ruwenzori, January 1999. (Press photo)

488   *Left*: with his bride-to-be Henrietta, and his daughter Furaha, Charles relocates his American home from Washington to Harrisburg where (*right*) the author visits him.

493   Batulomayu is visited by the author at Kitolu, in 2000.

495   Syayipuma Augustine, dressed for high altitude. 2001

496   Mudenge John, mountain guide.

498   An offering to Kalissia.

501   The giant *lobelia bequaertii* with human figure (boxed) alongside, at 12,000 ft.

511   Stanley's glaciers unveil beyond the giant *lobeliae wollastonii.*

506   Mudenge and Syayipuma approaching the snout of Elena glacier. 2001

508   The author and Mudenge befogged on Stanley. 2001

510   Re-united with his full Bakonzo escort, the author is photographed at Lake Kitandara, where he has been joined by Gustavo Corti (*right of centre*). The author's swollen face betrays mountain sickness. 2001

512   Top cutting: *The Monitor* breaks the touristic scandal. Bottom cutting: *New Vision* reports the author's arrest

517   News of baboons raiding the plantains send old and young scampering to their crops' defence in highland Bwamba. 1954

518-9   Top left: club mosses (*Lycopodium saururus*) dominate the giant heathers (*Phillipiae johnstonii*) at 11,500 feet. *Top right*: the giant groundsel, *senecio johnstonii advinalis*, and the *helichrysum stuhlmannii* turn alpine Ruwenzori into an endless and often impenetrable garden. (G. Yeoman) *Lower picture*: Lake Bujuku, from the ascent to Stanley.

522   Crossing the Freshfield pass, between Kitandara lakes and the upper Mubuku valley, in a snowstorm. (Syayipuma)

Index

The order in which the two or more parts of the names of Bakonzo characters is listed is, on the whole, determined by that part of the name that is most commonly used in the text.

Tom Stacey's earlier works have invariably evoked commendation from a wide range of voices.

On *The Living and the Dying*, Barbara Burke wrote in *The Irish Times:*

'It is Tom Stacey's belief that writers ought not to produce novels until they are certain that they have something worthwhile to tell. His last novel was published sixteen years ago... Finding *The Living and the Dying* among this week's new books was like finding a crocus alive and well in Arctic wastes...

'At the core of the book is not an idea, nor even a fusion of ideas, but a sound and deeply-reasoned philosophy that, if separated from the novel with which it is intricately bound, could merit publication in its own right. Ideally, I should like to say not more than that I have read it twice in ten days, will read it again, and advise you, very strongly, to try it...

'It is in Ed that Tom Stacey has put the mechanism that elevates this novel from the common rank to the master class. He is the filter through whom not only all the action and the highly-charged emotion of the novel passes, but who also functions as a sounding board for the reader's reaction to Jim's behaviour. Ed is subtly and brilliantly made by Mr Stacey to combine objective condemnation with subjective compassion and understanding. Nearing the end of the illness, he recalls that Jim "was growing more distant, but the air of secret certainty stayed.

'"How wise one gets," he exclaimed one, "when it's too late to pass it on."

'There is the same air of secret certainty throughout this novel and fortunately, Tom Stacey has not left it too late to pass on his wisdom. Sixteen years was a long time to wait, but it was worth it.'

And Dick Stanford in *The Scotsman*:

'How gratifying it is... to encounter a writer who stays silent in fiction until he has really something to say. Tom Stacey, of course, is well known as correspondent, columnist and publisher, but "The Living and the Dying" is only his second novel, following "The Brothers M" in 1960 which gained him golden opinions...

'Jeremy Taylor in the seventeenth century – and era of more

inward consciousness – could write a whole book on "holy dying", and Mr Stacey's novel can be regarded as a sort of secular fictional equivalent of this. He makes us reflect on the nature of death, the stages of its approach, and the way in which it may change the relationship between the living and the dying. He implicates us, also, in the question of profane and sacred love; whether the two spring from the same source, and whether, in the long run, all love is not open-ended, directed, that is, even in unconsciously, beyond its immediate object to the ultimate (as St Augustine believed).

'Metaphysical though this novel often is, it in no way lacks the satisfactions of a deeply dramatic story...'

Dr Myrna Blumberg, in *The Times*:

'Tom Stacey's second novel is uncommonly confident about love and death. Published 16 years after his first, its maturing has been worth waiting for: the orderly writing, robust intelligence and honesty are steadily enlivening...

'Can the living judge the dying? Mr Stacey is brilliant on Jim's apparent withdrawal symptoms from a comfortable live, his open-heartedness towards death, his attempts to make others begin not to miss him: "By courtesy of all creation... [people] are lent to one another." Penetrating and justly observed, the book ends with inspired energy.'

On his earlier novel, *The Brothers M*, Christopher Hill wrote in *The Spectator*:

'Africa, to Mr Stacey, is not only white whale and magic mountain but the Marabar caves, the failure of our passage to India and more than India. Like Forster's novel, his admission of defeat is an advance. He has to leave the centre of his novel unknown, but he gets closer to Africa than any English writer I have read before.'

Or *Time Magazine*, which wrote of 'this deeply felt and disturbing novel. Tom Stacey knows the depths and shallows of African politics. As a trained anthropologist (*The Hostile Sun*), he has a strong sense of what it must be like to live in a primitive society...'

Or Michael Davison, writing in the *East African Standard*:
'For vivid descriptive powers and adventure, it rivals Rider Haggard, but it is much broader in interest by reason of the remarkable insight of its characters and into the meaning of life itself... Tom Stacey leaps fully accoutred into the very front rank of contemporary writers.'

And in similar vein from the *Oxford Mail*:
'A fascinatingly authentic tale. As a novelist, Tom Stacey has acquired a mantle of majesty.'

The New Statesman perceived:
"... a great talent... He organises his material splendidly and maintains the same level right through this long book... Some of the African scenes, beautiful and terrible, are marvellously visualized. This book is a very considerable achievement.'

Or Ann Duchene in the *Guardian*:
'Mr Stacey writes always with authority, intelligence and the desperation of helpless love.'

Or John Barkham, in *The New York Times*:
'It is a deeply impressive work, complex, poetic, profound, which breaks new ground.'

Janice Elliott wrote on Tom Stacey's *The Pandemonium* in The *Sunday Telegraph*:
'Not only the subject but the beauty and simplicity of the style reminded me of Brian Morris' "Catholics", though Mr Stacey reached perhaps even deeper. His theme [the nature of love, spiritual and carnal] is great, but his approach is through the wonderfully detailed minutiae, observation of the people and of this "half-Norse world" belonging to the sea.'

Likewise on *The Pandemonium* in the *Hampstead and Highgate Express*:
'Tom Stacey writes better about loving than almost any other living writer. He comes to terms with the essence of the human condition,

that loving without wanting is like meat without salt, and that it is better to die admitting it than live denying it.'

Isabel Quigly writes on *Decline* in the *Financial Times*:

'"What is happening to England?" asks Tom Stacey's *Decline*... A moral tale without moralising, showing old values and new ones, it has a James-like quality at once tender and brisk: no over-writing, no sentimentality, above all the ability to show, with the right artistic detachment, a complex reality that has no visible solutions.'

Or Brendon O'Keeffe in *The Tablet*:

'One rarely finds an author who can so adroitly move about all classes, write to assuredly about the big questions, and stylishly find distinctive and credible voices for many different characters... A stylist whose prose we savour as long as we can.'

And William Green, writing in *The Spectator*:

'Stacey's decision to combine the story of a family with that of a nation is recklessly ambitious, yet somehow he pulls it off... It is the range and complexity that makes *Decline* such an impressive novel.'